RIGHTEOUS RĀMA

RIGHTEOUS RĀMA

The Evolution of an Epic

J. L. BROCKINGTON

DELHI
OXFORD UNIVERSITY PRESS
BOMBAY CALCUTTA MADRAS
1985

Oxford University Press, Walton Street, Oxford OX2 6DP
London New York Toronto
Delhi Bombay Calcutta Madras Karachi
Kuala Lumpur Singapore Hong Kong Tokyo
Nairobi Dar es Salaam Cape Town
Melbourne Auckland
and associated companies
Beirut Berlin Ibadan Mexico City Nicosia

Oxford is a trade mark of Oxford University Press

British Library Cataloguing in Publication Data
Brockington, J.L.
Righteous Rāma: the evolution of an epic.
1. V–alm–iki. Ramayana
I. Title
294.5'922 PK3661
ISBN 0-19-815463-1

Filmset by South End Typographics, Pondicherry
Printed by All India Press, Pondicherry
Published by R. Dayal, Oxford University Press
2/11 Ansari Road, Daryaganj, New Delhi 110002

PREFACE

This book seeks to set the Rāmāyaṇa of Vālmīki in its total context, thus providing a comprehensive study of the epic. Starting from a close linguistic study of the text, it establishes the relative chronology of the different layers of its composition and on that basis investigates the material, cultural, social and religious milieux as they are revealed at different periods. Previous studies of these aspects of the Rāmāyaṇa have tended to rely on rather subjective criteria for their assessment of the relative date of particular features, or else uncritically to assign the whole work to a single period. In this work, the careful analysis of the language and style of the epic in relation to the transition from earlier to classical Sanskrit is the basis for charting the various layers of composition on internal and relatively objective evidence. The linguistic data presented in the second chapter are therefore central to the argument of the book but equally may safely be omitted by those readers whose interests are cultural rather than linguistic, provided that they are willing to take on trust the division into stages propounded in the final part of that chapter (and summarised in the Appendix).

By means of this division into stages, the information which can be drawn from the Rāmāyaṇa on cultural aspects is significantly enhanced and we are able to see how the Rāmāyaṇa, like the even more extensive Mahābhārata, reflects the changing culture. We can discern in its different layers the last stages of Vedic religion, exemplified in particular by the early prominence of Indra, followed by the rise and eclipse of the relatively short-lived importance of Brahmā, which gives way in the latest stages to an incipient Vaiṣṇavism; thus, new light can be shed on the transition between the religion of the Vedas and later Hinduism. Similarly, the Rāmāyaṇa reflects a social pattern at a transitional phase between that of the Aryan expansion across northern India and the settled pattern of village-based agriculture which is so much a feature of modern India—the change from a heroic age to caste society.

Comparison with the Mahābhārata and the Purāṇas contributes to a fuller understanding of the textual history of the Rāmāyaṇa. The new light shed on the text also prompts a reconsideration of its influence on later Sanskrit and vernacular literature, as well as its spread outside India. For, as Rāma developed into a figure for veneration, and more particularly came to be seen as an *avatāra* of Viṣṇu, later generations of Indian poets continued to retell and adapt the legend down to the present day.

I owe my thanks to many individuals who have helped me in one way or another in the writing of this book. To my parents I am indebted for the example which encouraged me in an academic career, as well as for regularly accommodating me when working in the Indian Institute, Oxford; I am grateful also to my aunt, Miss R. Woodward, for providing me with a room to work in on one such extended visit. To Professor T. Burrow I am indebted for first introducing me to the Rāmāyaṇa and for supervising my doctoral thesis, out of which this present work has grown. Many others have helped me by the provision of information and offprints, which has been acknowledged at the relevant points. Those to whom I am grateful for discussion of the material or advice which goes beyond that, or is not otherwise acknowledged, are Professor R. E. Asher, Paul Dundas, Professor Minoru Hara, Dr R. S. McGregor, Dr Saveros Pou, Dr Peter Schreiner, Dr Nilmadhav Sen and Dr U. P. Shah (whose hospitality at the Rāmāyaṇa Department, Baroda, puts me particularly in his debt). Finally and particularly, I owe to my wife Mary the largest thanks for all her help and encouragement, expressed in her involvement throughout, from the collection and co-ordination of the data, through revision of earlier drafts, to the typing of the final version.

J. L. Brockington

October 1981

CONTENTS

Preface v

Abbreviations ix

1 The Background 1
The subdivisions of the work—a summary of the story—earlier views on its date and nature

2 Composition 16
The verbal system—the nominal system—sentence construction—figures of speech—stereotyped expressions—the stages of growth of the text

3 The Setting: Economic and Material Culture 62
The economy—roads and transport—employment—towns and buildings—clothing and ornaments—food and drink

4 The Setting: the Wider Environment 88
Fauna, including domestic animals—agriculture—flora—geographical data

5 The People: King, Court and Army 124
The king, his courtiers and political theory—armies, armour, weapons and the conventions of warfare

6 The People: the rest of Society 153
The population and its subdivisions—family relationships, marriage and the position of women—education and the arts

7 The Religious Pattern 194
Indra and the rest of the pantheon—Asuras and demi-gods—ascetics and their hermitages—ritual aspects—the increase in emphasis on ethics and religion—the more elaborate pattern of the third and fourth stages—Rāma's humanity and ultimate identity with Viṣṇu

8 Adaptations in Sanskrit 226
Allusions in the Mahābhārata—the Purāṇas—Classical Sanskrit literature—later Sanskrit Rāmāyaṇas

9 Adaptations in other Languages 260
Early Buddhist adaptations—Jain Rāmāyaṇas—South Indian versions—North Indian versions—the spread of the story in South-east Asia

10 Evolution of the Epic 307
The dating of the stages of growth—a survey of the cultural background of each stage—the development of the figure of Rāma

Appendix 329

Bibliography 347

Indices: 349
Ancient texts and authors 349
Modern authors 355
General 358

Abbreviations

General

BhG.	Bhagavadgītā
Bibl. Nat.	Bibliothèque Nationale, Paris
Hv.	Harivaṃśa
KA	Kauṭilīya Arthaśāstra
[l.v.]	verse in longer metre
Mbh.	Mahābhārata (Critical Edition)
Pāṇ	Pāṇini
Rām.	Rāmāyaṇa
Śat. Br.	Śatapatha Brāhmaṇa
U.P.	Uttar Pradesh
Vāj. S.	Vājasaneyī Saṃhitā

Periodicals

ABORI	Annals of the Bhandarkar Oriental Research Institute, Poona
AJPh	American Journal of Philology, Baltimore
AORM	Annals of Oriental Research, Madras
BEFEO	Bulletin de l'École Française d'Extrême Orient, Paris
BSOAS/BSOS	Bulletin of the School of Oriental (and African) Studies, London
HR	History of Religions, Chicago
IHQ	Indian Historical Quarterly, Calcutta
IIJ	Indo-Iranian Journal, 's-Gravenhage
IT	Indologica Taurinensia, Torino
JA	Journal Asiatique, Paris
JAOS	Journal of the American Oriental Society, New Haven, Baltimore
JIH	Journal of Indian History, Kerala University, Trivandrum
JOIB	Journal of the Oriental Institute, Baroda
JORM	Journal of Oriental Research, Madras
JRAS	Journal of the Royal Asiatic Society, London
NG	Nachrichten von der Kgl. Gesellschaft der Wissenschaften zu Göttingen, Phil.-hist. Klasse

RO	Rocznik Orientalistyczny, Kraków
WZKSA/WZKSO	Wiener Zeitschrift für die Kunde Süd- (und Ost-)asiens
ZDMG	Zeitschrift der deutschen morgenländischen Gesellschaft, Wiesbaden

1
THE BACKGROUND

> With a smile, Brahmā said to Vālmīki: 'You have indeed invented the *śloka*. ... O best of seers, compose the entire Rāma story.' (1.2.29–30)

THE Rāmāyaṇa enshrines the legend of Prince Rāma and his adventures when exiled to the forest. It is a long epic poem, composed mostly in the *śloka* metre, ranging from accounts of intrigue at court to wanderings among ascetics in the forest; it culminates in the great battle when the Rākṣasa Rāvaṇa is defeated and punished for his abduction of Rāma's wife, Sītā. Tradition has it that the original version was composed by a sage called Vālmīki and then transmitted orally; but the version of the Vālmīki Rāmāyaṇa now extant was undoubtedly composed over several centuries between perhaps 500 BC and 300 AD, during which period it was also committed to writing. It is now divided into seven *kāṇḍas*, or books, each comprising between 66 and 116 sargas, or chapters, whose contents and style enable several successive stages of composition to be determined.[1]

The original story began no doubt with some version of the court intrigues which open the Ayodhyākāṇḍa, now the second book of the epic. Here we are introduced to the aging king of Ayodhyā, Daśaratha, his wives Kausalyā, Kaikeyī and Sumitrā, and the four princes: Rāma, son of Kausalyā, Bharata, son of Kaikeyī, and Lakṣmaṇa and Śatrughna, sons of Sumitrā. Daśaratha determines, amid general approval, to install Rāma as *yuvarāja*, 'young king' or heir-apparent (sargas 1–6), but Kaikeyī, urged on by her servant Mantharā (7–9), contrives to have him supplanted by Bharata and banished to the forest for fourteen years (10–12). Daśaratha feels forced to give in to her petulance in fulfilment of two boons he has previously granted her, but his agony of mind in doing so is touchingly portrayed; so profound is

[1] For detailed discussion see chapter 2 and Appendix. All references are to the Critical Edition published at Baroda (*The Vālmīki-Rāmāyaṇa, Critically edited for the First Time*, 7 vols., G. H. Bhatt and U. P. Shah *gen. eds.*, Baroda, 1960–75), using its system of notation for references to text and rejected material (* passages). Short rejected passages are given in the *apparatus criticus* at the appropriate point in the text (e.g. 2.1*1) and longer ones in Appendix I of each volume (e.g. 2 App.I.1.1).

his grief that he dies shortly after Rāma's departure from Ayodhyā, attributing his death, separated from his son, to retribution for having accidentally killed an ascetic (57–8). His distress is shared by almost all the inhabitants of the town, but not by Rāma himself, who accepts the decree with absolute submission and with the calm self-control which regularly characterises him (16). The more completely to fulfil his father's commands, he suggests sending messengers to recall Bharata, who, with Śatrughna, is away from Ayodhyā on a visit, and so innocent and ignorant of his mother's machinations; Rāma then makes preparations for his departure with no protest whatsoever, accompanied at their insistence by his wife Sītā and his brother Lakṣmaṇa (17–35). The trio soon evade the huge crowd of mourning citizens who flock after them (40–1), and make their way, first by chariot, then on foot, to mount Citrakūṭa, visiting *en route* the Niṣāda chief Guha (44–5) and the ascetic Bharadvāja (48). On Citrakūṭa they erect a hermitage (50), where they live happily for a while, enjoying the beauties of nature (88–9).

Meanwhile, to avert the graphically predicted evils of a kingless state (61), Bharata has been recalled to Ayodhyā (62–5), where he confounds his mother's schemes by angrily rejecting the profferred kingdom (67, 73) and setting off, accompanied by the three queens and a huge retinue, to fetch Rāma back (76). They too meet Guha (78–81), and are entertained to a miraculous banquet by Bharadvāja (84–5). Rāma greets Bharata with none of the rancour displayed by the excitable Lakṣmaṇa (90–1), but enquires calmly about his conduct of public affairs (94, the *kaccit* sarga); but he insists on carrying out to the letter his father's express wish, undeterred alike by Bharata's impassioned pleas and offers to change places with him (97–9), by the cynical materialism expressed by the courtier Jābāli (100), and by the defence of orthodox traditional values put forward by the court chaplain, Vasiṣṭha (102). Eventually Bharata and his train return to Ayodhyā, taking with them Rāma's sandals as a symbol of his authority (104–5); Bharata retires to nearby Nandigrāma, from where he administers the country as Rāma's regent (107). Meanwhile Rāma and his companions decide to leave Citrakūṭa for a more remote part of the forest, by way of the hermitage of Atri and Anasūyā, who listen to their story and present them with handsome gifts of clothing and ornaments (109–11).

Book three, the Araṇyakāṇḍa, narrates the exiles' life amongst the hospitable, respectful sages and the hostile Rākṣasas of the Daṇḍaka forest. Despite Rāma's resolve to live like an ascetic, it is his role as the perfect kṣatriya, or warrior, which now comes to the fore. The brothers have to rescue Sītā from the clutches of a Rākṣasa, Virādha (2–3), and the sages extract a pledge from Rāma to protect them against the depredations of the Rākṣasas (5). Sītā (or, more realistically, a relatively late redactor of the poem) feels that such conduct may lead to a charge of aggression, but Rāma counters this argument with an appeal to his duty to protect the ascetics (8–9). For ten years Rāma and his party wander among the sages; we have specific accounts of their visits to Śarabhaṅga (4), Sutīkṣṇa (6–7), and to Agastya, who gives him divine weapons and advises him to build a hermitage in nearby Pañcavaṭī (10–12); on the way there, they meet the vulture Jaṭāyus, who narrates his lineage and offers them his protection (13).

While they are living in the hut they have built in Pañcavaṭī, the hideous but none the less amorous Rākṣasī Śūrpaṇakhā makes advances to the brothers; infuriated by their disdain, she attacks Sītā, and Lakṣmaṇa mutilates her as a punishment (16–17). Her brother Khara attempts to avenge her, first by sending a posse of fourteen Rākṣasas to kill the brothers (19), and then, after they have all been killed, by leading an army of fourteen thousand to attack them; Rāma alone defeats them all, killing the generals Dūṣaṇa (25) and Triśiras (26), and finally Khara himself (27–8), to the delight of the Daṇḍaka sages (29). Śūrpaṇakhā then seeks a different kind of vengeance from another brother, Rāvaṇa, king of Laṅkā, whom she incites to abduct Sītā (30–2). He compels the aid of the unwilling and timorous Mārīca (33–9), whose disguise as a golden deer and feigned call for help induce Sītā to send both brothers after it (40–3); Rāvaṇa, disguised as a mendicant, thus has no difficulty in seizing her (44–7). Jaṭāyus is fatally wounded when he attempts to intervene (48–9), and Sītā is taken to Laṅkā, where, having vehemently rejected all Rāvaṇa's blandishments, she is confined in a grove of *aśoka* trees (51–4).

Rāma and Lakṣmaṇa meanwhile are in great distress (55–62); the dying Jaṭāyus tells them what has happened (63–4), and the monster Kabandha advises them to ally themselves with the Vānara leader Sugrīva, who will help them to recover Sītā (65–9). On their way to find him they meet a Śabarī ascetic-woman (70).

Book four is the Kiṣkindhākāṇḍa, for it concentrates on events in or relating to the Vānara capital Kiṣkindhā. The beautiful lake Pampā revives Rāma's longing for his wife (1); there the two princes are accosted by the exiled Sugrīva's minister, Hanumān, who takes them to his master (2–4). Rāma and Sugrīva make a solemn pledge of alliance (5), and Rāma is encouraged by the sight of some of Sītā's clothes and ornaments which, seeing a group of Vānaras, she had thrown down as Rāvaṇa abducted her (7). Sugrīva next enlists Rāma's help in ousting his usurping brother Vālin (8), and recounts the history of their quarrel (9–11). Encouraged by Rāma, Sugrīva challenges Vālin to single combat, and finally, with Rāma's covert assistance, Vālin is mortally wounded (12, 14–16). He dies reproaching Rāma (17), who justifies his action (18), mourned by his wife Tārā and his son Aṅgada (20–3), and is cremated with elaborate ceremonial (24). Sugrīva is now installed as king, taking over Vālin's harem, including Tārā and his own former wife Rumā, with Aṅgada as his heir (25).

The onset of the rains prevents any further search for Sītā (26–7); afterwards Hanumān (28, 31) and then Lakṣmaṇa (33) remind Sugrīva of his promise to help. A vast army of Vānaras is mustered (36, 38), divided into four, and sent off with instructions to search for Sītā in every direction (39–42). Rāma places most faith in the party led by Hanumān and Aṅgada, and entrusts his ring to Hanumān as a token for Sītā (43). The other three parties return without success (46), but after much searching and several bouts of suicidal despair (48–54), Aṅgada and Hanumān's troop meet Saṃpāti, Jaṭāyus' brother (55); from him they learn that Sītā is on the island Laṅkā (57), and Hanumān resolves to leap over the sea to find her (65–6).

Book five, called the Sundarakāṇḍa after its account of the beauties of Laṅkā, opens with a long account of Hanumān's fantastic leap (1), after which he alights unnoticed in Laṅkā and wanders about the city, dazzled by its splendours (2–5). Entering Rāvaṇa's magnificent palace, he searches in vain for Sītā (6–9), but eventually discovers her in the *aśoka* grove (13), and overhears her rebuff Rāvaṇa's entreaties and threats (18–20). Her guards also try to persuade her to accept Rāvaṇa, though one, Trijaṭā, cheers her by recounting an auspicious dream (21–5). Hanumān gently reveals himself to the incredulous Sītā (28–33) and proves his identity by producing Rāma's ring (34). Sītā refuses to escape with Hanumān, preferring to be liberated by Rāma in person, but gives the Vānara a jewel as a token for Rāma (35–6). Instead of hurrying back in secret, Hanumān then embarks upon a course of ostentatious and wanton destruction (39, 41), kills a number of Rākṣasa champions (42–5) and finally, curious to see Rāvaṇa, allows himself to be captured by Indrajit, Rāvaṇa's son (46). The angry Rāvaṇa is dissuaded from killing Hanumān outright by his virtuous brother Vibhīṣaṇa's reminder of the inviolability of envoys (50), so he merely sets fire to the Vānara's tail (51). This does not have the desired effect: Hanumān uses it as a brand to complete the destruction of Laṅkā (52). Reassuring himself of Sītā's safety (53–4), he recrosses the sea (55) and reports to his eager companions (56–8). Overjoyed, they rampage through Sugrīva's private orchard, the Madhuvana, to the discomfiture of its guards (59–61) before returning to Kiṣkindhā with the news of the success of their mission (62–6).

Book six, the Yuddhakāṇḍa, concerns the final battle between the armies of Rāma and Rāvaṇa. While Rāma and the Vānaras march southwards (4), the Rākṣasas prepare for war (6–8), but Vibhīṣaṇa defects when his conciliatory advice is refused (9–10). After some debate, he is welcomed into Rāma's camp, and consecrated king of Laṅkā (11–13). The problem of how to cross the sea is solved by Nala's construction of a causeway (15). Rāvaṇa receives information from his spies about the size of the besieging army (16–21) and after trying in vain to frighten Sītā into submission by showing her the illusion of Rāma's severed head (22–4) and rejecting Rāma's ultimatum delivered by Aṅgada (31), joins battle (32–4).

Disaster soon strikes. Indrajit puts Rāma and Lakṣmaṇa out of action (35), to the despair of the Vānaras (36) and the watching Sītā (37–8), but eventually the brothers are restored by the divine intervention of the bird Garuḍa (40). Then follows a long series of duels, resulting in the eventual deaths of all the most fearsome Rākṣasa champions at the hands of Rāma, Lakṣmaṇa and the Vānara chiefs (41–86). During this time, Rāma overcomes Rāvaṇa but spares his life (47). One of the most terrible of the Rākṣasas is another brother, Kumbhakarṇa, who is under a curse of deep sleep (49); the elaborate efforts of his desperate comrades to wake him (48) provide some much needed comic relief from the tension of the battle scenes, but after causing initial havoc among the Vānaras even he is slain by Rāma (55). Indrajit repeatedly resorts to magic to strike terror into the Vānaras: one of his stratagems is to show Rāma and Lakṣmaṇa the illusion of Sītā being executed (68); he also embarks upon a sacrifice to ensure victory (69), but is prevented from completing it by Lakṣmaṇa (73), who eventually kills him (78). Only Rāvaṇa is left, and at last he takes the field again amid bad omens (83). His duel with Rāma is protracted, but finally, after Rāma receives divine help in the form of Indra's chariot and driver, Rāvaṇa too is killed (97), and Vibhīṣaṇa installed as king (100).

Little trace remains of what was no doubt the original simple happy ending of the story: there is no reason to suppose that Rāma and Sītā were not joyfully reunited and lived happily ever after. In the version now extant, however, later qualms about Sītā's virtue cause Rāma to be made coldly to spurn her, saying (for the first time) that he undertook the quest and combat simply to vindicate his own and his family's honour, and not for her sake (103). In desperation, Sītā undergoes an ordeal by fire (104). The gods appear to Rāma and reveal that he is in fact an incarnation of Viṣṇu (105) and Agni hands Sītā back to her delighted husband, unhurt and exonerated (106). Daśaratha now appears, blesses his sons, and tells Rāma to return to Ayodhyā and resume his reign (the fourteen years of exile have, it seems, just expired) (107). At Rāma's request, the dead Vānaras are restored to life by Indra (108); then Rāma, Lakṣmaṇa and Sītā, and all the Vānaras, and Vibhīṣaṇa and his counsellors, all climb into Rāvaṇa's chariot Puṣpaka, and—surveying as they go the scenes of their earlier adventures—they fly back to Ayodhyā (109–11).

After greeting Bharadvāja (112), Rāma sends Hanumān to find Bharata, who is living the life of an ascetic (113). Bharata is delighted by the news of Rāma's triumph and return (114), and restores to him the kingdom. This is followed by an elaborate ceremony of installation, and the epic is rounded off with a eulogy of Rāma and his righteous ten-thousand-year reign (116).

Popular stories, from the *Iliad* and the *Chanson de Guillaume* to Sherlock Holmes and the *Forsyte Saga*, have never lacked for sequels and prologues, and the Rāmāyaṇa is no exception. Now forming the first book of the poem, the Bālakāṇḍa is a late addition composed to narrate Rāma's birth, youthful exploits, and marriage. Some of its incidents develop suggestions in the main narrative, others are purely fanciful, with a distinct tendency towards the miraculous and the mythical: interpolated into the history of Rāma are the legends of Ṛśyaśṛṅga (8–10), Kuśa, Brahmadatta and Viśvāmitra (31–3), Gaṅgā (34, 41–2), Umā (35), Kārtikeya (36), Sagara (37–40), the churning of the ocean (44), Diti (45), Indra and Ahalyā (47–8), Vasiṣṭha, Viśvāmitra and the cow, Śabalā (51–5), Triśaṅku (56–9), Śunaḥśepa (60–1), and Viśvāmitra's attainment of brāhman status, despite the distractions of Menakā and Rambhā (62–3).

The birth of Rāma and his three brothers is narrated in miraculous terms: Daśaratha is childless, and in his anxiety for an heir performs first an *aśvamedha* (11–13), then a *putreṣṭi* sacrifice (14). At the gods' request, Viṣṇu decides to become incarnate as Daśaratha's four sons as the only means of destroying Rāvaṇa (14–15), and the other gods procreate the Vānara heroes (16); Rāma, then Bharata, then Lakṣmaṇa and Śatrughna, are born amongst great rejoicing (17).

We are told nothing of their childhood, until Rāma is fifteen, and the sage Viśvāmitra comes to court to ask for Rāma to protect his sacrifice against the attacks of the Rākṣasas Mārīca and Subāhu (17–20), an incident obviously suggested by Mārīca's speech to Rāvaṇa in the Araṇyakāṇḍa; with Daśaratha's reluctant permission, Rāma and Lakṣmaṇa accompany the sage and drive off his persecutors (21–9).

The account of Rāma's marriage is another Bālakāṇḍa expansion. Viśvāmitra takes Rāma and Lakṣmaṇa to attend King Janaka's sacrifice at Mithilā (30). We learn of Sītā's miraculous birth, and of Śiva's bow, which no man has strength to string (65); Rāma not merely bends but breaks the bow (66), and with Daśaratha's consent, Rāma is married to Sītā, Lakṣmaṇa to her sister, and Bharata and Śatrughna to her cousins (72).

As the party return to Ayodhyā at the close of the book, Rāma's status is further enhanced by an encounter with the belligerent Rāma Jāmadagnya, whom he frightens away (73–5). At a very late date, two summaries of the whole story were added to the beginning of the Bālakāṇḍa (1, 3), and its composition ascribed to the sage Vālmīki (2, 4).

The seventh book of the Rāmāyaṇa is the Uttarakāṇḍa, or 'Further Exploits.' It is set in Ayodhyā after Rāma's victorious return, but despite its title, the first third details Rāvaṇa's misdeeds before his encounter with Rāma, as told to Rāma by Agastya (1–36). Among the many miscellaneous incidents we are told how the Rākṣasa brothers practise penance, and are granted boons by Brahmā: Rāvaṇa becomes invincible except to man, Vibhīṣaṇa obtains virtue, and Kumbhakarṇa deep sleep (10). We also learn how Rāvaṇa expelled Kubera from Laṅkā, taking his Puṣpaka chariot as booty (11, 14–15), how his attack on Vedavatī leads her to prophesy her reincarnation as Sītā for his destruction (17), and how his incestuous rape of Rambhā provokes the curse which is to prevent him from raping Sītā (26); in a fight with Indra, his son is granted the name Indrajit, together with the promise of inviolability unless interrupted in a sacrifice (30), explaining his death at the hands of Lakṣmaṇa. Other incidents, such as Rāvaṇa's attempt to lift mount Kailāsa (16) and his fight with Yama (20–2), are irrelevant to the main story. Agastya's narrative concludes with an account of Hanumān's exploits (35–6).

The rest of the book deals with events subsequent to Rāma's installation. After his guests depart, Rāma lives happily with Sītā for a while, and the country prospers under his rule (40–1), but slanderous gossip about Sītā's virtue while a prisoner of Rāvaṇa compels Rāma reluctantly to order her exile to Vālmīki's hermitage (42–4), an order which is carried out only by means of a subterfuge (45–8). On his way to conquer the Asura Lavana and found the city Madhurā (53–62), Śatrughna stays the night at Vālmīki's hermitage and learns of the birth of Rāma's twin sons, Kuśa and Lava (58).

The general prosperity of Rāma's subjects is shattered by the untimely death of a brāhman boy (64); attributing this disaster to the fact that austerities are being performed by a man of inferior caste, Rāma summarily executes the culprit, restores the dead boy to life and re-establishes his righteous rule (65–7). A number of legends are narrated, including those of Śveta (68–9), Daṇḍa (70–2), Indra and Vṛtra (75–7), and Ila (78–81). Then Rāma prepares an *aśvamedha* (horse sacrifice) (82–3), at which Kuśa and Lava are recognised by their singing of the Rāma story (84–6). Sītā is recalled, and publicly affirms her purity by calling upon the Earth to swallow her in testimony; the Earth embraces Sītā and disappears with her (87–8), and Rāma is left to mourn her loss, using a golden statue of her as a substitute at sacrifices (89). After a long and prosperous reign, and the death of Lakṣmaṇa (96), Rāma settles the kingdom on Kuśa and Lava (97), and publicly immolates himself in the river Sarayū, along with the other two brothers and the Vānaras (100).

We have followed in this summary the divisions into *kāṇḍas* or books and sargas or chapters found in the Critical Edition, which basically in this matter follows the Southern Recension. The analysis of the text in ensuing chapters will also use these divisions as units of analysis, but they are in fact secondary, though recognised by the end of the poem's growth.[2] The considerable divergence between the recensions on the point at which one book ends and the next begins is in itself sufficient evidence of this. It has long been recognised that there are two main lines of transmission of the extant text, usually termed the Northern and Southern Recensions; but it is possible also to discern certain affinities within each of these, and the Critical Edition divides the Northern Recension into Northeastern, Northwestern and Western sub-recensions.[3]

[2] See p. 189.

[3] The Critical Edition does not use the term sub-recension (and hereafter I shall simplify to recension) but tends to speak of groups or versions, terms which it also employs for its grouping of manuscripts by the script employed into, for example, Śāradā and Malayāḷam versions. The manuscripts in a particular script may quite often be more closely related than others but not necessarily so. The Critical Edition has not in reality gone further than the subdivision of the N. recension into NE., NW. and W. in the construction of a *stemma codicum* nor in all probability is it possible to do so at present, given the degree of contamination apparent between mss. and recensions. Indeed, it is open to question whether the W. recension should really be distinguished from the NW. (cf. G. H. Bhatt, Araṇyakāṇḍa, Introduction pp. XXIII-XXV and my 'Sanskrit Epic Tradition I. Epic and Epitome (Rāmāyaṇa and Rāmopākhyāna)', IT 6, 1978,

These several recensions are each to a considerable extent divergent in their contents as well as their internal divisions.[4] This is due no doubt in part simply to the long time-span over which the epic has been transmitted but another factor must have been the method of transmission. For it is clear that both the epics, the Rāmāyaṇa and the much longer Mahābhārata, were composed against an oral background of heroic ballads and were transmitted through recitation by bards (*sūtas*). The earliest stages in the development which led to the epics may possibly be seen in the *ākhyāna* hymns of the *Ṛgveda* and more certainly in the songs of praise of heroes, legends and ancient stories (*gāthānārāśaṃsī, itihāsa, purāṇa*), the recitation of which formed part of the rituals discussed in the Brāhmaṇas. The next stage must have been the coalescence of such brief compositions into longer ballads and cycles of ballads around some central focus, either a particularly outstanding hero or events of special importance. The two extant epics would constitute the culmination of such an evolutionary process in the recitations of the *sūtas*, whose duties included not only the recital of their rulers' praises but also acting as their charioteers in battle or the hunt, thus giving their descriptions a basis in first-hand experience. Later on, itinerant ballad-singers (*kuśīlava*) played a role in the dissemination of these heroic lays and the epics among the population at large; the myth of their origin connects them with the recital of Vālmīki's poem by Rāma's sons Kuśa and Lava.[5]

The significance which such heroic poetry has for the Vedic literature is highlighted when the *Chāndogya Upaniṣad* (7.2.1) speaks of a fifth Veda composed of legendary tales and ancient stories (*itihāsa-purāṇa*), in a dialogue between two figures who are themselves significant for the growth of the epic, Nārada and Sanatkumāra. This fluid mass of tales, which must have represented a tradition parallel to that of the Vedic literature rather than a part of it, in the case of the Mahābhārata

pp. 79–111 esp. p. 82). Incidentally it should be noted that H. Wirtz (*Die westliche Rezension des Rāmāyaṇa*, Bonn, 1894) is concerned with what is now called the NW. recension (first stated by W. Ruben, *Studien zur Textgeschichte des Rāmāyaṇa* (Bonner Orientalistische Studien 19), Stuttgart, 1936, pp. X and 43). Ruben's suggestion (pp. 1, 32–4) of dividing the S. recension into two sub-recensions does not seem warranted, although the uniformity of the S. recension is certainly not complete.

[4] For a convenient listing of the main divergences of content between the recensions see C. Bulcke, 'The Three Recensions of the Vālmīki Rāmāyaṇa', JORM 17, 1947–8, pp. 1–32 and 18, 1948–9, p. 191.

[5] Charlotte Vaudeville comments on the low status of *kuśīlavas* and suggests that the story of the birth of the *śloka* from Vālmīki's observation of a Niṣāda killing a *krauñca* (1.2) was prefixed to the epic as part of their claim to respectability ('Rāmāyaṇa Studies I: The Krauñca-vadha episode in the Vālmīki Rāmāyaṇa', JAOS 83, 1963, pp. 327–35).

gradually coalesced around the story of the war between the Kurus and the Pāṇḍavas, which may possibly have a basis in the situation in the Delhi area and northwards about 900 BC. Whether this process was due to the unifying influence of a single poet, Vyāsa, is more problematic. But the role of the Bhārgavas in its amplification and in particular its brahmanisation is clear enough.[6]

In the case of the Rāmāyaṇa the situation is rather different. The greater uniformity of the language compared with that of the Mahābhārata and the evidence of a compact vocabulary and style strongly suggest that the traditional ascription of the Rāmāyaṇa to Vālmīki is valid, in so far as it affirms that the core of the work was composed by a single individual; naturally there is no means of showing whether or not this was the Vālmīki of legend.[7] Vālmīki himself figures directly in the action of both the Bāla and Uttara kāṇḍas, at the beginning of the Bālakāṇḍa receiving inspiration to narrate the epic and in the Uttarakāṇḍa providing shelter for Sītā when she is abandoned by Rāma. He is however conspicuously absent from the other books. Efforts were made subsequently to remedy this supposed defect and so, for example, the Southern recension inserts a passage in which Rāma, Sītā and Lakṣmaṇa visit Vālmīki when first they go into the forest (2.1200*), introducing thus typically an inconsistency by locating Vālmīki's hermitage on mount Citrakūṭa and not on the river Tamasā as in the Bāla and Uttara kāṇḍas.

[6] Still in many respects the best study of the Mahābhārata is Hopkins' *Great Epic*. Modern studies include J. A. B. van Buitenen *tr.* and *ed.*, *The Mahābhārata* vols. 1–3, Chicago and London, 1973–8 and B. A. van Nooten, *The Mahābhārata*, New York, 1971. For an interesting survey of the development of the epics see O. Botto, 'Origini e Sviluppo dell'Epica Indiana', Accademia Nazionale dei Lincei, *Problemi attuali di scienza e di cultura*, quaderno n. 139, 1970, pp. 655–77. On the Bhārgavas see V. S. Sukthankar, 'Epic Studies VI. The Bhṛgus and the Bhārata: A Text-Historical Study', ABORI 18, 1936–7, pp. 1–76, also R. P. Goldman, *Gods, Priests, and Warriors: The Bhṛgus of the Mahābhārata*, New York, 1977.

[7] In speaking of the various layers of composition of the Rāmāyaṇa, I shall use the name Vālmīki to denote the original author of the Rāmāyaṇa, as contrasted with later reciters or interpolators, but this in itself implies no further assertion about the date and nature of the work than that the original appears to be traceable to one man, who no doubt used and to some extent incorporated older material in his epic. On the traditions concerning Vālmīki as a person, see C. Bulcke, 'About Vālmīki' and 'More about Vālmīki', JOIB 8, 1958–9, pp. 121–31 and 346–8; however A. Bloch, in 'Vālmīki und die Ikṣvākuiden', IIJ 7, 1963–4, pp. 81–123, questions the view, going back to Jacobi, that Vālmīki was the court poet of the Ikṣvāku dynasty, while E. Hofstetter on the basis of the story of the Niṣāda and the *krauñca* sees Vālmīki as a 'Lord of Animals' (*Der Herr der Tiere im alten Indien* (Freiburger Beiträge zur Indologie 14), Wiesbaden, 1980, pp. 97–9).

There can thus be no question of accepting the historicity of the story in its present amplified form; but there is still room for the possibility that there is a kernel of historical or semi-historical fact around which the epic has developed. Just as the Mahābhārata may reflect the political situation near the beginning of the first millennium BC, the Rāmāyaṇa might be based on actual conditions in the Gaṅgā basin slightly later. In fact, there has been, especially in the latter part of the nineteenth century, considerable controversy over the origin and influence of the Rāma story. Opinions put forward then include: influence from the poems of Homer advanced by Weber and rebutted by Telang; its interpretation by Henry as an allegorical narration of a solar myth; by Lassen, and following him Weber, as an allegorical representation of the Aryans' first attempt to conquer South India; and by Jacobi as a transposition of Vedic mythology about Indra.[8]

More recently, the theories of Georges Dumézil have been brought to bear on the Mahābhārata and to a much lesser extent on the Rāmāyaṇa. Dumézil himself has seen underlying both the Mahābhārata and the Scandinavian *Ragnarök* an ancient eschatological conflict played out in three phases: a rigged game by which Evil triumphs for a lengthy period displacing the representatives of Good, a great battle in which the Good takes revenge and decisively eliminates the Evil, and the government of the Good.[9] In such general terms, this analysis could almost as well be applied to the Rāmāyaṇa, for there is undoubtedly an element of trickery or the deceitfulness of fate in the claiming of Kaikeyī's boons. Dumézil has also drawn attention to the three Rāmas known in Indian tradition, suggesting a possible trifunctional relationship between the brāhman Paraśurāma, the kṣatriya Rāma Dāśarathi and the plough-bearing Balarāma with his obvious

[8] A. Weber, *Uber das Rāmāyaṇa*, Berlin, 1870, and K. T. Telang, *Was the Rāmāyaṇa copied from Homer? A reply to Professor Weber*, Bombay, 1873 (A. Lillie, *Rama and Homer*, London, 1912, argues the contrary thesis that Homer found the theme of his poems in the Sanskrit epics); V. Henry, *Les Littératures de l'Inde*, Paris, 1904, pp. 162–7; C. Lassen, *Indische Alterthumskunde*, 2nd ed., Leipzig, 1866–74, vol. 1, pp. 647–8 and vol. 2, pp. 501–6; Jacobi, *Das Râmâyaṇa*, pp. 130–9 (rejected by W. Pax, 'Zum Rāmāyaṇa', ZDMG 90, 1936, pp. 616–25, in favour of European parallels for Sītā's abduction). To these could be added the view of it by J. Talboys Wheeler as the struggle of the Buddhists of Ceylon overwhelmed by brahmanic reaction (*The History of India from the earliest ages*, vol. 2, London, 1869, pp. 227–34). But even more fanciful views have been put forward, such as the identification of Rāma as Rameses II, Sītā as Sit-amon, sister of Akhenaton, and Rāvaṇa as a Hittite ruler (Malladi Venkata Ratnam, *Rāma, the Greatest Pharaoh of Egypt*, 2 vols., Rajahmundry, 1934).

[9] See G. Dumézil, *Les dieux des Germains*, Paris, 1959, p. 89 and *Mythe et épopée* I, Paris, 1968, p. 227, also A. Hiltebeitel, *The Ritual of Battle*, Ithaca, 1976, p. 301.

agricultural links, who furthermore appear in this order.[10] Heino Gehrts sees the Rāmāyaṇa as based on the oriental form of the folk-tale motif of two brothers and one bride (the role of one brother leading to death, of the other to marriage), where the bride is abducted and later freed, a sequence of events equivalent in meaning to the loss and recovery of royal power in the consecration rituals of the *rājasūya* and *aśvamedha*.[11] He holds that the ritual meaning of the tale is confirmed by the sacrificial imagery of the epic but there seems very little basis for this notion of a ritual of brotherhood; in addition it requires him to consider that two of the four brothers are a later addition—a drastic simplification of the story, though admittedly one made in an extra-Indian folk version of the Rāma story. In general, it does seem that such transformational interpretations are more readily applicable to the developed stages of the epic than to its origins.[12] Basically I would support the view propounded for other epic poetry also that myth is a final stage in the development of a hero, whose historicity and particularity are transmuted in the popular memory into a mythical and universal form.

Such divergence of view has been accompanied by equal dispute about its dating. Weber placed the date of its composition as late as the third or fourth century AD, whereas Jacobi considered that the core must be before the fifth century BC, probably between the eighth and sixth centuries. Keith's view was that the poem probably belonged to the sixth century BC and Macdonell suggested that its kernel was composed before 500 BC, while the more recent parts were not added till the second century BC or later. More recent estimates have inclined to be somewhat lower. Thus, Bulcke suggests a date towards the end of the fourth century BC, or less probably in the third, Gonda suggests the fourth century BC for its origin and the second century AD as its closing date, Grintser suggests for both epics a period of formation approximately from the fourth century BC to the third century AD, and Guruge simply places it somewhere before 300 BC. However Bhargava, after a re-examination of earlier views, proposes a dating of 600 BC.[13]

[10] Op. cit. p. 113. Jacobi had already of course speculated on the relationship of the three Rāmas, seeing it in their links with ploughing (*Das Râmâyaṇa*, pp. 134–5). For an attempt to discern elements of Dumézil's tripartite structure in the Rāmāyaṇa, see M. Molé, 'Deux notes sur le Rāmāyaṇa', *Homages à Georges Dumézil*, Bruxelle, 1960, pp. 140–50.

[11] H. Gehrts, *Rāmāyaṇa*: *Brüder und Braut im Märchen-Epos*, Bonn, 1977.

[12] Gehrts does in fact see his original ritual brotherhood as further developed ethically during the epic and thus the true brotherhood of the Rāghavas as a contrast to the other pairs of fratricidal brothers and, less plausibly, to the Pāṇḍava brothers in the Mahābhārata.

[13] See also A. B. Keith, 'The Date of the Rāmāyaṇa', JRAS 1915, pp. 318–28, A. A.

One thing that has been generally agreed upon is that the first and last books are later additions. There has also been a growing awareness that the original poem, contained in books 2–6, has over the centuries undergone alterations and additions. The bards who recited it from memory, responding to the expectations of their audience, felt the need to embellish and complete the original story with the insertion of episodes, descriptive digressions, praise of local deities and sacred places, and with geographical descriptions. The majority of the additions to the core are repetitions of events, of pathetic passages or additions of marvellous and supernatural deeds. A good deal of this material has been excluded from the Critical Edition on purely textual grounds and some even had been recognised as interpolated (*prakṣipta*) by the commentators who, between the twelfth and eighteenth centuries, wrote commentaries on the Southern recension explaining any difficulties of language or vocabulary and indicating the religious significance of the text.[14] There have also been attempts by most of the scholars just mentioned to distinguish such passages on criteria—sometimes rather subjective—of relevance, or consistency, or relationship to other versions of the Rāma story, or the degree of development of the narrative, in its transformation from an originally heroic epic into a Vaiṣṇava work. It is worth stressing that, far from being a Vaiṣṇava epic, Vālmīki's Rāmāyaṇa is no religious epic at all. It is lamentable that misunderstanding of this point (often perhaps attributable to oversimplification rather than downright error) should still persist so long after Hermann Jacobi's explicit declaration, which may be paraphrased thus:

Rāma's deification and identification with Viṣṇu are constantly present in the mind of the poet of the first and last books. But in the five genuine books, apart

Macdonell, *A History of Sanskrit Literature*, London, 1900, p. 309, C. Bulcke, *Rāmkathā* (*utpatti aur vikāś*), 2nd ed., Prayāg, 1962, pp. 27–47, 138–51, and 'The Rāmāyaṇa; its history and character,' *Poona Orientalist* 25, 1960, pp. 36–60, J. Gonda, *Die Religionen Indiens I* (*Die Religionen der Menschheit II*), 2nd ed., Stuttgart, 1978, p. 220, Grintser, *Epos*, pp. 136–52, A. Guruge, *The Society of the Rāmāyaṇa*, Maharagama, 1960, p. 38, and P. L. Bhargava, *The Date of Vālmīki's Rāmāyaṇa* (Rajasthan University Studies 1), Jaipur, 1965.

[14] In general, the commentators endeavoured to interpret the text to their contemporaries, presumably relying quite often on such a tradition of interpretation for their views. For information on both extant and lost commentaries see G. H. Bhatt, 'Rāmāyaṇa Commentaries', JOIB 14, 1964–5, pp. 350–61 and Uttarakāṇḍa Appendix III, also V. Raghavan, 'Uḍāli's commentary on the Rāmāyaṇa: the date and identification of the author and the discovery of his commentary', AORM 7.2, 1943, pp. 1–8 and W. Ruben, *Studien zur Textgeschichte des Rāmāyaṇa* (Bonner Orientalistische Studien 19), Stuttgart, 1936, pp. 2–33, who includes some remarks on Lokanātha, the only extant N. commentator (on NE.), not utilised by the Critical Edition.

from a few interpolated passages, this concept is absent and by contrast Rāma is thoroughly human. Such a transformation of Rāma's character could only have taken place over a long span of time.[15]

Such a transformation is operative not only with regard to Rāma's character but also with regard to Sītā's portrayal, for instance, the question of her birth, and to many other features of the story.

Rāma develops from the ideal figure of the dutiful son and prince through the embodiment of dharma to the stage ultimately of identification as an *avatāra* of Viṣṇu found regularly in the Bāla and Uttara kāṇḍas, though not constantly as Jacobi implies. This development will be taken up again subsequently and need not be elaborated on here. However, to a lesser extent it is accompanied by a similar process of mythologisation in respect of several of the other characters, the most obvious of which is the question of Sītā's parentage. From within the Rāmāyaṇa itself, there is absolutely no warrant for supposing that Sītā is the daughter of Rāvaṇa or the sister of Rāma or the like, as she is presented in certain other versions.[16] Only two views are possible: either she is the daughter of Janaka and his wife or she was found in his furrow by Janaka as he was ploughing. Both views can be supported by a number of references, but they are obviously incompatible and some explanation must be found. Adherence to the view of Sītā as foundling involves dismissing the references to normal parentage as mere accidental lapses by the poet or reciter. While this is certainly possible, though hardly flattering to either, the number of such references is against it and especially their tendency to occur mainly in earlier parts, whereas the foundling references occur more often later.[17] This strongly suggests that the story of Sītā in the furrow is a later development, which no doubt was influenced by the etymology of the name and by the fact that the minor Vedic goddess was especially associated with Indra.[18]

[15] *Das Râmâyaṇa*, p. 65. See further in chapter 7. For a contrary view see R. Antoine, *Rāma & the Bards*: *Epic Memory in the Ramayana*, Calcutta, 1975, who questions whether the poem was ever without its religious outlook and sees its compilers as the authors of the introduction to the Bālakāṇḍa producing a consciously literary work and fathering their efforts onto Vālmīki; he even sees the major figures as temporal representations of the Hindu triad: Rāvaṇa and Vibhīṣaṇa of Brahmā, Rāma of Viṣṇu and Indrajit of Śiva (p. 76). In fact, later mythologising tends to link Rāvaṇa with Śiva.

[16] The development of the Rāma story both within and beyond India will be surveyed in chapters 8 and 9.

[17] However, later texts can still refer to Sītā as born; for example the *Vāmana Purāṇa* speaks of her as born in king Janaka's house (*tato jātā gṛhe rājño janakasya mahātmanaḥ / sītā nāmeti vikhyātā rāmapatnī pativratā, Saromāhātmya* 16.10).

[18] On this last point, cf. Gonda, *Early Viṣṇuism*, p. 29. More generally, see C. Bulcke, 'La naissance de Sītā', BEFEO 46, 1952, pp. 107–17. In a later development still, the N. recension adds to Sītā's account of herself to Anasūyā that Janaka saw the Apsaras

Similarly Hanumān, who is regularly called the son of the wind (*vāyuputra, mārutātmaja*) as a metaphor for his speed and legerdemain, is provided at the end of the Kiṣkindhākāṇḍa with an elaborate story of how he was born to Añjanā, the wife of Kesarin, raped by Vāyu.[19] Rāvaṇa too, originally a relatively obscure figure, had to be made commensurate in stature with his opponent as Rāma increased in significance. Thus his titles or names, Daśagrīva and Daśānana, 'ten-necked' and 'ten-headed', originally also perhaps metaphorical for his strength, are taken more literally and he is described as having not only ten heads but twenty arms. The inconsistency between allusions to one or ten heads, two or twenty arms appears present throughout, but the stress on his supernatural abilities certainly tends to be later.[20]

Thus it can be seen that the questions of the dating, nature and significance of the Rāmāyaṇa are all inter-related. With the increasing religious significance of the work comes also its increasing adaptation to brāhman values, possibly under the influence of those same Bhārgavas responsible for the transformation of the Mahābhārata into its present encyclopaedic form.[21] But our understanding of the precise mechanisms involved and our interpretation of the information which the epic can provide on many aspects of the culture is obviously dependent on an accurate and reliable discrimination of the successive stages of growth and adaptation which the work has undergone. While many attempts have already been made to do this, the problem has been that a particular view of the work's evolution has been adopted and the evidence viewed in the light of it. In order to avoid the pitfalls involved in this type of approach, our analysis will start from an examination of the text itself, from a study of its language and style, to which we shall turn in the next chapter.

Menakā flying over, and being childless wished for a child by her, who is Sītā (2.2385* and 2388*).

[19] Cf. C. Bulcke, 'The Characterization of Hanuman', JOIB 9, 1959–60, pp. 393–402.

[20] There have been various explanations propounded for Rāvaṇa's ten heads. S. N. Batra ('Daśagrīva or Daśānana of the Rāmāyaṇa (The Ten-Headed Rāvaṇa)', JOIB 23, 1973–4, pp. 40–53) suggests the use of skulls and masks as helmets in explanation of other Rākṣasa names as well, while T. Goudriaan has incidentally pointed out that Rāvaṇa is not necessarily associated with the number ten in popular tradition ('Khaḍga-Rāvaṇa and his worship in Balinese and Indian tantric sources', WZKSA 21, 1977, pp. 143–69). A. Wurm (*Character-Portrayals in the Rāmāyaṇa of Vālmīki; a systematic representation*, Delhi, 1976, p. 246 n.) suggests that the confusion goes back to Vālmīki.

[21] So N. J. Shende, 'The Authorship of the Rāmāyaṇa', *Journal of the University of Bombay* 12, 1943, pp. 19–24. Certainly the term Bhārgava occurs twenty times in the Bāla and Uttara kāṇḍas but only twice in the earlier books (at 2.102.16a and 6.4.42d, both in fact later passages); it is also frequent in the * passages, where Vālmīki himself is termed a Bhārgava (7.1328* 2).

2
COMPOSITION

'I will use ordinary cultivated language. If I declaim like a brāhman, Sītā will be afraid, thinking me Rāvaṇa.'
(5.28.17c–18)

A complete description of the linguistic features of the core of the epic is therefore the best starting point for a proper analysis of the work. Since the Bāla and Uttara kāṇḍas are generally recognized as later additions, the first task is to examine the core books 2–6, after which the features in them can be compared to those in the first and last books. However, to anticipate the conclusions which will be drawn in the later part of this chapter, it is apparent that the core books do not display everywhere the unity which might be expected if they were the work of one man, although in general they do show a uniform and homogeneous language and style. Pāṇini's grammar, which has become the norm for classical Sanskrit, provides by its completeness of description a convenient shorthand method of indicating the distinctive features of any other form of the language, which may be noted simply as divergences from his analysis. This method will therefore be followed here but it is not intended to imply thereby that the language of the Rāmāyaṇa is simply an aberration from Pāṇinian norms or that Vālmīki must or should have conformed to those norms.[1] The intention is

[1] I cannot therefore accept as it stands the approach of L. A. van Daalen (*Vālmīki's Sanskrit*), who starts from the assumption that Vālmīki wrote 'correct' Sanskrit, discounts every divergence from Pāṇini with less than effectively total manuscript support, and, having thus disposed of the evidence, concludes by reaffirming his postulate. The pattern of transmission is just not that simple. Van Daalen assumes that Vālmīki wrote Pāṇinian Sanskrit and that irregular features are usually attributable to copyists; he therefore castigates what he calls the 'polishing-theory' (the assumption that some mss. show a form of the text which is grammatically more correct than the original) and suggests that those who accept it have no rational grounds for doing so. But in fact it is well known that for instance the text of the *Ṛgveda* is presented in an occasionally metrically impossible form just because later practice with regard to sandhi and orthography have been followed. Surely it is methodologically preferable to assume that the majority of mss. have the correct i.e. original reading, until there is some evidence to controvert the assumption, than to assume that a Pāṇinian form, even if found in only a small minority of mss., is inherently superior and original.

simply to note as briefly and simply as possible the characteristic linguistic features of the Rāmāyaṇa as they are apparent in the text presented by the Critical Edition.

The number of verbal roots employed in each of these books is somewhat over three hundred (for example 353 in the Ayodhyākāṇḍa and 305 in the Araṇyakāṇḍa) but the number used at all frequently in each is around two hundred (for example, 233 in the Ayodhyākāṇḍa and 190 in the Araṇyakāṇḍa occur more than three times).[2] The roots used are substantially the same throughout, with no more than 7% being exclusive to any one book. Many of the infrequent roots occur only in the form of past participles passive, which is the form of the verb from which the widest range of roots is found (typically 70% of those occurring). Moreover, the distribution of some of these infrequent roots is very uneven (e.g. √*van* at 2.10.5d, 88.25c, 27a[l.v.] and 89.15c), while several occur also not infrequently in * passages, suggesting that in many instances they belong to a later stage of the language. Roots are regularly compounded with up to two preverbs but the only example of a root doubly compounded with the same preverb is supplied by √*viś* with *upa*, found only occasionally. Compounds with three preverbs are rare and always include *sam*, usually first; however, their distribution again indicates that they belong on the whole to a more developed stage of the language, as indeed their nature would suggest.[3] Certain moods and tenses tend to use a different proportion of compound verbs from the average. The imperative and perfect in particular tend to use a much higher proportion of simple verbs, presumably because the definition implied by the use of preverbs is alien to the spirit of the imperative and is rendered unnecessary by the inclusiveness of the perfect. Conversely, the past participle passive shows a high proportion of forms from compound verbs (especially with more than one preverb), compensating perhaps for its loss of verbal character.

[2] Fuller details on this section can be found in my article VS, a complete description of the verbal system of the Ayodhyā and Araṇya kāṇḍas with further examples from the other books. It also contains full bibliographic information, to which may now be added Nilmadhav Sen, 'Irregular Treatment of the Augment in the Rāmāyaṇa', *S. K. De Memorial Volume*, ed. R. C. Hazra and S. C. Banerji, Calcutta, 1972, pp. 268–73. The Ayodhyā and Araṇya kāṇḍas will usually be cited as examples; besides being the first two books of the nucleus of the work, they represent approximately its range of lengths. The Araṇya and Kiṣkindhā kāṇḍas are the shortest with around 2000 *ślokas* each, while the two longest books are the Ayodhyā and Yuddha kāṇḍas with over 3000 and 4000 respectively.

[3] For example, in the Ayodhyākāṇḍa two-thirds of such forms occur in sargas which I shall suggest are later.

There is some divergence from classical norms in the use of voice, although the Rāmāyaṇa is less free in this respect than the Mahābhārata. In general, the *ātmanepada* is more frequent, especially in participial forms, often with no real difference of meaning, since the same verb may often be used in either the *parasmaipada* or the *ātmanepada*, sometimes within a very short space. But there are also instances where the reflexive sense of the *ātmanepada* is present, and there is also some variation between the moods and tenses in this respect: for instance √*gam* occurs only in the active in the indicative tenses but the middle is also used in the imperative. This difference in use of voice is evenly spread throughout and thus seems part of the original epic usage.[4] There are also sporadic instances of change of conjugation, of confusion of strong and weak stems of √*brū*, and of transference of verbal stem. Infrequently, a multiple subject occurs with a singular verb but is usually of the additive type, where the verb follows a singular noun and the remainder of the subject may better be regarded as a further clause with ellipse of its verb.[5] In the first person plural (and occasionally dual) of the present and future indicative, the secondary endings instead of the primary are not uncommon, especially in the future and in the present of √*as* (where *sma* is actually commoner than *smaḥ*). There are also some instances where what is formally a first person plural of the present indicative could be translated as an imperative, but this is a matter of usage rather than of inflection.

The present indicative is the commonest of the finite verbal forms, although the past tenses are more frequent in aggregate; this tense shows a wider spread of roots used than any other except the past participle passive, and one common root, √*arh*, occurs only in the present indicative. There is some variation in its frequency between the books depending on their subject-matter. It is also used occasionally, either with the particle *sma* or without any such indication, to indicate a past tense.[6] The present imperative is rather less than half as frequent as the indicative, and the commonest form, *paśya*, is often

[4] Indeed, there is some evidence that forms divergent from Pāṇini are more frequent in the earlier parts. Although van Daalen seeks to exclude all non-Pāṇinian forms from the text, he hesitates—rightly in view of the evidence—before deciding in most cases to exclude such 'cases of irregular voice' (*Vālmīki's Sanskrit*, pp. 186–8).

[5] The two exceptions in the Ayodhyā and Araṇya kāṇḍas (at 2.2.23 and 3.10.8) are undoubtedly late.

[6] In the Ayodhyā and Araṇya kāṇḍas the present indicative with *sma* in a past sense occurs 17 and 5 times respectively, and without such indication 8 and 12 times respectively, out of 1115 and 678 occurrences in total; there are also two instances of the present with *sma* in a present sense in later parts of the Ayodhyākāṇḍa.

just an exclamation. Most imperatives are found in simple form or with one preverb, in line with the directness of the mood, but reiterated imperatives occur sporadically, with an emotional or intensive force. The second person forms are much the commonest but among the third person forms a substantial proportion are passive, in contrast to the extensive occurrence of the active in the infrequent first person forms. The optative is again only about half as frequent as the imperative; from both moods a higher proportion are found in the Ayodhyākāṇḍa as a result of the relatively more extensive dialogue there. Divergences from the Pāṇinian norms are most infrequent in both moods, of which the usage is also regular. There are two-thirds as many present participles as indicatives, with active forms over three times as common as middle and only a small number of passive forms. There are a number of instances of the use of *-antī* to form the feminine stem where Pāṇini gives *-atī*, and *vice versa*; obviously, the language of the Rāmāyaṇa is much less restricted in this matter. Similarly, the use of *-āna* for *-māna* is frequently extended from the athematic conjugations to tenth class and causative verbs, a feature shared with the Mahābhārata.

The simple future is slightly less frequent than the present imperative and is similar to it in that uncompounded forms are more frequent than in other indicative tenses, with a few common roots providing a high proportion of the total. The tense shows similar variation in frequency due to subject-matter to the present indicative. There are numerous divergences from Pāṇini's description with regard to the use of the union-vowel *-i-*; the use of both *seṭ* and *aniṭ* forms from the same root is found, for example *nayiṣyati* and *neṣyati*. However, the forms *nayiṣyati* and the like begin to appear from the *Jaiminīya Brāhmaṇa* onwards and occur also in the Mahābhārata. Another variation from classical usage is the occurrence of *vadhiṣyati* to the exclusion of *haniṣyati* (cf. Pāṇini 2.4.42–3). There is also a tendency towards the use of the middle in the future, but this tendency is not confined to the epic language. The periphrastic future is extremely uncommon in these books, apart from the Ayodhyākāṇḍa, but is less rare in the Bāla and Uttara kāṇḍas and in * passages.[7] However, four-fifths of the instances in the Ayodhyākāṇḍa occur in the first 27 sargas and the rest of the book shows a similar scarcity of the form to the other books. Almost all

[7] There are 7 periphrastic futures in the Bālakāṇḍa, 20 in the Ayodhyākāṇḍa (16 in 2.1–27), 2 each in the Araṇya and Sundara kāṇḍas, 4 in the Kiṣkindhākāṇḍa, 6 in the Yuddhakāṇḍa and 14 in the Uttarakāṇḍa; the proportionate figure for the Bāla and Uttara kāṇḍas would be 11 (or about 7 if the early part of the Ayodhyākāṇḍa is discounted) against the 21 actually occurring.

the forms occurring are from simple verbs; for example, in the Ayodhyākāṇḍa the only exceptions are *abhiṣektā* and *abhiṣecayitā* (twice), in which the compound has a highly specific meaning. The future participle is even rarer and the imperative of the future (a form almost confined to the epics) occurs only once each in the Bāla, Araṇya, Kiṣkindhā and Uttara kāṇḍas.

The three past tenses are used without any real distinction with regard to duration of action or result; any two or occasionally all three are found used together in a single context. Nor are the classical restrictions about the employment of the different past tenses in situations of varying actuality observed with any regularity; thus, there are several occurrences of the first person perfect which ignore the Pāṇinian rule that it may only be used when the speaker wishes to make an emphatic denial or cannot recall the past event or action owing to some mental distraction. If there is any real distinction in use, it is in which roots occur in which form of the preterite, since, although many roots are found with more than one past tense, usually one form is much commoner. The causative and denominative conjugations rely on the periphrastic perfect and, to a lesser extent, on the imperfect for preterite forms. Unaugmented forms of both the imperfect and aorist occur; in the case of the imperfect these are used in a preterite sense and in the case of the aorist they are used with *mā* to form a prohibition.[8]

The least frequent of the past tenses is the aorist, especially if the unaugmented forms with *mā*, which amount to roughly a quarter of its occurrences, are discounted. It is formed from a limited number of roots and the rare examples of the reduplicated aorist are causative in sense, in contrast to the usage of the Mahābhārata. The imperfect is substantially more frequent but forms from √*brū*, 'to say', preponderate, comprising over a third of the total occurrences. The perfect is the commonest past tense and, although *uvāca* and its compounded forms are frequent, they do not comprise so high a proportion of the total as *abravīt* does of the imperfect. For metrical reasons, the third person plural of the middle is favoured. Use of strong verbal stem rather than weak in the third person dual or plural is extremely rare in the text but there are numerous instances in the * passages. Almost as uncommon are instances of middle forms with passive meanings. The periphrastic perfect functions simply as the perfect for tenth class and

[8] There is one exception to each in the Ayodhyākāṇḍa: an augmented imperfect with *mā* at 2.9.16cd and an unaugmented aorist in a preterite sense at 2.81.15a. There are also instances of a prohibition with *mā* and an augmented aorist in the Bālakāṇḍa (1.2.14ab) and in Kiṣkindhākāṇḍa (4.29.48d = 33.18d), a usage which is not uncommon in the Mahābhārata. Otherwise the distinction is completely observed.

causative verbs, which cannot make the simple perfect, and the auxiliary is almost invariably *āsa*. The perfect participle active is uncommon but even so several forms functioning as finite verbs fall outside the limitations of Pāṇini 3.2.108–9. However, a substitute made from the past participle passive with *-vat* is a little more common in the text (with 54 occurring in books 2–6, although many are attested in the Southern recension only) and becomes much commoner in the * passages; these forms also sometimes function as finite verbs.

Among the non-finite forms, the past participle passive is by far the commonest—it is indeed much the most frequent verbal form. But many of its occurrences are entirely adjectival, while in others it retains its full verbal significance, and many lie somewhere in between. Forms occur from a particularly wide range of roots, some of which appear only in this form; many are found with the negative prefix and there are no seriously anomalous forms. The past participle passive is very frequently used appositionally and is quite frequently so used to link the action of one sentence with another, picking up the main verbal idea in the previous sentence. It is also used instead of a finite verb or sporadically as one accompanied by an auxiliary; the latter feature is restricted to certain passages.

The absolutive is about half as frequent as the past participle passive. There is a tendency towards complementary distribution for a given root of its absolutive and past participle, which share between them the function of linking sentences. The major feature of its formation is the tendency to the use of the *-ya* ending for simple verbs and conversely of *-tvā* for compound verbs, especially causatives and tenth class verbs; *gṛhya* in particular is not uncommon.[9] The negative prefix, though found, is less common than with the past participle. Although the absolutive is generally verbal in sense, a few forms have come to act virtually as prepositions.

There are about one fifth as many gerundives as absolutives. Many of them, especially those formed with *-ya*, have become entirely adjectival. Gerundives can be used instead of finite verbs, normally replacing *arhati* + infinitive, but this usage is not frequent, for not only

[9] Van Daalen devotes a section of his book (*Vālmīki's Sanskrit* § 6, 18, pp. 214–22) to the question of irregular gerunds, laying stress on the fact that, whereas some mss. usually have variants for *gṛhya* which is grammatically incorrect according to Pāṇinian norms, in most cases variants for the regular form *gṛhītvā* were lacking. But this is just what might be expected from transmission by grammatically well-trained copyists; the normalising tendency must have been strong. Moreover, the predominance of *gṛhya* and to a lesser extent *uṣya* both in the Rāmāyaṇa and in the Mahābhārata suggests that this is a genuine feature.

is the gerundive mainly adjectival but in many, though not all, cases it has lost its obligatory sense.

The infinitive is of much the same frequency as the gerundive. Almost half the total are dependent on *icchati* or *arhati* and most of the remainder are dependent on various other verbs; infinitives dependent on adjectives and those to be construed with the whole sentence are rare. Apart from the not infrequent *seṭ* and *aniṭ* variants, irregularities of formation are very rare.[10]

Agent nouns are rare, except for *bhartṛ*, the relative frequency of which is due to the specialisation of sense. As with the periphrastic future formed from it, the distribution of the agent noun tends to be concentrated in certain sargas.

Among the secondary conjugations, the passive is about a third as frequent as the causative. The frequency of the past participle passive helps to explain the smaller number of finite forms, but it is also noteworthy that over a quarter of them are third person singular imperatives, commonly used impersonally without any agent expressed but having to be inferred from context. The only anomalies of the passive are instances of forms with active endings, but these are most infrequent; there is also one instance of a passive form used in an active sense (*paricaryāmahe*, 5.33.24c).

The causative is much the most frequently employed of the secondary conjugations and examples of it are found from all the more commonly occurring roots that admit such an extension of their meaning; it is especially frequent in the form of the past participle passive. Although the reduplicated aorist and the periphrastic perfect are linked with the causative, the imperfect is commoner than either. This tendency towards the imperfect no doubt results from avoidance of undue complication and accords well with the character of the causative as a conjugation markedly free from irregularities of form. However, very occasionally a causative formation seems not to have any causative meaning and conversely a causative meaning is required for a simple form. The use of causative formations with the meaning of the simple form is not unknown at any period of the language.

Verbal forms from desiderative bases are slightly more frequent than desiderative nouns or adjectives, but desiderative forms are nonetheless a rare feature, and the commonest desiderative base is *śuśrūṣā* which has achieved greater currency by developing a specialised

[10] For example, in the Ayodhyā and Araṇya kāṇḍas there are only *viṣīditum* at 2.98.43d (cf. *avasīditum* 5.1.77d and Mbh. 4.27.6c), *baddhum* at 3.53.24b, *pratikūlitum* at 3.23.12a and *dhāritum* at 3.51.20c, the last two of which are probably causative forms with loss of a syllable for metrical reasons.

sense. The number of roots from which desiderative forms are made is very restricted and there are no anomalies, not unexpectedly with a form so nearly aritificial in use. A quasi-desiderative adjective of the type *vaktukāma* is also found, even from roots making a true desiderative, and in addition the form *bhoktumanas* occurs once; these forms are rather more than half as frequent as the true desiderative adjective.[11] Inevitably the distribution of all desiderative forms is patchy but again there is a marked concentration in the first thirty sargas of the Ayodhyākāṇḍa.

Intensive forms are extremely rare, if one excludes *jāgṛ*, which appears to be felt as an independent base, in view of the wide spread of its forms and especially the occurrence of a form showing change of conjugation (*anvajāgrat* at 2.44.26c). One adjectival form, *lālasa*, has also in reality become an independent form. Otherwise, the few forms occurring are almost all present participles. Finally, the denominative is of such rare occurrence as to play no significant role in the verbal system, apart from those stems which are clearly denominative in origin though no longer classified as such.

The declension of nominal forms presents few remarkable features and, as is the case at all periods of Sanskrit literature, the main feature is the extent of nominal composition.[12] Instances of irregular declension are extremely rare, but there is occasional confusion between nominative and accusative plural. There are a certain number of instances of transfer of nominal stems, usually conditioned by metre, although the predominant direction of change is from consonant to vowel stems in accordance with a natural tendency towards simplification of the language. However, the occurrence also of shortening or lengthening of vowels in accordance with the requirements of the metre suggests that this is not simply Prakritisation. The largest number—though still small—are instances of the transfer of *-an*, *-as* and *-in* stems to vowel stems, but there are a few instances of the reverse process and such transfer is much commoner in the * passages than in the text.[13]

The enclitic forms of the first and second person pronouns are

[11] See further below, p. 27.

[12] Again, fuller details, including bibliographic information and complete lists of certain features, may be found in my article NS, of which this section presents the major features in a simpler form.

[13] This feature is therefore less frequent than has often been supposed by previous writers on the basis of older editions of the text. Transfer of *-us* stems to *-u* stems occurs in only two words: *avaṣṭabdhadhanum* at 3.24.1a and sporadically in the proper name Jaṭāyus, of which the *-us* forms are much better attested.

occasionally used for the oblique cases as well as the genitive and dative sanctioned by Pāṇini.[14] The use of *ātman* as a reflexive is quite frequent. Instances of geminated pronouns of pronominal bases of all types have the normal indefinite sense found at other stages of the language, but there is a tendency towards greater frequency of these geminated pronouns in later passages. Occasionally, the higher numerals agree in case with their substantives but other divergences from the classical pattern are extremely rare.

The syntax of the cases is also simple and basically regular and there is restricted use of prepositions or prepositional substitutes and of periphrases expressing case relations, indicating a comparatively unevolved stage of the language. The accusative of the object is of very wide extent; several verbs which are normally intransitive may take an object, usually with a slight difference in connotation, of which one form is the use of cognate accusatives. The double accusative with verbs of speaking and the like occurs quite often and entirely regularly, as does a double accusative with the causative of certain transitive verbs. The accusative of end of motion is not uncommon.

There are still some traces of the use of the unaccompanied instrumental in a sociative sense, although it is normally accompanied by some indicator. Use of the instrumental instead of the ablative of comparison is also found; this somewhat unexpected feature seems to be a survival from older forms of the language. Certain other idiomatic uses of the instrumental occur sporadically. The usage of both the dative and the ablative is very regular, although the dative of the aim or final dative is not infrequently paraphrased by other constructions. The genitive is widely used and in a few instances occurs instead of other cases, a first sign of its more general use as the main oblique case in later stages of the language. The genitive absolute, however, is much less frequent than the locative absolute. The locative, used basically to indicate the place where, is not uncommonly extended to indicate the place whither, and there occur also various other nuances of meaning. Although periphrastic expressions of case relations are also found, none of the idioms involved is at all common, with the possible exception of *artham* for the dative, any more than the use of absolutives in a prepositional sense is a regular feature. The use of adverbial suffixes with nouns as substitutes for case endings is, apart from a few common instances, largely confined to later passages. Thus

[14] These forms occur a number of times to express the agent with the past participle passive; since the genitive to express the agent of the passive voice does not otherwise occur, these are presumably instrumental.

it is clear that the cases in general retain their original functions, obviating the need for substitutes.

In the area of nominal composition the Rāmāyaṇa shows a relatively simple pattern and in many respects it holds an intermediate position between the Brāhmaṇas and early Sūtras on the one hand and the classical literature on the other. There are many minor divergences from Pāṇini's description, but these present the appearance of being dialectal variations rather than carelessness in conforming to accepted rules. The older portions of the Mahābhārata show much the same picture as the Rāmāyaṇa but its later parts approach more nearly the classical norm, though admitting many pseudo-archaisms and epicisms. The length of compounds is on the whole limited in comparison with the luxuriance later manifested and many of the larger compounds found occur also in the Mahābhārata, indicating that they belong to a stock of forms familiar to all. There is little trace in the earlier parts of any tendency to coin new compounds merely for the sake of displaying verbal dexterity. The metrical shortening of the final long vowel of the first member of a compound is an occasional feature, especially in words which thereby acquire a metrically more convenient form, but it is also very frequent in the Sūtras, and even in classical Sanskrit such shortening is found in the formation of technical terms.

Although the co-ordinative compounds, *dvandvas*, include some of the longest compounds, the great majority are of the oldest type with two members only. The Rāmāyaṇa does, however, show a certain proportion of multi-member *dvandvas*, unlike the older Upaniṣads from which such forms are almost completely absent.[15] It also shows a smaller proportion of *samāhāra dvandvas* than the early Upaniṣads but nevertheless retains a higher proportion than the Mahābhārata which, at least in its later parts, goes much further in eliminating *samāhāras* in favour of *itaretarayogas*. *Itaretarayoga dvandvas* fall into three main groups—gods and men, animals, objects—of which the first is the largest and most formalised, supplying many of the longest compounds found.

The large proportion of compounds with verbal roots as final member which are not in accord with Pāṇini's rules is a major aspect in which the language of the Rāmāyaṇa differs from that described by Pāṇini. The majority of the forms not provided for by Pāṇini are from √*dhṛ*, but are not otherwise remarkable in any particular; such forms occur also

[15] For these and other comparative figures from the Upaniṣads see W. Kirfel, *Beiträge zur Geschichte der Nominalkomposition in den Upaniṣads und im Epos*, Bonn, 1908. Kirfel surveys the Ayodhyā and Araṇya kāṇḍas only of the Rāmāyaṇa.

in the Mahābhārata but are virtually absent from the earlier Upaniṣads. The suffix *ṇini* (Pāṇini 3.2.51 and 78–86), producing forms such as *vanavāsin*, is an excellent example of a suffix which has a much wider application in the epic language than is allowed by Pāṇini, but there are many other instances of discrepancy between Pāṇini and the language of the Rāmāyaṇa among the compounds from verbal roots.

Among *tatpuruṣa* compounds, ablative *tatpuruṣas* are rare, while accusative and locative *tatpuruṣas* are not much more frequent, but nevertheless a number of forms, especially locative, fall outside Pāṇini's somewhat limiting rules for their formation. The most frequent final member of accusative *tatpuruṣas* is *gata*; a very few forms have a desiderative adjective as final member but their distribution indicates that the type is late. Dative *tatpuruṣas* are a little more frequent again, but forms with *artha* as final member supply over half the total number. Instrumental *tatpuruṣas* are fairly common. Most frequently the final member is a past participle passive and a very wide range of forms is found; the instrumental *tatpuruṣas* with nouns as the final member are rare (such forms are unusual in the Mahābhārata also). Genitive *tatpuruṣas* are by far the commonest form. A sizable number of forms ending with evaluative terms (*adhama, indra, uttama, mukhya, vara, śreṣṭha, sattama*) are found contrary to Pāṇini 2.2.10.[16] There are also a few instances of the objective genitive compounded with nouns in *-tṛ* and *-aka* (mostly not in accord with Pāṇini 2.2.16–17), but instances with agent nouns can be found from at least some of the Upaniṣads.

Karmadhāraya compounds may be divided for analysis into those with a noun as prior member, those with an adjective or numeral, and those with an adverb, preposition or negative particle. Forms such as *puruṣavyāghra* 'tiger among men', which have a metaphorical sense, are frequent, and another type with noun as prior member, that where the two members stand in apposition, is not uncommon, though technically irregular. Forms with an adjective as prior member present no major divergences, but many of those with a numeral are plural (whereas Pāṇini 2.4.1 allows only the singular). Various adverbial forms, especially *su-* and *dus-*, are compounded with both nouns and adjectives, but preposition and noun compounds are rare and compounds of preposition and adjective are confined to *ati*.

Genitive *bahuvrīhis* are by far the commonest form of *bahuvrīhi*, and indeed of any compound. The commonest form is that with an

[16] Three compounds only in the whole of the Ayodhyā and Araṇya kāṇḍas have an active participle as final member (excluded by Pāṇini 2.2.11), but they are grouped in the first few sargas of the Ayodhyākāṇḍa (2.2.14a, 14.2a, 16.60d), clearly indicating that the usage is not part of the original Rāmāyaṇa.

adjective or past participle passive as the prior member, such as *mahātman* or *viśālākṣa*; forms with a numeral as prior member are not infrequent; various adverbs are found as the prior member, and forms with the negative particle are also frequent. However the use of a gerundive as prior member, which appears to be pre-eminently a feature of Buddhist Sanskrit, is of very rare occurrence in the Rāmāyaṇa.[17]

Forms with a noun as prior member constitute a substantial group, with the members standing in a nominative, locative or genitive relationship. Within the first there is a very considerable class of what may be called *upamāna bahuvrīhis*, expressing a comparison. The simplest form of this is the type *padmākṣa*; in a very few the point of resemblance is included in the compound. The largest class, though, is that where the subject of the comparison lies outside the compound, as in *sūryavarṇa*. There is also a third type where the whole comparison is expressed in the compound with a word of comparison as the middle member; however, the distribution of these forms shows that they are commoner in the more ornate and less original passages. A special class consists of forms of which the first member is an infinitive, producing a quasi-desiderative adjective; these forms are an innovation in the language—they are absent from the Upaniṣads and not recognised by Pāṇini, though provided for by Kātyāyana (*vārtikas* 1–4 on Pāṇini 6.1.144).

Other types of *bahuvrīhi* are much less frequent than genitive forms. Instrumental *bahuvrīhis* with a past participle passive as first member are roughly two-fifths as frequent as the equivalent genitive type. However, instrumental forms theoretically include the common compounds with an initial *saha-* or *sa-*, such as *sahalakṣmaṇa* or *salakṣmaṇa*. Locative *bahuvrīhis* are infrequent, the majority having a past participle passive as prior member, while ablative forms are very rare. There also occur (with approximately the same frequency as locative *bahuvrīhis*) forms which have the same meaning as genitive or locative *bahuvrīhis*, made by the addition of the suffixes *-vat* or, more commonly, *-in*; similar are the forms with the suffix *-maya*.

The commonest *avyayībhāvas* are those with *yathā* as the prior member and other types are rare. Overall however the *avyayībhāva* compounds are only sporadic and the commonest type with *yathā*

[17] For example, only five instances (from three forms) occur in the Ayodhyā and Araṇya kāṇḍas, but a number are to be found in * passages. By contrast even such a brief—though admittedly late—passage of the Mahābhārata as the *Nalopākhyāna* has nine such forms. Even rarer, and also a later innovation, are *bahuvrīhis* with a present participle as prior member.

might equally be regarded as the adverbial use of a genitive *bahuvrīhi*.

Another method of making derivative formations is the use of *vṛddhi*. Its use in the formation of patronymics is an old-established feature of the language and certain common ones, such as *rāghava* and *vaidehī*, are very widely spread through the text, but others have a more restricted distribution. There is a tendency for other vṛddhied derivatives to occur in later passages,[18] and this appears especially true of forms where *vṛddhi* has been used in connection with a suffix. Probably again a distinction should be made between certain common forms occurring widely and other less frequent and predominantly later forms.

A more specialised feature of nominal composition consists of the long compounds, under which term I include all compounds of three members or more, excluding prepositions attached to verbal bases and *a*- privative but resolving compounds within compounds into their component parts. A high proportion of them are of pāda length or else combine with another word regularly to form a pāda-length phrase, and in this respect they share certain affinities with the stereotyped phrases discussed later; there is a tendency for a compound to be reused within a short space of its first appearance. The proportion of long compounds shows a steady increase from the Ayodhyākāṇḍa to the Sundarakāṇḍa, with the Yuddhakāṇḍa having almost exactly the mean proportion, whereas the Bāla and Uttara kāṇḍas have a similar proportion to each other, lower than the average for the other books.[19] While the increase in proportion may be due in part to differences of subject-matter, it is more likely that it is due to the greater amount of interpolated or reworked material present. In fact, it would support the view that, while the main portion of the Ayodhyākāṇḍa is in something like its original form, subsequent books have been greatly filled out by later narrators' liking for the supernatural and the exotic;

[18] For example, a fifth of all the vṛddhied derivatives in the Ayodhyā and Araṇya kāṇḍas occur in eight sargas (2.20, 65, 85 and 98, 3.8, 10, 15 and 60), and it is surely not coincidental that all of these eight are abnormal in other respects and in all probability subject to considerable interpolation.

[19] The exact figures are: the Ayodhyākāṇḍa shows a frequency equivalent to 28.24 long compounds in each 100 *śloka* stanzas (or 30.25 if verses in longer metres are included), the Araṇyakāṇḍa 34.63 per 100 *ślokas* (35.96% with longer verses), the Kiṣkindhākāṇḍa 40.26% (42.88%), the Sundarakāṇḍa 46.45% (51.83%), the Yuddhakāṇḍa 36.61% (42.62%), an average for these five books of 36.59% (40.47%), whereas the Bālakāṇḍa has 32.02% (32.68%) and the Uttarakāṇḍa 31.06% (32.61%). In addition to the increase in proportions due to inclusion of longer verses, it may be noted that the proportion of long compounds tends also to be higher in the N. recension than in the S. in their respective * passages.

certainly, the peak in the Sundarakāṇḍa is consistent with this. Within each book, there is substantial difference in proportions between individual sargas. There tends to be a scarcity of long compounds in narrative and unemphatic portions and deliberate employment of them in speeches (though not in conversations), descriptions and other passages of an emotional character.[20] There is also a subsidiary pattern visible in the relative elaboration of the beginnings and endings of the books. Some of the variation is due simply to difference of subject-matter, but some is due to the more elaborate styles of later authors adding to or reworking the text.

Naturally, many of these compounds occur only once, but there are a considerable number which are repeated exactly several times and are obviously stereotyped; in addition, there are a good many which vary only in the final member. Few compounds are as fixed as *nimeṣāntaramātreṇa* (*passim* in Rāmāyaṇa and Mahābhārata) but there are several which are obviously regularly used, of which a considerable proportion occur also in the Mahābhārata. Over one in ten of the long compounds occurring in the Rāmāyaṇa as a whole is paralleled exactly in the Mahābhārata and, since these include many of the commonest, the figure in proportion to occurrences rather than forms is about one in eight. About twice as many show close similarity and may be regarded as variant forms of the same basic expression common to both epics. Thus perhaps a third of all long compounds are in some degree standard formations rather than new creations. There is also a tendency to employ more than one of these long compounds in a single stanza, which both serves to emphasise the stereotyped nature of some of them and indicates the way in which some of these descriptive verses are built up out of ready-made units.

Another point which may be mentioned here is that in a few cases these long compounds exceed pāda length, thus causing the disappearance of the caesura; all instances of lack of break between pādas found in the text are so caused. The numbers involved are extremely small and tend to cluster in a way that implies a metrical innovation of the later stages only. There are four instances each in the Ayodhyā and Araṇya kāṇḍas (half in one sarga in each book, in 2.88 and 3.71), one only in the Kiṣkindhākāṇḍa, sixteen in the Sundarakāṇḍa (but five in the first sarga and three in each of sargas 7–8 and 54–5), and twelve in the Yuddhakāṇḍa (half of which are in sargas 60–3, including one in a

[20] Genealogies regularly produce low proportions of long compounds and, for example, 2.102, which consists largely of a genealogy, has less than half the average frequency for the book. This is a factor in the lower proportions for the Bāla and Uttara kāṇḍas. However, it is doubtful how far genealogies constituted part of the original epic.

longer verse at 6.60.7ab[l.v.]); for comparison, there are two instances in the Bālakāṇḍa and six in the Uttarakāṇḍa. The instances are very much associated with the sargas which have a high proportion of long compounds, belonging to the more ornate style of the second stage of the epic's growth.[21] There are of course numerous examples of such compounds exceeding eight syllables in longer verses (e.g. 14 in the Ayodhyākāṇḍa), which tend anyway to be more elaborate in style, but there is only the one example of a compound spanning pādas in a longer verse.

Those aspects of syntax which relate to the use of the various verbal forms and to the employment of cases have been briefly discussed already, but there are also some more general aspects of sentence construction worth noting.[22] There is a fairly uniform use of the relative forms in all situations, with a relative clause appearing in approximately one in six of all stanzas. However, a string of relative clauses in successive stanzas occurs as a type of stylistic device in a few passages, in some of which the relative clause has become so stylised as to form a refrain, while in others it is an emphatic device. Clauses following relative pronouns are somewhat more frequent than those following relative adverbs and conjunctions, but pronominal adjectives and certain similar forms are rare. The order of the relative and main clauses is inevitably freer than in prose, but nevertheless the general pattern of the relative clause preceding unless causal or consequential in character is observable. Similarly, the use of the demonstrative as a correlative is regular and almost obligatory with certain forms.[23]

The use of a doubled relative to express an indefinite sense is rare; somewhat commoner is the construction of the relative pronoun with *kaścid*, but often only the context indicates the indefinite sense. There is considerable use of *yad* as a causal conjunction, but compounds of *yad* are commoner in later passages, though never very frequent. The most frequent of the relative adverbs is *yathā*, but over half its occur-

[21] Nilmadhav Sen has surveyed long compounds of six or more members found in the Bombay Text ('The Vocabulary of the Rāmāyaṇa (III): Long Compounds', *Vāk* 5, 1957, pp. 142–6). Neither that list (as Sen acknowledges) nor therefore that of van Daalen specifically listing instances of lack of caesura between pādas (*Vālmīki's Sanskrit*, p. 76) is complete; to be added to the latter list (and some to Sen's also) are the instances at 5.7.41ab, 8.18cd, 12.23ab, 6.62.46ab, 7.32.22ab, 34cd, 36.2ab and 8ab.

[22] For fuller details on this section see my article *Syntax*.

[23] In a few instances the correlative does not have the same form as the relative, although such instances occur predominantly, if not exclusively, in later passages.

rences are to introduce similes and these are almost exclusively dependent on the main verb and are not separate clauses. Its use to express comparisons or the sense of 'according to' is about as frequent as that of *yadi*, which naturally is chiefly employed in the protasis of conditional sentences. The other relative adverbs or conjunctions are less common.

Questions are normally introduced by some form of the interrogative pronoun or occasionally an interrogative adjective; the use of *api* or the absence of any indicator are so rare as to be of no significance in any discussion of the use of interrogatives. The use of various particles with the interrogative is found occasionally and *cit* is quite frequent, especially in the form *kaccit*, which is often used in asking a general question and particularly a whole series of questions (as most notably in 2.94, often called the *kaccit* sarga). Compounds with an interrogative as the first member are not uncommon; a few have lost their interrogative meaning or have an indefinite sense, but all the *bahuvrīhi* compounds retain their interrogative meaning. As in the classical language, the use of interrogatives in rhetorical questions is an occasional idiom. The indefinite sense of the interrogative is normally marked by the addition of another particle, either *cit* or *cana*, but it also appears in compounds with *a-* privative, which are however uncommon.

Co-ordination, both between and within sentences, is regularly expressed by *ca*, but there is also relatively frequent use of the device whereby the verbal idea of the preceding sentence is repeated before adding the next statement; both absolutives and participles are employed for this purpose. Other types of anaphora are also sometimes used for linkage in this way. On occasion, however, parataxis is preferred to syntaxis, especially in questions, where the brevity thus achieved heightens their impact. Certainly, in cases where both positive and negative expressions of the same idea are given, parataxis tends to be preferred in order to bring out the antithesis. The use of *ca* with both parts of a closely linked pair is quite frequent, especially where this enhances the symmetry of the pāda, but less commonly asyndeton may be used or one final *ca*; instances of *ca* with each of three items are also found. It may be noted that all proverbial expressions show a marked predilection for asyndeton (a phenomenon by no means confined to Sanskrit). As a sentence copula, *ca* may rarely express an adversative sense. The connective particle *uta*, which is fairly frequent in the Mahābhārata, is rare in the Rāmāyaṇa and its few occurrences are mainly in later passages possibly influenced by the Mahābhārata.[24]

[24] It is found at 1.17.34b, 41.4f, 2.110.13d, 3.8.3b, 47.33b, 4.28.23d, 30.32d, 5.2.41d,

The use of *tathā* as a copula is confined to linking nouns. A common feature of the use of *vā* is the occurrence of *vā yadi vā* with pairs of opposites, giving within the pāda what is in effect a chiasmic order.

The particle used in the vast majority of cases to express antithesis is *tu*, but very occasionally *api* is used, and a stronger adversative sense is expressed by *kiṃ tu*. The causal particle is *hi*, which is extremely common but often of slight emphasis; if the causality needs to be stressed, then *yasmāt* ... *tasmāt* are used. Forms of the demonstrative are also used in a causal or conclusive sense. The emphatic particles commonly occurring are *eva* and *api* and all others are infrequent.[25] The commonest particle of exclamation is *hā*, and all others are rare, *bata* in particular being characteristic of later passages.

The negative particle *na* more commonly follows its verb and is not usually initial unless emphatic. The negative is regularly put with the first of two negative clauses only, but the use of *na* after each of two or more substantives with the meaning 'neither ... nor' is a regular feature.

The Rāmāyaṇa employs generally a direct verbal construction, but it is always possible for an absent auxiliary or copula to be understood and it is not uncommon for the verbal idea of a sentence to be expressed by a past participle passive or other predicatively used attribute. This is even possible when there is strong emphasis placed on such a word, and there also sometimes occurs a whole string of such clauses. Sometimes, however, an auxiliary is used with the past participle passive, although instances of this and other verbal periphrases tend to come from later passages. Thus, with regard to the sentence construction as well as to other aspects of the language, it is clear that the earlier parts of the Rāmāyaṇa were composed in what is basically a simple, straightforward style, although certain more complex constructions become more frequent in later parts of the text.

The style of the Rāmāyaṇa is also relatively undeveloped, particularly by comparison with classical Sanskrit, despite its frequently being termed the *ādikāvya*.[26] The more sophisticated *alaṃkāras* are largely

40.6d and 7.31.3a. For the frequency of various particles in the Mahābhārata see B. A. van Nooten, 'Redundancy in Mahābhārata Verse Composition', JAOS 89, 1969, pp. 50–8.

[25] In order of diminishing frequency they are: *nūnam, khalu, vai, kila, nāma* and *jātu*; they tend to be commoner in later passages. The particle *ha*, in origin emphatic, is used in the Rāmāyaṇa solely to fill out a line after a perfect tense.

[26] Fuller details on this section can be found in my article FS; comparisons with the Mahābhārata both in that article and here are based mainly on Ram Karan Sharma,

absent. Similes are the commonest figure and, as befits a poem belonging to the oral poetic tradition, many of them are extremely simple and can be shown to be constituents of the traditional stock, evidenced also in the Mahābhārata. As such they are valuable for a fuller understanding of the author's poetic techniques and methods of composition, as well as showing in the early stages of its formation that corpus of standard imagery which is such a feature of classical Sanskrit literature.

The vast majority of similes are simple comparisons offering only one point of likeness and expressed without the use of a separate verb. Examples of developed similes are very few and occur typically in the verses in longer metres and in a few, more elaborately worded sargas.[27] Similes, along with other figures of speech, tend to be used most in dramatic or emotional situations and at such points to be piled up almost without regard to their relations with each other, while in the Araṇya and Yuddha kāṇḍas another trend apparent is the frequency of similes in descriptions of fighting. However, the frequency with which the shorter similes occupy the fourth pāda of a verse, as well as the conventional nature of many used in battle scenes, suggest that they share the formulaic character of the various stereotyped expressions which will be examined subsequently. For this reason, coupled with their greater overall frequency, the tendency to accumulation at certain points is somewhat less marked in the case of similes than of other figures.[28] On the other hand a not infrequent feature is the repetition of the same *upamāna* in similes close to each other, with few or no instances elsewhere. Redundancy in the presentation of similes is rare.

The frequency of similes differs markedly between the different books, from just over one in ten stanzas in the Ayodhyā and Kiṣkindhā kāṇḍas to twice that figure in the Sundarakāṇḍa and only marginally less in the Araṇya and Yuddha kāṇḍas. The Bālakāṇḍa shows an even lower proportion of one in twelve stanzas, while the Uttarakāṇḍa shows an intermediate proportion which conceals, however, the marked divergence between its first thirty-six sargas with as high a proportion

Elements of Poetry in the Mahābhārata, Berkeley, 1964, in addition to my own reading. Cf. also S. L. Neveleva, *Voprosi Poetiki Drevneindiyskogo Eposa. Epitet i Sravnenie*, Moskva, 1979.

[27] Thus, in the Ayodhyākāṇḍa, the majority of examples occur in sargas 98, containing self-sacrificing speeches by Rāma and Bharata, and 106, containing the well-known description of the mourning city of Ayodhyā.

[28] Nevertheless certain sargas do contain a much greater proportion of similes than the average, in particular 2.38, 74, 87 and 106, 3.24–8, 30, 45 and 50, 5.4, 6–8, 13, 15, 17, 19, 27–8, 45, 47 and 53, 6.18, 53, 55, 57–9, 63–4, 75–6, 81, 86–7 and 106; also 1.6, 53 and 73, and 7.4–5, 7, 31–3 and 41. It may also be noted that the proportion in speeches may be as high as 75%, at least in the S. recension, cf. Söhnen, *Reden*, p. 321.

as any and the remainder of the book with a proportion even lower than the Bālakāṇḍa.[29] There is a similar variation in the proportion of similes having exact parallels or close similarity of wording to similes in the Mahābhārata, from for example a sixth in the Ayodhyākāṇḍa to over a quarter in the Araṇya and Yuddha kāṇḍas, where the frequency of battle scenes encourages the use of standard images; indeed a few similes are proverbial in nature.

Although requirements of subject-matter and other factors mean that certain types of simile are conspicuously more or less common in one book than another, the pattern of imagery overall is broadly similar to that found in the Mahābhārata. Over half the similes are drawn from the natural world, but the most frequent single *upamāna* is Indra (including his weapons, banner and abode) and similes involving comparisons with the gods form a sizable group. Indra and his weapons are particularly prominent in the Araṇya and Yuddha kāṇḍas and in the Yuddhakāṇḍa there is particular reference to his battle with Vṛtra; several similes also refer to his position as king of the gods. Yama is even more particularly concentrated in the Araṇya and Yuddha kāṇḍas (with 20 and 35 similes respectively out of 78 in all books), while the simile of the doomsday fire is also quite common in battle scenes. However, other deities are relatively little mentioned in similes, but in some respects the list of gods mentioned shows similarities to the Vedic pantheon rather than to later stages, for example in the presence of Parjanya and Garuḍa and the infrequency of mention of Viṣṇu and Śiva.[30] Similes taken from sacrifice, ritual and the like are also very infrequent, reflecting the relative absence of religious considerations from the basic narrative.

Among animal similes those referring to cattle are fewer than those referring to elephants, snakes or lions; even those which do occur show no signs of veneration of the cow and are equally concerned with bulls and bullocks. Elephants in fact provide the material for a considerable number of similes, several of which are variants on the highly formalised *totrārdita iva dvipaḥ* occurring equally in the Mahābhārata, but similes with snakes are slightly more frequent overall, being particularly frequent in the Yuddhakāṇḍa. Lions are a regular type of courage and strength in any literature and so are naturally popular here. Other

[29] The totals (and percentages) of similes in each book are: Bālakāṇḍa 164 (8.31%), Ayodhyā 340 (10.34%), Araṇya 390 (18.58%), Kiṣkindhā 239 (11.92%), Sundara 562 (22.09%), Yuddha 899 (20.02%) and Uttara 378 (13.90%), with 1–36 having 301 (21.39%) and 37–100 having 77 (5.87%).

[30] In this respect the text differs markedly from the * passages, which in general use more similes than the text and in particular are quite often sectarian Vaiṣṇava expansions.

animals, birds, insects and so forth are less common. Similes referring to trees and plants, of which the largest single group is those mentioning lotuses, are also not a very large category.

Much the commonest similes drawn from the natural world, mainly because of their frequency in the Yuddhakāṇḍa, are those involving mountains, which regularly symbolise immovability and are especially apt in episodes of fighting. The sun, which primarily symbolises brilliance, power and might, shows a steady increase in frequency of employment in similes from the Ayodhyākāṇḍa to the Yuddhakāṇḍa, partly explicable by the fact that the tawny colour of the Vānaras is quite often compared to the sun's hue. Many of the similes involving both the sun and the moon are extremely stereotyped in character, as indeed are most of those drawn from the other entities or forces of nature: stars, sky, rivers and the earth. Similes relating to human beings and situations are only a minor category, along with ornaments and jewels.

Whereas similes, as by far the most frequent figure of speech, occur fairly generally, the other *alaṃkāras* are used much more sparingly and virtually only at the more dramatic points of the narrative. The figures occurring are naturally in the main the simpler ones, of which the more frequent are *utprekṣā, rūpaka, atiśayokti* and *svabhāvokti* in order of frequency.[31] Metaphor (*rūpaka*) is in one sense the commonest figure, if all the compounds such as *puruṣarṣabha* 'bull among men' are included, but is not otherwise nearly so frequent. Metaphors contained in compounds have usually become mere clichés and are therefore discounted, unless a particular example retains the vividness of its imagery. The commonest metaphor is the sea of sorrow (*śokasāgara*), followed by the burning of an arrow; developed metaphor (*sāṅga rūpaka*) is extremely rare in the text.

The figure of *utprekṣā*, 'ascription', is not easy to define and is not altogether distinguishable from simile, while some instances have more than a little affinity with *atiśayokti*, hyperbole. It is the commonest figure after simile and there is perhaps an element of it more generally than the definite examples might imply. One stock specimen, *dārayann/cālayann/kampayann iva medinīm*, is shared with the Mahābhārata and there are a few others nearly as formalised. Examples

[31] It is in the field of these other *alaṃkāras* that the greatest difference is found between the text and * passages (the additional * passages being involved to a greater extent than the substitute ones). Whereas the number and variety of *alaṃkāras* in the text is limited, though still forming an important part of it, the * passages consist often of an amplification of some detail or incident by the use of a figure of speech.

of *utprekṣā* with verbs or participles are much commoner than those with adjectives. Hyperbole (*atiśayokti*) may also be a subsidiary element of other figures of speech but is more often found alone, especially in the Araṇya and Yuddha kāṇḍas, where the boastings of the Rākṣasas provide ample scope.

A certain number of passages of *svabhāvokti*, 'descriptive characterisation', some of considerable length and elaboration, occur in the text but it is much more frequent in the * passages. However, it is doubtful whether it was felt to be a distinct figure by the author or authors, just as the description of Rāvaṇa showing Sītā round his palace (3.53.7–12) is very similar to some instances of *svabhāvokti* and in fact reflects the same love of description. Even less frequent figures are *arthāntaranyāsa* (apodeixis), *samāsokti* (concise declaration), *nidarśana* (indication), *śleṣa* (double-entendre), *viṣama* (incongruity), *parisaṃkhyā* (delimitation) and *yathāsaṃkhya* (enumeration); yet others occur in the * passages, as well as more elaborate examples of these.

Chiasmus, or at least inversion of word order, though not recognised by the Sanskrit writers on poetics, occurs often enough in the text to suggest that the instances are not accidental but consciously produced by the poet for emphasis, especially since many instances occur in conjunction with a future tense and come from speeches; but another not uncommon use of chiasmus is in enumerations or other series of parallel utterances, presumably to avoid monotony.[32] As a figure, chiasmus links more perhaps with the *śabdālaṃkāras* of alliteration and the like. Alliteration is one of the more frequent stylistic features and is thus less confined to the highlights of the narrative than certain rhetorical devices, though often used to enhance the effect of similes. There is little trace of any attempt to use it affectively but constant employment for emphasis, although the frequent alliterative compounds probably have little if any emphatic function. Such naïve use of alliteration is often linked with the use of cognates, while the figure of *lāṭānuprāsa* (repetition of a word in different grammatical relationships) obviously owes some of its frequency to the same tendency. A particu-

[32] A list of all occurrences noted in the Ayodhyā and Araṇya kāṇḍas was given in FS, pp. 452–4, to which Söhnen has recently suggested certain additions (*Reden*, pp. 302 and 310). The instance at 2.27.17ab should certainly be added to my listing, 2.97.20 is chiastic if certain extra words are ignored, but the other examples she gives (2.97.2–3, 22cd with 23cd and 99.17cd[l.v.]) scarcely satisfy my own understanding of chiasmus as complete inversion of grammatically parallel wording between two clauses. However, Söhnen clearly accepts the role of chiasmus and indeed sees a more extended principle of parallelism operating within the structure of speeches (see further below).

larly common type of *lāṭānuprāsa* consists of personal name and epithet, such as *lakṣmaṇaḥ śubhalakṣaṇaḥ*, of which some have become stereotyped. Etymologising of various kinds and other forms of simple word-play are quite frequent and indicate a considerable preoccupation with the actual words used to express the narrative quite apart from their immediate function or euphony. On the other hand, the more developed *śabdālaṃkāras* are conspicuously absent from the text but again are to be found in the * passages.

An expression such as *lakṣmaṇaḥ śubhalakṣaṇaḥ* owes its frequency not only to the tendency to *lāṭānuprāsa* but also to its exactly fitting a pāda, for the pāda-length phrases comprising a personal name and a standard epithet of one sort or another are the most frequent of the various stereotyped expressions and have a definite narrative function in emphasising the aspect of the person's character relevant to the occasion.[33] In general, the various epithets and stock phrases either fill a pāda or else leave room for a word of two or three syllables; indeed, there are sometimes variants allowing all three possibilities. This is of obvious practical importance for an oral poem, since it allows the poet or reciter to fill out a line without effort. Thus formulae are to be found preponderantly in the second and fourth pādas, the only major exception being the formulae used after the end of a speech; in addition, as a result of the standard metrical pattern of the *śloka*, there has to be a different set of formulae for the odd pādas from those for the even pādas (although the change in wording involved may be slight).[34] Formulaic phrases do not necessarily conform to exactly the same wording on every occasion, but the variations are all obviously linked—'variations on a theme.'

and mount Meru; on the main road, he passes the fine houses of

[33] Fuller details on the material of this section may be found in my article SE. A major study of the formulae in the Mahābhārata and Rāmāyaṇa is now available in Grintser, *Epos*.

[34] I alluded briefly to this last point in my 'Note on Mrs. Sen's Article about the Rāmāyaṇa', JAOS 89, 1969, pp. 412–4; however a fuller treatment in relation to the Mahābhārata material is contained in Ya. V. Vasilkov, 'Elementi ustno-poeticheskoy techniki v "Mahabharatye" ' *Literatury Indii*, Moskva, 1973, pp. 3–23, developing the groupings of formulae propounded by Grintser in an earlier article, to which I have not had access. In an earlier article Vasilkov demonstrates the function of certain formulaic expressions in introducing the theme of a particular section ('Mahabharata i ustnaya epicheskaya poeziya', *Narodi Azii i Afriki*, 1971 no. 4, pp. 95–106). I am grateful to Dr Vasilkov for copies of his articles.

Although such forms of repetition are a feature common to many, if not all, epic traditions, their roots in oral composition do not mean that the epic was always an oral production. As has been recognised in Greek literature,[35] the traditional phraseology does not disappear immediately and the diction of a non-oral production continues to show formulaic patterns. This no doubt accounts for the tendency towards greater frequency of stock pādas in the later parts of both the Rāmāyaṇa and the Mahābhārata, a tendency already noticed by Hopkins.[36] Probably this exaggerated use of stock pādas in the later parts accounts, at least to some extent, for the steady rise in the proportion of stereotyped pādas from the Ayodhyā to the Yuddha kāṇḍa. The proportion in the Ayodhyākāṇḍa is about one in twenty-two pādas (4.53%) completely stereotyped and in the Yuddhakāṇḍa almost one in ten (9.25%).[37] Within this trend, however, there are variations between the books. Refrains are commoner in the Ayodhyākāṇḍa than elsewhere, no doubt because of their greater frequency in the construction of speeches;[38] repeated pādas and pāda-length long compounds are particularly frequent in the Kiṣkindhākāṇḍa; and the Yuddhakāṇḍa has a large proportion of stereotyped phrases which can be paralleled in the Mahābhārata, partly but not wholly because of the frequency of battle scenes.[39]

The inclusion of pādas with a marked formulaic character in a substantial part of their wording would raise the proportion to between 30% and 40%. Even these latter figures are lower than those given by Grintser of 50% in narrative chapters and 63% in battle chapters, but lower in didactic parts.[40] However, he is willing to consider even a disyllabic word as formulaic, whereas I would wish to see over half a pāda completely fixed before including it as a formula or stereotyped expression. This agrees with de Jong's view that 'It would be preferable to extend the length of a formula to a group of words or a compound of at least five syllables, in order to make a clear distinction between

[35] See for example G. S. Kirk, 'Formular Language and Oral Quality', *Yale Classical Studies* 20, 1966, pp. 153–74.

[36] *Great Epic*, p. 70.

[37] The former figure is an upward revision through further research of that given in SE (p. 210).

[38] On this point, see the comments by Söhnen (*Reden*, pp. 287–91), who gives a figure of 13% for the speeches studied by her, though recognising that some instances may have been made more pronounced by later interpolation, in which respect it is significant that her study is based on the Bombay edition, basically the S. recension.

[39] Cf. my SET III.

[40] *Epos*, pp. 71–95.

traditional vocabulary and formulaic diction.'[41] This is not to deny the usefulness of the concept of the 'supporting word' developed by Grintser and Vasilkov but to distinguish it from fully formulaic diction (as Vasilkov does in separating 'supporting words' from the much smaller number of 'pure formulas').[42] Thus *lakṣmaṇaś ca mahābalaḥ* is a stereotyped expression, whereas *mahābala* in itself is not, although its metrically preferred position at the end of even pādas is obviously significant in terms of the patterns of oral composition.

The different types of formulae may be classified into the following categories: personal epithets, introductions and conclusions of speeches, certain verbal formulae expressing emotion or emphasis, certain descriptive and often hyperbolic phrases, stock expressions for the events in battles, phrases of time, place and number, repeats and refrains, proverbs and similar expressions, and stereotyped similes or other figures of speech.[43] Personal names are regularly qualified by an adjective occupying the remainder of the pāda and to a considerable extent there is a common pool of adjectives available of suitable lengths to complete the pāda, although the choice is not unrestricted. Certain adjectives are for one reason or another specific (e.g. *rāmo daśarathātmajaḥ*, since the names of the other sons are trisyllabic, or *bharataḥ kekayīsutaḥ*, since only Bharata was born to Kaikeyī), but others display at the most a tendency to preferential use with a particular individual. Thus the various *dharma*- compounds are most frequently applied to Rāma but are by no means exclusive to him, whereas the patronymic *rāghava*, which could designate most of the major figures, is almost invariably used of him. Of the various *mahā*- compounds, *mahātapas* is used only of sages and *mahābala* of warriors, while *mahātman* is of general application but is more frequent in later stages.[44] It should be stressed that attributive epithets in general are relevant to the situation in which they occur and that the purely ornamental epithet is not common, although this is not to say that they

[41] J. W. de Jong, 'Recent Russian publications on the Indian epic', *Adyar Library Bulletin* 39, 1975, pp. 1–42, esp. p. 38.

[42] Op. cit.

[43] The last two categories are treated in detail in my articles *Proverbs* and FS, the others in SE. Grintser (op. cit., pp. 32 ff.) proposes a rather different grouping based more on function into attributive (roughly my personal epithets), narrative, auxiliary (mainly phrases of time, place and number), formulae of direct speech, maxims, and similes.

[44] In this respect there is a complete contrast between *mahābala*, which is found most often in the first stage and declines in frequency to the third stage, and *mahātman*, which steadily increases in frequency to the third stage (on the stages, see later in this chapter).

are vital to the narrative—rather their use is to point a contrast or heighten an effect. This is one respect in which the poet shows a controlled and skilful use of the techniques at his disposal.

Daśaratha is characterised by the two pādas *rājā daśarathaḥ*˘ ⁻and *vṛddhaṃ daśarathaṃ nṛpam*, while two of his wives are linked in *kausalyā ca sumitrā ca*, but none of these is very common. Rāma is naturally distinguished by the greatest variety of epithets, many of which stress his virtue, such as *rāmo dharmabhṛtāṃ varaḥ* and *rāmaḥ satyaparākramaḥ*; the commonest expression, however, is *rāmasyākliṣṭakarmaṇaḥ*, followed by *rāmo daśarathātmajaḥ*. Sītā is most often referred to as Janaka's daughter, *maithilī / vaidehī janakātmajā*, but also commonly as *sītā surasutopamā*. Lakṣmaṇa's name offers a natural opportunity for word play in pādas such as *lakṣmaṇo lakṣmivardhanaḥ* and *lakṣmaṇaḥ śubhalakṣaṇaḥ*. However, the largest group of stereotyped pādas including Lakṣmaṇa's name contain compounds with *mahā-* as the initial member; the most frequent is *lakṣmaṇaś ca mahābalaḥ*, which is almost twice as frequent as *lakṣmaṇasya mahātmanaḥ*, whereas with Bharata the only frequent pāda is *bharatasya mahātmanaḥ*.

Rāvaṇa's name also combines occasionally with a punning or etymologising epithet, in *rāvaṇo lokarāvaṇaḥ* and *rāvaṇaḥ śatrurāvaṇaḥ*, but the commonest pāda incorporating his name is *rāvaṇo rākṣasādhipaḥ*, with its variant *rāvaṇo rākṣaseśvaraḥ*. Hanumān is most frequently *hanumān mārutātmajaḥ*, and Sugrīva *sugrīvaḥ plavageśvaraḥ* or *sugrīvaḥ vānareśvaraḥ* (with *plavagādhipaḥ* and *vānarādhipaḥ* as less frequent variants). The minor characters are most commonly qualified in stock pādas by the various *mahā-* compounds. The Rākṣasas are regularly referred to as *rākṣasāḥ piśitāśanāḥ* and *rākṣasāḥ kāmarūpiṇaḥ*; stock pādas of this type are less frequent with the Vānaras but *vānarāḥ* (also *kapayaḥ/harayaḥ*) *kāmarūpiṇaḥ* is in fact the commonest. Stereotyped pādas referring to other groups include *ṛṣīṇāṃ ca mahātmanām, munayaḥ saṃśitavratāḥ* and *brāhmaṇāḥ vedapāragāḥ*. It is obvious that, although some epithets have a restricted application, many are freely adaptable to the formation of standard pādas and may be used in any appropriate situation.

The need in an oral tradition for clear markers of the beginnings and endings of speeches to distinguish them from the recitation of the surrounding narrative hardly needs stressing.[45] It is natural therefore that formulaic expression is particularly marked in the pādas used to introduce or to conclude speeches; thus, for instance approximately

[45] For a clear statement of this requirement and exceptions, as well as a discussion of the verbs used in this connection, see Söhnen, *Reden*, pp. 7–23.

half the occurrences of *abravīt* (or *abruvan*) are in one of the four formulae *idaṃ vacanam abravīt*, ⏑– – *vacanam abravīt*, x x x *vākyam abravīt* and x x x *idam abravīt*. These four formulae occupy the fourth (occasionally the second) pāda and significantly in the shorter forms the name of the speaker or the person addressed normally completes the pāda. Variant forms are also found for use in the first or third pādas, or to accommodate names of four syllables. Formulaic expression with the perfects *uvāca* and *pratyuvāca* is not so well defined, for these forms occur as often in the first and third pādas as in the second and fourth, but certain standard phrasings do occur. From another root entirely comes *ākhyātum upacakrame* (with variants *vyāhartum* and *pravaktum*), used to introduce more narrative accounts. The introductions to speeches are to a large extent common to the Mahābhārata, despite its regular use of *extra metrum* announcements of the speaker.

There are two well used types of stock phrase with *śrutvā* employed after a speech, both normally preceded by the genitive of the speaker and differing only in the length of the word which can precede (with compounding instead of the genitive increasing the possibilities further): x x x *vacanaṃ śrutvā* and x x x x *vacaḥ śrutvā*. Even commoner, but on the whole lacking any pronounced turns of phrase, are the past participle passive and absolutive of √*vac*; the most formulaic is *evam uktas* (*uktā*/*uktau*) *tu* x x x. Exceptionally the phrase *bāḍham ity eva* x x x, which is twice as frequent in the Uttarakāṇḍa as in the whole of the rest of the text, may be used in any pāda, although in the Mahābhārata it is restricted to the first or third.[46]

The verbal formulae which express emotion or emphasis include *praharṣam atulam lebhe*, *krodham* (*roṣam*/*kopam*) *āhārayat tīvram*, *vismayaṃ paramaṃ gatvā*/*gataḥ*, *dīrgham uṣṇaṃ viniḥśvasya*, *vilalāpa suduḥkhitaḥ*, *nāhaṃ jīvitum utsahe*, *na tvaṃ śocitum arhasi* and *ājñāpayitum arhasi*; all except the last are frequent in the Mahābhārata also. Of the descriptive phrases, some are similar to the personal epithets but of more general application and some consist of standardised descriptions of, for instance, jewellery or the forest. Those with most analogy to personal epithets are the variations around *siṃhaskandho mahābhujaḥ* and the group of phrases *vīryavatāṃ varaḥ*, *satyavatāṃ varaḥ*, *vedavidāṃ varaḥ*, *vadatāṃ varaḥ* and *jayatāṃ varaḥ* (but *śreṣṭhaḥ* in the prior pāda), but also similar and somewhat hyperbolical are *prāṇebhyo 'pi garīyasī* (and related phrases), *sarvabhūtahite rataḥ*, *rupeṇāpratimā bhuvi* and *adṛśyaḥ sarvabhūtānām*. The stan-

[46] See further in SET III.

dardised descriptions include the large group of pādas ending *vividhāni ca* (of which the commonest is *ratnāni vividhāni ca*), *śubhāny ābharaṇāni ca, puṣpāṇi/mūlāni ca phalāni ca* and x x x *vividhā drumāḥ*.

Among the stereotyped expressions connected with battle, x x *devāsure yuddhe* is a specific reference to a mythological event which has been made integral to the story. All others, however, are general in application. Two, as is natural in such a context, show marked hyperbole: *nayāmi/neṣyāmi yamasādanam*[47] and *sendrair api surāsuraiḥ* (with variants). Other standard formulae describe the start of conflict, weapons and their employment, and the fall of warriors: *abhyadhāvat susaṃkruddhaḥ* (with variants),[48] *tataḥ sutumulaṃ yuddham*; *śarāḥ kāñcanabhūṣaṇāḥ, sasarja niśitāñ śarān/bāṇān* and the shorter forms *niśitaiḥ śaraiḥ/bāṇaiḥ, vavarṣa śaravarṣāṇi*; *papāta* (*pātito/nipetur*) *dharaṇītale* and *papāta sahasā bhūmau* (both mainly in battle scenes but occasionally in other contexts), *rudhireṇa samukṣitaḥ* and, commonest of all, *raṇamūrdhani*.

Phrases of time include several to indicate the passage of a day or night (*kṛtvā paurvāhṇikaṃ karma* and variants, *anvāsya paścimāṃ saṃdhyām, rajanī cābhyavartata, prabhātāyāṃ tu śarvaryām, tasyāṃ/atha/tato rātryāṃ vyatītāyām* and *lambamāne divākare*), two to express the length of Rāma's exile (*nava varṣāṇi pañca ca* and *caturdaśa hi varṣāṇi*) and a few more general phrases or covering an extended period (*etasminn antare*—⏑̄ and *atha dīrghasya kālasya* occurring generally; *etasminn eva kāle tu, tataḥ kālena mahatā, kasya cit tv atha kālasya* and *pūrṇe varṣasahasre tu* restricted to the Bāla and Uttara kāṇḍas). Place names readily form the nucleus of stock pādas, of which the commonest are *ayodhyāṃ punar āgataḥ, kiṣkindhāṃ vālipālitām* and *laṅkāṃ* (*purīṃ*) *rāvaṇapālitām*, but life in the forest and locations within it produce several formulae: *vane vanyena jīvataḥ, vanāny upavanāni ca, ramaṇīye vanoddeśe, aśokavanikāmadhye* and *giriprasravaṇāni ca* (and variants). A certain degree of stereotyping is seen in *dakṣiṇāṃ diśam* (beginning odd pādas and concluding even pādas), and also in *diśo daśa* (usually concluding an even pāda). The seven seas find occasional mention in varying but usually alliterative wording, seen also in *samudraḥ saritāṃ patiḥ*, and the three worlds are especially referred to hyperbolically in the formulae *trayāṇām api*

[47] This formula and the related *gamiṣyāmi yamakṣayam* are infrequent in the Mahābhārata, whereas *yamasya sadanaṃ prati*, common in the Mahābhārata, occurs only at 2.58.31b and 7.21.1d; cf. SET III.

[48] On the frequency of *kruddhaḥ* at the end of the line leading up to fully formulaic pādas, see Ya.V.Vasilkov, 'Elementi ustno-poeticheskoy techniki v "Mahabharatye" ', *Literatury Indii*, Moskva, 1973, pp. 3–23, esp. pp. 7–8.

lokānām and *triṣu lokeṣu viśrutaḥ/vikhyātaḥ*. Numerals also appear in the alliterative *śataśo 'tha sahasraśaḥ* (also *sahasreṇa śatena ca*) and in *śatayojanam āyataḥ* (also *daśa-* etc.), *sahasrāṇi caturdaśa, rākṣasās te caturdaśa* and similar pādas.

The frequency with which a phrase or passage is repeated within a short space of its first occurrence—not infrequently a complete line is repeated virtually without alteration—is in part due to the naïve repetition of the original wording when a message is relayed or a situation occurring in the main narrative is recounted to another character. As such it is very much a feature of the epic language and a mark of its oral character.[49] Similarity of situation can also lead to identity of wording and mention twice in quick succession of a given locality is often couched in identical terms. Occasionally, however, such repetition seems to be due rather to textual corruption than to an original oral or popular style, indicating subsequent conflation of divergent developments; however, even here there may be an element of deliberate repetition by the original poet as a connecting device or simply to incorporate two versions of a traditional topic. Parallelism within the stanza could be regarded as the extreme form of such repetition but unlike it its function is emphatic and consequently it occurs predominantly in speeches; for example, the most extensive examples in the Araṇyakāṇḍa are contained in Sītā's reply to Rāvaṇa (3.45.34–9 and 40–5). This same speech also contains a refrain, *ahaṃ rāmam anuvratā* (3.45.29–31 and 891*), and refrains are even more clearly a device employed to heighten the dramatic effect of speeches.[50] However, there are signs that some speeches have been expanded in the course of transmission with attendant enhancement of the refrain element. It nonetheless remains true that there is obvious use of rhetorical devices to increase the impact of speeches and perhaps also further to mark them off from the surrounding narrative.

A not inconsiderable body of proverbial material serves to indicate the extent of the corpus of traditional material available to the poet, although naturally enough, in view of its nature, the Rāmāyaṇa contains less in the way of gnomic utterances than the Mahābhārata with its substantial didactic portions. Proverbial sayings are found on almost one hundred occasions in the text (with a further forty or more in * passages) but there are only three each in the Bāla and Uttara kāṇḍas. Several instances are repeats of the same proverb and a substantial

[49] See the discussion by Grintser on themes, repetitions, catalogues and inserted episodes (*Epos*, pp. 96–120).

[50] See Söhnen, *Reden*, pp. 287–91 for the role of refrains in speeches as part of a more general tendency to symmetrical construction of speeches around a central point (*Ringkomposition*, pp. 292–307); for her discussion of Sītā's speech see pp. 132–4.

number consist of citations in later anthologies only, which means that just over seventy are paralleled in the older literature. Over fifty occur also in the Mahābhārata, of which more than a third seem not to occur in other Sanskrit texts, whereas only half as many are paralleled in the *kathā* literature and as few as sixteen are found in the *dharmaśāstra* literature. Thus it is clear that the proverbial matter incorporated in the Rāmāyaṇa is drawn from the general epic tradition rather than from any other part of the literary tradition.

The distribution of the proverbial material is also of interest. It is clear that comparatively little use was made of proverbial expressions in the earliest stages but that there are concentrations in certain passages within books 2–6 which show evidence of expansion or alteration. There are, for instance, several in 2.98, which elaborates Rāma's previous refusal to return to Ayodhyā, in 2.101, Rāma's retort to Jābāli's casuistry, in 4.17–18, containing the moralising over the slaughter of Vālin, and in 6.70, where Lakṣmaṇa inveighs against the inefficacy of dharma. These and similar passages display a little of the tendency so obvious in certain parts of the Mahābhārata to introduce a moralising and didactic element, which lends itself to a gnomic form. By contrast, the Bāla and Uttara kāṇḍas contain so few because of the puranic character of much of their narrative. A considerable number of proverbs and the like is again, however, apparent in the next stage of the * passages, when they seem to have been a feature of the Northern recension, since twice as many occur there as in the Southern. This undoubtedly reflects the more polished text of the Northern recension, shown also in the greater frequency of *alaṃkāras*.

Some remarks on stereotyped similes and other figures of speech have already been made above. As we noted, the most stereotyped similes are those used in describing fighting and its results, of which a high proportion are shared with the Mahābhārata. They include both those drawn from mythology, such as *vṛtravāsavayor iva* and *vyāttānana / vyāditāsya ivāntakaḥ*, and a larger number taken from nature, such as *savidyud iva toyadaḥ, totrārdita iva dvipaḥ*, x x *āśīviṣopamam, siṃhaḥ kṣudramṛgaṃ yathā, vajrabhinna ivācalaḥ* and *chinnamūla iva drumaḥ*. Another common comparison is of a warrior or his arrows to a blazing fire (*śarān agniśikhopamān, jvalantam iva pāvakam* and *vidhūma iva pāvakaḥ*[51]). Two stereotyped similes for women's reactions to grief are *krośantīṃ kurarīm iva* and *pravāte kadalī yathā*, both drawn from

[51] On this last simile and its variants, see the discussion by L. A. van Daalen ('A note on *vidhūma* or *sadhūma iva pāvakaḥ* at *Rāmāyaṇa* 1, 54, 28 and 1, 55, 19', IT 7, 1979, pp. 171–80), to which should be added the instance at 3.68.4b of *vidhūmo 'gnir ivotthitaḥ* (noted at SE p. 446).

nature, as are several others which are slightly less formalised. The commonest metaphor of the sea of sorrow, itself formulaic, builds a complete stereotyped pāda *nimagnaḥ śokasāgare* (also verbal forms of √*masj*). There is also, as already mentioned, one stereotyped specimen of *utprekṣā* (*dārayann iva medinīm* and variants), while two instances of hyperbole (*sendrair api surāsuraiḥ* and *trayāṇām api lokānām*) have been included in the appropriate categories above.

The metrical pattern of the Rāmāyaṇa was much studied towards the end of last century,[52] when the much greater regularity of the *śloka* in the Rāmāyaṇa compared with the Mahābhārata was established. Metrical anomalies are extremely sporadic and in many such cases metrically more regular variants have virtually as much support, making it extremely difficult to determine the degree to which these very occasional irregularities are original. However, it is probably significant that the Bāla and Uttara kāṇḍas exhibit a slightly freer pattern, for Jacobi pointed to a series of irregular pādas in the Viśvāmitra episode (1.50–64), which are irregular third *vipulās* unless a consonant group with a liquid second fails to lengthen the preceding vowel, and to a more miscellaneous series in the narrative of Agastya (7.1–36).[53] On the other hand, the tolerance of hiatus between pādas, when taken in conjunction with its rarity within pādas, points to the partial survival of the older division of the *śloka* into four pādas alongside the division into two lines.

It is clear from the preceding surveys that, apart from the metrical pattern, the linguistic and stylistic features of the central books of the Rāmāyaṇa show considerable variation around a basically simple and fluent style. A measure of this variation is undoubtedly due to the differing subject-matter of various parts and to factors like the contrast between speeches or dialogue and narrative passages. On the other hand, a picture emerges basically of a clear-cut and cohesive language,

[52] Besides his treatment in *Das Râmâyaṇa*, pp. 25–31, Jacobi also included significant remarks in 'Über den Śloka im Mahābhārata', *Gurupūjākaumudī, Festgabe . . . Albrecht Weber*, Leipzig, 1896, pp. 50–3 (cf. also 'Zur Lehre vom Śloka', *Indische Studien* 17, 1885, pp. 442–51) as did Hopkins in his *Great Epic*, pp. 194–272 and 446–58. More recent treatments, utilising this older material, are found in Grintser, *Epos*, pp. 47–52 and van Daalen, *Vālmīki's Sanskrit*, pp. 67–71, 77–80.

[53] *Das Râmâyaṇa*, pp. 26–9.

which appears to be independent of, though possibly a little later than, the language described by Pāṇini and thus to form, together with the older parts of the Mahābhārata, a genuinely separate epic Sanskrit. Similarly, the evidence of style and vocabulary point to a single authorship for the core of the narrative, welding the separate elements centred on Ayodhyā, Kiṣkindhā and Laṅkā (which may represent pre-existing cycles of ballads) into a coherent and artistically effective epic.

It is therefore reasonable to postulate that the original Rāmāyaṇa was composed in this basically simple and fluent style, from which may be distinguished those passages which show marked divergence in linguistic and stylistic features, suggesting that they have been interpolated or greatly expanded. Hereafter I shall designate those sargas which from their simple and direct language appear to belong relatively unaltered to the original work of Vālmīki as the first stage of the text. In speaking of an original Rāmāyaṇa, I am not unmindful of the assertion by Hopkins that 'There can be no plausible original reconstructed and practically there was from the time of, let us say, the first repetition of the text, no original Rāmāyaṇa.'[54] Undoubtedly the poem was varied in details in succesive recitations (and even after it was written down) and this is the main reason why I have not engaged in any detailed textual criticism in this work. In general, I have not attempted to examine the status of individual verses but have taken sargas or groups of sargas as the unit. The reason for this is purely practical in order to reduce the complexities of the situation to manageable proportions; there is no particular value in the sarga as such—indeed, as already noted, there is reason to doubt whether the division is original—except in so far as it roughly corresponds to the successive events or episodes of the narrative. Certainly, many individual verses which have less than full manuscript support would probably be better removed from the text. The Critical Edition tends in particular to include in its text verses attested by the Southern recension if there is any Northern support at all, when they occur in isolation in a longer fully attested passage. Rigorous examination of such instances would in fact substantially reduce the number of apparent exceptions to the distinctiveness of the various stages in terms of vocabulary, concepts and cultural aspects.

This method does have limitations. For example, it would fail to

[54] E. W. Hopkins, 'The Original Rāmāyaṇa', JAOS 46, 1926, pp. 202–19, esp. p. 219. However, the very example which Hopkins gives (pp. 211–12) to illustrate this variation, *vipra* for *dvija*, confirms that certain broader trends do persist; cf. p. 156.

register interpolation through duplication either of a message or of an incident, if such duplication adhered reasonably closely to the wording of the original. In fact, however, such naïve repetition, which is often literal, is regularly a feature of epic or oral style. It is not therefore reasonable to maintain that any repeated passage is unauthentic, as Jacobi tends to do.[55] On the other hand, Grintser perhaps goes too far in seeing not only such stylistic repetitions but also contradictions of meaning and inserted episodes as belonging to the basic features of oral epic poetry, at any rate as far as the Rāmāyaṇa is concerned.[56] Anyway, while the detection of such possible interpolation obviously affects a literary or aesthetic appreciation of the text, it is irrelevant for examination of the linguistic or cultural changes, precisely because of the repetition of the original.

More generally, the method is designed, not to determine exactly what was the shape or extent of the epic composed by Vālmīki, but to show what was the type of poetic technique he used and the nature of the society and culture he described. Without the later episodes and the elaboration characteristic of the second stage and without the interruption of the verses in longer metres, the first stage of the Rāmāyaṇa exhibits a continuous narrative flow. The action concentrates on essentials and is not held up by passages of *svabhāvokti* and purely pedantic chronological details.[57] For instance, in Daśaratha's giving way to Kaikeyī's petulance Vālmīki gives a clear psychological motivation for Rāma's banishment which thus provides an effective link between the two separate parts of the story—the court intrigues at Ayodhyā and Rāma's war on Rāvaṇa over the abduction of Sītā—whereas the later interpolation of details about the curse pronounced on Daśaratha, by emphasising the supernatural at the expense of the realistic, reduces the dramatic intensity of the work.

Extending this relatively homogeneous material of the first stage, there are then a considerable number of passages in the second to sixth books which suggest from their language and style that they have been

[55] *Das Râmâyaṇa*, pp. 40–2.

[56] *Epos*, p. 96 ff.

[57] Vittore Pisani's theory ('The Rise of the Mahābhārata', *A Volume of Eastern and Indian Studies presented to Professor F. W. Thomas*, Bombay, 1939, pp. 166–76) that inserted episodes do not appear at random but are intended to cover the major temporal hiatuses in the main narrative, is at least as applicable to the motives of later redactors as to the earliest stages of the Mahābhārata. There is usually a reason for the expansions and interpolations in the Rāmāyaṇa.

interpolated or expanded; these will be designated the second stage of growth of the text. The first and second stages therefore comprise the whole of the Ayodhyā to Yuddha kāṇḍas, with almost exactly half belonging to each.[58] However, it should be remembered that the original poem would have included not only the material of the first stage but also that underlying the expansions (as opposed to insertions) of the second stage. There have been various previous attempts to isolate the interpolations in the Rāmāyaṇa, most notably by Jacobi and by Bulcke,[59] but the criteria used have been those of subject-matter and supposed relevance or otherwise to the narrative. Jacobi, indeed, was well aware of the significance of language and achieved a great deal in the analysis of the recensions and the elimination of extraneous material. But such criteria of relevance necessarily contain an element of the subjective and fail to pinpoint passages which are central to the narrative and for that very reason have subsequently been embellished. However, in many instances, passages already considered suspect on grounds of content can clearly be shown from the linguistic data to be aberrant from the norm; in such instances a look at the subject-matter will indicate the reason for the amplification.

Just as there are two types of addition to the text, expansion or modification of the existing text and addition or interpolation of new material, so there are two phases with distinctive characteristics. The earlier is an amplification of the literary aspects of the narrative, the inclusion of elements of *svabhāvokti* in descriptions, and the insertion of extraneous episodes and proverbial matter; the later is almost its antithesis, being the incorporation of didactic and moralistic material, often similar to that in the Mahābhārata, and often prompted by the desire to justify the heroes in those episodes where they do not conform to later ethical standards. These didactic and moralistic elements are written in a plain, unadorned style and indeed are almost deliberately non-stylish. Thus, the earlier expansions or interpolations tend to show a much more elaborate style than the rest of the text with high proportions of long compounds, vṛddhied derivatives and similes,

[58] Anyone unconvinced by the analysis here made can amalgamate subsequent statements about the first and second stages to arrive at the collective evidence of these books as contrasted with that of the Bāla and Uttara kāṇḍas and the passages rejected from the text of the Critical Edition. The first stage comprises 37.10% of the text, the second stage 38.32% and the Bāla and Uttara kāṇḍas 24.57%; however, if their longer verses are included, first-stage sargas comprise 38.49% of the total, almost exactly reversing the small difference in length between the first and second stages.

[59] Jacobi, *Das Râmâyaṇa* and C. Bulcke, *Rām-kathā* (*utpatti aur vikāś*), 2nd ed., Prayāg, 1962.

whereas some of the later ones show lower than normal proportions.

Whereas the Mahābhārata in its process of growth kept its content and plot but these were increasingly treated from an ethical standpoint, the Rāmāyaṇa was transformed from a heroic to a literary epic with the primary emphasis on the emotional and lyric aspects, becoming—as Indian tradition insists—the precursor of the artificial, literary epic as the *ādikāvya*. This change from the poetry of action to the poetry of feeling is marked not only by much greater use of *alaṃkāras* and lyric descriptions of nature but also in its later stages by what Grintser has termed the collapse of formulae.[60] Although in general formulae continued to be used, even overused, sometimes a formula loses its functional role of helping to construct metrically correct verses and is used purely for ornament, undergoing consequential elaboration of wording.

Some of the purely extraneous episodes included later within the Rāmāyaṇa are the story of Trijaṭa Gārgya at 2.29.22–7, the story of Vātāpi and Ilvala at 3.10.53–64, the narration of Garuḍa's exploits at 3.33.28–34, and the episode of the Vānaras' meeting with Niśākara and his prophecy at 4.59–61. Others have a degree of connection with the main narrative, such as Daśaratha's account of his former misdeed and the resultant curse at 2.57–8, Bharadvāja's miraculous entertainment of Bharata's army at 2.85, and the sending of the four search parties at 4.39–42. Proverbial matter is included conspicuously in, for example, the description of the evils of a kingless state at 2.61 and the *kaccit* sarga at 2.94; the inclusion of traditional matter is also seen in the occurrence of genealogies as at 2.102 and 3.13. Instances of inflation or insertion for the sake of introducing *svabhāvokti* and similar figures include Bharata's return to Ayodhyā at 2.65 and the description of the mourning town at 2.106, Lakṣmaṇa's description of winter at 3.15 and Rāma's of the rainy season at 4.27, and the splendours of Laṅkā revealed to Hanumān's gaze at 5.1–8. Expansion for the sake of ethical justification is seen at 3.8–9, where Sītā seeks to dissuade Rāma from killing the Rākṣasas and he justifies this on the basis of the protection owed to the hermits, and at 4.17–18, where Vālin reproaches Rāma for killing him by stealth and Rāma gives a rather laboured justification; basically similar is Sītā's appearing before the victorious Rāma and undergoing the fire-ordeal at 6.102–4.

These passages and certain others share various syntactical and stylistic features, absent or not so strongly marked in the general body

[60] For a discussion of the whole process of transition from heroic epic to literary epic, see Grintser, *Epos*, pp. 331 ff.

of the text, which point to a dating perhaps two to four centuries after the first stage.[61] Among the more pronounced features, all of which are not necessarily to be found in any one of these passages, are an exceptionally high proportion of stereotyped phrases of one kind or another, a high proportion of patronymics and other vṛddhied derivatives, an unusually high proportion of long compounds or in a few instances a very low proportion, certain marked differences in the types of nominal composition found, frequent or developed similes, the frequent occurrence of *svabhāvokti, utprekṣā* or other less common figures of speech, metrical irregularities or grammatically irregular forms used *metri causa*, and the occurrence of less common or irregular verbal forms, such as intensive or desiderative forms, aorists, periphrastic futures and future participles, unaugmented imperfects and changes of conjugation. The usage with regard to the relative pronouns and adverbs shows certain differences from that found in the remainder of the text. Certain of these passages also display a tendency towards poetic licence and indiscriminate use of supposedly epic forms.

Despite various attempts to prove the indispensability to the narrative of the verses in longer metres which are usually appended to each sarga,[62] these too should be included in the second stage on grounds of language and style. Most simply recapitulate the action of the sarga to which they are attached, or paraphrase the preceding *śloka* stanza (or less commonly the opening of the following sarga). Many are obviously redundant, and ignored by the narrative thread and often by the construction. In particular, in several cases where different recensions divide the sargas differently, such a tag stanza (or more than one) occurs only in the recension or manuscripts dividing the sargas at that point.

Although there is usually a single verse in a longer metre at the end of a sarga, the number decreases from the Ayodhyākāṇḍa to the Yuddhakāṇḍa, with the exception of the Sundarakāṇḍa. Conversely, there are instances of several at the end of a sarga but again the proportion decreases in the same fashion. No doubt the later redactors, who were endeavouring to make the Rāmāyaṇa fit the classical pre-

[61] A detailed survey of these later passages will be found in the Appendix. All second-stage passages are discussed there and accordingly no further references to it will be given.

[62] Cf. for example R. Narayana Aiyar, 'On the Longer Verses in the Rāmāyaṇa', *C. Kunhan Raja Presentation Volume*, Madras, 1946, pp. 82–112. On the other hand C. V. Vaidya suggests that all verses in other than *śloka* metre should be treated as later interpolations and holds that they were added to make the Rāmāyaṇa conform to the definition of a *mahākāvya* (*The Riddle of the Rāmāyaṇa*, Bombay, 1906, pp. 37–8).

scriptions for *kāvya* in this matter, slackened their efforts the further through they got, but the generally more ornate subject-matter and style of the Sundarakāṇḍa rekindled their enthusiasm. That the addition of tag verses in longer metres was part of the early literary embellishment of the Rāmāyaṇa is also suggested by their comparative absence in the Bāla and Uttara kāṇḍas.[63] In some cases where there is no tag verse in the text of the Critical Edition, none of the manuscripts used has one; in many more cases only one or two manuscripts have one. Again this tends to support the view that these tag verses are of doubtful authenticity in other cases than those rejected from the text of the Critical Edition. In general all verses in longer metres may be considered to belong to the second stage although, as is clear from the point just mentioned, the process of adding them to the text was a continuing one.

The commonest metres employed in the tag stanzas are the *upajāti* form of the *triṣṭubh* and the *vaṃśastha* form of the *jagatī*; unlike the Mahābhārata, the Rāmāyaṇa does not use other forms of the *triṣṭubh* and *jagatī* metres, as Hopkins observed.[64] Approximately 58% of verses in longer metres are *triṣṭubh*, 36% *vaṃśastha* and the remaining 6% other metres.[65] A certain number of the *triṣṭubh* stanzas are pure *upendravajrā* or rarely *indravajrā* rather than the *upajāti* which forms

[63] The exact figures are as follows: the Ayodhyākāṇḍa has 17 sargas lacking a tag verse and 30 with multiple tag verses, the Araṇyakāṇḍa has 24 lacking and 11 multiple, the Kiṣkindhākāṇḍa has 28 lacking and 9 multiple, the Sundarakāṇḍa has 22 lacking and 16 multiple, and the Yuddhakāṇḍa has 36 lacking and 18 multiple, whereas the Bālakāṇḍa has 65 lacking and 1 multiple and the Uttarakāṇḍa has 83 lacking and 7 multiple (thus both of these have only 10 sargas with one tag verse).

[64] *Great Epic*, p. 276; cf. also H. Oldenberg, 'Zur Chronologie der indischen Metrik', *Gurupūjākaumudī, Festgabe . . . Albrecht Weber*, Leipzig, 1896, pp. 9–12.

[65] Out of a total of 858½ verses in longer metre in the whole Rāmāyaṇa, 497 are *triṣṭubh*, 310½ *vaṃśastha*, 27 *puṣpitāgrā*, 11 *aparavaktra*, 6 *rucirā*, 4 *praharṣiṇī* (all in the Ayodhyākāṇḍa), 1 *vaiśvadevī*, and 2 anomalous (2.108.25–6), of which the first is *asaṃbādhā* and the second unidentifiable (for discussion, see Hopkins, op. cit., p. 332). An examination of the * passages in longer metres appended to the first twenty-five sargas of the Ayodhyā, Araṇya and Kiṣkindhā kāṇḍas yields some useful figures for comparison. In this section of the Ayodhyākāṇḍa there are 53½ stanzas in the following metres: 17½ *triṣṭubh*, 23 *vaṃśastha*, 1 *mālinī*, 1 *puṣpitāgrā*, and 1 mixed *puṣpitāgrā* and *aparavaktra* stanza. The 29½ stanzas of the Araṇyakāṇḍa section comprise 9 *triṣṭubhs*, 17½ *vaṃśasthas*, and 1 each of *aparavaktra*, *puṣpitāgrā* and *rucirā*. The Kiṣkindhākāṇḍa has 25½ stanzas in these metres: 10 *triṣṭubh*, 13 *vaṃśastha*, 1 *aparavaktra*, ½ *puṣpitāgrā*, and 1 in mixed *vātormi* and *śālinī*. Thus, the decline in frequency of stanzas in longer metres visible in the text is reflected in the * passages, indicating that this feature is common to all recensions. Also, the more elaborate metres are commoner in the * passages than in the text. However, these samples show proportions of long compounds little different from the tag verses admitted into the text, unlike the * passages in general

three quarters of the total, but there does not usually seem to be any real distinction sufficient to class them separately; possible exceptions are 4.30.1–5, where an initial *upajāti* is followed by 4 *upendravajrās*, 5.46, which consists of 31 *ślokas* interspersed with 28 longer verses comprising 3 *vaṃśasthas*, 5 *upajātis* and 20 *upendravajrās*, and 5.59.14–22, with 2 *upajātis* to 7½ *upendravajrās*, but significantly all three passages are portions in longer metre within sargas, which seem to be the latest among the longer verses. Similarly, although the *vaṃśastha* stanzas are usually pure (with initial *brevis*), occasionally some *indravaṃśā* pādas are found (e.g. 2.28.29) and thus strictly those verses should be classified as *vaṃśamālā*.

The verses in longer metres of the Ayodhyā to Yuddha kāṇḍas contain on average more than one long compound in each verse, a proportion virtually three times that for the *śloka* verses of these books (105.6% against 36.6%). The Ayodhyā and Araṇya kāṇḍas, which have no passages in longer metres within sargas, have somewhat lower proportions than the other books but still more than double the average for their *śloka* verses. The frequency of similes and of alliteration in these longer verses is also particularly noticeable. One striking instance of the artificiality toward which the tag verses tend is provided by 3.45.40–5, where three *vaṃśastha* stanzas are followed by three *triṣṭubh* stanzas and contain an elaborate series of similes for the difference between Rāma and Rāvaṇa worked out by means of parallelism and alliteration. Various types of *yamaka* and rhyme occur sporadically among the longer verses, of which the most extreme example is found at 5.4.

Whereas the norm in early parts of the Rāmāyaṇa is a direct verbal construction, with in addition the use of the past participle passive (which is still however used attributively rather than predicatively), in the verses in longer metres various verbal periphrases are apparent and the frequency of the form made from the past participle passive with *vat* is striking. Desiderative and intensive forms occur more commonly in these verses: for example, seven of the forty-nine desiderative forms in the Ayodhyākāṇḍa are found in tag verses (that is, a seventh of all desideratives is found in a twenty-second part of the whole) and in both the Ayodhyā and Kiṣkindhā kāṇḍas one of the two intensive forms found occurs in a tag verse. Such figures are too small

which show a significantly higher proportion of long compounds than the text. Yet, even within so small a sample are found a desiderative adjective (3.259*), a future participle (2.638*), *upeyivān* (4.504*) and *sabhājyamāna* (2.329*). The profusion of *alaṃkāras* and especially of *śabdālaṃkāras* in these passages is very marked and indeed might almost be said to provide their *raison d'être*.

for much reliance to be placed on them, but the relative frequency of such forms in these verses is one further indication of their lateness. Various anomalies of the nominal and verbal systems also occur with greater frequency than one might expect.[66]

It appears that two main stages are discernible in the addition of the stanzas in longer metres to the Rāmāyaṇa; in the earlier stage, the tag verses were composed in *upajāti* or *vaṃśastha* metre and the language and style, though more elaborate than the text, does not reach such extremes as in the second stage, when the use of more elaborate metres is found side by side with great elaboration of ornament; a third stage is perhaps discernible in the addition of passages in longer metres within sargas.

Excision of these tag verses helps to demonstrate the artificiality of the present division into sargas, for the epics were originally composed for oral recitation and transmission, and any such divisions would not be apparent. They must have been introduced fairly early in the text's history, however, for many of the demonstrably expanded or interpolated sargas are of much greater than average length; obviously the new material was added after the division into sargas had become established. It is significant that among the top 10% of sargas in length the great majority are listed in the Appendix as belonging to the second stage (forty-seven out of fifty-six). The exceptions are 3.41, 4.1, 11, 5.11, 24, 6.11, 40, 78 and 88; it is a reasonable inference that these too have been expanded, but with less effect on their style.[67] Equally, there is evidence that the present division of the work into *kāṇḍas* is not original, since there is wide discrepancy on this point between the recensions.

The first and last books, the Bāla and Uttara kāṇḍas, dealing as they do with events before and after the main story, have long been recognised to be later additions to the original Rāmāyaṇa of the Ayodhyā to Yuddha kāṇḍas; together they are hereafter referred to as the third stage of growth.[68] Even without a detailed analysis, there are sufficient points of evident difference to illustrate amply how great are the

[66] For some examples see VS pp. 3, 12, 18, 30, 32–3 and NS pp. 381–2.

[67] Note, however, the comments on 4.1 at p. 103, as well as those on 3.41, 5.11, 6.78 and 88 in the Appendix.

[68] For the sake of clarity, I would point out that this represents a change from the nomenclature adopted in my articles RA and 'Rāmo dharmabhṛtāṃ varaḥ', IT 5, 1977, pp. 55–68, where both the second and the third stage as here given were included as the second stage, though with acknowledgement of some chronological difference.

differences between these two books and the genuine Rāmāyaṇa. On the whole the trend is towards greater regularity and artificiality, but there are two aspects of the versification in which they are less regular than the genuine books, evidently because they had by then become part of the hall-mark of an epic, as it were. Half of the examples of hiatus between pādas which Böhtlingk collected from the first four books of the Bombay text came from the Bālakāṇḍa (thirty-eight out of seventy-five instances) and a hardly smaller proportion of the instances of lack of caesura between pādas (twenty-three out of fifty-three).[69] By contrast, long compounds extending beyond a pāda, though not common in the earlier books, are extremely rare in these two later books, with just two in the Bālakāṇḍa and four in the Uttarakāṇḍa.

Various stereotyped phrases occurring in the earlier books are not found in the Bāla or Uttara kāṇḍas and various others occur only in the Bāla and Uttara kāṇḍas. In many cases these phrases are taken from the Mahābhārata stock, demonstrating the great familiarity of the authors of these books with the other epic. A conspicuous example of this is *etasminn eva kāle tu*, which occurs five times in the Bālakāṇḍa and no less than fifty-one times in the Mahābhārata but is not found in the earlier books, where the equivalent phrase is *etasminn antare* – ⏓, occurring once in the Bālakāṇḍa, sixteen times in the Ayodhyā to Yuddha kāṇḍas, and seventeen times in the Uttarakāṇḍa—the difference is that in the early books the pāda may be filled out with *vīrāḥ* (four times) but in the Uttarakāṇḍa with *śūraḥ* (six times).[70] Again, the very similar phrase *kasya cit tv atha kālasya* occurs four times each in the Bāla and Uttara kāṇḍas (and seventeen times in the Mahābhārata) but only elsewhere at 2.1.1a. Similar is the use of two *yathā*- compounds in one pāda, which occurs mainly in the Bālakāṇḍa with eight occurrences against four in the whole of the Ayodhyā to Yuddha kāṇḍas; this usage is prominent also in the later parts of the Mahābhārata.[71]

The usage of the perfect tense is much more regular in the Bālakāṇḍa than in the earlier books. Thus, no instance is found in the Bālakāṇḍa of the use of the perfect for the immediate past or of its linkage with a present tense in the same sentence, and there is complete avoidance of

[69] See O. Böhtlingk, 'Bemerkenswerthes aus Râmâjaṇa, ed. Bomb. Adhj. I–IV', *Ber. Sächs. Akad. der Wiss. Phil.-hist. Klasse* 39, 1887, pp. 213–27. Similarly there are 18 instances of hiatus between pādas in the second half of the Uttarakāṇḍa.

[70] See my 'Note on Mrs Sen's Article about the *Rāmāyaṇa*', JAOS 89, 1969, pp. 412–4, SE p. 221 and Hopkins, *Great Epic* App. A. 30; *etasminn antare* – ⏓ occurs twenty-six times in the Mahābhārata.

[71] See my 'Note to Mrs Sen's Article about the *Rāmāyaṇa*', also SET III.

the first person in narration, in accordance with Pāṇini's descriptions; both these features occur in the earlier books, although admittedly they are not very common. The use of the dative for the genitive of the first and second person pronouns, which is very rare if not unknown in the earlier books, is an occasional idiom of the two later books.[72] There are also occasional instances of indiscriminate use of *bhavān* and *tvam* in one sentence, as at 1.65.3. Other features show a rise in frequency: the past participle passive with *-vat* is two and a half times more frequent than in the early books, periphrastic futures are approximately twice as frequent, and the use of adverbs made with *-ī* from nouns (e.g. *bhasmī* with √*kṛ* or √*bhū*) is over half as frequent again.

In keeping with their basically non-literary, puranic character, both books show a slightly lower proportion of long compounds than that for the earlier books as a whole, while the proportion of similes in the Bālakāṇḍa is only half that of the earlier books, and below their average in the Uttarakāṇḍa. Other figures of speech, however, occur quite prominently, and alliteration tends to be more emphatic than in the earlier Rāmāyaṇa.[73]

Despite this apparently overwhelming linguistic evidence for the lateness of these two books, Jacobi postulates an early date for a small part of the Bālakāṇḍa, because of lingering doubts about the apparent abruptness of the opening of the story in the Ayodhyākāṇḍa.[74] His 'Reconstruktion des ursprünglichen Anfangs' is in fact a brief passage which he believed was prefixed to the present Ayodhyākāṇḍa; such an introduction is in my view not necessarily required, since there is ample dramatic justification for being plunged *in medias res* (as would be the case if the epic opened with the present beginning of the Ayodhyākāṇḍa), especially in the case of a well-known story such as this presumably was when Vālmīki gave it its distinctive form. The passage reconstructed by Jacobi appears in the Critical Edition as 1.5.1–9, 6.2–4, 17.10, 11c–12d, 14, 13 and 7.[75] This passage obviously

[72] See Nilmadhav Sen, 'Un-Pāṇinian Pronouns and Numerals in the Rāmāyaṇa', JOIB 5, 1955, pp. 266–71.

[73] One instance of alliteration in the Bālakāṇḍa, *gaganād gāṃ gatāṃ tadā*, 42.8d, is completely different from anything in the earlier portions in its restriction of the consonants employed to *g* and the dentals, and approaches the artificiality of classical Sanskrit.

[74] *Das Râmâyaṇa*, pp. 50–9. Cf. also the arguments in support of Jacobi by J. Vekerdi, 'On the *Bāla-kāṇḍa* of the *Rāmāyaṇa*', *Acta Orient. Hung*. 19, 1966, pp. 13–24.

[75] It may be noted that 1.17.13 is similar to 2.1.10 and 1.17.7 is identical to 2.10* 3–4; this probably represents an attempt by the redactors of the S. recension to tie back the

is an introduction, but to the Bālakāṇḍa alone.[76] A mere glance shows that its style is quite alien to that of the early Rāmāyaṇa and similar to the more elaborate style of the second stage. Vekerdi in fact suggests that sargas 5–7, though having undergone some expansion, should be aligned with the older books, noting both their more elaborate style and the verse in longer metre concluding each in the standard pattern of the older books.[77] The contrast with the immediately following Ṛśyaśṛṅga episode (1.8–10) is indeed very marked, for these three sargas show a very low proportion of long compounds, a virtually total absence of figures of speech, and no concluding longer verses.

Certainly, it is possible to discern something of the process whereby both the Bālakāṇḍa and the Uttarakāṇḍa have been built up out of a number of virtually independent episodes, many of which have links with other literature and are indeed markedly puranic in character. Such links have often been used to date the various parts and inferentially the entire books. Thus, Lüders indicated that the form of the Ṛśyaśṛṅga episode just mentioned was later than the versions in the Mahābhārata (3.110–3) and the *Padma Purāṇa*.[78] Even earlier, Lassen had pointed to the awkwardness with which the *putreṣṭi* (1.14) supervenes on the *aśvamedha* (1.11–13) in the account of Daśaratha's sacrifices, as well as to the abrupt insertion of the Paraśurāma episode (1.73–5);[79] both, as he noted, have the purpose of asserting Rāma's nature as an *avatāra* of Viṣṇu, which is not otherwise explicitly claimed in the Bālakāṇḍa. Vekerdi also points out that this whole group of sargas (1.14–18) containing the legend of Viṣṇu's incarnation as Rāma all, except 15, conclude with a longer verse, as do the original intro-

beginning of the Ayodhyākāṇḍa to the birth of Daśaratha's sons, by then included in the Bālakāṇḍa.

[76] So G. H. Bhatt clearly indicates in his Critical Notes on the Bālakāṇḍa (pp. 424 and 435) for the first part of this passage.

[77] J. Vekerdi, op. cit.; he would also date it no later than the second century AD. The proportion of long compounds in all three is higher than the average (very high in 5) and so is the frequency of similes in 5 and 6, with a longer simile in each.

[78] H. Lüders, 'Die Sage von Ṛṣyaśṛṅga', NG 1897, pp. 87–135 and 'Zur Sage von Ṛṣyaśṛṅga', NG 1901, pp. 28–56; cf. also D. Schlingloff, 'The Unicorn, Origin and Migrations of an Indian Legend', *German Scholars on India*, vol. II, Bombay, 1976, pp. 294–307. On the other hand the association of Ṛśyaśṛṅga with a vow which links the twelve names of Viṣṇu with the twelve months and fulfils all wishes, especially that for sons, is found in *Ṛgvidhāna* 3.27–8. It may also be noted that the episode is considerably more developed in the N. recension.

[79] C. Lassen, *Indische Alterthumskunde*, vol. 1, 2nd ed., Leipzig, 1866, pp. 586–7; cf. also J. Muir, *Original Sanskrit Texts*, vol. 4, 2nd ed., London, 1873, pp. 164–78 and Satyavrat Shastri, 'Putreṣṭi in the Rāmāyaṇa: was it really necessary', IT 6, 1978, pp. 279–82.

ductory sargas 5–7, the subsequent introduction 1–4 (except 3), and the last sarga (1.76), all of which are connected to the basic story of the Rāmāyaṇa in a way that most of the Bālakāṇḍa is not.[80].

The whole of the Viśvāmitra episode (1.31–64) lacks direct relevance to the main story of Rāma and could be omitted.[81] Alternatively, it could be argued that it too accreted in stages, with for instance the story of Sagara (1.37–43) and Śatānanda's account of Viśvāmitra's history (1.50–64) as two of the units. With regard to the first, Lesný pointed out the correspondence of parts to the *Harivaṃśa* (10.56–64 with 218*, 219*, 220*) and the *Viṣṇu Purāṇa* (4.4.1–3), and Kirfel independently to the *Brahmāṇḍa* and *Vāyu Purāṇas* (also Mbh.3.106);[82] Kirfel argues that the author of this passage was acquainted with the *Vāyu Purāṇa* in something like its present form and therefore assigns the Bālakāṇḍa as a whole to the second half of the fourth century AD or later. With regard to the latter, Jacobi pointed out a series of irregular pādas within it,[83] and the number of puranic accounts—of Vasiṣṭha's cow, of Triśaṅku, of Ambarīṣa's sacrifice and of Menakā—certainly are suggestive of a relatively late date; on the other hand, in the last-mentioned episode, Viśvāmitra abruptly abandons Menakā (1.62/1173*) and there is no mention of Śakuntalā's birth, which may imply that the Bālakāṇḍa account is earlier than the *Śakuntalopākhyāna* (Mbh.1.62–9). As to the process of growth, it may be noted that 1.49, which displays a somewhat more elaborate style from the proportions of its similes and long compounds, is relevant for the arrival in Mithilā and that part of it (1.49.23–4) alludes back to the events narrated earlier including those contained in the later part of sarga 46 up to 48, whereas 1.50.18–28 is a repetition of sarga 33 and may well therefore mark the start of renewed interpolation. Similar textual repetition between the last sarga of the Bālakāṇḍa and the first sarga of the Ayodhyākāṇḍa presumably points to the separation of what once formed a single passage.[84]

[80] Vekerdi, op. cit.

[81] So indeed G. H. Bhatt, the editor of the Critical Edition, suggests (p. 456). It may be noted that none of these sargas is vouched for in the Bālakāṇḍa's own two summaries, the *Rāmopākhyāna* or the *Bhaṭṭikāvya* (unless BhK 2.41 is based on 1.49 rather than 1.65).

[82] V. Lesný, 'Über das Purāṇaartige Gepräge des Bālakāṇḍa', ZDMG 67, 1913, pp. 497–500 and W. Kirfel, 'Rāmāyaṇa Bālakāṇḍa und Purāṇa', *Die Welt des Orients* 1, 1947, pp. 113–28. Apart from the passage noted by Lesný also (1.37.3–22b), Kirfel also demonstrated the parallelism of 1.31.1ef, 45.1–46.18, 1277* 2 and 69.28 and 70.3c–13 with those Purāṇas; cf. the discussion of these passages in van Daalen, *Vālmīki's Sanskrit*, pp. 224–35.

[83] *Das Râmâyaṇa*, pp. 26–9, noted above.

[84] Many mss. read 2.1.1–5 and 11–14 after 1.76.12 and 1.76.13 is virtually identical to

Within the Uttarakāṇḍa, the most obvious stylistic difference is between Agastya's narrative (7.1–36) and the remainder of the book: not only is the average length of its sargas nearly double that of the rest, but it contains many more verses in longer metres and has substantially higher proportions of similes and long compounds.[85] The whole impression is of a much more ornate style, not dissimilar from the elaborated passages of the second stage, from which it may not differ too greatly in date. All but the last two sargas of Agastya's narrative relate the previous exploits of Rāvaṇa and his ancestors (termed by Jacobi therefore 'die Râvaṇeïs'), and corresponding material occurs in the *Rāmopākhyāna*, the oldest reworking of the Rāmāyaṇa material;[86] the last two, lengthy sargas (35–6) narrate the history of Hanumān and, despite their no doubt independent origin, show the same stylistic elaboration.[87] However, apart from this first part, the Uttarakāṇḍa in general displays every sign of being later than the Bālakāṇḍa, for example in regularly viewing Rāma as divine, and in

2.1.10; the priority between the extant parts can no longer be determined. In addition, it may be noted that 1.70 expands Janaka's genealogy already briefly given in 1.65 and that Daśaratha's genealogy in 1.69 is largely similar to that in 2.102. On the growth and dating of the Bālakāṇḍa see also C. Bulcke, *Rām-kathā* (*utpatti aur vikāś*), 2nd ed., Prayāg, 1962, pp. 122–5 and 'The Genesis of the Bālakāṇḍa', JOIB 2, 1952–3, pp. 327–31, and W. Ruben, *Studien zur Textgeschichte des Rāmāyaṇa* (Bonner Orientalistische Studien 19), Stuttgart, 1936, pp. 61 ff.

[85] The total length of 1–36 at 1407½ stanzas (average 39) exceeds that of 37–100 at 1312½ (average 20½); it contains 29 longer verses (several multiple) against 5 in the remainder, 301 similes (21.39%) against 77 (5.87%) and 561 long compounds (39.86%) against 326 (24.84%). On the other hand the frequency of periphrastic futures is lower (6 against 13), but the proportion of them increases with lateness.

[86] See pp. 228–9 and my 'Sanskrit Epic Tradition I. Epic and Epitome (Rāmāyaṇa and Rāmopākhyāna)', IT 6, 1978, pp. 79–111. R. Antoine (*Rāma & the Bards: Epic Memory in the Ramayana*, Calcutta, 1975, pp. 46–54) considers that both this account of Rāvaṇa by Agastya (7.1–34) and that of Viśvāmitra by Śatānanda (1.50–64) 'might well have been independent epic songs'. This view has considerable plausibility so far as Rāvaṇa's exploits are concerned.

[87] J. Vekerdi ('On the *Uttara-kāṇḍa* of the Rāmāyaṇa', *Acta Orient. Hung.* 17, 1964, pp. 187–95) comments that this version of the story of Hanumān's birth and childhood is essentially the same as that in 4.65, itself belonging to the second stage. For other assessments of this book, see M. V. Kibe, 'Is the Uttara Kanda of Valmiki Ramayana Un-Historical?' JIH 20, 1941, pp. 28–34 and A. K. Chatterjee, 'A Note on the Uttarakāṇḍa of the *Rāmāyaṇa*', JOIB 22, 1972–3, pp. 304–15. Kibe argues that the Uttarakāṇḍa is a necessary part of the Rāmāyaṇa, basically on grounds of piety, whereas Chatterjee argues for its lateness from the developed religious and social pattern apparent but nevertheless regards it, along with the rest of the Rāmāyaṇa, as pre-Buddhist and so belonging to the middle of the sixth century BC.

showing markedly less divergence between the recensions. It is significant, therefore, that Kālidāsa's *Raghuvaṃśa* apparently alludes to certain incidents narrated in it, for this would imply a date before the fourth century AD, earlier than Kirfel's dating of the Bālakāṇḍa.

Apart from the accounts of Rāvaṇa and Hanumān, which in fact fill out the background to the main story of the Rāmāyaṇa, the remainder of the Uttarakāṇḍa attempts in the main to fill out some of the questions left unanswered at the end of the Yuddhakāṇḍa; indeed it might almost be seen as the actualisation of the prediction made there by Maheśvara (who is in fact Agni or Brahmā, not Śiva), when he declares that Rāma, after resuming the kingdom, establishing the Ikṣvāku dynasty, celebrating an *aśvamedha* and gaining unparalleled fame, will deservedly go to heaven (6.107.1–6). All of it is narrated in a bare, unadorned style, with the sole exception of sarga 41 where the subject-matter—Rāma and Sītā in the pleasure-garden—absolutely requires some stylishness. Otherwise, there is no real difference between the narration of obviously puranic insertions, such as the stories of Śveta and Daṇḍa (7.68–72) or of Ila (7.78–81), and episodes such as the banishment of Sītā (7.42–7) which are central to its plot.

Accordingly, no attempt will normally be made to subdivide the stage of growth represented by the Bāla and Uttara kāṇḍas, even though they too undoubtedly reached their present form over a considerable period; they will be taken together as the third stage. Equally, apart from occasional remarks, no systematic investigation is made of the precise relationship with different passages of the second stage, although there must be a possibility—indeed a probability in a few cases—that there is some overlap chronologically. A further dimension to the attempt to separate into stages what was undoubtedly a continuing process of evolution of the text is that the separation may be not only chronological but also geographical and therefore in part cultural. Geographical divergence ultimately of course led to the emergence of the Northern and Southern recensions and this may indeed have occurred by the second century AD.[88]

The later stages of the divergence into recensions is attested in the material relegated by the Critical Edition to its * passages and Ap-

[88] As just noted, the Uttarakāṇḍa shows much less sign of this divergence. More importantly, the search party accounts of the second stage with their *Harivaṃśa* parallels suggest this; cf. p. 113 n.40.

pendix I.[89] Those additions or substitutions which are common to all or most manuscripts will be regarded as the fourth stage of growth, while those found only in a few or even just one manuscript will be designated the fifth stage, on the assumption that in general the more poorly attested a passage is the later it is likely to be. These two stages also manifest the two opposing trends visible in the second stage (and to a more limited extent in the third) of elaboration on the more dramatic and lyrical aspects of the story and of the narration in an unliterary puranic style of various extraneous episodes loosely inserted into the plot. However, the significant differences of style are those between the recensions, which are to a large extent masked in the text itself by the tendency to adopt Southern readings in cases of verbal disagreement. It is therefore useful to conclude with a brief survey of the more obvious differences between the recensions visible in passages belonging to the fourth and fifth stages.

The Northern recension presents in almost all aspects a more polished version than the Southern. There seems to be little difference between the Northwestern and Northeastern recensions with regard to style, despite the degree of divergence in readings, although if anything the Northeastern is more polished. The avoidance of irregular forms and of hiatus in the Northern recension is very marked, various *alaṃkāras* are much commoner and more developed, and it has many fewer instances of certain less sophisticated traits such as playing on personal names and parallelism of structure. Certain features, such as a preoccupation with numerals, seem to be a mark of lateness rather than a characteristic of any one recension.

The proportion of long compounds tends to be higher in the Northern recension than in the Southern in those places where it can be determined with sufficient certainty. A study of the verbal forms also reveals certain statistical differences. Change of voice is three times as common in the Southern passages as in the Northern passages and the text of the Araṇyakāṇḍa; the proportion in the Northern passages is almost the same as in the text.[90] If the text of the Ayodhyākāṇḍa is compared with the passages in Appendix I, it can be seen that finite forms are much commoner in the Southern passages from Appendix I than in either the Northern passages or the text; in the text non-finite forms are one and a fifth times as common as finite forms, in the Northern passages non-finite forms are one and a half times as frequent

[89] The distinction between * passages and those in Appendix I is purely one of length. Therefore, as a matter of convenience, I use the term * passage to designate both, on those occasions when the terms fourth and fifth stage are not employed.

[90] The form *prasvāpayata* at 3 App.I.12.19, showing both change of voice and lack of augment, is poorly supported by the mss. containing the passage.

as finite forms, whereas in the Southern passages finite forms are as frequent as non-finite forms. But these proportions conceal the trend towards nominal construction in the Northern recension, since they make no allowance for past participles contained in compounds or for greater use of verbal substitutes and do not distinguish between the attributive and predicative use of past participles passive. In particular, the gerundive, the causative and the periphrastic perfect are more frequent in the passages from Appendix I read by the Northern manuscripts; however, the gerundive is also slightly commoner in later portions of the text, especially 2.1–30, 85, 94, and 3.10 and 45.

Altogether, it may be said that the Northern recension shows a verbal pattern more like that of the classical literature. It is inclined to use the more elaborate and classical *alaṃkāras*, such as *rūpaka, svabhāvokti* and *dīpaka*, to a much greater extent than the Southern. Alliteration is also more frequent in the Northern recension, but it is common in both, since it occupies an intermediate position between the *alaṃkāras* found preponderantly in the Northern recension and the parallelism and punning epithets found in the Southern recension. Similes are naturally ubiquitous and it would be practically impossible to discover any major variations between the recensions in the use of them. One point of interest is the persistence of similes even in those cases where any other similarity between the readings of the two recensions has vanished; this is, of course, linked with the stereotyped nature of many of the similes already remarked on. Metaphors tend to be more elaborate in the Northern recension, which very often inserts them in additional * passages. Even where the same metaphor is found in both recensions, the version of the Northern recension is normally the more stylish. Parallelism of construction and similar phenomena, though found also in the Northern recension, are very much a mark of the Southern recension. Indeed, the Northern manuscripts may actually have eliminated some cases.

If this analysis of the growth of the text into successive stages has any validity, then its application to the study of the content of the text might be expected to yield useful results. Examination of the general setting of the poem in its physical environment, both natural and man-made, of the pattern of society it depicts and of the religious attitudes incorporated into it, in the light of this analysis, should reveal the culture presupposed by the successive authors for, as in the case of all pre-modern literatures (unless strongly influenced by an older treatment of the subject), the poets tend to describe the features of their own time without regard for anachronism. It is to these aspects of the text that we turn in the next chapters.

3
THE SETTING
ECONOMIC AND MATERIAL CULTURE

'A pleasant city encircled by a shining white rampart, with golden courtyards and arches of cat's-eye, thronged with elephants, horses and chariots, . . .' (3.46.11–12a)

Economic life is very meagrely presented in the Rāmāyaṇa, for of course its interests are not those of the mercantile or trading community. In addition, what evidence there is suggests that the economy was relatively undeveloped. There is no clear evidence for the use of coinage: even the term *niṣka*, originally a gold chest ornament but later used as money, occurs exclusively in the former sense, although the transition may be seen in the incident when Bharata's grandfather presents him with gifts of elephants, blankets, hides, two thousand *niṣkas* and six hundred horses (2.64.17–18), the whole being termed *dhana*, wealth. In other instances, a certain figure in gold is stated but the understood term may as well be a weight as a coin. However, in such use of numerals may be seen the evidence of an incipient money economy.

The term *dhana*, wealth or property, is the term most commonly employed but two other terms, *nidhāna* and *vitta*, occasionally occur. All in fact mean to a large extent simply a store of anything valuable, being nearly synonymous with *kośa*, a store-room or store, and the term *dhana* is several times linked with jewels (e.g. 2.29.15 and 66.9) or consists of jewels and gold (e.g. 3.41.30). It therefore easily bears a metaphorical meaning, as when brāhmans say that the Vedas are their wealth (2.40.23) or ascetics are described as 'rich in austerities' (*tapodhana*, which occurs especially in the Bāla and Uttara kāṇḍas and is half as frequent as *dhana*). It is also significant that—not just for the sake of alliteration—it is linked with *dhānya*, grain, in a quarter of its occurrences, either in the compound *dhanadhānya* or otherwise (e.g. 2.32.6). Thus one might say that it signifies reserves, whether of valuables or of foodstuffs. The only reference possibly to its functioning as capital is one allusion to merchants as having much wealth (*vaṇijaś ca mahādhanāḥ* 2.32.3b).

There are only a handful of references to merchants, *vaṇij* or *naigama*, in the Ayodhyākāṇḍa, the book which contains most about city life, and of these two terms, *naigama* is predominantly a late word, occurring mostly in the Uttarakāṇḍa, although seven references in the text to guilds or their leaders (*śreṇī, śreṇīmukhya*) might suggest a more developed pattern of economic activity than the rest of the evidence indicates. However, the standard descriptions of towns, whether Ayodhyā, Kiṣkindhā or Madhurā, mention trade or business, *nigama* and *paṇya*, and markets, *antarāpaṇa* or *āpaṇa*, although details are generally lacking (2.6.12, 13.2, 106.13, 4.32.5 and 7.62.11–12; cf. 2.61.17); the term *vīthi* for a market stall occurs twice in the Uttarakāṇḍa. Evidence for long-distance trade is found in one reference to merchants not travelling when there is no king (2.61.17) and in three similes—all from the second stage—of an individual joining a caravan of merchants (*sārtha*, 2.98.28), of the hardships of relatives while the caravan is gone (3.58.31), and of a traveller separated from the caravan in the wild (4.66.43); the overall picture is hardly favourable, besides being late.

The means, therefore, by which the king could replenish his treasury (*kośa*, rarely and only later *koṣṭhāgara*, literally 'store-house') must have been primarily taxation in kind on the agricultural community. In part this is implied by the linkage of *dhana* and *dhānya*, valuables and grain, already referred to. Even more, perhaps, the only term for taxation or the like, *bali*, points in this direction, for it has also—indeed, largely indistinguishably—the meaning of an offering, especially of food, to minor deities; a translation 'tribute' to some extent covers the semantic area better. There are in fact three brief passages dealing with the king's right to tax which, though spanning all the stages of growth, have very similar wording to the effect that a king who takes a sixth part as tribute (*baliṣaḍbhāga*) and fails to protect his subjects incurs *adharma*, sin (2.69.18, 3.5.10–13, and 7.1112* with 1113* and 1114*). It is obviously a traditional saying, which may indeed be paralleled from the Mahābhārata (12.137.96 and 13.24.78)[1] and *Manu* (8.308), but notably less precise than the treatment of taxation elsewhere in *Manu* or in Kauṭilya's *Arthaśāstra*. The earliest of the three passages does in fact go on to say that 'Of the supreme dharma which a sage eating roots and fruit performs, a quarter belongs to the king who protects his subjects righteously' (3.5.13). There are also a couple of references to the king balancing income and expenditure (2.1.21 and 94.45), both from the second stage.

[1] Mbh. 1.2015* is also virtually identical to *Manu* 8.308.

One expedient attested from other sources by which a king could obviate the lack of cash to pay for government works is the use of the *corvée*, forced labour (*viṣṭi*). However, the only references to this in the Rāmāyaṇa are late and allude to its use in making roads, one (from the late second stage) for Rāma's return (6.115.4) and the other (from the fourth stage) in connection with Bharata's expedition to persuade Rāma to return (2.1899*)

The various terms for roads and streets are somewhat commoner overall in the second and later periods but the individual terms show varied distributions. The two commonest terms, *pathin* (in composition, *patha*, as in *mahāpatha*) and *mārga*, show a somewhat greater frequency in the first stage than the average, whereas the less common *adhvan* occurs most frequently in the second stage. More specialised terms are commoner in the second and later stages; these are, in order of frequency: *rājamārga*, 'the king's way', the highway, *rathyā*, a road suitable for chariots or carriages, and *caryā*, (road for) driving about, carriage-road. Their order also indicates the relative size and importance of the roads; similarly, in the fourth stage we find *rathyā* and *uparathyā* 'main and side road' (e.g. 5.1072*). Two terms for crossroads, *śṛṅgāṭaka* and *catuṣpatha*, each occur once in the text, in the first and second stage respectively, too rarely to have any real significance.

In certain passages from the second stage onwards, there occur references both to sprinkling roads with water, presumably to lay the dust (1.5.8, 6.115.6 and 2 App.I.6.25), and to hanging lamps on trees to provide illumination at night (2.6.18 and 5.3.19). These suggest quite a concern for communications, which is also indicated by the description of the road for Bharata's journey (2.74), which is specially constructed by felling trees in wooded areas, planting them in others, levelling hollows, digging wells and placing a curb round them, and paving the road itself. However, the latter at least is undoubtedly an idealised picture and the reality is rather that alluded to in another passage of the second stage—roads impassable to vehicles in the rains (4.27.16[l.v.]). By contrast, the construction of Nala's causeway over the ocean is described very soberly: the Vānaras gather trees and rocks to hurl into the sea until a sufficiently solid platform is made. In this instance, however, the elaboration occurs in the fourth stage, where there are enumerations of the amount constructed in each day's work as well as long lists of different trees (6.280*–303*, App.I.13.1–2 and App.I.14).

The regular means of transport along these roads for the principal characters is the horse-drawn carriage or chariot—the same term *ratha* is used indifferently to describe the carriage used to convey one over long distances and the war-chariot from which one warrior fights while another drives. Approximately 70% of all references to vehicles and other forms of transport are to the *ratha*, for which the term *syandana* is a very occasional variant. Vehicles in general are denoted by the infrequent terms *yāna* and *vāhana*, while the *ratha* is also occasionally said to be drawn by donkeys and there are a couple of mentions of bullock-carts (*goratha*). Also used for conveyance, for example by Bharata on his expedition (2.86.34), is the palanquin or litter (*śibikā*), although most allusions to it are in its other role as bier.

It seems however that there were roads fit to drive on only as far as the Gaṅgā, which had to be crossed by boat (e.g. 2.46 and 83, and 7.46) or the like, for Bharata's army crosses it partly by boat, partly by raft (*plava*), partly with floats made of pitchers (*kumbhaghaṭa*) and partly by swimming (2.83). Rāma and his companions also have to construct their own raft in order to cross the Kālindī or Yamunā by cutting up Sītā's seat (2.49.3, 9–12) or in the more elaborate Northern version by binding timbers with creepers (2.1172*, which uses the term *uḍupa* for the raft). A particular, presumably large, boat is named *svastika* in this context (2.83.11a, 12a), but otherwise the simple term *nau* is always used, apart from one late occurrence of *pota*; thus it is clear that *nau* regularly denotes a river boat, although it also occurs in a few similes referring to ships at sea.

Apart from a few lists in the Ayodhyākāṇḍa, different occupations or employments are rarely mentioned and in fact are dominated by groups who are really various categories of royal servants. Only about a dozen occupations are mentioned in early passages outside such lists. Those such as *sūta* and *dūta*, which are clearly part of the royal entourage are considered elsewhere; others which closely resemble them are the *māgadhas* and *bandins*, minstrels and bards, and the general term for soldier, *yodha*. The fishermen or ferrymen (*dāśa*) who help travellers across the Gaṅgā are referred to seven times in the Ayodhyākāṇḍa, where the term *kaivarta* for fisherman is also found (2.78.7b). In addition we have references to fortune-tellers and astrologers (6.38.2a and 5b, *lakṣaṇika* and *kārtāntika*), mahouts (*gajāroha* 3.49.29c and 6.44.23a), riders or grooms (2.90.15d and 6.59.18c), guards (2.73.13a), craftsmen (2.73.13a), cooks (3.54.22f) and a butcher (2.42.24d). Even the later parts of the early books do not add further occupations, but only a couple of synonyms: *daivajña* (2.4.18c) for fortune-teller and *nāvika* (2.46.65d) for boatman.

Only if we include the evidence of certain lists does the picture change. One of these is in a sarga already noted as late (2.74.1–3) and lists the various skills needed to construct the road for Bharata while the other found in the text enumerates the different tradesmen and artisans who accompany him on his expedition (2.77.12–15). The latter is a random list interposed abruptly between the 'respected people, traders and all the subjects' and 'brāhmans knowing the Vedas' of the preceding and following stanzas, which suffice to indicate the whole population without detailed enumeration. Its authenticity is thus dubious. However, significantly, this list is then expanded—in a still more random fashion—in additions of the Northern recension; these are presented as two separate * passages (2.1904* and 1905*) but their attestation does not follow the usual division into Northeast and Northwest recensions and there is in fact a common core with some further expansion in one and rather more in the other.

The construction of the road requires the use of scouts or guides, surveyors, diggers or navvies, engineers, artisans, master builders, men skilled with machines, carpenters, pioneers, tree-fellers, well-diggers, plasterers or white-washers (presumably to mark out the route in some way), makers of bamboo work, and spies or scouts. Those who set out on it comprise jewellers, potters, weavers (carpenters?), armourers, peacock-catchers, sawyers, glass-workers, gem-piercers, ivory-workers, plasterers, vendors of perfumes, goldsmiths, blanket-washers, bathers, coverers (?), doctors, perfumers, wine-vendors, washermen, tailors, headmen, actors and their wives and fishermen. This in itself is a fuller and obviously much later list than that of occupations properly attested in the text. However, the Northern recension adds to it eulogists, equerries, minstrels and bards, basket-makers, workers in reed, sellers of grain, water-sellers, flower- fruit- and root-sellers, leather workers, blacksmiths, coppersmiths and tinkers, dealers in birch-bark, makers of sugar-candy, and heads of guilds—to cite only those occurring in the common core. The longest list (2.1905*) would in fact add another sixty terms to the twenty-three of the text, but there are some repetitions and several apparent synonyms or at least very closely related terms (e.g. two terms for carpenter and two for sawyer). Elsewhere in the fourth stage, various other occupations are mentioned, such as hunters and magicians.

Even the Bāla and Uttara kāṇḍas broadly reflect the earlier pattern in their texts, although general terms for artisans or craftsmen (*karmāntika, śilpin*) are a little more frequent and the term for wages (*niṣkraya*) makes its first appearance. Throughout, terms for servants are commoner than those for artisans. Two terms for servants (*dāsa* and *preṣya*) are most frequent in the first stage, and a third (*bhṛtya*) occurs predominantly in the second and third stages, with another term (*kiṃkara*) becoming common by the third stage; other terms (*ceṭī, paricāraka* and *parivāra*) are rare, or not attested at all until the fourth stage (*anujīvijana*). One of the terms is often translated 'slave' (*dāsa*) and is the term most often used to denote the personal servants at the court of Ayodhyā,[2] but there is no real evidence that their condition is one of slavery in any of the circumstances concerning them, and in fact Hanumān is content to declare to Rāvaṇa that he is Rāma's *dāsa*. There is certainly no reference to the buying or selling of individuals, apart from the sale of Śunaḥśepa as a sacrificial victim narrated only in the third stage (1.60–1), which is in any case a Vedic story (cf. e.g. *Aitareya Brāhmaṇa* 8.13–18)

If craftsmen are rarely mentioned in the earlier parts of the Rāmāyaṇa, so too are their products; but the writers of the later stages showed a natural tendency to produce elaborate descriptions of jewellery, buildings and vehicles. Even such a frequently mentioned material as gold is therefore found nearly twice as often in passages of the second stage as in the first stage. But the commonest terms, *kāñcana* and *hema*, are also more frequent in the first stage than the other terms, suggesting that they are part of the original vocabulary. By contrast, *kārtasvara* for example does not occur before the second stage, *hairaṇya* not before the third stage, and *kaladhauta* not before the fourth. No less than twenty synonyms for gold are found but, in addition to *kāñcana* and *hema*, the only ones occurring with any frequency are *suvarṇa, kanaka* and *jāmbūnada*. The last term originally at least meant '(gold) from the river Jambu'; this river is mythical, and was supposed to flow from the equally mythical mount Meru, yet use of the term may possibly preserve a memory of the northeast being the source of gold, rather than the Deccan mines which were brought within the ambit of North India probably from early Mauryan times.

[2] Dev Raj Chanana claims that, in contrast with the societies of Kiṣkindhā and Laṅkā, the society of Ayodhyā did know slavery, since it was agriculturally based whereas the other two were still at the food-gathering stage (*Slavery in Ancient India*, New Delhi, 1960, p. 29). The evidence is really insufficient either to substantiate or to invalidate his argument, although we may note that Sītā refers to the Rākṣasīs set to guard her as *dāsīs* (6.101.30, 32).

Certainly there is no reference to the mining of gold, although one later passage (4.39.22) refers to the earth as the source of silver. However, a term for ores, *dhātu*, is found occasionally, for example elephants are once described as streaked with gold, silver and copper ores (3.14.15), but it is not common and occurs preponderantly in later passages. On the other hand the refining of gold in the fire is alluded to (e.g. 3.28.20 and 4 App.I.14.66[l.v.]). There also occurs in the Bālakāṇḍa a myth of the origin of metals from Śiva's seed cast off on the Himālaya by Gaṅgā, which also grades the metals: gold superior, copper and iron middling, and tin and lead inferior (1.36.18–19). Interestingly, silver is absent from this list and the commentators, noticing the omission, suggest blandly that one of the two terms for gold means silver. In fact, its omission here is in line with its rarity throughout the text by comparison with gold, for it occurs only one tenth as often. Possibly this reflects the different methods necessary to win each metal; alluvial gold was obtained by panning, and so was more accessible to primitive technology than silver, which must be mined; it is also true that silver has always been scarcer relative to gold in India than it has in Europe. Incidentally, there are also references to the sea as the repository of jewels (2.76.7, 1.154* 12, 6.247* 3 etc.), obvious references to pearl-fishing.

To return to the Bālakāṇḍa myth, we may also note that this is the only mention of tin (*trapu*) in the text and one of only two references to lead (*sīsa*), the other reference also carrying an evaluation when Sītā declares that the difference between Rāma and Rāvaṇa is that between iron and lead (3.45.41[l.v.]). These two passages, both late, are also the only two in the text where the term *loha* is used for iron. Elsewhere that metal is termed *kārṣṇāyasa* or *kālāyasa*, 'black metal', and all three terms together are just over two-thirds as frequent as the term *tāmra* for copper (or its derivatives, brass and bronze), for which in later passages are found in addition the terms *ārakūṭa* and *kāṃsya*. This raises the question of the meaning of the terms *ayas* and *āyasa*, usually translated 'iron' but cognate with Latin *aes* 'copper' as well as with *iron*; their distribution pattern is similar to that for *tāmra*, with almost as many occurrences in earlier passages as later, whereas the terms for iron already mentioned have a later distribution pattern than other metals as a whole, which tend in any case to be commoner later. Thus, while the number of occurrences is too small for certainty to be reached, the balance of probability is that *ayas* 'metal' designates copper or bronze in the Rāmāyaṇa and that iron is distinguished as 'the black metal'. If so, the early phases of the poem are showing great conservatism, for recent opinion among archaeologists suggests that the use of iron in India was becoming general around 800 BC.[3] However, adherence to the older pattern on precisely this point is a well-known feature of Homer.

Certain other minerals are mentioned because of their use as gem-stones, of which the commonest, especially in later passages, is the *vaidūrya* 'cat's-eye gem', a sort of chrysoberyl. In addition, the redness of *gairika*, probably a form of arsenic, is occasionally used as a comparison for blood, and *manaḥśilā*, realgar or red arsenic, is thrice mentioned as a pigment, used along with a yellow pigment, *rocanā*, in marking the *tilaka* on the forehead.

So far as the Rāmāyaṇa is concerned there are only three cities—Ayodhyā, Kiṣkindhā and Laṅkā. Other cities are incidentally mentioned, but it is only these three that are described in any detail. Indeed, it is of Laṅkā that we are given the fullest description, especially of its fortifications, but also of Rāvaṇa's palace and other prominent buildings. However, all three cities are described in broadly similar terms and, although much of the detail is relatively late, Kiṣkindhā is still just as affluent and urbane as the other two, despite the growing tendency to depict the Vānaras as uncouth monkeys. In fact, the later the description the more idealised it is and it must be considered uncertain how far any of the cities are depicted from life. Indeed, the suggestion of the bystanders when they hear of Rāma's exile, that they should accompany him to the forest and thus turn it into the city (2.30.15–20, cf. App.I.15.21–30), indicates a much simpler way of life.

The fullest description of Ayodhyā comes early in the Bālakāṇḍa (and thus is very late), where it is described as created by Manu, being twelve *yojanas* by three in extent, with its main highway well-constructed and regularly sprinkled with water;[4] inhabited by Daśaratha, it possesses arched doorways, well laid out markets, every kind of engine

[3] See for example Dilip K. Chakrabarti, 'The beginning of iron in India', *Antiquity* 50, 1956, pp. 114–24, 'Distribution of Iron Ores', *Journal of the Economic and Social History of the Orient* 20, 1977, pp. 166–84 and 'Iron in early Indian literature', JRAS, 1979, pp. 22–30.

[4] The *yojana* is a measure of distance, commonly said to be around four miles. The evidence of the Rāmāyaṇa would suggest a much smaller unit. See p. 117. The antiquity of Ayodhyā as a historical site is now further established by a find of Painted Grey Ware during excavations in March-April 1975 by B. B. Lal; see H. D. Sankalia, 'Ayodhyā of the Rāmāyaṇa in a Historical Perspective', ABORI 58–9, 1977–8, pp. 893–919.

and weapon, lofty watch-towers and flag-staffs, hundreds of catapults, parks and mango groves, a girdle of *sāl* trees, an impregnably deep moat, mansions adorned with gems, pitch-roofed houses, palaces and houses, with a draughtsboard layout as well as being thronged with all sorts of people (1.5.6–22). Early in the Ayodhyākāṇḍa, as part of the preparations for Rāma's installation, flags and banners are raised in or on the temples, crossroads, highways, *caityas*, watch-towers, traders' shops, householders' residences, assembly-halls and trees of Ayodhyā (2.6.11–13), while further on, in the late *kaccit* sarga, Rāma enquires about the city's mansions, *caityas*, temples, reservoirs and ponds, and boundaries (2.94.36–8). At the end of the story, it is the white mansions and broad courtyards of Ayodhyā that first catch the eye of the Vānaras (6.111.31[l.v.]), Within the city Daśaratha's palace is obviously the most extensive building and some reference is made in the early part of the Ayodhyākāṇḍa to its courtyards (*kakṣyā*, e.g. 2.15.13) and its inner apartments (*antaḥpura*), from which those of Kausalyā are apparently separate (2.17.1–4 and 8), but the fullest detail is not found until the fourth stage (e.g. 2.349*—lofty mansions and palaces ornamented with jewelled lattice-work). The fullest account in the text at this point is of Rāma's residence, which is like Kailāsa in splendour and like Indra's residence, filled with great doors and embellished with balconies, having golden statues on its façade and its arches inlaid with gems, and hung with garlands of fine flowers (2.13.24–6, elaborated further in the fourth stage in 300*), as well as having three courtyards (2.5.4, cf. 14.1). The regular number of such successive courtyards or enclosures is three but as many as seven are occasionally mentioned (2.51.15 and 2.307*). Another prominent building, presumably also part of the palace complex, was the assembly-hall (*sabhā*) described as made of gold, studded with jewels and containing a golden throne strewn with rich coverings (2.75.8–10). But, just before, even Bharata's camp possesses, besides moat, gateways, ramparts, roadways and flags, also mansions and sky-scraping dovecots and seven-storey buildings (2.74.16–19), where the inappositeness of such a description is only too apparent.

When Lakṣmaṇa enters Kiṣkindhā to deliver Rāma's reproof to Sugrīva (4.32), he first passes the gate-keepers and then sees the jewelled, divine retreat crowded with mansions and palaces and adorned with varied shops and all sorts of flowering trees, its roads fragrant with various scents, and having multi-storey palaces rivalling the Vindhyas and mount Meru: on the main road, he passes the fine houses of various Vānara leaders before reaching Sugrīva's palace which is half-encircled (*parikṣipta*) by a white rock and is pleasant like Indra's residence, adorned with towering palaces, flowering trees, its door guarded by armed Vānaras and having a golden archway. Previously, the ramparts and moat surrounding the town have been mentioned in the context of Lakṣmaṇa's first approach (4.30.27), while for the installation of Sugrīva and Aṅgada it was adorned with flags (4.25.37). Elsewhere, Kiṣkindhā's gateways are mentioned (e.g. 4.11.26–30) and it is described as impregnable (e.g. 4.30.16). Its location is regularly given as being in the forest (e.g. 4.11.27, 12.14, 13.5–11 and 14.1) or in an isolated retreat (*guhā* e.g. 4.24.20, cf. 32.4 above[5]), specifically a mountain fastness or defile (e.g. *girigahvara* 4.25.37d, *girisaṃkaṭa* 30.16d), and in general the impression is given that its defence consisted mainly of its inaccessibility.

The first description of Laṅkā is when Rāvaṇa describes it to Sītā as lying across the sea, encircled by a shining white rampart, with golden courtyards and archways of cat's-eye, and adorned with parks full of fruiting trees (3.46.10–12). In the early sargas of the Sundarakāṇḍa, all much expanded, there is a much fuller description of Laṅkā, of its situation and fortifications (5.2.14–22), the city itself (especially 5.3.3–13, 20–37 and 5.6.1–15[l.v.]), and Rāvaṇa's palace (especially 5.7) seen through the wondering eyes of Hanumān as he searches for Sītā. Laṅkā has a moat filled with lotuses, a golden rampart and hundreds of watch-towers, it is wreathed with flags and banners and filled with wonderful golden archways (5.2.14–17, cf. 22–3 and 3.6–7). Here, as repeatedly, the city is declared to have been designed by Viśvakarman, the gods' own architect (5.2.19, cf. 4.57.20 and 7.5.20, also 5.113* and 6 App.I.16.50). Its extent is given in an addition of the fourth stage as twenty *yojanas* by ten (6.606*). Rāvaṇa's palace itself extends one *yojana* by half a *yojana* (5.7.2) and includes the inner apartments for the women, large mansions, banquet-halls, drinking-dens, pleasure-houses, arbours, and *caitya* buildings as well as the *aśoka* grove where Sītā is confined (5.12–13); among the architectural features of its buildings are pillars, pitched roofs, staircases to upper floors, daises and lattice-work of precious stones or gold. Incidentally, we learn in the battle scenes that the gates were oriented towards the compass-points (e.g. 6.28.10–13, 25–30 and 31.25–30), implying that the city was laid out on a grid pattern.

[5] That *guhā* means in the Rāmāyaṇa an isolated retreat, being derived from √*guh* 'to hide or conceal', and not a cave, as sometimes translated, is apparent not only from the way that Kiṣkindhā is described as containing ordinary buildings and fortified with walls and moat, but also from the fact that the term is used, for example, to describe Kumbhakarṇa's residence in Laṅkā (6.48.18–19).

To generalise from these undoubtedly conventional descriptions of cities gives the following picture of towns and architecture as envisaged at the different periods of the text. A city was regularly at all periods fortified with a moat, ramparts and gateways. Although moats (*parikhā*) are not all that frequently mentioned, not only do Ayodhyā, Kiṣkindhā and Laṅkā all have one but it is the only feature of Rājagṛha mentioned (2.64.1) and Bharata's camp is protected by one (2.74.17); however, it is only in the description of Laṅkā's defences that bridges over the moat are mentioned, as well as the four types of fort defended by a river, a mountain, a forest or an excavated ditch or moat (6.3.15–16, 19, cf. 49.33). The ramparts or city-wall (*prākāra*), which form the next line of defence, are more frequently mentioned and with equal frequency at all periods; a rarer term *vapra* denotes the mound on which the *prākāra* is then erected, forming a parapet-wall. The gateways are the most commonly mentioned of these three; the terms *dvār* or *dvāra* are very common especially in the earliest period, whereas the term *gopura* is uncommon, with most of its occurrences in the second stage, and the term *pratolī* rarer still.[6] The archways (*toraṇa*), commonly mentioned at all periods, seem generally to be a feature of the interior of the city rather than part of the gateways. Characteristic of the second stage are watch-towers or turrets (*aṭṭa, aṭṭāla, aṭṭālaka*) and cisterns or tanks (*prapā*). But overall, different aspects of fortifications are as common in the first stage as the second, and indeed to refer to a city simply as fortified or as a fort (*durga* as adjective or noun) is much more common in the earliest period than in the second.

References to buildings and parts of buildings are nearly twice as frequent in the later parts of the main books as in the earlier, which reflects the tendency of the second stage to include elaborate descriptions of all kinds; however by the third stage such terms are less frequent, again reflecting the shift away from poetic elaboration to mythological and didactic episodes. This is seen very clearly in the general terms for dwellings of varying grandeur—although the commonest term *gṛha* is relatively evenly distributed, the majority (*ālaya, niveśana, bhavana* and *vimāna*) are roughly twice as common in the second stage as the first and one term (*veśman*) is four times as common, whereas both *śālā* and *harmya* are as frequent early as late but have virtually disappeared by the third stage; in addition, though

[6] J. Ph. Vogel has examined this term and demonstrated its meaning as being that of a gateway, 'lofty and massive structures comprising rooms . . .' ('Errors in Sanskrit dictionaries', BSOAS 20, 1957, pp. 561–7. Cf. also D. Schlingloff, 'Arthaśāstra-Studien II. Die Anlage einer Festung (*durgavidhāna*)', WZKSO 11, 1967, pp. 44–85, esp. p. 62.

only sporadically, are found *āvāsa, geha, mandira* and *vasati*. Also the shelter Lakṣmaṇa puts up is several times described as a hut or cottage of leaves (*parṇaśālā*) and this is, as might be expected, an early feature; however, another term for such a shelter, *uṭaja*, literally 'produced from leaves', is distinctly late, and *kuṭī* is very rare.

The courtyard of a house or palace is quite commonly mentioned and must have been an original feature, since it is as frequent in early passages as late; the usual term *kakṣyā* in fact denotes as much the enclosure-wall, perhaps emphasising therefore privacy or seclusion, while the two other terms *catuṣka* and *catvara* could be translated 'quadrangle' and show therefore the standard shape for the courtyard. The inner apartments (*antaḥpura*) were regularly situated within several such courtyards. In connection with Rāvaṇa's palace are mentioned, in separate buildings apparently, a drinking-hall (*āpānabhūmi* or *āpānaśālā*), pleasure-houses (*krīḍāgṛha*) and picture-galleries (*citragṛha* or *citraśālā*), conservatories (*puṣpagṛha*) and arbours (*latāgṛha*), underground chambers and *caityas*. Some kind of dovecot or aviary (*viṭaṅka*) at the top of a building is also referred to a few times.

The text is virtually silent about the materials used for building, since any references are usually to the gold and precious stones used for ornament. There is a reference in a verse in longer metre to houses built of stone (5.39.16[l.v.]) but this appears to be the only definite statement in the text, for references to bricks in the Bālakāṇḍa are to their use for an altar, although the fourth stage does add a reference to bricklayers to the construction of the road for Bharata (2.1905* 10). We may suspect that wood was common but carpenters (*vardhaki*) are mentioned only in the last two contexts and timber (*dāru*) only sporadically. Occasional references to houses with pitched roofs (*kūṭāgāra*) and, in the fourth stage, to the roof-ridge (3.1048* 4) presumably indicate the standard type of roof in the absence of any counter indications. Equally, references to windows (*gavākṣa* or *vātāyana*) are rare and they must have been filled with a grille or lattice-work (*jāla*), which is in fact mentioned more often. Also more frequently mentioned than windows—because more relevant to aspects of the story—is the dais or raised platform (*vedikā*) which gave emphasis to the king's seat and the like, though the term can be used quite widely, for instance for the curb round a well. Door-panels (*kapāṭa*/*kavāṭa*) are mentioned occasionally at all periods, this term distinguishing a house-door from the gate that *dvār* or *dvāra* also signify; a bolt or pin (*argala*) to fasten them is once mentioned in the Bālakāṇḍa. The floors are very occasionally referred to as paved (*kuṭṭima*) from the second stage onwards.

The main rooms or halls are quite often described as supported by pillars (*stambha*) and the not infrequent mention, especially with regard to Rāvaṇa's palace, of a staircase (*sopāna*) demonstrates the existence of upper floors, which are implied by the traditional but rather suspect characterisation of a *vimāna* as sometimes at least seven storeys high; however, it should be noted that pillars occur proportionately less often in early passages than other architectural terms and staircases occur only from the second stage onwards. So rarely mentioned as to be of doubtful value are verandah (*vitardi*), balcony (*valabhī*) and canopy (*vitānaka*).

Thus, the picture of a house or palace presented in the first stage is simply that of a building or buildings set in one or more (up to seven) courtyards, probably with pitched roofs, a fair amount of ornament in gold and gems, a raised dais and possibly pillars. Only from the second stage and later does the description include any certain indication of multi-storey buildings with the mention of staircases or any suggestion of elaboration in flooring.

The furniture within these houses must have been of the simplest, even if richly ornamented at times. By far the commonest terms at all periods are the general terms for a seat (*āsana*) and a bed (*śayana*). The seat is sometimes qualified as excellent (*paramāsana, varāsana*) to designate a throne or seat of honour, which was usually ornamented with gold, while an occasional alternative term is *pīṭha* or *pīṭhikā* without any real difference in meaning. The bed doubled also as a couch, as seems more particularly to be indicated by the alternative term *paryaṅka*, whereas *talpa*, another occasional variant, is more definitely the bed or mattress, and *saṃstara* indicates its origin in a scattering of leaves or grass. Coverlets (*āstaraṇa, uttaracchada* and *paristoma*), blankets (*kambala*, the earlier term, and *kuthā*, from the second stage onwards) and cushions or pillows (*bṛsī*, or in the fourth stage *upadhāna*) complete the furnishings, except for the hints in Sītā's longing for the golden deer that skins were used in this way (e.g. 3.41.16, cf. 34), confirmed by the description of Rāvaṇa's bed as having coverlets of hides and sheepskins (5.8.4). However, the fourth stage also adds a door-curtain.

Clothing is normally referred to in the most general terms. Words for clothes or garments are followed in frequency at all periods by terms for belts and girdles, indicating the type of clothing as simply a loose piece of cloth draped and secured by a belt; loose enough, for instance, for Rāma to wipe his eyes with the end of his garment (4.7.14). The terms for clothes are, in order of frequency: *ambara, vastra, vāsas, veṣa, vasana, ācchāda(na), nivasana* and *śāṭī* (2.29.25a);[7] while those for girdles are: *dāman, kāñcī, raśanā, mekhalā* and *śroṇīsūtra*. Occasional use of the dual suggests that two layers of clothing were normal, as does reference to individuals wearing only a single garment (*ekavastradhara* 3.36.11, *ekavāsaḥsaṃvīta* 5.57.10, cf. 4.10.21, 5.13.20 etc.). One of these is the outer garment (*uttarīya*), perhaps no more than a shawl or wrap, which Sītā sheds along with some of her ornaments (3.52.2, 4.6.9–18, 5.13.43); the term is also once (5.31.22) used for clothes in general. The only other specific form of clothing mentioned occurs in the fourth stage—a loin-cloth (*kaupīna*, 1.209* 3). There are also two terms for footwear, no doubt sandals, of which *pādukā* is considerably commoner than *upānah* but the majority of their twenty or so occurrences are connected with Bharata taking Rāma's sandals as his symbol of authority.

Although Sītā's single robe in captivity (e.g. 5.13.20) is due to her having discarded her *uttarīya* where it may provide a clue for her rescue and is also symbolic of her wretchedness then, women perhaps quite often wore a single garment, for Hanumān's mother Añjanā seems to be wearing just one garment when Vāyu strips her (4.65.12–13). Certainly the descriptions, for example, of Sītā as she is carried off by Rāvaṇa (3.50.13–24) and of the dishevelled state of Rāvaṇa's sleeping women (5.7.41–53) are elaborated thus in the second stage not by minute description of different articles of clothing but by the variety of ornaments—necklaces, bracelets, anklets, girdles and so forth—with which they are adorned. Of course, in the forest Rāma, Lakṣmaṇa and Sītā would be dressed relatively simply, although in the scene where they doff their fine clothes and don bark-cloth (*cīra*) Sītā in fact puts hers on over her *kauśeya* garment.

The definition of the material is indeed the main description often given of clothing. The commonest material mentioned is the bark of the ascetics' garments, which Rāma, Lakṣmaṇa and Sītā adopt also for their exile; the earlier term for this is *cīra* but by the third stage the term *valkala* takes over. Next in frequency come the skins or hides (*ajina* and *kṛṣṇājina*) which are the alternative dress of ascetics and one of their distinctive badges. Only after these come the ordinary woven fabrics, of which the most frequent is *kauśeya*, with twenty occurrences

[7] Another group of terms—*cela, celikā* and *cailika*—is found only from the fourth stage onwards; two are general terms but *celikā* (v.l. at 5.9.5b) is usually held to denote a bodice.

of which marginally more are in early passages. This term is regularly held to mean silk and certainly does so in post-epic literature, but large-scale trade in silk from China seems to have developed only in the first century BC to the first century AD, which is much later than the period postulated for the early Rāmāyaṇa; such an isolated item seems entirely inadequate grounds for bringing down the date of the poem against the weight of other evidence, so we must assume either that there was sufficient trade in silk at a considerably earlier period than usually thought for it to be the mark of well-dressed ladies, or that originally the term was applied to some other substance and only later came to mean silk.[8] It may be noted that the description of Sītā as 'clothed in yellow silk' (*pītakauśeyavāsin*) is found only in the second stage (3.44.12b, 15b, 50.13b, 58.13b; cf. 58.25a). It is also perhaps significant that *kauśeya* is the only term in the text for silk.

A dozen references to linen, *kṣauma*, show that it also was used by the nobility and their servants (e.g. Kausalyā, Bharata, Rāvaṇa, Añjanā and Mantharā) and was obviously a prestige material; however, all but one of the references are from the second or later stages. Other fabrics, mentioned less frequently, are: from the first stage onwards cotton (*kārpāsaka* and *tūla*), woollen cloth (*praveṇī*) and jute (*paṭṭa*), from the second stage hemp (*śaṇa*) and from the fourth stage a cloth made from the hair or wool of a certain deer (*rāṅkava*) and once a sacred thread of muñja-grass (*mauñjī*, 1.209* 2).

Clothes are often described as bright or white (*śukla*, etc.) but otherwise quite commonly as red (*rakta*, etc.), which is sometimes compared to the colour of blood, while there are also a few references to a brownish-red colour (*kāṣāya*), to blue (*nīla*) and to yellow (*pīta*). Although *kāṣāya* is used of Rāvaṇa's disguise as a mendicant (3.44.3) and of Sītā in exile (7.88.9), it is also the colour of the dress of court officials in the second stage (2.14.3 and 6.113.30) and so is not then in any way the badge of ascetics, but does seem to be so in two passages of the fourth stage (1.209* 5 and 2 App.I.9.187). Yellow is especially

[8] In one passage of the fourth stage (3.790* 80) *kauśeya* is apparently distinguished from *patrorṇa*, which normally means woven silk, though perhaps not by much, since the same line also distinguishes between *praveṇī*, a type of coloured woollen cloth, and *āvika*, sheepskin (cf. equivalent text passage 3.41.34ab, also *pravāra* 'woollen cloth' of 3.789* 54). H. D. Sankalia (*Rāmāyaṇa—Myth or Reality*? New Delhi, 1973, pp. 56–7) definitely identifies *kauśeya* as silk and uses it as an argument for a relatively late date; however, he is in error in stating that 'Sita alone among all the persons who figure in the Ramayana wears a *Kausheya vastra*', although admittedly the majority of its occurrences relate to her.

associated with Sītā, echoing her own golden colouring (e.g. 3.50.21–2).[9] The actual dyestuff used is mentioned in a few passages of the second stage; in one Vālin lying in a pool of blood seems as though lying on a coverlet the colour of, that is dyed with, the lac-insect (*kṛmirāga-paristoma*, 4.23.13c) and in another the blood issuing from Devāntaka's mouth is the same colour as lac (*lākṣārasasavarṇa*, 6.58.15c), while madder, *māñjiṣṭha*, is mentioned a couple of times for its colour-value without any reference to clothing (2.88.5 and 5.1.4). But of course the poets were not particularly interested in such mundane details and so, for example, there is no mention of weaving in the text, only one to a needle (3.45.36) and a handful to thread.

Whereas there is relatively little difference in frequency of reference to clothing between the first and second stages, ornaments and other accessories are twice as frequent in the second stage, but the frequency then dramatically declines again in the third stage with its different interests. Most of the general terms for ornaments or jewels (*ābharaṇa, bhūṣaṇa, maṇi, ratna*) conform to this pattern of distribution, but two relatively infrequent terms (*alaṃkāra* and *vibhūṣaṇa*) are about as frequent in the first stage as the second, while *ratna* is the commonest term in the third stage. However, there are very varied distributions for different types of ornament. Garlands or wreaths of flowers are nearly as common in the first stage as the second and are indeed the commonest specific adornment mentioned in the first stage. By contrast, and presumably in consequence, terms for necklaces are virtually absent from the first stage but one (*hāra*) is common from the second stage onwards and another (*graiveya*) is very rare,[10] while in the third stage a term for the central gem of a necklace (*tarala*) occurs once. Another term, *niṣka*, denotes a golden ornament worn on the breast (6.64.5),[11] which was probably some kind of brooch rather than necklace.

There are three terms for bracelets or armlets (*aṅgada, keyūra* and *valaya*) but the frequency of *aṅgada* is conditioned by the play on Aṅgada's name, for he is several times described as having golden armlets. Two of the terms, *aṅgada* and *keyūra*, several times occur in

[9] However, Janārdana, a form of Viṣṇu or Kṛṣṇa is called *pītavāsas* at 7.6.28b, as is Viṣṇu at 1.457*.

[10] There is one occurrence of *hāra* in a passage of the first stage at 5.9.15c, but this follows immediately the elaboration of 5.1–8, of which it may contain elements, and is omitted by much of the NE. recension; *hāra* is found over twenty times in the second stage.

[11] See p. 62.

the same context and once all three terms do (2.29.5); this suggests that there may well be some degree of differentiation between them, such as whether they were worn on the upper or lower arm, but there are no clear indications from within the text. Anklets, *nūpura*, occur predominantly in the second stage and are especially a woman's ornament, whereas armlets are worn at least as much by men. Ear-rings (*kuṇḍala*) also are common to both sexes and, while most frequent in the second stage, are mentioned in all. A diadem or tiara (*kirīṭa*), mainly found in the second stage, is especially linked with the Rākṣasas, with Mārīca, Rāvaṇa, Kumbhakarṇa, Triśiras and Atikāya; a rare alternative term, *mukuṭa*, is also used of Rāvaṇa's headdress but also once in the Bālakāṇḍa of ordinary citizens, when it is said that under Daśaratha's rule there is no-one in Ayodhyā without ear-rings, tiara, garland, bracelets or *niṣka* (1.6.10–11). Even more interestingly the jewel worn on the head (*cūḍāmaṇi*) seems specific to Rāma and Sītā—Sītā gives hers to Hanumān as a token for Rāma (5.36.52, 38.7 and 63.21) and recognises the counterfeit head of Rāma by one (6.23.2)—but its precise nature is rather uncertain for Sītā takes hers from her dress and Hanumān puts it on his finger since his arm will not fit. Equally, the finger-ring (*aṅgulīya, aṅgulīyaka*) which Rāma entrusts to Hanumān is the only example in the text, being mentioned in the Bālakāṇḍa summary, when Rāma gives it and when Sītā receives it (1.3.18, 4.43.11 and 5.34.2); it is described as some kind of signet-ring being marked with Rāma's name but is anyway unique in itself.

Apart from the extensive use of gold in such ornaments, various precious or semi-precious stones are mentioned, though often in relation to their employment in the decoration of buildings. In order of frequency, these are cat's-eye (*vaidūrya*, a sort of chrysoberyl), pearl (*muktā* and once *gulikā*), crystal (*sphaṭika* or *sphāṭika* and *galvarka*), coral (*pravāla* and *vidruma*), diamond (*vajra*) and sapphire (*indranīla* and *masāra*); all are substantially more frequent in the second stage, which contains two thirds of all occurrences in the text. One list of different ornaments includes gem-stones threaded on gold (2.29.5c, cf. 7a), which must have been a skilful exercise.

Two accessories mentioned with some frequency, particularly in the second stage are umbrellas and fans. The common term for umbrella is *chatra*, denoting its covering or concealing quality, but also, though rarely, distinguished like the French *parasol* and *parapluie* as protecting against sun (*ātapatra*) or rain (*varṣatra*); it is also described on several occasions in somewhat stereotyped fashion as having many, or a hundred, ribs. Fans (*vyajana*) are more often designated by the material most commonly used, the hair of the yak's tail (*cāmara, cāmaravyajana* and *vālavyajana*); these are especially a symbol of court life or more exactly an indication of the presence of servants to wield them.

Hairstyles are only rarely alluded to, apart from the matted locks (*jaṭā*) of ascetics. This style is, however, in part a reaction against the normal orderliness of hair, though even so deliberately achieved, once with the use of banyan juice to set it in place (2.46.55); loose or untidy hair is always unusual. Thus Bharata, when he has an inauspicious dream about Daśaratha, sees him as having his hair undone (*mukta-mūrdhaja* 2.63.8b) and, with a rather different connotation, a young woman after love-play is dishevelled (5.12.18a), while warriors when exhausted or dying in battle also have loosened hair (e.g. 6.42.14 and 44.32). Conversely, Rāma is described as having beautiful hair (*sukeśānta* 2.55.8a) and the gods have fine hair and figures (7.6.27). The few references to hair and hairstyles are in fact equally frequent in the first stage as the second, but this is really an indication of the lack of elaboration on this topic in the second stage, by contrast with the treatment of jewellery. A braid or plait of hair is most frequently alluded to, because of the fact that Sītā adopts the single plait as a sign of mourning during her captivity. The widow's single plait is also metaphorically attributed to the city of Ayodhyā after Rāma's departure (2.100.8). Incidentally when Saramā, reassuring Sītā, declares that Rāma will come to undo her plait, it is described as reaching to her hips (6.24.32), so she evidently has really long hair, as is also implied in her threat to hang or throttle herself with her plait (5.26.17b[l.v.]); however both these passages elaborating on the basic point belong to the second stage.

The parting in the hair (*sīmanta*), once used because of its straightness as a comparison for Nala's causeway (6.15.26, also App.I.14.4*), was especially the mark of a pregnant woman since parting the hair was one of the twelve ceremonies of pregnancy laid down in the *Gṛhyasūtras*; thus the derivative *sīmantinī* is used to denote a pregnant woman once in the second stage (2.47.21) but more generally of married women once in the fourth stage (2.327* 13). Similarly, the tuft of hair left when the head is shaved at initiation becomes the mark of the student and so Mārīca, recalling his defeat by the young Rāma, calls him not only a handsome, beardless boy but also tonsured (*śikhin*, 3.36.11), while it also forms part of Rāvaṇa's disguise as a wanderer when he approaches Sītā (3.44.3). However, someone completely bald (*muṇḍa*) is inauspicious and thus Trijaṭā's dream of Laṅkā's destruction includes the bald and black-clad Rāvaṇa entering a lake of mud (5.25.18–19) and

Mālyavān, counselling making peace, cites the apparition of the bald and hideous figure of Kāla (6.26.30).

Hair, then, was normally worn fairly long and there are a couple of references in the text to the turban (*uṣnīṣa* 6.67.5 and 102.20), which would help to keep it in place, as well as several more references from the fourth stage. One particular style is alluded to only in the Bālakāṇḍa, where Rāma, once together with Lakṣmaṇa, is described as having crow's wings, that is side-locks (*kākapakṣadhara* 1.18.8c, 21.6c and 49.21c).[12] There is also one isolated reference in the text to wearing flowers in the hair, said explicitly to be a custom of Southerners (2.87.13), and in at least one passage of the fourth stage Rāma puts flowers in Sītā's hair (2 App.I.26.41–2, cf. 61–4); however this practice was evidently not widespread.

The wearing of beards, though mentioned extremely rarely in the text, or even in later additions, was probably normal; both text references noted belong in effect to the third stage, for one is the description of the supernatural figure issuing from Daśaratha's sacrifice as amply bearded and with glossy, fine hair (1.15.10) and the other mentions barbers, literally 'beard-trimmers' (*śmaśruvardhaka* 6.116.13), to prepare Rāma for his long-delayed installation in the final sarga of the Yuddhakāṇḍa. The term usually translated razor, *kṣura*, in fact denotes the sharpened point of a weapon such as an arrow in the Rāmāyaṇa, except perhaps where Sītā scornfully says to Rāvaṇa: 'You are wiping your eye with a needle and licking a razor with your tongue when you want to approach Rāma's dear wife' (3.45.36). Even brushes and combs are only mentioned in the second stage once in the list of toilet articles conjured up by Bharadvāja for Bharata's army (2.85.71). The total absence of any of these from the first stage merely indicates that the topic was not part of the poet's concerns.

So too such toilet articles as toothbrushes, cosmetics containers and mirrors are found in the account of Bharadvāja's entertainment (2.85.69–70) but not otherwise, and this same passage refers to seven or eight young women bathing and massaging Bharata's soldiers (50–1). Outside such obviously secondary episodes, there are simply inci-

[12] In fact this compound *kākapakṣadhara* occurs also in the fourth stage (2.2400* 1), in a late addition to the Mahābhārata (Mbh. 2 App.21.776, 791) and in the *Harivaṃśa* (49.26a and 52.2d); it is clearly late, as well as providing intriguing glimpses of the interrelations of the epics; cf. E. W. Hopkins, 'Allusions to the Rāma-story in the Mahābhārata', JAOS 50, 1930, pp. 85–103, esp. p. 89. Another point is that this description of Rāma as possessing side-locks before and after protecting Viśvāmitra's sacrifice is at variance with Mārīca's description of him, when he recalls his attempt to disrupt the sacrifice, as having a hair-tuft (*śikhin*); each probably denotes a different—and incompatible—style of initiatory tonsuring.

dental references to bathing (*snāna*), anointing (*anulepana*) and the use of scents (*gandha* or rarely *dhūpa*), of which there are anyway nearly twice as many from the second stage as from the first. From the relative frequencies of such references, it is clear that bathing was regularly followed by anointing with sandal-paste (*candana*) or less commonly aloe-wood (*agaru/aguru*). Scents or perfumes are also quite commonly referred to but probably include the use of sandal or other fragrant unguents. Allusion to the *tilaka* on a woman's forehead is mostly made in relation to the incident when Rāma makes it on Sītā's forehead with realgar (*manaḥśilā*), which then forms part of the message transmitted through Hanumān (5.38.5 and 63.21, also 2 App.I.26.33–40 and 5.834* and 835*). Terms are also found for cosmetics generally (*aṅgarāga*), for collyrium (*añjana, āñjanī*) and in the fourth stage for making up. Perhaps surprisingly, there is one reference to the custom of women painting their feet red (2.54.15, the Southern version, and 1311*, the Northern version) when Kausalyā laments that Sītā's feet will no longer be red but the colour of the lotus bud; this seems to come from the first stage—a very early period for this custom to be attested; we should therefore not stake too much on an isolated reference.

Allusions to food and drink are spread very evenly across the first three stages of growth of the epic, but this conceals a considerable shift in the type of reference made, which becomes still more apparent in the fourth stage. The evenness of spread is in fact largely due to the frequency of reference throughout to the ascetics' diet, typically given as fruit and roots (*phala* and *mūla*, often in the stereotyped compound *phalamūlāśana* and the like). After that, the first stage makes by far the most references to meat-eating, with many allusions to Rāma and Lakṣmaṇa killing game for their consumption, whereas by the third and fourth stages various sorts of gruel or mash form the standard diet and frequent mention is made of the appropriate foods for oblations, for feasting brāhmans and so forth,[13] while there are not a few condemnations of meat-eating implicit in some of the mythological incidents.

From the start of their exile in the forest, Rāma and Lakṣmaṇa kill animals for food (2.49.14) or for sacrifice (2.50.16) and, even after

[13] Inviting brāhmans to a *śrāddha* is central to the Vātāpi and Ilvala episode, a particularly late insertion of the second stage. Otherwise, references to feasting brāhmans at Daśaratha's *aśvamedha*, Rāma's planned installation and similar ceremonies all belong to the third and fourth stages.

Rāma has just killed the fabulous golden deer which Mārīca has become and is worried about the consequences, he stops to kill another *chital* and take its meat (3.42.21). Not only is this their practice but it is automatically assumed for them; for example, Kabandha says that Rāma can easily kill the birds and fish for food on his way to Sugrīva (3.69.8–11). Similarly, Guha offers Bharata himself fish, meat and honey (*matsyamāṃsamadhūni*) and his army roots, fruit, fresh and dried meat and forest produce (2.78.9 and 16). Lower classes have always of course been meat-eating and thus Guha's boatmen are naturally described as eaters of meat, roots and fruit (*māṃsamūla-phalāśana* 2.78.6), that is of whatever they could come by, and Bharata's army is regaled with meat and wine by Bharadvāja (2.85.17).

However, by the second stage the attitude is more equivocal. On the one hand, the dying Vālin continues to accept the slaughter of animals for food, though also introducing the legalistic maxim about the five types of five-nailed animals which may be eaten (4.17.33–5),[14] and Rāma and Lakṣmaṇa are shown hunting in the same way as in the first stage (e.g. 2.46.79[l.v.]).[15] But on the other hand, Rāma breaking the news to Kausalyā says: 'I shall dwell for fourteen years in the unpeopled forest, living on honey, roots and fruit (and) abandoning, in hermit fashion, meat' (2.17.15), and Hanumān describing Rāma's behaviour to Sītā says that 'Rāghava does not eat meat nor does he use honey (or "liquor")' (5.34.39), while Lakṣmaṇa is referred to as looking for fruit (4.29.14). The provision of a suitably gargantuan meat meal for Kumbhakarṇa (6.48.24–6) probably simply continues the same pattern as the description of the varied dishes left half-eaten in Rāvaṇa's banquet-hall: deer, buffalo, boar, peacock and junglefowl, rhinoceros, porcupine, partridge, brahminy duck, a kind of fish (?) and goat (5.9.11–14). The latter passage, though otherwise apparently of the first stage, is elaborated in the way more typical of the second, but both passages basically depict these leading Rākṣasas on the same model as the leading members of Rāma's family. But a rather different aspect appears in the episode of Vātāpi and Ilvala which Rāma hears from Sutīkṣṇa and narrates to Lakṣmaṇa, where Ilvala serves up his brother in the form of a ram to brāhmans as a means of destroying them, until they meet their match in Agastya (3.10.53–62). This episode, un-

[14] This maxim is found also at Mbh. 12.139.66 and *Manu* 5.18 (cf. my *Proverbs* p. 147).

[15] Here, as at 2.49.14 and 50.16, the animals are categorised as pure or clean (*medhya*), which no doubt reflects the same type of restrictions (cf. also 2.85.49 and 3.14.19).

doubtedly from late in the second stage, anticipates in the way it conflates meat-eating and cannibalism episodes occurring in the Uttarakāṇḍa, such as Vālmīki's narration of the story of Sudāsa or Kalmāṣapāda cursed to eat human flesh (7.57) and Agastya's narration of the story of King Śveta compelled to eat his own body (7.68–9). Here the disapproval by then felt for meat-eating is expressed under the stronger form of disgust for cannibalism. Another phobia finding expression in the third stage is the horror of eating dog's flesh expressed in Viśvāmitra cursing first Vasiṣṭha's sons and then his own to such a diet (1.58.20 and 61.13–16). By the fourth stage, Bharata's imprecations include among despised categories those who trade in lac, honey (or liquor), meat, iron and poison (2.1795* 1).

It should not be thought that this development is uniform and consistent. For example, in the first stage Rāma seems at one point to present himself as eating only fruit and roots when he rejects Guha's offered meal (2.44.20) and accepts sustenance—of water only in the Northern recension—from Lakṣmaṇa after sunset (2.44.24), but this may be a continuation of the fast where he vows to take only water that night (2.41.8), although in recounting his reception of Rāma to Bharata, Guha does ascribe Rāma's refusal to kṣatriya custom (2.81.14–15).[16] More certainly, the habit of meat-eating continues sporadically to be portrayed in the third stage, when for example Rāma gives the pregnant Sītā different sorts of wine (*madhu* and *maireya*) and servants bring him meat and fruit (7.41.13–14), and even in the fourth stage, for example when Rāma offers Sītā meat just before Bharata arrives (2.2091* 2–3). Nevertheless, the overall trend is unmistakable, with the frequency of the terms used for meat (*māṃsa, āmiṣa*) steadily declining after the first stage, even though they inevitably occur in those later passages which condemn the practice of meat-eating.

Fish was not such a regular article of diet but there does not seem initially to have been any prejudice against it, as Kabandha's remark already cited indicates, with the declaration that there are plenty of edible fish in the river Pampā (3.69.9–11); there is also at one point a simile of a fish caught on a baited hook (3.49.22). The Niṣāda chief, Guha, offers Bharata fish along with meat and honey (2.78.9) and

[16] Hopkins (*Ruling Caste*, p. 92) regards this as exemplifying the kṣatriya attitude of not being beholden to anyone in deliberate contrast to the brāhman eagerness to accept gifts. Thus even in this form taboos on acceptance of food from lower castes need not be involved. Fasting, which is mentioned fewer than fifty times in the whole text, is as much a sign of grief or despair (e.g. the Vānaras at the end of the Kiṣkindhākāṇḍa) as a religious practice; however, Bharata threatens to use it as a weapon to persuade Rāma to return (2.103.13–14).

another tribal group, the Kirāṭas, are characterised as eaters of raw fish (4.39.26). All but the last reference, which is anyway disparaging, come from the first stage and we may perhaps infer that eating fish, being always more restricted in popularity, fell into more rapid and complete disfavour than eating meat. However, this shift of attitudes is an index not so much of changing social patterns, for there is considerable evidence that kṣatriyas continued to eat meat, as of the transition of control over the epic from the *sūtas* its traditional reciters to brāhmans, among whom vegetarianism became the norm at an early date.

Vegetarianism as such is ascribed only to the ascetics in the forest and even then is more an expression of their rejection of society and organised labour than of respect for animal life. For example, Kausalyā sorrowfully contemplating Rāma's departure ponders how one used to the fine fare and service of court life will cope with roots and fruit, and with gleaning, that is gathering only what is available (2.21.2–3, cf. 2.55.5), and the fourth stage adds to Rāma's attempt to dissuade Sītā from accompanying him the need to be content with the fruit fallen from the trees (2.646*). Most fully, Agastya is described as collecting fruit and roots, herbs and vegetables in his hermitage (7.73.3).

The various grains are not named directly as foods, although there is ample evidence of their being grown,[17] but three dishes prepared from rice and milk in one way or another are named. However, none is very frequently mentioned and they are absent from the first stage. The most frequent of them is *pāyasa*, used of the preparation which Daśaratha is to give to his queens to overcome his childlessness (1.15) and of that provided by Bharadvāja for Bharata's army (2.85.38, 49, 64, 67); it was presumably something of a symbol of luxury or prosperity, since Bharata's imprecations include the wish that the malefactor may eat it and *kṛsara*, a rather similar dish of rice boiled with sesamum, in vain (2.69.22). This is the only reference to *kṛsara* in the text but it also occurs in the fourth stage, for instance along with *pāyasa* and other foods which Kausalyā offers as an oblation (2.410*). The third term, *odana*, also rice boiled in milk, appears as one of the foods produced by Vasiṣṭha's cow Śabalā (1.52.3) and in connection with the Ocean of Milk in the search party accounts (4.39.43), both of which—perhaps significantly—are decidedly mythological episodes. Two other terms for grain, one for unhusked grain (*akṣata*) and one for parched grain (*lājā*), are uncommon in the text and confined to use in oblations (e.g. 2.13.7) or otherwise ceremonially, as to welcome someone by scattering

[17] See p. 99.

parched grain like confetti (2.38.13) and as auspicious items for Sugrīva's installation (4.25.24). For this reason both terms are much commoner in the fourth stage, when numerous ceremonial details are interpolated (e.g. 2.410* and App.I.6.22).

Dairy products are only infrequently mentioned but occur at all periods, especially the fourth, both milk itself (*kṣīra, payas*) and its by-products, clarified butter (*ājya, ghṛta, sarpis*) and curds (*dadhi*). Again, use in ritual accounts for more frequent mention in later stages (e.g. 6 App.I.3.17). Even rarer is the mention of sauces or condiments (*sūpa* or *niṣṭhāna*) to accompany food, virtually only in the two elaborate magical banquets provided by Vasiṣṭha through Śabalā for Viśvāmitra's army (1.52.3) and by Bharadvāja for Bharata's army (2.85.62). As so often, the poem is little concerned with practical and pedestrian details, a good example of which is the rarity of mention of a cook (*sūda*) to prepare these dishes or of the utensils in which food or drink is prepared or served. In fact, the first stage mentions only jars or pitchers (*kalaśa, kumbha, ghaṭa*), to which are added in the second stage bowls (*pātra*), cups (*śarāva*), pans (*piṭhara, sthalī*) and another term for a pitcher (*bhṛṅga*), but there are only just over fifty references to these various utensils in the entire text. Significantly, Rāvaṇa's threat to Sītā that his cooks will chop her into little pieces for his breakfast occurs in different locations in both recensions, which suggests secondary insertion: it appears in the Southern recension at 3.54.22 (omitted by most Northern manuscripts) and in the Northern recension as a variant for 5.20.9. In the Uttarakāṇḍa the term also occurs in the episode of Kalmāṣapāda serving human flesh to Vasiṣṭha (7.57.24).

Both honey and sugar are mentioned but with striking differences in distribution: honey (*madhu, kṣaudra*) occurs most commonly in the first stage and with diminishing frequency thereafter, whereas sugar, either in its refined form (*śarkarā*) or the growing cane (*ikṣu*), is distinctly rare and late. There is a reference to refined sugar in the description of Rāvaṇa's banquet-hall (5.9.19), from which the elaborate list of meats has already been quoted[18] and in which also occurs the only reference to *sochal* salt (*sauvarcala* 5.9.13); thus, it is reasonable to consider this reference a later elaboration. Apart from this, the only text references to sugar are to both forms in Bharadvāja's entertainment (2.85.13, 52 and 67) and to sugar-cane in the Bālakāṇḍa (1.5.17 and 52.2). Sweets or confectionery are also preponderantly late, apart

[18] See p. 82. Both *śarkarā* and *aikṣava* occur in one passage of the fifth stage, along with terms for drinks (5 App. I.3.33), in an alternative description of Rāvaṇa's banquet-hall.

from one mention in connection with Vibhīṣaṇa's installation (*modaka*, 6.100.16) and one in the description of Rāvaṇa's banquet-hall (*ṣāḍava*, 5.9.15); a third sort is mentioned in the Bālakāṇḍa (*gauḍa*, 1.52.4). One slight complication with regard to honey is that the usual term, *madhu*, can also be used to designate an alcoholic drink, no doubt originally a sort of mead but more generally employed in the Rāmāyaṇa. Fermented honey can occur spontaneously from the action on the sugar in nectar, of the yeast naturally present in some flowers, or on the skins of certain fruits; possibly this was a factor in the Vānaras' destructive rampage in the Madhuvana (5.59–61).[19] However, context generally makes clear which meaning is appropriate and there are plenty of undoubted instances of the meaning 'honey' at each stage.

In fact the distribution pattern for the term *madhu* is broadly similar to that for terms for drink, of which the majority are for alcoholic drinks, for the highest frequency is found in the first stage and the proportions slowly decline thereafter. But, whereas honey tended to be superseded as a sweetener by sugar, alcohol, like meat-eating, was disapproved of by the more religiously-minded redactors of the later Rāmāyaṇa. Indeed, exceptions to the overall early pattern are *madirā* and *madya* which do not occur in the first stage but significantly mean 'intoxicating drink', being linked closely with *mada* 'exhilaration, intoxication', and so contain some hint of disapproval. But in the first stage and even in parts of the second several kinds of drink are mentioned and with approbation, for instance Sītā in her diatribe against Rāvaṇa contrasts fine wine (*surā*) with fermented rice-water (*sauvīraka*) among the many pairs of opposites by which she characterises Rāma and Rāvaṇa (3.45.40[l.v.]). The two most frequently mentioned sorts of drink are *madhu* and *surā*, but others found are *maireya, vāruṇī, mādhvīka, śauṇḍā, āsava* and *sīdhu*, of which the latter two are distilled liquors. On a number of occasions several terms are used together (e.g. 1.52.1, 2.85.13, 4.32.7, 5.9.19) which indicates that they are not synonyms but designate different varieties. However there is not really sufficient internal evidence to determine precisely which, except that Rāvaṇa's banquet-hall contains wine and *kṛtasurā* (perhaps = 'fermented'[20]), *mādhvīka*, and distillations from sugar, flowers and fruit (5.9.19).

[19] Fermented honey was well-known in the ancient world (cf. e.g. Xenophon, *Anabasis* 4.8.20 and Pliny, *Naturalis Historia* 21.13); however it should be noted that Kauṭilya defines *madhu* as the juice of grapes (*mṛdvīkārasa*, by contrast with *maireya*, made from molasses, KA 2.25.22–4). Incidentally, the Vānaras at one point pelt each other with beeswax (literally 'leavings of honey', *madhūcchiṣṭa*, 5.60.9).

[20] See Om Prakash, *Food and drinks in ancient India, from earliest times to c.1200 A.D.*, Delhi, 1961, p. 118.

Disapproval of drinking is already expressed in a proverb inserted into a passage of the first stage when Lakṣmaṇa reproaching Sugrīva says that expiation is possible for a brahmanicide, a drinker (*surāpa*) and a thief but not for an ingrate (4.33.12, cf. Mbh. 12.166.24 and *Pañcatantra* 3.157). But more typical of the first stage or even the second are descriptions of Ayodhyā, Kiṣkindhā and Laṅkā as all fragrant with liquor (2.106.14 and 21, 4.32.7 and 5.9.19). Expressions of disapproval are readily found from the fourth stage (e.g. 2 App.I.9.139). However, non-alcoholic drink is comparatively little mentioned, as we have already noted with reference to milk,[21] and the general term *pāna* for drinking or a drink is often applied to alcohol. Water is mentioned: for example Kabandha in directing Rāma to Sugrīva says that the water of the river Pampā is clear and good to drink (3.69.11–12); and its importance is recognised, for example, in the fourth stage addition to Lakṣmaṇa's imprecations, which includes a fouler of drinking water (2.1802* 15–16). Distaste for drinking water or wine already tasted is clearly expressed (e.g. 2.24.6 and 2.55.14) and is probably closer to such natural abhorrence of fouling (as other similes at 2.55.11–14, such as the tiger not eating another's prey, would suggest) than to later taboos on commensality.

[21] See above p. 85.

4
THE SETTING
THE WIDER ENVIRONMENT

'The plains, hidden in haze after sunrise, are filled with barley and wheat and bright with crying cranes.'
(3.15.16)

For the same reasons that meat-eating is most often mentioned in the first stage, with numerous allusions to killing game, the category of fauna which has the majority of its occurrences in the first stage is that of deer and antelopes; this category also shows a lower proportion in the third stage than other types of fauna. The most frequent term (comprising over 85% of the total occurrences) is *mṛga*, a general term for deer and indeed for wild animals in general, but no doubt usually denoting the blackbuck or Indian antelope, Antilope cervicapra (L.), also but rarely termed *kṛṣṇamṛga, hariṇa* and *eṇa / aiṇeya*; in modern times at least this animal is found on grass plains in herds and so is not perhaps the most natural inhabitant of the Daṇḍaka forest, but this may only indicate that *mṛga* is being used in a fairly general sense to mean game animal. The only other deer mentioned with any frequency is the *pṛṣata*, the modern *chital*, Axis axis (Erxleben), which inhabits forests throughout India up to 4,000 feet, and near water. The *nilgai*, Boselaphus tragocamelus (Pallas), *syn*. Antilope picta Pallas, is just occasionally mentioned under various names (*ṛśya, gokarṇa, ruru* or *mahāruru*), mostly in the second stage. In addition the *chinkāra* or Indian gazelle, Gazella gazella (Pallas), is mentioned a couple of times as *rohi* and other unidentified deer or antelope occurring once or twice are *kuraṅga, priyaka* and *śarabha*.[1]

[1] One of these unidentified deer possibly conceals the otherwise unmentioned *barasingha* or swamp deer (Cervus duvauceli Cuvier), which has much the same distribution as the *sāl* tree, so commonly mentioned. The wool of the *raṅku* deer has already been noted in connection with clothing (p. 76); this deer has not been identified but is possibly the long-haired Tibetan gazelle or *ragao*, Gazella picticaudata (Hodgson), *syn*. Procapra picticaudata Hodgson, since at Mbh. 2.47.9, 22 it is linked with the Northwest. Because of uncertainties over identification and more particularly the substantial changes in scientific nomenclature (especially of the flora) since the compilation of most dictionaries, synonyms will regularly be given in order to facilitate comparison with different works.

In general most animals and birds are slightly commoner in the second stage, but there are wide variations, as the category of deer and antelopes demonstrates. Basically the reason for greater frequency in the second stage and for a low one in the third, which is even more apparent for the flora, is that many names were added in the type of aesthetically motivated expansion found in the second stage but notably absent from the third, of the descriptions of nature at large or of the surrounding scenery. Indeed, were it not that horses and other equines, being part of court life, warfare and kingly ritual, show a distribution much more in line with the relative lengths of the different stages of the text, the frequency as well as the variety of animals mentioned in the third stage would be even less.

The commonest term for horse is *aśva* but the term *haya* is nearly as frequent in the first stage whereas *vājin* occurs somewhat more in the second stage than the first; words meaning basically 'quick-going' (*turaga, turaṃga, turaṃgama*) occur a few times, especially in the first stage, and so do terms for a mare (*vaḍavā*) and a colt (*kiśora*) which are however commoner in the second stage. Asses (*khara*, once *gardabha*, Equus hemionus Pallas) are mentioned not infrequently as mounts or drawing chariots, usually simply as an alternative to horses without any difference of esteem,[2] although in the second stage a simile compares an ass's gait disparagingly to a horse's (2.98.6a = 6.116.5a); on the other hand among the presents which Aśvapati gives to Bharata on his departure are swift, well-harnessed asses (2.64.20, not however in most N. mss.). The latter instance follows the sarga in which Bharata has dreams of foreboding which include seeing Daśaratha on a chariot drawn by asses explicitly stated to be a presage of death (2.63.14–16). But Rāvaṇa's chariot in the Araṇyakāṇḍa is regularly drawn by asses (3.33.6 etc.) and at that stage in the story this is scarcely an omen of his death. Moreover Khara is described as driving to his death in a chariot drawn by dappled horses (3.21.16), despite the apparent opportunity to pun on his name (as when his voice is harsher, *kharatara*, 3.21.1d), and Rāvaṇa himself in the Yuddhakāṇḍa drives a chariot drawn by horses. The she-mule is mentioned in a couple of similes, one expressing the belief that her offspring kills her, apparently in parturition (3.41.39), but is obviously therefore peripheral to the

[2] R. S. Chakravarthy ('Some aspects of the Rāmāyaṇa of Vālmīki', ABORI 53, 1972, pp. 204–11) also notes that horses and asses are not yet much differentiated for size and speed, regarding it as a sign of early date along with the fact that elephants were domesticated but not yet used for warfare and the mention of the breeding of dogs.

actual background of the epic, reflecting if anything the knowledge of later redactors.[3]

Elephants (Elephas maximus L.) are most frequently mentioned in battle contexts, even more so than horses, and in consequence an absolute majority of references to them occurs in the second stage, since their use in battle is a later feature.[4] Indeed elephants occur more frequently in the second stage than horses, though slightly less frequent overall. Only two terms are more frequent in the first stage than later, *kuñjara* and *dvipa* or *dvipāyin*; the latter, literally 'drinking twice', alludes indirectly to the trunk which provides two other names *hastin* and *karin*, both literally 'having a hand'. But much the most frequent term at all stages is *gaja*. Other terms occurring with any frequency in the text are *kareṇu* for a female elephant and *nāga, mātaṅga* and *vāraṇa*, all three of which are more frequent in the second stage than the average. One passage of the second stage describes two-, three- and four-tusked elephants, as well as one mention of an ivory worker (2.77.13), but in general its tusks are not so much alluded to as its trunk.[5] In the majority of instances elephants are domesticated but there are passages of natural description which include them among the wildlife of the forest (e.g. 3.10.4–6).

Cattle are referred to only half as often as either horses or elephants, reflecting the martial, rather than pastoral, interests of the epic. The standard term is *go*, meaning specifically the cow, but terms for bull (*ṛṣabha, vṛṣa, vṛṣabha*) are not infrequent in similes as a symbol of strength, while the milch-cow (*dhenu*) is occasionally employed along with her calf (*vatsa*) as a type of maternal affection. Were it not for such similes, cattle would be very little mentioned at all.[6] Other bovines are rarely mentioned. The commonest is the buffalo (*mahiṣa*, Bubalus bubalis (L.)), occurring sixteen times in the first and second stages, which is however always a wild animal, mentioned for example along with deer, boars and lions, and sometimes killed for its meat.

[3] See p. 184.

[4] See p. 137.

[5] However, the term *dantin* 'tusked' occurs rarely to denote an elephant, and another term for a female elephant, *gaṇikā*, appears in the fourth stage. Other rare terms are: *aindraśira* (denoting an esteemed type or quality of elephant, 2.64.20a), *kalabha* (a young elephant, 6.77.5d) and *śiśunāga* (a young elephant, 3.69.24d, 27a), from the first stage and *vāśitā* (a cow elephant in heat, 7.32.24b, 28e, 51b) in the third stage.

[6] In the second stage there occur once each terms for a young bullock (*damya*, 2.67.13) and an ox (*balīvarda*, 2.68.22). In the fourth stage further terms for bulls occur: *anaḍvāh, ukṣan* and *ukṣāṇa*.

The yak (*camara*, Bos grunniens L.) is rarely mentioned directly and mention of the fan made from its tail, the *cāmara*, occurs only in the second and fourth stages and not often then. In fact the *sṛmara*, with which the *cāmara* is linked in all its occurrences, is commoner since it occurs in a few other passages also; however, the occurrence of both together in lists seems to rule out the usual identification of the *sṛmara* as the yak while suggesting that it is a similar type of animal.[7] The *gayal (gavaya*, Bos frontalis L., *syn*. B. gavaeus) occurs once in the second stage and the *gaur* (*gauramukha*, Bos gaurus H. Smith) once in the fourth.

Other domestic animals of any kind are relatively uncommon in the first stage and more frequent in the third stage compared with other animals, but their total number of mentions is not much over fifty. This is due to the particular interests of the text, reflected even within this group by the fact that camels (*uṣṭra*) are more frequent than goats (*aja, chāga*) or sheep (*meṣa*) because camels are used for transport and so also for warfare, whereas sheep and goats are reared for their meat. There is one mention of a flock of goats (*bāstika*, 2.71.2c but not in the Northern recension) and in the fourth stage a term for sheep and goats (*ajāvika*). Although camels naturally belong to the drier northwestern parts of India, they are nonetheless mentioned in connection with the Laṅkā forces (6.48.38 and 53.28) in descriptions of the second stage, illustrating the aritificiality of much of this expansion. Dogs are tame but used basically for hunting. This is suggested by the description of the dogs which Aśvapati gives to Bharata as 'fighting with their teeth and large-bodied' (2.64.21) and confirmed by similes alluding to a doe surrounded by dogs in the hunt (3.53.5 and 5.13.23), although other similes put limits to their bravery by declaring that dogs cannot face a tiger (5.19.27) and that dogs flee from a leopard as cats from dogs (7.7.20). On the other hand their presence around habitations is shown by the fact that ill omens seen in Laṅkā include dogs gobbling up the food-offerings, *bali*, thrown to the ground (6.26.26). In the third stage there also occurs the taboo on eating dog's flesh, or more exactly the loathing and contempt for those who do (1.58.20, 61.13 and 16). But cats (*mārjāra, biḍāla*), which are mentioned only eight times in the text, are invariably wild; the nearest to domesticity is that cats and owls

[7] One of these passages is Jaṭāyus' genealogy (3.13.23) which is paralleled in the Mahābhārata (1.60.60) where van Buitenen translates *sṛmara* as 'marsh deer', which is clearly based on the definition of it as an animal frequenting damp places, but in his notes to the text gives with a query the identification Bos grunniens.

inhabit the desolate Ayodhyā (2.106.2).[8] Presumably therefore the terms refer to either the leopard-cat (Felis bengalensis Kerr) or the jungle cat (Felis chaus Güldenstaedt). A Rākṣasī has eyes like a cat's from anger (5.21.9), which expresses a similar view to the British notions about the wild cat.

In addition to the deer and antelope, buffaloes and cats, a considerable number of wild animals are mentioned. The commonest is the lion (Panthera leo (L.), *siṃha* or rarely *kesarin* 'the animal with a mane'), which as in many cultures is a symbol of courage and strength; the term is not infrequently also found as the final element of compounds to denote pre-eminence and valour, as is the tiger (Panthera tigris (L.), *vyāghra, śārdūla*), which however occurs much less frequently as the animal itself. A third big cat, the leopard (Panthera pardus (L.), *dvīpin*) occurs once in the second stage (3.44.28) and occasionally in later stages.

Other land mammals that occur with any frequency in the first and second stages are bears (*ṛkṣa*, Melursus ursinus (Shaw), the sloth bear, *or* Selenarctos thibetanus (G.Cuvier), the Himalayan black bear), monkeys (*golāṅgūla* and *śākhāmṛga*, rarely *valīmukha* and *gopuccha*; most probably the common langur, Presbytis entellus (Dufresne), but possibly including other species also),[9] jackals (*gomāyu, śivā*, rarely *śṛgāla* and *jambuka*, Canis aureus L.) and wild boar (*varāha*, occasionally *sūkara*, Sus scrofa L., *syn.* S. cristatus). Less common are wolves (*īhāmṛga, koka* or *vṛka*, Canis lupus L.), hyenas (*tarakṣu*, Hyaena hyaena (L.)), porcupines (*śalya, śalyaka* or *śvāvidh*, Hystrix indica Kerr), rhinoceros (*vārdhrāṇasa*, Rhinoceros unicornis L.), mongoose (*nakula*, Herpestes edwardsi (Geoffroy), *syn.* Viverra ichneumon), hare (*śaśa*, Lepus nigricollis F.Cuvier) and rat or mouse (*mūṣika*, also in the third stage *ākhu*, probably Rattus rattus (L.) and Mus musculus L., the house rat and house mouse, which are very

[8] One problematic exception is Hanumān's form on entering Laṅkā to reconnoitre, having the size of a *pṛṣadaṃśaka* (5.2.46e). Both the commentaries and the indigenous lexica consider this (or its variant *vṛṣadaṃśa*, also once in the fifth stage) to be a cat, but the subsequent versions (examined in chapters 8 and 9) put the matter in a different light. The change of size is omitted altogether in the *Rāmopākhyāna*; Kampaṉ and the *Adhyātma Rāmāyaṇa* refer only to his assuming a minute form, echoing what was said a couple of verses earlier (*rajanyāṃ hrasvatāṃ gataḥ*, Rām. 5.2.44b); Bhaṭṭi says that he assumed the size of a hare, in Guṇabhadra he has the form of a bee, in Tulsīdās he is like a gnat and in the Thai version as small as a beetle. It is obvious that the animal's identity was later unknown and that the authenticity of the stanza is questionable.

[9] These terms, though applied to the Vānaras, appear specifically to identify them as monkeys; however, the terms *kapi* and *hari* 'tawny', as well as *vānara* 'forest-dweller', have not in this context been taken as denoting monkeys.

similar in appearance apart from size). There is no obvious difference between the first and second stages in the occurrence of these mammals, some terms only occurring in the first stage and some only in the second, apart from less frequent mention of the jackal in the second stage. But the third stage has a much shorter list: only lions, tigers, leopards, bears and boar occur more than once, with single occurrences of jackal, langur, hare and rat or mouse. It is perhaps worth remarking that, although most of these animals have a fairly general distribution throughout India, the lion has apparently always been restricted to the northern part, not penetrating south of the Narmadā, and the tiger is not found in Ceylon.[10] A greater oddity is that the sole occurrence of the rhinoceros, now more or less confined to Assam and Nepal though once more extensively distributed in the Gaṅgā basin, is as one of the items in the banquet that Hanumān sees spread in Rāvaṇa's dining hall (5.9.13).

Whereas general terms for animals are uncommon, those for birds are quite frequent. For animals, apart from *mṛga* in some of its occurrences (especially in the compounds *mṛgadvija* and *mṛgapakṣin*, meaning animals and birds), there are under ten occurrences of *śvāpada*, a wild beast, and a couple of *potaka*, a young animal. But for birds there are several groups of terms: the largest group refers to their aerial mode of life (*khaga, vihaga, vihaṃga* and *vihaṃgama*), the next refers to them as flying (*pataga, pataṃga*) or winged (*pakṣin, patatrin, patraratha* and *suparṇa*), another defines them as oviparous (the rare *aṇḍaja* directly, *dvija*—commonest in the second stage—as born twice in the laying and hatching of the egg); there is also a term for a large bird (*śakuna* or *śakuni*).

While these general terms for birds as a whole show effectively the same distribution pattern as for the fauna as a whole, names of different species are rather more frequent in the second stage, with its passages of nature description, and much less common in the third stage than average. The birds more commonly mentioned in the first stage are vultures (Gyps bengalensis (Gmelin) and Gyps indicus (Scopoli), *gṛdhra*), geese (Anser indicus Latham, *haṃsa*, the bar-headed goose), crows (Corvus splendens Vieillot, *vāyasa* or less commonly *kāka*), peacocks (Pavo cristatus L., *mayūra*, so named from the male's call), herons (Ardea cinerea L. or A. purpurea Meyen, *kaṅka*) whose feathers were used to flight arrows, ospreys (Pandion haliaetus h. (L.), *kurara*) and cranes (*krauñca*). The usual identification of the *krauñca*

[10] Cf. R. I. Pocock, *Fauna of British India: Mammalia*, vol. 1, London, 1939, pp. 206–7 and 219.

is as the demoiselle crane, Anthropoides virgo L., which is in fact a winter visitor to India, as is the curlew, Numenius spp., with which it is also sometimes identified. However, the behaviour attributed to it in the third-stage story of Vālmīki observing the pair of *krauñcas*, one of which the Niṣāda kills, is much more typical of the sarus crane (Grus antigone a. L., *sārasa*) which performs its courtship openly and demonstrates great affection for its mate.[11] Moreover, the demoiselle crane's winter quarters and migration routes largely overlap those of the common crane, Grus g. lilfordi Sharpe, so that the two are usually found together and cannot readily be told apart.[12] Probably the term *krauñca* denotes both the demoiselle and common cranes, but certain characteristics of the *sārasa* have been erroneously transferred to it. There is an interesting passage where Sampāti, alluding to his descent from Garuḍa, the king of the birds, classifies birds according to their flight. The lowest group is the drongos and grain-eating birds, the second is crows and fruit-eating birds, the third hawks, cranes and ospreys, the fourth eagles, the fifth vultures and the sixth geese, while the path of Garuḍa is loftier than all (4.57.25–7).[13]

Geese, vultures, peacocks (also *barhin* or *barhiṇa* and once each *arjunaka* and *nīlakaṇṭhī*), crows and cranes remain quite common in the second stage, in which some other birds, especially aquatic or water-frequenting ones, are also quite common: coot (Fulica atra L., *kāraṇḍava*, once *kāraṇḍa*), ruddy sheldrake (Tadorna ferruginea Pallas *syn*. Anas casarca, *cakravāka*[14]), sarus crane, large egret (Egretta alba (L.), *balāka*), as well as the cuckoo (Eudynamys scolopacea sc. (L.), *kokila*).

Of the less common birds, the following are mentioned in the first stage: *kapota* (Columba livia Gmelin, blue rock pigeon), *kalahaṃsa* (also *kādamba* in the second stage, Anser a. rubirostris Swinhoe, *syn*. A. cinereus, greylag goose), *kukkuṭa* (Gallus g. murghi Robinson & Kloss, red jungle fowl), *kuliṅga* and *bhṛṅgarāja* (Dicrurus paradiseus (L.), racket-tailed drongo), *kṛkara* (a type of partridge, Francolinus

[11] Cf. Sálim Ali and S. D. Ripley, *Handbook of the Birds of India and Pakistan*, 10 vols., Bombay, 1968–74, vol. 2, pp. 142–3. (The nomenclature of the birds throughout is based on the *Handbook*). Cf. also P. Thieme, 'Kranich und Reiher im Sanskrit', *Studien zur Indologie und Iranistik* 1, 1975, pp. 3–36 and C. Vaudeville, 'Rāmāyaṇa Studies I: The Krauñca-vadha episode in the Vālmīki Rāmāyaṇa', JAOS 83, 1963, pp. 327–35.

[12] Cf. Sálim Ali and S. D. Ripley, op. cit., vol. 2, p. 146.

[13] J. Ph. Vogel (*The Goose in Indian Literature and Art*, Memoirs of the Kern Institute 2, Leiden, 1962, p. 17) noted the passage in connection with the Indian view of the goose as the high-flying, remote and even mysterious bird.

[14] Also twice in the second stage by play on its name called the bird 'named after a part of a chariot' (i.e. wheel, *cakra*).

spp., or bustard-quail, Turnix spp.), *dātyūha* and *natyūha* (also *jalakukkuṭa* from the second stage, Gallinula chloropus indica Blyth, Indian moorhen), *plava* (Amaurornis phoenicurus Pennant, white-breasted waterhen), *bhāsa* (a hawk, probably Accipiter nisus (L.), sparrow-hawk), *vañculaka* or *vañjula* (a kind of aquatic or water-haunting bird), *śuka* (a parrot, probably Psittacula eupatria (L.), large parakeet), *śyena* (an eagle, Aquila or Haliaeetus spp.), *sārikā* (Acridotheres tristis t. (L.), mynah, and probably also Gracula religiosa intermedia A. Hay, hill mynah) and *stokaka* (*sāraṅga* in the second stage, Clamator jacobinus (Boddaert), pied crested cuckoo). All these names, except *kuliṅga, dātyūha* and *stokaka*, also appear occasionally in the second stage, in which mention is also found of *ulūka* (an owl, probably Athene brama (Temminck), spotted owlet), *koṇālaka* (unidentified), *koyaṣṭi* (Vanellus indicus (Boddaert), *syn*. Sarcogrammus i., redwattled lapwing), *madgu* (probably Phalacrocorax niger (Vieillot), little cormorant), *rājahaṃsa* (either synonymous with *haṃsa* or more probably Phoenicopterus roseus Pallas, flamingo[15]) and *śatapatra* (a woodpecker, probably Dinopium benghalense (L.), goldenbacked woodpecker).

Far from adding any new species, the third stage sees a comparatively restricted list of birds, with only the *haṃsa, gṛdhra* and *krauñca* at all frequent and occasional mention of *kaṅka, kāka, kāraṇḍava, kokila, cakravāka, jalakukkuṭa, barhiṇa, bhṛṅgarāja, mayūra, vāyasa* and *sārasa*.

By contrast the fourth stage includes almost all the birds mentioned in the first and second stages with in addition *kirīṭaka* (an unidentified, presumably crested bird), *kṛkavāku* (another name for the peacock), *jṛmbha* (unidentified), *ṭiṭṭibha* (another name for a lapwing, Vanellus indicus), *tittira* (partridge, Francolinus spp.), *putrapriya* (unidentified, also e.g. Mbh. 3.107.8), *priyaṃvada* (unidentified), *baka* (another name for Egretta alba (L.)), *bhāradvāja* (Alauda gulgula Franklin, small skylark), *lāvaka* (quail, Perdicula or Turnix spp.), *vāghrīṇasa* (probably another name for the common crane) and *śarāri* (Ardea cinerea L., grey heron). The number of alternative names for species occurring in earlier stages is in itself a mark of the considerable development of the vocabulary and thus of the time interval involved.

Snakes, other reptiles and amphibia are slightly more frequent in the second stage than the average for the fauna as a whole. This is because they are almost entirely peripheral to the story, occurring either in

[15] The latter identification makes much more appropriate Kaikeyī's comparison of the hunchbacked Mantharā with a *rājahaṃsī* (2.9.33). On the other hand, a fourth stage passage (3.1074*) pairs a *rājahaṃsa* and a *haṃsī*.

similes and other figures of speech or as one item in the lists of wildlife in descriptive passages. None of the terms is as specific as those for mammals and birds; in fact the total of occurrences for this class is much the same as that for general terms for birds. The hostility between Garuḍa, king of the birds, and snakes is alluded to in a number of similes. Other pieces of traditional lore included are the fatal result for a certain lizard of swallowing a hailstone (*brāhmaṇī karakād iva*, 3.28.5d) and the invisibility of a snake's legs to all but other snakes (*ahir eva aheḥ pādān vijānāti na saṃśayaḥ*, 5.40.9cd). Similes involving snakes occur especially in two rather stereotyped forms—the comparison of the hand to a five-headed snake and of someone angry to a hissing snake.

There are a large number of terms for snakes, of which four are commoner in the first stage than elsewhere (*ahi, uraga, vyāla* and *sarpa*) whereas the remainder are commoner in the second stage (*āśīviṣa, nāga, pannaga, bhujaga* and *bhujaṃga*) or found only there and later (*brāhmaṇī* and *sarīsṛpa*). The term *nāga* probably denotes the cobra (Naja n. L., *syn*. N. tripudians) but other terms are applied to any snake. After snakes, the next most frequent are crocodiles, *grāha* (twice *graha*, Gavialis gangeticus Gray) and *nakra* or *makara* (Crocodilus palustris Lesson *or* C. porosus Schneider), but simply as regular inhabitants of rivers or the sea along with fish. Tortoises (*kacchapa* and *kūrma*, once each *kāmaṭha* in the fourth and *kamaṭha* in the fifth stage, Kachuga spp.) occur preponderantly in the second stage, since six of their eight occurrences are there including two in connection with Garuḍa's exploits (3.33.28, 31) and one in the traditional maxim about permissible types of meat (4.17.34), where the iguana (Varanus monitor (L.), *godhā*) is also listed, though not otherwise occurring before the fourth stage. The term *brāhmaṇī*, found once in the simile above, denotes, according to the commentators, 'a sort of lizard with a red tail',[16] Kubera turns himself into a chameleon in one third-stage episode (*kṛkalāsa*, Chamaeleon zeylanicus Laurenti, 7.18.5, 31) and frogs occur once in the first stage (*maṇḍūka*), once in the second (*bheka*) and a few times in the fourth (*dardura, maṇḍūka*); however, none of these can really be said to be part of the fauna regularly noted in the text.

Fish and other aquatic creatures are mentioned only about a hundred times; moreover, nearly 40% of these consist of the conch (*śaṅkha*,

[16] Satya Vrat notes that it is 'still called *bamani*, evidently a derivative from it, in the Bhojpuri dialect', without giving any precise identification (*The Rāmāyaṇa—A linguistic study*, Delhi, 1964, p. 6 n.).

Xancus pyrum (L.), *syn*. Turbinella p. Auct.), whose shell was used as a trumpet, and therefore occurs commonly in the battle scenes of the Yuddha and Uttara kāṇḍas. However, descriptions of the sea occasionally include the conch, linking it thrice with the pearl-oyster (*śukti*, Pinctada vulgaris)—the only mentions of this shellfish, although pearls as an item of jewellery are not infrequently mentioned. The sea is also occasionally thought of as inhabited by whales (*timi*; Balaenoptera musculus (L.), blue whale) in the first stage, and also by 'whale-swallowers' (*timimgila*, probably in fact another term for the blue whale) and other sea-monsters (*yādas*) in the second and later stages. Another aquatic mammal mentioned is the freshwater dolphin (*śiṃśumāra*, Platanista gangetica (Lebeck), *syn*. P. indi, Gangetic dolphin) but three of the five references to it come from the third stage. Fish, whether marine or freshwater, are denoted by the terms *matsya* and *mīna*, with a further term for large fish, *jhaṣa*. Individual species are not named except for one passage (3.69.9) where it is said that in lake Pampā *rohita* (Cyprinus rohitaka, a member of the carp family), *vakratuṇḍa* ('with a curved beak', unidentified) and *nalamīna* ('reed-like', perhaps an eel or spiny eel) can be killed with arrows. This is one of only three references to catching fish, the others being similes for Rāvaṇa's destruction at Rāma's hands as being like a fish caught on a hook (3.49.22 and 64.13), although another simile uses the fact that a fish lifted out of the water will soon die (2.47.31).[17]

Insects and the like form an even smaller group, of which two thirds of the occurrences are in the second stage. Bees (*bhramara*, once *madhukārin*, Apis indica F.) are the commonest, being mentioned ten times in the text, but are nonetheless rare compared with their frequency in classical poetry. Next in frequency come a general term for insects, meaning six-legged (*ṣaṭpada*, once *ṣaṭcaraṇa*), and another, *śalabha*, which means either a locust or a moth. The former term presumably indicates that the author recognised six legs as the distinguishing factor of an insect, although there is no evidence within our text to prove it; however, the term is much more frequent in the fourth stage than in the text and so is clearly relatively late. In some contexts, *śalabha* seems more naturally to mean locust (Oedipoda migratoria), as when the massing of armies is compared to them hiding the earth (4.44.1, 6.31.39–40 and 7.7.3), but elsewhere the imagery lies in their attraction by flames, which perhaps suits better the meaning of moth (3.13.36d[l.v.], 6.45.42d[l.v.], 53.36d and 7.34.44d). Another term for

[17] For the eating of fish see pp. 83–4. There is also an interesting maxim, apparently based on some kind of folk-tale, at 3.36.22: 'Like fish in a snake-pond, even though they do not sin, the pure are, through association with sin, destroyed by the sins of others.'

insect, *kīṭa*, appears only in relation to the drawbacks of forest life first in Kausalyā's blessings (2.22.6) and then in Rāma's speech to Sītā (2.25.12), where gnats (Culex pipiens, *daṃśa*), mosquitoes (Culex mosquito, *maśaka*), and scorpions (order Scorpionida, *vṛścika*) also find their only mention in the first and second stages. In addition, the firefly (Lamprophorus spp., *khadyota*) occurs in the first and second stages, the lāc-insect (Laccifer lacca, *kṛmi*) and its product (*lākṣā*), crickets (*jhillikā*), a fly (*makṣikā*) and an anthill (*valmīka*) are each mentioned once in the second stage and occasionally later, and a rain mite (probably genus Acarus of Trombidiidae, *indragopa*) thrice in the fourth stage.[18]

The relative lack of emphasis on animal husbandry and agriculture throughout is susceptible to two explanations: either the practice of agriculture was then little developed or the interests of poet and audience did not lie in that direction. The latter is clearly correct since by the time of the poem the Gaṅgā valley was undoubtedly well colonised—apart from anything else, the location of Daśaratha's capital at Ayodhyā demonstrates this—and this would have necessitated advanced agricultural techniques. Nevertheless specific reference to these techniques is commoner in later parts of the poem, although references to all facets of agriculture, including crops and cattle, are more evenly spread across the successive periods of the epic's growth. There are just over one hundred occurrences of terms specific to agriculture in the whole of the text and references to crops and domestic animals (excluding horses) are well under four hundred. The only terms which are at all frequent are the very general ones for cattle (*paśu*), ploughing and cultivation in general (*karṣaka, karṣaṇa, √kṛṣ, kṛṣi*), fields (*kṣetra*) and grain (*dhānya* and *sasya*).

Terms for a plough are predominantly late: among the five occurrences of *hala*, one is from the first stage, but *lāṅgala* is found only in the second and third stages and *phāla* not before the fourth stage. The use of bulls for ploughing—and their ill-treatment by the farmer—forms the subject-matter of one late simile; the few references to draught animals are concentrated in the second stage. Several of the references to ploughs are connected with the late myth that Janaka finds the baby

[18] On the accurate identification of the *indragopa*, not uncommon in the Pali canon and classical Sanskrit *kāvya*, see S. Lienhard, 'On the meaning and use of the word *indragopa*', IT 6, 1978, pp. 177–88. I am grateful to Professor Lienhard for an advance copy of this article.

Sītā in a furrow (*sītā*) while ploughing. It is of interest that *sītā* is not the only agricultural term which is reflected in the name of one of the Rāmāyaṇa's protagonists: *śūrpa*, a 'winnowing fan' is the prior element of Śūrpaṇakhā's name; however, unlike the names, both terms are strikingly late, found only from the fourth stage (2.2389* 2 and 2.1904* 2 respectively). But while attempts have been made to see the heroine as a euhemerised agricultural goddess,[19] I am not aware that anything of the sort has been undertaken for the villainess. There may indeed be some reflection of agricultural terms in the women's names, for such a tendency is found in many cultures; the lateness of the terms themselves is no doubt due to the fact that the original Rāmāyaṇa was a martial epic, and that the idyllic, rustic elements were introduced only later.

Rice is clearly the principal crop, but the few references to a wet-crop field (*kedāra*) are from the second and third stages (e.g. 6.5.11). There is no direct reference to the process of irrigation, only a casual allusion in Rāma's catechism to the population not being dependent on rain (*adevamātṛka*, literally 'not having the gods as mothers' i.e. providers, 2.94.39; cf. Mbh. 2.5.67 and KA 5.2.2). There are two early passages indicating the importance of rain at the end of the Ayodhyākāṇḍa (2.104.12, a simile of farmers longing for rain, and 109.9, a ten-year drought eased by Anasūyā's powers). The regular appearance of the rains is part of the proper ordering of affairs, and thus there is no rain and no sowing in a kingless state (2.61.8–9, cf. 16) but trees are ever in flower and Parjanya rains on time during Rāma's ideal rule (6.116.88), both passages coming from the second stage, as do other allusions (e.g. 5.27.6cd[l.v.] and 6.24.25).

The only specific grain mentioned in early parts of the text is rice (*kalama, nīvāra* or *naivāra*, later *śāli*), apart from the sole reference to one millet (*priyaṅgu*, Panicum italicum L., *syn.* Setaria italica Beauv.), but references to other grains occur in later stages: wheat (*godhūma*) and barley (*yava*) in the second stage and another millet (*śyāmaka*, Panicum frumentaceum Roxb., *syn.* Echinochloa frumentacea) in the fourth stage.[20] However, none is at all frequently mentioned at any stage. Legumes or pulses are mentioned only from the second stage

[19] Jacobi, *Das Râmâyaṇa*, pp. 130–1; often repeated since, e.g. Gonda, *Early Viṣṇuism*, p. 29. It is relevant to add that Draupadī shares with Sītā many features, including having arisen from the earth (Mbh. 1.189.34[l.v.]); others are identification with Śrī (Mbh. 1.189.48), an unusual birth—from the altar (Mbh. 1.57.92, 153.10 and 155.41), and being won by a contest with the bow (Mbh. 1.176–9).

[20] For as far back as can be traced, the different cereal crops have shown a characteristic distribution: rice centred on the Gaṅgā basin, wheat on the Panjab and millets (especially sorghum nowadays) on the Peninsula.

onwards: dal (*āḍhakī*, Cajanus indicus Spreng, *syn.* C. cajan, C. bicolor and Cytisus cajan Roxb.) and black gram (*māṣa*, Phaseolus mungo L.) from the second stage, green gram (*mudga*, Phaseolus radiatus L., *syn.* Ph. mungo Roxb. and Ph. aureus) from the third stage, horse-gram (*kulastha*, Dolichos biflorus L., *syn.* D. uniflorus Lam.) and chick-pea (*caṇaka*, Cicer arietinum) from the fourth. Other crop plants mentioned are: sesamum and its oil (*tila* and *taila*, Sesamum indicum DC, *syn.* S. orientale, not infrequent in connection with Daśaratha's funeral), cotton (*kārpāsaka*, Gossypium obtusifolium, twice mentioned, once early and once late), sugar-cane (*ikṣu*, Saccharum officinalis L., references in the second, third and fourth stages) and sunn hemp (*śaṇa*, Crotalaria juncea L., a fibre plant, rather than Cannabis sativa L., *syn.* C. indica Lamk., the drug). Mention of fodder for horses (*khādana, yavasa*) is surprisingly rare (2.41.10 and 44.15,21).

Terms connected with flora, if words for forests are included, are slightly more frequent than terms connected with fauna and, as already noted, even more concentrated in the second stage with half the total, by contrast with the third stage with only a ninth. In fact forests, being directly connected with the narrative, are more frequently mentioned in the first stage than other categories. The commonest term, with four-fifths of the total occurrences, is *vana*; *araṇya* and *kānana* have the same frequency but *araṇya* occurs mainly in the second stage whereas *kānana* is most frequent in the first;[21] another term for forest, *aṭavī*, occurs only rarely, as does a term meaning a grove, *ṣaṇḍa*, which is decidedly late in distribution. Trees are mentioned half as often as forests, the two commonest terms being *vṛkṣa* and *druma*; the next most frequent is *pādapa* and other occasional terms are *taru, naga, mahīruha, vanaspati, viṭapin* and, in the fourth stage only, *śākhin*. However, general terms for trees, like general terms for plants and their parts and names of individual species, occur mainly in passages of natural description and so tend to occur most frequently in the second stage.

Commercial exploitation of the forests is hardly alluded to at all at any stage. Two incidental references to charcoal (*aṅgāra*) from the second stage attest a more systematic use for fuel than the piles of firewood near *āśramas*. The common comparison of a warrior's fall to that of a tree[22] can usually refer as naturally to a tree uprooted by a gale

[21] This therefore provides another indicator of the lateness of the division into books; see pp. 8 and 189. If this were early, the third book would naturally have been named Vanakāṇḍa not Araṇyakāṇḍa.

[22] See my FS p. 448.

(this is certainly the case with the plantain in the Rāmāyaṇa) as to deliberate felling; occasionally the latter is suggested, however (e.g. *nikṛtta iva pādapaḥ* 4.17.1d, cf. 6.22.25d and 6 App.I.26.58 post.), and the fourth stage has allusions to felling *sāl* trees with an axe (2.425* and 1685*), which definitely suggests timber production. The details of the destruction of the Madhuvana (5.59–60) show that this area was the private preserve of the Vānara chief but it would be too far-fetched to see in this anything resembling a commercial orchard. Indeed, it is by no means clear which trees, if any, were actually cultivated. Abundant references to sandalwood (*candana* and *raktacandana*) show that this was a valued commodity, as was the *aguru* (aloe wood) with which it is not infrequently linked, while there is also one late reference to camphor (*karpūra*, 6.116.51, Cinnamomum camphora Vees, *syn.* Camphora officinarum Bauh. and Laurus camphora). However there is no direct evidence for whether such trees were actually cultivated or their products gathered from wild specimens.

The term for a creeper (*latā*) is the most frequent of the general terms for plants, with almost fifty occurrences; grass (mostly *tṛṇa* in the first stage and *śādvala* in the second), bushes or shrubs (*gulma*) and medicinal herbs (*oṣadhi, oṣadhī, auṣadha*) also occur not infrequently, the last mainly when Hanumān fetches them from the Himālayas (6.61).[23] The roots (*mūla*) and fruit (*phala*) of wild plants form a major part of the diet of ascetics and are commonly mentioned; both terms also have metaphorical uses which contribute to their frequency and general distribution.[24] Flowers (*puṣpa*, occasionally *kusuma* and *sumanas*) are naturally also quite frequent, along with adjectives for 'flowering, in flower' (*puṣpita, phulla* or *utphulla*, and *kusumita*) but other parts of plants are less frequently mentioned; they include branch (*śākhā*) and twig (*pallava*), bud (*kuḍmala, koraka*), petal (*palāśa*), leaf (*dala*), stalk (*nāla*), peduncle (*vṛnta*), pericarp (*karṇika*), filament (*kañjākiñjalka, kesara, mṛṇāla*), shoot (*aṅkura*) and bulb (*kanda*).

Of individual species mentioned, the most frequent are the various types of lotus or waterlily. The majority of the names occurring probably denote the Indian or sacred lotus (Nelumbium speciosum Willd., *syn.* Nelumbo nucifera Gaertn. and Nymphaea nelumbo L.); those commonly occurring are *kamala, nalina/nalinī, paṅkaja, padma* (and *padminī*, lotus-pond), *puṇḍarīka* and *puṣkara*, while less common

[23] Rare terms are *vallarī* (3.19.24f and 6.103.25d[l.v.]) and *vallī* (2.74.6a) for creepers, *śaṣpa* (3.41.19c and 7.18.30d) and *yavasa* (2.41.10c) for grass, and *vīrudh* (4.66.16a) for plants.

[24] For ascetics' diet see p. 81.

terms, mostly from the second stage and later, are *ambuja, aravinda, kuśeśaya, rājīva, śatapatra* and *saugandhika*. Other names apply to Nymphaea species, *utpala* and *nīlotpala* to the blue N. caerulea Savign., *syn*. N. cyanea Roxb., *indīvara* (once *kuvalaya*) to N. stellata Willd., and *kumuda* and *kahlāra* (both rare) to N. lotus L., although the last may be N. pubescens Willd.[25] The lotus figures a number of times in similes, especially as a comparison for the shape and colour of eyes, but its use in this way is much less frequent than in later literature.

Of the remaining flora, a dozen trees and plants occur with some frequency in the first stage:[26] *aśoka* (Saraca indica L., *syn*. Jonesia asoca Roxb., also rarely called *vañjula*), *iṅgudī* (Balanites roxburghii Planchon *or* Terminalia catappa L., Bengal almond),[27] *karṇikāra* (Pterospermum acerifolium Willd.), *kiṃśuka* (also occasionally *palāśa*, Butea monosperma (Lam.) Taub., *syn*. B. frondosa Roxb., Erythrina monosperma Lam. and Plaso m. Kuntzle, the 'flame-of-the-forest'), *kuśa* and *darbha* (Eragrostis cynosuroides Retz., Beauv., *syn*. Poa c. Roxb.), *candana* (Santalum album L., *syn*. S. myrtifolium Roxb. and Sirum myrtifolium L., sandalwood), *tāla* (Borassus flabellifer L., the palmyra or toddy-palm), *nyagrodha* (also once each in the second stage, *bhaṇḍīra* and *vaṭa*, Ficus bengalensis L., *syn*. F. indica Roxb., the banyan), *śiṃśapā* (Dalbergia sissoo Roxb.), and *sāla* (also quite often *aśvakarṇa* and once *sarja* in the second stage, Shorea robusta Gaertn. f., *syn*. Vatica robusta Steud.). The terms *aśvakarṇa* and *sāla* are usually held to refer to the same tree. However, in the Rāmāyaṇa the two names almost always occur in close proximity (only at 1.23.14a and 6.44.20–1 does *aśvakarṇa* not occur close to *sāla*). Either this indicates a relic of the time when *aśvakarṇa*, literally 'horse-eared', was simply an adjective, misunderstood by later poets, or the *aśvakarṇa* is a different tree from the *sāla*.

The habitat of the *sāla* nowadays is basically the sub-Himalayan belt

[25] In these identifications I mainly follow the indications noted by W. Rau, 'Lotusblumen', *Asiatica: Festschrift Friedrich Weller*, Leipzig, 1954, pp. 505–13, with which the more limited Rāmāyaṇa evidence is in agreement. Some authorities regard Nymphaea caerulea and N. stellata as synonymous.

[26] Identifications of trees mainly follow D. Brandis, *Indian Trees*, London, 1906.

[27] The *iṅgudī* (also once in the second stage *aiṅguda* and in the fourth stage *iṅguda* for its fruit) is especially mentioned in connection with the memorial rites for Daśaratha which Rāma performs and which involve an oil-cake (*piṇyāka*) made from the *iṅgudī* (2.95–6). Thus the identification as Terminalia catappa would seem more probable since it has oil-rich seeds, except that it is not regarded as indigenous; also, modern names for Balanites roxburghii in Hindi, *hiṅgu, hiṅgan* or *hiṅgota*, are apparently derived from *iṅguda*. Its identification must therefore remain in doubt.

and Central India north of the Godāvarī, especially the Chota Nagpur plateau, and must once have included much of the Gaṅgā basin; an important timber tree, it often occurs in pure stands, as the Rāmāyaṇa several times implies. A comparison of the distribution and habitat of the more frequently occurring trees in the first stage seems to indicate a relatively dry area towards the northeast as the common background. Certainly there is nothing to suggest any acquaintance with the distinctive flora of peninsular India.

Most references in the first stage are to one or two plants or trees at a time, but two passages contain longer lists of the kind typical of the second stage and are in fact probably also subsequent insertions into otherwise early sargas. Thus, in the description of Pañcavatī are included three stanzas (3.14.16–18) containing the names of twenty-four trees and of wild rice (*nīvāra*), and the Kiṣkindhākāṇḍa opens with a description of Pampā containing thirty-nine names of trees (4.1.35–40), somewhat similar to that which closes the Araṇyakāṇḍa, and certainly belonging to the second stage (3.71.15 and 21–2). These two lists both contain the names of several trees not occurring elsewhere in the first stage: *ketaka* (Pandanus tectorius Solander, *syn.* P. odoratissimus Roxb., screwpine), *kharjūra* (Phoenix sylvestris Roxb., *syn.* Elate s. L., wild date), *nīpa* (Anthocephalus cadamba Roxb. Miq., *syn.* A. morindaefolius Korth. and Nauclea c. Roxb., also in the second stage *kadamba* and *priyaka*), *pāṭala* (Stereospermum suaveolens DC, *syn.* Bignonia s. Roxb. and Spathodea s. Benth. et Hook f., trumpet-flower tree) and *syandana* (only in these two passages, elsewhere in the first and second stages, as well as in both of these passages, *timiśa* or *tiniśa* q.v.); in addition each contains several other trees not otherwise occurring in the first stage.[28] As is often the case with similar lists of trees from the second stage the species mentioned range from those requiring fairly dry conditions to moist and from hilly to low ground or littoral.

[28] Whereas the description of Pañcavatī contains only two trees not otherwise attested in the first or second stages (*lakuca*, Artocarpus lacucha Roxb., monkey-jack, and *śamī*, Acacia suma Kurz, *syn.* Mimosa s. Roxb. and A. sundra DC, *or* Prosopis spicigera L.), the description of Pampā has nine: *kuraṇṭa* (Marsilla quadrifolia L.), *kurabaka* (Barleria cristata Nees), *cūrṇaka* (Zizyphus rugosa Lamk.), *nāgavṛkṣa* (Mesua ferrea L., *syn.* Ochrocarpus longifolius Benth. & Hook, ironwood), *pāribhadra* (and also in the fourth stage *pārijāta*, Erythrina indica Lam., coral tree), *mallika* (Jasminum sambac Aiton, perennial jasmine), *mādhavī* (Hiptage madhoblata Gaertn. *syn.* Gaertnera racemosa Roxb.), *vāsantī* (identical either with *mādhavī* or *pāṭala*, both in this passage) and *śirīṣa* (Albizzia lebbek Benth., *syn.* Mimosa sirissa Roxb., Acacia s. Buch.-Ham. and Acacia speciosa Willd.).

One list of the second stage where habitat is largely immaterial is that of the different woods collected for Daśaratha's funeral (2.70.16), which are clearly listed chiefly for their aromatic properties, although in fact they mostly come from the Himālayas or the foothills; they are *candana, agaru, sarala* (Pinus roxburghii Sargent, *syn.* P. longifolia Roxb., chir pine), *padmaka* (Costus speciosus Sm., *syn.* C. arabicus *or* Prunus cerasoides D. Don, *syn.* P. puddum Roxb. and Cerasus puddum, Himalayan wild cherry) and *devadāru* (Cedrus deodara Laws, *syn.* C. libani var. deodara Hook f. and Pinus devadaru, deodar). But the description of Citrakūṭa (2.88), for instance, which should be that of a particular place, includes in one line the *puṃnāga*, which is a decidedly littoral species of central and southern India, and the *tagara* (Tabernaemontana coronaria Willd., grape jasmine) and *bhūrja* (Betula utilis D. Don, *syn.* B. bhojapatra Wall., birch) both of which require a markedly northern habitat; the latter two, along with *kuṣṭha* (Costus speciosus Sm., *syn.* C. arabicus) in this same line (2.88.24ab), do not occur elsewhere in the text. So too, when Hanumān views Laṅkā, thirteen trees are listed (5.2.9–10): one is definitely Himālayan (*sarala*) and two belong to hilly areas (*karṇikāra* and *nīpa*), whereas two grow on low ground (*kharjūra* and *ketaka*); one grows in semi-arid conditions (*karavīra*, Nerium odorum Ait.) and one cannot grow in arid conditions (*priyāla*, Buchanania latifolia Roxb. *syn.* B. lanzan Spreng). The description is obviously literary and does not refer to any specific locality. It may also be noted that the description of Rāvaṇa's *aśoka* grove mentions the *sāla* and contains the mango under two different names (*āmra* and *cūta*, Mangifera indica L.) as well as several trees of scarcely compatible habitat (5.12.3–4 and 42). Other lists of this sort appear in connection with Bharadvāja's entertainment (2.85.27, 46–8, 77), Agastya's hermitage (3.10.72), Rāma's grief-stricken ravings (3.58.12–19), the meeting with Kabandha (3.69.3 and 15), the description of the rainy season (4.27.4–9 and 18–27[l.v.]), the Vānaras' entry into Ṛkṣabila (4.49.20), the construction of Nala's causeway (6.15.16–17), the description of Laṅkā (6.30.3–4) and, in the third stage, Rāma and Sītā in the pleasure-garden (7.41.2–3).

In keeping with this tendency to include descriptive passages, twice as many trees or plants occur with some frequency in the second stage as in the first.[29] A few that were reasonably common in the first stage decline in frequency and so drop out of the list (*aśvakarṇa, iṅgudī, kiṃśuka* and *nyagrodha*), while many are added. The new ones are

[29] For this purpose the lists contained in 3.14 and 4.1 are regarded as belonging to the second stage. Five or more occurrences are regarded as frequent.

agaru or *aguru* (Aquilaria agallocha Roxb., aloewood or eagle wood), *arjuna* (Terminalia arjuna Wt. & A., *syn*: Pentaptera a.), *āmra, uddāla* (Cordia myxa L., *syn.* C. obliqua Willd., also once in the third stage *śleṣmātaka*), *kadalī* (Musa paradisiaca L., *syn.* M. sapientum, plantain), *ketaka, campaka* (Michelia champaca L., *syn.* M. aurantiaca Wall.), *cūta, tamāla* (Garcinia xanthochymus Hook f., *syn.* Xanthochymus pictorius Roxb.), *tiniśa* or *timiśa* (Dalbergia ougeinensis Roxb., *syn.* Amerimnus o. and Ougeinia dalbergioides Benth.), *tilaka* (Clerodendron phlomoides L.f.), *dhava* (Anogeissus latifolia Wall. *or* Woodfordia floribunda Salisb., *syn.* Grislea tomentosa Buch.-Ham. and W. fruticosa Kurz.), *panasa* (Artocarpus integrifolia L.f., jackfruit), *puṃnāga* (Calophyllum inophyllum L.), *bakula* (Mimusops elengi L.) and *raktacandana* (Pterocarpus santalinus L.f., red sandalwood).

With four exceptions (*uddāla, campaka, bakula* and *raktacandana*), these frequent names of the second stage also appear occasionally in the first stage and there are a number of names occurring in both stages only infrequently. Common to both stages, but infrequent, are *aśvattha* (Ficus religiosa L., the sacred fig tree or *pīpal), iṣīkā* (a reed or cane), *kuṭaja* (Holarrhena antidysenterica Wall., *syn.* H. codaga D. Don, Echites a. Roxb. ex Flem., Wrightia a., Chonemorpha a. G. Don and Nerium a. L. *or* Millingtonia hortensis L.f., mountain jasmine), *kovidāra* (Bauhinia spp., B. acuminata L., purpurea L. or variegata L.). *khadira* (Acacia catechu Willd. L., *syn.* Mimosa c. Roxb.), *jambī* or *jambū* (Eugenia jambolana Lam., *syn.* Syzygium cuminii L. (Skeels) and S. jambolanum DC, jambolan), *tiniśa* or *timiśa, tinduka* (Diospyros embryopteris Pers. *or* D. melanoxylon Roxb., ebony), *devadāru, naktamāla* (Pongamia pinnata (L.) Merr., *syn.* P. glabra Vent., Galedupa indica Lam., Dalbergia arborea Willd. and Cytisus pinnatus L.), *nārikela* or *nālikera* (Cocos nucifera L., coconut), *padmaka, palāśa* (= *kiṃśuka*), *priyāla, badara* or *badarī* (Zizyphus jujuba Lam., *syn.* Z. sativa Gaert., Z. vulgaris Lam., Z. zizyphus Karst. and Rhamnus zizuphus L., jujube tree), *bilva* (Aegle marmelos Correa, *bel* or wood-apple tree), *madhūka* (Madhuca latifolia (Roxb.) MacBr. *syn.* M. indica Gmel. and Bassia l. Roxb., *mahua*), *rodhra* or *lodhra* (Symplocos racemosa Roxb.), *vaṃśa* and *veṇu* (Arundo bambos L. or Bambusa spp., bamboo), *viśalyakaraṇī* (a medicinal herb), *śālmalī* (Bombax ceiba L., *syn.* B. malabaricum DC, B. heptaphyllum Cav. and Salmalia m. Schott & Endl., silk-cotton tree), *śaivala* (Blyxa octandra, *syn.* Vallisneria o., eel-grass), *saptacchada* or *saptaparṇa* (Alstonia scholaris Brown, *syn.* Echites s. L., milkwood) and *sarala*.

In addition the first stage contains the following infrequent names absent from the second stage: *uśīra* (Andropogon muricatus Retz., *syn.* A. squarrosus L., *khas-khas* grass), *kiṃpāka* (fruit of Trichosanthes palmata, snakegourd), *gajapuṣpī* (Arum campanulatum Roxb., *syn.* Amorphophallus c. Blume, elephant-flower, elephant-foot yam), *japā* (Hibiscus rosa-sinensis L., China rose, is the usual identification but this is not indigenous), *plakṣa* (Ficus infectoria Roxb.), *bhallātaka* (Anacardium occidentale L.), *madhūka* and *maskara* (Bambusa arundinacea Willd., bamboo). There is naturally a rather longer list of infrequent names only from the second stage (often also occurring in the fourth stage): *aṅkola* (Alangium decapetalum Lam., *syn.* A. lamarckii Thwaites, A. hexapetalum Roxb., A. tomentosum Lam., A. salviifolium Wangerin and Grewia s. L.f.), *atimuktaka* (Hiptage madhoblata Gaertn., *syn.* H. benghalensis Kurz. and Gaertnera racemosa Roxb.), *ariṣṭa* (Sapindus mukorossi Gaertn., *syn.* S. detergens Roxb. and S. saponaria, soap-nut), *asana* (Terminalia tomentosa Wt. & A., *syn.* T. crenulata Kurz., T. alata var. typica Heyne and T. glabra var. tomentosa Dalz., Indian laurel, *or* Bridelia retusa Spreng), *āmalaka* (Phyllanthus emblica L. *syn.* Emblica officinalis Gaertn. and E. myrobalan, Indian gooseberry), *kakubha* (Terminalia arjuna Wt. & A., *syn.* Pentaptera a., Rangoon ivy), *kapittha* (Feronia elephantum Correa, *syn.* Limonia acidissima, elephant-apple), *kāśa* (Saccharum spontaneum Mant.), *kāśmarī* (Gmelina arborea L.), *kīcaka* (Arundo karka, bamboo), *kunda* (Jasminum pubescens Willd., *syn.* J. multiflorum Andr.), *kuṣṭha, kharjūra, gośīrṣaka* (Phlomis zeylanica, *syn.* Leucas spp.), *ciribilva* (= *naktamāla*), *takkola* (unidentified[30]), *tagara, tuṅga* (Mallotus philippinensis Muell. Arg., *syn.* Rottlera tinctoria Roxb.), *nāgavṛkṣa, nicula* (Barringtonia acutangula Gaertn.), *dhanvana* (Grewia asiatica L. *syn.* G. elastica Royle), *pippalī* (Piper longum), *priyaka* (Anthocephalus cadamba Roxb. Miq., *syn.* A. morindaefolius Korth., A. indicus A. Rich and Nauclea cadamba Roxb. *or* Terminalia tomentosa Wt. & A.), *priyaṅgu* (Aglaia diepenhorstii Miq., *syn.* A. odoratissima Blume, A. roxburghiana Hiern and Miluca r. Wt. & A.), *bibhītaka* (Terminalia bellerica Roxb.), *bimba* (Momordica monadelpha Roxb.), *bījapūra* (Citrus medica L., citron), *bhaṇḍīra, bhavya* (Dillenia indica L., sandpaper tree), *bhūrja, marica* (Piper nigrum L., pepper shrub), *mālatī* (Jasminum grandiflorum L.), *mucukunda* and *muculinda* (Pterospermum suberifolium Lam.), *vañjula* (= *aśoka*), *vaṭa, varaṇa* (Crataeva roxburghii Kurz., *syn.* C. religiosa

[30] This cannot be Pimenta acris, bay-rum tree, with which Monier-Williams (*A Sanskrit-English Dictionary*, new ed., Oxford, 1899) identifies it, since that originates in the West Indies.

Forst), *vīraṇa* (= *uśīra*), *vetra* (Calamus spp., especially tenuis Roxb. and viminalis Willd.), *śalya* (Vangueria spinosa Roxb.), *śukladruma* (= *lodhra*), *sarja* (= *sāla*) and *hintāla* (Phoenix paludosa Roxb., marshy date tree).

The Third stage, lacking descriptive passages for the most part, shows a much more restricted flora. As already noted, there is one passage of nature description analogous to those typical of the second stage, where Rāma enters the *aśoka* grove with Sītā (7.41.1–10). This passage lists a dozen trees notable for their scent or their fruit: *candana, agaru, cūta, tuṅga, kāleyaka* (= *raktacandana* according to the Tilaka commentary, this is its only occurrence in the text), *devadāru, priyaṅgu, kadamba, kurabaka, jambū, pāṭali* and *kovidāra*. Apart from this passage, there is very little detail. Only two trees are at all common, the *aśoka* and *sāla* (once *aśvakarṇa*), and one grass, *kuśa* (once *darbha*), obviously because of its religious use. Some others of the flora occurring in the first or second stages are mentioned once or twice: *āmra, kakubha, kadamba, karavīra, karṇikāra, khadira, japā, tinduka, dhava, pāṭala, plakṣa, badarī, bilva* and *śaivala*. In addition three names besides *kāleyaka* occur for the first time once each: *tumba* (Lagenaria siceraria, *syn.* L. vulgaris Ser. and L. cucurbita l.L., bottle-gourd, 1.37.17), *śara* (Saccharum bengalense Retz., *syn.* S. arundinaceum Retz and S. sara Roxb., penreed grass, 7.31.7) and *śleṣmātaka* (= *uddāla*, 1.13.18).

By contrast, the fourth stage, often amplifying the descriptive passages of the second stage, reveals a very extensive flora. Not only do all the flora mentioned in earlier stages, with insignificant exceptions, occur in this stage also, but there are a considerable number of new names appearing. In some cases these are synonyms for plants or trees already found and so mark simply the evolution of the vocabulary. Thus, in the Northern recension we find the following synonyms: *karmaraṅga* (= *bhavya*), *kesara* (= *tuṅga*), *timīra* (= *timira*), *navamālikā* (= *mallika*), *pārijāta* and *mandāra* (= *pāribhadra*), *bālaka* (= *uśīra, vīraṇa*), and *vānīra* (= *vetra*), for which the Southern recension has *vetasa*, as well as *kandala* (= *kadalī*), *karañja* (= *ciribilva, naktamāla*), *surakta* (= *raktacandana*) and *sphūrjaka* (= *tinduka*).[31]

Among the species appearing for the first time, only the pomegranate

[31] Several more such synonyms appear only in the fifth stage, for example *kolla* (= *badarī*), *jambīra* (= *bījapūra*), *dhātakī* (= *dhava*), *dūrvā* (= *kuśa, darbha*), *rajju* (= *uddāla*), *rambhā* (= *kadalī*), *sahakāra* (= *āmra*) and *haridraka* (yellow sandal) in mss. of the N. recension, and *jāti* (= *mālatī*) in one S. ms. Also, some N. mss. introduce *bandhūka* (Pentapetes phoenicea) and *rohitaka* (Amoora rohituka Wt. & A., *syn.* A. polystachya Wt. & A. and Andersonia rohituka Roxb.) for the first time and one S. ms. adds *kuṅkuma* (Crocus sativus L.).

(*dāḍima*, Punica granatum L.) occurs in both recensions; it is particularly interesting to note that a fruit so widely cultivated in antiquity is first recorded at so late a stage. Presumably it spread from its original habitat in Iran more rapidly towards the classical world than towards India.

In addition the Northern recension introduces *akṣoḍa* (Juglans regia L., walnut), *āmrātaka* (Spondias mangifera Willd., hog plum), *uḍumbara* (Ficus glomerata Roxb., *syn*. F. racemosa Wall., wild fig), *kuṭhāra* (probably a misreading for *kuṭhera*, Ocimum sanctum L., *tulsī*), *tālīśa* (Flacourtia cataphracta Roxb.), *pīlu* (Salvadora oleoides Decne), *baka* (Sesbania grandiflora, *syn*. Agasti g., pea-tree), *lavalī* (Averrhoa acida) and *somavṛkṣa* (Acacia nilotica Del. subsp. indica Benth., *syn*. A. arabica Willd. and Mimosa a. Lam.); several of these species are distinctly northern in distribution indicating that again the poets' descriptions were based on their own local scenery. However, the two additions of the Southern recension are widespread: *agnimukhya* (Semicarpus anacardium L.f., *syn*. Anacardium zeylanica, marking nut) and *nimba* (Azadirachta indica A. Juss. *syn*. Melia a. L. and M. indica Brandis, *nīm*).

While the majority of the species common in the fourth and fifth stages were common also in earlier stages (*agaru, arjuna, āmra, karṇikāra, kuśa, ketaka, candana, campaka, tamāla, tāla, dhava, nyagrodha, panasa, puṃnāga, bakula* and *sāla*), a considerable proportion were rare in earlier stages. Some, the *kuṭaja* and *nāga*, are characteristic of southern India and this is no doubt why they were infrequently mentioned at earlier stages; for the remainder the explanation for greater frequency presumably lies in the frequency of descriptive passages and changes in favoured vocabulary (*kadamba, kharjūra, jambu, tinduka, tilaka, nīpa, lodhra* and *vetra*).

Although the fourth stage does include a few trees characteristic of southern India, the text as a whole shows little acquaintance with the distinctive flora of the south. The same is true of its allusions to climate. The two most extensive passages are Lakṣmaṇa's description of winter (3.15) and Rāma's description of the rainy season (4.7), both belonging to the second stage. The former in particular is typically northern with its references to frost and snow, mist shrouding the moon and lotuses shrivelled by the frost; there is also an allusion to winter as the time for the start of military campaigns. There is some variation in the duration given for the rains, either three months (as implied at 4.27.3) or four (4.25.12), but nowhere is there any mention of the more complex pattern of rainfall occurring in the south. Thus, presumably Daṇḍakāraṇya and Kiṣkindhā lie towards the north, or rather were described in terms of the northern climate by poets whose geographical horizons were limited to the area basically of the Indus and Gaṅgā basins.

In the past, discussion of the geographical data of the Rāmāyaṇa has tended to centre around the question of the location of Laṅkā, with basically two parties involved, one that seeks to uphold the traditional identification of Laṅkā with Ceylon (now renamed Śrī Laṅkā) and one that seeks to locate it somewhere in the Madhya Pradesh area. Such emphasis has rather obscured the fact that there is mention of other journeys than Rāma's exile and of other towns than Ayodhyā and Laṅkā in the poem. Consideration of these details may well throw fresh light on the original milieu of the poem as well as on the vexed question of Rāma's wanderings. However, we must again be careful to distinguish the differing amount of geographical knowledge at the various stages of the epic's growth and in particular to recognise the apparent wealth of information contained in the search party accounts (4.39–42) as not only relatively late but also contradictory.

If we set aside for the present the contentious locations connected with Rāma's exile, it is clear that the first stage shows an exclusively north Indian horizon. The only features mentioned south of the Mahendra mountains in Orissa are the river Godāvarī and the Malaya mountains, although two peoples or areas at the same distance southwards occur—Aparānta once (2.76.7) and a woman of the Śabara tribe at the end of the Araṇyakāṇḍa. The only town south of the Gaṅgā and Yamunā rivers mentioned—and then once in a proverb, which may well be a subsequent addition—is Gayā (2.99.13).[32] By contrast, many places to the northwest of Ayodhyā (later Oudh, modern Faizabad) are mentioned in the upper Gaṅgā basin, the Panjab and even beyond. A good illustration of this is the direct route taken by the messengers sent to recall Bharata from Rājagṛha (2.62.10–14), identified with Girijāk, modern Jalalpur, on the Jhelum.[33] Here it is briefly and

[32] There is only this one mention of Gayā in the Rāmāyaṇa. However, Gayā is mentioned as early as Yāska (*Nirukta* 12.19, possibly fifth century BC) and linked with Viṣṇu. The proverb occurs also in the Mahābhārata (3.82.85ab and 13.88.14ab) and in several Purāṇas.

[33] It may be noted that there is no mention in the Rāmāyaṇa before the third stage of the otherwise better known Rājagṛha in Bihar and none at all of its successor as capital of Magadha, Pāṭaliputra. It could be argued that this is because of their unorthodoxy as strongholds of Buddhism and Jainism but, at least in the case of Pāṭaliputra, it seems more likely to indicate that the origins of the story predate its foundation in the fifth

naturally indicated (the places given start only at some distance from Ayodhyā, as though it were superfluous to mention what would be familiar to all) that the messengers cross the Gaṅgā at Hastinapura (c. 57 miles northeast of Delhi), reaching the Pañcāla region and Kurujāṅgala, hurry across the Śaradaṇḍa river, enter the city of Kuliṅgā, reach Abhikāla after Tejobhibhavana, go through the middle of the Bāhlīkas past mount Sudāman, seeing Viṣṇu's footprint and the rivers Vipāśā and Śālmalī (or the river Vipāśā Śālmalī; the Vipāśā is the Beās), and arrive at Girivraja (= Rājagṛha). While some of the villages are unidentifiable, the major points are quite clear and form the natural and most direct route, which was obviously appropriate to the circumstances. The rather longer description of Bharata's return journey (2.65.1–13), which may well have been somewhat expanded along with the rest of the passage in which it is contained, makes him take a more northerly arc after his initial crossing of the Śatadrū river at Eladhāna (river Sutlej, Ludhiana[34]), passing closer to the foothills and going through more forested country. Elsewhere in the first stage, there are multiple occurrences of the countries or peoples of the Kosalas, Niṣādas, Videhas and Śabaras, the towns or villages of Ayodhyā, Kiṣkindhā, Prayāga, Mithilā, Rājagṛha (once Girivraja), Laṅkā and Śṛṅgaverapura, the rivers or lakes Gaṅgā (also Jāhnavī and Bhāgīrathī), Godāvarī, Gomatī (modern Gūmtī), Tamasā (modern E. Tons), Pampā (near Kiṣkindhā), Mandākinī (probably modern Paiśuni in Madhya Pradesh or a tributary, also once called Mālyavatī), Yamunā (also Aṃśumatī and Kālindī) and Sarayū, and the mountains Ṛśyamūka (near lake Pampā), Kailāsa, Citrakūṭa, Prasravaṇa (with which Mālyavat is probably to be identified), Malaya (roughly the Western Ghāts), Mahendra (a range in Orissa), Vindhya, Suvela (a peak overlooking Laṅkā) and Himavat (= Himālayas).[35]

century BC; such was indeed the opinion of Jacobi ('Über das Alter des Rāmāyaṇa', *Festgruss an Otto von Boehtlingk*, Stuttgart, 1888, pp. 44–5; also *Das Râmâyaṇa*, p. 101). The people of Magadha are mentioned first in the search party accounts, then in the third stage.

[34] See O.P. Bharadwaj, 'The Identification of Ludhiana on the basis of the Epics and the Purāṇas', *Purāṇa* 17, 1975, pp. 106–17.

[35] There are single occurrences in this stage of the countries or peoples Aparānta, Kurujāṅgala, Koṭya, Pāñcāla, Bāhlīka and Sāmudra, the towns or villages Abhikāla, Kuliṅgā, Gayā, Tejobhibhavana, Nikumbhilā and Hastinapura, the rivers Vipāśā (= Beās), Vedaśrutī (small river near Ayodhyā, either modern Bisuri or Chaukā), Śaradaṇḍā and Syandikā (modern Sai, near Jaunpur), and the mountains Añjana, Uśīrabīja, Ṛkṣavat (Eastern Vindhyas), Oṣadhi, Kāñcana, Trikūṭa (in Laṅkā), Droṇa, Dhūmra, Padmatāla, Pāriyātra (Western Vindhyas), Maināka (near Laṅkā), Sālveya and Sudāman (in Bāhlīka).

The ocean is known from the first stage and indeed is alluded to almost as frequently then as in the second stage, although the terms used vary in their distribution. The commonest term *sāgara*, for which we have an etymological legend provided in the Bālakāṇḍa in the form of Sagara's sons digging for his lost sacrificial horse (1.37–40), is slightly more frequent in the second stage than the first, whereas *samudra*, the next term in order of frequency, is most frequent in the first stage; other terms are *arṇava* (commonest in the second stage), *udadhi* (evenly distributed) and less commonly *varuṇālaya*. However, though known, the ocean is certainly not familiar to the poet and is mainly referred to in purely formal terms as the husband or lord of rivers (e.g. *samudraḥ saritāṃ patiḥ, nadanadīpati*), or in the stereotyped grouping of the seven seas (*sapta samudra*). Its saltiness is mentioned a few times (e.g. 3.21.2, 4.57.31 and 6.40.34–5), and its waves and tides are alluded to occasionally but with somewhat greater frequency and precision in later stages; the link between the moon and the tides is first clearly expressed in the fourth stage (e.g. 2.239*7 and 4.1375*), although the *parvan*, the 'node', is alluded to earlier as the time of the ocean's waxing (e.g. 2.6.27, 16.7 and 38.11).[36]

The forests are not sharply differentiated from each other. Daṇḍaka seems the most extensive and reaches up to the Gaṅgā, since Guha's territory is said to lie in it (2.78.11), although at times its boundary seems to be put further south, as when Rāma and his companions are said to enter Daṇḍaka in the opening verse of the Araṇyakāṇḍa, while it is also said to be north of the Godāvarī in a later passage (4.40.12); the most exact definition, which is also the latest, describes it as the former territory of king Daṇḍa, located between the Vindhya and Śaivala mountains (7.70.16–17 and 72.17).[37] Janasthāna is frequently mentioned in a way that suggests that it is on or around mount Citrakūṭa (e.g. 2.108.11) but it may also be more or less identified with Daṇḍaka; there is at times real inconsistency, as when Khara's forces come out of Janasthāna to attack Rāma (3.21.19) but the conflict itself takes place in Janasthāna (3.34.2, 9), while it is also said that Khara had gone to Janasthāna for Śūrpaṇakhā's sake (3.48.14) and Rāma himself returns to Janasthāna after killing Mārīca (3.42.21, cf. 55.10, 18). However,

[36] Hopkins had already noted that there were more detailed allusions to the ocean in Gorresio's edition than in the Bombay edition—a definite mark of lateness—while establishing that both epics were acquainted with the ocean ('The Ocean in Sanskrit Epic Poetry', AJPh 21, 1900, pp. 378–86).

[37] The latter are identified by Paramasiva Iyer (*Rāmāyaṇa and Laṅkā*, Bangalore City, 1940, pp. 103–4) with the Panna range, making the Daṇḍaka a plateau about twenty-five miles wide and nearly a hundred miles long.

since the name literally means 'the place of people' it is natural both that it should be applied to Rāma's abode and that it could have a shifting meaning; indeed, there is a play on the name once when Rāvaṇa orders Janasthāna to be made a place of slaughter (3.52.19). There is one reference to Krauñcāraṇya as three *krośas* distant from Janasthāna (3.65.5), that is, contiguous. In one passage of the second stage (3.12–14), the trio go on two *yojanas* from Agastya's *āśrama*, meet the vulture Jaṭāyus and erect a hut in Pañcavaṭī, which cannot be very far from the Godāvarī since they go there to bathe; Pañcavaṭī is therefore another sub-division of the Daṇḍaka forest, but it is this same hut to which Śūrpaṇakhā and then Khara come and which is elsewhere described as in Janasthāna. Thus, Pañcavaṭī is just an alternative designation in this passage alone for Janasthāna.

Not only Pañcavaṭī but also Agastya's *āśrama* occur only from the second stage onwards, although Agastya himself is occasionally alluded to at all stages as the protector of the southern direction. The story of his request to the Vindhyas not to rise till his return is briefly given in connection with his *āśrama* (3.10.83, cf. Mbh. 3.102.1–13, *Brahma Purāṇa* 118.1–8 etc.), which must therefore be south of the Vindhyas, as the other details of their journey suggest and as the Mahābhārata confirms, though assigning it to different locations in different passages.[38] Indeed, the main part of the second stage, apart from the search party accounts, does not add a great deal to the picture either in the north or the south. Multiple mentions are found of the countries or peoples of the Kekayas (Kaikeyī of course is referred to throughout but her people only from the second stage) and Mlecchas (foreigners, barbarians), of the settlements at Agastya's *āśrama* and Nandigrāma (modern Nandgaon, eight or nine miles south of Faiẓabad), of the river Kauśikī (modern Kośī), of the mountains Asta (the mythical 'sunset' mountain in the west), Maināka (Śivālik range, distinct from Maināka of first stage) and Sahya (Western Ghāts, especially the central section), and of the lake Mānasa (on mount Kailāsa in the Himālayas).[39]

The geographical data of the search party accounts (4.39–42) are

[38] Nevertheless Agastya, along with other sages of the south, visits Rāma at Ayodhyā in the first part of the Uttarakāṇḍa; the untoward consequences of such a journey seem to have escaped the author's attention.

[39] In addition, a large number of places or features occur only in the description of Bharata's return journey (2.65): the Śatadrū (river Sutlej), Eladhāna (Ludhiana), the Aparaparpaṭas, mount Ākurvatī, Śalyakartana, river Kuliṅgā, Jambūprastha, Varūtha, Ujjihānā (modern Ujhani in Budaun District, U.P. or Ujjhan in Derapur *tahsil*, Khanpur District), Sarvatīrtha, river Uttānakā, Hastipṛṣṭhaka, river Kuṭikā (also occurring in the variant form Kuṭilā in the fourth stage), river Kapīvatī at Lauhitya, river Sthāṇumatī at Ekasāla, Vinata and Kaliṅganagara. There are also single occurrences in this stage of the peoples Tālajaṅghas, Śaśabindus and Haihayas, the town Vaijayanta, the *tīrtha* Gokarṇa,

obviously late compared with the rest of the second stage, approximating to the position of the third stage, and apparently arranged systematically in that each party searches one of the four compass points. Lévi first established a *terminus ante quem* for these sargas by demonstrating that they provide the source for the description of Jambudvīpa in the *Saddharmasmṛtyupasthānasūtra*, a Buddhist work translated into Chinese in 539 AD, which he considers to have borrowed from the Northwestern recension, presumably in Kashmir.[40] Without excluding the possibility of interpolation, he held that these passages could not be much earlier than the second century BC nor much later than the first century AD. Nevertheless Mankad, having pointed out the similarity of some lines to the *Matsya Purāṇa adhyāya* 163, deduced that the Rāmāyaṇa 'has taken several stanzas verbatim' from the *Matsya Purāṇa*.[41] While the *Matsya Purāṇa* is quite an early Purāṇa, this would place the search party accounts much later than anything else in the text. However, Mankad's arguments do not suffice to establish the direction of borrowing. Indeed other evidence for the *Matsya Purāṇa* being familiar with the Rāmāyaṇa would suggest the opposite direction.[42] The passage fits no more directly into its context in the *Matsya Purāṇa*, where it amplifies the statement that Hiraṇyakaśipu terrorised the whole world, than the longer accounts of the Rāmāyaṇa. Much of the similarity lies simply in the occurrence of particular names, which is quite compatible with borrowing by both from a common source.[43]

the river Vasvaukasārā and lake Pañcāpsaras, the forest Śvetāraṇya, and the mountains Ariṣṭa, Indrakīla, Kauraja, Dardura (Nilgiri Hills), Mahāruṇa and Sunābha.

[40] S. Lévi, 'Pour l'histoire du Rāmāyaṇa', JA 1918, pp. 1–160. He also pointed out the similarity of two *Harivaṃśa* passages (App.I.42.196–297 and App.I.42A.425–93), of which the latter is closest to the NE. recension. It may also be noted that part of the description of the north is paralleled in the Mahābhārata, in the *Anuśāsanaparvan's* description of the world won by the gift of cows (Rām. 4.42.40–4 incl. 933*, cf. Mbh. 13.80.20–1, 23–6). See also W. Ruben, *Studien zur Textgeschichte des Rāmāyaṇa* (Bonner Orientalistische Studien 19), Stuttgart, 1936, pp. 46–52.

[41] Introduction to Kiṣkindhākāṇḍa, pp. XXXV-XLIV, comments in the Critical Notes on sarga 43 (p. 461) and 'The Matsya Purāṇa and the Rāmāyaṇa', *Purāṇa* 8, 1966, pp. 159–67. Cf. also V. S. Agrawala, *Matsya Purāṇa—a study*, Varanasi, 1963, p. 261. See also van Daalen, *Vālmīki's Sanskrit*, pp. 56–66; however, he tends to favour the originality of four search parties against the present emphasis on Hanumān and the signet-ring in 4.43 (pp. 141–2).

[42] See p. 234.

[43] The difference in order of the items, which is not in reality so great, is then readily explicable in terms of the different thematic arrangements, the Rāmāyaṇa by direction, the *Matsya Purāṇa* by type of feature (broadly rivers 60–4, countries and peoples 66–7 and mountains 77–89). Another indicator is that one *Harivaṃśa* passage (App.I. 42A.425–93), which is in general very close to the *Matsya Purāṇa* readings, nevertheless

The eastern direction, apart from the anomalous mention of the Sarasvatī and Sindhu rivers in the Southern recension, contains features centred on the lower Gaṅgā, stretching northwards as far as the sub-Himālayan tribe of the Kirātas and eastwards across the sea to Yavadvīpa (i.e. Java) and the islands in the ocean.[44] The southern direction starts with the river Narmadā and the peoples of the Daśarṇas, Mekhalas and Utkalas who stretch across Central India from just north of the Narmadā through to Orissa, although the Vaṅgas and Puṇḍras of Bengal stray into this list as well as the eastern one. In the far south are mentioned the Colas, Pāṇḍyas and Keralas. Avantī (modern Malwa) is mentioned in both the southern and western accounts but in the main the identifiable western toponyms are located in the Sind and Kathiawar areas, for the Sindhu itself (river Indus) is mentioned where it meets the sea and the Bāhlīkas, usually located in the northwest, are explicitly linked with the people of Surāṣṭra. In the northern direction are found a long list of peoples, Mlecchas, Pulindas, Śūrasenas, Prasthalas, Bharatas, Kurus, Madrakas, Kāmbojas, Yavanas (Greeks), Śakas, Āraṭṭakas, Bāhlīkas, Ṛṣikas, Pauravas, Ṭaṅkaṇas, Cīnas, Paramacīnas, Nīhāras and Daradas; these belong to the Panjab and extreme northwest, but alongside the ancient Bharatas and Kurus we find the Yavanas and Śakas of the mid-second century BC to first century AD, though not the Pahlavas (added in a * passage a little further on).[45] The centre from which the four directions are surveyed lies by implication in the Gaṅgā-Yamunā doab or slightly to its north or south. This is in fact consonant with Ayodhyā as standpoint but less so with Kiṣkindhā, where Sugrīva issues these instructions, even in its more probable location in the central Madhya Pradesh area, still less in

sometimes has readings nearer to those of the Rāmāyaṇa (lines 432, 437–8, 443 and 452; cf. Rām. 4.754*, 39.22b, 21d, 38b and 40.13ab) and includes one line absent from the *Matsya Purāṇa* but occurring in the Rāmāyaṇa (line 443 = Rām. 4.39.38ab; also 40*, cf. Rām. 4.40.8ab). Furthermore, as appears from Mankad's own lists, the majority of the names in the Rāmāyaṇa passage do not occur in the *Matsya Purāṇa*, despite his statement that 'most of these names are also found in the Matsya Purāṇa 163', while a fifth of the *Matsya Purāṇa* names do not occur in the Rāmāyaṇa text. He has, however, correctly indicated that the similarity is greatest with the N. recension.

[44] Mankad, on the basis of several variant readings, wishes to replace Yavadvīpa with the Jambudvīpa (= India) of the *Matsya Purāṇa* parallel, thus destroying the sense of the passage and ignoring the fact that some variants in fact tend to confirm Yavadvīpa—the *lectio difficilior*—as the original Rāmāyaṇa reading (cf. S. Lévi, op. cit., pp. 80–5 and 148–9). Similarly, though retaining Sarasvatī and Sindhu in his text (4.39.20a), in his introduction he accepts the N. recension's variant of mount Mekala (Maikal range) as the original reading.

[45] Cf. S. Lévi, op. cit., pp. 149–50.

its traditional location at or near Hampi on the river Tungabhadrā about 60 miles from Bellary. In reality, the compiler of the search party accounts is envisaging India from the viewpoint of a North Indian of the early centuries AD.

The most noteworthy feature of the topography of the third stage is the way in which it reflects the growth of urbanisation. Half the new names found are of towns and villages, including the great urban centres of Kauśāmbī (modern Kosam, a village near the confluence of the Betvā with the Yamunā), Girivraja or Vasumatī (= Rājagṛha, the first great capital of Magadha), Takṣaśilā (Taxila, about 20 miles northwest of modern Rawalpindi), Pratiṣṭhāna (modern Paithan, on the river Godāvarī south of Aurangabad), Madhurā (= Mathurā), Mahodaya (modern Kanauj) and Viśālā (or Vaiśālika, modern Basarh, 27 miles north of Patna), while the ancient town of Kāśī first appears under its other name Vārāṇasī. This aspect is perhaps also reflected in the legends of the foundation of cities by the sons of Rāma and Lakṣmaṇa: Aṅgadīyā and Candrakāntā by Aṅgada and Candraketu respectively in the Kārāpatha and Malla territories (7.92.1–9), Kuśāvatī and Śrāvatī by Kuśa and Lava in Kosala and Northern Kosala (7.98.4–5).[46] However, the majority of these places are located in the Gaṅgā basin, extending now into the Bengal area with the mention of the Aṅga country (around modern Bhagalpur) and the Maladas (probably Malda district, West Bengal).[47] Two major exceptions are particularly interesting, for Puṣkara (1.60–2, modern Pokkhar, 5 miles west of

[46] None of these places can be certainly identified. The Mallas probably occupied the area between the Gaṇḍak and little Gaṇḍak rivers in north Bihar and the Kārāpatha region was apparently just west of them. The cities of Kuśāvatī and Śrāvatī are reminiscent of the Kuśīnagara (modern Kasia on the little Gaṇḍak in Deoria District) and Śrāvastī (modern Saheth-Maheth, eleven miles from Balarampur, U.P.) familiar from the Buddha's travels; however, the statement that Kuśāvatī is in the Vindhyas seems to rule this out. The same objection applies to a traditional identification of Kuśāvatī with Kusabhavanpur (an older name for Sultanpur, Faizabad District, U.P.), while another tradition that Kuśāvatī and Śrāvatī are Kasur near Lahore and Lahore itself in the Panjab is totally implausible. D. C. Sircar (*Studies in the Geography of Ancient and Medieval India*, 2nd ed., Delhi, 1971, p. 270) would locate Kuśāvatī in the Raipur-Bilaspur-Sambalpur region of Madhya Pradesh.

[47] There must be certain reservations about these identifications. The regular location of Aṅga is as around Bhagalpur, but the Bālakāṇḍa at one point (1.22.14) seems to locate it between the Gaṅgā and the Sarayū, as has been noted by M. S. Pandey (*Historical Geography and Topography of Bihar*, Delhi, 1963, p. 95), who also suggests (p. 60) that 'During the age of the Rāmāyaṇa, the Sarayū joined the Gaṅgā opposite modern Buxar, which is located as the hermitage of Viśvāmitra.' Also, the Maladas are closely linked in the text with the Karūṣas, who lived in the area to the west of the river Śoṇa (Shahabad District, S.W. Bihar).

Ajmer, Rajasthan) is noted as the main—indeed only surviving—*tīrtha* of Brahmā, whose cult belongs especially to the early centuries AD,[48] and Pratiṣṭhāna had its greatest prominence in the first and second centuries AD under the Sātavāhanas; together they give a clue towards the period of composition of this stage. This is reinforced by the appearance of the Gāndhāras and the Pahlavas for the first time, also lying outside the Gaṅgā basin but to the northwest. The Pahlavas appear in the legend of the origin of various impure peoples in the northwest of originally foreign provenance who are emitted in self-defence by Vasiṣṭha's wonder cow: the Pahlavas, Śakas, Yavanas, Kāmbojas, Mlecchas, Hārītas and Kirāṭas (1.53.18–54.3, cf. Mbh. 1.165.35–7). As noted in relation to the search party accounts, the domination of the northwest and the Panjab by the first three belongs to the second century BC to first century AD. Although the legend implies that this domination has collapsed, it should probably be dated at no great interval after the event, which seems in general to have faded rapidly from the Indian consciousness.[49]

In the fourth and fifth stages a large number of place names are added, partly to expand existing lists such as those of the routes of the envoys to fetch Bharata and his return and of the search parties, but partly also to give greater definition at other points. The changing situation in the northwest is reflected in the appearance of Kāśmīra, Puṣkarāvatī (modern Charsada, 20 miles northeast of Peshawar) and Śākala (modern Sialkot) to join the Gāndhāras and Takṣaśilā already found in the third stage, while greater familiarity with south India as it

[48] See p. 198; cf. also S. M. Bhardwaj, *Hindu places of pilgrimage in India: a study in cultural geography*, London, 1973, p. 41.

[49] In addition to the places already mentioned, the following occur for the first time in the third stage: the countries or peoples of the Vanāyus, Saurāṣṭra (south Kathiawar) and Sauvīras (to the east of the lower Indus), the towns, villages or *tīrthas* Aśma, Kāmpilyā (modern Kampil, on the old Gaṅgā between Budaun and Farrukhabad), Kuśaplavana (according to the Tilaka commentary a penance grove east of Viśālā), Gokarṇa (here, modern Gomukhi, two miles beyond Gangotri, Tehri district, U.P.), Gopratāra (the site of Rāma's suicide in the Sarayū near Ayodhyā), Dharmāraṇya (like Kauśambī, Girivraja and Mahodaya, founded by a son of king Kuśa), Madhumanta (king Daṇḍa's capital), Māhiṣmatī (on the river Narmadā) and Sāṃkāśya (modern Sankissa, on the north bank of the river Kālīnadī, forty-five miles north-west of Kanauj), the rivers Ikṣumatī (modern Kālīnadī, tributary of the Gaṅgā which it joins at Kanauj) and Sumāgadhī (flowing past Girivraja), the mountains Bhṛgutuṅga or Bhṛguprasravaṇa (in the Himālayas), Śaivala (the Panna range in Bundelkhand) and Śvetaparvata (possibly in Assam), the forests Naimisāraṇya (modern Nimsar, forty-five miles north-west of Lakhnau, twenty miles south-west of Sitapur) and Śaravaṇa (near Śvetaparvata) and the lake Bindusaras (two miles from Gangotri in the Rudra Himālaya).

really exists is shown by mention of the Drāviḍas in the fifth stage. The Gaṅgā-Yamunā doab, earlier defined by mention of the Pāñcālas, now appears as the Antarvedi; the Panjab appears as Pañcajana, and the Thar Desert as Maru. A third of the new names occur also in the text of the Mahābhārata, indicating the way in which the two traditions were mingling, though it may well be that both epics are sometimes reproducing traditional lists from some other source. However, the addition of the Ānartas, Dvāravatī (= Dvaraka) and Prabhāsa (a *tīrtha* in Kathiawar, = Somnath) is obviously directly due to the growing importance of the Kṛṣṇa legend.

As well as the identification of the locations mentioned, another clue to the evaluation of the geographical knowledge of the text is the assessment of the measurement of distance. It will therefore be helpful to examine this point before moving on to the question of the major locations of Kiṣkindhā and Laṅkā. There are effectively just two units of distance occurring in the Rāmāyaṇa, the *yojana* and *krośa*.[50] The *yojana* is commonly held to be a distance of between 2½ and 9 miles, its value fluctuating somewhat as with the roughly equivalent league, and the *krośa* to be a quarter or an eighth of a *yojana*. However, it is soon clear that, so far as they have a fixed value in the Rāmāyaṇa, both in fact denote substantially shorter distances. Thus, in the Bālakāṇḍa, the city of Ayodhyā is described as 12 *yojanas* long and 3 broad (1.5.7); we know that in the Mauryan period the city of Pāṭaliputra was 9 miles long and 1¾ wide and it is hardly likely that Ayodhyā was even as big, implying a value for the *yojana* of no more than about half a mile. Incidentally both cities were thus elongated because they were built alongside the river bank, and the distance to the bank of the Sarayū from the city or from the royal palace is given on two separate occasions as 1½ *yojanas* (1.21.9 and 7.100.1); since the city was actually beside the river, this can be no great distance. Similarly, descriptions of Laṅkā give its size as 30 *yojanas* in extent (7.5.22) or 20 *yojanas* by 10 (6.606*), while Rāvaṇa's palace is half a *yojana* by one (5.7.2) and his brother Kumbhakarṇa's twice the size at one *yojana* by two (7.13.3–4). Equally, when Bharata is on his expedition after Rāma, he halts and leaves his army behind before meeting Bharadvāja and then Rāma. On the first occasion the distance (from which he can see Bharadvāja's hermitage) is described as being only a *krośa* (2.84.1) and on the second as 1½ *yojanas* but he can nonetheless be seen by Lakṣmaṇa from his vantage point in a *sāl* tree (2.91.14–16).

[50] The length of a pasture (*gavyūtimātra*), held to be two *krośas*, occurs once in the fourth stage, as well as in later parts of the Mahābhārata.

While the distances need not be the same they are presumably of the same order and also quite small. Indeed, the term *krośa*, derived from a root meaning 'to shout', clearly is a short distance, occurring normally in the form 'only a *krośa*' (*krośamātre*), and on other occasions also such places are within sight of each other (3.65.21, 6.113.25–6, 7.90.5).

These measurements are obviously intended to be realistic, as are the early ones in the account of Rāma, Lakṣmaṇa and Sītā penetrating the forest. The forest begins virtually immediately south of the river and surrounds Prayāga, at or near which is Bharadvāja's *āśrama* and also the famous banyan (2.48.6–8, 49.4–5 and App.I.25.11, 35–6, 44).[51] From there to Citrakūṭa the distance is 10 *krośas* in the Southern recension or 3 *yojanas* in the Northern (2.48.25), subsequently also given as 2½ *yojanas* (2.86.10). The inaccuracy of this statement may suggest that the poet is already in unknown territory, for the distance from Allahabad to the peak now identified as Citrakūṭa is about 65 miles and the *yojana* is certainly not as long as 20 miles or more. However, as Pargiter pointed out,[52] the name may well have denoted the range rather than just the one peak, reducing the distance to about 20 miles, but this still produces a higher value for the *yojana* than the passages previously discussed.

As they now proceed further into the forest, the distances tend to be expressed as often in terms of a long journey as of a definite unit; the units in effect become the day's journey. From the hermitage at Citrakūṭa the trio go on to Atri's hermitage (2.109.1–5) for one night. They next enter Daṇḍaka and stay a night at a hermitage before going on. The following day they kill Virādha and go on from there 1½ *yojanas* to Śarabhaṅga's *āśrama* (3.3.22). Śarabhaṅga directs them to Sutīkṣṇa, whose hermitage Rāma and his companions reach after a long journey across rivers in full spate (3.6.2). Sutīkṣṇa directs them to another hermitage in the Daṇḍaka forest; on the way, after a long journey, at evening they see a lake a *yojana* in extent which is Pañcāpsaras (3.10.5). Subsequently they return to Sutīkṣṇa's hermitage before departing to visit Agastya; the hermitage of Agastya's brother is four *yojanas* south of Sutīkṣṇa's and it is one *yojana* further to

[51] As P. V. Kane noted (*History of Dharmaśāstra*, vol. IV, Poona, 1953, p. 597), the Rāmāyaṇa does not say much about Prayāga and certainly there is no hint of its significance as a *tīrtha*, so prominent in the Mahābhārata (e.g. 3.83.65–83).

[52] F. E. Pargiter, 'The geography of Rāma's Exile', JRAS, 1894, pp. 231–64, esp. p. 239. A different method of reducing the distance is adopted by M. V. Kibe ('Further Light on Rāvaṇa's Laṅkā located in Central India from Vālmīki's Rāmāyaṇa', ABORI 17, 1936, pp. 371–84) who asserts that 'the shortest distance between the bank of the Yamunā and Citrakūṭa is between 20 and 30 miles' (p. 373).

Agastya's (3.10.36, 40), with Pañcavaṭī two *yojanas* from there (3.12.13).

Thereafter, significantly, it is not the distance between places on their journeying that are mentioned, but rather the size of various features. Thus, Garuḍa seizes a branch 100 *yojanas* long (3.33.28, 31) and Mārīca ruefully recalls Rāma pitching him into a sea 100 *yojanas* wide at their first encounter (3.36.16). The only exception is the very late search party accounts but here too it is noticeable how many of the distances are expressed in the round figures of 10 or 100 *yojanas*, which obviously merely express vague ideas of great size. So the mountains Udaya and Pāriyātra each measure 100 *yojanas* (4.39.49 and 41.16, so also mount Vajra at 872*), the island on which Rāvaṇa dwells is 100 *yojanas* in extent and set across a sea 100 *yojanas* wide (4.40.24–7), and the barren area before mount Kailāsa measures 100 *yojanas* (4.42.18–19), while mounts Saumanasa and Kuñjara are a *yojana* wide and 10 high (4.39.51 and 40.35); an even higher figure is the sun crossing 10,000 *yojanas* in half a *muhūrta* to reach mount Meru (4.41.37). However, these accounts also include a few more specific figures: 13 *yojanas* in connection with the Golden Mountain of the far north (4.39.45), 14 *yojanas* for mount Sūryavān (4.40.31) and 64 for mount Varāha (4.41.24). Elsewhere also the round figures of 10 and 100 are used of mountains, for example mount Ariṣṭa (5.54.26) and mount Trikūṭa (6.30.18–19).

It is in the sense of this vague hyperbole that we are to understand the allusions to the sea in front of Laṅkā as being 100 *yojanas* wide and Hanumān's leap as therefore also 100 *yojanas*; this is mentioned repeatedly at the end of the Kiṣkindhākāṇḍa and beginning of the Sundarakāṇḍa, with frequent subsequent allusions. We may however note that Hanumān grows enormously to make the jump, reaching 10 *yojanas* in height (5.1.69, also 56.28), and that Nala's causeway is 10 *yojanas* wide (6.15.20), in each case a tenth of the distance to be covered. Similar exaggeration is clearly involved in the statements that Vālin hurled the dead Dundubhi one *yojana* whereas Rāma manages 10 (4.11.40 + 50), and that Kabandha's arms are a *yojana* long (3.65.19, 67.13 and 6.111.18).

In the light of these very vague notions in the earliest stages of distances south of the Gaṅgā and of the clear evidence for a steadily growing knowledge of India, and particularly for only a late acquaintance with south India, we are in a better position to assess the problem of the location of Kiṣkindhā, Laṅkā and related features. In the first stage, the real limit of Aryan settlement southwards is that of the

Yamunā and Gaṅgā rivers, with some vague knowledge of the country to the south as far as the Vindhyas and the Mahendra mountains. In fact the name Vindhyas may well have been somewhat less exact in connotation than later, referring to the whole complex of mountain chains to the northwest of the Deccan. At this period then, both Kiṣkindhā and Laṅkā would have lain in the upland areas approximately between Jabalpur and the Chota Nagpur plateau; whether we can ever identify the localities intended is more problematical.[53] It does seem clear that Laṅkā has become a proper name from a term meaning simply an island or an isolated hill and that there are several Godāvarī rivers, if indeed that was not also a descriptive term. Quite apart from the inherent improbability of the traditional identification of Laṅkā as Ceylon, there is no evidence for the currency of the name until long after the composition of the Rāmāyaṇa, although possibly too early for it to be through acquaintance with the epic; however, if it is in origin a general term, this does not present any particular difficulty.[54]

With Kiṣkindhā and Laṅkā placed in the Jabalpur area, the view that the Vānaras and Rākṣasas are mythologised aboriginal tribes of this area is given added cogency, for in the early stages of Aryan advance southwards such peoples would have posed serious obstacles or been potentially important allies. To begin with the first such group met, the Niṣādas are depicted as being friendly towards Daśaratha and his family. Their chief, Guha, refers to such traditional friendship and welcomes Rāma with an embrace, when Rāma's party reach the Gaṅgā (2.44.9–12). Thus, in the first stage, the Niṣādas are allies and more or less equals of the people of Ayodhyā, though tribal in structure. Guha

[53] Two detailed studies which place them in this area are those of M. V. Kibe ('Rāvaṇa's Laṅkā located in Central India', IHQ 4, 1928, pp. 694–702 and 'Further Light on Rāvaṇa's Laṅkā located in Central India from Vālmīki's Rāmāyaṇa', ABORI 17, 1936, pp. 371–84) who locates Laṅkā on the Amarakaṇṭaka mountain, and T. Paramasiva Iyer (*Rāmāyaṇa and Laṅkā*, Bangalore City, 1940), who locates Laṅkā on the Indrāṇā hill about eighteen miles north of Jabalpur. More recently H. D. Sankalia (*Rāmāyaṇa—Myth or Reality?* New Delhi, 1973) has supported Paramasiva Iyer's identification and U. P. Shah ('The Sālakaṭaṅkaṭas and Laṅkā', JAOS 96, 1976, pp. 109–13) has adduced new evidence from the third stage, the Uttarakāṇḍa, in support of Kibe's view, while V. V. Mirashi ('Location of Rāvaṇa's Laṅkā', JOIB 24, 1974–5, pp. 357–68) has reasserted the traditional view on minimal evidence. Other locations for Laṅkā have been propounded, including an attempt to provide India with its own version of Atlantis by making the Maldives the last vestiges of a sunken Laṅkā (V. H. Vader, 'Situation of Rāvaṇa's Laṅkā: On the Equator', IHQ 2, 1926, pp. 345–50).

[54] Paramasiva Iyer (op. cit., p. xiii) makes the interesting suggestion that this identification was made at the period when the Coḻas were becoming a great naval power, even conquering Ceylon for a time, in the tenth to eleventh centuries AD.

not only embraces Rāma but also offers him food, which is refused not because of commensality barriers but on the grounds of their ascetic vows; Guha subsequently prepares food for Bharata (2.78.9). However, by the third stage, the Niṣādas are definitely inferior and even despised, as is illustrated most graphically in the legend of the Niṣāda shooting the *krauñca* and prompting Vālmīki into poetry (1.2.9–14), and also by Viśvāmitra cursing Vasiṣṭha's sons to such status (1.58.21).[55] The Śabaras (modern Saoras) occur in the person of the Śabarī ascetic, whose way of life testifies to some degree of adoption of Aryan customs. Although there are Nāga tribes to the present day in India (nowadays in Assam but earlier in Central India), the Nāgas are probably the most mythologised tribal group in the text, being homologised partly with the snakes that the term may also denote and partly with semi-divine groups such as the Yakṣas and Gandharvas. However there are Nāga girls in Rāvaṇa's harem (5.10.21–2) and mention is made of his defeat of them (6.7.8). The brothers Jaṭāyus and Saṃpāti are called vultures (*gṛdhra*) and definitely depicted normally as winged, but some details have been held to indicate that the term was in origin a tribal name or totemic device; in particular Rāma and Lakṣmaṇa perform the full cremation ritual for Jaṭāyus as for a respected relative (3.64.26–35) and Saṃpāti has taken the ritual bath which ends the studentship stage of life (4.59.1).

The ambiguity in the depiction of the Vānaras runs through all the stages of the epic—now they are treated as basically human, now as mere monkeys. The commonest term *vānara*, deriving ultimately from *vana* 'forest', simply denotes their habitat and is quite compatible with their being a forest tribe, two other common terms, *kapi* and *hari*, probably both denote a tawny colour and so are ambivalent, while terms definitely denoting monkeys are much less frequent. We note elsewhere that Kiṣkindhā is described in the same terms as Ayodhyā and Laṅkā and that their political structure is basically identical,[56] to which may be added that, among several allusions to clothing (e.g. 4.10.21, 25.1, 65.10–12), the citizens of Kiṣkindhā are well dressed and ornamented (4.32.23); indeed, Kiṣkindhā is civilisation in terms of Rāma's vow to remain in the forest (4.25.9). The degree to which human and even Aryan attributes are predicated of them can be seen from such examples as that the installations of Sugrīva and Aṅgada

[55] It is interesting to note that the Niṣādas, who first appear extensively in the later Vedic literature, were already by the time of Yāska (possibly fifth century BC) a despised group (*Nirukta* 3.8).

[56] See pp. 69–72 and 127–8.

include gifts to brāhmans (4.25.26), Sugrīva alludes to the Vedas (4.6.4) and in the fourth stage knowledge of the Vedas and grammar is ascribed to Hanumān on separate occasions by Rāma and Sītā (4 App.I.3.1–12, 6.3181*), while Tārā mourns Vālin as *āryaputra* (4.19.27) and the term *vīrya*, 'manliness, heroism', is quite frequently used of them. On the other hand for example, Hanumān, reproving Sugrīva, says that his monkey nature is clear from his levity of mind (4.2.16), and Rāvaṇa declares that a tail is a monkey's chief ornament before ordering that Hanumān's be set alight (5.51.3, 29–30). Further examples in each direction could be cited, but in fact such unequivocal statements are in the minority and in the main the assumption is that the Vānaras are intelligent, if somewhat volatile individuals with normal emotions and behaviour and following standard customs and rituals; the only exception is possibly the tendency to ascribe great prowess in leaping to them, but this is true of Hanumān more than of the Vānaras in general. Equally, questions of ethics are of significance in relation to them: Vālin accuses Rāma of underhand behaviour in killing him (4.17) and Tārā declares that Sugrīva will be true to his word since no Vānara chief is not (4.34.2–3), while much of the justification for Sugrīva lies in his brother having seized his wife.[57] Their greater use of rocks and stones as weapons is a trait shared with the Rākṣasas and would be quite natural for forest tribes as well as for monkeys.[58] Presumably, in the earliest stage of the legend the Vānaras were simply a forest tribe but, as knowledge of these increased and they were held in ever lower esteem, the Vānaras came to be regarded as monkeys, just as, as geographical horizons enlarged, Kiṣkindhā and Laṅkā were pushed ever further away until they came to be identified as in Karnataka and Ceylon respectively. From the ambivalence in attitude of the text at all stages, we should infer that the transition from human to monkey antedates Vālmīki's transformation of the legend into an epic.

It is interesting to note that, because Sugrīva sides with Rāma, there is a tendency for Vālin, the brother whom Rāma slays for him and whom he thus replaces, to be portrayed in somewhat similar terms to the Rākṣasas and by the third stage even to be regarded as allied with Rāvaṇa (7.34), although in a passage of the second stage he declares that he could have delivered Rāvaṇa bound to Rāma (4.17.41). The essential difference between the Vānaras and the Rākṣasas is that the former are friendly to Rāma and the latter are hostile. Thus, just as the forces of good tend to be compared to Indra and other gods, so Rāvaṇa

[57] See pp. 174 and 178.

[58] See p. 149.

and the Rākṣasas tend to be compared to Indra's opponents. Even their ability to change shape at will is shared almost equally with the Vānaras and no doubt reflects the uncanny ability—for a settled agricultural people—of such tribal peoples to appear and disappear out of their surroundings.

The hostility of the Rākṣasas to the ascetics is very clearly portrayed at all stages. It is noteworthy that Agastya's claim to patronage of the southern region includes his having pacified the Rākṣasas (3.10.79–82), for, when combined with the way in which Rāma's championship of the ascetics is stressed, this highlights the extent to which the Rākṣasas are feared or hated because of their resistance to Aryan penetration southwards; it is only in the third stage that the story of the setting up of Rākṣasa control in the Daṇḍaka forest is given (7.24.31–5) along with the supposed derivation of the name from king Daṇḍa (7.70–2), no doubt as an indirect justification for the southward expansion by suggesting that it is in fact reassertion of legitimate control (as the name Daṇḍa, literally 'stick', may be translated).

Despite their opposition to such Aryan penetration, the Rākṣasas are not portrayed as low or despicable, although their contempt for men is mentioned (e.g. 3.20.16–17, 38.4–5 and 6.99.16). Rather their cultured behaviour is alluded to and they are placed on a level with the northerners; thus, Indrajit insults his uncle Vibhīṣaṇa by calling him *anārya* ('ignoble' or 'non-Aryan', 6.68.26d) and Rāvaṇa is called *āryaputra* (e.g. 6.23.34a and 98.4a). The Rākṣasas therefore may be considered to reflect, not so much a forest-tribe like the Vānaras, but rather another relatively advanced culture to the south with whom the Aryans were just coming into contact. It is tempting to speculate and to attempt to link the bloodthirstiness of the Rākṣasas with the warlike strain apparent in some early Tamil poetry, but there is not really enough evidence on which to base any meaningful conclusions.[59] The occasional differences in the customs and behaviour of the Rākṣasas—or for that matter the Vānaras—which we shall observe in the next chapters are perhaps pointers in the right direction but are overlaid in any case with the mythologising element which increasingly dominates the later stages of the epic.

[59] The suggestion has been made from time to time (e.g. F. E. Pargiter, *Ancient Indian Historical Tradition*, Oxford, 1922 (repr. Delhi, 1962), p. 242 n.5; G. L. Hart III, *The Poems of Ancient Tamil; their milieu and their Sanskrit counterparts*, Berkeley, 1975, p. 13) that Rāvaṇa's name is a sanskritised version of the Tamil *iṟaivaṉ* 'king, sovereign, lord'; is plausible but not decisive.

5
THE PEOPLE
KING, COURT AND ARMY

> 'Being a quarter of Indra, a king protects his subjects, o Rāma; therefore he enjoys a good life and the world's esteem.' (3.1.18)

The king surrounded by his courtiers forms the natural focus of society throughout the epic, not just in the Ayodhyākāṇḍa where the narrative concentrates on the machinations at court. Indeed, the centrality of the ruler to orderly society is well illustrated by the two pictures of ideal society with which the epic in effect starts and ends, as well as being negatively exemplified by the dirge on the evils of a kingless state, on literally anarchy (2.61). For among the opening chapters of the Bālakāṇḍa is included an idyllic picture of life under Daśaratha's rule, in which everyone is prosperous, virtuous, happy and handsome, religion flourishes and the due order of society is observed under his powerful and benign sway (1.6), while the Yuddhakaṇḍa reaches its conclusion and climax in the description of Rāma's righteous rule, when there are no widows mourning and no untimely death, people are joyful and righteous, long-lived and blessed with sons, and even nature obliges with trees perpetually in flower and fruit and the rains appearing on time 'when Rāma governs the kingdom' (*rāme rājyaṃ praśāsati*, a regular refrain in the passage, 6.116.80–90). Such formalised passages are of course relatively late but the basic attitude is found at all stages.

By far the most frequent term for the ruler is *rājan* (= Latin *rex*, etc.), a term which might denote anything from a tribal chieftain to an absolute monarch. The only other terms that are really frequent—but less common even so than *rājan*—are its derivative *mahārāja, pārthiva*, '(ruler) of the earth', *mahīpati*, 'lord of the earth', and *nṛpa*, 'protector of men', the last of which becomes notably more frequent in the third stage. The vastly more elaborate titles of later Indian history are strikingly absent, as are effectively the technical terms of the political handbooks such as those for emperors or paramount rulers (except *cakravartin*, 5.29.2, *samrāj*, 2.195*1 and *sārvabhauma* in this sense only at 2.82.16a). Nor are *janādhipa* and similar terms at all common or early, as might be expected if the view were valid that such terms in the epics preserve a memory of the tribal basis of kingship.[1] Nonetheless, the general impression is of a ruler intimately in contact with his people and responsive to their feelings, even though mechanisms for popular participation in government were rudimentary, if indeed they really existed at all.

In fact, it is possible to trace the gradual transition from the ruler accorded respect and affection of the first stage through claims to divine status first made in the second stage to hyperbolic statements of the king's absolute power in the fourth stage. The first phases of the transition can be seen in such instances as that where Rāvaṇa in a piece of special pleading stresses to Mārīca that kings are to be honoured and respected in all circumstances, prefacing this with a proverb to the effect that kings partake of the nature of five gods for various aspects of their character (3.38.12–13), and that where Bharata urging Rāma's return declares that the king, though human, is regarded like a god (2.95.4). Then, for example, to Vālin's point that kings should act in a disciplined fashion and not from passion, Rāma replies that kings, being gods in human form, should not be harmed or slandered (4.17.28–30 and 18.38) and even according to some Northern manuscripts uses the same proverb as Rāvaṇa to make his point (4.404*). This identification of the king with various gods is made more lengthily and explicitly in another fourth-stage passage which is closely modelled on a *dharmaśāstra* passage (2 App.I.29, cf. *Manu* 9.303–11). Other proverbs cited in the fourth stage emphasise the king's absolute and arbitrary authority, saying for example that a king can kill by a mere smile (2.610*) and that he is the maker of things or people and their destroyer (7 App.I.8.367). In the light of this clearly expressed view of kingship, it is ironic to note that Daśaratha and Rāma actually behave in a way quite at variance with it. Daśaratha, the earlier, and supposedly more constitutional monarch, banishes Rāma arbitrarily, consulting no-one, and against the wishes of the populace; indeed, though the citizens openly grieve to hear the decision, and threaten to depart with Rāma, they make no direct representations to the king. In the third stage, however, Rāma's rule is in some ways much less authoritarian. He is anxious to know public opinion, and his sacrifice of both love and

[1] This is based on *jana* meaning originally 'clan, tribe' rather than 'people'. A recent statement of this view is by Ram Sharan Sharma, 'From Gopati to Bhūpati (A Review of the Changing Position of the King)', presented at the Fourth World Sanskrit Conference, Weimar, May 1979.

justice in banishing Sītā, otherwise parallel to his father's, is made to placate his subjects' prejudice (7.42–4).

The king's power is matched by his obligations to his subjects, a point clearly made in relation to his right to levy taxes.[2] This is the basis of the appeal made to Rāma by the sages of the Daṇḍaka forest for protection against the Rākṣasas' depredations (3.5.7–18). Lakṣmaṇa calms the grieving Rāma with the assertion that kings as wielders of punishment should be merciful (3.61.9) and Hanumān, describing Rāma to Sītā as the ideal of kingship, declares that he is the protector of his people and of dharma (5.33.10). Such is the view of the first and to a large extent the second stage. Later, the king's punitive role is given greater prominence, with the third stage even propounding an aetiological myth about king Daṇḍa being told by Manu to use *daṇḍa* 'punishment' (literally 'rod', both as means of inflicting punishment and as symbol of authority, cf. Latin *fasces*, 7.70.8–10).

However, we do not in general find any clearly articulated theory of kingship presented. The nearest to it is in the fourth stage when Agastya narrates to Rāma how in the primeval age, the *Kṛtayuga*, people begged Brahmā, the creator, to give them a king and he in granting their request endowed him with the attributes of the *lokapālas* (7 App.I.12; these four 'regents of the quarters' are largely the same as the five gods of the proverb already cited). Implicit in these statements is the view that the individual should be fit to rule.

The general expectation is that the king's eldest son will succeed him on the throne and allusions to this principle are found at all stages in the epic's growth. Even Mantharā accepts it as she rouses Kaikeyī to take action on behalf of her son Bharata (2.8.13–14). But such succession is not automatic, as the declarations of others in this opening part of the Ayodhyākāṇḍa make clear. Thus, Rāma explains to Sītā that kings abandon their own sons if evil and appoint capable individuals in their place (2.23.33) while the aged counsellor Siddhārtha narrates the story of Asamañjas, who so outrages the people that they say to the king, 'Choose him or us', and is exiled to placate them (2.32.15–19); the latter story is also alluded to in the Bālakāṇḍa which adds that Asmañjas was Sagara's eldest son (1.37.16 and 20–1).

There is a strong suggestion at the beginning of 2.61 that the group of named brāhmans called *rājakartāraḥ*, literally 'king-makers', do genuinely have some choice in whom they elect as Daśaratha's successor. They go to the *sabhā* along with the *amātyas* and run over the state of events, but then launch into the long dirge on the evils of a kingless

[2] See pp. 63–4.

state, which is undoubtedly secondary and must therefore cast some doubt on the opening of this sarga. In any case, when Bharata arrives in response to Vasiṣṭha's summons, he remonstrates with them that the family custom is for kingship to go to the oldest and that Rāma should therefore be ruler (2.73.7–8). Incidentally, we may note that Vasiṣṭha, the *purohita*, is not one of this group, but it is he who takes the decisive step of sending for Bharata. Overall the impression is that the succession is not a completely automatic process, but this must be due in part at least to the special circumstances produced by the exile of the eldest son. However, some kind of endorsement by the *sabhā* or the group of ministers seems to have been necessary. Sugrīva, narrating his story, says that Vālin was made ruler by the *mantrins* after their father's death and he himself was installed by them after Vālin's presumed death (4.9.2 and 20).

Emphasis on the hereditary principle in general is only slight. The term *pitṛpaitāmaha* 'ancestral' is relatively infrequent and can refer as much to inherited possessions; for instance, Sugrīva refers to the Madhuvana thus in the Sundarakāṇḍa (5.60.30 and 62.29). More specifically, the much commoner term *rājaputra* is used to emphasise membership of a royal family and is thus an exact equivalent of 'prince' or 'princess', applied in most of its occurrences to Rāma and his brothers or Sītā; there is no trace in the text nor even, so far as I have been able to establish, in the fourth and fifth stages of its later extended usage to signify a member of a clan of royal descent, a Rājput.

The Ayodhyākāṇḍa opens of course with Daśaratha making plans to install Rāma as *yuvarāja*, literally 'young king', and it is that which prompts Mantharā to instigate Kaikeyī's machinations. This would not merely have meant his naming as heir apparent but also his active association with government; he would from that point be consecrated as king, even though the junior partner to his father during the latter's lifetime.[3] Hence the urgency of the situation at this point for Kaikeyī, perhaps reinforced by the hint that Daśaratha has deliberately removed Bharata from the scene by sending him and Śatrughna to their uncle's before Rāma's installation (2.4.25–6). This practice explains the solicitude with which Vālin urges his brother Sugrīva to accept Aṅgada, Vālin's own son, as his *yuvarāja* (4.22.8–10); thereafter, Aṅgada is several times alluded to by this title and certainly plays a major role at his uncle's court. The vital part of the ceremony for installation, whether as *yuvarāja* or *rājan*, is the sprinkling or anointing, *abhiṣeka*,

[3] That such a custom was not confined to Indian notions of kingship is shown by the coronation of prince Henry by Henry II of England during his own lifetime.

which is therefore the normal term for the ceremony, as coronation is in Western cultures. Indeed, neither in references to Rāma's or Bharata's installation in the Ayodhyākāṇḍa nor in those of Sugrīva and Aṅgada in the Kiṣkindhākāṇḍa is much detail beyond this given in the text. Nor are there many passages where the appropriate behaviour for a ruler is explored, except in the terms already noted.

While we find the basic terms of political theory appearing from time to time there are comparatively few passages where any character develops his views on the subject. As part of his reminder to Sugrīva of his duty to aid Rāma, Hanumān discourses on the importance of friends or allies, *mitra*, but does not really go beyond general moral principles (4.28.9–12), although Rāma in sending his ultimatum to Sugrīva refers to kings eager for conquest (*jigīṣu*, 4.29.30b). Again, when contemplating the destruction of the Aśokavana, Hanumān runs through the four 'means of success', *upāya*—conciliation, bribery, sowing dissension and use of force (*sāman, dāna, bheda, parākrama*)—and decides on the last; however, while the first of these two verses is a *śloka* (5.39.2), it merely mentions four means and the listing of them is in the following, no doubt secondary, *vaṃśastha* stanza. There are a number of other incidental references to these *upāyas*, either singly or in combination, in other parts of the Rāmāyaṇa, especially to conciliation (*sāman*, sometimes *sāntva*), several times urged on Rāvaṇa as his best policy by members of his court (for example by Mālyavān at 6.26.6–10). These four means, though occurring in the *Kauṭilīya Arthaśāstra* at 2.10.47–56, are not as characteristic of that tradition as the *ṣāḍguṇya* 'sixfold policy', which is however only referred to in the Rāmāyaṇa in a Southern insert into the late *kaccit* sarga (2.2165*3),[4] and in an even later addition to the Uttarakāṇḍa, where a dog (identified as Yama's watchdog Sārameya) is admitted to audience with Rāma and discourses on politics and morals (7 App.I.8.348).

In addition to the four means, Kumbhakarṇa actually mentions *arthaśāstra*, the science of politics, in his rather unwelcome advice to Rāvaṇa (6.51.15); the term also occurs in the *kaccit* sarga (2.94.9b), in the discussion over the golden deer between Rāma and Lakṣmaṇa (3.41.32c) and several times in the fourth stage. However, the *kaccit* sarga also mentions *dharmaśāstra*, the legal or moral tradition

[4] Cf. O.Botto, 'Dvaidhībhāva in the Kauṭilīyārthaśāstra', *India Maior* (Gonda vol.), Leiden, 1972, pp. 46–56. But the first two lines of this insert give several lists by their numerical totals very much in the style of Manu, and in fact the *Tilaka* commentary actually quotes *Manu* 7.47 and 48 in explanation of two of them.

(2.94.33a), and the views implicit or explicit in the Rāmāyaṇa at all stages are on the whole nearer to that tradition, for example, the view that a king who, after uprooting a dynasty, does not establish another ruler instead goes to hell (7.54.18; cf. *Manu* 7.202–3). Indeed, the later the stage the more nearly they coincide and so in the fourth stage Vibhīṣaṇa arguing policy with Rāvaṇa in fact treats him to a discourse on morals (6 App.I.2.288–329; cf. also 6 App.I.5), whereas in the first stage his warning to Rāvaṇa includes referring to Rāma as *vijigīṣu* 'desirous of victory or conquest' (6.9.10b), a standard term of the *arthaśāstra* tradition, which Hanumān also uses to describe Rāma to Sītā (5.34.16c). It is particularly interesting that this term should be applied to Rāma early on. However, it is in line with the general tendency for all terms relating to policy (*naya* or *nīti*) to decline in frequency with later stages, being replaced by terms drawn from the *dharmaśāstra* tradition.

Daśaratha's court is naturally the centre of action in the first half of the Ayodhyākāṇḍa but the text does not furnish any very detailed description of its functioning. The few details given of other courts, Guha's, Sugrīva's or Rāvaṇa's, are indistinguishable from those given of the court at Ayodhyā; obviously, just one model of courtly life is present to the poet's mind. Ayodhyā is described very occasionally as the king's seat or capital, *rājadhānī*, a term used also once each of Rāvaṇa's capital and of Yama's and Indra's abodes. Assemblies seem to be referred to by interchangeable terms, and their membership is not fixed. The usual term is *sabhā*, for which an occasional, though mainly late, alternative is *pariṣad*, definitely equated with it in a Northern insertion of the fourth stage (2.1897* 1–4), whereas *saṃsad* is a more general term, also late, for any crowd or other group of people, and *samiti* occurs only in the epithet *samitiṃjaya* ('victorious in battles' rather than 'eminent in the assembly') apart from one obviously aritificial revival in the fourth stage (6 App.I.3.139[l.v.]).[5] Indeed, the term *sabhā* means the assembly-hall as much as the body assembled; for example, when Vasiṣṭha enters the *sabhā* of the Ikṣvākus, which is golden, jewel-encrusted and like Indra's hall Sudharmā, and then orders the *dūtas* to summon various groups to it (2.75.8–11, cf. Rāvaṇa's assembly-hall 'well fashioned by Viśvakarman', the divine architect,

[5] P. C. Dharma however regards *pariṣad, sabhā, samiti* and *saṃsad* as synonyms for a 'Popular or Representative Assembly'. Equally, *ārya* 'noble' simply describes members of the *sabhā* (cf. 2.76.1ab) and is not another term for them, as she considers (*The Rāmāyaṇa Polity*, Mylapore, 1941, pp. 35–6). Hopkins regards *sabhā* as basically denoting any type of assembly (*Ruling Caste*, pp. 148–51).

6 App.I.3.94–8). Here and in many other passages the *sabhā* or *pariṣad* consists of leaders of the community but occasionally is said to consist of kings, presumably vassals, as for example when Daśaratha announces to the *pariṣad* his intention of installing Rāma as heir apparent (*yuvarāja*) and the kings reply urging him to proceed (2.2.1–15). More generally it appears that both ministers and *sabhā* should be consulted on all major matters.

There is very little evidence within the text concerning the administration of justice. Indeed, much the fullest information comes from a lengthy passage in the fourth stage (7 App.I.8), in which Rāma summons and then enters his *sabhā*—here clearly a judicial body in addition to its other functions—along with his *purohita*, learned brāhmans, ministers who know affairs, lawyers and so forth (306–10), taking his place on the seat of justice (*dharmāsana*, 102*) in order to hear plaintiffs (*kāryārthin* or *kāryin*, 10, 46–7, 315–7); but, although there is the episode of the dog which presents itself to lecture Rāma on dharma (331–465, cf. the dispute between a vulture and an owl adjudicated by Rāma in 7 App.I.10), the passage is mainly a pretext for the inclusion of various narratives, *ākhyānas*. However, among these the story of king Nṛga and the curse he suffers emphasises the necessity for the king to be accessible to litigants (13–82), although the main point of the story is the vengeful power of slighted brāhmans, as it is of the following story of Nimi who was sleeping when approached with a complaint by Vasiṣṭha and so was cursed by him (83–123). It is only within this passage that we find a term for lawyer (*dharmapāṭhaka*, 309 and 426).

Elsewhere, Aṅgada envisages the punishments, or perhaps more exactly retribution, that await an unsuccessful return from seeking Sītā (4.54.10–11) and Sītā compares her state in captivity to that of a thief condemned to death by royal command at the end of his last night (5.26.7[l.v.]); the latter is from a particularly elaborate expansion of the second stage. But in general the position of the epic is typified by the proverb with which Lakṣmaṇa reproaches Sugrīva: 'For a brāhman-slayer, wine-drinker, thief or vow-breaker expiation is laid down by the good, for the ingrate there is no expiation' (4.33.12). In other words the situation is still one of religious penances rather than judicial penalty. In this respect the third-stage incident where Rāma summarily executes a śūdra whose unauthorised performance of penance has subverted the natural order presents special difficulties to the modern Westerner. What seems to us arbitrary despotism is seen by the text as a further example of Rāma's justice and his anxiety for the welfare of his people as a whole in response to a justified grievance (7.64–7).

The most prominent court officials, to judge from the frequency of their mention, are the *sacivas, mantrins* and *amātyas* but in all probability the terms are synonymous, at least in the earlier stages, although by the third stage the term *mantrin* is ousting the others.[6] The only argument against their synonymity is one occurence of *amātya* and *mantrin* side by side (2.104.17), and possibly one of *mantrin* and *saciva* distinguished (5.47.13), but in its favour is the fact that Sumantra is called successively *amātya* and *mantrin* (1.7.2d and 8.4b, at a still later stage Sumantra is one of Rāma's eight named *sacivas*, 7 App.I.10.52–4), and that other passages indicate identity of *mantrin* and *saciva* (e.g. 4.6.1) and *saciva* and *amātya* (6.31.63–5). The traditional number of ministers seems to have been eight (e.g. 1.7.1–2, 2.61.2–3), a pattern reflected also in the *dharmaśāstras* (e.g. *Manu* 7.54, laying down seven or eight *sacivas*). Nevertheless, the *kaccit* sarga, using a term for official not otherwise found in the text (*tīrtha*), suggests setting spies to keep watch on the eighteen ministers of the other side and fifteen of one's own (2.94.30 = Mbh.2.5.27; also 18 *tīrthas* at KA 1.12.20).[7] There is reference to hereditary office from the second stage onwards: the *kaccit* sarga refers to ancestral *amātyas* (2.94.21) and a fifth-stage passage terms Vasiṣṭha and the other brāhman advisers as from of old (*paurvaka*, 1.251*3). However, the term 'minister's son' (*amātya-putra/mantrisuta*, 5.42.19c[l.v.], 43.1b, 44.1a, 46.7c) means literally that and does not have its later connotation of hereditary official.

By contrast the term *sūta* is rather more frequent in the earliest stages and less common in the third, with the same type of distribution and much the same frequency as *saciva*, marginally the commonest of the three terms for minister or courtier in the first stage. Daśaratha's *sūta*, Sumantra, is an important figure who well exemplifies the two roles of the ancient *sūta*, of confidant and eulogist and of charioteer.[8] He is by implication one of the major officials at court—indeed the

[6] The terms *mantrin, saciva* and *amātya* are not differentiated in the Mahābhārata either, according to B. P. Roy, *Political ideas and institutions in the Mahābhārata*, Calcutta, 1975, p. 190. This reinforces Hopkins' statement that 'Absence of defined titles and functions among the ministers makes it impossible to differentiate strictly the different values of these titles' (op. cit., p. 101). However the *Kauṭilīya Arthaśāstra* seems to make *amātya* a more inclusive, and therefore inferior, designation to *mantrin* (e.g. 1.8.29 and 1.10.1).

[7] For P. C. Dharma they are 'Departmental Heads of State' (op. cit., pp. 56–7). The lists of officials given by one fifth-stage passage (2.2149*) and by commentators on both epics bear no relation to the officials actually mentioned in either text.

[8] W. Ruben rightly emphasises the *sūta's* role as friend and adviser of the king as well as eulogist (*Studien zur Textgeschichte des Rāmāyaṇa* (Bonner Orientalistische Studien 19), Stuttgart, 1936, pp. 253–63).

Bālakāṇḍa makes this explicit by listing him among the *amātyas* and *mantrins* (1.7.1–2 and 8.2–4)—and is learned in traditional matter, being called not only 'knowing ancient matters' (*purāṇavid*, 2.13.17b and 14.1d) but also 'knowing the Vedas' (*vedavid*, 2.29.4a), yet it is also he who drives Rāma, Lakṣmaṇa and Sītā as far as the Gaṅgā at the start of their exile, and he is called *sārathi* 'charioteer' again at the conclusion of the whole story (6.116.19b). In fact, the term *sārathi*, though less frequent than *sūta*, is commoner than many others for the king's courtiers and also occurs predominantly in earlier parts.

The next most frequently mentioned official is the *dūta*, messenger, envoy or ambassador, sent on various errands but enjoying a definite status. Five *dūtas* sent by Vasiṣṭha to summon Bharata from Rājagṛha are named at 2.62.5, although we may note that the names overlap with the list of eight *amātyas* at 1.7.1–2. The inviolability of envoys is several times alluded to and is of direct relevance to the story when Hanumān is captured in Laṅkā and brought before Rāvaṇa, for Rāvaṇa in anger orders his execution but is persuaded by Vibhīṣaṇa urging the unparalleled enormity of the action (5.50.1–7) to substitute the lesser punishment of setting fire to his tail. The *kaccit* sarga declares the need for envoys to give their message exactly (2.94.29cd), echoed by the spy Śuka in the fourth stage when he pleads for immunity as an envoy (6 App.I.10.35–46). The king's chaplain, the *purohita*, is carefully distinguished from the *mantrins*, and Daśaratha's *purohita*, Vasiṣṭha, is prominent in the arrangements for Rāma's installation and takes the lead in sorting out procedure following Daśaratha's death, but he is not otherwise particularly prominent in the earlier parts. His prominence is related to these ritually important occasions and he does not have the role of special adviser in the way that later developed. An alternative form of the title—*purodhas*—is found in the third stage (also once in the Ayodhyākāṇḍa) where the term *ṛtvij* is also applied to the same individuals, for example, Vasiṣṭha and Vāmadeva listed as such following the list of eight *amātyas* (1.7.3). Elsewhere also brāhmans as the king's advisers are distinguished from *amātyas* (2.61.3).[9]

The commander-in-chief, *senāpati*, completes the list of early court officials but is relatively infrequently mentioned, though a little more

[9] A few more officials are mentioned when, on the eve of his departure from court, Rāma asks Lakṣmaṇa to reward certain individuals. Agastya and Kauśika, a teacher of the Taittirīya school, and Citraratha, the *sūta* and *saciva*, are mentioned in the text (2.29.12–15), but then the N. recension adds a list of more or less personal servants: bards, attendants, launderers, barbers, jesters, servants, bathers, anointers, masseurs, cup-bearers and reciters (2.753*) and wrestlers, fighters, masseurs, players and Kausalyā's servants (2.755* 1–3).

common in earlier than in later parts. Indeed in the Ayodhyākāṇḍa the office is mentioned only in connection with Bharata's expedition to find Rāma and in the late *kaccit* sarga with which Rāma then catechises Bharata. In subsequent books some individuals are named: thus, Dūṣaṇa and Triśiras are Khara's generals, and the term is applied to Sugrīva before (and also occasionally after) he regains the throne, while subsequently Nīla is the Vānara *senāpati*, just as Prahasta is Rāvaṇa's. *Senāpati* is the most usual term, and commonest in the earlier parts, but *vāhinīpati* is also found and, in passages of the second stage, also *camūpati*. The *senāpati* is superior to the *balādhyakṣa*, literally 'superintendent of forces', perhaps roughly equivalent to divisional commander. This term, the only other denoting a rank,[10] is almost exclusively found in the first stage, though not common even there. At one point four are mentioned (6.83.26a) and at another Prahasta as *senāpati* addresses Rāvaṇa in front of the *balādhyakṣas* and then gives them orders (6.45.17–19), while Makarākṣa, when selected as the Rākṣasa champion, tells a *balādhyakṣa* to fetch his chariot and army; on the other hand, in one of the two occurrences of the term in the third stage, Dūṣaṇa is described at the point when he is sent to guard Daṇḍaka as a *balādhyakṣa* (7.24.31). Thus all the indications are that this is a very senior rank but nonetheless subordinate to the *senāpati*. Interestingly, a technical term found once only in the Rāmāyaṇa is given a meaning different from the one it bears in the technical literature: *pārṣṇigrāha* (7.92.12d) is used to denote the ally or commander keeping up the rear and not, as in the *Kauṭilīya Arthaśāstra*, an enemy in the rear.

The siege of Laṅkā and the great battle scenes of the Yuddhakāṇḍa, 'Book of the Battle', form of course the culmination of the second half of the plot of the Rāmāyaṇa, the period of exile; but at the start also of that period of exile, in the first half of the Araṇyakāṇḍa, there are warlike encounters between Rāma and the Rākṣasas. These are naturally the main areas where terms for warfare, armies and weapons occur, but the generally heroic nature of the epic means that such terms have a wide distribution throughout the text and a high frequency too, with nearly six thousand occurrences of terms denoting military action. However, in general the first stage shows the highest frequency and the third the lowest, although there is a certain tendency for such terms to

[10] However, the term *nāyaka*, denoting literally a leader, is occasionally used to indicate military leaders.

occur more often in early passages of books 2–5 and in late passages of book 6, no doubt because the elaborated parts of books 2–5 are not usually battle scenes whereas they are in the Yuddhakāṇḍa. But there are interesting variations within this overall pattern both for individual terms and more significantly for different types of weapon.

Terms for battles and combat, with over one thousand occurrences, follow fairly closely the average distribution. The commonest term is *yuddha*, followed closely by *raṇa* and then, with roughly half the number of occurrences, by *samara*; all three terms are frequent at each stage and obviously belong to the original vocabulary of the epic. Less common terms occurring preponderantly in the first stage are *saṃyuga, mṛdha, vimarda, saṃprahāra* and *saṃmarda*. More frequent terms in the second stage than the average are *āhava* (with *mahāhava*), *saṃkhya, saṃgrāma* and *saṃyat*. The distribution of *saṃyat* is particularly striking, for twelve of its fifteen occurrences are in verses in longer metres from the second stage, with another in such a verse added to a sarga of the first stage. The late second to third stage adds the term *āyodhana* and the fifth stage *abhiyuddha*, but these later stages tend on the whole to simplify by ceasing to use certain of the terms found earlier; for example, *vimarda* and *saṃyat* are absent from the third stage, *mṛdha* and *saṃprahāra* are very rare in the fourth and fifth stages.

There is one reference in the first stage to Rāma taking up the Garuḍa formation (*vyūha*), a couple of references to the drawing up of battle-formations in the second stage and a few more in the fourth, but there is no description of their exact form. So too there are general allusions to the mobilisation of an army for war in the account of Khara's expedition against Rāma (3.21) and in the summoning and arrival of the Vānara armies (4.36 and 38), but no concrete details of procedure are given. However, the use of drums to summon troops is mentioned in the Yuddhakāṇḍa (6.23.41, cf. 24.18–26). Also there is a suggestion in the account of Bharata's expedition to find Rāma that encampments were regularly burnt on being vacated, presumably to prevent their use by the enemy (2.83.15).[11]

The commonest term for army, *sainya*, is over twice as frequent as the simple term *senā* from which it is derived but, although it is the commonest term even in the first stage, its highest frequency is in the second, illustrating once again the tendency for vṛddhied derivatives to appear more often in the more ornate later language. The term *senā*

[11] The term for camp here is a general one for a dwelling (*āvāsa*). A more specific term occurs once but is attested only by the S. recension (*śibira* at 6.49.29b).

undoubtedly belongs to the first stage of the language, whereas the less common *camū, vāhinī* and *anīka* are more frequent in the second stage, and *akṣauhiṇī*, denoting a massed army, occurs predominantly in the third, with five occurrences there, two in the second stage, and one in the fourth. This extreme rarity of the term *akṣauhiṇī* in the Rāmāyaṇa contrasts with the Mahābhārata where it is not uncommon and is the more interesting as the word has been cogently explained as a hypersanskritism from a Prakrit form and thus linguistically not very early.[12]

There is in fact nothing in the Rāmāyaṇa corresponding to the passages in the Mahābhārata where the various units of an army are named and their gradations of size explained (Mbh. 1.2.15–23, 5.152.1–25, etc.). All the terms occurring in the Rāmāyaṇa, apart perhaps from *akṣauhiṇī*, are used interchangeably. However, occasionally armies are described as having four limbs (e.g. *senā caturaṅginī*, 1.68.6b, *caturvidhabalā camū*, 2.32.2b) or the presence of elephants, horses and chariots is indicated (e.g. 2.107.11 and 3.28.2) but these are all of the nature of formal descriptions, mostly from later stages, and there is little in the battle scenes to indicate the participation of either elephants or cavalry. There is even in a variant reading mention of a six-membered army (*ṣaḍaṅginī*, v.l. at 1.50.21b for *varūthinī*, a term for army not otherwise occurring in the Rāmāyaṇa). Once in the third stage we find figures given for the different parts: Śatrughna's army against Lavaṇa consists of 4,000 horses, 2,000 chariots and 100 elephants (7.56.2). But in a fourth-stage passage Sugrīva gives a different classification into allied, tribal, standing, mercenary and enemy forces (*mitra, aṭavī, maula, bhṛtya* and *dviṣat*, 6.177* 11–12; cf. KA 9.2.1).

Two other terms of very wide meaning may also denote armies: *daṇḍa* (basically 'stick', hence also 'punishment, coercion, power, forces') and *bala* ('strength', hence 'power, armed forces'). In addition, armies are denoted rarely, but mostly in the first stage, by their possession of flags or standards, with the term *dhvajinī*. Flags or banners are also used to distinguish the chariots of individual heroes and form the rallying points for the ordinary soldiers. The banners were distinguished by various devices: Śambara's has a whale (2.9.10d), Bharata's a *kovidāra* tree (2.78.3b), Prahasta's a snake (6.45.26a),

[12] Cf. J. Charpentier, 'Revue de Louis Renou, *Grammaire Sanscrite*', *Le Monde Oriental* 24, 1930, pp. 176–85, esp. p. 178 and P. Tedesco, 'Notes to Mayrhofer's Etymological Sanskrit Dictionary', JAOS 80, 1960, pp. 360–6.

Indrajit's a lion (6.47.15a[l.v.]) and Rāvaṇa's a human head (6.88.14c). For Rāma, who leads no troops of his own, no banner is recorded. Śiva however has a bull on his banner (1.35.15b, 6.82.34c and 105.2b). The commonest term is *dhvaja* but *patākā* and *ketu* also occur, though with slightly greater frequency in the second stage, and once *vaijayanta*.

Terms for soldiers in general are uncommon. The most frequent is *mahāratha*, denoting a chariot-warrior, also rarely termed *atiratha* or *rathin* (both mainly late), contrasted with the foot-soldier *padāti* or *pādāta*, mentioned little more than a score of times; also distinguishing the type of soldier is the term *iṣvāsa* 'archer' which is very rare compared with the frequency of mention of individuals holding bows. There are a few occurrences of terms based on √*yudh* 'to fight' as general terms for soldiers (*yudhin, yodha, yodhaka, yodhin*) but the two other general terms are very rare and late: *bhaṭa* occurs once in the second stage only (3.8.14d) and *sainika* five times in the text but more often in the fourth and fifth stages. In the actual accounts of battles the common soldiery is almost completely ignored, apart from a few references to the Vānaras and Rākṣasas assailing each other indiscriminately.

As the relative frequency of *mahāratha* indicates, the type of combat most frequently depicted is that of warriors riding in chariots. Most duels (*dvandvayuddha*) are in fact instances of combat between two warriors mounted on chariots and there is even a specific, though rare, term for a chariot-duel (*dvairatha*), used only in the context of Rāma's last combat with Rāvaṇa (6.90.13b, 94.13c and 95.1c).[13] During this combat the gods, seeing Rāma fighting from the ground while Rāvaṇa is still mounted on his chariot, exclaim that this is an unfair fight (6.90.4c) and send Mātali with Indra's chariot to right the balance; this particular passage belongs to the second stage but probably reflects the gods' partisanship rather than any chivalrous regard for fair tactics. Certainly, there are several instances from the first stage of combats continuing when one contestant's chariot is put out of action and he continues to fight without it (*viratha*); for example, Khara after losing his chariot continues to fight Rāma with his club (3.27.27–9), Jaṭāyus destroys Rāvaṇa's chariot and attempts to continue the fight (3.49.14–36, cf. 4.56.10), Rāma smashes Makarākṣa's chariot but Makarākṣa grabs a pike to continue the fight (6.66.29), and Indrajit despite the slaughter of his horses and charioteer assails Lakṣmaṇa with a shower

[13] However, since the term *dvairatha* is not uncommon in the Mahābhārata, it has possibly been borrowed from there, for the first reference certainly belongs to the second stage, the second is in a probably interpolated verse, and the third could well be an expansion.

of arrows (6.77.29–37). This persists into the third stage also, for example Mālin, after leaving his chariot, seizes a club to continue his fight with Garuḍa (7.7.33). The death or disabling of the charioteer has of course the same effect as the destruction of the chariot but nonetheless in the fourth stage Indrajit twice is said to manage the feat of steering and fighting after the loss of his charioteer (6.1702* and App.I.47); earlier stages—more realistic—have nothing comparable. Equally, references to chariots rising into the air belong to the more elaborate passages of the second stage and later, obviously reflecting the mythologising of the story.[14]

Terms for chariots, horses and related items in fact form the third largest category after terms for arrows and for battles. Their distribution is close to the average but with rather fewer in the third stage. This is in line with the well-known decline in the importance of chariots compared with elephants for warfare.[15] A striking illustration of this change was first adduced by Hopkins, who noted that on one occasion Indra actually abandons his chariot to mount his elephant Airāvata for battle (7.29.26).[16] There are two allusions in the Yuddhakāṇḍa to Indra riding Airāvata for war, once in a simile of the second stage (6.4.15d) and once in an account by Vibhīṣaṇa of Kumbhakarṇa's battle with Indra, when he tears out one of Airāvata's tusks (6.49.17); the latter is probably in fact secondary, as the preceding three sargas certainly are, though it does not show any marked stylistic variation. The elephants guarding Laṅkā are said to equal Airāvata in battle (5.5.30b), Vibhīṣaṇa identifies Indrajit and Mahodara to Rāma as riding on elephants (6.47.14[l.v.] and 17[l.v.]) and Mahodara mounts an elephant Sudarśana in battle (6.57.19), which is killed by Aṅgada who tears out one of its tusks for a weapon (6.58.14); again these belong to the second stage and are exceptional compared with the frequency of chariots.

The chariot was no doubt usually drawn by a pair of horses but there

[14] Nevertheless, Miss Dharma declares: 'There are many references to the use of Vimāna (aeroplane of some sort) and Puṣpaka (Airship), and to air fights in the Rāmāyaṇa. The science and art of aerial navigation has been lost since a long time in India' (P. C. Dharma, *The Rāmāyaṇa Polity*, Mylapore, 1941, pp. 85–6). Regretfully, I cannot follow her in such flights of fancy.

[15] Cf. Hopkins, *Ruling Caste*, pp. 266–7. Sarva Daman Singh (*Warfare*, pp. 35–6) suggests that this shift is already visible in the Pali canon and that the epics thus show an older pattern than these early Buddhist works.

[16] E. W. Hopkins, *Epic Mythology*, Strassburg, 1915, pp. 126–7; cf. J. Gonda, *Change and continuity in Indian religion*, Disputationes Rheno-Trajectinae 9, 's-Gravenhage, 1965, p. 92.

are a very few explicit references to four horses, both in battle (3.26.14d, 27.27b, 6.77.29d, 96.8d) and for peaceful purposes (2 App.I.10.25); in the Mahābhārata also two horses are usual but four are mentioned on a fair number of occasions.[17] Even more rarely eight horses are mentioned (5.44.26—S. only—, 45.4d[l.v.] and 6.83.26) or a purely fanciful thousand (6.59.11; cf. a thousand asses at 6.57.4). But asses are not infrequent (e.g. 5.42.5 and 6.41.26). There is only ever one charioteer (*sūta, sārathi*) in the Rāmāyaṇa, even when four horses are mentioned, in contrast to the Mahābhārata, where two additional drivers for the extra horses are mentioned.[18] The standard term for the chariot is *ratha*, which is thirteen times as common as *syandana*, proportionately more frequent in the third stage.[19] Of the terms for horses *aśva* is slightly more frequent than *haya*, both of which are early, whereas *vājin* is less frequent again and definitely later in distribution. Apart from occasional listing of the parts of a chariot to indicate its completeness (as of Prahasta's chariot at 6.45.24–6 or of Indra's at 6.90.5–7), the individual parts are very rarely mentioned. In order of frequency we find the felly or rim of the wheel (*nemi*), the axle (*akṣa*), the wheel itself (*cakra*), the driving-box (*rathopastha*), the pole (*kūbara*), the 'drag' or stay (*anukarṣa*), the triangle-piece (*triveṇu*), the general equipment (*apaskara*), the charioteer's stance (*nīḍa*), the seat (*bandhura*) and the guard-rail (*varūtha*); even with the help of the evidence of the Mahābhārata the meaning of several of the terms is still not certain.[20] The horses' harness is only occasionally referred to as *bhāṇḍa* (in fact any kind of equipment) or *jāla* (literally 'net', also 'chain-mail'), with single references to ornaments on it of chaplets (*āpīḍa*) and tufts of hair (*prakīrṇaka*). To these may be added the whip (*kaśā*) or goad (*pratoda*) used to control the horses, also both very rare. Altogether the poets of the Rāmāyaṇa at all stages were very little interested in the mechanics of the chariot's action or construction, compared with the exploits of the warriors fighting from them. Even the various types or manœuvres that the charioteer could execute are alluded to only rarely (e.g. 6.96.3).[21]

It is perhaps the same concentration on the warrior's exploits to the

[17] Cf. Hopkins, *Ruling Caste*, pp. 235–7 and Singh, *Warfare*, pp. 36 and 42.

[18] Cf. Hopkins, loc. cit. and Singh, op. cit., pp. 44–5.

[19] When it is necessary to distinguish the war-chariot from the ordinary vehicle, it is specifically—but rarely—designated *sāṃgrāmiko rathaḥ*, a phrase found also in the Mahābhārata and the *Kauṭilīya Arthaśāstra*.

[20] See the discussions by Hopkins, op. cit., pp. 237–42 and Singh, op. cit., pp. 36–45.

[21] Hopkins noted this instance only from the Rāmāyaṇa and called it 'a doubtful passage' (op. cit., p. 253 and n.).

exclusion of mundane details that accounts for the infrequent mention of protective armour, the various terms for which occur well under a hundred times in the entire text; however, it is worth noting that over half the occurrences are in the first stage, which might be expected to show somewhat more realism. The item most often mentioned is the *kavaca*, breastplate or cuirass, which is however sometimes used almost asageneral term for armour, occurring on occasion interchangeably with the *varman*, coat of mail or body armour (e.g. 3.27.15–16). Since there is a specific term for breastplate (*uraśchada*), it seemspreferable to assume that *kavaca* denotes the complete cuirass, for which however a late synonym *kañcuka* also exists. While *varman* may well denote chain-mail, its use is established by the, admittedly late, use of *jāla* which basically means a net, lattice or grille to denote an item of armour (6.62.42a; cf. *jālikā*, 3.384* 7). The cuirass is referred to as being ornamented with gold (6.76.19b), which in the fourth stage develops into cuirasses made of gold (e.g. 6.710* 2 and 2080* 4); the basic material must have been bronze or iron but this is not stated as it is in the Mahābhārata.[22] A further general term occurring twice in the second stage means literally 'body-protection' (*tanutrāṇa*, 6.57.55a and 2.734* 1, and *tanutra*, 6.62.8a, 3.384* 7 and 6.1407* 8; cf. *marmatra*, 2.85.71c).

After the cuirass the next most frequent item of armour mentioned is the shield (*carman* or rarely *phalaka*) with a score of occurrences. The material used is indicated by the basic meaning of *carman* as hide or skin, which is occasionally further identified as tigerskin (2.13.4d, 3.2.6a, 4.25.25a) or cowhide (5.1.22c, 6.84.21a).[23] The shield is also regularly linked with the sword in a way that suggests that it was not worn when the warrior was using his bow but was picked up with the sword for use at close quarters. There are only a handful of references for the remaining items—finger-guard, arm-guard and helmet—but all are attested in the first stage. The finger-guard (*aṅgulitra* or *aṅgulitrāṇa*) and arm-guard or vambrace (*godhā*) were used together by the archer

[22] Cf. Hopkins, op. cit., p. 304. Singh (op. cit., p. 116) comments on gold being unsuitably soft for armour but not on the more intractable problem of its weight. At one point in the Yuddhakāṇḍa the N. recension describes Lakṣmaṇa as wearing gold chain-mail as well as his cuirass (6.1610*), instead of the still more implausible gold bow of the S. recension (6.72.23b). While it would be possible to regard gold as denoting only gilding in such passages, it seems more likely that it is used literally in these late flights of fancy, for there are ways of expressing ornamentation with gold found not uncommonly in the first stage, though rarely of weapons.

[23] The use of cowhide for this purpose is one of several indications that cows were not yet venerated at the period of the early Rāmāyaṇa.

to protect him from the impact of his own bow-string; the latter at least was also made of cow-hide. The helmet (*śirastra, śirastrāṇa*) is mainly mentioned in connection with the fall of a decapitated head, which interestingly is also described as wearing ear-rings (6.78.33ab, 85.27cd, 86.15–16) presumably indicating that the helmet was fairly short and lacked ear-flaps or the like. There are also very occasional references to the use of armour on horses and elephants (e.g. 3.60.31 and 6.1407* 7–8).

Overall, the total references to weapons show a distribution identical to that for warfare in general, though individual weapons show particularly interesting differences. It is also instructive to note the relative frequency of different weapons. Terms for weapons in general show some increase in the second stage, but are proportionately much more frequent by the third, obviously reflecting the greater distance of the later stages from the military background; however, one of the terms, *praharaṇa*, is commoner earlier than late while the other three, *astra, āyudha* and *śastra*, are relatively more frequent later. Indeed, *astra* occurs very often in the third stage, since it is the regular term for the various divine or mystical weapons that occur there with some frequency, in contrast to their virtually complete absence from the first stage.

Arrows on their own comprise almost a third of all mentions of weapons and with bows and quivers make up more than half the total. Moreover, by comparison with other weapons, the arrow is much more frequent in the first stage than in the third. The shift away from archery is not as dramatic as that might suggest, though nonetheless real, for bows and quivers show more nearly the standard distribution for military terms and, while less than half as frequently mentioned as arrows in the first stage, are as frequent by the third. Again, the greater immediacy of the first stage accounts for the frequency of the arrow itself, referred to in its flight and reaching its target, by contrast with the more theoretical approach of later stages. There are an exceptionally large number of terms for arrows and their parts, which also illustrates their centrality to the early epic. The standard term is *śara*, accounting for almost half the total, with the next most frequent term, *bāṇa*, comprising a further quarter; a third, much less frequent, general term is *sāyaka* which, though meaning in origin simply a missile, is used in the Rāmāyaṇa only of arrows, but occurs most frequently in the second stage. All three terms are sometimes used interchangeably within a single context (e.g. 3.26.13–15), showing their synonymity. Other passages similarly establish the identity of *śara, bāṇa* and *iṣu* (e.g. 2.57.17–19), *bāṇa, iṣu* and *nārāca* (e.g. 2.58.13–16) and *bāṇa* and *pṛṣatka* (6.78.6–7); the last term *pṛṣatka* is very rare. Another general term is *mārgaṇa* 'the seeker', which, though less common, is predominantly early.

The material normally used for arrows was no doubt reeds (the original meaning of both *śara* and *bāṇa*) or bamboos, as the references to joints suggest (e.g. *śaraiḥ saṃnataparvabhiḥ*, 3.26.14b and 27.20b *et passim* in the Mbh.; cf. 3.37.12d, 6.59.71b and 7.61.10d); the rare late term *aiṣīka* specifically denotes a reed used as a missile, while in the fourth stage the term for an arrow-maker (*kāṇḍakāra*) is compounded from another term for a reed. But there are just a few references to ones of metal (*āyasa*, 5.44.20, 6.59.40, 63.14) and it is commonly held that *nārāca* denotes an iron arrow.[24] That the *nārāca* is a type of arrow was suggested above and is established by the phrase *jyāmukta iva nārācaḥ* (5.12.4c and 55.9c), but it is also used adjectivally with *śara* (e.g. 6.75.26) indicating that it in fact denotes a specific type, presumably one with a metal shaft; it is rather commoner in the Mahābhārata. In the Araṇyakāṇḍa only, there occurs a compound linking *nārāca* with another weapon *nālīka* and *nālīka* is once substituted for *nārāca* by the Northern recension (6.753* for 6.35.23ab); in view of its rarity, it is obviously impractical to identify the exact nature of the *nālīka* but it is clearly an arrow and presumably similar but not identical to the *nārāca*.[25] The term *vaitastika* occurs only from the fourth stage, though it is found in the relatively late *Droṇaparvan* (Mbh. 7.98.50c, 51a, 164.150a), and from its derivation denotes a short arrow only a span long; the term *ardhanārāca* or *ardhanālīka* (6.35.23a/753*) probably also denotes a short arrow, but it is obvious that short arrows are not original and probably never common.

Many of the terms for arrows in fact indicate different types of arrow-head. Thus, to take them in order of frequency, the *bhalla* has a broad head, the *ardhacandra* a crescent-shaped one (once linked with a *candra* 'moon-shaped' arrow), both *karṇin* and *vikarṇin* denote a wide-eared point, and *kṣura* or *kṣurapra*, literally 'razor-edged', indicate a particularly sharp point, as perhaps does *śilīmukha* if this term means 'whetted on the stone' rather than 'stone-tipped'. This last term occurs only once in the text (but several times in the fourth and fifth stages) and is therefore of slight significance, which is even more true

[24] See Hopkins, op. cit., p. 279 and Singh, op. cit., pp. 104–5.
[25] See Hopkins, ibid. and Singh, ibid.

of two other terms attested from only one verse, *añjalika*, apparently denoting a broad point, and *vatsadanta* 'calf-toothed' denoting on the evidence of the Mahābhārata a particularly sharp point.[26]

At the other end of the arrow, there was the *puṅkha*, a metal end containing the notch for the bow-string; it is regularly spoken of as being made of gold, presumably in fact gilded, even though it may well have had a function as a weight in balancing the arrow. The feathering is also alluded to in general terms (*patrin, patatri*) and in particular heron-feathers were used (*kaṅkapatra, kaṅkavāsas*), references to this in the text coming exclusively from the first stage. But there are also a few references, predominantly from the first stage, to unfeathered arrows (*viśikha*), and single references from the second stage to arrows flighted with peacock-feathers (3.3.12) and vulture-feathers (6.87.26).

Nearly half the references to bows and related items are to the term *dhanus* (or *dhanvan*, in origin the same word), which is over twice as common as the next most frequent term *cāpa*. A third, less frequent term, *kārmuka*, commoner in the second stage than elsewhere, denotes the material used, the wood of the *kṛmuka* tree (not found otherwise in the Rāmāyaṇa and not satisfactorily identified).[27] Infrequent and mainly late are the somewhat artificial terms *bāṇāsana* and *śarāsana* 'seat for the arrow', established certainly as meaning bow by use interchangeably with the other terms (e.g. 6.78.28–9). The bow was regularly unstrung when not in use and thus the stringing of the bow was a mark of bellicose intentions, of which a further development was the deliberate twanging of the bow-string as a challenge or warning

[26] The first line of the verse in question is identical with one from the Mahābhārata (6.35.23ab = Mbh. 7.37.22cd); the weapons common to the two verses include not only *añjalika* and *vatsadanta* but also the only occurrence of *ardhanārāca/ardhanālīka*, noted above, and—in a variant reading—of *vipāṭha* (also at 6 App.I.43.8 and Mbh. 4.38.26a). It is clear therefore that these terms are a late borrowing from the Mahābhārata. For some discussion of their meaning, see Hopkins, op. cit., pp. 278–80 and Singh, op. cit., pp. 104–6. Hopkins mentions the *varāhakarṇa* 'boar-ear' as occurring in the Mahābhārata (4.38.27) meaning a barbed arrow; the term is found in the Rāmāyaṇa in the fourth stage (3.537*6).

[27] There is one passage in the *Kauṭilīya Arthaśāstra* (2.18.8) which defines bows (*dhanus*) as made from *tāla, cāpa*, wood and horn and as called *kārmuka, kodaṇḍa* and *drūṇa*; if the names (including *dhanus* as the fourth) are regarded as corresponding with the materials, then the *kārmuka* bow was made of palmyra wood. This interpretation was adopted by Meyer in his translation but is viewed with reserve by Kangle in his edition of the text. Against it is the fact that there is no other evidence that *dhanus* means specifically a horn bow and indeed some to the opposite effect, since *dhanus* is a common term whereas horn bows appear to have been exceptional, even though particularly effective.

signal, alluded to a dozen times in the text, mostly in the second stage. The regular term for the bow-string is *jyā*; *guṇa* is very rare and *maurvī*, meaning one made of *mūrvā* grass (Sanseviera zeylanica), is found only in the third stage.

The type of bow is nowhere exactly described but there are various indications that it was of the longbow type. The very rare mention of short arrows implies that normally the arrow was of considerable length, requiring a large bow; there are a few mentions of drawing the arrow or the bow back to the ear, coming from all stages, and found also in the Mahābhārata; and there may be a reference to Rāma leaning on his bow or even fixing it in the ground (*avaṣṭabdhadhanuṃ rāmam*, 3.24.1a), though this could be interpreted simply as his grasping it. Again, the use of one particular type of wood, indicated by the term *kṛmuka*, seems to rule out a compound bow. And Śiva's bow which Rāma lifts and breaks at Sītā's *svayaṃvara* in the Bālakāṇḍa is too heavy for ordinary men, suggesting a premium on sheer size. Against the last two points can be set the group of references in the Uttarakāṇḍa (7.7.7–18)—also the third stage, like Śiva's bow—to Viṣṇu's bow of horn (*śārṅga*), which is on the whole most easily interpreted as some kind of compound bow, whether its name indicates the material used or the shape of the bow when slack.[28] Also, Rāma's bow is described once as triply-curved (*trivinata*, 3.42.2a), when he picks it up. However, the great majority of the evidence is in favour of a long bow held vertically, of which the string was drawn back to the face, specifically the ear, for aim and release.

Incidentally, the bows of warriors are several times, six times in books 2–6, compared to Indra's bow in a way which suggests that it was still seen as a real bow rather than as the rainbow, as was to become its standard meaning in classical Sanskrit literature;[29] the only instance of the rainbow image is significantly from a passage of the second stage (6.59.14d + 17c). The six examples are split evenly between Rāma's or Lakṣmaṇa's bows and those of Rākṣasas.

[28] This is for example the view adopted by M. B. Emeneau, 'The Composite Bow in India', *Proceedings, American Philosophical Society* 97, 1953, pp. 77–87. Emeneau distinguishes the self or simple bow, the compound bow of two or more pieces, usually of wood or horn, and two types of sinew-backed bow: one reinforced with sinews on the side of the bow away from the archer and the other also having a band of horn on the other side. Viṣṇu's bow would presumably be of the last type. Representations of composite bows occur among the sculptures at Bharhut (*c.*150 BC).

[29] Cf. S. Lienhard, 'On the meaning and use of the word *indragopa*', IT 6, 1978, pp. 177–88. It is therefore particularly interesting to note his comment that 'Rāma's bow' has become a term for a rainbow in Bengali.

Quivers are mentioned only rather infrequently as part of the mundane equipment rather than actual offensive weapons. The commonest term is *tūṇī*, but *iṣudhi, kalāpa, tūṇīra* and *śarāvara* also occur. Most commonly these terms occur in the dual, reflecting the normal practice of a pair of quivers strapped to the back, although there is one reference in the second stage to as many as thirty-eight quivers lying with other weapons in a chariot (6.59.19b).[30] But the regular pattern is that of the stock phrase about quivers with an inexhaustible supply of arrows (*tūṇī cākṣayasāyakau*, 1.1.34d, 2.28.13b, 110.38d, 3.11.30d).

An ample supply of arrows would be needed to sustain the feats of continuous shooting often alluded to, especially in the Yuddhakāṇḍa, and graphically indicated by the standard compounds for 'networks of arrows' (*śarajāla, bāṇajāla*) and 'showers of arrows' (*śaravarṣa*, less commonly *bāṇavarṣa* and *śaravṛṣṭi*) which occur predominantly in the first stage, whereas the somewhat less apposite 'flood of arrows' (*bāṇaugha, śaraugha*) has a higher frequency in the second stage than other terms for arrows. Obviously therefore dexterity and speed with the bow were more highly prized in battle than carefulness of aim. Consequently we find warriors described as bristling with arrows and as lying on a bed of arrows (*śaratalpa*, occurring five times).

After bows and arrows, the category of weapons next most frequently mentioned are spears, javelins and the like, with approximately 300 occurrences in the text—less than a fifth as frequent. It is also noteworthy that in the second and third stages such weapons occur relatively more frequently than the average for all weapons. Whereas European warfare tended to distinguish between those that were hurled—javelins and spears—and those that were thrust—lances and pikes—, this difference is not so clear-cut in ancient Indian warfare, which makes distinctions more perhaps according to size, though several of the weapons are poorly defined in either epic, occurring only in lists.[31] The commonest, especially in the second stage, is the *śūla* which is specifically a pike used mainly for thrusting and generally described as held or brandished, but also occasionally hurled; it is four times described

[30] The use of the dual only when Rāma and Lakṣmaṇa are donning their equipment at 3.7.18–19 is presumably by oversight and in fact the NE. recension reads the plural, as do most manuscripts in a parallel situation at 4.3.15. However, the term *śarāvara* occurs only in the singular in the text (3.49.12b and 63.17b, both referring to Jaṭāyus' attack on Rāvaṇa) and is explained by the commentators variously as 'quiver' and 'armour'; either would be possible in this context but the first is needed at 3.1176* 1 where the dual is used (*śarāvarau śaraiḥ saṃpūrṇau*).

[31] On the Mahābhārata evidence, see Hopkins, op. cit., pp. 287–92 and Singh, op. cit., pp. 108–9.

as made of metal (*āyasa*, cf. *ayomukha*, 3.45.39a) and also quite often as large. On one occasion when a Rākṣasa, Makarākṣa, hurls a *śūla* (6.66.29–32), Rāma uses three arrows to destroy it. Since usually if the number of arrows is mentioned it corresponds to the number of targets, this perhaps suggests that the *śūla* was also thought of as a trident; the latter weapon specifically though rarely designated as *triśūla* (which is an ordinary weapon of war and not linked with Śiva) and in the fourth stage only as *trikaṇṭaka*.

Next in frequency comes the *śakti*, a spear or javelin, which is especially connected with warriors fighting in chariots and occasionally called accordingly a chariot-spear (*rathaśakti*, 6.59.13c and 95.9c); there are quite a few explicit references to it being thrown and none that conflict with its being a casting weapon. Rāvaṇa is described as throwing two particularly elaborate specimens, one of which is garlanded with gold and the other adorned with eight bells (6.88.21b and 30b; cf. 91.25b and 2004* 5). The material used for it is not specified, although it is perhaps significant that it is never described as metal. Exceptionally in this group, the *paṭṭasa* or *paṭṭiśa* occurs overwhelmingly in the first stage but even so mainly in lists of weapons which do not permit us to ascertain its individual characteristics. Three other less common weapons are the *prāsa, tomara* and *bhiṇḍipāla*. The *prāsa*, occurring mainly in the second stage, is several times linked with the *tomara* in both the Rāmāyaṇa and the Mahābhārata and presumably is broadly similar to it; the standard interpretation of its meaning is a barbed missile or dart. Besides being linked with the *prāsa*, the *tomara* occurs once in a *dvandva* compound with an elephant goad (*aṅkuśa*, 2.68.28b) and once is itself used against an elephant (3.27.22), which confirm its meaning as a type of lance. The *bhiṇḍipāla* occurs almost exclusively in lists and so the only clue to its identity is provided by the reference to Vānaras pierced by *bhiṇḍipālas* (6.42.19b), from which it appears to fall into this group.[32] There are also a few more rarely mentioned weapons of this group: *ṛṣṭi, kuṇapa* and *kunta* in addition to *trikaṇṭaka* and *triśūla* already mentioned. The *ṛṣṭi*, a type of javelin, is not uncommon in the *Ṛgveda* and in all probability is a lingering survival in the Rāmāyaṇa named by force of tradition rather than importance of use, but despite its rarity it occurs in all stages. By

[32] It may be noted that the *Kauṭilīya Arthaśāstra* includes these three—*prāsa, tomara* and *bhiṇḍipāla*—with *śakti, śūla* and certain others in one group of weapons with piercing points (KA 2.18.7). However, the *bhiṇḍipāla* is also interpreted by commentators on some texts as a kind of sling and is translated by van Buitenen as 'slingshot' at Mbh. 5.19.3.

contrast, the *kuṇapa* and *kunta*, both types of spears, occur only in the fourth stage, apart from one occurrence of *kunta* in the second (6.73.21b); although they are not frequent in the Mahābhārata, where also their distribution tends to be late, they have no doubt been borrowed from there.

Clubs, maces and the like are a little less frequent than spears and javelins but show more or less the standard distribution for weapons. It is therefore particularly interesting to note that of the two common terms *parigha* is most frequent in the first stage and *gadā* in the third, indicating that the *parigha* rapidly went out of fashion compared with the *gadā*. Both are large clubs but there is some suggestion that the *parigha* is the larger of the two and it is more often described as made of metal (*āyasa*) than any other weapon in this group. Such iron clubs must have been exceptional and more usually the club or mace is of wood, sometimes bound with iron. One of the fullest descriptions is of Dūṣaṇa's *parigha* as bound with golden braids and studded with sharp iron nails (3.25.5), while a *gadā* is described as having many spikes (*bahukaṇṭaka*, 6.42.33b), indicating the way in which these weapons were made more fearsome. The club was above all Vibhīṣaṇa's weapon and he is several times described as club in hand (*gadāpāṇi*). Other terms for clubs are *musala, mudgara* and *kūṭamudgara*. The term *musala* also denotes—though not in the Rāmāyaṇa—the pestle used for grinding grain and the like and is presumably a long, tapering wooden club, though twice described as *āyasa*. The *mudgara* is a type of hammer or mallet, of which the relatively rare *kūṭamudgara* is usually explained as a concealed, therefore necessarily smaller, version but, while its exact nature is not clear from its ten occurrences in the text, combatants are several times described as holding it in their hands; this argues against concealment and the commentators evidently regard it as a kind of iron hammer, presumably simply another kind of hammer.[33]

Swords and related items are mentioned only about half as frequently as either spears or clubs but they occur mostly in the first and second stages with a marked decline from the third stage onward. The commonest term, providing over half the total, is *khaḍga*, the general epic

[33] It is apparently not mentioned in the Mahābhārata, according to Hopkins (op. cit., p. 291) who suggests that in the Rāmāyaṇa it 'seems to be a hatchet rather than a hammer', adding 'It may be, in the usual sense, concealed, a trick-weapon, but is possibly another kind of hammer.' This is perhaps also supported by the occurrence of *kūṭa* in the sense of a hammer or mallet in Vedic literature (cf. M. Mayrhofer, *Kurzgefasstes etymologisches Wörterbuch des Altindischen*, 3 vols., Heidelberg, 1953–68).

term for sword, while *asi*, the Vedic term, persists into the epic period to provide about a third of the references; the remainder consists of a third term for the sword itself *nistriṃśa* and terms for the hilt, *tsaru*, and sheath, *kośa*. All three terms for sword are used interchangeably in certain passages which indicates that there is at least no great distinction of type between them.[34] As to their length, the only indication is that Atikāya's sword, huge like him, is ten *hastas* long with a hilt of four *hastas* (6.59.20); since the *hasta* is equivalent to the cubit, these lengths are roughly fifteen feet and six feet (five and two metres) respectively. Apart from this instance, the hilt is mentioned only in order to be described as of gold and the sword in general is several times referred to as being ornamented with gold and once as having a silver sheath (3.11.31). Since the sword is regularly referred to as being bound or strapped on, the use of a sword-belt is obviously standard, but there is not any separate term for it. Swords are evidently of the broadsword or cutlass type not the rapier, since their action is invariably described as cutting and never as piercing; apart that is from a few lists of weapons described as thrown which, presumably through carelessness, include swords as well as other hand-held weapons such as axes (e.g. 3.24.23).

Battle-axes are in fact only infrequently mentioned, with just twenty-five occurrences of *paraśvadha*, five of *paraśu*, and one each of *kuṭhāra* (6.59.103c[l.v.]) and *kuliśa* (7.35.46d); the latter two terms are therefore of marginal significance as weapons. Indeed, *kuṭhāra* really denotes a woodman's axe, being found once in that sense (2.74.7c), in addition to its one occurrence as a weapon where we find in the same stanza a plough as an offensive weapon (*hala*, also a weapon at 6.83.24b). So too *paraśu* denotes a woodman's axe once (2.95.9e) and twice refers to Rāma Jāmadagnya's weapon. However, *paraśvadha* exclusively denotes a battle-axe in its occurrences in the Rāmāyaṇa.[35]

The *vajra* or *aśani*, traditionally Indra's weapon and often translated as 'thunderbolt', is occasionally found as an ordinary weapon, as well as being referred to as actually used by Indra, for example against Kabandha (3.67.10), and described as having a hundred joints; more

[34] There may be some distinction in their use in the Mahābhārata, although both Hopkins (op. cit., p. 285) and Singh (op. cit., p. 109) are very hesitant about making one.

[35] Hopkins (op. cit., p. 291) suggests that an unknown distinction is made between *paraśu* and *paraśvadha* in the Mahābhārata; in the Rāmāyaṇa *paraśu* occurs only in the prior pāda of the line and *paraśvadha* (with one exception) only in the posterior pāda, suggesting simply alternation for metric reasons.

often, it occurs in similes or metaphors to dramatise the impact of ordinary weapons.[36] So too the *cakra*, often, especially in the third stage, linked with Viṣṇu, is also an ordinary weapon, evidently by etymology some sort of discus or quoit but nevertheless once described as coming from Rāvaṇa's bow (6.88.7). Two other weapons which tend to be associated with particular deities are the noose, *pāśa*, of Varuṇa and the staff or stick, *daṇḍa*, of Yama, both of which are found very occasionally as weapons. Another term for a stick or staff, *yaṣṭi*, also appears as a weapon very rarely in the Yuddhakāṇḍa.[37] There are also occasional references to the *yantras* which formed part of the defences of all three cities, Ayodhyā, Kiṣkindhā and Laṅkā, although it is only in connection with Laṅkā that we have any description of their use; here they are placed over or at the gates in order to tumble the enemy from the bridges into the moat and are made to take stones (6.3.11–16)—evidently they are a type of large catapult or *ballista*, a sense well in accord with the term's basic meaning of a mechanical contrivance, an 'engine'. Linked with the *yantras* here and elsewhere are *śataghnīs*, which however also occur as hand-held weapons; since the term literally means 'hundred-killers', it is reasonable to suppose that the *śataghnī* was covered with multiple spikes or protuberances and might be either a large device, something like a caltrop, to roll down from the walls, or a particular knobbly club or cudgel.[38] However, both *yantras* and *śataghnīs* are mentioned only rarely.

[36] In a recent work Wilhelm Rau has sought to establish that the Vedic *vájra* was a kind of harpoon (*Metalle und Metallgeräte im vedischen Indien* (Abh. d. Ak. d. Wiss. u. der Lit., Geistes- und Sozialw. Kl., Jg. 1973, Nr.8), Wiesbaden, 1974). In a subsequent article B. Schlerath ('Vedisch vájra—"die Keule des Indra" ', *Orbis* 24, 1975, pp. 493–518) has criticised this view, as well as commenting briefly on T. K. Das Gupta, *Der Vajra, eine vedische Waffe*, Alt- und Neu-Indische Studien 16, Wiesbaden, 1975, and has reaffirmed the traditional view of the *vajra* as a club, in large measure on the basis of the parallel Iranian evidence. In a brief rejoinder ('Erwiderung auf B. Schlerath: Vedisch vájra—"die Keule des Indra" ', *Orbis* 25, 1976, pp. 356–8) Rau has pointed out certain inaccuracies in Schlerath's article but not made any real reply to the main points.

[37] Even more marginal are the sling, *kṣepanī*, twice in the second stage (also in the fourth), two other terms for plough, *lāṅgala* and *sīra*, each once as a weapon in the third stage, and an unidentified weapon, *karpara*, in the fourth stage. There is also the intriguing *musuṇḍī* (so once in the second stage) or *bhuśuṇḍī* (so several times in the fourth and fifth stages), regarded by Hopkins as 'a projectile hand-weapon' (op. cit., p. 292) on the evidence of the Mahābhārata, but translated by van Buitenen as 'catapult' or 'flame-thrower'; the etymology proposed by T. Burrow ('Sanskrit words having dental -*s*- after *i*, *u*, and *r*', *Studies in Greek, Italic and Indo-European Linguistics offered to L. R. Palmer* ed. A. Morpurgo Davies and W. Meld, Innsbruck, 1976, pp. 33–41) from *musaṃ-dhi- 'having (or delivering) a punch' obviously suggests some kind of club.

[38] Both terms are discussed by Hopkins (op. cit., pp. 177, 299–302; also 'On Fire-

In addition to these orthodox weapons, however, other things might be pressed into service at need. The Vānaras especially are often depicted as seizing branches or complete trees and rocks or boulders to fling at their opponents, as well as using their teeth, nails and fists, or pulling hair and ears. These practices are not confined to the Vānaras, for even Rāvaṇa in the final combat with Rāma fights with rocks and trees (6.95.17–18), while lesser Rākṣasas do so on several occasions. Nor are these natural weapons necessarily a last resort: Mahodara and Sugrīva in their combat begin with clubs, then resort to fisticuffs and then to swords and shields (6.85). In general a combat begins with the antagonists shooting at each other with arrows, particularly in the first stage of growth, or hurling spears, which becomes more frequent later. Then, when dismounted from their chariots either by accident or voluntarily, they resort to clubs or swords or various other hand-held weapons.

Also, there is occasional reference, in addition to the various divine or magical weapons employed on both sides, to the worship of weapons, but this only appears in the second or later stages and is not frequent. However, at one point Sītā is said to honour Rāma's bow regularly with perfumes and garlands (6.23.17) and the same respect was accorded Janaka's bow (1.750*), Rāma's bow is fetched from his *ācārya's* house (2.28.14) where in the Northern recension it was honoured (2.735*), and Rāvaṇa receiving the sword Candrahāsa from Śiva is told not to despise it (7.321*).

By contrast with the frequency of mention of weapons, the strategy and conventions of warfare are scantily referred to, for the same reason that the common soldiery rates little mention: concentration on the spectacular set pieces of the major duels at the expense of the less dramatic. Nevertheless, enough incidental reference is found to enable us to piece together some general principles. Campaigning inevitably stops with the coming of the monsoon. It is for this reason that Rāma is urged by Sugrīva to stay with him in Kiṣkindhā and Rāma recognises the force of the argument, while insisting on staying outside the city to comply with the conditions of his exile, and explicitly defines the rainy season as lasting four months, declaring that they will resume activity

Arms in Ancient India', JAOS 13, 1889, proceedings, pp. cxciv-cxcviii) and Singh (op. cit., pp. 112–4), making essentially the same conclusions from the Mahābhārata evidence.

in the month Kārtikeya (4.25.12–15). His second-stage lyric description of the rainy season also states that then kings' expeditions are halted and men abroad go home (4.27.15[l.v.]). Despite the arrangement, Rāma has to send a stern message to Sugrīva reminding him when the rains are over that the time for action has arrived (4.29.30–2; cf. App.I.16.37–40[l.v.]). This episode, integral in spite of some inflation to the story, reveals the standard pattern of Indian warfare that campaigns start in the autumn after the cessation of the monsoons that rule out all travel. This is a fact of life, one might say, rather than a convention of military behaviour. Indeed, its very universality is the motive for the incident in the third stage which is a deliberate breach of it: Lavaṇa, the Rākṣasa ruler of Madhuvana, is invincible, unless he can be caught off his guard and away from his weapons, and so Rāma orders Śatrughna to march against him during the rainy season (7.56.10–12).

So too it is natural for fighting to stop for the night and, for example, Khara when facing Rāma cuts short his boasting lest the sun should set and prevent the battle (3.28.23cd). Equally, this convention is not invariably observed, for at one point the fight between the Vānaras and Rākṣasas continues after nightfall (6.34); the glinting of the weapons like fireflies and the sound of drums revealing the combatants' positions are graphically described, and suggest that it is exceptional.[39]

All other conventions alluded to in the text are honoured as much in the breach as in the observance. This is most marked with the supposed inviolability of women.[40] In theory this immunity is extended to a warrior when accompanied by women but Arjuna Kārtavīrya's ministers plead the point in vain to Rāvaṇa (7.32.28); Dundubhi, challenging Vālin to fight in the presence of his women, gives him till the morning on the grounds also that it is a sin to kill someone drunk or distraught or asleep or destitute (presumably unarmed, 4.11.34). Basically, these amount to a reluctance to take advantage of an enemy's weakness, which is most clearly exemplified in the actual action by Rāma's sparing of Rāvaṇa when he is exhausted and his bow is broken (6.47.132), an incident however which has been added or expanded in order to enhance Rāma's moral prestige. More usually no quarter is given once battle has been joined, although the third and fourth stages

[39] Singh (op. cit., p. 20) notes two instances of fighting at night in the Mahābhārata (4.32.1–3 and 7.138–61). The allusion in the third stage to a battle lasting seven nights (*saptarātraṃ kṛte saṃkhye*, 7.22.13c) no more indicates night-fighting than would the use of fortnight in English.

[40] See p. 179 for details.

begin to introduce the idea of clemency for those who surrender, if not its practice (7.8.3 and 6.330* 4). However, in the somewhat different context of Vibhīṣaṇa's arrival and the discussion of whether to receive him, Rāma propounds the view which formerly was declared by Kaṇḍu son of Kaṇva that anyone seeking protection, however unworthy, is to be protected to the best of one's ability for otherwise his sins accrue to the one who fails to protect him (6.12.14–18): this clearly reflects a much more archaic attitude.

On the other hand, the view is widespread that retreat in battle is shameful, being found implicitly in the general commendatory description of warriors as not retreating in battle (*samareṣv anivartiṇām*, 3.21.8d etc.) and explicitly in for example Aṅgada's and Hanumān's chiding of the Vānaras fleeing before Kumbhakarṇa and Indrajit (6.54.3–6, 16–24 and 69.3–4). Aṅgada includes among his urgings the rewards of death in battle, which are more fully spelt out elsewhere in a fourth-stage passage (7 App.I.1.147–53). So too, in the fourth stage Rāma consoles Vibhīṣaṇa for Rāvaṇa's death in terms of the kṣatriya ethos of either victory or defeat (6 App.I.67.63–74). But discretion is sometimes the better part of valour and this is in effect what Rāvaṇa's charioteer replies to Rāvaṇa's upbraidings for having withdrawn him from combat; his justification develops into a more general homily on the need to know the time and place for attack or retreat (6.93.11–23)

To return to Vibhīṣaṇa's arrival at the Vānara encampment, the immediate reaction by the Vānaras is naturally distrust and Sugrīva for example voices the suspicion that Vibhīṣaṇa is a spy or a kind of Trojan horse (6.11.17–20, more fully in 177*). Here and elsewhere the opinion is expressed that spies (*cara, cāra, cāraka* land in the fourth stage *praṇidhi*) may freely be punished or killed, by contrast with the inviolability of envoys. The use of deceit in war is in fact a fairly regular tactic of the Rākṣasas but one which draws remarkably little condemnation from anyone; for example Garuḍa's remark, as he frees Rāma and Lakṣmaṇa from Indrajit's arrows, that the Rākṣasas are always crooked fighters (*kūṭayodhin*, 6.40.53) is more of a statement of fact and a warning to be more careful in future than a moral judgement. Furthermore, while Indrajit renders himself invisible in combat on two occasions (6.34 and 60), Hanumān considers disguise before entering Laṅkā to reconnoitre and then becomes some kind of animal (*pṛṣadaṃśaka*, 5.2.31–3 and 46).

Nevertheless, one thing that is fairly universally condemned is intervention by a third in a duel, which as we have already seen is to a large extent the standard form of combat. Yet this of course forms part of

Vālin's dying accusations against Rāma (4.17), whereas Hanumān refrains from attacking Rāvaṇa while he is engaged with Nīla for this reason (6.47.69–70). Another item of Vālin's complaint is that Rāma's attack was without provocation and this has close analogies with another moralising passage of the second stage where Sītā counsels Rāma against attacking the Rākṣasas without direct provocation (3.8). In both cases, of course, the charges have been brought in order that Rāma may rebut them. Yet once again we see the actual events narrated at variance with the theory expressed in later stages. The rules or conventions of war were evidently not formulated in detail in the first stage, and indeed nowhere in the Rāmāyaṇa do we find the detailed codes of conduct included in the Mahābhārata (e.g. 6.1.27–32).[41] Instead, we find expressed general and rather vague notions of fair play based essentially on the idea that combat should be between equals.

[41] Interestingly, one such passage in the Mahābhārata (12.96.7–97.23) on the principles of fair combat is extended in its S. recension by a reference to Rāma using Indra's chariot in the final contest with Rāvaṇa (Mbh. 12.228* 6–9). But, as I noted earlier, the principle involved here is several times infringed in the Rāmāyaṇa without remark.

6

THE PEOPLE

THE REST OF SOCIETY

The people inside and outside the city, citizens and rural dwellers, women old and young ... (2.2.31)

Although the Rāmāyaṇa obviously envisages a stratified society, the broad picture presented is that of the ruler, surrounded by his court or army, contrasted with his other subjects; mention of the four *varṇas* is not found until the second stage and more particularly the third. The subjects at large are not infrequently referred to as *prajā, jana* or *janapada*; a somewhat more systematic reference is that to the inhabitants of town and country (*paura jānapada*, either qualifying *jana* or alone) to stress the totality of the population—a concept quite as frequent as that of any kind of constituent assembly.[1] Naturally enough the townsfolk, *paura*, are more commonly referred to alone—frequently turning out *en masse* for some celebration—than are the countryfolk, *jānapada*, particularly from the second stage onwards. Alongside these terms for the population as such, there is the very common term *rājya* 'kingdom' (also 'kingship'), frequent terms for cities (*purī, pura, nagara* and *nagarī*) and less frequently overall three terms for country or territory (*deśa, rāṣtra* and *viṣaya*).

On many occasions when one might have expected an enumeration of the *varṇas* to define the totality of the population, lists of different groups occur. For example, drawn just from the Ayodhyā and Yuddha kāṇḍas, a few instances covering the first four stages occur thus: for the earliest stage, brāhmans, kṣatriyas, soldiers, courtiers and heads of guilds (*gaṇavallabha*) in the Southern recension (2.75.11ab), or counsellors, merchants and other principal citizens in the Northern recension (2.1888* 2), are summoned to attend Bharata's *sabhā*; for

[1] P. C. Dharma (*The Rāmāyaṇa Polity,* Mylapore, 1941, pp. 36–8) attempts to make out of the *paurajānapada* a representative body, through a misunderstanding of *abhyantaraś ca bāhyaś ca paurajānapado janaḥ* at 2.2.31ab, 'the people both inside and outside (the city), the citizens and rural dwellers' (cf. *rāṣṭre puravare tathā* at 30d). She wishes to take *abhyantara* and *bāhya* as the inner body of representatives and the group at large, declaring that 'Unless we interpret Paurajānapada as the representative body there is no force in the use of the words Ābhyantara and Bāhya.'

the early second stage or perhaps also first stage, from the prior part of the Ayodhyākāṇḍa (2.13.1–2), brāhmans, courtiers, generals and leading merchants assemble in readiness for Rāma's installation; while in the late second stage, when the whole population turns out to greet Rāma's return to Ayodhyā, Bharata is surrounded by leading brāhmans, leaders of guilds with other merchants, and counsellors (*dvijātimukhyaiḥ, śreṇīmukhyaiḥ sanaigamaiḥ, mantribhiḥ*, 6.115.13); but just before in the narrative an insertion of the Southern recension, belonging therefore to the fourth stage, lists brāhmans with *rājanyas* (= kṣatriyas) and groups of guild leaders (6.3548*).[2] What is perhaps most striking about all such listings is the relative prominence of the leading merchants, a situation only paralleled in the early Buddhist texts and presumably reflecting a comparatively short-lived phase of society before the pressures of orthodoxy reasserted themselves. Yet this feature is apparent only in such incidental listings and is nowhere reflected in the narrative of the Rāmāyaṇa.

There is of course inevitably a tendency operative to regularise any mention of *varṇas* to the standard four-*varṇa* pattern. Thus, in the examples already mentioned, single manuscripts or perhaps two or three, have produced variant readings to achieve this result. Again, when Rāma questions Bharata about his conduct of government the text has him asking whether brāhmans, kṣatriyas and vaiśyas are devoted to their own duties (2.94.35ab) but one Bengali manuscript introduces śūdras in one way and three Devanāgarī manuscripts in another, so as to complete the list. Here, their own duties are clearly those of each separate *varṇa* and presumably the same is true when it is said that all will be satisfied with their own duties in Rāma's perfect rule (6.116.89), which may be linked with the other statements from the text's second and third stages of growth declaring that Rāma will protect the four-*varṇa* system (e.g. 1.1.75, 5.33.11 and 6.113.29; cf. also 1.6.16–17, 12.12, 24.15, 25.5, 2.15.11 and 98.57), or listing the four *varṇas*, not necessarily in order (e.g. 1.12.17cd and 2.76.30b[l.v.]). Perhaps the clearest expression in the text of the different functions and privileges of the *varṇas* is found in four late passages. The first of these lists the blessings from reading the Rāmāyaṇa in terms of success in their respective spheres for *dvija, kṣatriya, vaṇigjana* and *śūdra* (1.1.79[l.v.]). The second, which forms part of a vignette of the ideal

[2] There is also an incidental mention of headmen of villages and hamlets (*grāmaghoṣamahattarāḥ*, 2.77.15b) among the many occupations accompanying Bharata's expedition, but significantly this is part of a list intended to be comprehensive; in general the text ignores the lower levels of administration and their interaction with the general population.

society made possible under Daśaratha's rule, lists the four *varṇas* in their standard pecking order, which is clearly stated as part of the list in both the text and the Northern variant (1.6.17/248* 31). The third, as part of Jaṭāyus' genealogical and cosmogonical discourse, reproduces the tradition based on the *Ṛgveda* (10.90) thus:

> Manu bore men by noble Kaśyapa—brāhmans, kṣatriyas, vaiśyas and śūdras, o bull among men. From the mouth were born brāhmans, from the chest kṣatriyas, from the thighs were born vaiśyas, from the feet śūdras, according to scripture. (3.13.29–30)

The last is a dirge by Nārada on the decline of dharma in successive *yugas* as the other *varṇas* usurp the privileges of brāhmans (7.65.8–26); there is also a much briefer remark in the same vein by Agastya to Rāma (7.67.10).

Tension or conflict between the *varṇas* is not expressed in either the first or second stage. However, in addition to Nārada's dirge from the Uttarakāṇḍa, there is also from the third stage the extended treatment of the rivalry between Vasiṣṭha and Viśvāmitra in 1.52–64, which recounts first their struggle over the cow Śabalā (1.52–5) and then the process by which Viśvāmitra becomes a brāhman from a kṣatriya, including within the latter the episode of Triśaṅku's ascent to heaven (especially at 1.58.14–15). We also find a rather pale reflection of the traditional hostility of the brāhman Rāma Jāmadagnya towards kṣatriyas (1.73–5), when he comes to challenge Daśaratha and party and the brāhmans with Daśaratha express the hope that he will not again exterminate the kṣatriyas, but in the rest of this narrative of how he tamely submits to Rāma Dāśarathi and is banished to mount Mahendra there is no further overt allusion to this hostility. However, presumably we may see in the very presence of the episode an implicit counter to the pretensions of the Bhārgavas in the other epic.[3]

One of the most striking illustrations of the change of attitudes during the growth of the epic is provided by the terms for members of the *varṇas*. In each case the majority of references numerically come from the Bāla and Uttara kāṇḍas, which are barely a quarter of the

[3] Cf. V. S. Sukthankar, 'Epic Studies VI. The Bhṛgus and the Bhārata: A Text-Historical Study', ABORI 18, 1936–7, pp. 1–76; S. S. Janaki, 'Paraśurāma', *Purāṇa* 8, 1966, pp. 52–82; R. P. Goldman, *Gods, Priests, and Warriors: The Bhṛgus of the Mahābhārata*, New York, 1977; and Gail, *Paraśurāma*. However, Gail also draws attention to the fact that, in another group of references in the Mahābhārata, Rāma Jāmadagnya tutors Bhīṣma, Droṇa and Karṇa in weapons (p.34); this weaponry aspect may also provide a clue to the reasons for the inclusion of this episode. As to chronology, it may be noted that Rāma Jāmadagnya is carrying an axe (1.73.18a)—a feature found in the text of the other epic only at the late Mbh. 13.14.137–8 (cf. Gail, op. cit., pp. 43–4).

total length of the text, and within the earlier books a higher proportion occurs in the second stage. Thus, there are only about forty references to brāhmans in the first stage, but the frequency in the second stage is well over twice as great and by the third stage well over four times. Not only that, but the terms employed change: *brāhmaṇa*, which is the commonest term in both the first and second stages, is eclipsed in the third by the term *dvija*, which there is twice as common, while *brahman*, whether for individual or caste, is extremely rare outside the third stage but within it is nearly twice as frequent as *brāhmaṇa*. Of the two other less common terms *dvijāti* tends to be early and *vipra* late (preponderantly third and fourth stages). It may be noted that *dvija* and *dvijāti*, literally 'twice-born', are always used in the more restricted sense of brāhman and not of the three upper *varṇas*.[4]

The majority of references in the first stage are simply to brāhmans as one group within the court set-up (e.g. 2.62.1 and 83.14) or of the population, as when the whole city it seems accompanies Bharata on his expedition after Rāma (2.77.16), while others are simply part of the description of individuals, for example when the sage Bharadvāja is also designated a brāhman (2.86.14). Their position is normally one of respect but equally peripheral to the main story in most instances. Vasiṣṭha as court chaplain, *purohita*, is however an influential figure, as we have seen elsewhere,[5] and for example Daśaratha rises from his seat to greet him (2.5.22, cf. 101*), but exaggerated respect automatically accorded to any brāhman seems a late feature (e.g. 6.104.23 and 7 App.I.4.26). Even so the episode of the comic and impecunious brāhman Trijaṭa Gārgya (2.29.22–7, also 763*) presents their eagerness for alms in a rather unfavourable light. The practice of giving gifts to brāhmans is alluded to several times in the context of Rāma's departure for the forest (2.29.12–17 and 22–7, 30.1 and 31.3), but this incident is the longest devoted to it. Elsewhere in the Ayodhyākāṇḍa gifts to brāhmans figure in Sītā's vow to Gaṅgā (2.46.73) and the obsequies for Daśaratha (2.71.2–3). Linked with the obligation to give alms to brāhmans is that to provide hospitality, of which one instance is central to the narrative, since it is for this reason that Sītā feels obliged to receive Rāvaṇa when he comes disguised as a wandering brāhman (3.45.1–2); this motif is presumably original, although the passage has been much remodelled in transmission. A feast for brāhmans is detailed in the Bālakāṇḍa (1.12.9–10, cf. 13.11–13).

[4] So too in the early chapters of *Manu*, which enumerate the duties of the *dvija*, he is in fact the brāhman.

[5] See p. 132.

Other aspects of the status and function of brāhmans only come to the fore from the second stage onwards. Thus, the heinousness of the crime of killing a brāhman, though found once in the first stage in a simile expressing Daśaratha's sorrow at the hurt he has done Rāma (2.37.11a), occurs otherwise in later stages (e.g. 2.18.24, 1415* 8, 4.17.32a, 7.75.3 and App.I.8.422–32), while also from the second stage comes Bharata's seeking the reason for Rāma's banishment in various crimes, including that of robbing a brāhman (2.66.37ab and 40ab). The duty of brāhmans is to study and not to rule (1.13.40) and a mountain in its fixity is compared to a brāhman studying (4.27.10), while it is legitimate for a brāhman but not for a kṣatriya to fast as a means of coercion (2.103.17). In a kingless state brāhmans do not perform sacrifice (2.61.12) and Bharata, as he approaches Ayodhyā, considers brāhmans sacrificing as one of the characteristics of the city (2.65.16). Similarly, Ayodhyā is elsewhere described as thronged with learned brāhmans (1.5.23[l.v.], cf. 6.12–13 and 13.7) and their presence at court is alluded to (2.2.22), but these references are late. Later still is the elaborate eulogy of brāhmans added to the opening of the Ayodhyākāṇḍa in the Northwestern and Western recensions (2 App.I.2.16–24).

Cows and brāhmans are linked in the fashion typical of later Hinduism in the Bālakāṇḍa (1.24.13c and 25.5a), which also points to food taboos in the story of Triśaṅku as *caṇḍāla* inviting brāhmans to a sacrifice and their horror at this (1.58.15), together with the mention of dog-eating *muṣṭikas* (another despised group, 1.58.20).

The kṣatriyas also are mentioned more often in later parts, although the rise in frequency is not so spectacular as with the brāhmans, except for the abstract or generic term *kṣatra*. The Vedic term for members of this *varṇa, rājanya*, has dropped out except for purely artificial late revival (2.76.30b[l.v.] and 6.3548*). However, this does point to one feature which might otherwise be misleading: the apparent neglect of kṣatriyas in a poem predominantly about regal and martial values. Quite simply, the major figures are normally referred to as kings and princes (*rājan* and *rājaputra*) and discussion of their rights and duties is in terms of their family traditions and a king's obligations, not usually, at least until the later stages, in terms of the conduct of the kṣatriya *varṇa* (*kṣatradharma*). Accordingly we find several allusions to the king's right to taxes based on his duty of protection (2.69.18, 3.1.18–19, 5.11–13, etc.) or to the latter alone (e.g. 2.2.4, 94.41, 3.9.3, 6.12.4, cf. 1.596* and 4.105*), but even these statements are commoner in later passages, with this tendency to moralising and didactic elaboration of what in the earliest stage is left implicit. In the second stage the qualities needed in a king are listed (4.17.25; cf. *kaccit* sarga 2.94) and his duty of giving to brāhmans emphasised (2.12.5). The king's duty to rule is explicitly contrasted with the brāhman's duty to study in the Bālakāṇḍa (1.13.39–40). In the fourth stage Rāma, to console Vibhīṣaṇa for Rāvaṇa's death, discourses on *kṣatradharma* as the necessity to win or lose, kill or be killed (6 App.I.67.63–74).

Vaiśya is the term exclusively used in the text for the third *varṇa*, the sole exception being *vaṇigjana*, 'the trading class', in the very late *phalaśruti* at the beginning of the Bālakāṇḍa (1.1.79 [l.v.]); occasionally in the fourth stage the simple term *viś* is found (e.g. 1.248* 31 substituting for 1.6.17). The vaiśyas are mentioned almost exclusively in lists of the *varṇas* (e.g. 3.13.29–30) in the second and later stages or in an equivalent context in Nārada's lament about the *yugas* and the status of the *varṇas* (7.65.18–21). The only exception is the mention that the ascetic youth killed by Daśaratha was born to a vaiśya father by a śūdra mother (2.57.37). In fact there is slightly more emphasis placed on the fourth *varṇa* and even lower groups in the later stages. It is instructive to compare this incident of the ascetic killed by Daśaratha, where the act, or rather the father's curse which follows it, is adduced to account for Daśaratha's sorry state (2.57–8), with the incident of Rāma slaying a śūdra ascetic Śambūka, where the act is considered creditable to Rāma and the śūdra's actions are viewed as inimical to society (7.67; cf. 7.65). There has been an enormous shift in attitudes between the period of the former, among the earlier additions to the story, and the latter, among the latest parts included in the text, which can only reasonably be explained as the result of the infiltration and eventual dominance of strict brāhman attitudes. This is illustrated also in the legend of Triśaṅku cursed to become a *caṇḍāla* (1.57.8–15), whereas the earlier more liberal attitude is also seen in Rāma's friendly encounter with the Śabarī ascetic (3.70, especially 6–9).[6]

The four *varṇas* are of course regularly linked with the four stages of life in the *varṇāśramadharma* of the legal literature. However, the only reference in the text appears to be from the second stage where Bharata, putting pressure on Rāma to return, refers first to the duty of protecting the four *varṇas* and then says that the householder's stage is the best of the four stages of life (2.98.57–8; cf. e.g. Mbh. 12.12.11 and 23.2–5). There are a few references to the studentship period, as when Sītā slightly inappositely says that she will enjoy herself with Rāma in

[6] The status of the Śabarī woman will be commented on later; see p. 177. D. P. Vora, *Evolution of Morals in the Epics*, Bombay, 1959, pp. 165–6 comments on her and on Rāma slaying the *śūdra* ascetic.

the forest as a *brahmacāriṇī* (2.24.10), or when others refer to *brahmacarya* in relation to Rāma's exile (2.46.10a, 76.10a and 5.33.12b; also 2 App.I.9.150 and App.I.13.49). Apart from these, all other references are to individuals becoming ascetics or to those who already are.

Such ascetics participate in the action to a considerable extent, but their portrayal is perhaps unexpected, in that they are *vānaprasthas* rather than *sannyāsins*, maintaining the sacred fire and performing sacrifice. Indeed, Agastya greets Rāma 'in the manner of hermits' (*vānaprasthena dharmeṇa*, 3.11.24c), and Hanumān, when he contemplates renouncing the world on the apparent failure of his search for Sītā, uses the terms *vānaprastha* and *tāpasa* as synonymous (5.11.40–5, cf. 356*); Rāma too, immediately before drowning himself at the end of the Uttarakāṇḍa, takes the great vow of going forth (*cakāra ... mahāprasthānikaṃ vidhi*, 7.99.3cd). So also Lakṣmaṇa refers to the custom of former kings who retired to the forest after handing over their subjects to their sons (2.20.20–1). The term *saṃnyāsin* does not occur in the text and *saṃnyāsa* occurs only when Hanumān, in greater despondency, considers giving up his life (*prāṇasaṃnyāsa*, 5.53.8c). Indeed Jacobi suggests that the *vānaprastha* as a religious institution is apparently the brahmanised form of an originally social custom of banishment of the elderly or at least their withdrawal from active participation, an equivalent of retirement; certainly, in the Rāmāyaṇa, the *vānaprastha* stage is less overtly religious than might be anticipated.[7]

Family relationships are obviously significant in the society depicted in the early stages and much emphasised in later parts, but the early attitude is implicit rather than spelt out in detailed genealogies or the like. Indeed, so far as the main plot is concerned it is striking how restricted the family grouping is. Daśaratha is effectively without ancestry,[8] and the action concentrates entirely in the first part of the plot upon the relationship between him, his wives and his sons. It is symptomatic of this trend that the commonest term for relatives (*bāndhava*) occurs only forty-two times in the first and second stages, while terms for grandparents are found fewer than a dozen times. In point of fact, the narrative of the Rāmāyaṇa is concerned simply with

[7] Jacobi, *Das Râmâyaṇa*, p.61n. For the more religious aspects see my RA p.120 and below (pp. 205–7).

[8] It is not until late in the second stage that Vasiṣṭha recites the Ikṣvāku genealogy (2.102).

the family across two generations and, unlike the Mahābhārata, does not trace its problems any further back or forward. Such a statement must of course be modified when the third stage is reached. Then we are introduced at an early point (1.3) to the sons of Rāma and Sītā, Kuśa and Lava, soon after to Rāma's ancestor Sagara and his sons (1.5 and especially 1.37–40), to Sītā's adoptive father (1.49 and 1.65), to Sītā's former incarnation as Vedavatī (7.17) and so on.

In the main story, however, Rāma identifies himself and is described by others as the son of Daśaratha and a member of the Ikṣvāku dynasty; these two regularly but not invariably go together. Bharata, in accordance with the narrative requirements of the plot, is especially referred to as Kaikeyī's son and for the same reason Lakṣmaṇa is regularly Rāma's younger brother. Sītā is regularly depicted as Janaka's daughter and Rāma's wife, and just occasionally—though mainly in later passages—as Daśaratha's daughter-in-law. Thus by far the commonest terms for relations are those for father, mother, brother, sister, son or daughter, husband and wife. Grandparents, grandchildren, uncles, cousins and relatives by marriage are all only sporadically mentioned, particularly in the earlier parts of the text.

Nevertheless, within the commoner relationships some interesting shifts of vocabulary occur. Father is normally *pitṛ* but the term *tāta* is also found mainly in the second stage (somewhat more generally used in the vocative as an honorific).[9] Mother is normally *mātṛ* but also occasionally *jananī* at all periods (the corresponding *janayitṛ* and *janitṛ* for father are very rare) and the term *ambā* is characteristic of later parts. Sons and daughters are usually expressed by *putra* which is roughly twice as common as the next most frequent term *suta*, which is however actually commoner in verses in longer metre as well as occurring rather more commonly elsewhere in the second and third stages; other occasional terms are *ātmaja*, which is commoner in compounds, *apatya*, found in the second and more especially third stages, *tanaya*, characteristic of the third stage, and *prasava*, found exclusively there; the sexually specific terms *duhitṛ* and *sūnu* are most uncommon and even rarer are the terms *tanūja, dāraka* and *putraka*. We may also note that *bhaginī* has virtually replaced *svasṛ* as the standard term for sister, whereas *bhrātṛ* remains the standard term for brother, and other terms, which are much less common, are more specifically younger/older/step brother (*agraja, anuja, avaraja, pūrvaja, vaimātra*).

[9] The use of terms of relationship as forms of address is quite frequent, alongside patronymics and personal names or status designations such as *rājan* and, more commonly later, *prabho*. The employment of such honorifics and the types of greetings used (*añjali*, embrace and circumambulation in particular) merit a separate study.

Obedience to and respect for parents is one of the cardinal virtues, alluded to regularly and also used as the standard against which to judge other loyalties. Thus, in the Ayodhyākāṇḍa, Kāśyapa is cited as going to heaven through obedience to his mother as well as practice of austerities (2.18.20), and other references to obedience to parents are found at 559* 9 (a Southern addition to Kausalyā's benediction on Rāma), 27.29 (Rāma explains to Sītā that he must go into exile, expanded on in the Southern insert 705*), 97.17–18 (Rāma's advice to Bharata to forgive his mother), 103.2–3 and 9–11 (Vasiṣṭha and Rāma argue about his return, Vasiṣṭha citing Kausalyā's wish and Rāma Daśaratha's) and App.I.11.1–11 (Kausalyā urges her claims to Rāma's obedience against Daśaratha's—a Southern elaboration); these examples span the development of the epic and reflect continued adherence to this pattern. Its use as the absolute standard is well seen in Sītā's declaration that Lakṣmaṇa treats Rāma like his father and her like his mother (5.36.46).

Parents' affection for their children and concern for their welfare is also well depicted. The regular marks of affection are smelling the head and embracing; the term for kissing (√*cumb*) is very rare and late. Daśaratha's pleasure in Rāma is very apparent as he proposes to install him as heir apparent (2.3.21–4, cf. 4.13–14) and his first reaction to Kaikeyī's ultimatum is to declare that Rāma is dearer to him than she is and to refuse to part with him (2.10.17 and 37–40, also 200*). Equally, Kausalyā mourns Rāma's departure as being equivalent to barrenness through loss of her only son (2.17.20–2, expanded on in 17.32[l.v.], 443*[l.v.] and App.I.11.15–18) and Bharata upbraids his mother for causing such distress to Kausalyā, comparing her to the mythical cow Surabhi weeping for her two sons (2.68.14–25). The imagery of cow and calf also appears earlier when all Daśaratha's queens mourn Rāma's exile 'like cows missing their calves' (2.36.7), while the universal sorrow at his departure is stressed *inter alia* by the assertion that it eclipses a mother's joy in her eldest son (2.42.4). Later in the story Sītā in captivity mournfully speculates that Kausalyā may kill herself at Rāma's death (6.80.46–8).

Such is the attitude in the first and second stages but in later stages a different emphasis tends to predominate. Although Daśaratha proposes in the Bālakāṇḍa to offer an *aśvamedha* to fulfil his desire for a son (1.11.8–9) and his joy at the births is expressed in the context of the naming ceremony (1.17.11–20), these have been preceded by the statement that Daśaratha lacks a son to continue the dynasty (1.8.1).[10]

[10] There is no reference to Daśaratha's previous childlessness in the first two stages,

Again, Viśvāmitra declares that fathers beget sons to ensure their well-being in the other world (1.61.8). The same type of concern is given expression in the offering of water to the dead (2.95.6–7) and the proverbial etymology for *putra* as 'the one who saves (√*trā*) from the hell called Put' (2.99.12). One may compare also the implicit contrast in the story of Sagara's sons between Keśinī's 'single son to continue the dynasty' and Sumati's 60,000 sons (1.37–40, especially 37.8–14). This is not to say that natural parental affection and concern are later ignored; for example, to take one instance each from the Bāla and Uttara kāṇḍas, Daśaratha declares—with perhaps unconscious irony in view of later events—that Viśvāmitra's arrival is as welcome as the birth of a son to a childless father by a wife of equal status (1.17.33ab), and of the women carried off by Rāvaṇa some wonder what will happen to their children, whilst others are concerned for other relatives (7.24.7–8).

Another aspect is the natural tendency to talk of children taking after their parents. This is said constantly of Rāma, also of Bharata (e.g. 2.105.17) and Lakṣmaṇa (e.g. 3.14.27), of Hanumān taking after Vāyu (e.g. 4.65.28) and Nala after Viśvakarman (6.15.12–13). It is reversed in Lakṣmaṇa's puzzled enquiry about how Kaikeyī can be so cruel with Daśaratha as her husband and Bharata as her son (3.15.33)—which one may note belongs to the second stage—and is given formal expression in the fourth stage when Sumantra comments to Kaikeyī: 'This proverbial saying seems to me true, that men take after their fathers and women their mothers' (2 App.I.14.55–6). This is reduced by Jābāli to the purely biological role of parents in reproduction, when, in an insertion of the fourth stage (2.2239*), he is trying to persuade Rāma that his continued adherence to Daśaratha's wishes is pointless after his death. In somewhat the same way, the physical likeness, 'like reflections', of Kuśa and Lava to Rāma is stressed as part of their recognition and acceptance as his sons (7.85.7–8).

Elsewhere, in earlier stages, the biological role is rather played down in the polygamous setting of Daśaratha's court, for example Bharata calls Kausalyā his senior mother (2.67.7ab) and Rāma calls Kaikeyī his middle mother (3.15.35a), while it is stressed that Rāma behaves to the other queens exactly as to his own mother (2.110.5; cf.

not even in his narration of the curse for killing the ascetic youth (2.57–8). Equally, there is no evidence outside 1.15–17 for the more or less simultaneous birth of Rāma and his brothers. Nor are Lakṣmaṇa and Śatrughna ever referred to as twins (unlike Kuśa and Lava in the Uttarakāṇḍa); yet Kālidāsa calls them so explicitly at *Raghuvaṃśa* 10.71. Only the use of the dual *saumitrī* of them at 1.508* 2 may perhaps imply it.

Daśaratha's assertion that Rāma has treated Kaikeyī just like his mother at 2.10.34).

The relationship between the brothers is regularly depicted as one of warm affection and closeness, the sole apparent exception being Lakṣmaṇa's flare-up of anger against Bharata for usurping Rāma's place, when he is pacified by Rāma. In Lakṣmaṇa's devotion to Rāma there is a strong element of deference to the elder.[11] We have already noted his declaration that Rāma and Sītā are like father and mother in his regard, and in the later stages this is sometimes put even more emphatically, as when Lakṣmaṇa declares that he will serve Rāma like a slave (2.1737*). But the affection is mutual and for example Lakṣmaṇa can be described simultaneously as devoted to Rāma and as dear to him (3.32.12–13), and when Rāma sees Lakṣmaṇa first wounded and then, as he thinks, killed, he asks what is the use of Sītā or his own life, for, while he can find another wife equal to Sītā he cannot find a brother to equal Lakṣmaṇa as a companion (6.39.5–12 and 89.7–8; the latter expanded in many manuscripts by 2029* which in part repeats material from 6.39). Equally, Rāma's selflessness in saying that he would willingly give everything to Bharata of his own accord (2.16.33) is matched by Bharata's efforts to persuade Rāma to return and take up the throne (2.97–8).

There is however a strong contrast in the fraternal relationships of the Vānaras and of the Rākṣasas. Vālin and Sugrīva are shown as bitterly jealous and quite ready to use force against each other. To some extent Sugrīva is portrayed as the innocent victim of Vālin's suspicious nature but he then eagerly solicits Rāma's help in killing his brother (4.8–16), even though he has presented himself as having been subservient to Vālin (4.9.1–3).[12] The situation is much the same among the Rākṣasas. Śūrpaṇakhā, when she reports the defeat of the Rākṣasas in Daṇḍaka to Rāvaṇa, has some harsh words to say about his competence as a ruler (3.31). Rāvaṇa, angrily rejecting Vibhīṣaṇa's advice to placate Rāma and return Sītā, has strong words to say about relatives as a source of danger, even quoting a supposed proverb

[11] Indeed in the fourth stage Lakṣmaṇa in his devotion to Rāma (or the better to point up Rāma's calm acceptance) is made to urge Rāma to seize or kill the king (2.454*) or himself to vow to kill his father (2.458*) because of Rāma's banishment. However, in the text Daśaratha himself suggests that Rāma should stage a coup (2.31.23).

[12] J. M.Masson stresses very much Sugrīva's fear of Vālin, regarding it as paranoia, and suggests that he is acting out a fratricidal phantasy ('Fratricide among the Monkeys: Psychoanalytic Observations on an Episode in the Vālmīkirāmāyaṇam', JAOS 95, 1975, pp. 672–8). He makes the worthwhile point that Rāma sides with Sugrīva very impetuously on the basis of their common loss (only implied in the text, cf. below). But what lies behind Masson's own repeated muddling of Vālin and Sugrīva?

current among the elephants (6.10.1–11). Later, when the exigencies of battle force Rāvaṇa to wake another brother Kumbhakarṇa out of his extended sleep, Kumbhakarṇa chides Rāvaṇa for his lack of political acumen and Rāvaṇa sharply reminds him of the respect due to an elder and criticises his presumed lack of affection (6.51.1–26). In more general terms, the split between the Vānara brothers, Vālin and Sugrīva, is paralleled by the breach between Rāvaṇa and Vibhīṣaṇa; in both cases, too, Rāma sides with one brother and performs the *abhiṣeka* installing him as rightful ruler. However, the quarrel between Vālin and Sugrīva antedates Rāma's arrival and the rights and wrongs of it are by no means clear-cut in the early form of the story. By contrast the clash between Rāvaṇa and Vibhīṣaṇa is presented as springing from the moral issue of Rāvaṇa's seizure of Sītā, and to a lesser extent the political one of whether or not to oppose Rāma and his allies; Vibhīṣaṇa, therefore, being as one might say, the white sheep of the family, finds himself ostracised and goes off to join the side of morality. There then follows the interesting episode where Sugrīva, seeing Vibhīṣaṇa approaching their camp, is suspicious and advises Rāma not to have any truck with him but rather to kill him immediately simply on the grounds that he is Rāvaṇa's brother, while Hanumān suspects that Vibhīṣaṇa's motive is self-interest, having heard how Rāma helped Sugrīva and wanting the same short-cut to the throne for himself (6.11). It seems probable, therefore, that this parallelism is not intended as a commentary on different patterns of family relationships but rather as an expression of the contrasting attitudes to power of Rāma—and by extension his brothers—and of the world at large. Indeed, there is an attempt made in the fourth stage to homologate Rāma's and Sugrīva's situations on the basis of common undeserved exile and common loss of their wives to another (4 App.I.4), which certainly suggests that no basic distinction between Aryan and non-Aryan fraternal behaviour is being drawn either consciously or unconsciously.

The same contrast between hero and villain obviously colours any picture of marital relationships that can be assembled. Rāma and Sītā are from the start of the epic's development seen as models of conjugal fidelity, whereas Rāvaṇa is portrayed by contrast as an epitome of licentiousness; to a lesser extent all other characters have their weaknesses. However, it is possible from casual references and from maxims quoted in the context of the basic story to disentangle what is the general attitude at the various stages of the epic's growth to the relationship of husband and wife. Most basically, this is expressed in the terms most commonly employed (*bhartṛ* and *bhāryā*) as that between the one who supports and the one requiring support. Both other terms for husband (*nātha* and *pati*) also express the concept of the husband as dominant partner, but neither is nearly as common as *bhartṛ*. Almost as frequent, especially earlier, for wife is the term *dāra*, whereas the only other terms at all frequently employed, *patnī* and *yoṣit*, tend to be later.

The role of husband as protector of his wife is implicit throughout. As part of Sītā's efforts to persuade Rāma to let her accompany him to exile, she proclaims her confidence in his ability to protect her there as elsewhere (2.24.11), while towards the end of the story and from the fourth stage comes her affirmation as she is abandoned in the forest that a husband is not only a woman's deity but also her refuge (7.888* 1). Jaṭāyus censures Rāvaṇa as he carries off Sītā saying that other men's wives are to be protected just like his own (3.48.7). But this line cannot be pursued too far without raising questions about Rāma's protection of Sītā and this may be one reason why it is not much stressed, although undoubtedly one motive in the elaboration of the story of Mārīca becoming a golden deer is implicitly to absolve Rāma of any blame in this respect.

The mutual affection and companionship of Rāma and Sītā is clear throughout but tends to be more explicitly presented from the second stage onwards. For example, when Rāma discourses to Sītā about the beauties of Citrakūṭa he says that part of the attraction is being there in her company (2.88–9) and subsequently he declares that he would be willing to stay by the Mandākinī and forget Ayodhyā if only he could recover Sītā (4.55*, cf. 35* and 46*); in between, in the immediate aftermath of Sītā's disappearance, he has expressed his apprehension and sorrow, declaring that he could not live a moment without Sītā (3.56.4ab), leading up to the elaborate depiction of his distraught roamings (3.58–60) of which the greater part belongs to the second stage. Later again, when his army is encamped before Laṅkā, Rāma gives expression to his ardent longing for Sītā (6.5.4–20). Incidentally, these and similar passages which could be cited serve to highlight how out of character with the early story is Rāma's cold rejection of Sītā after the defeat of Rāvaṇa (6.103). Still, the companionship aspect is by no means limited to Rāma and Sītā, as may be seen by looking at Tārā's lament for the slain Vālin (4.23.2–16) which includes reference to the husband as friend. An expansion of the Southern recension makes Tārā put this still more emphatically in her pleadings to Rāma, during which she says that on scriptural authority a wife is the man's identical or inseparable self (4 App.I.26.143–4). Interestingly, this echoes what in another expansion of the fourth stage Vasiṣṭha says to Kaikeyī, that since a wife is the self of all married men, Sītā should rule in Rāma's absence (2 App.I.15.19–20). There is of course an element of special pleading in both but the fact remains that this view is given as almost a stock saying in what is a fairly late stage of the Rāmāyaṇa's development.

Such closeness is also perhaps reflected in those passages which indicate wives' influence on their husbands. Sometimes this comes out in purely incidental allusions, as when Rāma speaks, urged on by Sītā, when he bestows jewellery on Suyajña (2.29.6), but at other points is the focus of a whole episode, as when Sītā delivers her moral homily to Rāma urging him to lay aside arms in the forest, including the significant utterance: 'Out of affection and esteem I remind you—I am not instructing you—that under no circumstances should you kill without provocation ... ' (3.8.20). Mostly such allusions are to groups of wives, for example, to cite just a few from the first stage, the women of Ayodhyā reproaching their husbands for Rāma's departure (2.42.5–25), the soldiers' wives hurrying their husbands to mobilise (2.76.23), or the Vānaras liable to scorn from their wives, if they fly from battle (6.54.18).

However, in general and especially in the later stages, the accent is placed on a wife's devotion and subservience to her husband. There are two main ways in which this is done, either by stereotyped statements that a husband is his wife's deity (e.g. 2.26.14d, 34.27d, 56.5, 109.23–4, 3.54.3d, 5.546* and 547*, 26.12a[l.v.], 7.86.10, 888*) or by comparison with various mythical models. Occasionally both are combined as for example when Sītā herself says to Anasūyā, Atri's wife, that she knows that the husband is the woman's *guru* (here of course used in its older sense of someone senior and respected, especially parents and by extension one's teacher; cf. 5.22.7f) and that obedience to her husband is the wife's *tapas*, for which Sāvitrī and Rohiṇī are renowned (2.110.2–12). Sītā is compared in faithfulness to Rohiṇī by others (1.1.24, 5.13.20–1 and 6.80.50) and herself cites Sāvitrī when she is persuading Rāma to let her accompany him to the forest (2.27.6). But it is no doubt significant that all these instances belong to the second and third stages and that so far only Rohiṇī and Sāvitrī are instanced. However, in the fourth stage further names occur, for instance in one list besides these two are named Suvarcalā, Śacī, Arundhatī, Lopamudrā, Sukanyā, Madayantī and Damayantī (5.548*).

A subsidiary aspect of this duty to her husband is that of providing him with children, but this is remarkable for its rarity in the Rāmāyaṇa. There is included in the *kaccit* sarga by the fourth stage the question whether as part of the general well-being of the state, the wives of the citizens are fruitful (2.2165* 10). The only occasions from the earliest stages are Kausalyā's lament at Rāma's exile that she is as good as barren as a result (2.17.20–1) and Sītā's lament when she thinks Rāma and Lakṣmaṇa killed that the fortunetellers lied in foretelling that she would have children and not be a widow (6.38.2–3). However, both these suggest rather the joys of parenthood than the duty.

Similarly, there is no detailed reference at all in the early stages to pregnancy. Before the third stage the only major reference is the simile of a foetus being cut up in the womb in the late passage giving Sītā's first lament (5.26.6[l.v.]), although another simile from the second stage compares the period of the rains gathering for nine months to a pregnancy (4.27.3). However in the third stage are narrated the birth of Skanda (1.36.12–27), the destruction in the womb of Diti's foetus by Indra (1.45.5–22), the birth of Viśravas to Tṛṇabindu's daughter (7.2.28), Sītā's pregnancy longing (7.41.13–27) and the birth of Kuśa and Lava (7.58.1–6).

The absence of wifely subjection is one of the marks of the breakdown of society listed in the sarga on the evils of a kingless state (2.61.9–10), whereas by extension the wife ought properly to show the same respect to her husband's parents (2.23.26–30; cf. 34[l.v.] and 611*). Implicit in the latter is the wife's going to reside with her husband's family in the extended family pattern which has been standard at most if not all periods of Indian society. This is also alluded to in a simile, again coming from the second stage, which compares Sītā's wretchedness in captivity with the lot of a woman from a good home who is as it were born into a bad family at marriage (5.17.9). We may, however, note incidentally that the woman's role as housewife is virtually ignored at all periods, a clear indication of the aristocratic and then religious pre-occupations of its redactors. A wife's position as part of her husband's family is spelt out more clearly in the third stage, where Sītā is welcomed after marriage by her mother-in-law (1.76.8–11) and Sumālin alludes to the three lineages of a girl: her mother's, her father's and that into which she is married (7.9.7). Sītā's staying within Daśaratha's palace is simply assumed without overt remark in the Ayodhyākāṇḍa and elsewhere in the earlier books.

Most of the references to marriage as an institution are indeed to be found in the third stage, which has tended in the past to produce a rather distorted and over-definite picture, despite the fact that its evidence is contradictory and confusing. In general, for example, the age of marriage seems to be older in the earliest passages than in the later ones, but there are also certain passages in the Uttarakāṇḍa in particular which suggest adult marriage, most probably because it is simply reproducing material from an older period. The most notorious crux here is the question of Rāma's and Sītā's ages on marriage, where the evidence is particularly tangled as previous scholars have noted.[13] When Viśvāmitra comes to Daśaratha's court to secure Rāma's services in guarding his sacrifice, Daśaratha exclaims in distress that Rāma is only fifteen (*ūṇaṣoḍaśavarṣa*, 1.19.2a and 3.36.6a) and is still unskilled in warfare. However, Viśvāmitra takes Rāma and Lakṣmaṇa off on this mission and after its successful completion they go to Mithilā, on the way visiting Sumati who asks the identity of these two handsome young warriors (1.47.2–6). Thus presumably Rāma is fifteen or sixteen when they arrive at Mithilā and he breaks the bow which wins him Sītā's hand, when Janaka refers to Sītā as growing up (*vardhamānām*, 1.65.16b). Sītā, when describing her wedding to Anasūyā, talks about her father's worries when she reached 'the age suitable for union with a husband' (*patisaṃyogasulabhaṃ vayaḥ*, 2.110.33a), a turn of phrase which implies, as do other passages, that cohabitation followed the ceremony directly (e.g. 1.76.11). Rāma and Sītā then have a year of married life before the exile; this is attested both by the statement that Rāma was seventeen at the time of his planned installation, which precipitates the crisis (2.17.26), and by Sītā's recapitulation of their history to Rāvaṇa when she receives him in their hut, for in the reading given in the text she explicitly says that she lived a year with Rāma before their exile (3.45.4–5). Yet in the same passage, in a verse which fits the context badly and in an insertion (3.45.10 and 874*), she gives their ages then as Rāma twenty-five and herself eighteen, which, if combined with the totalling of their exile to date as at least ten years (3.10.23–5) and even more if combined with the variant here—in fact the majority reading—of twelve years of marriage before exile (also at 5.31.13) would make absolute nonsense.[14] Quite simply the original

[13] For example A. S. Altekar (*The Position of Women in Hindu Civilization*, 3rd ed., Delhi, 1962, pp. 52–3) rejects the implication that Sītā is a child at marriage by suggesting that one passage has been interpolated. However, there are many more references than those he cites, although obviously his explanation is basically correct. A contrary view is expressed by A. Guruge, *The Society of the Rāmāyaṇa*, Maharagama, 1960, pp. 197 ff. The most recent discussion is by van Daalen (*Vālmīki's Sanskrit*, pp. 209–14).

[14] The commentators recognise the fact and therefore carefully explain that the ages Sītā gives refer to the start of their exile, thereby distorting the obvious meaning. (Cf. the Critical Notes on 1.76.11). P. A. Grintser has examined these chronological discrepancies

poet and his audience were not interested in chronological exactitude and most probably did not mention any ages. The general impression is that Rāma and Sītā were adult or nearly so at marriage and at the time of exile, which were not far apart. The references to Rāma as fifteen when he goes off with Viśvāmitra and seventeen on the eve of installation may be regarded as the rendering precise of this general impression during the second stage, although it is possible that the remark that Rāma was seventeen at the time he was to be installed is original. Later still, there occur references to Rāma and Sītā being married as child to child (6.23.20 and 104.16).

Equally, a passing reference in the second stage suggests that Daśaratha was adult before he married Kausalyā, for as he is dying he tells her about his sin of killing the ascetic youth which happened 'while you were still unmarried and I was heir apparent' (2.57.10ab). Several episodes in the Uttarakāṇḍa also suggest adult, or at any rate post-puberty, marriages. The Rākṣasa Sumālin tells his daughter Kaikasī that it is time she was married as her youth is passing (7.9.4); Vedavatī is clearly fully developed when molested by Rāvaṇa as she was engaged in penance (7.17.2–5 and 18–21), and Arajā too is old enough to excite Daṇḍa's lust while still living with her father (7.71.4–15).

Nevertheless, the initiative for arranging the marriage is normally with the fathers. Sītā's account of her marriage is that Janaka arranges the *svayaṃvara* (2.110.23 and 37), and that when Rāma has won her he seeks Daśaratha's permission first (2.110.49–50). However the majority of instances are found in the third stage. Thus in the Bālakāṇḍa Daśaratha starts to think about his sons' marriage (1.17.22–3), evidently when they are fifteen, since he is interrupted in his deliberations by Viśvāmitra coming to claim Rāma's help; Janaka arranges the contest for Sītā's hand and has to defend his city against the forces of disappointed suitors (1.65.15–27); and Viśvāmitra suggests that, since Sītā's sister Urmilā is to be married to Lakṣmaṇa, the set of marriages should be completed by the giving of Janaka's nieces, his brother Kuśadhvaja's daughters, to Bharata and Śatrughna (1.71.1–11; cf. 2.110.51). In the Uttarakāṇḍa, when Tṛṇabindu's daughter becomes pregnant as a result of accidentally infringing Pulastya's curse while roaming freely, and it seems alone, in the forest, the father's reaction is to marry her as soon as possible to Pulastya (7.2), and Bharadvāja gives his daughter as wife to the son who is born of this union (7.3.1–4); the first part of this episode implies very considerable freedom for unmarried girls even after puberty. However, other episodes suggest

caused by the constant use of a 12-year period as a unit of time-reckoning in the epics (*Epos*, pp. 111–12).

either free choice or a mixture of arranged marriage and free choice. Thus in two successive sargas of the Bālakāṇḍa there occur both the story of Kuśanābha's daughters, who are wooed by Vāyu but tell him that their father will arrange their *svayaṃvara*, and the tale of the Gandharvī Somadā who persuades the sage Cūlin to marry her (1.31–2). In the Uttarakāṇḍa, similarly, there is the story of Sumālin who decides to marry his daughter to Viśravas but it is the daughter herself who then accosts Viśravas and persuades him to accept her (7.9.1–20), while later Arajā responds to Daṇḍa's advances by referring him to her father (7.71.4–15 and 1170*). However, it would be unwise to place much reliance on these episodes as indicators of the contemporary pattern, for the authors of these two books are quite clearly envisaging an earlier, indeed mythical, age whose rules are almost axiomatically at variance with contemporary practice.

Indeed, some of these could also be regarded as instances of mixed marriages. Thus, Pulastya is referred to as a *brahmarṣi* and Tṛṇabindu as a *rājarṣi*, while Bharadvāja is also a brāhman; Sumālin is a Rākṣasa and Viśravas a brāhman; and Daṇḍa is a kṣatriya and Arajā daughter of a Bhārgava brāhman. The last would therefore be a *pratiloma* union, that is unnatural, because the wife was of higher status than the husband, but this is not among the objections to it. Another example of such a union occurs in a later stage still, when king Yayāti, a kṣatriya therefore, has two wives, one of whom is the daughter of Uśanas, a brāhman (7 App.I.8.227–8). Examples of *anuloma* marriages, with husband of higher status than the wife, can be found outside the Uttarakāṇḍa but none come from the first stage. The ascetic Ṛśyaśṛṅga is enticed to Aṅga and given king Romapāda's daughter in marriage, an example of brāhman and kṣatriya (1.9.30–1), the ascetic youth killed by Dásaratha reassures him that his parents are a vaiśya and a śūdrā woman (2.57.37), and the inmates of Rāvaṇa's harem include the wives and daughters of royal sages, *pitṛs, daityas* as well as Rākṣasīs (5.7.65), and *vidyādhara* and *nāga* women (5.10.20–2), captured in war. Yet Sītā gives as a subsidiary reason for her rejection of Rāvaṇa that a human ought not to marry a Rākṣasa (5.23.3ab), although such an objection is not brought up when Śūrpaṇakhā makes advances to Rāma and Lakṣmaṇa (3.16–17).

As to the form of the marriage ceremony and such related matters as a dowry or bride-price, the evidence is really confined to the details of the multiple wedding of Rāma and his brothers with Sītā, her sister and cousins, given towards the end of the Bālakāṇḍa. For Sītā, in recalling her marriage to Anasūyā in fact gives very little information: after Rāma had broken the bow, she was given to him by Janaka, who held up the water for sprinkling, but Rāma would not accept her without Daśaratha's permission and, when this is given, her younger sister Urmilā also was given to Lakṣmaṇa as wife; such was her *svayaṃvara* (2.110.47–52). The information in the Bālakāṇḍa expands on this presumably somewhat earlier passage but in part conflicts with it. First there comes the fixing of an auspicious day (1.71.12, cf. 70.24), then the actual wedding is performed by joining hands, explicitly repeated for each of the four couples (1.72.8–23), for here the cousins are included as brides for Bharata and Śatrughna. There is no mention of water in the text, although expansions by the Southern recension include both this and the ceremony taking place in the presence of fire (1324* and 1327*). The whole occasion ends with Janaka giving large presents as dowry (*kanyādhana*, 1.73.3–6). Previously, in the context of the bending of the bow, Janaka has referred to Sītā as *vīryaśulkā*, 'the prize of heroism', that is of the strength to bend the bow, but the second element of the word means, besides prize, also nuptial gift. The term also occurs in a reference to Kaikeyī's marriage, when Rāma explains to Bharata that Daśaratha had pledged the succession as dowry (*śulka*) in his maternal grandfather's presence; however this appears merely as an auxiliary explanation to the usual two boons which Kaikeyī can claim (2.99.3–4). Whether from their dowry or not, wives could have their own independent property—in the case of Kausalyā once mentioned as a thousand villages (2.28.7)—but allusions to this are meagre and late (e.g. 6.116.69-73 and App.I.72.25). Other brief references to the marriage ritual are to Daśaratha marrying Kaikeyī by taking her hand and leading her round the fire (2.37.8ab) and to Rāvaṇa marrying Mandodarī by taking hands over the fire (7.12.17).

Quite apart from the respect and subservience that a wife once married was expected to show to her husband, her position must have been rendered less secure by the possibility or in many cases actuality of competition from other wives, for polygamy seems to have been regular, at least for kings. This was of course traditional and even institutionalized in the ritual, in particular in the horse sacrifice, which finds a place in the Bālakāṇḍa (1.13.28).[15] The insecurity is well illustrated by Daśaratha's reaction of abandoning Kaikeyī as soon as he has kept his promise (2.12.11 and 37.6–9; cf. also 2 App.I.9.173–5 and 6.107.24–6) and even more graphically by Rāma saying that he can find another wife like Sītā but not another brother (6.39.5–6; cf. 796*), which on repetition in a more elaborate lament for Lakṣmaṇa becomes

[15] The names here given—*mahiṣī, parivṛktī* and *vāvātā*—are indeed drawn from the Vedic literature (e.g. *Vāj.S.* 23.24–8 and *Śat.Br.* 13.4.1.9).

effectively that wives are two a penny (6.2029* 5–6). Three of Daśaratha's queens are regularly named because they are the mothers of his sons—Kausalyā, Kaikeyī and Sumitrā—but they are not his only wives or concubines. The remainder may be added as an afterthought (e.g. 1.78.8: these three 'and the king's other women'), but several times a total is given. For example, Daśaratha summons his wives to say farewell to Rāma and three hundred and fifty women come surrounding Kausalyā (2.31.10–11) but just afterwards there is the wailing of a thousand women in the king's residence (2.31.16)—either a simple inconsistency or else the first figure is that of wives and concubines and the second includes all female attendants. However, the first figure occurs again when Rāma, saying farewell to his mother (*jananī*), sees there three hundred and fifty mothers (*mātaraḥ*, 2.34.32). References to the plurality of Daśaratha's wives are too numerous to list and occur at all stages of the text. Similarly there are references to numbers of wives for Vālin and Sugrīva (e.g. 4.16.10, 20.20, 24.28–9, 37.5) and to the extent of Rāvaṇa's harem (e.g. 3.36.26, 53.14–31, 5.7–8, 19.7, 22.31, 6.102.8), which even reaches seven thousand women.

The possibilities of tension and conflict in such a polygamous household were clearly considerable and play a significant part in the development of the plot. Mantharā plays on the jealousies and fears of Kaikeyī if she is no longer the favourite of the reigning king but only a step-mother (2.8.17 and 26; cf. 2.134*), and Rāma, as they leave Ayodhyā, talks sorrowfully to Lakṣmaṇa of the tensions between Kaikeyī and the other wives (2.47.15–16), while later elaborations of the story make Kaikeyī, as part of her tactics for getting her own way, accuse Daśaratha of preferring Kausalyā (2 App.I.9.67) and Kausalyā mourn the loss of Daśaratha's esteem and becoming a part of Kaikeyī's retinue (2.433*). One practical means of lessening such tensions was that of maintaining separate establishments; this is made explicit when Bharata, not finding his father in his own mother's residence decides to try Kausalyā's (2.66.12–13), besides being implied for example when Rāma going to Kausalyā goes in past doorkeepers and female attendants (2.17.4–5). Equally there is a strong emphasis on seniority among the queens and Kausalyā is frequently referred to as Daśaratha's chief queen, just as Sītā declares that she was handed over to Janaka's senior queen to bring up (2.110.32). So too Rāvaṇa in his infatuation with Sītā offers that she shall become mistress of all his wives (3.53.17; cf. 5.22.31).

More interesting, however, in terms of the way that the story developed over the centuries, is the question whether the marriage of Rāma and Sītā was from the beginning the monogamous union of later piety.

Obviously, it came to be so regarded and this is clearly presented in the Uttarakāṇḍa through the declaration that Rāma did not take another wife after banishing Sītā but used a golden statue of her as substitute in his sacrifices (7.89.4).[16] On the other hand, Sītā lamenting in the *aśoka* grove regrets the uselessness of her devotion to her husband (*ekapatnītva*) and speculates that Rāma will upon his return from exile enjoy the company of lovely women (5.26.13–14[ll.vv.]). It could be objected that this is only speculation but there are at least two other passages—also from the second stage—which explicitly speak of Rāma's wives and in fact come from virtually the beginning and the end of the main narrative. Mantharā, as she seeks to rouse Kaikeyī, says: 'Assuredly Rāma's excellent women will be delighted and your daughter-in-law will be saddened at Bharata's fall' (2.8.5). Then, in the preparations for Rāma's installation after his return, Śatrughna dresses up Rāma and Lakṣmaṇa, Daśaratha's wives adorn Sītā, and Kausalyā Rāghava's wives (6.116.16–18); Rāghava, 'descendant of Raghu', normally means Rāma, although it could signify Daśaratha except that his wives have been mentioned immediately before, but, despite the obvious symmetry of the passage a substantial number of manuscripts read instead the Vānaras' wives—who are quite out of place here—evidently to avoid the obvious implication, just as in the previous passage many manuscripts substitute a verse giving Rāma and Bharata just one wife each (2.139*). There does not seem to be any passage indisputably belonging to the earliest stage that gives an unambiguous declaration either way, although it is obviously the case that Rāma's and Sītā's union is effectively monogamous during their stay in the forest and the not infrequent description of Sītā as *dharmapatnī* (e.g. 3.32.14b, 47.28d, 48.5b, 5.7.68b[l.v.], 6.101.39b) may point in the same direction. The nearest to an explicit statement is when Rāma rejects Śūrpaṇakhā's advances on the grounds that she would not want a rival in Sītā and refers her on to Lakṣmaṇa as 'a handsome young bachelor' (3.17.1–5), for the implication is undoubtedly that only Sītā stands in Śūrpaṇakhā's way and that is certainly how it is taken since she goes on to attack Sītā; but it is doubtful whether too much should be read into this banter.

While polygamy is then the norm for the males of ruling families, adultery is very much castigated for both parties. Thus, Bharata, when trying to think of a reason for Rāma's exile, considers the possibility of adultery among crimes which he might have committed (2.66.38) and Sītā in her moral homily includes it among the two or three gravest sins

[16] Rāma's use of a golden image as surrogate is alluded to in *Gobhilasmṛti* 3.10 (= *Karmapradīpa* of Kātyāyana, fourth to sixth century AD.) and was presumably by then a well-known tale.

(3.8.3–5, also 122*), while among the elaborations introduced into Kausalyā's curse is abandoning one's own wife for another's (2.1802* 11–12)—a somewhat unnecessary elaboration since she already includes the one who violates his *guru's* bed (*gurutalpaga*, 2.69.26b), to whom Daśaratha also compares his crime of killing the ascetic youth (2.57.22d), both the crime and the term being redolent of the *dharmaśāstras* (e.g. *Manu* 9.235). These incidental examples belong to the second and fourth stages, after the start of brahmanical influence. It is seen also in the story of Indra's adultery with Gautama's wife Ahalyā, which appears in both the Bāla and the Uttara kāṇḍas (1.47.15—48.10 and 7.30.20–8).[17] In the latter, Indra is presented as bringing adultery into the world by his evil example. One interesting point about the Bālakāṇḍa account is that Ahalyā rejoins Gautama on the expiry of the curse laid on her for the offence (1.48.20–1). Indra's punishment of impotence in the first account is soon remedied by the gods and that of capture by an enemy in the second is mitigated by Brahmā's intervention.

Appeal to *smṛti*, tradition, and in particular the lawbooks, is made by Rāma when he gives as Vālin's crime, his incestuous union with Rūma, saying that death is laid down as the punishment for the man who out of lust approaches his own sister or his younger brother's wife (4.18.22; cf. *Manu* 11.171). Equally, Vālin in the course of his accusation against Rāma mentions among those who go to hell the *parivettṛ*, the younger brother who marries before his elder brother (4.17.32; cf. e.g. *Manu* 11.60 and *Viṣṇusmṛti* 37.15–16), while Aṅgada later brings up the accusation that Sugrīva has appropriated his elder brother's wife who should properly be treated as a mother (4.54.3; cf. e.g. *Manu* 9.57). The first two of these passages certainly belong to the second stage and all presumably reflect the beginning of brahmanical moralising. However, it is noticeable that there is in fact little condemnation of this taking over by the succeeding ruler of his predecessor's harem. Thus, at the end of the story, Vibhīṣaṇa enters the inner apartment and encourages Sītā with his women—obviously Rāvaṇa's who are now his; indeed, several manuscripts see the point and substitute the statement that he sent a message through the superintendents of his brother's harem (6.102.8cd and 3197*). Presumably such a practice was normal in the period of the epic's first stage but condemned later. From a later period still comes the incident in the Uttarakāṇḍa where Rāvaṇa's roving eye is caught by Rambhā's beauty as she passes, she resists his advances on the grounds that she is pledged to his nephew Nalakūbara, but Rāvaṇa counters by saying that as an Apsaras she is available to

[17] For translation and some comment see W.D.O'Flaherty, *Hindu Myths*, Harmondsworth, 1975, no. 28.

anyone; the result, which clearly provides the rationale for the episode, is that Nalakūbara curses Rāvaṇa that his head will split in seven pieces if he forces another woman against her will (7.26). A variant, with exactly the same purpose but different characters, is found in an addition to the Yuddhakāṇḍa in which Rāvaṇa rapes Puñjikasthalā as she is on her way to Pitāmaha (6 App.I.3.248–60).

Within the context of the main narrative, and in the first stage, we have Sītā's castigation of Lakṣmaṇa when she suspects his motives for staying with her rather than going after Rāma (3.43.21–3) and her reproof of Rāvaṇa for seeking another man's wife (e.g. 5.19.3–16); but both of these may as readily be considered condemnations of abduction and rape. Sītā many times warns Rāvaṇa of the dangers of seizing her (e.g. 3.46.22, 51.3–7 and 54.17; cf. Jaṭāyus' condemnation at 3.48.5–6). However, at least part of the objection is that he has seized her by trickery and not in fair fight (3.51.5); this reminds us both of Arjuna's capture of Kṛṣṇa's sister in the Mahābhārata and much later of Rājput traditions of winning a bride by force of arms.[18] Two other mythological examples of rape narrated are that of Añjanā, Hanumān's mother, stripped of her clothes and raped by the wind, Māruta (4.65.12–19), narrated purely factually to explain Hanumān's capabilities, and that of Arajā violated by king Daṇḍa (7.71.4–15), which is strongly denounced but also, as we have already seen,[19] involves a *pratiloma* union. One general comment, from perhaps a slightly unexpected angle, is contained in the late *kaccit* sarga, where it is said that women hate a man who uses force (2.94.22).

Emphasis on a wife's chastity is found prominently in the second stage expressed in terms of avoiding even the touch of a stranger. Thus, the thought of Sītā's being touched by another is terrible to Rāma (3.2.19) and she herself declares to Hanumān that she will not voluntarily touch another male (5.35.62–3); eventually this is put dramatically that she would not touch a Rākṣasa even with that least auspicious member, her left foot (5.24.9ab, omitted in several manuscripts and so in reality representative of the fourth stage). Public opinion on this point is made the reason for Rāma's rejection of Sītā twice over in the late second and third stages (6.103.18–24 and 7.42. 17–20).

[18] Marriage by capture (the *rākṣasa* form) is recognised as one of the eight types of marriage in the *dharmaśāstras*, provided that the woman's guardian is defeated in fair fight; however, it tends to fall into disfavour in later legal theory. The equivalence of earth (i.e. territory) and woman as legitimate conquests for a kṣatriya is one of the interesting points made by Minoru Hara in his article, 'The Rākṣasa Form of Marriage', JAOS 94, 1974, pp. 296–300.

[19] See p. 170.

Other aspects of sexual mores are of slight significance even in the later stages of development of the text. Despite the frankness of the descriptions of the physical beauty of various women, especially in the context of Rāvaṇa's approaches to them, there is virtually no description of love-play, the only exceptions being a few similes, all from the second stage—one describing the bashfulness of newly-married brides (4.29.28), one a young girl bearing the nail-marks and other signs of an amorous encounter (5.12.18), and a group of similes about a lovers' tiff and reconciliation (5.12.29–31). Indra's adultery with Ahalyā includes ignoring the proper times for intercourse (1.47.18), which also appear in a late addition to Kausalyā's curse (2.1802* 9–10), while a rationalization of menstrual impurity—not otherwise alluded to at all, by contrast with the Mahābhārata—is provided in the Uttarakāṇḍa where it comes by transfer of a quarter of Indra's sin of brahmanicide (7.77.14; cf. 4 App.I.14.45–8[l.v.]).[20]

The growing strictness of sexual mores is reflected also in the shift from women's active participation in public life to their virtually complete seclusion within the home and especially the inner apartment of the king's palace. This shift must have been a gradual one and have affected different strata of society at a varying rate, with the main impact first felt among the royal household. However, basic features of the story show that seclusion was by no means regular at the earliest period, since, for example, Sītā is able to accompany Rāma to the forest freely, driving openly through the town as they depart, and Daśaratha's wives go out with Bharata to persuade Rāma to return (2.77.6) and again to greet him on his triumphant return (6.115.10). Again, embedded in passages of the second stage but probably reflecting older conditions, we find that unmarried girls are among the auspicious items on parade for Rāma's planned and actual installations (2.13.11 and 6.116.57; cf. 2 App.I.10.24 and 6.116.35). Kaikeyī has tended Daśaratha on the battle-field, thereby gaining the two boons which form the lynch-pin of the narrative (2.9.12–13), and we learn incidentally that Mandodarī has travelled widely with Rāvaṇa (6.99.19–20). Mention is also made of women in the crowds thronging the streets on various occasions (e.g. 1.13.9 and 398*, 2.5.13 and 18, 2.327*, 2.60.19 [l.v.], 6.115.26, 7.82.13 and 18–19) in elaborations of the second to fourth stages, so clearly even by then seclusion was not regular for ordinary women. This is also presumably implicit in the miraculous entertainment provided by Bharadvāja, when the trees of his *āśrama* become women to tend and delight Bharata's soldiers (2.85.44–54). The presence of wives at some of the great public rituals or other

[20] Cf. O'Flaherty, op. cit., pp. 77–90.

ceremonial occasions is another common feature (e.g. 1.13.26–7, 21.2, 2.69.9, 70.19–21, 95.21–2, 6.80.48).

On the other hand, indications of seclusion are not lacking. The king's inner apartment (*antaḥpura*) is mentioned about fifty times in the text of the earlier books and twice as many references are in early as in later passages; but this need not necessarily imply very rigid seclusion and there is only one reference to a superintendent of women (*stryadhyakṣa*) in all the detail about Daśaratha's palace (2.14.3d) and three, in the fourth stage, to such officials in Vibhīṣaṇa's palace (6.3201* 1, 3203* 3 and 3204* 2), whereas we also find old and young women as the doorkeepers of Kausalyā's apartment (2.17.4–5), but eunuchs as harem guards only in a late part of the third stage (7.99.10). This is not the only inconsistency in the early sargas of the Ayodhyākāṇḍa: within one sarga it is recorded that Sītā goes freely to see Daśaratha and that she had till then not been seen even by the beings of the air (2.30.1 and 8), of which the former is more in accord with the general pattern. However, the Bālakāṇḍa mentions theatres for women (1.5.12a) in its elaborate and very late description of Ayodhyā. Perhaps a transition between freedom and strictness may be seen in another passage of the late second stage when Rāma insists that it is all right for women to be seen on various special occasions but does so in response to Vibhīṣaṇa's attempt to clear the place of men before Sītā comes (6.102.19–27).[21] Another feature of the later inferior position of women is introduced in the fourth stage when Sītā serves Rāma and Lakṣmaṇa and herself eats afterwards (2 App.I.26.73–6). Later still, in the fifth stage comes the declaration 'Happy sleeps the man in whose family a girl is not born to break his pride' (2.2396*), no doubt by the burden of marrying her.

An archaic feature still present in both the first and second stages is the presence of women in *āśramas* and actually as ascetics. Sītā herself is readily welcomed at the *āśramas* of Bharadvāja, Atri, Śarabhaṅga and Agastya (2.48.10–13, 109.6, 3.4.22, 10.21–6, 11.1–4, 12.1–8) and she is received into Vālmīki's *āśrama*, when exiled by Rāma, in a late expansion of the story (7.46–8). At Vālmīki's *āśrama*, however, the female ascetics live near the main hermitage, by implication in separate quarters (7.48.11 and 14), which sets this apart from other instances. Even in the Uttarakāṇḍa reference is also made to sages accompanied by their wives (7.82.13d). Seven individual female ascetics are mentioned, such as Atri's wife Anasūyā (2.109), Śabarī (3.70),[22]

[21] Cf. A. S. Altekar, *The Position of Women in Hindu Civilization*, 3rd ed., Delhi, 1962, p. 168.

[22] However, Śabarī is carefully stated to have been the attendant (*paricāriṇī*, 3.69.19 and 70.24) of the Mataṅgavana sages, presumably because of her lowly status either as a woman or perhaps more probably as belonging to a tribal group.

Svayamprabhā (4.50) and Vedavatī (7.17), and Sītā herself in her distress and emaciation is likened to one (*niyatā tāpasī*, 5.13.29d). On the other side can be set only Virādha's question about why Rāma and Lakṣmaṇa have a young woman with them (3.2.11), with its possible implication that this is not normal. However, we also find in the third stage the traditional mythological role of women as temptresses to distract ascetics in the stories of Ṛśyaśṛṅga (1.9) and Pulastya (7.2.7–9), or the Apsaras Rambhā sent to tempt Viśvāmitra (1.63).

The women who tempt Ṛśyaśṛṅga are identified in this version of the legend as prostitutes (1.9.5 and 7; cf. 1.8.21 and 309* 9–10). There are also references to the presence of prostitutes in the streets on various festive occasions (2.32.3, 45.9, App.I.2.56, App.I.10.31, 6.3457* 2), and Sītā says to Rāma that his leaving her behind is like an actor giving his wife to other men (2.27.8cd; cf. 77.15c), while the Bālakāṇḍa refers to the Apsarases as divine prostitutes (1.44.19–20). The concept of prostitutes as auspicious seems to be a relatively early feature in Indian society and is attested also, for instance, in some of the older parts of the Pali canon, so it is the more striking that the references in the Rāmāyaṇa tend to be among its later passages.

In its attitude to widows, also, the text shows a very ancient character. The standard terms for widows and widowhood (*vidhavā* and *vaidhavya*) are much commoner in the earliest stage and by the late second stage there is no sign that widows are inauspicious, since Daśaratha's widows take a full part in the celebration of Rāma's return (6.115–6); later still, however, widowhood is the greatest calamity that can befall a woman (7.514*). Even clearer is the absence of any reference to the custom of *satī*, of the wife burning herself on her husband's pyre, until the third stage when Vedavatī's mother immolates herself on Kuśadhvaja's death (7.17.13); later still a Southern addition has Kausalyā contemplate becoming a *satī* (2.1534*) and a Northeastern addition likens Laṅkā to a woman adorned and ready to die (6.607*). In all the various laments of Sītā, Tārā and Mandodarī for the supposed or actual deaths of their husbands there is no hint of it (e.g. 4.23.10, 5.18.8, 6.38.21, 99.23–4) and the nearest approach is when Sītā asks Rāvaṇa to kill her too along with Rāma (6.23.28–9), which comes from the second stage. A parallel to this from the fourth stage is when Tārā says to Rāma that to kill her would not be the sin of killing a woman but a kindness (4 App.I.14. 140–4). Instead, the possible remarriage of even such high-caste widows is envisaged or actually occurs, for the possibility of it underlies Sītā's harsh words to Lakṣmaṇa (3.43.21–3), Sugrīva takes over his brother's widow Tārā, who becomes his chief queen, and Vibhīṣaṇa similarly takes over Rāvaṇa's harem. More specifically these are instances of *niyoga*, remarriage with the brother-in-law, accepted in the *dharmasūtras* but increasingly restricted and discouraged in later legal works.

Of course, besides the question of producing a son to perform his father's obsequies, there was involved in such a custom the need to provide a woman with a guardian. There are several references to the need for women to be protected and to their lack of independence, such duty of protection falling, as one passage makes clear, on husband, then son, then other relatives, and as last resort on the king (2.55.18; cf. 2.47.3–4, 94.42, 3.48.5–7, 6 App.I.68.67, 7.24.2).

Another feature of the special position of women—common to most cultures—is their inviolability, which quite often is interpreted as simply stopping short of killing. This is naturally enough found at all stages: in the first stage Rāma and Lakṣmaṇa only disfigure Śūrpaṇakhā (3.17.17–22, cf. 32.11), of which a fourth stage doublet is Lakṣmaṇa's disfiguring of Ayomukhī (3 App.I.17.19–22); in the second stage, when the battle is going badly, Rāvaṇa prepares to kill Sītā but is dissuaded by Supārśva (6.80.29–56); in the Bālakāṇḍa Viśvāmitra cites mythological parallels to overcome Rāma's reluctance to kill Tāṭakā, especially that Indra once slew Virocana's daughter and Viṣṇu killed Bhṛgu's wife, mother of Kāvya (1.24.13–19).[23] One fifth stage insertion (6.1552*) then makes Indrajit cite Rāma's killing of Tāṭakā to justify his own planned killing of Sītā—a somewhat unexpected development. Many further incidents or allusions could be cited (e.g. 2.72.20–2, 4 App.I.17.24, 5 App.I.42–6, 6.68.17–21 and 27). There is also the tendency to link old people, women and children whether explicitly or implicitly as all needing protection (e.g. 1.13.9, 2.5.18 and 69.24).

Related to the last is the matter of proper behaviour towards women. For instance, as they depart for the forest, Rāma and Lakṣmaṇa help Sītā into the chariot or boat and prepare a seat for her (2.35.12–14, 38.12, 46.62–3 and 49.9–10). Lakṣmaṇa's general attitude to Sītā is one of respectful service and he declares that he trusts her as a deity (3.43.26), but in later stages this becomes exaggerated, for example, when Rāma shows Lakṣmaṇa the clothes dropped by Sītā as she was carried off (4.6.18), in a later addition Lakṣmaṇa denies acquaintance with anything above Sītā's anklets (4.147*).

As elsewhere, however, such exaggerated respect coexists with a low opinion of women's personal qualities. Immediately after declaring that Sītā is a deity to him, Lakṣmaṇa goes on to call women fickle and

[23] It is interesting therefore to note the increasing emphasis on the inviolability of women shown in Bhavabhūti's censure of Rāma's action in his own literary version of the Rāma story (*Uttararāmacarita* 5.34).

divisive, eager to get their own way and given to fits of temper (3.43. 26–7), although it must be admitted that he has had some provocation from her. Also from the first stage probably, though not integral to the plot, is Agastya's praise for Sītā as not being subject to the usual womanly defects of fickleness and so forth (3.12.5–7). The prime example of a woman getting her own way is of course Kaikeyī (2.9.16–19, 10.16, App.I.9.68–71 and 190–1), to whom are also attributed in later passages the defects of temper and vanity (2.436*, 1710*, App.I.9.52 and 81–2). Emphasis on such defects is very much a late feature. Indeed, apart perhaps from Sītā coveting the golden deer (which is not commented on in this connection) the only examples of excessive curiosity are late—for example, Ahalyā's curiosity to experience love-making with Indra (1.47.19) and Kaikeyī's mother willing to cause her husband's death in satisfaction of her curiosity (2 App.I.14.35–52).[24]

In keeping with this general view of woman's role in life, there is very little in the text relevant to the education of women. In the first part of the Ayodhyākāṇḍa we learn that Sītā is 'well versed in royal duties' (*abhijñā rājadharmāṇām*, 2.23.4c) as she prepares to take part in Rāma's installation, and then, as they make ready to depart for the forest, she tells how as a girl she heard about forest-life from a *bhikṣinī*, after astrologers had predicted it for her, and claims scriptural authority for her assertion that it is women's duty to follow their husbands anywhere (2.26.6–15). This implies a certain amount of formal instruction for her and this is endorsed by Hanumān's assumption, when he ponders how to greet her, that Sītā would understand learned Sanskrit (5.28.17–19). Not even in the Bālakāṇḍa do we find any explicit statement about Sītā's education. Yet the female ascetics were expected to be learned: for example, the Śabarī ascetic is catechised by Rāma (3.70.7–8) and Svayaṃprabhā is *sarvajñā* (4.51.17a).

Allusions to formal education or study are extremely meagre in the first two stages, but the Bālakāṇḍa's account of Rāma's youth naturally includes rather more information and the third and later stages in general contain many more allusions to teachers and pupils. Rāma's own education seems to have had a distinctly practical slant. In the opening chapter of the Ayodhyākāṇḍa he is described as taking part in

[24] The latter incident is commented on by D. P. Vora, *Evolution of Morals in the Epics*, Bombay, 1959, p. 113. It may well provide the basis for an episode in the Khotanese version of the Rāmāyaṇa (see p. 265).

conversations with learned and respectable elders in the intervals of his weapon-training (2.1.17), as the best of those who know the science of the bow (*dhanurvedavidāṃ śreṣṭhaḥ*, 23c) and as versed in military tactics and various practical skills, while later Hanumān describes him to Sītā as being trained in royal learning and knowing the *Yajurveda* and *dhanurveda* (5.33.13–14). In both we see the close association of traditional learning and military training, natural for a kṣatriya, which is interestingly reinforced by Rāma's request to Lakṣmaṇa as they prepare for their departure to fetch him his weapons from the house of his teacher (2.28.14/735*). The very term *dhanurveda*, 'science of the bow', suggests that for the kṣatriya that is his proper field of learning, parallel to the three or four Vedas of the brāhmans, and it is no doubt significant that it is linked with the *Yajurveda*, whose more ritualistic emphasis might well be appropriate to a king's residual sacrificial duties. Although these allusions come from passages assigned to the second stage, they probably reflect the original pattern, which nonetheless persists to a large extent into the later stages where reference to Rāma's education is commoner. The Bālakāṇḍa opens with Nārada's declaration of Rāma as the ideal hero who 'upholds tradition, knows the truth of Vedas and Vedāṅgas and is skilled in the lore of archery' (1.1.13). Significantly, however, it passes from the birth of the four brothers to the arrival of Viśvāmitra in a single chapter (1.17), for Viśvāmitra's arrival and claiming of Rāma to help him signals the start of Rāma's exploits, although Daśaratha is loath to part with him and urges that he is still untrained, especially in weaponry (1.19.7). The text is content to say that the brothers are Veda-knowing heroes endowed with knowledge and good qualities (1.19.14) but the fourth stage feels compelled to add that Rāma was trained in elephant-riding, horse-riding and charioteering and skilled in archery (1.511*) and that all were proficient in recitation of the Vedas, obedience to their father and archery (1.513*). However, Viśvāmitra soon presents Rāma with the *vidyās* named Balā and Atibalā (1.21.14–18), where the term *vidyā* means as in several of its rather infrequent occurrences not so much 'wisdom, knowledge' as 'occult knowledge, spell'. Viśvāmitra's continued instruction of Rāma is then made the excuse for the inclusion of several stories in the next few chapters. Subsequently, it is narrated how Viśvāmitra secures the gift of divine weapons and instructs Rāma in their use, which consists in fact of giving their names (1.26–7); Viśvāmitra himself, it is later recorded, gained the lore of archery along with the Vedāṅgas and Upaniṣads from Śiva (1.54.16).

The role of the teacher is much less heavily emphasised than in much Sanskrit literature. The two main terms, *ācārya* and *upādhyāya*, between them occur just over thirty times in the text but with very different distributions, for *ācārya* occurs predominantly in the first stage and the commoner *upādhyāya* in the third; incidentally, as in other older Sanskrit literature *guru* is not restricted to teacher but means any respected senior and so can be used to describe rather than designate a teacher (e.g. 6.20.7a); indeed Vasiṣṭha urges his claims to Rāma's respect by citing the proverbial statement that a man has three *gurus*, his father and mother and his teacher, the last qualifying because he gives wisdom (2.103.2–3). Rāma gives a slightly different form of the saying in his defence of his actions to Vālin, declaring that there are three fathers—the older brother, the father himself and the one who gives wisdom—and three sons—the younger brother, the son himself and a worthy pupil (4.18.13–14). Later, with fine irony, Rāvaṇa upbraids his two spies, Śuka and Sāraṇa, declaring that teachers are of no avail if one will not learn (6.20.7–8). Apart from such aphorisms, the only mentions of teachers and pupils in the first or second stages are purely formal, in allusions to the ascetics' hermitages, and only become common from the third stage. References to learned men, though never frequent, also become much commoner in the third stage, where the term *vipra* is usual, by contrast with *paṇḍita* in the first two stages. The much later educational institution, the *maṭha* or college, occurs only in a passage without manuscript support found in the Kumbhakonam edition (2.1867* 1); it is no doubt significant that it occurs in this edition from South India where the institution of the *maṭha* first appeared.

In any case instruction was evidently entirely oral. The term *śāstra*, therefore, which is among the commonest in this field though still occurring under fifty times, should be understood in its general sense of the body of learning on a subject sometimes codified by one individual; it does not of course indicate a written textbook. We have just seen the role of story-telling in Rāma's upbringing and the flourishing of story-telling is one of the characteristics of a well-ordered state (2.61.14). The importance of memory in consequence is indicated in a passage from the second stage where Hanumān's hesitation and uncertainty as he first sees Sītā is likened to a vague memory only recalled by an effort (5.13.36). More definite allusions to learning by heart are found from the third stage onwards, such as Kuśa and Lava learning the Rāmāyaṇa by heart (1.4.11–12) and Bharata learning the Vedas as well as other subjects at his uncle's (2 App.I.4.13–24). When the many virtues of the inhabitants of Daśaratha's kingdom are extolled, they are described as learned by a term which literally means 'having heard much' (*bahuśruta*, 1.6.14b and 13.16b).

Recitation of the Vedas would no doubt also have been regular but it is noticeable that reference to it is virtually absent from the first stage. One exception is a reference to the *sāmans* chanted at Daśaratha's funeral (2.70.18/1812* 65–6).[25] From the second stage onwards, reflecting the gradual penetration of the epic by brāhman standards, allusion to it becomes steadily more frequent. For example, in the relatively ornate description of the hermitages in Daṇḍakāraṇya with which the Āraṇyakāṇḍa opens, they are described as 'echoing with the sound of recitation and ornamented by eminent brāhmans learned in the Vedas' (3.1.8, cf. 5), while Rāma's description of the rainy season includes the statement that the month of Prauṣṭhapada, the start of the rains, is the time for brāhmans to chant *sāmans* (4.27.34, cf. *Gobhila Gṛhyasūtra* 3.3). Reference to brāhman disputations is even more clearly late: the *kaccit* sarga puts the bad side with its condemnation of worldly brāhmans skilled in sophistry (2.94.32–3), while an addition to the dirge on the sorrows of a kingless state gives the absence of men learned in the *śāstras* debating as another bad sign (2.1566* 3–4). The only reference which is really in context comes from the third stage, where such disputations take place during the year of preparation for the *aśvamedha* (1.13.14).

Probably the fullest list of the subjects of study comes in the fourth-stage passage about Bharata's education at his uncle's, which describes Bharata as accomplished in the lore of archery, in the Veda, and in ethics, skilled in politics and also in athletics or gymnastics, familiar with elephant lore and chariot lore, painting and writing, jumping and swimming, and experienced in astronomy (2 App.I.4.54–8). In many ways the nearest parallel to this is the description of the audience for Kuśa and Lava as they recite the Rāmāyaṇa being made up of those who are learned in phonetics, metrics, poetics, ritual detail and astronomy, in argument and debate (7.1313*), and also in metre, the Purāṇas, music, painting, singing and dancing (7.1314* + 1315*). There is nothing comparable to these lists from the earlier stages.

Apart from the science of archery (*dhanurveda*) already referred to in connection with Rāma's education, there is surprisingly little evidence of formal military training in the earlier passages. This is undoubtedly due to the lack of interest in the brothers' youth rather than the absence of such training. A description of the inhabitants of Ayodhyā as practising archery and killing wild animals (1.5.20–1), though from

[25] However, as I note elsewhere (p. [162]), some details may well have been added to the description of the funeral. In any case, the context is exceptional in almost requiring such a mention.

the third stage, probably indicates the extent to which training in the chief weapons used was gained through the hunting of game, which for the ruling class would, as in other parts of the world, have combined sport and food.

Various practical branches of learning were clearly well developed, although we have no references to the formal learning processes. Thus, the number of allusions drawn from the field of medicine indicate considerable attainments in it. Doctors (*vaidya*) are listed among the various trades and professions in Bharata's entourage (2.77.14c) and occasionally elsewhere. Numerous similes refer to the role of herbs as medicines, even as antidotes to snakebite (5.1.19), while Bharata likens his mother's action in securing Rāma's banishment on top of the king's death to putting alkali on a wound (2.67.3). During the battle scenes, at one point Vibhīṣaṇa decides from their appearance that Rāma and Lakṣmaṇa are unconscious, not dead (6.38.31–2, 40.22–3), and that they can be revived by spells and herbs (6.40.28–30), while subsequently, when Rāma and Lakṣmaṇa are again senseless, Hanumān fetches herbs from the Himālayas (6.61); Suṣeṇa also heals Lakṣmaṇa twice (6.79.13–16 and 89.9–25). Some knowledge of embalming seems to lie behind the vat of oil used to preserve Daśaratha's body (2.60.12–14) and that of the brāhman youth (7.66.2–4).[26]

The care of animals also finds mention from time to time, such as the feeding and watering of horses in connection with Rāma's departure (2.44.15, 21–3). Also from the first stage comes a simile based on the popular belief that parturition is lethal to the she-mule (3.41.39d). Increasing later elaboration includes, for example, a catalogue of different breeds of horses and elephants (1.6.20–2). The practical value of this is obvious, although there is also evidence of quite a familiarity with wild-life which might be dignified with the term zoology.[27]

Similarly, the building of the altar for Daśaratha's sacrifice is described with some use of terms relevant to geometry drawn from the ritual treatises (*kalpasūtra*, 1.13.33b): thus the sacrificial posts are octagonal (*aṣṭāśri*, 20c) and priests skilled in mensuration (*śulbakarma* 'rope-work', 22d) build up the bricks. The reference in a fourth-stage passage to Rāma definitely laying out their *āśrama* (2.1213* 1–2) probably

[26] The use of oil to preserve a body in this way is known to the *Śrautasūtras*, two of which lay down that an *āhitāgni* (one who has maintained the sacrificial fire) who has died away from home should be placed in a vat of oil and brought home in a cart (*Satyāṣāḍhaśrautasūtra* 29.4.29 and *Vaikhānasaśrautasūtra* 31.23).

[27] See pp. 88–98.

points in the same direction. However, there is nothing comparable from the earlier stages.

From the number of similes alluding to the stars and planets at all stages of the epic, some basic astronomy was known at an early date. But the more detailed references are from the second or later stages, such as the fact that the sun shifts south in winter (3.15.8) or a long list of asterisms in similes (5.55.1–4). Later a growing interest in astrology motivates the insertion of various data, such as Rāma's horoscope (1.506*) and the auspicious moment for his return to Ayodhyā (6.3430*), but the mention of the asterism Puṣya in relation to his proposed installation in the early sargas of the Ayodhyākāṇḍa seems more or less integral to the narrative and may therefore be original, despite the considerable modification these sargas have undergone in transmission.[28]

The question of writing in the Rāmāyaṇa has been extensively discussed,[29] especially with regard to its bearing on the date of the poem. There are in fact very few references in the text but these are all to marking objects with a name, not to the use of writing for extended documents of whatever type. The better known are the two mentions of the ring marked with his own name which Rāma gives to Hanumān as a token for Sītā (4.43.11 and 5.34.2); most recently Sankalia, regarding this as a definite signet-ring, has argued that therefore this episode postdates the introduction of signet-rings via the Indo-Greeks. However, despite the expansion visible in the second passage, both references belong apparently to the first stage, as do two references to arrows marked with names, and it seems impossible to assign so late a date to the core of the work. Equally, it seems implausible to dismiss all four as later interpolations, especially since, as Sankalia rightly notes, the ring motif appears integral to the plot.[30] One of the references

[28] See pp. 210 and 218 and my RA pp. 121–2. Jacobi sought to use the reference to Puṣya in relation to winter at 3.15.12 as a means of dating, arguing that its shining all night at midwinter pointed to the seventh century BC. (*Das Râmâyaṇa*, pp. 108–9); however, this reference definitely belongs to the second stage. He also considers that the description of a solar eclipse as an omen at 3.22.11–14 owes its vividness to being based on actual observation, in this case in the sixth or possibly eighth century BC (ibid. pp. 109–11).

[29] E. g. Jacobi, op. cit., p. 38n. and H.D. Sankalia, *Rāmāyaṇa—Myth or Reality*? New Delhi, 1973.

[30] Op. cit., pp. 55–6. However, though the ring motif is central to the plot, its inscribing is not, and we may note that Sītā gives Hanumān as a return token for Rāma a jewel from her hair (*cūḍāmaṇi*, 5.36.52), for the individuality of the piece is here obviously its authentication.

to arrows uses exactly the same compound for 'marked with Rāma's name' as one of the ring references (*rāmanāmāṅkita*, 6.52.25d, cf. 5.34.2c), which serves to tie them together; the other is less unequivocal and could simply denote some mark of Rāma and Lakṣmaṇa's ownership (*iṣavo rāmalakṣmaṇalakṣaṇāḥ*, 5.19.21cd), but variant readings indicate that it was subsequently understood as indicating their names, thus definitely suggesting writing. However, the point that all of these references are to such specialised use may suggest that they are in fact archaic, belonging to the period when writing was known but not yet used for general communication, of which the first recorded instance is the Aśokan edicts of the third century BC.

Certainly, there is never any reference to a written message in any of the various accounts of messengers or ambassadors going back and forth. The messengers sent by Vasiṣṭha to bring Bharata back to Ayodhyā deliver their message orally (2.64.2), Lakṣmaṇa delivers Rāma's ultimatum to Sugrīva by word of mouth (4.29.50, 33.6, etc.), and the various embassies sent to Rāvaṇa all give their messages orally. Indeed, the first references actually to reading or writing are from later parts of the third stage, in the context of Kuśa and Lava's recitation of the Rāmāyaṇa called a novel form of composition (*pāṭhyajāti*, 7.85.2c), and in the *phalaśruti*, 'recital of benefits', which ends the opening chapter of the Bālakāṇḍa:

> Any who read this purifying, sin-cancelling, holy and Veda-equalling saga of Rāma will be freed from all sin. The reader of this life-giving tale, the Rāmāyaṇa, will be honoured in heaven after death, in company with his sons and grandsons and his retinue.
>
> Were the reader twice-born, he would attain eloquence,
> if a kṣatriya, attain temporal power,
> if a trader, an honourable fortune,
> if a śūdra, he would attain greatness. (1.1.77–9)

The verb for reading (√*paṭh*) or its derivatives also occurs in the other *phalaśrutis* at the ends of the Yuddha and Uttara kāṇḍas which are relegated to the status of * passages (e.g. 6.3703(F)* 7, 3703(G)* 5,8, 7.1520* 7, 1522* 4,6,9). These *phalaśrutis* also contain references to writing (√*likh*, 6.3709* 6, 7.1537* 1, 1540* 17) and to a manuscript or book (*pustaka*, 7.1527(C)* 7); there are also a very few other references to writing in other passages of the fourth or fifth stages (e.g. 2.1* 2, 63* 4, App.I.5.12). There is also one stanza in the Sundarakāṇḍa read by some Southern manuscripts in which Hanumān compares Sītā in her emaciated state to the wisdom of someone who is accustomed to read on the new moon day wasting away (5.1259* = 1356*).

That reading and writing are mentioned only in such late passages might indicate brahmanical abhorrence of its use, but this is evidenced only with regard to its religious use, and such an explanation is valid only if one is prepared to accept the Rāmāyaṇa as of brahmanical origin rather than a kṣatriya work later brahmanised. Altogether, the balance of the evidence is in favour of regarding the Rāmāyaṇa as belonging in origin to a period well before the general use of writing. Its own oral nature would anyway suggest this and it is interesting therefore to note that Minoru Hara has pointed to the story of Nārada's telling Vālmīki about Rāma (1.1.6–76 and 2.1–41) as evidence for Vālmīki himself as a bard, and equally the story of Kuśa and Lava (7.63 with App.I.9 and 84) as evidence for its transmission 'from the aged teacher to young pupils as is seen today in the living Slavic oral epic tradition.'[31] There may of course in both be an element of deliberate alignment with such tradition. On the other hand, we may note the frequency of occurrence of the reciter (*vācaka*) in the *phalaśrutis* as evidence of the continuance of the memory of the tradition, if not the tradition itself, while the Northern recension includes eulogists and reciters (*bandin, vācaka*, 2.753* 1+5) among those to whom Rāma makes gifts on his departure from court.

The question of language was also once discussed as much as that of writing. The position of the epic language in relation to other forms of Sanskrit has already been dealt with in detail, but it is perhaps appropriate at this stage to say a little about the supposed internal evidence on the point. Essentially these are a very limited number of occasions on which one of the characters is depicted as using a particular type of speech, either polished or colloquial. In some the polished form of speech is characterised as *saṃskṛta*, 'perfected', but this is never opposed to *prākṛta*, which always has its basic meaning 'of ordinary people, common' and is not used to denote a type of speech.[32] Perhaps the nearest in fact to the use of technical terms in the text is the occasion when Vibhīṣaṇa speaks in clear language, free from colloquialisms (*agrāmyapadavat*, 6.28.6); but there is by the fourth stage a reference to the study of grammar in its entirety, which Rāma takes to be one of Hanumān's accomplishments (4 App.I.3.3). One element of language study, phonetics or more simply correct pronunciation, is found in the second stage when Bharadvāja is described as using clear speech (2.85.19).

[31] 'Vālmīki, the Singer of Tales', in *S.K.De Memorial Volume*, ed. R. C. Hazra and S. C. Banerji, Calcutta, 1972, pp. 117–28.

[32] Jacobi was of this opinion (op. cit., p. 115) and it is confirmed by my own analysis of all occurrences of *prākṛta* in the text.

Even when *saṃskṛta* is used of language, it does not necessarily imply the later views. Thus, when Hanumān is pondering exactly how to speak to Sītā in order to avoid alarming her he decides in favour of 'human' polished speech (*vācaṃ . . . mānuṣīṃ saṃskṛtām*, 5.28.17cd, cf. *mānuṣaṃ vākyam*, 19b), in contrast either to his own monkey speech as Jacobi considered,[33] or more naturally to the polished speech of brāhmans (*dvijātir iva saṃskṛtām*, 18b) which risks confusion with Rāvaṇa; apparently here learned, brahmanised speech is contrasted with 'human', that is ordinary, speech but both called Sanskrit. The basic meaning of *saṃskṛta* as 'polished, perfected' is reflected in the use of the closely related *saṃskāra* 'embellishment' when Hanumān seeing Sītā unornamented because of her grief mentally compares her to an utterance devoid of embellishment which expresses its meaning (5.13.43); this passage belongs to the second stage and so quite naturally expresses the tendency to see suitable speech as being properly ornate. In a very late incident, when Ilvala addresses some brāhmans to tell them that the meal—of his brother's flesh, disguised as mutton—is prepared (*bhrātaraṃ saṃskṛtaṃ . . . meṣarūpiṇam*, 3.10.55ab), he is described as *saṃskṛtaṃ vadan* (54b) which could be taken to mean 'speaking refined' (as some commentators do) but in the context more naturally to mean 'saying that (the meal) was ready'. There is thus an awareness of different levels or styles of speech but none of really divergent languages.

While Vālmīki's enquiry to Nārada about the ideal man as the prologue to the whole Rāmāyaṇa suggests both the traditional story and its oral transmission, the next two sargas put rather a different slant on both aspects. For immediately afterwards Vālmīki observes the killing of a crane which moves him to compassion and leads him to give utterance to his feelings in a *śloka* (1.2.12–17), confirmed as a new invention by Brahmā's words (1.2.29–36); thus, however traditional the story, its form of expression is here presented as novel. Then, the third chapter opens with Vālmīki, in order to learn more of the story, having recourse to meditation (1.3.1–2), that is to excogitation of the narrative for himself. We seem in fact to have a more or less deliberate blending of innovation and tradition, which is maintained in the account of Kuśa and Lava learning the Rāmāyaṇa from Vālmīki—the traditional, oral element—and giving its first public performance before Rāma—the innovatory aspect (1.4.1–12 and 22–7). This recitation or chanting of the poem before Rāma is narrated again in greater detail in the Uttarakāṇḍa (7.84–5).

[33] Loc. cit.

In all these contexts, but nowhere else in the text, the epic is referred to as a poem (*kāvya*), a definite literary production, and there is also one allusion to poets (*kavi*, 1.4.20c/212* 2). However, the concept of the epic as the *ādikāvya*, the first literary production, does not appear outside the undoubtedly late *phalaśrutis*, 'recital of benefits', both those at the end of the Yuddha and Uttara kāṇḍas and one exceptionally added in the fifth stage to the Ayodhyākāṇḍa (2.2335* 6). Yet, in referring to the epic as a literary production, the Bālakāṇḍa enumerates the *rasas*, the aesthetic qualities recognised by literary theory (1.4.8/203* 15–16). Only in the Uttarakāṇḍa passage is there any reference to the subdivisions of the poem. There it is stated that Kuśa and Lava recited twenty sargas a day (7.84.9 and 85.11–12) and that the whole poem is 500 sargas long (7.85.20), to which insertions add 2400 *ślokas* and 100 episodes (7.1328*) and six books along with Uttara (7.1330*). The same type of additional details and the same equivocation over the status of the Uttarakāṇḍa are seen in the *phalaśrutis*, some of those at the end of the Yuddhakaṇda referring to the epic as complete at that point. Since such passages belong to a very late stage in the growth of the epic, this is strong internal evidence for only reluctant admission of the final book into the poem.

Although by its nature the Rāmāyaṇa is clearly an epic, this admittedly late stress on its literary character is justified—certainly by comparison with the Mahābhārata. However, unlike that epic, it does not include to anything like the same extent examples of other types of literature. There is scarcely anything corresponding to the lengthy didactic portions of the Mahābhārata that are closely connected with the *dharmaśāstras*, nor are there lengthy discourses on ethics and philosophy; the nearest approach is Jābāli's use of materialist arguments in an attempt to persuade Rāma to return and Rāma's firm reply (2.100–1, amplified in 2241*), although some other passages have also been expanded or added to provide moral justification or defence of elements in the narrative. There are a number of genealogies, especially of the Ikṣvākus (1.69.18–31, 2.102.5–29), but these are a natural outgrowth of the work's basic concerns. Equally, there are a certain number of allusions to folk-tales or other traditional stories, such as those of the crow and the palm tree (3.39.16), the elephant's view of the dangers from relatives (6.10.6–7) or the tiger and the bear (6.101.34), but none of these is told *in extenso*. There is also only one passage of Purāṇa-style prophecy provided by the Niśākara episode (4.61), in which the term Purāṇa as the title of that type of literature occurs (3a); otherwise the nearest is the description of the *sūta* Sumantra as *purāṇavid* 'knowing ancient matters' (2.13.17b and 14.1d) where the allusion is by no means necessarily to the extant class of texts. In any case both passages belong to the second stage and the Niśākara episode is altogether anomalous.

Another feature of the epic's presentation of itself in these passages is the inter-connection of recitation and music. This is indicated by Vālmīki's words on inventing the *śloka*: 'This saying of mine, in my sorrowful affliction, is metrical, with equal syllables and adapted to the rhythm of strings: it shall be the *śloka*, without dispute' (1.2.17). It is shown even more directly by the use of √*gā/gai* 'to sing' and its derivatives for the recitation of the text; the same term is used of the *sāmans* chanted at Daśaratha's funeral (2.70.18, cf. 4.27.34) and also more generally of singing together with dancing and acting (e.g. 2.6.14), while panegyric verses and eulogies (*gāthā, stuti*, 2.82.8) are mentioned along with the sound of singing and musical instruments. To underline the musical connections, when Kuśa and Lava recite the Rāmāyaṇa (1.4.7–9), it is again described as 'adapted to the rhythm of strings' (7d, cf. 7.84.14d and 85.3b) and as provided with the three lengths of note and the seven primary notes (7bc, cf. 7.85.3a and 1320*), while Kuśa and Lava themselves are described as knowing the essence of music and being skilled in practising registers and scales (9ab). Dr. te Nijenhuis has drawn attention to the fact that this passage uses the same musical terminology as Bharata, Dattila and the other ancient Indian musicologists.[34] Her translation here of the Bālakāṇḍa passage is:

> In a reciting and in a singing way they sang poetry, which was sweet, furnished with the three durations (i.e. the durations of notes and syllables, viz.: *laghu, guru* and *pluta*), based on the seven jātis, furnished with [the accompaniment of] stringed instruments and with speeds (7), endowed with the comic, erotic, pathetic, furious, heroic, terrible, odious and other sentiments (8). The two brothers, knowing the essence of music, being skilled in practising registers and scales, and being well-versed in producing notes, are like two Gandharvas (9).

These last are in fact the most technical of the musical allusions in

[34] E. Wiersma-te Nijenhuis, ed. and tr., *Dattilam: a compendium of ancient Indian music*, Orientalia Rheno-Traiectina 11, Leiden, 1970, pp. 62–3. Since Bharata's *Nāṭyaśāstra* and the *Dattilam* probably belong to the early centuries AD, this fits well with the date assumed for the third stage of the Rāmāyaṇa. The three registers (*tristhāna*), corresponding to high, middle and low octaves, are mentioned in a second stage passage describing the singing of Rāvaṇa's women and likening it to that of Apsarases in heaven (5.3.24) as well as in one much later passage (7 App.I.9.3* 1; cf. *Nāradīyā Śikṣā Sāmavedīyā* 1.1.7 and *Dattilam* 8).

the whole epic.[35] Much more typical are passing mentions of various musical instruments, both in the context of leisure and recreation and in battle scenes, where the conch in particular is much used as a signal. The sound of music or singing is part of the regular description of the three cities and also, in the later stages, of any festive occasion, such as Bharadvāja's entertainment of Bharata's army (2.85.40–6), or place for recreation, as in Rāma's *aśoka* grove (7.41.15). Bharadvāja's entertainment includes two terms for musicians—drummers and cymbal-players (*mārdaṅgika, śamyāgrāha*, 46ab)—as well as referring to several Gandharvarājas as singing, among whom it names Nārada, Tumburu, Gopa and Parvata (43, cf. Mbh. 5.11.12, 6.7.18, 12.311.15); the degree of detail is indicative of the lateness of this passage. As a result of this development of the Gandharvas into celestial musicians, seen more clearly in the Mahābhārata, the derivative term *gāndharva* can mean music; however it does so on only four of its ten occurrences in the text (1.4.9a, 6.42.23d, 7.23.43c and 85.10b), once more illustrating the lateness of this development.

In general, however, the frequency of occurrence of musical allusions increases steadily through the successive stages of development, but no term is really frequent at any stage with the limited exception of singing in the context of the recitation of the Rāmāyaṇa from the third stage. General terms for music or musical instruments (*vāditra, vādya*) are quite rare and there is only one occurrence of the related term for musician (*vādaka*, 2.14.26c), whereas the terms for songs (*gīta, geya*) and singers (*gātṛ, gāyaka*) are a little commoner. But there are as many as twenty-two individual instruments named, of which half are drums or related percussion instruments (*āḍambara, jharjhara, ḍiṇḍima, dundubhi, paṭaha, paṇava, bherikā, bherī, maḍḍuka, muraja* and *mṛdaṅga*),[36] but of these only three occur several times in the first stage (*dundubhi, bherī* and *mṛdaṅga*) and two others once (*paṇava* and *muraja*). However, the commonest instrument is the conch (*śaṅkha*)

[35] The attempt to see in *kaiśikācāryaiḥ* at 5.1.158c a reference to the *Kaiśika rāga* is totally implausible, even though the commentators agree on it; moreover, the reading is by no means certain. P. C. Dharma, 'Musical Culture in the Rāmāyaṇa', *Indian Culture* 4, 1937–8, pp. 445–54, was therefore right to mention it with reserve.

[36] There is no indication within the text of the precise nature of these instruments or how one differs from another; however, most of the terms are found in Bharata's *Nāṭyaśāstra*, which distinguishes the drums used to provide a variety of notes (*mṛdaṅga, paṇava* and *dardura*, 33.2cd etc.) from those for low notes only (*bherī, paṭaha, dundubhi* and *ḍiṇḍima*, 33.27) and mentions among minor instruments of the first class the *muraja* (11b) and *jhallarī* (13c, perhaps the same as the *jharjhara* of the Rāmāyaṇa), classing them all as percussion instruments (*ātodya*, 1a and 2a).

because of its use as a war signal. The *tūrya* also occurs several times in warlike contexts and once apparently the noise of conches is described also as the sound of *tūryas* (2.75.2–3), suggesting that it is some kind of horn or trumpet. The only other wind instrument is the bamboo flute, *vaṃśa* or *veṇu*, each of which is found once only in the text but more often in the fourth stage. One is in the description of Hanumān's search in Rāvaṇa's harem (5.8), where its sleeping inhabitants clasp various instruments, which include also three sorts of drum not mentioned elsewhere in the first three stages (*āḍambara, ḍiṇḍima* and *maḍḍuka*); these are summed up as percussion instruments (*ātodya*, 5.8.45a), another term found only here. In addition, fourth stage modifications to this passage include the only mentions of a particular type of *vīṇā*, the *vipañcī* (v.l. 5.8.34a, 5.277* 2), one of the two types given in the *Nāṭyaśāstra* (29.120). Another passage of the second stage mentions in a simile a *vallakī*, a kind of lute, but most Northern manuscripts omit this stanza (5.15.23), and the instrument is not otherwise attested before the fourth stage.

The *vīṇā* itself is not common and was evidently of the ancient arched harp type played with a plectrum, as an elaborate simile from the fourth stage comparing it with a bow demonstrates (6 App.I.16.117–20).[37] The term *koṇa* in fact denotes both plectrum and drumstick. Bells are also occasionally mentioned, both the larger *ghaṇṭā* and the small *kiṅkiṇī/kiṅkiṇīka* which was also worn as ornament by women. The latter term is clearly onomatopoeic, as are many of the terms for drums, but the high proportion of these terms for which a Dravidian or Munda origin has been suggested may possibly suggest that especially the percussion instruments were cultural borrowings;[38] a notable exception is the conch (*śaṅkha*, cf. Greek *kónkhē*), fulfilling the role of battle trumpet. The striking of the drum could also be a martialling signal (e.g. 6.23.21) and the noise of battle is occasionally likened to music; the most elaborate example is a metaphor worked out over a complete stanza (6.42.23), with the battle as music (*gāndharva*), the bowstring as the strings (of the *vīṇā*, hiccups as the beat or measure (*tāla*) and deep groans as songs (*saṃgīta*).[39]

Just as the Gandharvas are the celestial musicians, so the Apsarases

[37] On the original nature of the *vīṇā* see te Nijenhuis, op. cit., pp. 73–88.

[38] However, so many of these etymologies are contested that it is scarcely safe to draw any firm conclusions; cf. M. Mayrhofer, *Kurzgefasstes etymologisches Wörterbuch des Altindischen*, 3 vol., Heidelberg, 1953–68 and the literature cited there, also P. Tedesco, 'Notes to Mayrhofer's Etymological Sanskrit Dictionary', JAOS 80, 1960, pp. 360–6. In any case, as already noted, most terms occur also in Bharata's *Nāṭyaśāstra* and so must have been well established by that time.

[39] There are however several reasons for considering it a later addition: such extended

are the divine dancers, and thus both are alluded to for example in the descriptions of Bharadvāja's entertainment (2.85.23, 40–6) and of Rāma's *abhiṣeka* (6.116.62). The majority of such references, like these two, come from the second or later stages; one exception is the reference to Hemā, an Apsaras, as skilled in dance and song (4.50.17). However, it is quite clear that from the second stage onwards the presence of dancers and actors was a standard part of the urban scene, especially on festive occasions. Thus, among the evils of a kingless state is the absence of actors and dancers (2.61.13), Bharata's entourage includes actors and their women (2.77.15), actors and dancers are among those involved in preparations for the *aśvamedha* sacrifice (1.12.7, cf. 7.82.17), and a fourth-stage passage lists dancers and prostitutes as summoned to take part in the planned celebration of Rāma's installation (2 App.I.6.26). In this last instance we see the low estimation of the women involved in these activities, which is even more graphically expressed in the passage where Sītā, to persuade Rāma to let her accompany him into exile, chides him with wanting to give her to others like an actor does (2.27.8).[40]

The close links between acting and dancing are illustrated by the fact that the standard terms for actors and dancers are related and are also often compounded in such descriptions (*naṭa*, actor, *nartaka*, dancer); these and other derivatives of √*nṛt* 'to dance' are the most frequent terms, although none are at all common. The only other terms occurring in the first or second stages are *śailūṣa* for an actor and *tāla* for the musical measure which is characteristic of the dance. In the fourth stage a derivative of the latter, *tālāpacara* or *tālāvacara*, occurs meaning a dancer, as does another term *lāsaka* in a list of names of Śiva (7 App.I.1.339), while the term *raṅga* for a stage occurs both in a compound meaning one who earns his living on the stage (*raṅgopajīvin*, 2.1905* 1) and in an ornate metaphor of battle as a stage, which follows the elaborate comparison of bow and *vīṇā* already noted (6 App. I.16.121). At earlier periods, there was presumably no special location and so for example it is stated that, in order to cheer Bharata, courtiers present various plays and tell jokes in the assembly (2.63.4–5) and that Rāvaṇa's women, when Hanumān sees them in the inner apartments, are worn out by sporting, singing, dancing and drinking (5.9.4 cf. 8.30). That is, these activities were simply a natural outgrowth of court life.

metaphors are rare, this is the only use of *gāndharva* to mean music before the third stage, *tāla* occurs also at 6.116.34 but otherwise only in the fourth stage, and *saṃgīta* 'song' is only attested elsewhere in the fourth stage, as in the elaborate metaphor of the music of nature at 4.540* 1–8[ll.vv.].

[40] The term used here for actor, *śailūṣa*, is that used also at 2.77.15c but not elsewhere; the same overtones may well therefore be present there also.

7
THE RELIGIOUS PATTERN

Then gods, Gandharvas, Siddhas and supreme sages cheered Rāma's exploit: 'Bravo, bravo.' (6.81.33)

The same process of development which we have seen modifying the language, material culture and social structure of the Rāmāyaṇa may also be seen at work in the attitude to religion underlying the text, both in the practices described and in the character of Rāma himself.[1] This transformation may be summed up in the stereotyped expression *rāmo dharmabhṛtāṃ varaḥ*, 'Rāma, best of upholders of dharma'. Its original meaning might be paraphrased as 'a pillar of the establishment', with an emphasis on dharma as the correct social order, even political stability, entirely natural in a kṣatriya context; it is only in the later stages that we can discern a shift to regarding dharma as 'righteousness, moral values (only)' and the hero as 'righteous Rāma'. Indeed, too great emphasis on the religious aspect of the Rāmāyaṇa tends to distort the picture by focusing attention on what is, by Indian standards, of comparatively slight significance. The Vaiṣṇava elements to be found in the Rāmāyaṇa are definitely a later development, and the religious pattern of the core of the text is decidedly more archaic than has generally been recognized so far.

In general, mention of the gods is much more frequent in the later parts of the text—in itself an index of the way in which religious influence begins to make itself felt. Well over half the thousand or so occurrences in the text of terms for the gods are found in the third stage, more than twice as many as in the second stage and well over three times as many as in the first, both of which are considerably longer. However, the two commonest terms, *deva* and *sura*, are more frequent in the first stage than the overall proportion, though still commoner in the later stages; thus, these two terms, of which *deva* is nearly twice as frequent as *sura*, may reasonably be said to belong to the first stage. All other terms, in addition to being much less common, occur predominantly in the later stages; in diminishing order of fre-

[1] For more detailed discussion of the material contained in this chapter see my RA and 'Rāmo dharmabhṛtāṃ varaḥ', IT 5, 1977, pp. 55–68.

quency these are: *devatā, amara, daivata, tridaśa, vibudha* and *divaukas*. In the third stage we find the term *sura* (actually a back-formation from *asura*, interpreted as *a-sura*) explained by a sub-myth within the myth of the churning of the ocean which states that the gods drank wine (*surā*, but in this context actually termed *vāruṇī*) whereas Diti's sons, the Asuras, refused (1.44.21–3).

The major deities whose names occur with any frequency in the first and second stages are: Agni, the Aśvins, Indra, Kandarpa, Kubera, Garuḍa, Parjanya, Bṛhaspati, Brahmā, the Maruts, Yama, Lakṣmī, Varuṇa, Vāyu, Viśvakarman, Viṣṇu, Śiva and Soma. Both the deities mentioned and their relative frequency are closer to the Vedic pantheon on the whole than to classical Hinduism, for example in the continued presence of the Aśvins, Parjanya and Varuṇa and in the prominence of Indra coupled with the insignificance of Viṣṇu and Śiva. The commonest gods in order of frequency are: Indra, Yama, Brahmā, Garuḍa, Viṣṇu, Varuṇa and Vāyu; let us now look at these in a little more detail.

The frequency of Indra is particularly striking. In the first stage he is normally the most active and influential of the gods and their leader against the Asuras; his victory over Vṛtra is frequently alluded to, but the Yuddhakāṇḍa also depicts him as checked or worsted by Meghanāda, more commonly therefore called Indrajit, by Kumbhakarṇa and by Atikāya. Although Jacobi perhaps goes too far in proposing an identification of Rāma with Indra, Rāma is certainly often compared to Indra, and Sītā occasionally therefore compared to his wife Śacī, but no real identification is ever made, despite Jacobi's suggestion that Rāma's battle with Rāvaṇa is 'eine andere Form des Kampfes Indra's mit Vṛitra'.[2] Indeed, many leading figures are compared in heroism to Indra, including even Rāvaṇa in ten comparisons, as well as other Rākṣasas, and there are several standard compounds to express this idea.[3] The point is that Indra is the standard of comparison for any king *qua* king. Thus, in the Ayodhyākāṇḍa Daśaratha, Rāma and Bharata are all compared to Indra, and Rāma

[2] *Das Râmâyaṇa*, pp. 130–1. Jacobi's argument is that, since Sītā is in later Vedic literature the wife of Indra or Parjanya, Rāma must be a form of these gods. So too W. Caland, noting the assistance given to Indra by the Maruts against Vṛtra, suggests that the Vānaras helping Rāma were originally these wind and storm deities ('De incarnaties van den god Wishṇu', *Provinciaal Utrechtsch Genootschap v. K. en W.*, 1927, reported in Gonda, *Early Viṣṇuism*, p. 154). Hanumān of course is regularly called *mārutātmaja* 'son of the wind', because of his great strength and speed.

[3] See my FS p. 445.

acts towards Sītā as Indra to Śacī (2.88.2cd). At the beginning of the Araṇyakāṇḍa Lakṣmaṇa compares himself to Indra as wielder of the thunderbolt in his anger against Bharata (3.2.23) and Rāma replies to the sage Sutīkṣṇa 'as Indra to Brahmā' (3.6.12d). Even as late as the Bālakāṇḍa, Daśaratha, Janaka and Brahmadatta are compared to Indra as rulers, and Vasiṣṭha is like Indra because surrounded by other sages, whereas Rāma with Lakṣmaṇa is compared twice to the Aśvins, since he is still too young for kingly status. The comparison has become stereotyped in terms like *narendra* for king, and Indra himself can be addressed in the Uttarakāṇḍa as *devendra*, so formal has it become.

Whereas general terms for deities are over half as common again in the second stage as the first and more than three times as frequent in the third stage, the various names for Indra occur with virtually the same frequency in the first two stages and show an increase of a third in the third stage. This amounts to a relative decline in frequency, underlining the point that Indra is especially the deity of the early stages of the epic. The two commonest names are Indra and Śakra, which are about as frequent in the first stage as the second, whereas the more grandiose form Mahendra is twice as frequent in the second stage. The patronymic Vāsava is also fairly common and is fairly evenly distributed. Two epithets serving as names are decidedly earlier in their distribution, though rather uncommon; these are Puraṃdara 'destroyer of forts' and Maghavān 'bountiful', which clearly express the view of Indra going back to Vedic literature; the term Śatakratu, 'possessing a hundred powers/sacrifices', is also predominantly early. By contrast Sahasrākṣa 'thousand-eyed' (once Sahasracakṣus) with its puranic overtones of Indra's punishment for adultery is twice as frequent in the second stage as the first and five times in the third. Also late in distribution and relatively rare are titles such as *tridaśeśvara* or *vibudhādhipa*, both meaning 'lord of the gods', and the terms Pākasāsana 'punisher of Pāka', Śacīpati 'husband of Śacī' and Vajradhara, Vajrin, etc. 'wielder of the thunderbolt'.

Yama is basically a personified death, not overmuch thought about except on the field of battle; the stereotyped nature of the battle scenes means that the number of references to him outweighs his importance as a deity. However, the frequency of *nayāmi yamasādanam* 'I lead to Yama's abode' and similar pādas strongly suggests that, if the phrases are still meaningful, the view of life after death in the Rāmāyaṇa is that of an abode of the dead. In fact, the view of the after-life is very nebulous in the oldest parts of the text but gains a little in definition by the second stage, with ideas of Yama's abode being supplemented by the distinction between heaven and hell. Daśaratha is regularly referred to as having gone to heaven (*svarga*), which is clearly envisaged as the normal reward of the righteous, just as hell (*naraka* or *niraya*) is the punishment of the wicked. But how either is reached is not clearly indicated, although the southern region is that traversed by the dead (2.57.11) and a not infrequent phrase suggests the dissolution of the elements of the body into their correlates in nature (*mayi pañcatvam āpanne*, 2.57.24c etc.). There are also occasional allusions to various presages of death, of which the main one is seeing golden trees. However, there is remarkably little reference to the concept of *saṃsāra* in the first stage and not a great deal more even in the second; the early Rāmāyaṇa is not totally unaware of the concept of reincarnation but largely ignores it, which indicates either a very early date for it or a purely secular background or most probably a combination of both.[4] Indeed, the older idea persists even into the third stage, with both good and bad in Yama's realm (7.21.10cd, greatly expanded in 403* and 404*) and Yama himself called *pretarāja* (e.g. 7.15.17). Also in the third stage we find Yama himself distinguished from a personified Mṛtyu 'Death' (7.22) and portrayed as a *lokapāla*, an aspect first found at the end of the Yuddhakāṇḍa (6.105.1–5) and growing more frequent in the fourth and fifth stages. The Uttarakāṇḍa contains an elaborate account of his defeat by Rāvaṇa (7.21.2), though only after Brahmā's intervention, which is also alluded to in the fourth stage (e.g. 3.750* and App.I.11.68) and has possibly developed out of an allusion to Rāvaṇa having worsted death in his conflict with Kubera (6.7.13).

Brahmā occupies quite a prominent position, a significant feature in view of his later eclipse. He is mentioned nearly three times as frequently in the second stage as the first and over three times as frequently in the third stage; if allowance is made for the comparative lengths of the texts, his frequency in the third stage has increased not far short of fivefold. There is no significant difference between the different names—Brahmā, Svayaṃbhū and Pitāmaha or their derivatives—in this respect. The term Prajāpati, which usually but not invariably denotes Brahmā, is rare in the first or second stages but becomes frequent in the third and later stages. In fact Brahmā or his world is referred to only thirty-four times in the first stage, which certainly suggests that he was of slight significance then. It is therefore only natural that several of

[4] Benjamin Khan (*The concept of dharma in Valmiki Ramayana*, Delhi, 1965) affirms that the Rāmāyaṇa lacks any unequivocal assertion of transmigration (p. 121); he also notes that it seems completely unaware of *mokṣa* (p. 45; cf. A. Guruge, *The Society of the Rāmāyaṇa*, Maharagama, 1960, p. 274). The earliest use of *mokṣa* in its accepted meaning is not until the fourth stage.

the most striking references to him belong to the second stage, including one (2.102.2) on which Jan Gonda comments: 'In the Rāmāyaṇa it is Brahmā who becomes a boar, raises up the earth, and creates the whole world; before all was water only (2,110,3). Yet, in the NW. recension Viṣṇu's name has crept in.'[5] Brahmā is a generous bestower of favours and in particular weapons, which he distributes with a fine impartiality to Rākṣasas as well; indeed, once Indrajit is described as Svayaṃbhū's darling (6.61.12d). The story of his granting boons to Rāvaṇa only gains currency in the third and fourth stages (7.10.12–22, cf. 4 App.I.8.8 and 7 App.I.1.288–348), though first alluded to in a catalogue of Rāvaṇa's exploits found in the second stage (3.30.17–18). However, Brahmā does sometimes utter curses, as against Kumbhakarṇa (6.48.9c and 49.23–7), and engage in other activities, such as fathering the Vānara Jambavat (4.40.2 and v.l. 6.21.20c) and creating the aerial chariot Puṣpaka (6.115.23 and 29). At the end of the Yuddhakāṇḍa, when the gods gather to reveal Rāma's divinity to him, it is Brahmā who, after an initial chorus, acts as spokesman (6.105). However, in the Rāmāyaṇa it is Indra who then restores the dead Vānaras to life at Rāma's request (6.108), but, most interestingly, the *Rāmopākhyāna* substitutes Brahmā for Indra (Mbh. 3.275.40). Brahmā is particularly prominent in the third stage and for instance it is he who welcomes Rāma to heaven after his eventual self-immolation (7.100.6). Interestingly, a passage of the fourth stage portrays Brahmā dissuading Rāma from self-immolation following Sītā's swallowing-up by the Earth (7 App.I.13.22-45). The description of Brahmā as four-faced seems also to belong to the later stages; there are references to him as such occasionally in the third stage (1.2.22c, 7.5.11a, 35.65c[l.v.] and 36.22c) and in the fourth (5.1049* 18[l.v.], App.I.13.26 and 7 App. I.3.16). We also find in the third stage the first reference to him as born from the lotus (7.30.9–10). Altogether, there is ample evidence in both epics to confirm Hacker's suggestion of 'the existence, in the first centuries BC and the first centuries AD, of an influential Hindu sect that adored *Brahmā* as the highest deity.'[6]

[5] *Early Viṣṇuism*, p. 140.

[6] P. Hacker, 'The Sāṅkhyization of the Emanation Doctrine Shown in a Critical Analysis of Texts', WZKSA 5, 1961, pp. 75–112. A sculptural representation of a four-headed Brahmā occurs on the southern panel of the Deogaṛh temple of the fifth century AD. Descriptions of Brahmā as four-faced and as born from the lotus occur, for example, at Mbh. 3.194.12–16 (where Mārkaṇḍeya describes his birth from Viṣṇu's navel); on the position of Brahmā in the *Āraṇyakaparvan*, see S. L. Neveleva, *Mifologiya drevneindiyskogo eposa* (*panteon*), Moskva, 1975, pp. 38–45. I am grateful to Dr Neveleva for a copy of this work.

Garuḍa, the bird who becomes Viṣṇu's mount (*vāhana*) in classical Sanskrit mythology, appears both more freqeuntly than Viṣṇu and almost entirely independently of him. Part of the explanation is that he is a symbol of speed, a much prized quality of the Vānaras, esepcially Hanumān. In other similes of the first and second stages Rāma is compared to him (3.29.5d and 5.19.23b); particularly striking is Sītā's scornful double simile in which she categorises the disparity between Rāma and Rāvaṇa as that between Garuḍa and a crow (3.45.42a[l.v.]). Jaṭāyus mentions him as his uncle (3.13.32d), and subsequently we are told how he flew off carrying a huge branch, an elephant and a tortoise, ending up by smashing an iron grille and stealing the ambrosia (*amṛta*) from Indra's palace, an incident with Vedic reminiscences surprising in such an obviously interpolated passage (3.33.28–34).[7] Not so obviously late, though possibly inflated, is the passage during the siege of Laṅkā where Garuḍa intervenes personally to rescue Rāma and Lakṣmaṇa from the craft of Indrajit (6.40.33–59); here there is an undoubted reference to Garuḍa's traditional enmity towards snakes. A widely-attested fourth-stage insertion, however, introduces a hint of Rāma's future identity with Viṣṇu and relationship with Garuḍa by saying that Rāma will understand the reason for his friendship when he is victorious (6.835*), and a less well-attested addition, after Nārada's abrupt arrival to remind Rāma of his identity with Viṣṇu, makes Vāyu advise him to remember Garuḍa (6 App.I.25). In the third stage, Garuḍa appears in person in a fight with the Rākṣasa Mālin (7.7).

The most striking aspect of the appearance of Viṣṇu is the comparative lack of reverence accorded to him even at quite late stages in the transmission of the text. Thus the first stage contains only thirteen references to him, the majority of them incidental similes, and the only one which refers directly to Viṣṇu himself in fact denies Rāma's identity with him (5.48.5–11). In the second stage, the first twenty sargas of the Ayodhyākāṇḍa show a marked concentration of references to the Viṣṇu cult, but the Vānaras' boastful references to him at the end of the Kiṣkindhākāṇḍa (64.15, 65.35 and 66.22) do not indicate any great esteem. Elsewhere, he appears merely as one of a list of gods, and not even *primus inter pares* (e.g. 3.11.17–18, 5.32.28ab and 6.82.24). In a number of similes comparing Rāma and Lakṣmaṇa to gods (e.g. 6.24.29d, 79.4d and 87.9d), Rāma is compared to Indra and it is Lakṣmaṇa who is compared to Viṣṇu. Indeed, the range of individuals compared to him is catholic: not only Rāma and Lakṣmaṇa,

[7] See D. M. Knipe, 'The Heroic Theft: Myths from Ṛgveda IV and the Ancient Near East', HR 6, 1966–7, pp. 328–60; more doubtful is his suggestion of a reference in this passage to Garuḍa's other Vedic role as serpent-killer.

but Hanumān, another Vānara and even several Rākṣasas. In view of the importance of the Rāma story to later Vaiṣṇava tradition, the appearance of Viṣṇu in Vālmīki's text is clearly of great interest; it is particularly noteworthy that in many cases the Southern recension alone introduces his name. The pattern is one of increasing prominence, as he gradually assumes the role of chief of the gods, but more significant, perhaps, than his presence in the text is his absence from it, often coupled with greater prominence of Indra, at those very points where Vaiṣṇava emphasis is now apparent. For example, Agastya is commonly said to present Rāma with Viṣṇu's weapons in a passage elaborated, if not introduced, in the second stage, whereas the text itself gives Brahmā and Indra equal prominence with Viṣṇu (3.11.29–33, cf. 6.97.4–5). It is even more noteworthy that, of the two summaries added to the Bālakāṇḍa at the very end of the third stage of growth, the first refers only to Indra (1.1.34ab) while the second ignores the incident completely (1.3).[8]

Lakṣmī or Śrī, Viṣṇu's classical consort, appears fairly often as the royal fortune or good luck in general; for example, the subjects of Ayodhyā ask that Padmā Śrī attend Bharata because he wants to return the kingdom to his elder brother (2.73.15). Yet she is seldom linked in any way with Viṣṇu; in fact there are only three instances of this in the first two stages (2.110.19d, 3.11.32cd and 5.19.24cd), and she is also linked with Indra once (6.40.25).[9] Admittedly Sītā is compared to Śrī about half a dozen times in these books but this does not mean that Śrī is therefore Viṣṇu's consort. However, when Rāma's identity with Viṣṇu is revealed, Sītā is naturally also identified with Lakṣmī (6.105.25a), and this is also found in the fourth stage (e.g. 7 App.I.3.219, 361).[10]

[8] In fact the Bālakāṇḍa has its own episode of bestowal of divine weapons in Viśvāmitra's gift of arms to Rāma and instruction in their use (1.26–27/700*), where also Viṣṇu's *cakra* is only one of many (1.26.5c, cf. 55.10b). Either this bestowal through Viśvāmitra or that through Agastya is superfluous, not only to the narrative but also logically and theologically.

[9] Gonda (*Early Viṣṇuism*, p. 224) noted this as a reference to a myth given in the Purāṇas, remarking: 'Would it be too rash to consider this narrative a reminiscence of a former association between Śrī-Lakṣmī and Indra, which was broken off in favour of Viṣṇu when he came to be, in many respects, Indra's successor?'

[10] A coincidental juxtaposition of elephants and Lakṣmī among the decoration of the Puṣpaka *vimāna* (5.6.14[l.v.]) is seen as a definite Gajalakṣmī symbol, first sculpturally represented at Sāñcī in the second to first century BC by H. D. Sankalia, 'The Ur (Original) Rāmāyaṇa or Archaeology and the Rāmāyaṇa', *Indologen-Tagung*, 1971, *ed.* H. Härtel and V. Moeller, pp. 151–60; his attendant comment about *atlantes* is irrelevant, being based on a misunderstanding of *vyomacara* at 5.45.6[l.v.].

Little prominence is given to Viṣṇu's *avatāras*. In the second stage, references are found to Janārdana, Rāma Jāmadagnya, Kṛṣṇa and the boar (2.4.33d, 18.29, 4.27.22a[l.v.] and 6.105.12–16). In the Bālakāṇḍa, Paraśurāma actually participates in the action, though only to enhance the prestige of Rāma Dāśarathi (1.73–5), and the myth of the Vāmana 'Dwarf' *avatāra* is also narrated (1.28.2–11), but the name Vāsudeva is attributed, not to Kṛṣṇa, but to Kapila (1.39.2, 24). In addition, Narasiṃha, Baladeva, Hṛṣīkeśa and the tortoise appear in the fourth stage (e.g. 1 App.I.8, 6 App.I.25 and 7 App.I.1) but it is naturally the fifth stage which presents the most developed view, with references to the boar, Nṛhari (= Narasiṃha), Rāma (= Paraśurāma) and Kalki (3.1191(A)*). Even the terms *avatāra* and the earlier *prādurbhāva*, with the verbs from which they derive, are absent from the text in this specialized religious sense, although perhaps the first moves towards it may be seen in the use of *prādur* for the divine figure appearing to Daśaratha (1.15.9c); in the fourth stage much of the Northern recension uses *prādur* + $\sqrt{}$*bhū* of Viṣṇu's incarnation in Daśaratha's sons (1.462* 11 and 463* 3).[11]

Mention of Viṣṇu's discus is found occasionally in the second stage, alongside references to his bow, but standardised reference to his bearing the conch and discus (*śaṅkhacakradhara*) or also the mace (*śaṅkhacakragadādhara*) belong to the third and later stages. Equally his characteristic mark, the Śrīvatsa, apart from one mention in the late second stage (6.105.23d), does not occur until the fourth stage.

Varuṇa, on the other hand, appears as a lingering survival, owing to his being seen in three stereotyped aspects: his linking with Indra in the compound *mahendravaruṇopama* 'equal to Indra and Varuṇa', his residence in and lordship of the ocean, and his presence as regent of the west among the *lokapālas*, a formalised grouping characteristic of the later stages. Nearly half as common as mention of Varuṇa himself is mention of his abode (*varuṇālaya*), which in all but three of its occurrences denotes the sea in general, being often used in apposition to terms for the sea (usually *sāgara*, twice *samudra*); the three exceptions are all late—two in the Uttarakāṇḍa make Varuṇa's abode part of the underworld,[12] and one in the very late, perhaps equally late, search party accounts locates mount Varāha in the fathomless abode of

[11] The absence of the term *avatāra* in this context was already noticed by P. Hacker ('Zur Entwicklung der Avatāralehre', WZKSA 4, 1960, pp. 47–70).

[12] The first of these forms part of Agastya's narration of Rāvaṇa's previous deeds in the course of which he attacks the *lokapālas* successively, kills Yama and reaches Varuṇa's abode. F. B. J. Kuiper, in the latest study on Varuṇa in the epic in his *Varuṇa and Vidūṣaka: On the origin of the Sanskrit drama*, Amsterdam, 1979, pp. 74–93, is

Varuṇa (*agādhe varuṇālaye*, 4.41.24d), where however the details elsewhere in the sarga show that the western ocean and the subterranean waters are identical and that there on Mount Asta is the residence of Varuṇa, the bearer of the noose (4.41.39cd, cf. Mbh. 3.160.10–11). In addition, when the Vānaras are asking themselves how to get their army across to Laṅkā, the sea is in one second-stage expansion described as like Varuṇa's abode full of snakes (which may therefore be being considered as separate, i.e. the underworld) and as the fathomless abode of Asuras (6.2.79–80).[13] Subsequently, when Rāma prepares to discharge his arrows into the sea, which is termed Varuṇa's abode, snakes and Dānavas are terrified and from the middle of the sea Ocean himself, Sāgara, appears (6.14.13—15.1), thus preserving the distinction between the deity and the element, while apparently transferring to the latter some of the characteristics of Varuṇa's subterranean abode.

Varuṇa's noose is mentioned in the second and later stages (e.g. 4.41.39, 6.59.33c, 1.26.9a, 3.203* 1, cf. e.g. Mbh. 3.42.27, 190.60, 221.11) but in an artificial manner. However, in line with his former prominence, it is he who gave the famous bow to Janaka in the second stage (2.28.12 and 110.38), whereas usually in the third stage onwards the donor is Śiva (e.g. 1.65.7–13).[14] Also in the third stage, when the gods become birds in fear of Rāvaṇa's depredations, Varuṇa takes the form of a *haṃsa* and subsequently endows it with his own white colour (7.18.5 and 27–30). In a fourth-stage passage he is the progenitor of Vasiṣṭha in a pitcher, when aroused by the sight of Urvaśī, who is however pledged to Mitra (7 App.I.8.144–71). Mitra, his Vedic com-

therefore in error in placing this event after Rāvaṇa's killing by Rāma and seeing it as an illustration of Hopkins' statement that 'A dead or defeated demon goes to Varuṇālaya as naturally as a dead man goes to Yamasādana' (pp. 89–90). The error perhaps arose through too cursory a reading of Hopkins, who in fact cites in support of his statement (*Epic Mythology*, Strassburg, 1915, p. 119) the Uttarakāṇḍa passage, where the Asura Madhu at death 'after abandoning this world, entered Varuṇa's abode' (7.53.19ab).

[13] This is undoubtedly a late passage, these stanzas being followed immediately by an elaborate double simile (*upameyopamā*). Association of Varuṇa's abode with snakes (*nāgas*) and Asuras (Daityas or Dānavas) occurs also in the third and later stages (7.23.4–6, cf. 6 App.I.11.8), but Kuiper's view that 'In the epic the presence of serpents is a common feature in descriptions of Varuṇa's abode' (op. cit., p. 88) is hardly supported by the evidence for the Rāmāyaṇa. On Varuṇa in the Mahābhārata, see Hopkins, op. cit., pp. 116–22 and S. L. Neveleva, *Mifologiya drevneindiyskogo eposa* (*panteon*), Moskva, 1975, pp. 73–6.

[14] However we may note that some NE. mss. substitute Śaṅkara (= Śiva) in one passage (2.2392* for 110.38), just as in the Bālakāṇḍa, when the bow is just referred to as Janaka's, some NE. mss. explicitly mention Śiva as alone able to bend it (1.1220* for 66.8–9).

panion, occurs once in a list of deities from the second stage (6.60.7[l.v.]) but otherwise has almost completely disappeared, except for pedantic revival in a few other passages of the fourth stage and the reference in the third stage to his having gained the status of Varuṇa by performing the *rājasūya* (7.74.5).

Vāyu appears both in his declining anthropomorphic role, and as a symbol of natural forces.[15] He shares the fruit of a rite with Agni and Soma, two other Vedic deities who, though ritually important, are not frequent in the Rāmāyaṇa (2.101.28cd). By the second stage he is subordinate to Indra: his role as Indra's messenger is alluded to when Hanumān is called 'son of Indra's messenger' (*vāsavadūtasūnu*, 6.61.56b[l.v.]), and when he gives a garland to Rāma at Indra's urging (6.116.60–1). It is his position as Hanumān's father which largely accounts for his prominence. The story of his rape of Añjanā is narrated once each in the second and third stages (4.65.9–19 and 7.35–6); just like Bhīma in the Mahābhārata, another son of Vāyu, Hanumān shows the enormous strength symbolised by this parentage.[16] His form as a god is not really to be distinguished from his physical basis in the wind, and he appears frequently in similes as a symbol of speed and strength, particularly of destructive might but also as life-giving breath. He cannot be bound with fetters (3.53.24), and the term *prabhañjana* 'breaker, smasher' is used for a cyclone. In the Bālakāṇḍa appears the story of his attempted seduction of Kuśanābha's daughters and breaking of their limbs when they refuse (1.31.12–32.4, where he is called rather ironically the 'self of all', *sarvātmaka*); and in the Uttarakāṇḍa he is declared to be the breaths and the whole world (*vāyuḥ sarvam idaṃ jagat*, 7.35.61b = *Taittirīya Brāhmaṇa* 3.11.1.9 and Mbh. 3.1382* 4 post.), without whom creatures become like a log. As well as Hanumān, the vultures Saṃpāti and Jaṭāyus are described as equal in speed to Mātariśvan (= Vāyu, 4.59.19ab).

The Asuras as a class are characterised in the early Rāmāyaṇa by hostility to the gods and virtual equality with them; this feature is typified by the common phrase *devāsure yuddhe* 'in the war between the gods and Asuras'. Hiraṇyakaśipu is opposed to Indra, not Viṣṇu; his son Anuhlāda attracts Indra's wrath for deceiving Śacī, and Prahrāda is one of Indra's victims. Various groups of semi-divine beings are quite often mentioned, but usually purely formally in lists and in

[15] In determining the frequency of Vāyu, patronymics such as Mārutātmaja have been ignored; if they were included, Vāyu would come much higher in the list.

[16] It is interesting that in the encounter of these two sons of Vāyu in the Mahābhārata (3.147), it is Hanumān who is the stronger.

general they are of slight importance. The commonest are the celestial musicians, the Gandharvas, who are nearly as frequent in the first as in later stages, whereas the Apsarases, usually thought of as their companions and as dancers, scarcely appear before the second stage and are in fact much less commonly mentioned than the Gandharvas. However, from the second stage onwards, various individual Gandharvas and Apsarases are named. In the third stage, the legend of the origin of the Apsarases from the churning of the ocean includes an explanation for their supposed promiscuity in non-acceptance by either gods or anti-gods (1.44.18–20). However Rāvaṇa, when he rapes the Apsaras Rambhā, is cursed because she is the wife of his nephew (7.26).

Equally undeveloped in the epic's first two stages is the portrayal of the religious position of the Rākṣasas. As enemies of Rāma and his allies, they tend to be compared to Indra's opponents, but divine or demonic traits are mostly limited to their ability to assume any form at will. Once, however, an offering is made to them (2.38.5), and some of them know the Vedas and perform sacrifice (e.g. 5.16.2). Brahmā gives them weapons and grants them boons, often after the practice of considerable austerities; this is admittedly something of a commonplace on both sides, but it is perhaps a characteristic of the Rākṣasas that their austerities and other religious practices are engaged in for temporal ends not spiritual.[17] Probably the best known instance is Indrajit's sacrifice to secure invincibility (6.73). Not only are there brāhmans among the Rākṣasas (e.g. 1.11.17, 5.16.2 and 6.45.21) but the presence of *dīkṣitas* in Laṅkā (5.3.28) attests their maintenance of the sacrificial ritual. Thus, far from being the demons of later mythology, the Rākṣasas in the Rāmāyaṇa are mainly depicted as not merely human but also cultured.

Several groups of sages are mentioned at various points, mainly in passages belonging to the second and later stages, of whom the commonest are the Vaikhānasas and Vālakhilyas; although when the *vaikhānasa mārga* is mentioned once (2.48.58a), it appears to mean the ascetic way of life. Possibly we may discern in the prominence of the Vaikhānasas compared with other groups a first stage in the epic's transformation into a Vaiṣṇava work.[18]

[17] Cf. Ramashraya Sharma, *A socio-political study of the Vālmīki Rāmāyaṇa*, Delhi, 1971, p. 434.

[18] Some remarks on ascetics in relationship to the scheme of the four stages of life

The two terms regularly used for ascetics are *ṛṣi* and *muni* which are of approximately equal frequency, although *muni* is somewhat commoner in the third stage, where both terms are over twice as common proportionately as in the first and second stages. In addition, *tapasvin* and *tāpasa*, both specifically indicating the performance of austerities, are rather less frequent. Other terms (*parivrājaka, bhikṣu, yati, vānaprastha* and *śramaṇa*) are all very rare. Their characteristic item of dress is their bark-cloth, for which the standard term is *cīra*, although *valkala* is also employed from the second stage; for example, Rāma and Sītā put on bark-cloth to mark their retirement to the forest and *cīra* is repeatedly mentioned in this sarga (2.33). Much less frequent mention is made of matted hair (*jaṭā, jaṭila*) or of the skins also worn, whether goatskin (*ajina*) or antelope skin (*kṛṣṇājina*). The water pot (*kalaśa*), standard equipment for later Indian ascetics, is little mentioned and not at all in this sense in the first stage, while a skull as drinking vessel (*kapāla*) and a staff (*yaṣṭi, daṇḍa*) are rare. One full description is of Rāvaṇa as he approaches Sītā disguised as a mendicant: 'wrapped in a loose robe, tonsured, holding a parasol, wearing sandals, and duly carrying on his left arm his staff and drinking bowl' (3.44.3), but this belongs to the second stage at the earliest, for the Northwestern recension omits this description.[19]

A lyric description of a hermitage, *āśrama*, in the Daṇḍaka forest opens the Araṇyakāṇḍa, of which a significant part is that it is 'adorned with broad hearths, ladles and other sacrificial implements, hides, *kuśa* grass, fire-wood, pitchers of water, and roots and fruit' and 'resembling the abode of Brahmā, echoing with the sound of prayer (Brahman), ornamented by eminent brāhmans learned in the Vedas (Brahman)' (3.1.4 and 8). Here is implied both sacrifice and recitation of the Vedas. Various other hermitages possess sacrificial altars, one—Pratyaksthalī—in the Mataṅgavana is named (3.70.19a), and the altar in Rāma's own hermitage is obviously a conspicuous feature (2.93.23,

have already been made on pp. 158–9. Although the Vaikhānasas in more modern times are a South Indian Vaiṣṇava community, who claim descent from a Vedic school, the name is often applied in the *dharmaśāstra* tradition to *vānaprasthas* and, more significantly, two Brāhmaṇas term the Vaikhānasas 'seers dear to Indra' (*Pañcaviṃśa B.* 14.4.7 and *Jaiminīya B.* 3. 190).

[19] What is in effect another list is provided by the gifts of the *munis* to Kuśa and Lava expanded from the *kalaśa* and *valkala* only of the Bālakāṇḍa text (1.4.19) to *kṛṣṇājina, yajñasūtra*, sacrificial thread, drinking-gourd, thread of *muñja*, cushion, loin-cloth, axe, ochre robe, bark-cloth, hair-band, cord for firewood, sacrificial vessel, load of firewood and seat of *udumbara* wood in the fourth stage (1.209*); the artificiality of this list is very evident.

cf. 2.50.16–19 and 1213*). Other full descriptions of *āśramas* come from the third stage (Agastya's at 1.50 and Vālmīki's at 7.47–8). One point made clear from the earliest stage onward is that *āśramas* should be away from society (e.g. 2.47.2) and explicitly beyond the limits of cultivation (2.1107* 1), with which may be linked Rāma's refusal to enter Kiṣkindhā because of his vow of forest life (4.25.9). Especially, of course, the remoteness of the Himālayas was favoured and this is once referred to in Sugrīva's narration of his situation to Rāma (4.11.12 and 16–17). But on the whole the hermitages mentioned in the Rāmāyaṇa seem to have been the abode of a fair number of ascetics together, reflected for example not only in the descriptions just mentioned but also in the fact that telling stories was a common occupation in *āśramas* (e.g. *citrāḥ kathayataḥ kathāḥ*, 2.48.31d and similar phrases).

Among the activities of the hermitages the performance of rituals is more frequently alluded to in the first and second stages than the performance of penances or austerities, although by the third stage the emphasis has switched to austerities. Thus, performance of the *agnihotra* is mentioned in connection with the hermitages of Vasiṣṭha, Bharadvāja, Atri and Śarabhaṅga (1.51.4 and 52.13, 2.48.11, 86.2 and 111.6, 3.4.21; cf. 3.37.4), while Bharadvāja's hermitage also has a definite hut for the fire (*agniśālā*, 2.85.10). Vasiṣṭha performs various rituals in his *āśrama* for which the products of his magic cow Śabalā are needed (1.52.13–23). Rāma makes part of his justification for military behaviour that the Rākṣasas are interrupting the ascetics' rituals (3.9.11) but subsequently it is said that the ascetics are discomfitting the Rākṣasas by their penances and sacrifices (6.27.17–20).

Apart from an elaborate list of different types of ascetics, mainly classified by various austerities, who petition Rāma at one point (3.5.2–5, expanded in 84* and 85*), the only types of austerity mentioned in the early books are living on air, plunging into water and keeping the arms lifted (2.89.6–7 and 3.10.12).[20] Usually, and particularly in the early parts, the text is content just to mention *tapas*, austerities, without giving details. The goal of such asceticism is given in the earlier books as the winning of heaven (2.48.28, 3.4.26) or, in the Śarabhaṅga episode, the world of Brahmā (3.4.24–5), evidently synonymous. This episode is also interesting in that it presents Indra as eager to lead Śarabhaṅga thither (3.4.24, cf. 3.6.10) and not, as in puranic accounts, doing his best to hinder such attempts by putting temptation, usually

[20] Different austerities of this type are listed *in extenso* in the *dharmaśāstras* (e.g. *Manu* 6.16–26, *Yājñavalkyasmṛti* 3.45–52). The penance of the five fires is rarely mentioned (2.648* 6, in addition to 3.5.5 above) and probably late.

sexual, in the ascetics' way; an allusion to something of that sort is however found in Sītā's homily to Rāma where she tells the story of the ascetic led astray by the sword left with him by Indra (3.8.13–19).

Such ascetics, and brāhmans generally, are learned in the Vedas but the epic itself shows little knowledge of them; even the stock phrase *brāhmaṇā vedapāragāḥ* 'brāhmans steeped in the Vedas' is characteristic of the second stage rather than the first. The majority of references to the Vedas are in the most general terms, although we do find expressed the belief that the Vedas are not open to questioning (3.48.21)[21]. On the whole more emphasis is placed on the less formal aspects of religion. The phrase *sa hi dharmaḥ sanātanaḥ* (2.16.52d, 20.10d and 27.30d) or *eṣa dharmaḥ sanātanaḥ* (3.3.24b, 5.1.100b *et passim* in Mbh.) 'this is the eternal tradition' is used mainly of social duty and especially of filial obedience. A general pattern of religious observance is outlined when the accustomed usage of the Ikṣvākus is given as 'charity, initiation at sacrifices and laying down one's life in battle' (2.25.7), while the giving of cows as a fee or gift to brāhmans is mentioned thrice (2.46.73, 71.1 and 4.5.5cd).

The commonest ritual acts alluded to in the first stage are the morning and evening worship (*saṃdhyā*), but there is no mention at any stage of a midday *saṃdhyā*. In the second stage the commonest ritual is still the *saṃdhyā*, which interestingly Sītā is thought of as performing when alone (5.12.48), although the fullest descriptions of the morning and evening *saṃdhyās* occur in the third stage (1.22.2–3 and 7.72.20–73.2 respectively). There was evidently as yet no prohibition on women performing Vedic rituals independently, since Kausalyā too both performs *pūjā* to Viṣṇu and makes oblations into the fire (2.17.6–7). For there begins in the second stage a shift to more informal types of worship which may broadly be classed as *pūjā*, for example Kausalyā also worships the hosts of gods with garlands, perfumes and *stutis* 'hymns of praise' (2.22.12/576*),[22] as well as a

[21] Recitation of the Vedas has already been discussed at p. 183.

[22] However, Kausalyā's blessings pronounced over Rāma at 2.22.1–15 may well be particularly late; they share several verbal similarities with Kuntī's lament as she abandons the infant Karṇa at Mbh. 3.292.9–21. An analysis of the occurrence of √*stu* and its nominal derivatives (under thirty in the text, considerably more in * passages) by my friend Dr Peter Schreiner indicates three types of use. In the first category the king is praised, usually by professionals (*sūta, māgadha*, etc.), as part of court life; the majority of occurrences in the text belong here and come from all three stages. In the second category, apparently modelled on courtly routine, heavenly beings praise a hero or a god for his deeds; instances of this come from the third and later stages. In the third category, praising is part of a religious activity, either in connection with a Vedic rite or in revering

recognition of more localised deities in the terms *gṛhadevatā, vanadevatā* and *vanadaivata*, and, for example, in Sītā's worship of the Gaṅgā as they cross (2.46.67–73).

Sacrifice (*yajña*, occasionally *adhvara* or *kratu*), oblations (*homa*, occasionally *havis*), and the sacrificial altar (*vedī*) are mentioned in the first stage from time to time, as well as the best known of the individual sacrifices—the *agnihotra, aśvamedha, rājasūya* and *vājapeya*—of which the first is a daily ritual and the other three are closely associated with kingship; there are single mentions of a sacrificial session (*satra*, 6.76.27d, also found in later stages), a participant in it (*satrin*, 6.38.3b) and a particular oblation (*caru*, 6.67.8a). The only priest mentioned in the first stage is the *purohita* (in the third stage also *purodhas*) but then he is the king's personal chaplain; nonetheless he becomes more frequent in later stages. To these are added in the second stage the *agniṣṭoma, āgrayaṇa, paurṇamāsī* and *pauṇḍarīka* sacrifices, as well as a further general term for sacrifice (*ijyā*), one for the time of the Soma pressing (*sutyākāla*) and reference to expiation (*prāyaścitta*); the names of two officiating priests also appear once each in the second stage, the *praśāstṛ* and the *sadasya*. The role of the fire in carrying the offering to the gods and the way it blazes from the oblation are alluded to from time to time, but details of the sacrificial performance are in general conspicuously absent; indeed, the passage where Rāma and Lakṣmaṇa sacrifice a blackbuck to consecrate their newly-built hut (2.50.15–19) is marked by a striking air of informality, compared with the elaboration of detail in the Brāhmaṇa and Sūtra literature. Lakṣmaṇa kills and cooks the buck, then asks Rāma to officiate because he is suitably skilled, implying that this was not the first occasion on which the kṣatriya Rāma had assumed the priestly role.

There is little sign of any veneration of the cow in the first stage; indeed, Bharadvāja offers Rāma beef (2.48.16cd). But it does appear in the second and subsequent stages, for example Bharata's curse includes 'may he kick a sleeping cow' (2.69.15). Some details of funeral customs can be extracted from the accounts of Daśaratha's embalming and cremation (2.60 and 70–1), but the degree of divergence between the recensions indicates both the unreliability of such details and their small importance in the original work.[23]

a deity (into which group come Kausalyā's prayers); this begins to occur from the second stage onwards. We hope in the future to issue a joint publication on this and related topics.

[23] See pp. 183–4. W. Caland discusses in some detail the funerals of Daśaratha at

References to any fixed and constructed place of worship are virtually absent from the first three stages; one exception, belonging to the second stage, has Rāma and Sītā sleep in Viṣṇu's holy *āyatana* (2.6.4). By the fourth stage mention of *caityas* and *āyatanas* together is quite common.[24] *Tīrthas* are mentioned occasionally; for example in the Ayodhyā and Araṇya kāṇḍas there are two references in passages of the first stage (3.37.4a and 70.18c, just before the mention of the altar Pratyaksthalī) but four from the second stage (2.89.5c, 94.30d, 3.10.50a and 60.3a) and many more from the fourth and fifth stages. A separate room or hut for the fire is mentioned in three passages of the second stage (2.70.13b, 85.10a, 5.33.43d). The description of Rāvaṇa's palace as 'like the house of a god' (*devagṛhopama*, 3.53.6d) was taken by Hopkins as 'suggesting that a temple is meant',[25] but it is more likely that the reference is to a deity's heavenly abode.

There are references to *caityas* as cult spots in the text—a few from the first stage but mostly from the second. They are particularly associated with the Rākṣasas, who perform both orthodox and unorthodox rituals at them. The earlier references to *caityas* seem on the whole to be simply to non-brāhmanical cult spots, but the fourth stage, as I indicated before, mentions *caityas* and *āyatanas* together quite often, indeed in *dvandva* compounds, that is, linking but distinguishing them. However, in one second-stage passage a *caitya* building is described with a thousand pillars, a stairway or steps of coral, and a golden dais which seems to be a temple (5.13.15–17).[26]

While mention of any permanent shrine is very rare in the first stage, though a little more frequent in the second, references to images are totally absent. Yet in the third stage Rāvaṇa sets up and worships a golden *liṅga* with perfumes and flowers (7.31.38–9). There is greater elaboration then in the fourth stage, when, for example, the Northern recension inserts an allusion to images trembling (6.548* 1).

2.70 and of Rāvaṇa at 6 App.I.69 in their relationship to the ritual texts (*Die Altindischen Todten- und Bestattungsgebräuche*, Amsterdam, 1896, pp. 168–71).

[24] E. W. Hopkins (*Epic Mythology*, Strassburg, 1915, pp. 70–2) draws a distinction between the Mahābhārata and the Rāmāyaṇa on this point, suggesting that the latter does mention temples and other shrines, but the majority of the instances he cites have been relegated to * passages in the Critical Edition. For a more recent discussion see O. Viennot, *Le culte de l'arbre dans l'Inde ancienne*, Annales du Musée Guimet 59, Paris, 1954, pp. 88–9.

[25] Loc. cit.

[26] On the other hand, where *cetiya* occurs in Pali texts it refers to pre-Buddhist *yakṣa*

It is indeed to counteract such slight emphasis on moral and religious matters that some of the more notable additions or expansions to the text have been made, among them Daśaratha's account of his former misdeed and the resultant curse through which he is dying separated from his son (2.57–8);[27] the didactic moralising of the *kaccit* sarga (2.94); Rāma's meeting with Agastya and presentation with divine weapons (3.11), inserted to enhance the Vaiṣṇava element in the text; Sītā's reproof and Rāma's ethical justification of his aggression towards the Rākṣasas (3.8–9); and Vālin's reproach and Rāma's rather laboured excuses for killing him in an underhand way (4.17–18). Indeed, the *kaccit* sarga goes further in the cause of orthodoxy by condemning *lokāyatika* brāhmans, those that is whose values are worldly and who therefore are 'foolish though thinking themselves learned' (2.94.32), and the evil of atheism (*nāstikya*, 56a, also at 2.2240* 4, cf. 2241*). So too the evils of a kingless state include the presence of atheists (*nāstika*, 2.61.22) and, in the third stage, Ayodhyā under Daśaratha's benign rule is free of them (1.6.8, 14). However, impiety apparently consists of atheism or non-belief not of heterodoxy. The term *śramaṇa*, in other texts often denoting a Buddhist monk, occurs in the first stage to describe the Śabara woman (3.69.19 and 70.7, also 1.1.46), who follows more or less orthodox ascetic practices, in the second stage in an obscure reference to an incident of Māndhātṛ's career (4.18.31), and even in the third stage linked as worthy individuals with brāhmans (1.13.8); however, the Buddha is once mentioned and condemned in the fourth stage (2.2241* 13[l.v.]).

Astrology and the belief in omens begin to be included in the epic from its second stage onwards. Thus a favourable date is chosen for Rāma's installation (2.3.4 and 24, with 62* 1) along with favourable positions of the moon (2.4.21 and 23.8), while Kausalyā's blessing includes invocation of all the asterisms (*nakṣatras*, 2.22.5). Several asterisms are mentioned, of which much the most frequent is Rohiṇī, but only because she has become a standard comparison for a favourite wife. All the then-known planets are mentioned, though rarely, and descriptions of omens sometimes include the appearance of comets or meteors (*dhūmaketu* or *ulkā*) as a presage of gloom (e.g. 2.4.17–19); so too there is an eclipse as Rāvaṇa gains a temporary advantage over Rāma in their final duel (6.90.27–30). However, the astrologers who

centres, which is not dissimilar from the use of *caitya* in the earlier stages of the Rāmāyaṇa.

[27] The emphasis it places on *karma* is elsewhere found only in the fourth stage.

had, apparently falsely, predicted long life for Rāma and motherhood for Sītā are upbraided (6.23.12 and 38.2–14). The cries of birds are regarded as omens for good or bad (e.g. 3.50.3, 65.9–11, 4.1.24–5), a jackal's cry is always inauspicious (e.g. 6.31.11), while the throbbing of one's right arm is a good omen and of one's left a bad omen for a man and *vice versa* for a woman (e.g. 3.57.4 and 5.25.35–7, also 7.45.11–12).

Some minor cosmogonic elements are also included in the second stage, principally in Jaṭāyus' giving of 'his identity and lineage from the origin of creation' (3.13), but also in the Ikṣvāku genealogy (2.102; cf. 1.67.17–30); however, the few details given certainly do not amount to a definite cosmology. The end of the process is left equally vague, with only the fairly common simile of the doomsday fire as a comparison for the devastation of war to give any definition at all.

Whereas the first stage envisages individuals as responsible for their own situations and, even if they are in a difficult or painful situation, it is because of what they have done, by implication in this present life (e.g. 2.38.16–17, 3.47.26 and 49.26), by contrast the second stage sees both *karma* acting across lives and fate as explaining present ills. Thus Hanumān declares to Tārā that everyone reaps the reward of good or evil deeds after death and that therefore she is grieving unreasonably (4.21.2–3).[28] Equally, fate or destiny is invoked several times as a purely external force, sometimes in proverbial form ('fate is unavoidable' *kālo hi duratikramaḥ* or, in the third stage, *daivaṃ hi duratikramam*). Of the different terms used, *kṛtānta* probably is related to the concept of *karma*, but *kāla*, literally 'time', obviously expresses something more akin to predestination and the other common term *daiva* emphasises the fortuitous aspect or the intervention of the gods; the term *niyati*, with its strongly determinist ring, is very rare. However, *daiva* means rather 'chance' than 'fate' as when it is declared that misfortunes come to all for none can escape *daiva* (3.62.5–12) or reference is made to its unforeseeability (2.19.18 and App.I.18.64 cf. *Manu* 7.205c).[29]

[28] More exactly he says that she is grieving for those whom she should not grieve for, a sentiment identical to Kṛṣṇa's at *Bhagavadgītā* 2.11, although there is no coincidence of wording. However, an addition elsewhere of the fourth stage on this topic is virtually identical in wording to another stanza of Kṛṣṇa's discourse (2.1833* ≏ BhG. 2.27). Other coincidences of wording with the *Bhagavadgītā* appear accidental (e.g. *anāryajuṣṭam asvargyam*, 2.76.13a, BhG. 2.2c, and Mbh. 9.30.22c, probably a legal commonplace, and *svargadvāram apāvṛtam* 6 App.I.63.65 post., BhG. 2.32b and Mbh. 8 App.I.14.3 post., a phrase with several minor variants).

[29] For an interesting discussion of this phrase, *daivam acintyam*, see L. Rocher, 'The Purāṇa of Fate and Human Effort', ABORI 58–9, 1977–8, pp. 271–8.

In fact, the gods do not often participate in the action directly; the only major exception is their sending Mātali to act as Rāma's charioteer in the final battle. More commonly at all stages, though perhaps almost always through subsequent expansion, gods, sages and minor deities assemble to express horror at the Rākṣasas' audacity and support for Rāma in his opposition to them, thus forming a kind of divine chorus or audience;[30] indeed, towards the climax of the battle, in a passage of the second stage, we find the assembled divine spectators taking sides, with the gods cheering on Rāma and the Asuras Rāvaṇa (6.91.5–8). However, neither here nor elsewhere is there usually any suggestion of direct intervention by the deities. Nevertheless, such passive participation by the gods may well mark the start of the ethical polarisation which was to transform the story, especially when taken in conjunction with the rather uncommon epithet *nairṛta* applied predominantly in the second stage to the Rākṣasas (thirty-one times, against nine in the first stage and five in the third); whether *nirṛti* is simply 'destruction' or personified as occasionally in Vedic literature, the term obviously has moral overtones.

The religious pattern evident in the third stage is much more developed—the Bālakāṇḍa opens with the figure of Nārada (1.1.1—2.2),[31] the Uttarakāṇḍa closes with the first hints of *bhakti* (7.98.15 and

[30] For example, when Khara's army sets out amid evil portents, a few stanzas expressing the good wishes to Rāma of the gods and other divine beings are found at two points (3.22.26–9 and 23.17–18 + 420*) but the variation in manuscript support suggests that at least the first has been added later to this basically first stage passage; in addition, the inclusion of Siddhas and Cāraṇas in both and Guhyakas in the second is symptomatic of the pantheon popular later. Similarly, Söhnen, *Reden* vol. 1, p. 281, also p. 285, rightly questions the address by divine sages to Bharata at 2.104.1–8, with its anticipatory reference to Rāvaṇa's death, and assigns it to the period of composition of the Bālakāṇḍa.

[31] It may be too simple to see in the occurrence here of Nārada a first emphasis on *bhakti*, since he appears in Vedic literature from the *Yajurveda* onwards. Nevertheless, he is associated with Kṛṣṇa in the Mahābharata (e.g. 12.200.44–5) and subsequently becomes an example of the devotional life and teacher of the way of *bhakti*. Undoubtedly this is the reason for his greater prominence in some of the adaptations of the Rāmāyaṇa to be surveyed in chapters 8–9. Within the Rāmāyaṇa itself, Nārada appears only in Kausalyā's invocations (2.22.5a, a late, Vaiṣṇava passage) in the first two stages but elsewhere in the third stage to bemoan the decline of dharma across the *yugas* and to identify the śūdra practising asceticism as the cause of the brāhman boy's death (7.65), as well as dissuading Rāvaṇa from attacking men, which includes a reference to him as *samarapriya* (7.20.12b, perhaps a first hint of the role later assigned to him of a causer of strife), while in the fourth stage he arrives abruptly during the battle to remind Rāma of his identity with Viṣṇu (6 App.I.25).

100.15), and the positions of Viṣṇu and Śiva are both greatly enhanced—but older features still persist: much of the Bālakāṇḍa ignores Rāma's divinity; Rāma's reward for his exemplary life is to go to Brahmaloka (1.1.76d), where Vālmīki too is promised residence (1.2.36); but Viṣṇu incarnates as Rāma (1.14–15) and Paraśurāma recognises him as Viṣṇu (1.75.17–20). A number of the myths incorporated into the Bālakāṇḍa also betray later ideas, among them Viśvāmitra's and Vasiṣṭha's quarrel over Vasiṣṭha's cow Śabalā (1.51–5), with its strong overtones of veneration of the cow, and the stories of Gaṅgā, Umā and Kārtikeya (1.34–6); indeed, after an assertion that Gaṅgā is purifying (1.40.19–20), it returns to her story with a full account of her descent from heaven (1.42.15–21, also 934*; cf. also 43.13–20, 949*, 950*).

Increasing brāhmanisation of the work is shown by the prominence of Bhṛgu and various Bhārgavas in the Bālakāṇḍa and more particularly in the Uttarakāṇḍa. Daśaratha declares that his priest and preceptor Vasiṣṭha is his deity as he begs him not to take Rāma and Lakṣmaṇa (1.19.20d: *daivataṃ hi bhavān guruḥ*). Similarly, the summary execution of the śūdra whose penance has caused the death of a brāhman boy, resulting from the view that only a brāhman may perform penance (7.64–7), strikingly indicates the exaggerated emphasis on Rāma's moral rule to be found in these late passages; this concept is no doubt a developed form of the passages stressing Rāma's proper ordering of the four *varṇas* found in the Bālakāṇḍa (1.1.75, 6.17, 24.15).

Increased stress is laid on asceticism and its results. In addition to the types of austerity found in earlier stages and repeated here (e.g. 1.50.26–7, 62.22), mention is made of fasting and lying on ashes (1.47.29, cf. 1.898* and 1083*). Also the *ṛṣi* Cūlin is described as *ūrdhvaretāḥ śubhācāraḥ* (1.32.11c) indicating possibly tantric aspects to his chastity, although he soon has a son by the Gandharvī Somadā (1.32.18d called 'mental, from the mind (only)' by the Southern recension. In the third stage austerities are used to extract concessions from the gods or to compel them in various ways: Gautama castrates Indra by a curse (1.47.26–7), Viśvāmitra gains mastery of archery and other military skills from Śiva by his penances (1.54.12–19), Viśvāmitra uses his powers to thrust Trisáṅku bodily into the sky (1.57–9) and eventually, despite temptations, extorts from Brahmā his desire of becoming a brāhman (1.62.15–64.12), and Rāvaṇa and his brothers practise *tapas* and perform sacrifices in order to gain various boons from Pitāmaha (7.10.10–39). Their enhanced status is given unequivocal expression in the epithet 'gods on earth' (*ṛṣayaḥ . . . mahīsurāḥ*, 7.99.9ab), while their increasingly mythical aspect is reflected in allusions to seven great sages (7.1.5) and to Agastya's birth from a pot in his title Kumbhayoni (7.67.8 and 73.2). There are also a few references in these books to the use of yoga techniques to achieve clairvoyance (1.154* 7–8, 1.22.17, 7.48.5 and 10), sometimes quite banal, as when Kaikasī making advances to Viśravas says he ought to be able by his inherent powers to divine her purpose (7.9.14–16), but the only reference outside them is in the quite anomalous episode of Niśākara's prophecy (4.61.3c *dṛṣṭaṃ me tapasā*); admittedly, Saṃpāti just before sees things at a great distance (4.57.28–30), but this is merely an exaggeration of birds' keen sight. The ascription of such yogic powers is clearly a late feature.

Rituals, too, are much more elaborate: the royal horse sacrifice, the *aśvamedha*, is given in greater detail than would be natural for the core of the epic (1.11–13), but it does seem basic to the Bālakāṇḍa as a means for Daśaratha to achieve his aim of fathering sons (1.13.46), whereas the *putreṣṭi*, which contains the explicit details of Viṣṇu's incarnation as the four sons, is inserted awkwardly and unnecessarily at the end of the *aśvamedha* ceremony (1.14–16). It is incidentally in connection with Daśaratha's *aśvamedha* that many more sacrifices are mentioned which occur first in this stage. Altogether the third stage adds to those already mentioned the *gomedha*, the *jyotiṣṭoma* and its modifications, the *ukthya, atirātra* and *aptoryāma*, and components, *abhijit, upasad, pravargya* and *viśvajit*, as well as the *catuṣṭoma* as a part of the *aśvamedha* and the new moon ritual (*darśa*, 1.52.23c) to join the full moon ritual already found in the second stage (*paurṇamāsī*, now also *pūrṇamāsa*). Yet another *aśvamedha* recounted in the third stage is that planned by Sagara when the theft of the sacrificial horse leads to the excavation of the ocean (1.38.4–10). The term *iṣṭi* for sacrifice seems only to be used for the *putreṣṭi*. Officiants mentioned for the first time are the *adhvaryu, udgātṛ, śamitṛ* and *hotṛ*. Over half the references to rituals and worship in the text come from this third stage.

The *aśvamedha* is also prominent in the Uttarakāṇḍa, where two exemplars are narrated—that of Indra after killing Vṛtra (7.77) and that to secure Ilā's restoration to manhood (7.81)—before Rāma himself offers one. These two *aśvamedhas* also illustrate the enhanced prestige of Viṣṇu and Śiva in the Uttarakāṇḍa, for the first is offered to Viṣṇu by Indra on the advice of Viṣṇu himself, after he has declined to fight Vṛtra in person because of past friendship (7.76.3–7), whereas the second is offered to Śiva. Both Śiva and Viṣṇu appear as protectors of the other gods, who for example turn first to Śiva, but are sent on to Viṣṇu who agrees to act against Sukeśa's sons (7.6). The story of Dakṣa's sacrifice disrupted by Śiva is alluded to (e.g. 1.65.9–11) as well as Śiva's thrusting down of Kailāsa when Rāvaṇa attempts to uproot it (7.16). Besides the bow given to Janaka's ancestors, Śiva is in the third stage a notable granter of boons, for example to Viśvāmitra, to Rāvaṇa and to Madhu (1.54.13–18, 7.16 and 7.53.5–10), while Rāvaṇa is also depicted as worshipping the *liṅga* (7.31.38–40, also 660*). Śiva's position has improved as much as Indra's has declined, although Śiva remains ultimately subordinate to Viṣṇu. Their enhanced significance is reflected in their titles: both are called *devadeva* and *deveśa*, Śiva is *sarvabhūtapati* (7.53.12b) and Viṣṇu is *tribhuvanaśreṣṭha* (7.76.17c). Viṣṇu is referred to by a wide variety of names in the third stage, but their distribution is patchy: Nārāyaṇa occurs more or less throughout the Uttarakāṇḍa, but the rest, Indrānuja, Govinda, Janārdana, Padmanābha, Puruṣottama, Madhusūdana, Mādhava, Vāsudeva and Hari, are found in only one or two passages each (e.g. Hari at 7.6–8).

Indra has, however, by no means disappeared, although his portrayal now approaches the puranic view. It is Indra who leads the gods in battle (7.27–8), though first appealing to Viṣṇu as supreme deity, but he is fallible: captured and only released through Brahmā's intervention (7.29–30), he is lectured about his adultery with Ahalyā. Similarly, his performance of the *aśvamedha* already mentioned to free himself of the guilt of murdering a brāhman (personified as Brahmahatyā) has puranic overtones. His prestige has not altogether evaporated, however. Whereas at the end of the Yuddhakāṇḍa it is appropriately enough Agni who restores Sītā to Rāma after the fire-ordeal (6.106.1–9), when Rāma recalls this episode to his brothers in the Uttarakāṇḍa, he says that she was actually handed back by Mahendra (7.44.8), an all the more surprising discrepancy in view of the lateness of the fire-ordeal itself.[32]

Like Viṣṇu and Śiva, both Indra and Brahmā are called by such titles as *deveśa* and *īśāna* in the third stage; indeed, Indra is called *deveśa* by the second stage (e.g. 4.28.5a), though perhaps not in the later sense of supreme deity. In short, the third stage reveals a quartet of deities rather than a trio. Indra's continuing prominence results no doubt from his position as the kṣatriyas' god, just as Brahmā is the brāhmans'

[32] See Nilmadhav Sen. 'The Fire-Ordeal of Sītā—A later interpolation in the Rāmāyaṇa?' JOIB 1, 1952, pp. 201–6 and G. H. Bhatt, 'The Fire-Ordeal of Sītā—An interpolation in the Vālmīki Rāmāyaṇa', JOIB 5, 1955–6, p. 292.

and ascetics' deity (note e.g. *brahmā brāhmaṇavatsalaḥ*, 7.5.14d). This identification with particular castes can be seen already in similes from earlier stages, as when Bharata, come to persuade Rāma to give up living in the forest, greets him 'as devout Mahendra does Prajāpati' (2.96.27d[l.v.]), and may provide the reason for the ultimate eclipse of both Indra and Brahmā by Viṣṇu and Śiva.[33]

This eclipse has progressed further by the fourth stage, but it is not yet complete, for Indra and Brahmā both still appear; for example, Brahmā sends Indra to cheer Sītā in Laṅkā (3 App.I.12), and Rāma narrates to his *sabhā* the story of Brahmā issuing as a demiurge from the sleeping Viṣṇu (7 App.I.10.88–97, cf. 7 App.I.3.147). However, Viṣṇu and Śiva are regularly seen as supreme deities. One Southern insertion describes how a deputation of gods led by Pitāmaha petitions Viṣṇu, who decides to become incarnate in order to kill Rāvaṇa; here he is called *deveśa* and *devo devānām* (1.467* 7,15). Another depicts the gods turning to Śiva for help at the churning of the ocean and lists his names or titles in an elaborate series (1 App.I.8). The mantra of invulnerability which Brahmā gives to Rāvaṇa lists 108 names of Śiva, including Gaṇeśa, Laguḍī, Jharjharī and Brahmacārin (7 App.I. 1.301–46).[34] Nevertheless, it is of course Viṣṇu who is supreme, as can be seen from the story already mentioned in which Śiva thrusts back into position Kailāsa shaken by Rāvaṇa, where a few manuscripts introduce Viṣṇu (7.312*).

The fourth stage shows in other regards an enlarged pantheon by inclusion of some of the more abstract deities found in later Vedic literature: Tvaṣṭṛ, the artisan god, appears several times against once in the second stage (2.85.11b), Dhātṛ—who occurs with Vidhātṛ a few times in the second stage—, Pūṣan and Vācaspati also occur several

[33] A different explanation is suggested by F. B. J. Kuiper who sees the cause in the changed view of the cosmic dualism: 'The increasing emphasis laid on the gods of totality, who transcended this dualism, would seem to be the main reason why the importance of both Varuṇa and Indra, when considered in the context of the total mythological system, is no longer equal to what it was in the Vedic period' (*Varuṇa and Vidūṣaka: On the origin of the Sanskrit drama*, Amsterdam, 1979, p. 75). However, despite his arguments, Varuṇa has already declined more than Indra in the Rāmāyaṇa at least and Brahmā, whom he regards as one of the 'gods of totality', has only a brief period of prominence before he too is eclipsed.

[34] Gaṇeśa, even as a name for Śiva himself and not his son, is extremely late and apparently does not occur in the text of the Mahābhārata (but cf. *gaṇeśvaravināyakāḥ*, Mbh. 13.App.I.18.54 post.). However, in a *phalaśruti* at the end of the Yuddhakāṇḍa (6.3703(G)* 2) are mentioned a class of minor deities or demons, the Vināyakas, a term later used of Gaṇeśa, while in a passage of the fifth stage Gaṇeśa himself occurs under his title of Vighneśvara (6.1386* 1[l.v.]).

times, and formal groupings become commoner, especially the *vaiśvadevas* and the *lokapālas*. The *lokapālas*, 'world-protectors' (in fact regents of the four quarters) and even more the *diśāgajas*, 'elephants of the regions (= compass-points)', are characteristic of later, puranic Hinduism, although the *lokapālas* are for instance named in *Manu* as recipients of a *bali* offering (*Manu* 3.87). One Vedic deity who later undergoes something of a revival as the result of influence from Iran brought into the Northwest from the first century AD onwards under the Kuṣāṇas and later is Sūrya. This is reflected in the so-called *Ādityahṛdaya*, a litany of homage to the sun expounded to Rāma in a sudden unheralded appearance by Agastya, in which Sūrya is identified with Brahmā, Viṣṇu, Śiva and so forth (6 App.I.65); there are in fact several texts of this name, of which this is the best known.[35] It has been widely popular, although the commentator Govindarāja states that Uḍāli did not have it in his text of the Rāmāyaṇa. Mythological figures appearing for the first time include Dhanvantari, the divine physician, Nandi, Viṣvaksena, the Vṛkodaras, Śeṣa and Sārameya. The Bhārgavas achieve a more prominent, even inflated, position. The Vedas are referred to more often and in more detail, including references to specific texts such as the *Gāyatrī* (3.203* 2 and 6 App.I.25.61) and the *Śatarudrīya* (2 App.I.31.21), to specific schools (Kaṭha and Kalāpin, 2.754* 2), and to the exclusion of śūdras from hearing the Vedas (3.926*); the wisdom of one who recites them on the first day of the lunar fortnight wastes away (5.1259* = 1356*). By the fifth stage there is mention of the Nyāya and Mīmāṃsā systems along with the *dharmaśāstra* literature (5 App.I.6.31). There is also greater use of mantras as spells, as well as elaboration of the briefer ritual details of earlier stages, for example in the use of such a technical term as *anvāstaraṇika* 'to be chosen as secondary victim' (2.1812* 72, part of the more elaborate Northern alternative to 2.70 describing Daśaratha's funeral), and the mention of one sacrifice for the first time (*sautrāmaṇi*, 7.1383*). At the same time there is still more prominent mention of Hinduistic features. For example, the crossing of the Gaṅgā, already in the second stage accompanied by worship from Sītā, is now further marked by muttered invocations, sipping water and obeisance as they

[35] Bāṇa refers in his *Harṣacarita* to Prabhākaravardhana reciting an *Ādityahṛdaya* mantra daily. The Rāmāyaṇa passage has influenced another text of the same name assigned to the *Bhaviṣyottara Purāṇa* and, in Gail's opinion, forms the model for Paraśurāma's hymn to Kṛṣṇa at *Brahmāṇḍa Purāṇa* 3.35 which he dates after 800 AD (*Paraśurāma* pp. 167–8 and 193–7). One may also compare the late list of the 108 names of the sun at Mbh. 3.3.

enter the boat (2.1096*) and by more elaborate offerings of a thousand jars of wine and rice with meat (2.1101*); the growing sanctity of Gaṅgā is also shown by the fetching of jars of Gaṅgā water for the installation ceremony (2 App.I.10.20), and in one substitution belonging to the fifth stage she is called the purifier of the whole world (2.1099* 1). Alongside the Vedas and Purāṇas are mentioned Pañcarātra texts in Agastya's narration to Rāma of Sanatkumāra's discourse to Rāvaṇa (7 App.I.3.151). One fifth-stage addition even includes a Śaiva ascetic having a rosary of *rudrākṣa* berries and smeared with ashes (7 App.I.1.19*). Overall, brahmanical influence becomes very apparent.

The emphasis on astrology by now is seen for example in the inclusion of horoscopes for Rāma and his brothers (1.506* and 508*) and the assigning of a propitious moment for the consecration of the exiles' hut (2.1206* 7). Both horoscopes reveal their lateness by the inclusion alongside the older *nakṣatra* system of the signs of the zodiac Cancer (*karkaṭa* and *kulīra*, also 2.259* 1, both meaning 'crab', a translation from the Greek) and Pisces (*mīna* 'fish'), for the zodiacal system was borrowed from the Greeks of Alexandria, first in the middle of the second century AD.[36]

It is worth repeating that consideration of the religious pattern apparent in the text should not lead the reader to over-emphasise its importance. In its early stages at least, the Rāmāyaṇa is a martial epic with a kṣatriya background, and Rāma is its noble hero. As Jacobi put it, he is 'durchaus Mensch', 'thoroughly human'.[37] This is implied by Rāma's own statement that he is subject to fate (2.98.15), affirmed during the revelation of his divinity when—perhaps through modesty—he declares himself to be human (6.105.10ab), and reiterated both by his enemies,

[36] D. Pingree, in his edition of *The Yavanajātaka of Sphujidhvaja*, Harvard Oriental Series 48, Cambridge, Mass., 1978, stresses the link with specifically Alexandria (vol. 2, pp. 196–8), as well as noting the date of the work by Yavaneśvara on which it is based as 149/50 AD. He also rejects any possibility of the earlier appearance of the zodiac in India, as claimed for example by B. Barua, *Gāyā and Buddha-Gāyā*, Calcutta, 1934, vol. 2, pp. 83, 90–3 and 121. Pingree further notes (vol. 2, pp. 268–9) the implausibility of five planets in their exaltations—the entire horoscope is obviously a reflection of Rāma's greatness not a prediction of it. Nevertheless, a recent attempt has been made to compute actual dates for Rāma's horoscope, arriving at the following dates in order of decreasing astronomical probability: 11th March 200 AD, 16th March 745 AD, and 4th April 110 BC (K. Ferrari d'Occhieppo, 'Datierbarkeit des Horoskops im I. Buch des Epos Rāmāyaṇa', WZKSA 23, 1979, pp. 109–16). Thus, even acceptance of the most likely of these would imply a third century date for the passage.

[37] *Das Râmâyaṇa*, p. 65.

who scornfully call him a 'human footsoldier' (3.25.22d, 6.98.15d) and even by his admiring ally Hanumān, who denies Rāma's identity with Viṣṇu in successive sargas, explicitly calling him human on the second occasion (5.48.11 and 49.26). Rāma's superhuman abilities do not conflict with this status, for they reflect nothing more than the hyperbole appropriate to any epic tradition; that his prowess should sometimes lead those who witness it to compare him to a god is likewise understandable; for instance, to convince Sugrīva of his ability to defeat Vālin, Rāma pierces seven *sāl* trees in a row with an arrow which returns to his quiver (4.11.47–12.4), a feat which provokes Sugrīva to call him 'equal to Indra and Varuṇa' (*mahendravaruṇopama*, 4.12.10d). Even so, he obviously views Rāma as a man, though of superhuman prowess, as another statement makes clear: 'You are capable of killing with arrows all the gods along with Indra, o bull among men, how much more Vālin, o king' (4.12.8). The same idea lies behind Mārīca's terrified assertion that 'Rāma is dharma incarnate, pious, truly brave, and king of the whole world, as Vāsava of the gods' (3.35.13). So too in her lament over the dead Rāvaṇa Mandodarī, after saying that Rāma is only human, declares that after all he cannot just be human and must be Indra in the form of Rāma (6.99.5–11).[38] Rāma is being extolled for his martial abilities, with more than a hint of his kingly function, whether for protection or punishment, and so is frequently compared to Indra throughout the first two stages.

Among these frequent comparisons with Indra are the three instances in the Yuddhakāṇḍa where Rāma and Lakṣmaṇa are compared to Indra and Viṣṇu respectively. The two brothers are also once compared to Indra's two arms (5.19.28c), as well as to various pairs of deities, twice in the Balakāṇḍa to the Aśvins (21.7f and 47.3c), several times to Indra and Varuṇa, also to Brahmā and Indra (2.29.11d), Vāyu and Indra (5.36.40b), and Agni and Māruta (5.37.52c). Rāma alone is compared with various gods, for example Brahmā (2.1.10c and 93.27b), Śiva (3.23.27cd, 24.10cd, 26d and 61.2cd), Garuḍa (3.29.5d and 5.19.23b), Kandarpa (3.32.5c), Kubera (2.14.16a), and, most frequently after Indra, Parjanya (2.1.31d, 3.13cd, 14.21, 104.12d, 3.27.7d); as well as at least twice, in passages belonging to the second stage (2.1.32 and 5.33.9), to several deities at once for different aspects of his character. Rāma and Sītā are even compared to Rudra and Devī, once in the second stage (3.15.39[l.v.]) and at least once in the fourth stage

[38] However, the S. recension cannot leave it there and makes her continue that it cannot after all be so, since Indra cannot face Rāvaṇa, and Rāma must therefore be Viṣṇu (6.3114*).

(2 App.I.26.60). As well as direct comparisons, we may note Rāma's association with Indra to enhance his status. It is Indra who, in conversation with the sage Śarabhaṅga, predicts—in effect commissions—Rāma's future exploits (3.4.19).[39] The Śarabhaṅga episode belongs to the second stage and a similar, but briefer, passage, where Kabandha refers to Indra's promise of release for him by Rāma (3.67.15–16), is also secondary, being omitted by the Northwestern recension. Equally, in the supreme crisis of his duel with Rāvaṇa, Rāma receives the aid of Indra's charioteer, Mātali, and is thus implicitly equated with Indra (6.90–100).[40] Again, Rāma's lifting of the curse on Ahalyā indirectly links him with Indra, who caused it by his adultery with her. However, by the third stage Indra's moral degradation, which reaches its climax in the Purāṇas, has already begun, as noted earlier; this is incompatible with the growing stress on Rāma's upholding of dharma and must be a factor in the disruption of the association of Rāma with Indra. Accordingly, the association of Rāma with Indra can only have been a transitional phase in his evolution from hero to *avatāra*.

Nevertheless, these are the terms in which Rāma is viewed, not merely in the earliest parts but also to quite an extent in the third stage. There are at least sixty occasions on which Rāma is compared to Indra in the first two stages, against eight comparisons and four identifications with Viṣṇu. All four explicit identifications are in the Yuddhakāṇḍa, and all but one occur in the very late final section (6.26.31ab, 105.5–16, 107.17 and 30). In the third stage, during the course of Agastya's narration to Rāma of Rāvaṇa's background, Agastya declares to Rāma: 'You, sir, are the eternal four-armed god Nārāyaṇa, the invincible, imperishable lord, born to kill the Rākṣasas' (7.8.25). Though only a single verse added almost as it were as an afterthought at the end of its sarga, this in many ways sums up the implicit attitude of the Uttarakāṇḍa, whereas the Bālakāṇḍa is nearer to the core of the epic in tending to assume Rāma's humanity. The Bālakāṇḍa does of course contain the account of Viṣṇu's decision to become incarnate for the destruction of Rāvaṇa (1.14–15), but we may note that it is through the mechanism,

[39] F. Whaling (*The Rise of the Religious Significance of Rāma*, Delhi, 1980, pp. 80–1) notes that, significantly, this episode is not found in later Rāmāyaṇas. Śarabhaṅga himself but not Indra's visit occurs in the *Rāmopākhyāna* (Mbh. 3.261.39–40). Nevertheless, Kampaṉ in his version (see pp. 269–72) includes not only Indra's visit to Śarabhaṅga and invitation to him to go to the abode of Brahmā but also his praise of Rāma (3.2).

[40] In the Mahābhārata, Mātali comes to take Arjuna to Indra's heaven and then drives the chariot for him in his battles with the Nivātakavacas and the inhabitants of Hiraṇyapura (Mbh. 3.161–71); Arjuna is of course regarded as Indra's son.

in response to Daśaratha's sacrifice, of a dish of gruel presented by a divine figure to the king and shared by him among his wives (1.15.25–7); the logic of this is that all four sons are partial incarnations of the deity—a position that is not adopted elsewhere.[41] Identification with Viṣṇu grows more frequent with the fourth stage. For example at the beginning of the Ayodhyākāṇḍa both recensions separately make Rāma an *aṃśāvatāra* of Viṣṇu (2.1.9cd v.l., 10* 1–2). In the Sundarakāṇḍa, Southern manuscripts enlarge Hanumān's description of Rāma to Rāvaṇa, making him declare that Rāma is capable of emanating the entire world with its inhabitants and that he is equal in prowess to Viṣṇu (5.1048* 5–6, 11). In the Yuddhakāṇḍa, two Northern additions say that Viṣṇu, lord of the gods, has taken human form as Rāma (6.254* and App.I.17.40), and the *phalaśrutis* at its end also include an identification of Rāma with Viṣṇu (3703(G)* 10–11).

The recurrent epithets linked with Rāma's name mirror this development, with little interest in religious matters being shown by the early redactors. Much the commonest is *rāmasyākliṣṭakarmaṇaḥ* 'of ever-active Rāma' found twenty-three times in the first two stages; this adjective is virtually specific to Rāma in the Rāmāyaṇa but in the Mahābhārata characterises both Kṛṣṇa and Pārtha, i.e. Arjuna. Next most frequent, with eighteen instances each, are the simple patronymic *rāmo daśarathātmajaḥ and rāghavasya mahātmanaḥ* 'of noble Rāma', where he is called by an adjective applied to practically every individual that the metre allows, not excluding Rāvaṇa, though *rāvaṇasya durātmanaḥ* 'of ignoble Rāvaṇa' is commoner. 'The truly brave Rāma', *rāmaḥ satyaparākramaḥ*, occurs sixteen times, while *rāmo dharmabhṛtāṃ varaḥ* occurs a dozen times. These last two stress the kṣatriya values, firstly of truth and valour, secondly of upholding tradition, which form the moral basis of the original story. With the subsequent brahmanisation of the work and consequent shift in emphasis of dharma from 'tradition, social duty' to 'righteousness, religious duty' comes the desire to assign divine status to Rāma, at first usually expressed through comparison with Indra. The many examples of this tendency include 'the truly brave Rāma, equal to Indra in his divine qualities' (*divyair guṇaiḥ śakrasamo rāmaḥ satyaparākramaḥ*, 2.2.19ab) and 'Rāma, the best upholder of dharma and equal in prowess to Mahendra' (*rāmo dharmabhṛtāṃ śreṣṭho mahendrasamavikramaḥ*, 5.56.17cd).

[41] The divine *pāyasa* is definitely shared out between the wives, but there is room for dispute on the proportions, since this passage and that describing the birth of the sons (1.17.6–10) appear to differ; the commentators go to great lengths to reconcile the discrepancy.

Later passages chart the rise in status of both Brahmā and Viṣṇu in such similes as 'Rāma, the truly brave, renowned throughout the world, surpassed his brothers in qualities, as the Self-born [i.e. Brahmā] surpasses creation' (*teṣām atiyaśā loke rāmaḥ satyaparākramaḥ/ svayaṃbhūr iva bhūtānāṃ babhūva guṇavattaraḥ//*1.76.13); an almost identical verse at the beginning of the Ayodhyākāṇḍa, originally no doubt part of the same passage,[42] is followed by an insertion of the Southern recension declaring that Viṣṇu was born as Rāma to kill Rāvaṇa (2.1.10 and 10*). It is only in the fourth stage that this complete identification with Viṣṇu becomes frequent, for even when Rāma's divinity is revealed after the capture of Laṅkā (6.105), we may note that it is Kubera, Yama, Indra, Varuṇa, Śiva and Brahmā who do so and that the first words they address to Rāma, *kartā sarvasya lokasya* 'maker of the entire world' (5a), have just been applied to Brahmā (2c). It is also significant that the revelation takes place in two stages, strikingly similar to the successive stages of Kṛṣṇa's self-revelation in chapters 9–10 and 11 of the *Bhagavadgītā*, though much briefer; no doubt the same factors were at work in each case. In the first stage (stanzas 5–8) Rāma is identified with various deities, and only in the second (stanzas 12–16) is he identified with Viṣṇu and his various manifestations; even here the term *indrakarmā* 'having Indra's deeds' appears along with identification with Indra (16a), and it is not until two sargas later that he is eventually called *puruṣottama* (6.107.17d, 30d).[43]

Such is the picture which can be built up from a study of the incidental details of the text. On a broader canvas, the characters and actions of the individuals portrayed provide some interesting insights. The one word which governs the actions of Rāma and his family is 'fidelity': Daśaratha is faithful to his vow to Kaikeyī, Rāma faithfully performs his filial duty, Bharata refuses to usurp his elder brother's rights, Lakṣmaṇa behaves to Rāma more like a servant than a prince. Sītā accompanies her husband to a life of hardship and resists all Rāvaṇa's threats and blandishments, and Rāma undergoes great perils to rescue her.

It is one thing, however, to attempt to fulfil one's dharma, quite another to define it in such a way as to cover all contingencies, and inevitably conflicts arise. Whether the result of the exigencies of the

[42] On the artificiality of the present division into books, see p. 53.

[43] Similarly in the fourth stage Nārada's *māhātmya* (6 App.I.25.28–81) identifies Rāma with Indra (50) as well as with other gods, after first hailing him as Nārāyaṇa; whereas a Southern expansion of Trijaṭā's dream (5 App.I.5) emphasises Rāma's identity with Viṣṇu as the supreme (*paraṃ brahma paraṃ satyam*, 19).

original plot, or of the change in attitudes which took place in society during the long composition of the poem,it is these conflicts which give life to the characters and prevent them from appearing to be mere puppets. Daśaratha is (perhaps literally) heartbroken on the personal level at being parted from his favourite son, but sees it as his duty to keep his promise to Kaikeyī; what he does not see is that he is thereby infringing his duty to protect the defenceless from arbitrary tyranny, to give his people the best available ruler, and not to make rash vows.[44] This incident finds many parallels in the third-stage story of Rāma's banishment of Sītā to allay the suspicions of his people about her virtue while in Rāvaṇa's hands, an incident foreign to the spirit of the earlier parts of the story, and introduced as part of the brahmanisation of the work. Here, too, a monarch subjugates his personal happiness to his idea of duty, thereby knowingly inflicting cruel injustice on an individual.

Rāma is portrayed as a model of piety at all times. He makes not the least protest when told of his father's unexpected, harsh decree, and even goes so far as to advise that messengers be sent to recall his supplanter, Bharata. He entertains no rancour towards those who have caused his banishment, and automatically attributes his own purity of motive to others, refusing to suspect either Bharata or Vibhīṣaṇa when others find their approach alarming. One of his most frequently stressed attributes is his self-control, yet when this can be subordinated to the artistic desire to portray him as a credible man, a prey to normal human feelings, and he expresses his grief at the loss of Sītā in a series of emotional ravings from which Lakṣmaṇa has to calm him. Equally, though true to his pledged word down to the last detail, as shown by his refusal to leave the forest and pass the rainy season in Kiṣkindhā, he can be devious when he wishes to avoid a public display of emotion. Thus, he avoids the citizens of Ayodhyā who attempt to follow him into exile, and the method of Sītā's banishment in the Uttarakāṇḍa is nothing short of deceitful. It is in this third stage that the concept of 'righteous Rāma' is most stressed, but it does not seem to extend to the personal level. Equally, though he frequently bases his obedience to Daśaratha on an abstract piety, when the courtier Jābāli attempts to persuade him to return to Ayodhyā on worldly grounds, he counters expediency with an argument stressing the expediency of

[44] However, W. Ruben ('Vier Liebestragödien des Rāmāyaṇa', ZDMG 100, 1950, pp. 287–355) seeks to make out of Daśaratha's intention to install Rāma a pledge ('gegebene Wort') comparable to his vow to Kaikeyī and suggests that, in the situation where he therefore has to break one promise, Daśaratha weakly gives in to his favourite; this is to miss the real irony of the situation.

morality: since subjects copy their ruler's habits, a monarch must adhere to truth (2.101).

Rāma is viewed in the early stages as the perfect kṣatriya, a position which in no way conflicts with the religious ideals of his time, for each should do his duty within his own *varṇa*. He declares that he will live in the forest like an ascetic in a manner more usually associated with brāhmans, but it is when he seeks to carry out this resolve that his role as the perfect kṣatriya comes to the fore. When the sages complain of harassment by the Rākṣasas, Rāma immediately agrees to protect them. By the second stage, qualms about the morality of his position seem to have crept in. Sītā is made to put forward a limited version of the doctrine of non-violence (*ahiṃsā*), saying that he should not attack the Rākṣasas without direct provocation, and forcing Rāma to justify his action by asserting his duty both to protect the sages and to fulfil his pledged word (3.8–9).

Rāma's championship of Sugrīva and killing of Vālin provides further evidence of this conflict of opposing ideals. Although Sugrīva is presented by the text as the wronged brother, and unhesitatingly accepted as such by Rāma, the rights and wrongs of the matter are by no means clear-cut. For Rāma to interfere as he does in the duel between Sugrīva and Vālin is deceitful and a clear breach of the conventions of warfare,[45] as the dying Vālin points out in a second-stage insertion. To justify himself, Rāma claims the duty of punishing Vālin's crimes acting as Bharata's agent, and then rather lamely—and quite against the spirit of the earlier part, where the Vānaras are effectively human—adds that after all Vālin is only an animal and thus fair game (4.17–18). The point is that the original authors were concerned only with telling a story which extolled Rāma's martial qualities and abilities, and it was only later redactors who became worried by moral scruples. This is obviously the reason for Rāma's complete *volte face* after the siege of Laṅkā, where he suddenly announces that he has undertaken the quest for Sītā only to vindicate his own and his family's honour, not for her sake, and coldly spurns her until her virtue is exonerated by the fire-ordeal (6.102–4). This episode must be a later substitution for an original straightforward happy ending, for until it, Rāma's and Sītā's love for each other has always been portrayed in glowing terms, equalled only by their distress at her abduction.

Lakṣmaṇa, on the other hand, presents a totally different picture. In valour and prowess he is almost Rāma's equal, and his submission to

[45] See pp. 151–2.

Rāma parallels Rāma's obedience to his father, but here the resemblance ends. When Rāma is resigned, he is rebellious; when Rāma is trusting, he is suspicious; when Rāma is calm, he is irascible or fearful; but when Rāma raves, he reassures. This is obviously not intended as a realistic portrayal of his character, for he acts as a foil for Rāma, partly to heighten Rāma's virtues by contrast, partly to afford Rāma an opportunity to expound the correct values.

Sītā's character is rather more fully delineated: her actions, like Rāma's, do not always entirely correspond to her pronouncements. She is obviously devoted to Rāma and to his interests, and thus becomes in later Indian tradition the pattern of the ideal wife, but, at least in the first two stages, she is portrayed as far from meek and submissive, and clearly shares with her husband a relationship based more on mutual love and respect than on domination and fear. Indeed, on two crucial occasions, when she pleads to be allowed to accompany him into exile and when she persuades him to indulge her whim for the golden deer, it is her wishes which prevail against his better judgement. She feels able to criticise Rāma's aggressive behaviour towards the Rākṣasas, with respect but none the less freely, although this is of course merely a device of the redactors to allow Rāma to justify his actions; it would be wrong to attribute this dispute to any significant difference in moral outlook. Sītā remains devoted to Rāma, and this devotion fuels the flames both of her defiant, scornful resistance of Rāvaṇa and her spirited but mistaken denunciation of Lakṣmaṇa's motives in seeking to remain with her when Rāma goes after the golden deer. By the end of the second stage and the third, she is portrayed as more submissive but no less spirited: she makes no verbal remonstrance when Rāma rejects her after the capture of Laṅkā, nor when he later banishes her from Ayodhyā, but her actions, first in undergoing the fire-ordeal, then in calling upon the Earth to vindicate her, show that she has lost none of her old defiance. It is intriguing to note that the two ordeals, though for the same purpose, have different ends: in the first she will be restored to Rāma if she has been faithful to him, in the second she will be swallowed by the Earth. Is this second ordeal an act of defiant vengeance, preventing Rāma from again enjoying the wife he has so misused, or is it a final self-sacrifice from a still-devoted wife who realises that, because of public opinion, she can never make her husband completely happy? Neither her character nor Rāma's have been basically altered by the passage of time and the changing religious climate, for unlike the external observances, they are basic to the plot, and such developments as there are appear to have been grafted on in a less than skilful manner.

8
ADAPTATIONS IN SANSKRIT

'While ever mountains and streams shall endure upon earth, so long shall the Rāmāyaṇa story circulate about the worlds.' (1.2.35)

The increasing veneration of Rāma himself is obviously a factor in the popularity of the epic and its dissemination. Yet at least the first stages of the spread of the story into other literature seem to have preceded the deification of Rāma. Thus, the Mahābhārata contains passages alluding to or summarising the Rāma legend which reveal both attitudes to Rāma, as human and as divine. The most extensive of these Mahābhārata passages, the *Rāmopākhyāna* (Mbh. 3.257–76),[1] sees Rāma as an exemplary but basically human figure—the position reached by the middle of the second stage of the Rāmāyaṇa's growth—in most of its narration, but in one relatively brief section has Brahmā declare that Viṣṇu has descended to earth and tell the other gods to become incarnate as the Vānaras and so forth (Mbh. 3.260). Indeed, the logic of the *Rāmopākhyāna's* presence at that point in the Mahābhārata is that Rāma is human, for Mārkaṇḍeya narrates Rāma's story in answer to Yudhiṣṭhira's enquiry whether there was any man more unfortunate than he in suffering exile to the forest.

The *Rāmopākhyāna* is a relatively extended summary of the story and it is therefore all the more noteworthy that a substantial proportion of its wording is identical with that of the Rāmāyaṇa (approximately 15%). The distribution of such correspondences is noticeably even and their order of occurrence significantly close. Moreover, they demonstrate conclusively that the *Rāmopākhyāna* is in general closer to the Northern recension of the Rāmāyaṇa, suggesting that the *Rāmopākhyāna* is later and that this recension was well established before the fixing of the text of the Mahābhārata. Despite a significant number of agreements with the Southern recension, the *Rāmopākhyāna* is clearly not based on it, even in an earlier form, although this is

[1] See my article 'Sanskrit Epic Tradition I. Epic and Epitome (Rāmāyaṇa and Rāmopākhyāna)', IT 6, 1978, pp. 79–111, where references to earlier studies may also be found.

generally and rightly held to be the more conservative version of the Rāmāyaṇa. Sluszkiewicz, who listed some fifty-seven parallels according to the Rāmāyaṇa recension they follow most closely,[2] drew attention to the fact that he found twice as many correspondences to the Bengal recension as to the Bombay, while also pointing out that the author of the *Rāmopākhyāna* could not have relied exclusively on that recension, and he suggested rather hesitantly that the author of the *Rāmopākhyāna* might have drawn on a third recension which could in fact be the archetype of our present versions. In fact, further examination of *Rāmopākhyāna* parallels to passages with limited manuscript support in the Rāmāyaṇa shows clearly that the primary affiliation of the *Rāmopākhyāna* is in particular with the Northeastern recension, a point which is significant for the textual history of the Rāmāyaṇa.

On the other hand there are certain divergences which have sometimes been taken to indicate that the *Rāmopākhyāna* is independent of the Rāmāyaṇa. Several of them are instances of the addition of detail which is almost certainly secondary. Thus, the *Rāmopākhyāna* names the place where Rāvaṇa visits Mārīca as Gokarṇa (261.54), probably developed from its mention as the site of Rāvaṇa's penance in a fourth-stage passage of the Rāmāyaṇa (3.591*, further elaborated at 7.9.37 and 159*). Elsewhere also the *Rāmopākhyāna* shows a more developed geography than the Rāmāyaṇa. When Brahmā asks the other gods to become incarnate as Vānaras to help Viṣṇu in his form as Rāma, he orders a Gandharvī named Dundubhī to be born as the hunchback Mantharā (260.1–15). Another kind of divergence can be seen in the different tactics employed by Kaikeyī to get her way with Daśaratha. Since the king's reply is virtually identical in both texts (2.10.10 and 261.22c–23b), it seems likely that the discrepancy is simply the result of artistic licence. Similarly, in the episode of Rāvaṇa's abduction of Sītā, the *Rāmopākhyāna* has Sītā re-enter the hermitage (262.39); in the Rāmāyaṇa she has never left it (3.45–47).

Other discrepancies, often involving the names of minor characters, are frequent but of little significance. At one point the *Rāmopākhyāna* names Sugrīva's ministers as Mainda, Dvivida, Hanumān and Jāmbavān (264.23); the Rāmāyaṇa at the equivalent point has, as Raghavan accurately but misleadingly indicates, a 'list which is completely different from that given in the *Rāmopākhyāna*'.[3] In fact the *Rāmopākhyāna*

[2] E. Słuszkiewicz, *Przyczynki do badań nad dziejami redakcyj Rāmāyany*, Kraków, 1938, pp. 13–32.

[3] V. Raghavan, *The Greater Rāmāyaṇa*, Varanasi, 1973, p. 17. This work contains

takes these names from a longer list occurring in other contexts and so this is actually an instance of transposition demonstrating the closeness of the *Rāmopākhyāna* to the Rāmāyaṇa and not the converse. However, a list of eight *piśācas* and Rākṣasas (*Rāmopākhyāna* 269.2) is entirely new.

Another divergence lies in the *Rāmopākhyāna* treatment of the Yuddhakāṇḍa material: while some is abbreviated, other parts are treated more extensively, so that the author of the *Rāmopākhyāna* has devoted nearly half his space to under one third of his original and thereby shifted the emphasis of the story. Some of its elaboration consists of additions of names, such as we have just seen, some consists of details of strategy after the manner of the *arthaśāstra*, some is developed out of slight hints in the Rāmāyaṇa, and some arises through rearrangement of the order of events, involving at times some telescoping of individual incidents. After Rāma's victory, he repudiates Sītā, who appeals to the elements to vindicate her, and accepts her back only after reassurances from Brahmā, but the fire-ordeal as such is absent (275.1–36); the whole account ends with Rāma's installation and performance of ten *aśvamedhas* (275.65–9).

To place against such divergences, there are occasions on which the *Rāmopākhyāna* is scarcely intelligible without a prior knowledge of the story, for example the extreme brevity of its narrative of Bharata meeting Rāma and receiving the sandals. There are also occasions when the actual wording of the *Rāmopākhyāna* is more explicable in the light of the Rāmāyaṇa. Again, even where he has rearranged incidents, the author of the *Rāmopākhyāna* keeps closely to the text of the Rāmāyaṇa, whether using whole incidents or briefer parallels of one or two pādas, which he tends to group even when divorcing them from their Rāmāyaṇa context.

A major question is whether the Bāla or the Uttara kāṇḍa was in existence at the time that the *Rāmopākhyāna* was composed. Only one section from each, the genealogies and background of Rāma and Rāvaṇa respectively, appear as a prologue to the *Rāmopākhyāna*, and the evidence probably indicates that this passage is the source whence the Bāla and Uttara kāṇḍas have been expanded. At any rate, presumably Rāvaṇa's genealogy was included in the *Rāmopākhyāna* earlier than in the Rāmāyaṇa, since otherwise more of the story of the Uttarakāṇḍa

much useful information on the treatment of the Rāma story in the Mahābhārata and the Purāṇas. The first significant attempt to trace the different versions of the Rāma story is contained in A. Baumgartner, *Das Râmâyana und die Râma-Literatur der Inder* (Ergänzungshefte zu den 'Stimmen aus Maria-Laach' 62), Freiburg, 1894.

would have been included. Moreover, the *Rāmopākhyāna* seems to have pieced together its account of Rāvaṇa's activities from stray indications in the earlier parts of the Rāmāyaṇa, for there is a striking lack of verbal similarity to the equivalent part of the Uttarakāṇḍa (7.11–34). In conjunction with the previous evidence, this may be taken to indicate that not only is the *Rāmopākhyāna* based on the Rāmāyaṇa, being closest to the extant Northeastern recension, but also that its composition should be assigned, in terms of the stages of growth of the Rāmāyaṇa, to the middle of the second stage. Although, as its framework clearly indicates, the *Rāmopākhyāna* is one of the considerable number of expansions in the *Āraṇyakaparvan* of the Mahābhārata, it is certainly not among the latest additions to the Mahābhārata. As we have noted, in general it still sees Rāma as an exemplary but basically human figure, unlike some of the many other brief references to the Rāma story throughout the *Āraṇyakaparvan*, which see him as an *avatāra*.[4]

Within the Mahābhārata tradition, there is also a group of four passages which are obviously linked in being similar in subject-matter, and often wording, to the closing verses of the Yuddhakāṇḍa (6.116.80–90). These passages form two pairs, since two treat Rāma as one of the *avatāras* of Viṣṇu (Hv. 31.110–42 and Mbh. 2 App.21.492–582), whereas two include him among the sixteen kings of old (Mbh. 12.29.46–55 and 7 App. 8.437–82).[5] The relationships within each of the pairs seem clear enough; the *Sabhā* passage (Mbh. 2 App.21) is based on the *Harivaṃśa* and the *Droṇa* (Mbh. 7 App.8) form of the narrative of the sixteen kings is later than the *Śānti* account (Mbh. 12.29). The virtually complete lack of overlap between these four passages and the *Rāmopākhyāna* immediately excludes the possibility of their being derived from the Rāmāyaṇa through the *Rāmopākhyāna*. But the *avatāra* passages preface the common material from the end of the Yuddhakāṇḍa with a summary of the Rāmāyaṇa, which quite often uses its own wording, while the *Droṇa* passage has its own résumé which is quite separate and much briefer.

The available evidence supports the view that the *Sabhā* passage is

[4] Thus, Hanumān in his narrative to Bhīma calls him Viṣṇu in human form (Mbh. 3.147.28c) and Dhaumya comforts Yudhiṣṭhira by instancing even gods concealing themselves, including Viṣṇu living in Daśaratha's house (Mbh. 3.299.18).

[5] See my article 'Sanskrit Epic Tradition II. The Avatāra Accounts of Rāma', to be published in the proceedings of the Fourth World Sanskrit Conference, Weimar, 1979, by Akademie-Verlag, Berlin. For a discussion of the section on Rāma Jāmadagnya in the *Harivaṃśa* passage see Gail, *Paraśurāma*, pp. 46–7.

derived from the *Harivaṃśa* version and also indicates that both were familiar with the Rāmāyaṇa at the end of its third stage of growth. The *Droṇa* passage is particularly intriguing; it is much freer in its wording than any of the others, making its affiliations less easy to determine; the verses it shares with the *Śānti* version are simply a framework, and in the body of the passages there is no instance of agreement without agreement of the other two passages also. There is evidence—conflicting, unfortunately—to suggest that it does not derive solely from the *Śānti* passage but is also based on either the *Harivaṃśa* or the *Sabhā* version, or possibly both. Altogether, the *Droṇa* passage gives the impression of being an eclectic version standing at the end of the line of transmission.

All four of the passages share a common dependence on the closing verses of the Yuddhakāṇḍa, and again it is clear that the closest connection is with the Northern recension of the Rāmāyaṇa. The *Śāntiparvan* passage draws most directly on this Rāmāyaṇa passage and appears to be the earliest. The *Harivaṃśa* passage, despite some evidence of contact with the *Śāntiparvan* version, draws separately on the Rāmāyaṇa both for its summary of the story and for its section on Rāma's righteous rule. The *Sabhāparvan* version is expanded from the *Harivaṃśa* passage which, with occasional additions, it follows quite closely. The *Droṇaparvan* passage shares a common framework with the *Śāntiparvan* passage, treating Rāma therefore as a mortal hero, nonetheless showing acquaintance with the *avatāra* passages of the *Harivaṃśa* and the *Sabhāparvan*. Not only does it share common innovations with the *Sabhā* versions, its indebtedness to it is clear, making this the latest version.

Although the earliest version, that of the *Śāntiparvan*, shows little acquaintance with the Bāla or Uttara kāṇḍas and treats Rāma as a mortal hero, his legend was evidently by then well known and other parts of the *Śāntiparvan* are undoubtedly later than the complete Rāmāyaṇa; but the *Harivaṃśa* and *Sabhā* versions are familiar with the Uttarakāṇḍa, tending to corroborate a date for the final redaction of the Rāmāyaṇa well before the time when the Mahābhārata attained its present form. The priority has long been recognised—these details serve to emphasise the considerable interval involved.

Another brief account of the Rāma story, independent of either the *Rāmopākhyāna* or the four passages just examined, is Hanumān's account of the Rāma story to Bhīma, who meets Hanumān in the course of bringing the Saugandhika flower for Draupadī (Mbh. 3.147); here, by contrast with the Rāmāyaṇa itself, Hanumān explicitly declares that Rāma is Viṣṇu in human form (Mbh. 3.147.28), as well as actually naming the Rāmāyaṇa (11c).[6] Similarly, the account of Rāma's encounter with his namesake Rāma son of Jamadagni inserted by some manuscripts into the *Tīrthayātrā* section of the *Āraṇyakaparvan* (Mbh. 3 App.14) is a completely separable reworking—indeed substantial remodelling—of the Bālakāṇḍa episode (Rām. 1.73–5), although there are a few verbal reminiscences.[7]

It is noteworthy that the last two passages mentioned occur in the *Āraṇyakaparvan* of the Mahābhārata, as does the *Rāmopākhyāna*. In fact, there are no less than seven such passages definitely referring to characters or episodes of the Rāmāyaṇa in that book, and in addition there is the *Nalopākhyāna* which undoubtedly borrows verbally from the Rāmāyaṇa.[8] The next largest number is in the *Śāntiparvan*, which has five such passages, and there are two each in the *Droṇa* and *Śalya* parvans, as well as a further eight which are rejected from the text of the Critical Edition of the Mahābhārata. This pattern is of course entirely consistent with such passages having been incorporated into the Mahābhārata during its main phase of expansion, for it has long been held that the *Āraṇyaka* and *Śānti* parvans reached their present bulk as a result of it.

By contrast, there is no direct mention of any central character or incident of the Mahābhārata in the Rāmāyaṇa. There are several individuals only briefly appearing or alluded to in the Rāmāyaṇa whose stories are narrated at greater length in the Mahābhārata, usually in the *Āraṇyakaparvan*; however, these are clearly part of the traditional stock of tales independently and often secondarily incorporated into either epic.[9]

[6] Another such naming occurs in one late addition at the end of the *Harivaṃśa* (App.I.40.168–9, cf. Rām. 2.60*), while another actually refers to the acting of a play based on the Rāmāyaṇa (App.I.29F.236–48). One may surmise that mention of the text is later than narration of the story.

[7] Cf. V. S. Sukthankar, 'Epic Studies VI. The Bhṛgus and the Bhārata: A Text-Historical Study', ABORI 18, 1936–7, pp. 1–76, esp. pp. 20–1, V. Raghavan, *The Greater Rāmāyaṇa*, Varanasi, 1973, p. 10, and Gail, *Paraśurāma*, p. 50. Mbh. 3 App.14.33–4 may be compared with Rām. 1.74.28, 36 with 75.3ab, 42 with 75.4cd, 71 with 75.20cd, and 72 with 75.19ab.

[8] See V. S. Sukthankar, 'The Nala Episode and the Rāmāyaṇa', *A Volume of Eastern and Indian Studies presented to F. W. Thomas*, Bombay, 1939, pp. 294–303, and G. C. Jhala, ' "The Nala Episode and the Rāmāyaṇa" A Footnote', ABORI 48–9, 1968, pp. 295–8.

[9] Thus the *Āraṇyakaparvan* includes the stories of Nala and Damayantī (Mbh. 3.50–78, Rām. 5.548* 7), Ilvala and Vātāpi (Mbh. 3.94–7, Rām. 3.10.53–64), Sagara and Asamañjas (Mbh. 3.104–5, Rām. 2.32.15–20), Ṛśyaśṛṅga (Mbh. 3.110–3, Rām. 1.8–9),

As well as these instances of narrative passages showing links between the two epics, there is also of course a substantial common stock of proverbs, similes, long compounds and the various types of stereotyped phrase.[10] The majority of the proverbs occurring in the Rāmāyaṇa are also found in the Mahābhārata and about a fifth of the similes are common to both. They illustrate the richness of the common, underlying bardic tradition, as do many of the stereotyped expressions. These, however, may be divided into three groups: those found in both epics and thus most probably belonging to the common traditional stock, those found in the Mahābhārata but not in the Rāmāyaṇa or only in later parts, and those peculiar to the Rāmāyaṇa and lacking in the Mahābhārata or only in late passages. As a result, it is clear that the poets of the later parts of the Rāmāyaṇa were intimately acquainted with the Mahābhārata in something like its present form, whereas Vālmīki was not. In particular, later parts of the Yuddhakāṇḍa seem to show familiarity with the *Bhīṣmaparvan*, although this may in part be due to similarity of subject-matter. There is also a fair amount of evidence that the redactors of the Northern recension were more familiar with the Mahābhārata.

More substantial common passages include much of the didactic element in the Rāmāyaṇa. Thus, for example, the sarga on the evils of a kingless state (2.61) shows a large measure of agreement with a Mahābhārata passage which discusses the evils resulting if a king does not protect his people (Mbh. 12.67–8) and which probably derives from the Rāmāyaṇa version. Conversely, the story of Surabhi (2.68) is undoubtedly borrowed from the Mahābhārata (3.10). The *kaccit* sarga, however, though probably inserted later into the Mahābhārata, may well derive in both epics from an independent catechism. In addition, the Mahābhārata has borrowed certain other elements from the Rāmāyaṇa, of which one example has already been given in the *Nalopākhyāna*, where Sudeva's soliloquy (Mbh. 3.65) closely imitates Hanumān's soliloquy (Rām. 5.13–14 and 17).

Although the *dharmaśāstra* literature is broadly contemporary with the middle to later stages of the epic tradition (and there are many links

Cyavana and Sukanyā (Mbh. 3.122–4, Rām. 2.102.16, 5.548* 7, 7.1.2 etc.), Māndhātṛ (Mbh. 3.126, Rām. 1.69.22–3 etc.), Aṣṭāvakra (Mbh. 3.132–4, Rām. 6.107.16) and Sāvitrī (Mbh. 3.277–83, Rām. 2.27.6 and 5.548* 5). From elsewhere we have the story of king Nṛga changed into a chameleon (Mbh. 13.6.38c, 69 and 71.2, 14.93.74, Rām. 7 App.I.8.13–82).

[10] Some aspects of this have already been covered in chapter 2 and the Appendix. Cf. also my articles SE, FS, *Proverbs* and SET III.

between the *dharmaśāstras* and the didactic parts of the Mahābhārata), there is very little sign of any mutual influence between the *dharmaśāstras* and the Rāmāyaṇa. The relatively few verses in common are almost without exception found in the Mahābhārata also and may therefore be taken as part of the traditional corpus of proverbial material; certainly, they do not indicate any direct acquaintance of the Rāmāyaṇa with the *dharmaśāstras* nor *vice versa*. However, in its mainly later didactic portions, the Rāmāyaṇa does show similarity of outlook and terminology with the *dharmaśāstras* and by the fourth stage this is probably sufficient to suggest general awareness of that class of literature, although the term occurs once in the second stage (2.94.33). In the opposite direction, there is the allusion in the *Gobhilasmṛti* to Rāma's use of a golden image of Sītā at his sacrifice.[11] It is interesting to note, however, that for certain later writers on dharma the Rāmāyaṇa was authoritative; for example Ballāla Sena, the author of the *Dānasāgara*, a twelfth-century digest on *dharmaśāstra*, and Raghunandana, the sixteenth-century Bengali author of the *Smṛtitattva*, both quote the Rāmāyaṇa as a source.[12]

By contrast, the Purāṇas, which broadly continue the epic tradition as well as developing their own particular interests, show more considerable acquaintance with both epics, though with marked variation from one text to another. Chronologically, they undoubtedly postdate the main phases of composition of the epics, but there is also the possibility of influence by them on the latest parts of the epic tradition, with the *Harivaṃśa* in particular forming something of a transition between the two. However, in the present context, their chief value is to confirm the period by which certain episodes were included in the Rāmāyaṇa, and even more to show how the Rāma story has been modified and developed in the course of time. In this respect, their basically religious nature makes it easier to plot the theological developments in the depiction of Rāma than in the contemporary works of classical Sanskrit literature, which will also be surveyed subsequently; they thus form a transition to the later Sanskrit and vernacular Rāmāyaṇas. In their aspect as popular literature, they also form part of the background to the extra-Indian versions of the story.

[11] See p. 173 n.16.

[12] For details see Bhabatosh Bhattacharya, 'The Rāmāyaṇa and its influence upon Ballāla Sena and Raghunandana', JOIB 2, 1953, pp. 18–22, and Nilmadhav Sen, 'A note on "The Rāmāyaṇa and its influence upon Ballāla Sena and Raghunandana"', JOIB 2, 1953, pp. 232–5.

The *Vāyu Purāṇa* briefly deals with the stories of Rāma and Rāvaṇa in its genealogical sections, Rāvaṇa's descent through Viśravas being given (70.32 ff.), while the appearance of Sītā when Janaka was ploughing the sacrificial ground and a son Bhānumān are mentioned under Nimi's line (89).[13] The passage on Rāma concludes with the traditional lines on *rāmarājya* in virtually the same form as in the *Harivaṃśa*. That on Rāvaṇa makes him four-legged, in addition to his ten heads and twenty arms (70.42).

The *Viṣṇu Purāṇa* concentrates mainly on Kṛṣṇa and deals only very briefly, in prose, with the Rāma *avatāra* in its narrative of the solar dynasty (4.4), but none the less includes material from the Uttarakāṇḍa. It commences the account by explicitly declaring that Viṣṇu was born fourfold as Rāma, Lakṣmaṇa, Bharata and Śatrughna (4.4.40),[14] before summarising the main story from Rāma's youthful slaying of Tāḍakā and Mārīca to his taking back of Sītā after the fire-ordeal; there is no divergence from the Rāmāyaṇa narrative. It then devotes almost as much space to Bharata conquering the Gandharvas, Śatrughna killing Lavaṇa and the sons of the four brothers founding various cities, before listing the later members of the dynasty. In the next chapter, on the kings of Mithilā, as one member of Janaka's line, called here Sīradhvaja, is ploughing the ground for a sacrifice to secure children, his daughter Sītā springs up in the furrow (4.5.12), and a little later there is mention of Janaka's son Bhānumān (4.5.30).

The *Matsya Purāṇa* lacks any narration of the Rāma story, although it does mention Vālmīki's narration of it a couple of times (12.50–1 and 53.71–2). However, in view of the passage already discussed in which it parallels the search party accounts,[15] it is significant that it contains two descriptions of Śiva burning Tripura (140.58–75 and 188.15–56), which are evidently based on the burning of Laṅkā, first by Hanumān and later by the Vānaras during the battle (Rām. 5.52 and 6.62), as well as a description of a moonlit night and the pleasures of Tripura's inhabitants (139.15–47), clearly modelled on the opening of the Sundarakāṇḍa. It is obvious that the compiler of the *Matsya Purāṇa* was in fact well acquainted with the Rāmāyaṇa.[16]

[13] The *Viṣṇu Purāṇa* also states that Janaka has a son Bhānumān, while the Jain writer Vimalasūri in his *Paümacariya* makes twins of Sītā and Bhāmaṇḍala; the direction of influence is unclear.

[14] Earlier, it declares that when Viṣṇu was born as Rāghava, Lakṣmī was Sītā (1.9.41, cf. *Harivaṃśa* 31.117cd, *Brahmavaivarta Purāṇa* 2.14 and *Devībhāgavata Purāṇa* 9.16).

[15] See p. 113.

[16] Cf. V. Raghavan, 'Gleanings from the Matsya Purāṇa', *Purāṇa* 1, 1959, pp. 80–8 and 'Further Gleanings from the Matsya Purāṇa', *Purāṇa* 3, 1961, pp. 321–30.

In most Purāṇas the Rāma story is relatively brief, if present at all, but the *Padma Purāṇa* contains extensive narratives as well as some briefer allusions. While much of the material is based on the Vālmīki Rāmāyaṇa, there are a number of divergences and evidence of dependence also on Kālidāsa and Bhavabhūti. The *Pātālakhaṇḍa* contains a lengthy account of Rāma's *aśvamedha* (4.1–68), which opens with an explicit reference to the fact that there are many forms of the Rāma story. It also for the first time contains the idea that Rāma has incurred guilt for the killing of Rāvaṇa who is a brāhman though a Rākṣasa; Agastya therefore advises him to perform the *aśvamedha*. A whole series of episodes is then narrated concerning the wanderings of the sacrificial horse, leading up to its arrival at Vālmīki's hermitage. Here Śatrughna and the other guardians of Rāma's sacrificial horse manage to capture Lava, who is trying to steal it, after a tough fight, but in their turn they are defeated by Kuśa and taken prisoner; Sītā then brings about their liberation and that of the sacrificial horse. In Bhavabhūti's *Uttararāmacarita* Lakṣmaṇa's son Candraketu fights with Lava for possession of the sacrificial horse. There is no trace of such an encounter in the Uttarakāṇḍa, where Kuśa and Lava accompany Vālmīki as singers to the actual sacrifice; however in the Mahābhārata, Arjuna, as guardian of Yudhiṣṭhira's sacrificial horse, does battle among others with his nephew Meghasandhi (Mbh. 14.83)—a parallel situation.[17]

The narrative now includes, in effect as flashbacks, the story of Rāma's abandonment of Sītā and then the whole story of her life from her finding by Janaka. On the return of the party to Ayodhyā, Rāma sends for his sons who come and sing the Rāmāyaṇa before him. Then follows the story of the origin of the epic from the beginning of the Bālakāṇḍa. Thus, the narrative here is drawn principally from the Bāla and Uttara kāṇḍa events. We may note, however, that the narrative of Brahmā asking the Gandharvī Dundubhī to be born as Mantharā (4.15) is derived from the *Rāmopākhyāna* (Mbh. 3.260.9–15) and has no basis anywhere in the Rāmāyaṇa.[18] The *Pātālakhaṇḍa* also contains

[17] The capture of Lava and presumably therefore conflict over the horse occurred in one of the lost Rāma plays, the *Chalitarāma* (not later than the tenth century). The clash between the guardians of the sacrificial horse and Rāma's sons is further elaborated in the *Jaiminīya Aśvamedha*, the *Āśvamedhika parvan* of the *Jaimini Bhārata*, into an encounter between Śatrughna, Lakṣmaṇa and Bharata with their armies and Kuśa and Lava (25–36); this is much expanded from the Uttarakāṇḍa and is also acquainted with Kālidāsa's *Raghuvaṃśa* and Bhavabhūti's *Uttararāmacarita*. The passage is obviously late and theologically highly developed, laying stress on the recitation of Rāma's name (27.60). From it in turn is drawn the *Lavakuśaryuddha* of the fourteenth-century Assamese poet, Harivara Vipra.

[18] It is however alluded to by, for example, the *Tilaka* commentary which declares

some briefer allusions to the Rāma story. One of these includes, among the events following the *aśvamedha*, Rāma rescuing Vibhīṣaṇa from imprisonment by certain Drāviḍas, who objected to the *liṅga* erected by Rāma at the causeway (4.100.34 ff.). Elsewhere (5.27–8), it includes two interesting new incidents which appear also in virtually the same wording in the *Skanda Purāṇa* (5.1.31 and 7.111). In the first Rāma erects a *liṅga* and performs a *śrāddha* for Daśaratha, in the course of which Sītā disappears and afterwards explains her conduct by the shame she felt at being seen in her ascetic clothes of bark-cloth by Daśaratha who has actually appeared visibly to her. In the other, Rāma and Lakṣmaṇa each make wounding remarks to each other and this is put down to the influence of the place, an unexpected manifestation of human frailty.

The sixth book of the *Padma Purāṇa*, the *Uttarakhaṇḍa*, has an account of all the *avatāras* of Viṣṇu, including Rāma (6.269–71). This shows a developed form of the concept, for while Rāma himself is the *avatāra* of Viṣṇu, Bharata is the manifestation of his conch, Lakṣmaṇa of Ananta and Śatrughna of the discus Sudarśana; in addition, Kausalyā is said to have seen all deities and the universe within Rāma's form before he resumes his childhood, an obvious borrowing from the Kṛṣṇa legend. Despite the elaboration that certain episodes have undergone and the greatly developed theology, this account is based fairly directly on the original Rāmāyaṇa and even contains a number of verbal reminiscences. However, like the *Rāmopākhyāna*, it places the narrative of Rāvaṇa's past at the beginning of its treatment.

Some later Vaiṣṇava Purāṇas elaborate the *avatāra* aspect still further and correlate the four brothers with the four aspects (*caturvyūha*) of the deity in the Pañcarātra system, making Rāma an incarnation of Nārāyaṇa or Vāsudeva, Lakṣmaṇa of Saṃkarṣaṇa, Bharata of Pradyumna and Śatrughna of Aniruddha (*Nāradīya Purāṇa* 2.75.3–5, *Viṣṇudharmottara Purāṇa* 1.212.21–22). The *Viṣṇudharmottara Purāṇa* also includes a reference to the meeting of the two Rāmas (1.35.11–14b, cf. Rām. 1.73–6), as well as narrating the duel itself; its account is altogether more advanced theologically than that of the Bālakāṇḍa.[19] The story of Vedavatī from the Uttarakāṇḍa (Rām. 7.17) is narrated in the *Viṣṇudharmottara Purāṇa* (1.221.17–46) as well as in several other

that Mantharā was sent by the gods (*ad* 2.7.1.). The same commentary (*ad* 3.70.13) actually quotes the *Padma Purāṇa* innovation of Śabarī tasting the fruit she offers Rāma.

[19] It has been usual to assign the Vdh.P. a long period of growth between the seventh and tenth centuries. However, more recently Adalbert Gail has suggested that it was put together in a rather short time around 600 AD (*Paraśurāma*, pp. 98–101); this would imply that the Bālakāṇḍa must be substantially earlier than that date.

Purāṇas (*Vāmana Purāṇa*, *Saromāhātmya* 16.8–12, *Brahmavaivarta Purāṇa* 2.14.1–64, *Skanda Purāṇa* 1.8.105–10 and 2.5.18–30 and *Devībhāgavata Purāṇa* 3.30.6–12 and 9.16.3–53). The *Nāradīya Purāṇa*, as part of a narration by Rāma of Hanumān's story, includes the story of Vibhīṣaṇa's rescue by Rāma (1.79), found also in the *Padma Purāṇa*, as well as giving more precise timings than often, for example in Rāma and Lakṣmaṇa staying for a month with Viśvāmitra after his sacrifice, and in Sītā having been carried off in the thirteenth year of exile. Hanumān himself is said to be a Śaiva devotee reborn, which contributes to the substantial Śaiva element already present in Rāma's discourse on the worship of the crystal *liṅga* at Tryambak.

The *Garuḍa Purāṇa* includes in successive chapters two brief accounts of the Rāmāyaṇa narrative (1.142–3), neither of which shows any significant variation, although the first includes a passage glorifying Sītā's chastity after its seven-verse summary.[20] The *Varāha Purāṇa*, though lacking any account of the Rāma story, shows acquaintance with the Uttarakāṇḍa, since it traces the history of the Varāha image in the Kapilavarāha shrine at Mathurā back through Śatrughna who received it, as a reward for conquering Lavaṇa, from Rāma who had brought it to Ayodhyā from Laṅkā (163, *Mathurāmāhātmya*).

The various Śaiva Purāṇas often contain brief accounts of the Rāma story subordinated to their main themes. Thus, the *Kūrma Purāṇa* includes a brief summary in the dynasty of the solar kings (1.20.17–56), of which the only point of interest is the stress on Rāma establishing a *liṅga* in the middle of the causeway and worshipping it, thereby earning Śiva's blessing. Subsequently, when dealing with the various virtues, it illustrates devotion to a husband with the story of Sītā (2.33.110–40). An important development is that, when seized by Rāvaṇa, Sītā prays to Agni who in response creates a counterfeit of her for Rāvaṇa to carry off and takes the real Sītā to heaven with him; then in the fire-ordeal following the conquest of Laṅkā, Agni consumes the false Sītā and restores the real one to Rāma.[21] The *Śiva Purāṇa* even more decidedly adapts the story to its theological interests, for it

[20] There is a recent translation of the second passage in C. Dimmitt and J.A.B. van Buitenen, *Classical Hindu Mythology*, Philadelphia, 1978, pp. 85–8.

[21] The similarity thus produced to the legend of Helen of Troy has been examined by W. Printz, 'Helena und Sītā', *Beiträge zur Literaturwissenschaft und Geistesgeschichte Indiens, Festgabe Hermann Jacobi*, Bonn, 1926, pp. 103–13. He interprets this as a case of convergence in development, rightly rejecting any suggestion of influence (such as A. Weber had considered, *Über das Rāmāyaṇa*, Berlin, 1870, pp. 11–58), and regards the *Brahmavaivarta Purāṇa* version as the most naïve of the three examined by him (the third is the *Adhyātma Rāmāyaṇa*).

narrates simply a meeting of Śiva and Satī with Rāma and Lakṣmaṇa as they sorrowfully search for Sītā, with Satī at first rather dubious about Rāma's position, which provides the opportunity for Rāma to explain the spheres of responsibility of Brahmā, Viṣṇu and Śiva and the *avatāras* which he becomes (2.2.24–5). It is interesting to note that, whereas Śiva declares that Lakṣmaṇa is a partial *avatāra* of Śeṣa and Rāma a full *avatāra* of Viṣṇu (2.2.24.39), Rāma himself declares that he and his brothers are a fourfold incarnation of Viṣṇu (2.2.25.33). The *Śiva Purāṇa* also subsequently narrates the story of Hanumān (3.20), who is considered a manifestation of Śiva.[22] The story of his birth is interesting, for it is said that Śiva, aroused by the sight of Viṣṇu in his form as Mohinī, sheds some semen which is transferred to Gautama's daughter Añjanī through her ear and by which she conceives Hanumān.[23]

The *Skanda Purāṇa* in a similar fashion stresses the *liṅga*-worship of the Rākṣasas as the means by which they gained such powers, going on to describe the gods' appeal to Viṣṇu and his incarnation as Rāma (1.1.8); here an aspect of Śiva himself appears as Hanumān, whose celibacy is for the first time stressed. Subsequently, it also deals with the causeway and the Rāmeśvaram *liṅga* (3.1.1–2 and 43–7);[24] this account is notable for its close verbal coincidences with the *Rāmopākhyāna*, which is evidently its source, although the discourse that Rāma gives to Hanumān in connection with the establishment of the *liṅga* follows closely Rāma's discourse to Bharata (Rām. 2.98). Its next section, the *Dharmāraṇya*, again returns to the Rāma story, this time basing its narrative with its many chronological details on the *Padma Purāṇa* account (*Pātālakhaṇḍa* 36).

[22] Hanumān is also regarded as an *avatāra* of Śiva in the *Skanda* (5.2.79 and 3.84), *Mahābhāgavata* (37), *Bṛhaddharma* (18) and *Bhaviṣya* (2.4.13) *Purāṇas*, and the *Mahānāṭaka* (6.27). This view of him is then standard in the late Sanskrit Rāmāyaṇas and north Indian vernacular versions (*Ānanda Rāmāyaṇa* 1.11, *Tattvasaṃgraha Rāmāyaṇa* 4.12, Kṛttibās' *Rāmāyaṇ* and Tulsīdās' *Vinayapatrikā*. See C. Bulcke, 'The Characterization of Hanuman', JOIB 9, 1959–60, pp. 393–402.

[23] In addition to the rather modified form of this motif in the *Adhyātma Rāmāyaṇa* it occurs in very similar form, apart from the substitution of Rāma for Śiva, in the Malay version and in least changed form in modern Bhojpurī folktales, where Rāma pours Śiva's seed into Añjanī's body usually through her ear, and Vāyu, the wind, is just a foster father (see L. T. Wolcott, 'Hanumān: The Power-Dispensing Monkey in North Indian Folk Religion', *Journal of Asian Studies* 37, 1977–8, pp. 653–61).

[24] The *Saura Purāṇa*, in its brief account of the Rāma story (30.48–69), also emphasises Rāma's establishment of the Rāmeśvaram *liṅga* at the causeway, as well as making Rāma's *aśvamedha* an act of propitiation to Śiva.

The *Agni Purāṇa* begins with an account of the *avatāras* of Viṣṇu, devoting most space to Rāma and summarising the Rāmāyaṇa in seven chapters (5–11), each book being summarised in one chapter.[25] The text indicates its close dependence on the Rāmāyaṇa by introducing its narration as being in the way in which Nārada formerly related it to Vālmīki (*Agni P.* 5.1, cf. Rām. 1.1.1 - 2.2). The first chapter follows the Bālakāṇḍa quite closely, first of all tracing Daśaratha's descent from Nārāyaṇa (= Viṣṇu) through Brahmā, Marīci, Vivasvat and Manu, leading to Nārāyaṇa's decision to incarnate as Daśaratha's four sons to punish Rāvaṇa. However, in the account of the events of Rāma's youth, the episode of Ahalyā is lacking. In its summary of the Ayodhyākāṇḍa, Mantharā's hatred is explained by her having been dragged by the feet by Rāma (6.8), and the story of the crow which molests Sītā is included here (6.36–7) instead of in the Sundarakāṇḍa. The visit to Atri's *āśrama* and Sītā's conversation with Anasūyā from the end of the Ayodhyākāṇḍa form the start of the next chapter in the *Agni Purāṇa* as in the Northern recension of the Rāmāyaṇa, which, from this and other indications, the *Agni Purāṇa* appears to follow. Divergences include Indrajit's success in binding Hanumān being due to the *nāgapāśa* not the *brahmāstra* (9.18) and the account of Viśravas' wives (11.1–3), but there are no really major discrepancies. Subsequently, the *Agni Purāṇa* includes a sizable section on *rājanīti* (238–42) which is said to be what Rāma taught Lakṣmaṇa in the Rāmāyaṇa and especially on the battlefield. An analogous passage from the Mahābhārata (13.74.11–15) has Bhīṣma ascribe certain teaching at several removes to Rāma's instruction of Lakṣmaṇa, Rāma himself having had it from Daśaratha to whom it came from Pitāmaha through Indra. Are these perhaps separate attempts to endow Rāma with the teaching role of the even better known *avatāra* Kṛṣṇa?

The *Brahma Purāṇa* has several brief allusions to the Rāma story, of which one is of some interest for the way that it re-orders events to follow exactly their chronological order (ch. 123). Thus, it begins with Daśaratha's assistance to the gods in their battle with the Asuras and the granting of the boon to Kaikeyī and continues with the episode of Daśaratha's unwitting slaying of the ascetic youth. The major innovation of its account is that Daśaratha after death is tortured in different hells, from which he is rescued by Rāma's arrival at the Godāvarī, and the purpose of it is the enhancement of the greatness of the Rāmatīrtha on

[25] See A. N. Krishna Aiyangar, 'Agnipurāṇa and the Rāmāyaṇa', *Bhāratīya Vidyā* 25, 1965, pp. 9–17.

the Godāvarī. The *Brahma Purāṇa* also includes the narration of the *avatāras* of Viṣṇu, including Rāma (213.124–58), found in the *Harivaṃśa* (Hv. 31).

The *Brahmavaivarta Purāṇa* recounts in full the story of Vedavatī (2.14.1–64), though with some variations from the account in the Uttarakāṇḍa (Rām. 7.17); thus, her father Kuśadhvaja is a king rather than a sage and she herself is said to be Lakṣmī rather than having the form of Vāc (Speech). Immediately before the incident of the golden deer a brāhman, who is in fact Agni, tells Rāma secretly that he will remove the real Sītā for safekeeping and restoration after the battle, leaving meanwhile a duplicate (*chāyā*) Sītā behind; this develops further the story found in the *Kūrma Purāṇa*, where the exchange immediately follows Rāvaṇa's seizure of Sītā. Then, Mārīca, when killed by Rāma, is stated to go to Viṣṇu's heaven Vaikuṇṭha, resuming his true form as Jaya, one of its two gate-keepers. Elsewhere the Purāṇa narrates the story of Indra's adultery with Ahalyā (4.47.61) and follows it with a brief narration of the Rāma story, laying particular stress on Śūrpaṇakhā's lust; it also, as in some other Purāṇas, mentions Hanumān as a partial incarnation of Śiva (4.47.62–3).

The *Bhāgavata Purāṇa*, though naturally concentrating on Kṛṣṇa, includes a fairly extensive treatment, in the account of the kings of the solar dynasty, of the Rāma story (9.10–12). Its author states that the Rāma story has been sung by many sages, but seems nevertheless to follow basically the original Rāmāyaṇa. The most major divergence, obviously theologically motivated, is that after the fall of Laṅkā Rāma finds Sītā in the *aśoka* grove, takes pity on her and, lifting her into the *vimāna*, goes straight back to Ayodhyā; such a presentation obviously accords better with the *bhakti* outlook of the author and the attendant emphasis on the compassion and grace of the deity. However, the account of Sītā's banishment and final disappearance are retained.[26]

The *Narasiṃha Purāṇa* includes as part of its account of the *avatāras* of Viṣṇu Mārkaṇḍeya's narration of the Rāma story (47–52). Its extreme lateness is corroborated by its eclectic use of epic, puranic and literary sources. Thus it quotes more or less verbatim from the Rāmāyaṇa itself (5.1.1+7 at 51.1–2, 6.105.27 at 52.113), from Kālidāsa's *Raghuvaṃśa* (11.17 at 47.82, 12.34 at 49.40) and from a thirteenth-

[26] An unusual variant on Sītā's final disappearance occurs in one of the minor Purāṇas, the *Kalki Purāṇa*, which has Rāma suggest at this point that Sītā should undergo another fire-ordeal; this is the only noteworthy point in its treatment of the Rāma story (3.24–57).

century Rāma play, the *Dūtāṅgada* of Subhaṭa (at 52.21–32).[27] It is also acquainted with the *Ādityahṛdaya* (Rām. 6 App.I.65), both in this context (52.96–7) and elsewhere (20.1–6), and it transposes the suggestion of Rākṣasas impersonating Bharata and his troops found in another passage of the fourth stage (6.131*) from the start of the battle to the seizure of Sītā (48.78–83). But its lateness is even more clearly seen in its stress on the efficacy of reciting Rāma's name and on Rāma being Parabrahman (47.143–5).

The first stages by which the cult of Rāma was brought into connection with the worship of Devī are seen in the *Devībhāgavata Purāṇa*, which integrates the Rāmāyaṇa story with the worship of Devī during Śārada Navarātri (28–30). Rāma is regarded as an incarnation of Viṣṇu, Lakṣmaṇa of Śeṣa (30.55–6), Sītā of Lakṣmī (28.13 and 30.13) and the Vānaras as partial incarnations of the other gods. There are no major deviations in its narrative, although it is worth noting that it knows the episodes of Vedavatī's curse on Rāvaṇa (30.9–12, cf. Rām. 7.17) and of Indra's mission to the captive Sītā (30.16–17, cf. Rām. 3 App.I.12). So too the *Mahābhāgavata Purāṇa*, in a narrative which is reproduced almost verbatim in the *Bṛhaddharma Purāṇa*, sets it in the context of Śārada Navarātri, giving its mythological framework the appropriate slant. Thus, at the beginning Viṣṇu and the other gods seek the co-operation of Śiva and Pārvatī, since Rāvaṇa is a devotee of Śiva and Devī protects Laṅkā, and Śiva himself becomes Hanumān, who in his reconnoitring of Laṅkā discovers a shrine to Caṇḍikā and gets Devī to desert Laṅkā. As in the Śaiva Purāṇas mention is made of Rāma establishing a *liṅga* on the causeway, while the *Mahābhāgavata Purāṇa* also elaborates on Rāma's worship of Devī (43–6) and has the battle end with the death of Rāvaṇa on Daśamī (47), concluding with renewed emphasis on the worship of Devī during Śārada Navarātri and listening to the Rāmāyaṇa as part of the festival. Another feature of the *Mahābhāgavata Purāṇa's* account is the abrupt mention of Sītā as Mandodarī's daughter (42.64). The *Bṛhaddharma Purāṇa* also has another section which narrates Sarasvatī's manifestation through Vālmīki and his utterance of the first *śloka* (25.46–69) before summarising the main incidents of the story (26). Another Śākta Purāṇa, the *Kālikā Purāṇa*, expatiates even more fully on the link between Navarātri and Rāma's victory over Rāvaṇa (62.24–41), as well as narrating the origin of Sītā from the earth as Janaka was ploughing the ground for a sacrifice to procure offspring (38).

[27] See V. Raghavan, 'The Date of the Narasiṃha Purāṇa', *India Maior* (Gonda vol.), Leiden, 1972, pp. 239–40 and *The Greater Rāmāyaṇa*, Varanasi, 1973, pp. 60–3.

The Rāmāyaṇa, along with the Mahābhārata, has furnished the theme or plot of an enormous number of works of pure literature in Sanskrit or Prakrit, too numerous to deal with here in their entirety.[28] The earliest extant examples are two plays ascribed to Bhāsa, the *Pratimānāṭaka* and the *Abhiṣekanāṭaka*, perhaps of the third century AD. The *Pratimānāṭaka* begins with the ordering of preparations for Rāma's installation by Daśaratha, halted by a word from Mantharā. Rāma and Sītā are portrayed as from that point toying with the idea of ascetic life, even before the clarification of Kaikeyī's demands for the kingdom promised as her dowry. Bharata on his return discovers his father's death by entering a shrine in which are erected the statues of deceased Ikṣvākus, Dilīpa, Raghu, Aja—and Daśaratha. Rāvaṇa's arrival at the hermitage immediately follows the narration of Bharata's visit, although the killing of Khara is alluded to; Rāma is there, pondering what offering to make to his father, for which Rāvaṇa suggests certain golden-flanked deer who live in the Himālayas, and Rāma goes after one. The sixth act is then taken up with a report of events by Sumantra to Bharata, who reviles his mother over Sītā's misery, and Kaikeyī's revelation of the curse on Daśaratha for killing the ascetic youth. The last act then jumps to Rāma's victorious return to Ayodhyā and the meeting with Bharata. Thus the *Pratimānāṭaka* is a free and selective treatment of the events of the Ayodhyā to Yuddha kāṇḍas and makes no reference to anything contained in the Bāla or Uttara kāṇḍas.

The *Abhiṣekanāṭaka* in some sense fills in the lacunae in the story. Its first act depicts the conflict between Vālin and Sugrīva, Rāma's killing of Vālin and Vālin's reproach. The second act covers Hanumān's arrival in Laṅkā and overhearing of Rāvaṇa's wooing of Sītā. The third act presents Hanumān's defeat of Akṣa, Vibhīṣaṇa's remonstrance with Rāvaṇa and Hanumān being brought before Rāvaṇa. In the fourth act, Vibhīṣaṇa arrives as Rāma and his allies reach the sea, Varuṇa appears and parts the sea for them, and Śuka and Sāraṇa are captured. In the fifth Sītā is shown the feigned heads of Rāma and Lakṣmaṇa, Rāvaṇa receives the news of Indrajit's death and goes off in his chariot to fight Rāma. After a recapitulation of the duel between Rāma and Rāvaṇa, the sixth act depicts Sītā undergoing the fire-ordeal before coming into Rāma's presence and Agni recognising Rāma as Nārāyaṇa as he hands her back and declaring Sītā to be Lakṣmī to a

[28] For a listing of these works, see Juthika Ghosh, *Epic Sources of Sanskrit Literature*, Calcutta Sanskrit College Research Series 23, Calcutta, 1963 and V. Raghavan, *Some Old Lost Rāma Plays*, Annamalainagar, 1961.

chorus of divine approval; as the act and the play end Rāma, installed, is invited to rule the earth. Despite again some freedom of treatment, the Rāmāyaṇa is basically followed, as is not unexpected in the earliest literary treatments of the themes.

Among the treatments of the Rāma story in classical Sanskrit literature, the best known is undoubtedly Kālidāsa's *Raghuvaṃśa*, of the fourth or fifth century. As its name indicates, it sets the story within the whole history of the dynasty of Raghu, the Ikṣvākus. For the earlier figures in the dynasty Kālidāsa follows a genealogy different from any occurring in the Rāmāyaṇa but close to that given in the *Viṣṇu Purāṇa*. Kālidāsa reaches Daśaratha in the ninth sarga and recounts the story from the Rāmāyaṇa up to the fifteenth sarga.[29] The balance of his poem is at times very different; for example, the fire-ordeal is referred to in a single word in the closing verse of the twelfth sarga, while the thirteenth sarga displays Kālidāsa's descriptive talents in a depiction of the countryside seen on their flight back to Ayodhyā. Kālidāsa does not include any episode unknown to the Rāmāyaṇa and he is fully acquainted with the Uttarakāṇḍa.[30] On the other hand his brevity of treatment at some points means that no inference is permissible concerning any incident omitted.

Kālidāsa's fame evidently was soon so general that another of the narrative poems on the Rāma story, Kumāradāsa's *Jānakīharaṇa*, is largely modelled on the *Raghuvaṃśa*, as well as showing some indebtedness to his *Kumārasaṃbhava*.[31] There are no major innovations in his treatment, although there are occasional divergences, for example Bṛhaspati rather than Brahmā invokes Viṣṇu's incarnation, and amplifications, as in his picture of Daśaratha and his wives in the first canto. In contrast to Kālidāsa but like his near contemporary Bhaṭṭi, Kumāradāsa ends his treatment with Rāma's installation after his triumphant return to Ayodhyā. There is even more apparent than in Kālidāsa the tendency towards romantic and naturalistic description.

[29] As extant, the poem consists of nineteen sargas but it has often been thought incomplete. Whether it is or not, the story of Rāma is obviously its main theme.

[30] U. P. Shah in his introduction to the Critical Edition of that book (p. 51) interestingly suggests that *Raghuvaṃśa* 15.37, stating that Śatrughna avoided Vālmīki's *āśrama* on his return from Madhupurī, was intended by Kālidāsa to reject as inappropriate or interpolated Śatrughna's second visit to Vālmīki (Rām. 7 App.I.9).

[31] Cf. E. Słuszkiewicz, *Przyczynki do badań nad dziejami redakcyj Rāmāyany*, Kraków, 1938, ch. 3. Following A. Gawroński, he assigns the poem to the sixth century. He also shows that where it directly follows the Rāmāyaṇa it is based on a text intermediate between the present NE. and S. recensions.

Bhaṭṭi's *Rāvaṇavadha*, or *Bhaṭṭikāvya*,[32] could be regarded as a fairly full summary of the Rāmāyaṇa, on which it is clearly directly based, for it is almost exactly one tenth of the length of the original (1625 stanzas against 16,380 of the Bāla to Yuddha kāṇḍas), but in fact its treatment is decidedly uneven, with the greatest attention paid to certain erotic scenes added to the Sundarakāṇḍa and especially to the battle scenes of the Yuddhakāṇḍa, which occupies over half the total length of the poem. Like Kumāradāsa, Bhaṭṭi was acquainted with a text of the Rāmāyaṇa intermediate between the present Northeast and Southern recensions;[33] one notable feature is that it has nothing at all corresponding to the Uttarakāṇḍa and that it omits virtually all the mythological material from the Bālakāṇḍa (1.31–47 and 50–64) as well as the birth of the Vānaras (1.16). Bhaṭṭi also shows a definite Śaiva tendency and so at the beginning of his poem Daśaratha is declared to worship only Śiva and at its end Śiva, instead of Brahmā, reminds Rāma of his divinity.

Other passages omitted in the *Bhaṭṭikāvya* are those on Sītā's resolve to go to the forest (Rām. 2.24–7), the evils of a kingless state (Rām. 2.61), Bharata's consoling of Kausalyā (2.69), Jābāli's and Vasiṣṭha's speeches urging Rāma to return (2.100–2), Sītā's homily and the meetings with Agastya and Jaṭāyus (3.8–15), Sītā's diatribe against Rāvaṇa (3.45.28–45), the Saptajana hermitage (4.13), Tārā's advice to Vālin, Hanumān's consolation of her after his death and her subsequent intervention on Sugrīva's behalf (4.15, 21 and 34), the return of the unsuccessful search parties (4.46),[34] the Niśākara episode (4.59–61), Sītā's despair and thoughts of suicide (5.23–4), Hanumān's offer to rescue Sītā immediately (5.35) and his defeat of Jambumālin and the sons of Rāvaṇa's ministers (5.42–4), the first encounter between Rāma and Rāvaṇa (6.47), Mahodara's speech (6.52), and during the return to Ayodhyā the meeting with Bharadvāja and Hanumān's narration of

[32] The poem was composed in the reign of one of the Maitraka rulers of Valabhī, named Śrīdharasena; the dates of the four rulers so named range from approximately 490 to 650 AD.

[33] Cf. H. Wirtz, *Die westliche Rezension des Rāmāyaṇa*, Bonn, 1894 and Sluszkiewicz, op. cit. His purpose in writing the work was to provide an illustration of the rules of grammar and rhetoric, in which he has an imitator in Bhaumaka's (or Bhaṭṭabhīma's) *Rāvaṇārjunīya*, the subject-matter of which is Rāvaṇa's fight with Kārtavīrya Arjuna and which was composed before the eleventh century.

[34] Although it mentions the despatch of the search parties to north, west and east at 7.51–2, the *Bhaṭṭikāvya* does so in a way and at a point which suggests that it is drawing on Rām. 4.44 rather than 4.39 and 41–2, the main search party accounts.

events to Bharata (6.112 and 114). The *Bhaṭṭikāvya* also simplifies certain passages, such as the events at the end of the rains leading up to the reminder to Sugrīva (BhK. 7.14, Rām. 4.28) and the deliberations and boastings of the Vānaras about crossing to Laṅkā (BhK. 7.108–9, Rām. 4.64–6). On the other hand it greatly expands others, notably the combat between Hanumān and Indrajit (BhK. 9.46–95, Rām. 5.46), the building of the causeway (BhK. 13.8–30, Rām. 6.15) and Rāvaṇa's angry speech leading up to Indrajit's entry into the battle (BhK. 16.1–17.19, Rām. 6.67); it also gives at some length Vibhīṣaṇa's lament for Rāvaṇa, which is found in the fourth stage of the Rāmāyaṇa (BhK. 18.1–36, Rām. 6 App.I.67.27–94). It also adds certain entirely new passages: a meeting with several ascetics immediately after the killing of Tāṭakā (BhK. 2.24–31),[35] Rāvaṇa's boastings after receiving Śūrpaṇakhā's complaint (BhK. 5.23–9), Hanumān's bravado between his encounters with Akṣa and Indrajit (BhK. 9.39–45), and especially the description of the love-play of the Rākṣasas (BhK. 11.3–33), a lengthy erotic passage perhaps prompted by Hanumān's sight of Rāvaṇa's sleeping harem (Rām. 5.8.28–50) but if so transferred to a later stage in the narrative and to Laṅkā's inhabitants in general. However, despite such artistically motivated alterations, it is clear that Bhaṭṭi is following quite closely the Rāmāyaṇa as it had developed to include much of the Bālakāṇḍa, though not the Uttarakāṇḍa.

The *Setubandha* or *Rāvaṇavaha*, a poem in Prakrit by a king Pravarasena or a poet of his court, narrates—as its names between them indicate—the story of Rāma from the building of the causeway up to the death of Rāvaṇa, which forms the major part of the Yuddhakāṇḍa.[36] After these works of the sixth to seventh centuries, the narrative poem as a vehicle for the Rāma story seems to have become less popular, the only extant examples being Abhinanda's *Rāmacarita*, of unknown date, and Cakrakavi's *Jānakīpariṇaya*, of the seventeenth century.[37]

Bhavabhūti, early in the eighth century, wrote a pair of dramas on the

[35] It also transposes the killing of Tāṭakā and Viśvāmitra's gift of arms (BhK. 2.21–3, Rām. 1.23–7). There are also other minor transpositions.

[36] In so far as the work draws directly on the Rāmāyaṇa, it too appears to follow a form of the text intermediate between the present NE. and S. recensions, which presumably therefore had not diverged so far at the time of its composition (probably the sixth century AD) and that of the contemporary *Bhaṭṭikāvya* and *Jānakīharaṇa*; cf. E. Sluszkiewicz, 'Le Rāvaṇavaha et le Rāmāyaṇa', RO 3, 1927, pp. 107–32.

[37] Moreover, neither of these two works narrates the complete story. The *Rāmacarita* begins at the meeting of Rāma and Sugrīva and concludes in the middle of the Yuddha-

Rāma theme, the *Mahāvīracarita* and *Uttararāmacarita* ('The Deeds of the Great Hero' and 'Rāma's Later Deeds'); the first narrates the main events of the story up to the triumphant return to Ayodhyā and the second develops certain themes of the Uttarakāṇḍa centring round Sītā's banishment. In the *Mahāvīracarita* Bhavabhūti considerably develops the marriage of Rāma and Sītā; he introduces a feature which then becomes common to most of the Rāma dramas in the meeting between Rāma and Sītā before the *svayaṃvara* (which he locates in Viśvāmitra's *āśrama*, whereas other dramas place it in Mithilā), which is a real contest. Indeed, a messenger comes from Rāvaṇa to demand Sītā's hand for his master and retires in chagrin after the breaking of the bow. In his jealousy Rāvaṇa then, through his minister Mālyavat, incites Paraśurāma as a disciple of Śiva to punish Rāma for breaking the bow. The quarrel between the two Rāmas thus takes place immediately afterwards rather than on the return journey to Ayodhyā; no less than two of the seven acts of the play are devoted to it.[38] Bhavabhūti further turns the whole action into a feud between Rāma and Rāvaṇa by having Mālyavat despatch Śūrpaṇakhā disguised as Mantharā to secure Rāma's exile. Later also Mālyavat intrigues against Rāma with Vālin, who is presented as an ally of Rāvaṇa and is thus legitimately slain by Rāma.

The *Uttararāmacarita* opens with a recapitulation of the story through the device of the picture gallery, where Lakṣmaṇa shows to Rāma and the now pregnant Sītā a depiction of their previous adventures.[39] This is interrupted by the servant, whom Rāma has charged with ascertaining the people's feelings, with the news of the slanders about Sītā. Rāma's misery in banishing Sītā is graphically portrayed. After a prologue alluding to Vālmīki's rearing of Kuśa and Lava and his invention of the

kāṇḍa battles, following basically the Rāmāyaṇa story, though with some inventiveness of detail. The *Jānakīpariṇaya*, in accordance with its title, deals only with the episode of Sītā's marriage.

[38] In this too, Bhavabhūti starts a trend apparent in the later dramas also, cf. *Anargharāghava* act 4, *Bālarāmāyaṇa* act 4, *Prasannarāghava* act 4, and *Hanumannāṭaka* 2.44–71.

[39] This recapitulation includes Ṛśyaśṛṅga's marriage to Śāntā, who is declared to be the daughter of Daśaratha adopted by Lomapāda, as in the N. recension (1.322* and 331*), rather than Romapāda's daughter as she is in the S. recension (1.10.3 and 19); the N. version may be explained as an expansion arising out of a misunderstanding of 1.10.3 and certainly seems secondary compared with the S. version. Bhavabhūti's direct quotations (of 1.2.14, 1.1394* 3–6 and 2 App.I.26.11–12) show also that he was acquainted with a version similar to the N. recension.

śloka, to Rāma's releasing of a sacrificial horse under the custody of Lakṣmaṇa's son Candraketu and the untimely death of the brāhman boy, in the second act Rāma himself enters the Daṇḍaka forest to kill Śambuka. In the third act, Bhavabhūti introduces the very moving scene where Rāma, wandering distraught in the forest at the memories brought back, faints and is revived by Sītā, made invisible by the goddess Gaṅgā, touching him: both converse with their attendants, so near and yet so far from each other. The fourth act contains another innovation in the meeting at Vālmīki's hermitage of Vasiṣṭha, Arundhatī, Kausalyā and Janaka, upon which Lava happens before being hurried away by his youthful companions to view this novel creature, a horse. In the next act, Lava then engages Candraketu and his company in combat but is pacified in the sixth act by the arrival of Rāma, whom he comes to recognise as his father, as does Kuśa who now also arrives; Rāma himself gradually comes to realise who the twins are. In the last act, as in the first, Bhavabhūti uses an indirect device to fill in the story; here a play within a play, its presentation arranged by Vālmīki and its plot Sītā's throwing herself into the Gaṅgā, the birth of the twins and their protection by Gaṅgā and the Earth. Rāma again faints and is again revived by the touch of Sītā's hand, but this time she is restored to him and the play ends amid general reconciliation and rejoicing.

Indebtedness to Bhavabhūti is apparent in the *Āścaryacūḍāmaṇi* of Śaktibhadra, of perhaps the ninth century, especially in its attempt to provide dramatic unity through the theme of a long-standing feud between Rāma and Rāvaṇa. It takes its name from the prominence of the incident of the jewelled diadem given by Sītā to Hanumān for Rāma, and deals in seven acts with events from Śūrpaṇakhā's approach up to the fire-ordeal, but its only real novelty is in making Rāvaṇa disguise himself as Rāma in order to approach Sītā. So too the *Kundamālā* of Dhīranāga (or Vīranāga) is modelled on the *Uttararāmacarita*, taking its name from its distinctive feature, the use of a jasmine garland as a recognition token; it was composed before the twelfth century.[40]

Murāri's *Anargharāghava*, of the ninth or tenth century, though also derivative, is of some significance as a source for later versions. Thus,

[40] However, its editor Kali Kumar Datta (*Calcutta Sanskrit College Research Series XXVIII*, Calcutta, 1964), naming its author as Diṅnāga, assigns it to some time between the fourth and sixth centuries and therefore regards the *Uttararāmacarita* as borrowing from it, in which he is followed by H. D. Sankalia, 'Kundamālā and Uttararāmacarita', JOIB 15, 1965–6, pp. 322–34.

in his third and fourth acts, Murāri takes from Bhavabhūti the theme of Rāvaṇa's enmity for Rāma, beginning with his messenger's presence at Sītā's *svayaṃvara* and including Mālyavat's machinations, Śūrpaṇakhā's disguise as Mantharā, and Paraśurāma's intervention; this last includes the motif of Sītā's apprehension that by again bending his bow Rāma may gain another wife which occurs also in the *Hanumannāṭaka* and Kṛttibās' Bengali version. Murāri begins his play in the first two acts with Viśvāmitra seeking Rāma's help against Tāḍakā and her death, while in a dialogue interlude two of Viśvāmitra's pupils give the history of the Rākṣasas and Vānaras. The fifth act presents events in the forest, much of it by indirect narration. An innovation is that Vālin is made the aggressor in the quarrel with Rāma, the *casus belli* being Lakṣmaṇa's accidental dislodgement of Dundhubi's skeleton; this and Bhavabhūti's remodelling of the episode are clearly the forerunners of its complete suppression in Māyurāja's *Udāttarāghava* (although the incident is also suppressed in the earlier Jain *Paümacariya* by Vimalasūri). The entire sixth act consists of indirect narration: first the building of the causeway is told by Śuka and Sāraṇa, then off-stage voices announce the departure for battle and death of Kumbhakarṇa and Meghanāda and Rāvaṇa's taking the field, and finally two demi-gods describe the last combat.[41] The seventh and last act, modelled closely on the last act of the *Mahāvīracarita*, describes the aerial journey back to Ayodhyā, amplifying it with a visit to mount Sumeru and the world of the moon.

Murāri's work in turn, as well as Bhavabhūti's is the model for Rājaśekhara's *Bālarāmāyaṇa*, written at the end of the ninth century or beginning of the tenth. A prolix drama in ten acts, it makes Rāvaṇa's passion for Sītā the dominating feature,[42] spending the first four acts on the events of the Bālakāṇḍa, up to the duel of Rāma and Paraśurāma.

[41] This last dialogue has been closely imitated in the 13th century *Ullāgharāghava* of Someśvara, which contains other borrowings from the *Anargharāghava*, as well as from the *Raghuvaṃśa* and the *Uttararāmacarita*. There is a series of dramas with names ending in *-rāghava*, which seem to be linked; others are Māyurāja's *Udāttarāghava* (now lost), Virūpakṣadeva's *Unmattarāghava*, Bhāskara's *Unmattarāghava*, Bhīmaṭa's *Abhinavarāghava* (one of five lost Rāma plays), Śākalyamalla's *Udārarāghava* and Jayadeva's *Prasannarāghava* (see p. 250).

[42] In this it is followed by the *Jānakīpariṇaya* of Rāmabhadra Dīkṣita in the seventeenth century, of which the only other distinctive feature is an episode where Rāvaṇa and other Rākṣasas masquerade as Rāma and his associates leading to a comedy of mistaken identities. Rāmabhadra Dīkṣita also wrote several *stotras* or hymns to Rāma, as did many other authors of this period such as Appaya Dīkṣita (1554–1626), Nīlakaṇṭha Dīkṣita and Rāghavendratīrtha (1623–71).

Rāvaṇa appears in person at the *svayaṃvara* but declines to test himself against the bow.[43] In the third act, as Rāvaṇa pines for Sītā, some wandering players arrive and present a play on the betrothal of Sītā to Rāma, infuriating Rāvaṇa. The device is repeated in the fifth act, where marionettes with speaking parrots inside act the part of Sītā and others, and again in the seventh act, where such a head cast up on the shore lamely substitutes for the illusory killing of Sītā in the original. In the ninth act Indra himself describes the final duel and the last act describes the return, again revealing Rājaśekhara's indebtedness to his models.

Direct borrowing from Bhavabhūti, Murāri and Rājaśekhara is apparent in the huge and irregularly constructed drama, much of it narrative in character, known as the *Hanumannāṭaka* in its fourteen-act version and the *Mahānāṭaka* in its ten-act form.[44] Tradition ascribes its origin to Hanumān and its recovery from certain fragments to Bhoja; the latter may well suggest that it was compiled in the eleventh century.[45] If so the process of accretion probably continued, since there are also close similarities to the thirteenth-century *Prasanna-rāghava*. When Rāma bends the bow, both Sītā with her attendants and the other contestants are present, although Rāvaṇa's envoy has already retired. In the conflict with Paraśurāma Lakṣmaṇa plays a larger part than usual in provoking him. In the third act, the episode where a boatman is reluctant to ferry them over the Gaṅgā lest his boat suffer the same fate as the stone turned into a woman (i.e. Ahalyā) and a scene where certain peasants entertain them on their journey into the forest are taken over by Tulsīdās. Aṅgada's mission to Rāvaṇa is given some prominence, as are Mandodarī's attempts thereafter to get Rāvaṇa to return Sītā. In general, however, it shows no striking divergences from the other dramas on which it is based.[46]

[43] Rāvaṇa also comes to Sītā's *svayaṃvara* in the first act of the lost *Jānakīrāghava*.

[44] It also borrows verses from Kālidāsa, Vasukalpa, Dhīranāga's *Kundamālā* and the now lost play by Bhavabhūti's patron Yaśovarman, entitled *Rāmābhyudaya*. See S. K. De, 'The Problem of the Mahānāṭaka', IHQ 7, 1931, pp. 537–627 and 629–43 [709–23].

[45] A form of it must have been in existence by the beginning of the twelfth century, since a number of verses are ascribed to it in Vidyākara's *Subhāṣitaratnakośa*.

[46] Also of eleventh-century date are Sandhyākaranandin's *Rāmacarita* (a work which contrives to tell simultaneously the story of Rāma and of Rāmapāla of the Pāla dynasty, after the style of Kavirāja's *Rāghavapāṇḍavīya*, which narrates at one and the same time the Rāmāyaṇa and the Mahābhārata), Kṣemendra's *Rāmāyaṇamañjarī* (an epitome of the epic, based mainly on the NW. recension and useful for textual studies but having no independent value) and Bhoja's *Campūrāmāyaṇa*, which in the mixed prose and verse form of the *campū* narrates closely the story of the Rāmāyaṇa based on its S. recension and with some influence from Kālidāsa's *Raghuvaṃśa* (cf. E. Sluszkiewicz, 'Notes sur le Campūrāmāyaṇa de Bhōja', RO 3, 1927, pp. 107–32).

The *Prasannarāghava*, composed by Jayadeva son of Mahādeva probably around 1200 AD, is of greater significance than most of the later dramas, since it was evidently one of Tulsīdās' sources. As in the *Bālarāmāyaṇa*, in the first act Rāvaṇa comes in person to Janaka's court to gain Sītā's hand, disdains Śiva's bow and prepares to carry her off by brute force; another demonic contender, Bāṇāsura, arrives, quarrels with Rāvaṇa and fails to bend the bow, whereupon both in succession depart angrily. In the second act, as in other dramas, the meeting between Rāma and Sītā before the *svayaṃvara* is prominently presented; here, Rāma and Lakṣmaṇa are in a garden picking flowers for the evening offering, when Sītā passes by on her way to the temple of Pārvatī, and the two lovers are spellbound with mutual admiration. In the third act, Rāma and Lakṣmaṇa are formally presented at Janaka's court by Viśvāmitra and Rāma is on the point of bending the bow, when an ascetic arrives with a message from Paraśurāma commanding Janaka to avoid a humiliation to the bow of Śiva, his *guru*. At the start of the next act, Paraśurāma himself arrives to punish the to him unknown guilty one, is impressed nevertheless by the beauty of Rāma and Lakṣmaṇa but after a long argument with them, culminating in the duel, submits to Rāma. In the fifth act, a dialogue between various rivers and the ocean fills in some of the intervening detail before the sixth act, where Rāma magically witnesses events in Laṅkā.[47] In the seventh and final act, after a prologue alluding to Vibhīṣaṇa's breach with Rāvaṇa, Prahastaka and Mandodarī attempt to dissuade Rāvaṇa from battle, and the play closes with the return to Ayodhyā in the aerial car Puṣpaka.

Subhaṭa's *Dūtāṅgada* takes its title from Aṅgada's embassy, which it presents in four scenes, and is indebted for its theme to the *Mahānāṭaka*, showing acquaintance also with the *Bālarāmāyaṇa*. Aṅgada goes as an envoy to Rāvaṇa, Vibhīṣaṇa and Mandodarī also attempt to dissuade Rāvaṇa, Rāvaṇa endeavours to persuade Aṅgada that Sītā is in love with him with the device of an illusory Sītā, but Aṇgada is not deceived and departs with threats; the play ends with Gandharvas recounting Rāvaṇa's death. As already noted, it is quoted by one very late Purāṇa.[48]

At a later date for the most part than these two main streams of development of the Rāma story, in the Purāṇas and in classical Sanskrit literature, there come the later, sectarian recastings in Sanskrit of the

[47] This is evidently the origin of the motif of the magic mirror which shows Rāma what is happening in Laṅkā and which gives its name to Mahādeva's *Adbhutadarpaṇa* (seventeenth century).

[48] See pp. 240–1.

Rāmāyaṇa. These draw on both the earlier lines of development, which in any case show considerable mutual influence as we have already seen, but show a much more pronounced sectarian and theological emphasis, while adhering to the narrative pattern. In this they differ from the probably roughly contemporary sectarian Upaniṣads devoted to Rāma worship, which display no interest at all in the story of Rāma, though sharing the same theological outlook.[49]

In the Indian tradition the *Yogavāsiṣṭha Rāmāyaṇa* (also called *Mahārāmāyaṇa, Ārṣarāmāyaṇa* and *Jñānavāsiṣṭha*) passes as an original work of Vālmīki, being cast in the form of a dialogue between him and king Ariṣṭanemi reproducing Vasiṣṭha's instruction to Rāma; however, it also mentions that, because it fell into oblivion, the story has now been recited for the twelfth time. Obviously, numerous recastings lie between Vālmīki's version and the *Yogavāsiṣṭha*. Although its central theme is drawn from the Bālakāṇḍa the work is notionally concerned with the entire narrative of the Rāmāyaṇa, giving at one point in the form of a prediction by Viśvāmitra of Rāma's future actions a summary of the main incidents (VIa.128.68–74). Moreover, its narration of events from Viśvāmitra's arrival up to the expounding of his views by Vasiṣṭha is drawn in part verbatim from the Rāmāyaṇa (I.6–10 cf. Rām. 1.17.23–21.1).[50] Alongside this acquaintance with the Rāmāyaṇa, the author of the *Yogavāsiṣṭha* reveals familiarity with a very wide range of Sanskrit literature and philosophy, the scope and nature of its quotations indicating probably its composition in the twelfth or thirteenth century. Among these quotations is the reproduction of a hymn to Rāma as divine from Abhinanda's *Rāmacarita* (9.8–66 reproduced

[49] I shall not therefore discuss these Upaniṣads further, nor the *stotras*, mostly belonging to the sixteenth and seventeenth centuries, which as part of their praise of Rāma sometimes summarise the story. Texts of the *Rāmatāpanīya Upaniṣad* (both the *Pūrvatāpanīya* and *Uttaratāpanīya*) and the *Rāmarahasya Upaniṣad* are published in *The Vaiṣṇava-Upaniṣads ed.* A. Mahadeva Sastri, Madras, 1953; cf. also A. Weber, *Die Râma-Tâpanîya-Upanishad* (Abh. der K. Ak. der Wissensch. zu Berlin, 1864), Berlin, 1864.

[50] T. G. Mainkar argues for the dependence here of the *Yogavāsiṣṭha* on the NW. recension of Kashmir (*The Vāsiṣṭha Rāmāyaṇa: a study*, 2nd ed., New Delhi, 1977, pp. 5–21). This corroborates V. Raghavan's assessment that the *Yogavāsiṣṭha* was indebted to the Kashmiri recension of the *Bhagavadgītā* ('The Yoga-Vāsiṣṭha and the Bhagavadgītā and the place of origin of the Yoga-Vāsiṣṭha' and 'The Date of the Yoga-Vāsiṣṭha', JORM 13, 1943–4, pp. 73–82 and 100–128, and 17, 1947–8, pp. 228–31'). P. C. Divanji ('The Date and Place of Origin of the Yogavāsiṣṭha', a paper read at the 7th Oriental conference held at Baroda, 1933) argues that the work was composed in the first half of the tenth century in Kashmir; however, in another paper at the same conference on 'The Probable Date of Yoga-vāsiṣṭha', B. L. Ātreya concludes that it was written '*before Bhartṛ-hari and after Kāli-dāsa*' (repeated in his *The Philosophy of the Yoga-vāsiṣṭha*, Madras, 1936, and elsewhere).

at YV VIa.128.81–94). On the other hand it is quoted by Vidyāraṇya in his *Pañcadaśī* in the first half of the fourteenth century. Its purpose is, through this discourse by Vasiṣṭha to Rāma, to expound a philosophical viewpoint, which is basically Vedāntin but is also deeply influenced by Buddhist idealism. Apart from the attendant stress on Rāma as a *jīvanmukta*, one who has gained release in this life, the work does not show any novel features in its presentation of the Rāma story. However, among the numerous extraneous stories included is that of a visit by Vasiṣṭha to the crow Bhuśuṇḍa, who describes his long life during which he has seen among other things eleven births of Rāma and twelve compositions of the Rāmāyaṇa; this is presumably the starting point for the idea of Bhuśuṇḍi as the narrator of the *Bhuśuṇḍi Rāmāyaṇa*.

The *Adhyātma Rāmāyaṇa*, theoretically an integral part of the *Brahmāṇḍa Purāṇa*, is a retelling of the Rāma story, also from a definite philosophical or theological standpoint, since it teaches that the world is an allusion imposed on the eternally blissful Absolute, combining a form of Advaita Vedānta with belief in Rāma's saving grace.[51] It substantially abridges the story, while at the same time frequently interrupting the plot with philosophical passages. There are various divergences from the original Rāmāyaṇa.

The Earth, oppressed by Rāvaṇa, goes in the form of a cow to Brahmā who then induces Viṣṇu to incarnate himself as Rāma (1.2.6), whereas in the Bālakāṇḍa it is the gods who go to Brahmā. The narration of the childhood sports indulged in by Rāma (1.3.43–58) recalls those of Kṛṣṇa in the *Bhāgavata Purāṇa*. While Rāma is an incarnation of Viṣṇu, Lakṣmaṇa, Bharata and Śatrughna are incarnations of Śeṣa, the conch and the discus (1.4.16–18). When Rāma kills Tāḍakā, she is transformed into a beautiful Yakṣiṇī and goes to heaven (1.4.26–32). Ahalyā, restored to human form from a stone by Rāma's arrival (as in Kālidāsa's *Raghuvaṃśa* 11.34, *Padma Purāṇa* etc.), addresses to him a long *stuti*, hymn of praise (1.5.43–59) on his divine nature. Immediately afterwards Rāma hails a boatman on the Gaṅgā who is reluctant to ferry them over, fearing a like transformation for his boat (1.6.1–5), as in the

[51] See H. von Glasenapp, *Zwei philosophische Râmâyaṇas*, Wiesbaden, 1951, B. H. Kapadia, 'The Adhyātma Rāmāyaṇa', JOIB 14, 1964–5, pp. 164–70 and F. Whaling, *The Rise of the Religious Significance of Rāma*, Delhi, 1980, pp. 105–218. P. C. Bagchi (Introduction to *Adhyātmarāmāyaṇam, ed.* N. Siddhantaratna (Calcutta Sanskrit Series 11), Calcutta, 1935), considers that it was composed between 1490 and 1550 (p. 76). It is sometimes ascribed to Rāmānanda, and is probably connected with his sect, as a link with Varanasi (6.15.58) may imply.

Hanumannāṭaka. Before Rāma can be installed Nārada appears and says that he should not be installed but go into exile so as to fulfil his duty of killing Rāvaṇa (2.1), while Mantharā is instigated by the goddess of speech who has entered her (2.2.44–6, similarly in the *Ānanda, Bhuśuṇḍi* and *Tattvasaṃgraha Rāmāyaṇas*). As Lakṣmaṇa and Guha watch over the sleeping Rāma and Sītā near the beginning of the journey into exile, Lakṣmaṇa treats Guha to a discourse on the workings of *karma* and the illusoriness of existence (2.6.1–16). Then the visit to Vālmīki, found only in the fourth stage of the original (2.1200*), is made the occasion for a long discourse by the sage on Rāma's dwelling, that is his nature as the supreme (2.6.51–63). Similarly, Vasiṣṭha addresses to Bharata on his return to Ayodhyā from his uncle a long speech of consolation, concentrating on the philosophic argument of the ephemerality of human life (2.7.93–107). In the Virādha episode (3.1.17–46), Rāma kills Virādha before he can actually touch Sītā, a form of the story more acceptable to devotees since it preserves Sītā's purity. Rāma himself warns Sītā that Rāvaṇa will approach her and so she should enter the hut, allowing only a counterfeit of herself to remain outside; she is then to remain for a year with Agni (3.7.1–4), who destroys the false Sītā in the fire-ordeal following the capture of Laṅkā and restores the real one (6.13.20). This clearly theologically motivated development has already been noted in the *Brahmavaivarta* and *Kūrma Purāṇas* and also occurs in the *Adbhuta Rāmāyaṇa* and in Tulsīdās. Another such development is that opponents conquered by Rāma reach eternal bliss, such as Virādha (3.1.44–6), Mārīca (3.7.19–24), Vālin (4.2.71) and in particular Rāvaṇa himself (6.11.78–9), because their thoughts had been directed towards the deity even if in anger, as Nārada is made to explain to the jealous gods on the last occasion (6.11.83–8); this appears to be another borrowing from the *Bhāgavata Purāṇa*.

The meeting with Śabarī (3.10) is made the vehicle for emphasising the all-embracing grace of Rāma, who discourses to her on the nine aspects or stages of *bhakti*, while Svayaṃprabhā, after magically transporting the Vānaras to the edge of the ocean, goes to Rāma and receives from him the gift of *bhakti* (4.6.59–84). Hanumān assumes a diminutive form in order to penetrate Laṅkā (5.1.43 and 2.1) and, when brought before Rāvaṇa, delivers a long speech on the Vedāntin view of *avidyā* and the merits of devotion to Rāma (5.4). Vibhīṣaṇa is depicted very much as a devotee of Rāma and on his first arrival he also asks for the gift of *bhakti* (6.3.1–48). When the Vānaras begin building the causeway, Rāma erects a *liṅga*, called Rāmeśvara, and worships it

(6.4.1–4), as in the Śaiva Purāṇas. From mount Suvela Rāma sees Rāvaṇa's umbrellas and crown and shatters them with an arrow (6.5.41–4). The incident of Kālanemi sent by Rāvaṇa to prevent Hanumān gathering herbs on mount Gandhamādana from the fourth stage (6 App.I.56) is developed with Kālanemi lecturing Rāvaṇa on Vedānta (6.6.36–7.33). On the field of battle, Kumbhakarṇa congratulates Vibhīṣaṇa on having become a devotee of Rāma (6.8.8–16), an episode found in the fourth stage of the original (6 App.I.36), and following Kumbhakarṇa's death Nārada arrives to praise Rāma and prophesy that Lakṣmaṇa will next day kill Indrajit and the following day Rāma will kill Rāvaṇa (6.8.34–52, cf. Rām. 6 App.I.32). Lakṣmaṇa alone is able to kill Indrajit, because of his abstention from food and sleep throughout their exile (6.8.64–6). Rāvaṇa, as well as Indrajit, performs a sacrifice (6.10), which the Vānaras seek to disrupt and succeed when Aṅgada drags on the dishevelled Mandodarī, an incident again based on a fourth stage passage (Rām. 6 App.I.63).[52] After Rāvaṇa's death, Lakṣmaṇa at Rāma's bidding consoles Vibhīṣaṇa with a philosophical discourse (6.12). In addition the work contains extensive stories about Vālmīki's past (2.6.65–86) and about how Rāvaṇa's counsellor Śuka was formerly a brāhman *vānaprastha* cursed by Agastya to become a Rākṣasa (6.5.5–24). In its Uttarakāṇḍa, after the birth and exploits of Rāvaṇa, is narrated the birth of Vālin and Sugrīva (7.3.1–15); a male monkey created by Brahmā is turned by falling into a lake into a beautiful woman, on seeing whom Indra and Sūrya emit their semen onto her hair and neck to produce Vālin and Sugrīva respectively, with Sūrya then giving Hanumān as a companion to Sugrīva. The work then inserts an exposition by Rāma of the way of salvation (*Rāmagītā*, 7.5), obviously in imitation of the *Bhagavadgītā*; it brings together the philosophical and theological teachings scattered through the rest of the work and expounds the Vedāntin view of *mokṣa*, the performance of one's duties in a spirit of devotion, meditation on the formula *tat tvam asi*, detachment of the senses and merging in the Absolute.[53]

[52] The immediate source may, however, be the lost pre-ninth-century drama, the *Kṛtyarāvaṇa*, which on the evidence of the *Nāṭyadarpaṇa* describes Aṅgada seizing Mandodarī by her hair in its sixth act; the incident also occurs in Vimalasūri's *Paümacariya*. In the *Ānanda Rāmāyaṇa* Hanumān, not Aṅgada, carries Mandodarī to where Rāvaṇa is doing penance. An attenuated form of it may perhaps be seen in the Tibetan version, in which Naṇḍa (= Hanumān) disturbs Daśagrīva's mind by mounting his palace and talking to his wife.

[53] This *Rāmagītā* has often been transmitted and commented on separately and probably it is actually older than the work in which it is now included.

A curious footnote to these two philosophically oriented Rāmāyaṇas is provided by the even later *Adbhuta Rāmāyaṇa*.[54] It is distinctly Śākta in character and contrives to elevate Sītā above Rāma, making her into Devī. As its alternative name of *Adbhutottarakāṇḍa* indicates, it starts really with the events of the Uttarakāṇḍa and extends them, claiming to be an eighth *kāṇḍa* to Vālmīki's Rāmāyaṇa and further bolstering its status by asserting that it forms part of a much longer divine Rāmāyaṇa. The reasons for the incarnation of Viṣṇu and Lakṣmī as Rāma and Sītā are given as curses of Nārada and Parvata. Sītā's birth is narrated in elaborate and incredible detail. The sage Gṛtsamada's wife has begged for a daughter who will be Lakṣmī herself and the sage has been sprinkling milk and reciting mantras into a jar to invoke Lakṣmī's presence. Rāvaṇa arrives to demand submission from the ascetics in Daṇḍaka and in token of it collects a drop of blood from each, by chance using this jar to hold it. Mandodarī, to whom he gives it for custody, subsequently drinks the contents believing them to be poison but instead becomes pregnant with Lakṣmī. She buries the foetus secretly in Kurukṣetra and Janaka, coming shortly afterwards to sacrifice, turns up the infant with his plough and adopts her. This is clearly a much elaborated version of Sītā's birth as the child of Mandodarī and Rāvaṇa and subsequent abandonment, which is found in several versions, reaccommodated to the version of her appearing out of the furrow.

The work omits all other incidents from the Bālakāṇḍa and the first part of the Ayodhyākāṇḍa, apart from the encounter with Paraśurāma. It next takes up its summary of the story with the departure into exile for unexplained reasons. After Sītā's carrying off by Rāvaṇa, a river is formed from the flood of Rāma's tears, which becomes the Vaitaraṇī.[55] Later Hanumān explains that the abduction of Sītā is only illusory. Then follows a brief narration of the campaign against Rāvaṇa, leading up to a general concourse of celebration at Ayodhyā attended by many *ṛṣis*. Here Sītā announces that the killing of Rāvaṇa is not really much of an exploit while his thousand-headed brother and namesake remains terrorising the gods. Rāma promptly mobilises an army against this Rāvaṇa but is defeated, whereupon Sītā assumes the terrible form of Devī and gleefully destroys Rāvaṇa and all his forces. Her rage threatens

[54] See G. A. Grierson, 'On the Adbhuta-Rāmāyaṇa', BSOS 4, 1926–8, pp. 11–27.

[55] Since, in the Tibetan and Khmer versions, this motif of the river of tears is attached to Sugrīva, it seems probable that this folk element has only been rather loosely attached to the Rāma story, accounting for its sporadic and widely-separated occurrence and the variation of individual involved.

to annihilate the world, even with Mahādeva (i.e. Śiva) taking the form of a corpse under her feet, so Rāma, revived by Brahmā, praises her by reciting her thousand names and thus pacifies her. The extent to which this episode, which forms the *raison d'être* of the work, is modelled on the *Devīmāhātmya* and Śākta mythology is abundantly clear. It is interesting therefore to note the extent to which the few other events narrated in any detail are influenced by folk material.

A definite folk element is also prominent in the *Ānanda Rāmāyaṇa*, which in addition shows some signs of influence from the Jain versions; it should probably be assigned to the fifteenth century. Its account of Sītā's birth makes her an incarnation of Padmā (Lakṣmī), born of fire, who is taken to Laṅkā by Rāvaṇa and then abandoned, but found and adopted by Janaka. During Daśaratha's sacrifice for the birth of sons, a vulture (who is in fact an Apsaras under a curse) steals a portion of the *pāyasa* and deposits it on mount Añjana, from which Hanumān is produced;[56] Hanumān is consequently a partial incarnation of Viṣṇu, although elsewhere he is regarded as an *avatāra* of Śiva, as in some Purāṇas.

Rāvaṇa is mentioned as one of the kings who attempt to bend Śiva's bow in order to win Sītā, and Rāma and Sītā exchange glances before the bending of the bow. Both these episodes occur first in Bhavabhūti's *Mahāvīracarita* and are found in another of these late Sanskrit versions, the *Bhuśuṇḍi Rāmāyaṇa*. The folk motif of the line drawn round Sītā also appears, as does the belief that Vālin has a boon by which he appropriates half the strength of anyone who fights with him (first found in Kampaṉ's version and also occurring in the Thai version). The seven *sāl* trees pierced by Rāma as he demonstrates his ability to Sugrīva are supported by the king of snakes, a popular element which has found its way to the Khmer version, which also has a close parallel to the narrative where Rāvaṇa spreads his protective umbrella over Laṅkā but Sugrīva smashes it and brings down Rāvaṇa's crown.[57] Aṅgada, when no seat is offered him on his embassy to Rāvaṇa, coils up his tail and sits on it, a popular motif transmitted through Bengal to the Malay and Thai versions. Rāvaṇa, rather than Indrajit, beheads the illusory Sītā, which may well represent a borrowing from the Jain

[56] The motif of a bird stealing part of this sacred food is used in the Thai version to account for the birth of Sītā, and is presumably derived from the episode of the crow which molests Sītā and which subsequently is identified as Mārīca's mother. This has here been combined with the more usual traditions about Hanumān's birth.

[57] In the parallel incident in the *Adhyātma Rāmāyaṇa* and Tulsīdās, it is Rāma who brings down the umbrellas and crown with an arrow.

version of Guṇabhadra, just as the replacement of Rāma by Lakṣmaṇa as the slayer of the ascetic Śambūka probably derives from Vimalasūri. Hanumān molests Mandodarī in order to interrupt Rāvaṇa's penance, whereas in the *Adhyātma Rāmāyaṇa* the incident is ascribed to Aṅgada. The reference to a convention that a warrior revealing his vital spot when asked by an opponent will not be taken advantage of (5.8.94) may perhaps have some relationship to the folk motif of the misplaced, even external, vital spot or soul found in such diverse versions as the Tibetan and Khotanese, Tulsīdās' Hindi version and the Malay and Thai versions. The episode of Sītā drawing Rāvaṇa's portrait also appears; it first occurs in the Jain versions of Bhadreśvara and Hemacandra and becomes common in vernacular versions in India and Southeast Asia. Another motif shared with the Southeast Asian versions, as well as the Tibetan, is the birth of one son only to Sītā and the subsequent miraculous creation of Lava by Vālmīki. There is also reference to the tradition of Rāvaṇa lifting mount Kailāsa and demanding Umā from Śiva. As an indication of its theological attitude, it may be noted that the *Ānanda Rāmāyaṇa* contains the *Rāmarakṣā stotra*, which summarises Rāma's deeds through various epithets applied to him, an obvious transition between narrative and purely devotional literature. Even more revealing is Rāma's promise to some Apsarases that they may fulfil their desire for him in his *avatāra* as Kṛṣṇa and in particular his boon to a devoted maid-servant that she will take birth as Rādhā.

The influence of the *Bhāgavata Purāṇa*, already present in the *Adhyātma Rāmāyaṇa*, is even more pronounced in the *Bhuśuṇḍi Rāmāyaṇa*.[58] It narrates Rāma's childhood sports on the model of Kṛṣṇa's twice over and assimilates the river Sarayū and countryside nearby (which it terms Pramodavana) to the Yamunā and Vṛndāvana; numerous demons are sent by Rāvaṇa to destroy Rāma and are killed by him, just as Kaṃsa sends them against Kṛṣṇa; Rāma himself performs various exploits clearly based on those of Kṛṣṇa and dances the *rāslīlā* with Sītā and a multitude of *gopīs*. This last incident (1.130.73–4) reveals the influence of Jayadeva's *Gītagovinda* and Līlāśuka's *Kṛṣṇakarṇāmṛta*, belonging to the twelfth and thirteenth centuries; thus, the *Bhuśuṇḍi Rāmāyaṇa* probably belongs to the fourteenth century—it cannot be much later, since it is one of Tulsīdās' sources. Theologically, also like the *Adhyātma*, the work shows an integration of Advaita with fervent *bhakti* devotion of the erotic type. There is

[58] See *Bhuśuṇḍi Rāmāyaṇa, Pūrva Khaṇḍa, ed.* B. P. Singh, with an English introduction by V. Raghavan, Varanasi, 1975.

probably some tantric influence in the way that Sītā is regarded as Rāma's *śakti* and is termed Sahajā or Sahajānandinī, while Rāma's supreme abode is called Sītāloka or Sītāvaikuṇṭha.

The framework of the text is the narration of the Rāma story by Brahmā to the crow Bhuśuṇḍi, who becomes a devotee of Rāma. In addition to the extensive borrowings from the Kṛṣṇa story of the *Bhāgavata Purāṇa* and the free use of flashbacks and previews of the action, the work shows various specific developments of the Rāma story. The four sons of Daśaratha are correlated with the four *vyūhas* (though neither that term nor the name of the Pāñcarātra system occurs), Vāsudeva, Saṃkarṣaṇa, Pradyumna and Aniruddha (1.15–16), and their order of birth is made to correspond, with Lakṣmaṇa given as the second son and Bharata the third (1.12.30 and 15.1); thus, in another feature the story is made to conform to the theology. To parallel this, Janaka's wife Sunayanā prays to Lakṣmī who becomes incarnate as four daughters, who in due course marry Daśaratha's four sons. As in some other versions, Rāma and Sītā meet and fall in love before the contest for her hand, which Rāvaṇa also attends. As in the *Adhyātma*, Mantharā is induced by Sarasvatī to rouse Kaikeyī's jealousy. The motif of only the illusory Sītā being seized by Rāvaṇa while her real self resides with Agni, found first in the *Kūrma* and *Brahmavaivarta Purāṇas* and shared with the other late Sanskrit Rāmāyaṇas, is here combined with the circle drawn round Sītā to protect her found also in the widely separated Khotanese and Malay versions. The story of Śabarī is further elaborated, including not only the popular tradition of her first sampling the fruit she offers to Rāma (first found in the *Padma Purāṇa*) but also a famine resulting from the ensuing jealousy of the sages. In common with the *Adhyātma*, the text has the incident of Rāma, on first seeing Rāvaṇa afar in his palace, breaking his parasol and *chaurī* with an arrow. Sītā when pregnant retires voluntarily to the forest *āśrama*, although later an ascetic relays to her gossip about her stay with Rāvaṇa. The story closes, as in the Uttarakāṇḍa, with the arrival of Kāla and Rāma's departure for his permanent abode, but the theological emphasis is again apparent in the discourse in eighteen chapters on Viṣṇubhakti that Rāma gives to Durvāsas; an earlier discourse which Rāma gives to console the women of Pramodavana for his impending departure is actually entitled *Rāmagītā*. All in all, the Rāma story proper is nearly swamped by the inflow of elements from the Kṛṣṇa cult.[59]

[59] The influence of the Kṛṣṇa legend is even more apparent in a late Bengali version, Raghunandana's *Rāmarasāyaṇa* of the eighteenth century.

An interesting tailpiece to these devotional Rāmāyaṇas in Sanskrit is provided by the *Tattvasaṃgraha Rāmāyaṇa* written, probably in the seventeenth century, by Rāmabrahmānanda as a definite compendium of all forms of the Rāma story.[60] Rāmabrahmānanda names his sources as the *Dharmakhaṇḍa, Agastyasaṃhitā, Umāsaṃhitā, Adhyātma Rāmāyaṇa, Brahma Purāṇa, Brahmāṇḍa Purāṇa, Skanda Purāṇa, Bhāgavata Purāṇa, Viṣṇu Purāṇa, Rāmatāpanīya Upaniṣad, Hiraṇyagarbhasaṃhitā, Bhārata* (i.e. Mahābhārata), *Śeṣadharma, Puruṣārthasedhāsindhu, Itihāsasamuccaya, Purāṇasāra* and *Harimāhātmyadarpaṇa*. In fact, he ranges more widely still, mentioning for instance also the *Padma* and *Kūrma Purāṇas* for their differing views on Rāma's incarnation,and he also draws on popular traditions. Thus, among the numerous episodes narrated are the magic circle drawn round Sītā by Lakṣmaṇa, from which Rāvaṇa inveigles her by offering to read her palm, Rāvaṇa's lifting of the ground on which Sītā stands, the motif of Rāvaṇa's vulnerable point being his toe,[61] and Hanumān's dragging of Mandodarī by the hair (intermediate in form between the *Adhyātma Rāmāyaṇa* and the Khmer and Malay versions). The theological device of the illusory Sītā here takes a slightly different form: Rāma summons the goddess of death to become the false Sītā and conceals the real Sītā within his breast (where as Lakṣmī she always resides). The work also includes within its Uttarakāṇḍa the story of the thousand-headed relative of Rāvaṇa whom Sītā goes to destroy, found also in the *Adbhuta Rāmāyaṇa*; here, Hanumān plays quite a major role in the conflict and is identified with Śiva, as he had been already to a certain extent in the story of his birth from Gautama's daughter, to whom had been transferred the embryo conceived by Pārvatī as she and Śiva watch a Vānara couple. The episode ends with hymns on the thousand names of Sītā and on the five-faced Hanumān. Nevertheless, overall the work is quite definitely one of devotion to Rāma (*Rāmabhakti*), as is the author's similar *Rāmāyaṇatattvadarpaṇa*. Both this and the author's South Indian background are well illustrated by the story that Rāma presented Vibhīṣaṇa with an image of Raṅganātha and that Vibhīṣaṇa subsequently established it at Śrīraṅgam.

[60] See V. Raghavan, 'The Tattvasaṁgraharāmāyaṇa of Rāmabrahmānanda', AORM 10, 1952–3, Sanskrit pp. 1–55.

[61] The motif is here presented as a mere ruse of Rāvaṇa to get Jaṭāyus to reveal his weak spot; this seems a later, rationalised form of the simple form found in the Khotanese version.

9
ADAPTATIONS IN OTHER LANGUAGES

'While ever the story of Rāma you compose circulates, so long shall you be immortalised in my worlds, in heaven above and on the earth below.' (1.2.36)

As well as all these recastings of the Rāma story within the Sanskritic Hindu tradition, the story has passed into the popular culture of the Buddhist and Jain faiths, has been translated or rather adapted into every modern Indian language as part of the continuing Hindu tradition in its *bhakti* aspect, and has spread beyond India to become part of the culture of the whole of Southeast Asia, originally in a Hindu context but subsequently accommodated to Buddhism or Islam with consequent changes in emphasis. Chronologically, some of these developments precede many of the treatments within the Sanskrit tradition surveyed above; indeed, claims have been made for the canonical Buddhist version as the antecedent of all others.

The *Dasaratha Jātaka* gives a version of the Rāma story which appears more modern than the Rāmāyaṇa but which may go back to a separate source. One of the major differences is that in it Rāma, Lakṣmaṇa and Sītā are all children of Daśaratha, after whose death Bharata is born to another queen. Weber and some scholars subsequently have seen this as the oldest form of the legend, with the others developing from it.[1] But such an evolution would have taken a long time and would result in placing the Rāmāyaṇa at an improbably late date, for it is clear that the story of Rāma is unknown in the Vedic literature and so this period of development cannot be pushed backward in time. Rather, it is clear that the story in the *Dasaratha Jātaka* is relatively late and indeed the narration in the prose passages (which in their present form are a Pali translation of a fifth-century AD Sinhalese original) contradicts some details of the much older *gāthās* or has even misunderstood them. Thus Lüders argued that the first *gāthā* referred to the offering of water to the dead, clearly alluded to in the Rāmāyaṇa, but was misunderstood by the writer of the prose and turned into the

[1] A. Weber, *Über das Rāmāyaṇa*, Berlin, 1870 and J. Przyluski, 'Epic Studies', IHQ 15, 1939, pp. 289–99.

story of Rāma telling Sītā and Lakṣmaṇa to enter the water before revealing their father's death; equally *gāthā* 10 paraphrases the proverbial 2.110.3.[2] The *gāthās* themselves seem mostly to be a Buddhist adaptation of the *kaccit* sarga; certainly they do not contain anything incompatible with the Rāmāyaṇa. In fact, the *gāthās* of some other Jātakas contain allusions to aspects of the Rāmāyaṇa story.[3] Some other differences in the *Dasaratha Jātaka* are that Daśaratha is king of Varanasi, has 16,000 wives and dies nine years after Rāma's departure for the forest, the scene of Rāma's exile being the Himālayas.

On the other hand the question of Sītā's parentage is one motif by which it is possible perhaps to trace the linkages between the different versions of the Rāma story. The view that her father is Daśaratha seems in fact to make its appearance quite early in the Buddhist tradition, for there is a reference in the *Dīgha Nikāya* to a king Okkāka (probably = Ikṣvāku) banishing his elder children, who 'through fear of injuring the purity of their line' 'intermarried with their sisters' giving rise to the Sākya clan.[4] There are other Buddhist parallels for brother–sister marriages.

Within the Buddhist tradition, the next references to the Rāma story come from the Kuṣāṇa period of the early centuries AD. A philosophical

[2] H. Lüders, 'Die Sage von Ṛṣyaśṛṅga', NG 1897, pp. 87–135, esp. pp. 128–9. See also my *Proverbs*, p. 144. Cf. D. C. Sircar, 'The Rāmāyaṇa and the Dasaratha Jātaka', JOIB 26, 1976–7, pp. 50–5.

[3] The blessing pronounced by Rāma's mother on his departure for Daṇḍaka forest is mentioned in the *Jayadissa Jātaka* (513.17). The *Vessantara Jātaka* includes a *gāthā* where Maddī declares that she will never desert Vessantara, just as the devoted Sītā never deserted Rāma (547.541). The story of an ascetic youth slain by a king is found in the *Sāma Jātaka*; also for example twice over in the *Śyāma Jātaka* of Mahāvastu 2.208.2—231.6 (and in the *Haribhaṭṭajātakamālā*, which gives a version particularly close to the Rāmāyaṇa), in which Sāma, while looking after his blind parents, goes to draw water from the river and is accidentally shot by the king of Vārāṇasī (cf. *Sāmajātaka ed.* R.Čičak-Chand, Bonn, 1974, and E. Hofstetter, *Der Herr der Tiere im alten Indien* (Freiburger Beiträge zur Indologie 14), Wiesbaden, 1980, pp. 100–15). Since the episode in the Rāmāyaṇa of Daśaratha slaying the youth belongs to the second stage, it is possible that it was taken from Buddhist literature (as H. Oldenberg argued on the basis of the greater stylistic elaboration seen in the epic, 'Jātakastudien', NG, 1918, pp. 429–68, esp. pp. 456–9), but more probably both borrow separately from folk tradition.

[4] *Dīgha Nikāya* 3.1.15 (*Ambaṭṭha Sutta*). E. J. Thomas discussed the relationship of this passage to the *Dasaratha Jātaka* and the Rāmāyaṇa in *The Life of Buddha as Legend and History*, London, 1927, pp. 5–16; a king Okkāka also occurs in the *Kusa Jātaka* (531). However, more recently it has been suggested that this view of Sītā's parentage arose through confusion of Daśaratha and Daśakaṇṭha (= Rāvaṇa), which would imply that it is the last of the variants to appear (cf. J.W. de Jong, 'Three Notes on the Vasudevahiṇḍi', *Saṃjñāvyākaraṇa*, Studia Indologica Internationalia, 1954, Poona/Paris, p. 11).

text of the Sarvāstivādin school, unfortunately very fragmentary, gives briefly the story in these terms: Sītā, with her husband's welfare in mind, (followed him into exile,) living in the forest, and was carried off by Rāvaṇa, lord of Laṅkā; Rāma (while searching for her) met the king of the Vānaras and, making an alliance with him, attacked the Rākṣasas.[5] Aśvaghoṣa's *Buddhacarita* mentions Daśaratha's death shortly after Rāma's banishment and alludes to various other incidents, as well as containing several verses which may plausibly be seen as echoes of the Rāmāyaṇa.[6] Possibly also going back to the same period is a brief reference to the Rāmāyaṇa in the *Mahāvibhāṣa*, of which Hsüan-tsang's Chinese translation is: 'As a book called the Rāmāyaṇa, there are 12,000 *ślokas*. They explain only two topics, namely Rāvaṇa carries off Sītā by violence and Rāma recovers Sītā and returns.'[7]

There are two fuller Chinese versions of the Rāma story, which further illustrate the popularity of the Rāma story in Buddhist circles. One is the 'Story without Names' or '*Jātaka* of an Unnamed King' translated into Chinese from the Indian original by K'ang-seng-hui in 251 AD.[8] In this, the unnamed king, who is the Buddha in a former birth, withdraws from his own kingdom in order to avoid conflict with his maternal uncle, who is the king of the neighbouring country and out of greed invades the other's territory; there is no suggestion of intrigues at court but instead this direct appeal to the principles of *ahiṃsā*. Interestingly, the figure equivalent to Vālin is then specified as an uncle of the monkey chief (= Sugrīva) and the similarity of their sufferings unites the king and the monkey chief and motivates their mutual assistance; thus, this Chinese version preserves the parallelism of Rāma's and Sugrīva's situations by altering both sets of relationships. The queen's abductor (i.e. Rāvaṇa) is depicted as a king of dragons (*nāgarāja*)—an adaptation to fit in with the demonology of the different

[5] D. Schlingloff, 'The Oldest Extant Parvan-List of the Mahābhārata', JAOS 89, 1969, pp. 334–8, esp. p. 334.

[6] See E. H. Johnston, *tr.*, *The Buddhacarita*, Lahore, 1935–6. More recently, V. Raghavan ('Buddhological Texts and the Epics', *Adyar Library Bulletin* 20, 1956, pp. 349–59) has indicated such echoes in Aśvaghoṣa's other works and even in Mahāyāna works like the *Lalitavistara* and *Mahāvastu*.

[7] K. Watanabe, 'The Oldest Record of the Rāmāyaṇa in a Chinese Buddhist Writing', JRAS 1907, pp. 99–103.

[8] It is the forty-sixth tale of the *Liu-tu-tsi-ching*. See E. Huber, 'Le Rāmāyaṇa et les Jātakas', BEFEO 4, 1904, pp. 698–701; E. Chavannes, *Cinq cent contes et apologues* I, Paris, 1910, pp. 173–8, and Raghu Vira and Chikyo Yamamoto *eds.*, *Rāmāyaṇa in China* (Sarasvatī Vihāra Series 8), Lahore, 1938. A useful general survey of extra-Indian versions of the Rāma story is contained in V. Raghavan, *The Rāmāyaṇa in Greater India*, Surat, 1975.

culture—who has transformed himself into a sage. It also places considerable stress on the activities of a small monkey, into whom Indra has transformed himself and who is equivalent to Hanumān. It also tells of the queen's ordeal after the king has returned to his capital, apparently a conflation of Sītā's ordeals at the end of the Yuddhakāṇḍa and in the Uttarakāṇḍa, but otherwise does not refer to events narrated in the Uttarakāṇḍa.

The other, the *Nidāna* of king 'Ten-Luxuries' (i.e. Daśarata for Daśaratha), was translated into Chinese by Chi-chia-yeh in 472 AD.[9] It is a very abbreviated treatment, lacking anything on Sītā's seizure by Rāvaṇa or on the Vānaras, but virtually identical to the Rāmāyaṇa in its treatment of those components of the story found in it. Rāma (called Lomo) is exiled for twelve years (rather than fourteen) and leaves for the forest with Lakṣmaṇa, while Bharata, having failed to persuade him to return, enthrones a sandal and rules as regent; Bharata is made the third brother, following a common tendency to simplify the relationships between the brothers. At the end of the period of exile Rāma returns and is reluctantly persuaded to accept the throne. The story emphasises filial piety and personal integrity, again ending with the Buddha identifying Rāma (elsewhere described as having the power of Nārāyaṇa) as himself in a previous birth.

The Japanese versions of the Rāma story are not taken directly from an Indian original but came through the Chinese *Tripiṭaka* and others.[10] One is an abridged Rāma story related in the twelfth-century collection of popular tales, the *Hobutsushū* by Tairano Yasuyori. Like the earlier Chinese versions, to which the author of these tales refers as giving details of the story, the hero is unnamed and is identified as the Buddha in a previous birth. However, at certain points the Japanese version is closer to the Indian original than to the Chinese version, possibly under the influence of oral traditions brought by the occasional Indians who reached Japan from the eighth century onwards. The Japanese version agrees with the Chinese in making the king retreat to the woods through fear of killing people in battle—the more religious motive of *ahiṃsā* appropriate to a Buddhist context—but unlike it has an account of Sītā's earnest wishes to accompany her husband, echoing

[9] It is the first story of the first chapter of the *Tsa-pao-tsang-ching*. See also S. Lévi, 'La légende de Râma dans un avadâna chinois', *Album Kern*, Leiden, 1903, pp. 279–81.

[10] Minoru Hara, 'Japanese Versions of the Rāma Story', *The Ramayana Tradition in Asia, ed.* V. Raghavan, New Delhi, 1980, pp. 334–47. I am greatly indebted to Professor Hara for providing me with a copy of this paper before publication. Cf. also his 'Rāma monogatari to momotarō dōwa', *Ashikaga Atsuuji hakushi kiju kinen, Orientogaku Indogaku ronshū*, Tōkyō, 1978, pp. 523–39.

a striking feature of the original Rāmāyaṇa. It is perhaps significant, incidentally, that neither has any hint of a miraculous birth or unusual parentage for Sītā.

This Japanese version is also closer to the original in that the details of the queen's abduction are narrated by a sick bird (= Jaṭāyus) before the king's encounter with the monkeys rather than after, as in the Chinese version. Again it includes the incident, lacking in the Chinese version, of the small monkey (= Hanumān) going to the Himālayas to fetch a healing herb. It concludes with the king becoming ruler of both countries at the people's invitation, whereas the Chinese version tells of the queen's ordeal after the king has returned to the capital.

A second derivative from the Rāmāyaṇa occurs in another collection of tales, the *Sambo-ekotoba* by Minamotono Tamenori, belonging to the tenth century. This is a modification of the episode of Daśaratha's accidental killing of the young ascetic, a theme which apparently was popular in Buddhist circles, for the frame of this story is found in the *Sāma Jātaka* and the *Śyāma Jātaka* in the *Mahāvastu-avadāna* and was transmitted thence through versions in the Chinese *Tripiṭaka* to Japan. In all of these the story is provided with a happy ending, since the dead son is restored to life and so there is no need for the aged father to curse the king.

There seems to be no direct relationship between the Chinese versions and the Tibetan version most recently studied by de Jong or the Khotanese version studied by Bailey, although there are several points of agreement between the Tibetan and Khotanese stories.[11] The Tibetan version, found in the Tun-huang manuscripts and presumably written during the Tibetan occupation of Tun-huang (late eighth to mid ninth century AD), must be closely related to an unknown Indian original and does not show any Buddhist influence, unlike the first especially of the two Chinese Rāma stories.[12] It conflates two versions of Sītā's parentage: she is born to Daśagrīva (= Rāvaṇa) who, because of predictions that she will ruin her father, has her committed to the water in a copper box, and she is then found by an Indian peasant while he is channelling water in a furrow of his field and named accordingly. The first element

[11] J. W. de Jong, 'An Old Tibetan Version of the Rāmāyaṇa', *T'oung Pao* 58, 1972, pp. 190–202, also 'The Tun-huang manuscripts of the Tibetan Rāmāyaṇa story', IIJ 19, 1977, pp. 37–88, and H. W. Bailey, 'The Rāma story in Khotanese', JAOS 59, 1939, pp. 460–8 and 'Rāma' and 'Rāma II', BSOAS 10, 1940–2, pp. 365–76 and 559–98. For a French translation of one ms. of the Tibetan version see J. K. Balbir, *L'histoire de Rāma en tibétain d'après des manuscrits de Touen-houang*, Paris, 1963.

[12] Indeed, C. Bulcke (*Rām-kathā* (*utpatti aur vikās*), 2nd ed., Prayāg, 1962, p. 229) considers that it was partly based on the Jain version of Guṇabhadra.

is quite different from Vālmīki's Rāmāyaṇa whereas the second is reminiscent of its secondary version of Sītā's birth. Only two brothers are mentioned—Ramaṇa (= Rāma) and Lakśaṇa, who initially replaces Bharata and thus, when Ramaṇa retires to the forest (there is no mention of any intrigues), becomes king, but later is found in his own role, guarding Sītā while Ramaṇa pursues the deer, until her insinuations drive him to follow Ramaṇa. Another motif now first appearing is Rāvaṇa's vital spot here said to be his horse-head, although given away by his revealing the toe of his right foot, which is the vital spot in the Khotanese version. One son, Lava, is born to Sītā while she has been left with five hundred ascetics during Ramaṇa's expedition against Benbala; Lava is lost and, before he is found, a sage creates Kuśa from *kuśa* grass.[13] The banishment proper is narrated subsequently, and follows Ramaṇa listening to a Licchavi washerman and his wife, but there is a happy reunion owing to Hanumān's intervention.

The Khotanese version, perhaps of the ninth century AD, has been adapted by means of a prologue and epilogue to Buddhist teachings, and is cast in the form of a *Jātaka*, though written entirely in verse. Again, familial relationships are distorted. Rāma and Lakṣmaṇa are the sons of Sahasrabāhu, who is the son of Daśaratha, and this Sahasrabāhu is killed by Paraśurāma in revenge for the theft of his father's cow; evidently this is the result of a conflation of the Mahābhārata story of the 'thousand-armed' (*sahasrabāhu*) Arjuna Kārtavīrya with the Bālakāṇḍa episode of the meeting between the two Rāmas. Sītā is the daughter of Daśagrīva, as in the Tibetan version and various others, and abandoned in the great river in a box which is here recovered by a sage who brings her up until Rāma and Lakṣmaṇa arrive, fall in love with her and take her away with them, setting a magic circle round her to guard her whenever necessary. Rāma allies himself with Naṇḍa (= Vālin) and kills Sugrīva, thus reversing the original roles but still making use of a sign to distinguish them, in this version and in the Tibetan a mirror; Naṇḍa also corresponds to Hanumān in the siege of Laṅkā. In addition, this Khotanese version includes an episode of a king (here Nahauṣa) who knows the speech of animals and his wife who demands to be told the secret, even though it be the death of him; while this is essentially a common folk-tale motif, the same theme is assigned to Kaikeyī's father and mother in the fourth stage of Vālmīki's Rāmāyaṇa (2 App.I.14.36–52) and may well have been transposed from there in the Khotanese version.

[13] Since this motif also occurs in Somadeva's *Kathāsaritsāgara* (eleventh century) and the Kashmiri version of the Rāmāyaṇa by Divākara Prakāśa Bhaṭṭa it presumably derives from the *Bṛhatkathā*; it also appears in the Southeast Asian versions.

The Rāma story has also spread through Central Asia to Mongolia, where four versions of the story are extant,[14] and to Siberia. The Mongolian versions specifically have links with the Tibetan and include the development of the motif of Rāvaṇa's vital spot to that of the external soul, for the soul of the demon Mangus (= Rāvaṇa) is kept in a secret place and only when Rāma, having discovered it by a stratagem, destroys it is the demon killed.

By contrast with the Buddhist versions' tendency to turn Rāma into a Bodhisattva with the accompanying stress on his superhuman aspects, Jain versions of the story tend to adopt a reductionist approach. This is least pronounced in the *Vasudevahiṇḍi* of Saṅghadāsa, which probably contains the oldest Jain version of the Rāma story and presumably therefore was composed before the end of the third century AD, the date assigned to Vimalasūri's *Paümacariya*.[15] These two were written in Prakrit but the *Uttarapurāṇa* of Guṇabhadra, the third major Jain version, was written in Sanskrit, as were many later adaptations.[16]

In the *Vasudevahiṇḍi* (in *Mayaṇavegālambha*, 240–5), as in the other Jain versions, the Rākṣasas and Vānaras are depicted as Vidyādharas, masters of magic who in general are benevolent, a possible indebtedness to Guṇāḍhya's *Bṛhatkathā*.[17] Thus, the Rākṣasas

[14] C. Damdinsürèn, *Ramajana Mongold dèlgèrsèn n'*, Ulaanbaatar, 1976.

[15] See J. C. Jain *ed.*, *The Vasudevahiṇḍi* (L.D. Series 59), Ahmedabad, 1977, and J. C. Jain, 'An old version of the Jaina Rāmāyaṇa', *Sambodhi* 4, 1975–6, pp. 22–9, also K. R. Chandra, 'Sources of the Rāma-story of Paumacariyam', JOIB 14, 1964, pp. 134–47 and 'Extent of the influence of the Rāma-story of Paumacariyam', JOIB 15, 1966, pp. 341–9. On all the Jain versions, see V. M. Kulkarni, 'The Origin and Development of the Rāma Story in Jaina Literature', JOIB 9, 1959–60, pp. 189–204 and 284–304.

[16] From the *Paümacariya* are derived Raviṣeṇa's *Padmapurāṇa* (678 AD), Hemacandra's versions in his *Yogaśāstrasvopajñavṛtti* and *Triṣaṣṭiśalākāpuruṣacarita* (twelfth century) and Dhaneśvara's *Śatruñjayamāhātmya* (fourteenth century) in Sanskrit, in Prakrit Śīlācārya's *Caüpannamahāpurisacariya* (868 AD) and Bhadreśvara's *Kahāvalī* (eleventh century), and in A~abhraṃśa Svayambhū's *Paümacariü* (eighth to ninth centuries). From the *Uttarapuraṇa* are derived Puṣpadanta's *Mahāpurāṇa* (965 AD) in Apabhraṃśa and Kṛṣṇadāsa's *Puṇyacandrodayapurāṇa* (sixteenth century) in Sanskrit. There is, however, some cross influence, and some of the later versions follow Vālmīki more closely than earlier ones.

[17] Since the story of Rāma is included within the story of Vegavatī both in the *Vasudevahiṇḍi* and in the *Kathāsaritsāgara* (*Rāmāyaṇavṛttānta*, 107.12–26), there is some likelihood that this point of attachment is owed to their source, the *Bṛhatkathā*; Kṣemendra's *Bṛhatkathāmañjarī* includes a *Rāmākhyāyikā*. Also, the name of Vegavatī and even some aspects of her story resemble the Vedavatī of the Uttarakāṇḍa—was perhaps the story of Vedavatī taken into the Rāmāyaṇa from the *Bṛhatkathā*, which then reversed the borrowing by absorbing a summary of the Rāmāyaṇa?

are given a distinctly more favourable treatment. The *Vasudevahiṇḍi's* account is in general close to the Vālmīki Rāmāyaṇa but there are certain divergences. It begins with Rāvaṇa's genealogy (as does Vimalasūri's version) and closes with Rāma's installation, suggesting some link with the *Rāmopākhyāna*. Saṅghadāsa narrates the marriage of Mandodarī with Rāvaṇa, despite predictions that her first child will destroy the family; Sītā, when born, is enclosed in a box, which is not however committed to the waters (as in several forms of the story) but placed where it is discovered in front of Janaka's plough. The circumstances in which Daśaratha grants Kaikeyī two boons are slightly modified, removing the supernatural element from the help in battle and adding a second reason, presumably to coincide with the two boons. Śatrughna, incidentally, is depicted as Kaikeyī's son, as also in Vimalasūri's work, no doubt because of his close links with Bharata. When the two brothers first meet the Vānaras, it is Hanumān who proposes friendship with Rāma and makes a pact with fire as witness; this is clearly a symptom of Hanumān's increasing prominence at the expense of Sugrīva and the other Vānaras. Rāvaṇa is killed by Lakṣmaṇa not Rāma, and there is no mention of a fire-ordeal imposed on Sītā.

Vimalasūri in his *Paümacariya* reveals his indebtedness to the Vālmīki Rāmāyaṇa in his very divergences from it, for, without naming the work that he is attacking, he mentions various features of it which he regards as unbelievable and so modifies in his own account, such as the monkey nature of the Vānaras, the bloodthirstinesss of the Rākṣasas, Indra's defeat by Rāvaṇa, Rāma's killing of the golden deer and of Vālin, and the construction of the causeway. His rationalist attitude is very apparent. He renames the major characters, which accounts for the name of his poem, since Rāma is called Paüma (Sanskrit Padma), but not infrequently reverts to the original names. He is also concerned to increase the moral elevation of his characters and so passes over Kaikeyī's intrigues, omits the episode of the golden deer, makes Vālin resign the throne voluntarily to Sugrīva,[18] has Lakṣmaṇa not Rāma kill Rāvaṇa, omits Sītā's fire-ordeal after the capture of Laṅkā, and has Lakṣmaṇa kill Śambūka by accident;[19] the purpose of many divergences is to exonerate Rāma from killing even animals. Rāvaṇa is turned into

[18] However, the story of the false Sugrīva who ousts the real one from his kingdom, in which Vimalasūri is followed by Hemacandra, is nothing but a doublet of the enmity between the Vānara brothers, and supports his overall indebtedness to Vālmīki.

[19] Lakṣmaṇa's accidental killing of Śambūka is taken into several South Indian versions: the Kannaḍa *Pampa Rāmāyaṇa*, the Telugu version by Raṅganātha (3.4–5) and the Kannaḍa *Torave Rāmāyaṇa* (6.45).

a devout and pious Jain, whose only weakness is his passion for Sītā, and thus the incidents of the illusory head of Rāma and the beheading of the illusory Sītā are omitted. In addition, various episodes are introduced to buttress the Jain emphasis. There are also certain actual discrepancies from the original. Śatrughna is the son of Kaikeyī, as noted above. Janaka and his wife Videhā have twins, Bhāmaṇḍala and Sītā. Khara and Dūṣaṇa are made one individual, who is the husband of Rāvaṇa's sister Candraṇakhā, but on the other hand Indrajit is differentiated into two sons of Rāvaṇa, Indrajit and Meghavāhana.

Guṇabhadra in his *Uttarapurāṇa*, written in the ninth century, agrees with Saṅghadāsa in making Sītā the daughter of Mandodarī and Rāvaṇa, abandoned and found by Janaka and his wife Vasudhā (= Earth); the motivation is supplied by Maṇimatī's curse on Rāvaṇa which corresponds to Vedavatī's. He says that Daśaratha originally ruled at Vārāṇasī but then migrated to Ayodhyā after the annihilation of Sagara's family.[20] Janaka gives Sītā in marriage to Rāma, who has protected a sacrifice undertaken by Janaka (a conflation of Viśvāmitra and Janaka). Rāma, Sītā and Lakṣmaṇa then go off to Vārāṇasī to protect the subjects there—Kaikeyī's intrigues accordingly are absent. Rāvaṇa, as a result of the instigation of the sage Nārada, becomes enamoured of Sītā and sends his sister Śūrpaṇakhā as a go-between. When he seizes her, he dare not even touch her, since he would have been deprived of his magic art of flying through the air. It is then Daśaratha who informs Rāma of Sītā's abduction. Lakṣmaṇa, not Rāma, fights and kills Vālin, another device to place Rāma above any violence. On the other hand, Guṇabhadra retains for example the episode of the golden deer and, from the opposite side, the beheading of the illusory Sītā is performed by Rāvaṇa himself.

Although later Jain versions are largely derivative, certain innovations may be noted. Bhadreśvara in his *Kahāvalī* introduces the motif of Sītā drawing a portrait of Rāvaṇa at the urging of her co-wives, which forms the cause of her banishment;[21] this feature is adopted by Hemacandra in his *Triṣaṣṭiśalākāpuruṣacarita* and, through Kṛttibās' Bengali version, has spread into the Southeast Asian versions of the Rāma story. A further variant on Daśaratha's place of rule occurs in Hemacandra's *Triṣaṣṭiśalākāpuruṣacarita*, where after his marriage to

[20] This seems possibly an attempt to reconcile the traditions of the Rāmāyaṇa and the *Dasaratha Jātaka*.

[21] The first occurrence of this motif is apparently in an allusion to the Rāma story in the *Upadeśapada* of Haribhadrasūri (cf. 700–70 AD), according to Kulkarni (op. cit., p. 297).

Kaikeyī Daśaratha leaves Ayodhyā for Rājagṛha, living there out of fear of Rāvaṇa, and Rāma and Lakṣmaṇa are born there, but subsequently Daśaratha returns to Ayodhyā, where Bharata and Śatrughna are born. Also in Hemacandra's account, during the battle Nala and Nīla capture the two kings Samudra and Setu—a rationalist recasting of the subjugation of the ocean by building the causeway, like his explanation, derived from Vimalasūri, of the name Daśamukha for Rāvaṇa from his putting on as a child a necklace of nine rubies, in which his face was reflected. In a somewhat similar fashion, the Jain stress on the number of Lakṣmaṇa's wives may be a deliberate counter to the usual emphasis on his celibacy; Hanumān also is presented as somewhat of a philanderer, a feature which becomes more strongly marked in the Southeast Asian versions.

The story of Rāma was evidently current in South India from about the third century AD, since there are several clear allusions to episodes from it in early Tamil literature. However, the major background to Kampaṉ's great translation of the epic into Tamil was provided by the *bhakti* devotional poetry of the Āḻvārs, from which Kampaṉ even makes certain borrowings. The attitude of fervent devotion to an incarnate deity which characterises their poetry is reflected in the very name of Kampaṉ's work, the *Irāmāvatāram* 'The Descent of Rāma'. This attitude and the particular poetic qualities with which he endowed his work are what distinguish Kampaṉ from Vālmikī, whom he follows quite closely in his narrative.[22] Kampaṉ's date has still not been agreed on with any finality but must fall within the period from the ninth to the twelfth centuries. Thus, his is the first adaptation of the Rāmāyaṇa into a language other than Sanskrit or Prakrit in India (although the Old Javanese version belongs to the tenth century) and is the earliest devotional treatment of the story in the various living languages of India.

Kampaṉ's poem is divided into six books, following the original, for he omits the Uttarakāṇḍa, and is about half as long. He was nevertheless acquainted with the Uttarakāṇḍa for the story of Vedavatī is introduced as part of the warning that Vibhīṣaṇa gives to Rāvaṇa before their final breach. Kampaṉ further dramatises Vibhīṣaṇa's speech by drawing on other parts of Vaiṣṇava mythology, since Vibhīṣaṇa goes on to narrate the story of Hiraṇyakaśipu and Viṣṇu's incarnation as his destroyer, the man-lion Narasiṃha, as an awful warning to Rāvaṇa. Divergences

[22] See S. Shankar Raju Naidu, *A comparative study of Kamba Ramayanam and Tulasi Ramayan*, Madras, 1971.

from the original Rāmāyaṇa are not particularly major, but we may note some of the more interesting and important. In narrating Viṣṇu's promise to the gods to become incarnate as a son of Daśaratha, Kampaṉ makes Rāma himself Viṣṇu, Lakṣmaṇa Śeṣa, Bharata the *cakra* and Śatrughna the conch (1.5.22) as in several Purāṇas. The story of Ahalyā's release by the dust of Rāma's feet includes her turning to stone, derived from Kālidāsa, probably through the Purāṇas. As in the Sanskrit dramas, Rāma and Sītā are depicted as meeting before the actual bending of the bow: Kampaṉ has Viśvāmitra take Rāma and Lakṣmaṇa along a street in Mithilā from which Rāma catches sight of Sītā on a balcony, their eyes meet and it is love at first sight. When Sītā marries Rāma, the three daughters of Janaka's brother, Kuśadhvaja, marry the other three brothers, including Urmilā, who in the Bālakāṇḍa is Sītā's younger sister (Rām. 1.70.21–2). After Kaikeyī has demanded the two boons from Daśaratha, Kausalyā goes to him, helping him to regain consciousness, and it is at this point that he narrates his killing of the ascetic youth (2.4.74–90). In a similar telescoping of events, Daśaratha dies as soon as he has heard from Sumantra about Rāma's departure (2.5.60). Daśaratha has actually forbidden Bharata to make the funeral oblations over him (2.4.50, cf. 2.9.132) rather than expressing the wish that Bharata's offerings may not reach him (Rām. 2.37.9), and so Śatrughna performs the funeral ceremonies. Bharata, when he fails to persuade Rāma to accept the throne, swears that he will immolate himself if Rāma does not return on time when the period of exile is over (2.12.133; the motif first occurs in a fourth-stage insertion by the Southern recension, Rām. 2.2304*); this then provides a dramatic ending to the poem, for Bharata is actually making the necessary preparations when Hanumān arrives as Rāma's envoy to tell him that all is well.

Sutīkṣṇa, in directing them to Agastya, declares that he is imparting teachings in Tamil (3.3.41), a natural development of his link with the south. Agastya returns Viṣṇu's bow to Rāma who had entrusted it to Varuṇa after his encounter with Paraśurāma (3.3.55, cf. 1.22). Lakṣmaṇa mutilates Śūrpaṇakhā on his own initiative, cutting off her breasts as well as nose and ears, when she returns to seize Sītā; Kampaṉ highlights Śūrpaṇakhā's infatuation with Rāma and Rāvaṇa's with Sītā. Rāvaṇa, when he abducts Sītā, lifts hut and all, thus avoiding direct bodily contact with her (3.8.74).[23] The devotional attitude apparent here is also visible in the episode where Saṃpāti, having met the Vānaras and learnt about his brother Jaṭāyus' death for Rāma, gets the

[23] The motif of Rāvaṇa lifting the ground on which Sītā stands occurs also in the Tibetan version and in the *Tattvasaṃgraha Rāmāyaṇa*.

Vānaras to repeat Rāma's name, whereupon his wings, long ago burnt off, regrow to their original size and strength (4.16.48–9); so too for Hanumān in his leap to Laṅkā, repetition of Rāma's name is the only way of achieving success (5.1.88); already we begin to see the emphasis on the name which is to become so marked later. Earlier in the story, Rāma's sympathy with Sugrīva is aroused by Hanumān's explanation that Vālin has taken Sugrīva's wife, in response to his own observation of the absence of women; Kampaṉ thus portrays his characters in a better light. Similarly, he makes of Vālin an impressive figure, who can believe no ill of Rāma, but the only real innovation is that Vālin attempts to check and then draw out the arrow which kills him to ascertain its nature and its owner,[24] although it may also be noted that now Rāma reverses the argument about Vālin as merely a monkey to declare that if he can debate morals then he should be bound by them; but he still has no counter to the charge of underhand behaviour in shooting Vālin unawares, except the story that Vālin through a boon of Śiva appropriates part of any open adversary's strength. On the other hand, to clear Sugrīva of acting hastily, Kampaṉ emphasises the role of the Vānara ministers in persuading him to accept the throne and in themselves rolling the stone across the cave. Tārā, after Vālin's death, is depicted as an ideal widow and does not marry Sugrīva; indeed her widowhood, with its reminder of his mothers' widowhood, serves to pacify Lakṣmaṇa when he delivers Rāma's ultimatum (4.11.52). Kampaṉ is concerned also to justify the character of Vibhīṣaṇa, stressing the aspect of his devotion to Rāma and minimising his self-interest. Incidentally, the figure of Trijaṭā, Sītā's Rākṣasī jailer, is made Vibhīṣaṇa's daughter (5.6.22), presumably because she too is sympathetic to Rāma's cause;[25] her dream is narrated with great elaboration and some difference of detail (5.6). Hanumān's modesty is brought out not only when he prepares for his leap to Laṅkā but more particularly

[24] This must be the ultimate origin of the episode in the Khmer *Rāmakerti I* where Bālī catches the arrow, asks which god it belongs to and then, seeing Rām's name on it, places it on his head (2443–8).

[25] Trijaṭā is also Vibhīṣaṇa's daughter in the Old Javanese version, the Oriya version by Balarāmdās, Govindarāja's commentary on Rām. 5.?5.4 and the Malay *Sĕrī Rāma*. No doubt for the same reasons, she is his wife in the *Ānanda Rāmāyaṇa* (1.9.101) and the Khmer *Rāmakerti I* and his sister in the Marāṭhī *Bhāvārtha Rāmāyaṇa*. C. Bulcke ('Sītā's friend Trijaṭā', *Indian Antiquary Third Series* 1, 1964, pp. 55–63) suggests conflation of Trijaṭā with Vibhīṣaṇa's daughter Analā (also Nandā or Kalā, mentioned at Rām. 5.35.11). Already in the *Rāmopākhyāna* Sītā tells Hanumān that Trijaṭā came and gave her a message from Avindhya (Mbh. 3.264.53–5). Another sympathetic Rākṣasī, Saramā, originally separate (Rām. 6.24–5), becomes within the Rāmāyaṇa itself by the third stage Vibhīṣaṇa's wife (Rām. 7.12.22).

on his return, when he does not relate his exploits to the Vānaras, who however guess them from his wounds (5.15.9–10).

During Lakṣmaṇa's installation of Vibhīṣaṇa as ruler of Laṅkā, mention is made of Lakṣmaṇa's lack of sleep throughout their exile (6.4.144), a motif elaborated in later versions. Kumbhakarṇa participates in the debate preceding Vibhīṣaṇa's defection, but then is woken in the middle of the battle; in general, greater stress is laid on his adherence to duty as the motive of his loyalty to Rāvaṇa. There are various divergences in the battle scenes, including the innovation of an illusory Janaka brought bound before Sītā (6.16). Rāvaṇa sends for his reserve forces from throughout the world (6.29). Mandodarī utters laments on the deaths of her sons Akṣa and Indrajit, as well as her great dirge for Rāvaṇa, which culminates in her own death of grief (6.36.239–46). Kampaṉ ends his poem with the triumphal note of Rāma's installation after his joyful return, a fitting climax to his stress on loving service to the incarnate deity.

Evidence for the prestige of the Rāmāyaṇa in Karṇātaka is found in the Mahākūṭa inscription of 601–2 AD by the Cāḷukya ruler Maṅgaleśa, which echoes the definition of an ideal man in the opening sarga of the Bālakāṇḍa. Nevertheless, the first adaptation into Kannaḍa, the *Pampa Rāmāyaṇa* of Abhinava Pampa (a pseudonym for Nāgacandra), is in the Jain tradition, owing more to Vimalasūri (through Raviṣeṇa) and Guṇabhadra than to the Sanskrit quoted by Maṅgaleśa; it was probably composed around the end of the eleventh century. The basic story has undergone some very considerable modifications, and much extraneous matter in the form of the previous lives of various characters is included, as well as the location of several events in Jain shrines. Abhinava Pampa provides a lengthy background to the Bālakāṇḍa events with a genealogy of Daśaratha, his marriages first to Aparājite, Sumitre and Suprabhe (= Kausalyā and a duplicated Sumitrā, as in Raviṣeṇa's *Padmapurāṇa*[26]) and then to Kaikeyī, on which occasion Kaikeyī acts as his charioteer in his fight with her disappointed suitors and so gains the two fateful boons; similarly, an extended background is given to Sītā, who is here, as in Vimalasūri, Janaka's daughter by birth and has a twin brother, here kidnapped by Vidyādharas and (ignorant of their true relationship) a rival for Sītā's hand. Janaka promises Sītā to Rāma in marriage as a reward for his military help (cf. Guṇabhadra), but the

[26] Another indication that Raviṣeṇa is Abhinava Pampa's source is provided by their common telling of Vibhīṣaṇa's attempt to avert Rāvaṇa's fate by killing the fathers of Rāma and Sītā, which Daśaratha and Janaka frustrate by substituting images of themselves.

bending of the bow is nonetheless retained, ostensibly to decide between the claims of Rāma and the twin brother but in reality narrated as though it were the contest for her hand.

Daśaratha in fact abdicates and Bharata's attempt to persuade Rāma to return is prompted not by Daśaratha's death but by Kaikeyī's repentant urgings, and she herself endeavours to persuade Rāma. On the way south Lakṣmaṇa has various amorous and military adventures, while a Yakṣa ruler creates a magnificient city for them to spend the rainy season in. When they reach Daṇḍaka, ruled by Khara and his wife Candraṇakhī, Rāvaṇa's sister, Lakṣmaṇa finds a sword in a bamboo clump and accidentally decapitates Candraṇakhī's son Śambhuka who is performing penance there.[27] This enrages Candraṇakhī, who nonetheless becomes enamoured of Lakṣmaṇa, though not apparently of Rāma. Rāvaṇa is informed of events and arrives on the scene while Lakṣmaṇa is absent fighting Khara and Dūṣaṇa, sees Rāma and Sītā together in their hut (cf. Bhāsa's *Pratimānāṭaka*) and commands a demi-goddess to decoy Rāma away, which she does by mimicking Lakṣmaṇa's summons for help; the episode of the golden deer as such is lacking, and indeed Mārīca appears later to remonstrate with Rāvaṇa.

Sugrīva takes the initiative in seeking out Rāma and Lakṣmaṇa. His opponent is some evildoer who has falsely assumed his appearance and usurped his position, imprisoning Sugrīva's wife Sutāre. In the ensuing conflict Lakṣmaṇa seizes and destroys the false Sugrīva; Rāma is thus rendered passive as well as being freed of any taint of unethical behaviour, recalling Vimalasūri's version. Vālin does occur however (and is said to have resigned his throne to Sugrīva) in the context of Rāvaṇa's genealogy and exploits which follow next and in which, as in Vimalasūri, Rāvaṇa's ten heads are rationalistically explained as reflections in his mother's jewel-mirror. Hanumān is commissioned to go to Laṅkā and Rāma gives him his ear-rings; in Laṅkā he confers with Vibhīṣaṇa.

At one stage in the battle, in order to gain supernatural power, Rāvaṇa performs worship which the Vānaras seek to disrupt by various provocations, including seizing Mandodarī's jewels and tying together the hair of his women.[28] Rāvaṇa is killed by Lakṣmaṇa, although Rāma has taken part in combat, and Sītā's fire-ordeal is suppressed, as in older Jain versions, but her subsequent banishment and the birth of the twins are retained. When grown, Kuśa and Lava, discovering from

[27] Abhinava Pampa here again follows Vimalasūri. The motif of a bamboo-clump as a hiding-place is found also in a different context in the Malay version (see p. 295).

[28] This motif occurs with some variation in the Khmer version.

Nārada their history, go to Ayodhyā to challenge Rāma and Lakṣmaṇa before all are reunited, though not before Sītā has now passed through the fire-ordeal; Sītā then retires from the world. The story of Vedavatī is included in many stories of past lives narrated with much Jain emphasis.

The apparent popularity of Kampaṉ's Tamil version in the Kannaḍa-speaking area is perhaps explained by the Jain emphasis of the *Pampa Rāmāyaṇa*. Subsequently Battatīśvara wrote a *Rāmāyaṇa* in the *bhāmini ṣaṭpadī* metre, but it did not achieve the popularity of the *Torave Rāmāyaṇa* of Narahari alias Kumāra Vālmīki (mid seventeenth century); there is also an *Uttara Rāmāyaṇa* in Kannaḍa, written by Yogindra and Tirumale Vaidya.

In Malayāḷam literature, the earliest versions of the Rāma story are the *Rāmacaritam* and the *Rāmakathappāṭṭu*, probably little later in date than Kampaṉ's Tamil version. However, both of these are only partial versions, since they are based solely on the Yuddhakāṇḍa, although the *Rāmacaritam* does include a résumé of previous events when Bharata, on the eve of Rāma's installation, asks Hanumān to narrate to him all that happened during the exile. In this there are certain variations from the standard pattern: for example, Śūrpaṇakhā arrives to find Sītā alone and threatens to kill her, whereupon Rāvaṇa, arriving in the guise of an ascetic, offers to lead Sītā to Rāma. Slightly later come the *Kaṇṇaśśa Rāmāyaṇam* of Rāma Paṇikkar, which belongs to the fourteenth or early fifteenth century, and Punam's *Rāmāyaṇacampū*, probably of the fifteenth century. Rāma Paṇikkar's work is composed from a *bhakti* standpoint. He dramatises the meeting of the two Rāmas, possibly reflecting antagonism to Paraśurāma as a symbol of brāhman superiority. His description of Sītā dancing like a peacock when Rāma breaks the bow is taken over by the more famous later poet Eẓuttaccaṅ, who modifies the image to that of a peahen.

Eẓuttaccaṅ's *Attiyatuma Rāmāyaṇam* is the best known Malayāḷam version of the story, though based—as its name indicates—on the *Adhyātma Rāmāyaṇa* rather than on Vālmīki.[29] However, Eẓuttaccan treats various incidents in a novel and more poetic manner than his original, and does at times revert to the older narrative; indeed, the *Uttararāmāyaṇam* also, though less certainly, ascribed to him follows the *Kaṇṇaśśa Rāmāyaṇam*, which is based on Vālmīki, not the *Adhyātma*

[29] See C. A. Menon, *Ežuttaccan and his Age*, Madras, 1940.

Rāmāyaṇa. In the *Attiyatuma Rāmāyaṇam*, Rāma's childhood is described attractively and at some length. In the encounter with Paraśurāma, Eẓuttaccan depicts Rāma as being sarcastically polite to him, thus emphasising the correctness of Rāma's behaviour here and elsewhere, just as he stresses Rāma's filial obedience in connection with his banishment. Similarly, Bharata's attachment to Rāma is shown in the way that, when he is going after Rāma to persuade him to return, he rolls in the dust which bears the imprint of Rāma's feet and pours it over his head, whereas in the *Adhyātma Rāmāyaṇa* he simply extolls the dust trodden by Rāma. Eẓuttaccan also follows the *Adhyātma Rāmāyaṇa* in the story of how Vālmīki was transformed from a highway robber into a saint and the author of the Rāmāyaṇa by repeating the name of Rāma. Śūrpaṇakhā's attack on Sītā is attributed to despair at her unrequited love for Rāma, and Lakṣmaṇa's violent intervention is motivated by fanatical devotion to Rāma, who does not in any way commission it; thus, Rāma comes out of the episode more creditably than in most versions. Again, Sugrīva's closing of the cave on Vālin is interpreted as a tragic misunderstanding, caused by the Asura Māyāvin's magic, and Vālin is not accused of any misconduct with Sugrīva's wife, so both brothers are cleared of any stain on their character. Eẓuttaccan also amplifies on the *Adhyātma Rāmāyaṇa* in his emphasis on Vālin's immense power in the fight between the two brothers. His treatment of the battle scenes is vivid and relatively independent, and he reintroduces from a later stage of Vālmīki's Rāmāyaṇa Agastya's exposition to Rāma of the *Ādityahṛdaya*, which is omitted in the *Adhyātma Rāmāyaṇa*. On the other hand, he drops the long discourse which, in the *Adhyātma Rāmāyaṇa*, Lakṣmaṇa delivers to Vibhīṣaṇa as he mourns Rāvaṇa's death, and makes Rāma himself pay homage to his fallen enemy.[30]

When Rāvaṇa falls in battle, a light issues from his body and ascends to heaven, as it does in the case of all those killed by Rāma; Eẓuttaccan here remains truer to the understanding of Rāma as Viṣṇu in human form than the *Adhyātma Rāmāyaṇa*, in which the light merges with Rāma, symbolising the attainment by Rāvaṇa of union

[30] In south Indian tradition, especially in its more popular forms, Rāvaṇa is regularly a more important figure. Such enhanced prestige is already apparent in the *Laṅkāvatāra Sūtra*, which is cast in the form of a discourse between Rāvaṇa and the Buddha, and mentions the grandeur of Laṅkā and Rāvaṇa's great learning, as well as that of his counsellors Śuka and Sāraṇa; the work declares that Rāvaṇa belonged to the Mahāyāna but makes no mention of his encounter with Rāma.

with the supreme self. On the return journey to Ayodhyā, Tārā and the other Vānarīs are collected from Kiṣkindhā at Sītā's request—a motif very briefly alluded to in the *Adhyātma Rāmāyaṇa* (and found also in Kampaṉ's Tamil version), which is based on an addition of the North-western recension to Vālmīki (6.3399*).

In the remaining literary language of the Dravidian family, Telugu, there are three main tellings of the story but none has achieved unchallenged supremacy. The oldest is a *Rāmāyaṇa* in *dvipada* metre from the thirteenth century by Raṅganātha; the author was apparently court poet to a chieftain Buddharāju, whose sons later added an *Uttarakāṇḍa*. Next is the *Bhāskara Rāmāyaṇa* of Hulakki Bhāskara in the fourteenth century and the third is the *Mollā Rāmāyaṇa* of the sixteenth century. Raṅganātha's version contains the story of Lakṣmaṇa getting two boons from the goddess of sleep; the first is sleep for his wife Urmilā throughout the fourteen years of his absence and the other wakefulness for himself during that period (2.3–5; cf. Kampaṉ and Kṛttibās). Bhāskara's version is in *campū* form and includes contributions from his son Mallikārjunabhaṭṭa, his friend Ayyalārya, and his friend's disciple Rudradeva. It includes the episode, based on a passage of the fourth stage (Rām. 3 App.I.10), in which Akampana tells Rāvaṇa about Rāma's slaughter of the Rākṣasas, which anticipates Śūrpaṇakhā's arrival and duplicates Rāvaṇa's calling on Mārīca for help.

The first major adaptation of the Rāmāyaṇa into a North Indian language was that into Bengali by Kṛttibās, who probably composed his *Rāmāyaṇ* near the beginning of the fifteenth century; his version was then followed by a series of others in Bengali, by the poetess Candrāvatī towards the end of the sixteenth century, by Dvija Madhukantha and Kavicandra probably in the same century and from the end of the seventeenth century Nityānanda Ācārya's *Adbhut Rāmāyaṇ*. In the course of its transmission Kṛttibās' version has, because of its popularity, absorbed several passages from these other versions.[31]

Among the early episodes of Kṛttibās' poem is that of Raghu giving away everything in charity, a possible sign of the Buddhist influence which was still at his period to be fcund in Bengal. In the Rāma story proper, the Paraśurāma episode, besides emphasising Paraśurāma's

[31] See Dineshchandra Sen, *The Bengali Ramayanas*, Calcutta, 1920, also J. C. Ghosh, *Bengali Literature*, London, 1948 and D. Zbavitel, *Bengali Literature*, Wiesbaden, 1976.

Śaiva affiliations, has Sītā fear that by bending this bow too Rāma will gain another wife as a rival to her; this motif has already occurred in Murāri's *Anargharāghava* and the *Hanumannāṭaka*. Śaiva influence is also seen in the depiction of Rāvaṇa as a worshipper of Śiva and the adducing of encouragement by Śiva to validate Vibhīṣaṇa's desertion of his brother. This is at variance with the emphasis visible in the extant poem, but probably interpolated from Kavicandra's version, on Rākṣasas as devotees, especially the novel figures of Taraṇisena and Vīrabāhu who go into battle with the name of Rāma on their banners and seeking death and release at Rāma's hands. The same Śaiva tendency is seen in the *Śivarāmer Yuddha*, also attributed to Kṛttibās, in which Lakṣmaṇa's gathering roots and fruits in Śiva's garden leads to war between Rāma and Śiva, the outcome of which is that Śiva agrees to lend Rāma the services of his gate-keeper Hanumān, who thereafter becomes a worshipper of Rāma.[32] The establishment of the Rāmeśvara *liṅga* by Rāma is naturally also described, while Kausalyā, who is depicted in the second stage of the original Rāmāyaṇa as a worshipper of Viṣṇu, is turned by Kṛttibās into a worshipper of Śiva and Pārvatī.

Kṛttibās diverges in several other respects from the traditional narrative. Kaikeyī's crime of causing Rāma's exile is ascribed to a brāhman's curse. From the beginning of their exile, Lakṣmaṇa is supposed, by virtue of a boon exacted from the goddess of sleep, to have forgone sleep, eating and the sight of any woman's face; this is revealed only at the end of the story, when Agastya alludes to such abstinences as being required in Indrajit's conqueror and Rāma, incredulous, demands of Lakṣmaṇa that he substantiate the sage's statement, which he does by producing the fruit that had been his portion miraculously preserved by the touch of Rāma's hands and accounting for every day down to the pedantic listing of those crisis days when no food was gathered.[33] Similar banality, or perhaps more exactly influence of folk literature, is apparent in the Kālanemi episode, probably derived through the *Adhyātma Rāmāyaṇa*, which is developed by Rāvaṇa promising half his kingdom to Kālanemi for success and

[32] The Śaiva affiliations of both Paraśurāma and Hanumān have of course puranic antecedents; what is interesting is the persistence of this feature so strongly in a Vaiṣṇava oriented work.

[33] This motif of Lakṣmaṇa's abstention from food and sleep, which is taken over for example by the Khmer version, is obviously based on the vigil by Lakṣmaṇa and Guha over the sleeping Rāma and Sītā (Rām. 2.45.1–9) on their first night in the forest, investing an essentially peripheral incident with deeper significance. It occurs also in the Telugu version by Raṅganātha and the Kannaḍa *Torave Rāmāyaṇa* of Narahari.

Kālanemi busying himself planning the division of Laṅkā rather than the job in hand, thus providing a Bengali equivalent of counting one's chickens before they are hatched.

A later addition to Kṛttibās' poem, drawn from folk-tale material and found also in extra-Indian versions, is the story of Mahī Rāvaṇa, a son born to Rāvaṇa in the underworld.[34] In Rāvaṇa's extremity, Mahī Rāvaṇa comes to his aid and, despite Vibhīṣaṇa's warnings to Hanumān, tricks his way into the Vānara camp and magically carries off Rāma and Lakṣmaṇa back to the underworld. The wily Hanumān manages to penetrate there, learns of their imminent sacrifice to Kālī and, following Kālī's advice, fools Mahī into becoming the sacrifice himself. Another lengthy addition to the battle sections is the *Aṅgader rāybār* taken over from the *Adbhut Rāmāyaṇ* of Nityānanda Ācārya; in this Aṅgada's embassy to Rāvaṇa is vividly and dramatically narrated, with Aṅgada's defiance to Rāvaṇa typified by his curling his tail into a seat as high as Rāvaṇa's throne (a motif drawn from the *Ānanda Rāmāyaṇa* and transmitted to the Malay and Thai versions).

A minor innovation following the defeat of Rāvaṇa is that Vibhīṣaṇa offers the services of the women in his harem to anoint and otherwise serve Rāma, who reproves him for the suggestion on the grounds that he wants nothing to do with any woman but Sītā. From a Jain version of the story, Bhadreśvara's *Kahāvalī* or Hemacandra's treatment, Kṛttibās takes the motif of Sītā sketching Rāvaṇa's portrait, which rouses Rāma's jealousy and thus leads to her banishment. In Kṛttibās' version she draws the sketch on the floor of her bedroom to satisfy the curiosity of Rāma's brothers' wives. But in Candrāvatī's version this incident is given greater definition, for the instigator now acts out of malice and is named as a daughter of Kaikeyī; she gets Sītā to draw the portrait on a fan and, when Sītā falls asleep, places it on her breast before going to inform Rāma.[35]

In the neighbouring Assam the fourteenth-century poet Mādhava Kandali rendered the Rāmāyaṇa into Assamese, producing a poetic version quite close to the original but with some popular material

[34] The episode of Maiyārāb (= Mahī Rāvaṇa) is found in both the Malay *Ḥikāyat Srī Rāma* and the Javanese *Serāt Kāṇḍa* and forms, together with the episode of Sītā drawing Rāvaṇa's portrait (noted below), the main evidence for the transmission of the Rāma story through Bengal to Southeast Asia. However, it should be noted that this same story was current at the opposite end of India, in the Tamil legends of Mayil Rāvaṇan and the Malayāḷam poem on Pātāla Rāvaṇa in the seventeenth century by Vīra Kerala Varma.

[35] This latter version seems nearer to the form of the episode that has passed into Southeast Asian versions.

incorporated. Although he states that he translated all seven books, the first and last have since been ousted by the more Vaiṣṇava oriented versions of Mādhavadeva (1489–1596?) and Śaṅkaradeva (1449–1568?) respectively, while at the same period Durgāvara composed his *Gīti Rāmāyaṇa* in a popular form intended for sung performance but based mainly on Mādhava Kandali's rendering. Then in the eighteenth century Raghunātha Mahant wrote the first prose version in his *Rāmāyaṇa-kathā*, as well as certain other works treating parts of the story.

In Oriya the oldest extant version is Bālarāmdās' *Jagamohana Rāmāyaṇa* of the late fifteenth to early sixteenth centuries. Though referring to Vālmīki, the poet declares that he composed his poem as he had heard it from the narrations of *paṇḍits*. Nonetheless, his narrative adheres fairly closely in its contents to the original, including for instance the episodes of Ṛṣyaśṛṅga and Śabarī, the fire-ordeal and the chanting of the Rāmāyaṇa by Kuśa and Lava, but the style is naïve and to some extent events are localised in Orissa.

Although Tulsīdās was not the first to narrate the Rāma story in Hindī,[36] his version has become so much the standard that to many it is the Rāmāyaṇa. His *Rāmcaritmānas*, 'Lake of the Deeds of Rāma', was begun in 1574 at Ayodhyā and finished after some considerable period at Varanasi; in addition, he wrote several other works covering greater or lesser parts of the Rāma story.[37] Tulsī repeatedly states that his doctrine derives from the Vedas and Purāṇas and often refers to Vālmīki as the prime source for the Rāma story. However, it is clear that he has borrowed extensively from the *Adhyātma Rāmāyaṇa*, giving his work the same framework of a dialogue between Śiva and Pārvatī. Tulsī himself seems to have been a Rāmānandin, which may well link with his following of the *Adhyātma Rāmāyaṇa*. He is nevertheless fairly eclectic in his use of sources and is indebted also to the *Śiva* and *Bhāgavata Purāṇas*, the *Yogavāsiṣṭha*, *Adbhuta* and *Bhuśuṇḍi*

[36] The fifteenth-century poet Viṣṇudās from Gwalior wrote a complete version in his *Rāmāyankathā* (*ed.* Loknāth Dvivedī Silākārī, Ilāhābād, Sāgar, 1972), which Dr Stuart McGregor kindly brought to my notice. The work shows considerable influence from the Jain versions, as well as from Vālmīki and the *Adhyātma Rāmāyaṇa*. Interestingly, the work is divided into just three books: a Bālakāṇḍa (covering the story up to the Kiṣkindhā events), a Sundarakāṇḍa (up to Rāma's installation) and an Uttarakāṇḍa (from the genealogy of the Rākṣasas up to Rāma's ascent to heaven). Even earlier is the brief account of Rāma in the passage on the ten *avatāras* in Cand Bārdāī's *Pṛthvīrājarāso*.

[37] See W. D. P. Hill, *tr.*, *The Holy Lake of the Acts of Rama*, Bombay, 1952, F. R. Allchin *tr.*, *Kavitāvalī*, London, 1964 and *The Petition to Rām*, London, 1966, C. Vaudeville, *Étude sur les sources et la composition du Rāmāyaṇa de Tulsī-Dās*, Paris, 1955, and F. Whaling, *The Rise of the Religious Significance of Rāma*, Delhi, 1980, pp. 221–327.

Rāmāyaṇas and the Vaiṣṇava dramas, the *Prasannarāghava* and the *Hanumannāṭaka*.

The proportions of Tulsī's work are very different from Vālmīki's. The Bālakāṇḍa is the longest of the seven books and, with the Ayodhyākāṇḍa (which is only a little shorter), comprises about two-thirds of the total, whereas the Araṇya, Kiṣkindhā and Sundara kāṇḍas are much briefer. After a lengthy prologue, the Bālakāṇḍa continues with the story, closely modelled on the *Śiva Purāṇa*, of the meeting of Śiva and Satī with Rāma as he searches for Sītā , leading into the legend of Dakṣa's sacrifice and the marriage of Pārvatī taken from the same source,[38] before the dialogue itself between Śiva and Pārvatī, which is derived through the *Adhyātma* or *Bhuśuṇḍi Rāmāyaṇas* from the *Padma Purāṇa*.

Then, one third of the way through the Bālakāṇḍa, Tulsī moves on to the Rāma story proper with an account of the reasons for Viṣṇu's incarnation through the legends of Jaya and Vijaya, Jalandhara, Nārada, Manu and Śatarūpā, and Pratāpabhānu. The first of these develops the *Bhāgavata Purāṇa* story of Viṣṇu's doorkeepers, Jaya and Vijaya, becoming as the result of a curse the demons Hiraṇyākṣa and Hiraṇyakaśipu with their subsequent incarnation as Rāvaṇa and Kumbhakarṇa, thus further transforming the enemies of Rāma into devotees. Jalandhara also is incarnate as Rāvaṇa intent on revenging himself on Viṣṇu, who in the form of this legend found in the *Padma Purāṇa* seduces Jalandhara's wife in a mirror-image of Rāvaṇa's seizure of Sītā; the story had probably already been bowdlerised before reaching Tulsī.

As in the *Adhyātma*, the Earth in the form of a cow goes to Brahmā but Viṣṇu then, as in the original, through the divided oblation takes birth as Daśaratha's four sons.[39] In his account of Rāma's childhood and adolescence Tulsī follows the *Adhyātma*, itself modelled on the *Bhāgavata Purāṇa*, in assimilating Rāma to Kṛṣṇa, though with more discretion, just as he makes only a passing reference to the story of Ahalyā. The description of Mithilā on the arrival of Rāma and Lakṣmaṇa with Viśvāmitra is apparently based on that of Mathurā in the *Bhāgavata Purāṇa* (10.41). Rāma and Sītā meet before the *svayaṃvara*, as in most of the dramas, among which Tulsī seems to have followed most closely

[38] The last episode forms the theme of another of Tulsī's works, the *Pārvatīmaṅgal*, dated to 1585, which nonetheless appears to have formed the basis for the treatment of the episode in the *Rāmcaritmānas*.

[39] However, in the rest of the poem, Rāma alone is the incarnation of the Supreme Being and Lakṣmaṇa is several times identified with Śeṣa, as in the *Adhyātma*.

the *Prasannarāghava*. The contest over the bow and Sītā's *svayaṃvara* are described at length and, despite borrowings from the Rāma dramas, in an original manner, which enhances the individuality of the participants. The episode of Paraśurāma, which the dramas link closely with the *svayaṃvara*, is narrated similarly by Tulsī. The Bālakāṇḍa closes with the marriage celebrations, which as in the original are of all four brothers with Janaka's daughters and nieces, and the return to Ayodhyā.[40]

The Ayodhyākāṇḍa begins with the return of Rāma and Sītā to Ayodhyā and ends with Bharata's return there after his visit to Rāma in exile. Mantharā's incitement of Kaikeyī is ascribed to her being the goddess Śāradā (= Sarasvatī), as in the *Adhyātma*. From the same source Tulsī takes his treatment of Lakṣmaṇa's discourse to Guha, and of the boatman's reluctance to ferry them over the Gaṅgā; the latter, motivated by the story of Ahalyā, in the *Adhyātma* more naturally follows that episode immediately, but occurs in this position also in the *Hanumannāṭaka* (3.133–4). Between the visits to Bharadvāja and Vālmīki, Tulsī gives a description of various encounters along the Yamunā into which is abruptly inserted the arrival of an ascetic devotee; this has plausibly been seen as in a sense autobiographical, for in his more personal *Vinayapatrikā* Tulsī alludes to having visions of Rāma.[41] Vālmīki gives a long discourse praising Rāma and also affirming the divinity of Sītā and Lakṣmaṇa in a way frequent in the *Adhyātma* but exceptional in the *Rāmcaritmānas*.[42] The death of Daśaratha is narrated in a compressed manner, close to the original.

The second part of the Ayodhyākāṇḍa is taken up with Bharata's activities, to which Tulsī attaches exceptional importance and which he narrates with some novelty, though generally following Vālmīki. Vaśiṣṭha's long speech of consolation to Bharata is based on the *Adhyātma* but Tulsī emphasises Daśaratha's adherence to his caste duties and his sanctity as Rāma's father. Tulsī has a further innovation in Sītā's dream of Bharata's approach and then the news brought by the Kolas and Kirātas to Rāma. Rāma and Lakṣmaṇa greet Vaśiṣṭha,

[40] The narration of Rāma and Sītā's marriage is very similar to Tulsī's *Jānakīmaṅgal*, which in turn closely resembles in language and form the *Pārvatīmaṅgal* (which Dclosed the first half of the Bālakāṇḍa), and is probably based on it.

[41] So Vaudeville, op. cit., pp. 141–3. Another incident apparently due to Tulsī's own experiences is the intervention of Atri during Bharata's visit to Citrakūṭa and his presentation to Bharata of water from various sacred spots to deposit in a well, thereafter named Bharatakūpa, which presumably reflects some local legend collected by Tulsī in his travels.

[42] There is a distinct possibility that this passage has been interpolated, cf. Vaudeville, op. cit., pp. 144–6.

Guha and Daśaratha's queens, and Kaikeyī, full of remorse, is forgiven by Rāma. Rāma multiplies himself in order to embrace all the citizens of Ayodhyā and subsequently, when the Kolas and Kirātas provide a feast for them, Sītā multiplies herself to serve her mothers-in-law with equal respect. Tulsī also remodels the debate between Rāma and Bharata where each seeks to persuade the other to rule; he suppresses the figure of Jābāli, though mentioning him among those who soon take their leave, and adds Janaka, arriving from Mithilā. The book ends in accord with the original with Bharata establishing himself and enthroning the sandals at Nandigrāma. Indeed, by contrast with the other books, Tulsī seems often in the Ayodhyākāṇḍa to have based himself directly on Vālmīki with relatively little indebtedness to the *Adhyātma*. Also, in this book Rāma's deeds are attributed to himself and not to *māyā*, whereas in the rest of the poem they are called *līlā* 'play, sport'.

The Araṇyakāṇḍa opens with the subsequent events at Citrakūṭa and Tulsī includes here (3.2.3) the episode of the crow molesting Sītā found in the Sundarakāṇḍa of Vālmīki (but in the fourth stage also added to the end of the Ayodhyākāṇḍa, to which this passage corresponds); the occurrence of Bhuṣuṇḍi as narrator indicates the immediate source of this episode as the *Bhuśuṇḍi Rāmāyaṇa*, as also of the condemnation of women added to the Śūrpaṇakhā episode (3.17.3) and the loss by Rāvaṇa of his glory (*tejas*) after seizing Sītā (3.28.5). Tulsī's extremely concise account of the Virādha episode seems based on the *Adhyātma*, which he also follows in his narration of meetings with Atri, Sutīkṣṇa and Agastya, the story of the illusory Sītā (and the return of the real Sītā in the fire-ordeal), the meeting with Śabarī and Rāma's discourse to her on the nine types or stages of *bhakti*. However, in the battle with the fourteen thousand Rākṣasas he borrows directly from Vālmīki, from whom he presumably derives his narration of Rāma's laments near lake Pampā, for the *Adhyātma* ignores them; from an unknown source he then adds the arrival of Nārada and a discourse on the Name of Rāma, a theme he greatly favours.

The Kiṣkindhākāṇḍa is very brief, but still contains a strong didactic element owed to the *Adhyātma* in the hymns of Sugrīva and Vālin to Rāma and Rāma's discourse to Tārā. The descriptions of the Rains and of Autumn, though occurring in the same location as in Vālmīki's Rāmāyaṇa, in fact are modelled on the *Bhāgavata Purāṇa* (10.20). In the narrative, Tulsī follows the *Adhyātma* in making Svayaṃprabhā, after helping the Vānaras, go to Rāma, who grants her the gift of *bhakti*.

The Sundarakāṇḍa in its first part sees Hanumān particularly prominent. The narrative broadly follows Vālmīki but with frequent borrowings from the dramas, especially the *Prasannarāghava*, as in the dialogue between Rāvaṇa and Sītā overheard by Hanumān and in Sītā's subsequent despair. An innovation is that in his search of Laṅkā Hanumān sees signs of Vaiṣṇava worship and is thus led to Vibhīṣaṇa, with whom he has an edifying conversation; and when Hanumān sets fire to Laṅkā, Vibhīṣaṇa's house is spared. Tulsī also transfers to the second meeting of Hanumān with Sītā her giving him a jewel for Rāma and narrating the story of the crow; this is based on the narrative of the first meeting in Vālmīki.

In the Laṅkākāṇḍa, Rāma erects a *liṅga* at the causeway as in the *Adhyātma*, but most of the battle preliminaries, which are particularly developed compared with the rest of the book, show the influence of the dramas. Thus, Mandodarī's first efforts to dissuade Rāvaṇa from battle are based on the *Prasannarāghava* (7.27–74) and the *Hanumannāṭaka* (8.498) and the description of Rāma on mount Suvela on the *Prasannarāghava* (7.139.61); later the embassy of Aṅgada to Rāvaṇa is based on the *Hanumannāṭaka* (7.451–88) and Trijaṭā's informing Sītā of Rāvaṇa's state during the final battle on the *Hanumannāṭaka* (14.26). However, the shattering of Rāvaṇa's umbrella follows the *Adhyātma* and the ensuing discourse by Mandodarī (*Mandodarīgītā*) is modelled on a passage of the *Bhāgavata Purāṇa*; the repetition of certain incidents (with for example no less than three interventions by Mandodarī) is a feature of the Laṅkākāṇḍa, motivated no doubt by a wish to edify his audience. The incident where Hanumān, flying to collect the healing herbs, passes over Ayodhyā and is nearly shot by Bharata, until he reveals his identity and narrates Rāma's activities, is drawn from the fourth stage of the Rāmāyaṇa (6 App.I.57), since it is omitted in the *Adhyātma*, which also lacks Garuḍa freeing Rāma from the snake-arrows of Indrajit, taken therefore by Tulsī from the Rāmāyaṇa (6.40). On the other hand the intervening episodes of Vibhīṣaṇa's encounter with Kumbhakarṇa and Nārada's prophecy follow the *Adhyātma*, as does the subsequent episode of Rāvaṇa's sacrifice. Before the final duel between Rāma and Rāvaṇa, Vibhīṣaṇa explains to Rāma that Rāvaṇa has so far survived because his navel contains *amṛta* (6.102); there is no source for this in the versions drawn on by Tulsī but it is undoubtedly an adaptation of the folk motif of the external or otherwise misplaced and therefore inviolable heart.[43] The death of Rāvaṇa is followed by a series of *stutis*, hymns of praise to

[43] Thus probably the Tibetan motif of the horse-head, the Khotanese of the right toe and others are, like Tulsī's, all independent drawings on popular mythology.

Rāma, in which Tulsī models his work closely on the *Adhyātma*. However, he introduces an innovation into the return journey to Ayodhyā with a visit to Guha also on the way, used to underline the grace of Rāma even to the impure.

Tulsī postpones to the Uttarakāṇḍa the return to Ayodhyā itself, the reunion with Bharata and the installation, which form the end of the Yuddhakāṇḍa of the original and of the *Adhyātma*. Then Bhuṣuṇḍi abruptly takes up the narration and the hymns of the gods and sages to Rāma which he narrates to Garuḍa are doctrinally very different from the *Adhyātma* and obviously come from the *Bhuśuṇḍi Rāmāyaṇa*. Next comes a passage narrated by Śiva, not Bhuṣuṇḍi, describing his sacrifices and the birth of Kuśa and Lava (but Sītā's second repudiation is ignored); this is followed, after one verse where Bhuṣuṇḍi again is the narrator, by a kind of theological appendix, in which Rāma discourses to his companions, his brothers and Hanumān, and then to the entire city, on the distinctive qualities of his devotees and on the way to salvation; although similarly placed to the *Rāmagītā* of the *Adhyātma* and inspired by it, Tulsī presents a rather different teaching with all the stress on *bhakti*, regarded as a gift of the Lord.

The second half of the Uttarakāṇḍa begins with Umā asking Śiva how a crow became a devotee of Rāma, thus going back to the opening framework in the Bālakāṇḍa. However, though nominally introducing the story of the Garuḍa and Bhuṣuṇḍi, Śiva in reality introduces another Rāmāyaṇa narrated to Garuḍa by Bhuṣuṇḍi, who effectively becomes the narrator of the rest of the work; this is not just a résumé of the main work, for it omits certain episodes and gives others a greater importance. Although Bhuṣuṇḍi narrates the story of Rāma, his main aim is to instruct Garuḍa about *māyā* and salvation by devotion to Rāma; thus it is very much theologically oriented. The prime source for this section is clearly the *Bhuśuṇḍi Rāmāyaṇa*, as it is for the other occasions on which Bhuṣuṇḍi intervenes as narrator.[44]

Whereas in some areas, one particular adaptation enjoyed greater popularity, in others no one version achieved supremacy. In Marāṭhī Ekanātha's *Bhāvārtha Rāmāyaṇa*, though left incomplete at his death in 1599, is probably the best-known, as well as the earliest; Ekanātha, naturally enough as one of the leading figures in the *bhakti* movement

[44] However part of the passage dealing with the light of knowledge apparently draws on an earlier work of his own, the *Jñānadīpikā*; see F. R. Allchin, 'The reconciliation of *jñāna* and *bhakti* in Rāmacaritamānasa', *Religious Studies* 12, 1976, pp. 81–91, esp. p. 85, who cites S. L. Katre, 'Jñānadīpikā, an early work of Tulsīdās', *Munshi Indological Felicitation Volume*, 1963, pp. 401–11.

in Maharashtra, gives to his poem a strongly theological and philosophical tone and develops the theme of *rāmarājya*, the kingdom of god on earth, stressing the role of Rāma as an upholder of dharma.[45] Other versions also have their currency, however, from the roughly contemporary adaptation of the Yuddhakāṇḍa by Kṛṣṇadāsa Loḷyā, apparently inspired by Ekanātha's work, to the late eighteenth-century *Mantra Rāmāyaṇas* of Moropanta, a series of poems on the theme, each repeatedly incorporating a different mantra. In between come the *Saṃkṣepa Rāmāyaṇa* of Ekanātha's grandson Mukteśvara, which draws extensively on the *Adhyātma Rāmāyaṇa* and the *Hanumannāṭaka*, the *Pātāḷakāṇḍa Rāmāyaṇa* of Kānho Trimaladāsa, adaptations of the Sundara and Yuddha kāṇḍas by Rāmadāsa (1608–81), emphasising Rāma's role of liberator from the power of evil represented by Rāvaṇa, a *Sītāsvayaṃvara* and an incomplete Rāmāyaṇa by a female disciple of Rāmadāsa called Veṇābāī (1628–1700), adaptations of both the Rāmāyaṇa and the *Yogavāsiṣṭha* by another follower Mādhava, and the *Rāmavijaya* of Śrīdhara written in 1703.

In Gujarātī, episodes from the Rāma story were the earliest form used—by Bhālaṇa in his *Rāmaviraha* and *Rāmabālacarita* of the fifteenth century, by his sons, Udhava and Viṣṇudāsa, by the Jain writer Lāvaṇyasamaya in his *Rāvaṇamandodarīsaṃvāda* early in the sixteenth century, and by Premānand in his *Raṇayajña* on the battle between Rāma and Rāvaṇa. Premānand also composed, late in the seventeenth century, a complete version of the Rāmāyaṇa, based in part on these episodic treatments. Probably the best known version is that of Girdhar (1787–1852).

A Kāśmīrī version of the Rāma story was produced in the late eighteenth century by Divākara Prakāśa Bhaṭṭa.[46] It further develops the significance of Sītā's birth, for it claims that Mandodarī was originally a fairy (*parī*, i.e. *apsaras*) who took human form in order to achieve Rāvaṇa's destruction. Rāvaṇa marries her and in his absence she bears a daughter, Sītā, whose horoscope predicts that she will kill her father and marry a forest-dweller. She is therefore thrown into a river to drown but is washed ashore and found by Janaka. Subsequently, Indra despatches Sarasvatī to corrupt Kaikeyī (147), while Vasiṣṭha, consoling

[45] The feature of Bharata and Śatrughna as both sons of Kaikeyī is shared with the Jain *Paümacariya* of Vimalasūri, but the coincidence is probably accidental, since the motivating factor is obviously their close association, which goes back to the original.

[46] G. A. Grierson, *ed., The Kāshmīrī Rāmâyaṇa, comprising the Śrīrāmâvatāracarita and the Lavakuśayuddhacarita of Divâkara Prakāśa Bhaṭṭa* (Bibliotheca Indica 253), Calcutta, 1930.

Daśaratha for Rāma's departure, declares that Rāma is Nārāyaṇa, Lakṣmaṇa is Śeṣa, and Śatrughna and Bharata are Viṣṇu's conch and discus (222–4); both these features are found in the *Adhyātma* and *Bhuśuṇḍi Rāmāyaṇas*, with which the Kāśmīrī version shares its theological outlook. The episode of Jaṭāyus' attempt to prevent Rāvaṇa carrying off Sītā shows a strong similarity to the Khotanese version; in the Khotanese version Rāvaṇa throws lumps of tin red with blood before the vulture guarding Sītā and in the Kāśmīrī version Sītā persuades Rāvaṇa to hurl stones smeared with blood at Jaṭāyus, which he will swallow and so be unable to move (Sītā's hope is that thus Rāma will find him and discover what has happened, 412–4).

An unusual feature is that the history of Rāvaṇa's exploits is transferred from the Uttara to the Sundara kāṇḍa and inserted into the episode of Hanumān's visit to Laṅkā, during which he meets Nārada and learns from him the history of Laṅkā (590–618) and of Pulastya and his descendants (619–38), the former including also the story of Garuḍa, the elephant and the tortoise from the Araṇyakāṇḍa. Vibhīṣaṇa's advice is rejected by Rāvaṇa and he himself exiled only after Aṅgada's embassy (822–30). Rāvaṇa's attempted sacrifice is interrupted by Hanumān's taunting of Mandodarī (854–70). In the narration of the fire-ordeal it is declared that an illusory (*mohamāyā*) Sītā enters the fire, which burns for fourteen days, and then the real Sītā emerges (1077–88), although there is no previous mention of the illusory Sītā in the extant text; again, there are obvious links with the sectarian Sanskrit versions. Its Uttarakāṇḍa (1098–1137) then narrates the return to Ayodhyā and so forth from the end of the Yuddhakāṇḍa.

The events of the Uttarakāṇḍa are in fact related in the second part of the work, the *Lavakuśayuddhacarita*, the centre of which is, as its name shows, the conflict between Sītā's sons and Bharata and Śatrughna, who are guarding the sacrificial horse (1322–79). Not only Bharata and Śatrughna but also in turn Lakṣmaṇa and Rāma are killed by the boys before being restored to life by Vālmīki (1540–50). This part also includes the episode of the sister-in-law persuading Sītā to sketch Rāvaṇa (1145–63, cf. Candrāvatī's Bengali version), the birth of one son and the miraculous creation of the other (1258–1303, cf. the Tibetan and Southeast Asian versions), Sītā's appeal to and swallowing by the Earth (1692–1723), and the story of Durvāsas (1740–61).

The Rāma story not only spread throughout India in the various adaptations just surveyed but has also passed far beyond to spread throughout much of Asia. Its earliest spread seems to have been by the land routes which took traders and Buddhist monks through Central Asia to China and Japan; these and related versions have already been discussed, since chronologically they precede most if not all of the Indian vernacular versions. The growth of Indian influence in Southeast Asia, which began early in the Christian era and reached its peak around the tenth century, was carried by sea from the east coast initially but later also from the Gujarat area in the west as a result both of trade and of deliberate assimilation by the Indianised states flourishing there. The spread of the Rāma story was very much involved in this cultural diffusion, to the extent of becoming regarded as part of the national tradition in several countries. The production of these versions was taking place over the same period as the adaptations into Indian languages, with the earliest, the Old Javanese, being approximately contemporary with Kampaṉ.

The oldest evidence for the story of Southeast Asia comes from south Vietnam, the ancient Champa, where an inscription of the seventh century AD on a temple to Vālmīki mentions both the poem and the *avatāras* of Viṣṇu. It has been suggested that its founder, king Prakāśadharman, was indebted to Khmer culture for his attachment to the Rāmāyaṇa.[47] The inscription itself reveals close acquaintance with the opening of the Bālakāṇḍa. In north Vietnam, the ancient Annam, the story has been given a local setting with Annam itself as the kingdom of Daśaratha and Champa to the south as that of Rāvaṇa.[48]

In Indonesia archaeological evidence for the Rāma story is found in the ninth century AD in the bas-reliefs at Prambanan in Central Java, while the oldest literary version, the *Rāmāyaṇa Kakawin* of Yogīśvara, is not much later since it may be assigned to the early tenth century.[49] The first two thirds of the work are closely modelled on the *Rāvaṇavadha* of Bhaṭṭi, the *Bhaṭṭikāvya*, although it is clear that Yogīśvara was also acquainted with other versions of the story, and in the last third of the poem abandoned that source for an apparently eclectic drawing on

[47] See P. Mus, 'L' inscription à Vālmīki de Prakāçadharma (Trà-kiệu),' BEFEO 28, 1928, pp. 147–52.

[48] E. Huber, 'La légende de Rāma en Annam', BEFEO 5, 1905, pp. 168 ff.

[49] See C. Hooykaas, *The Old-Javanese Rāmāyaṇa Kakawin* (Verhandelingen van het Koninklijk Instituut voor Taal–, Land– en Volkenkunde 16), 's-Gravenhage, 1955 and 'Old Javanese Rāmāyaṇa', JORM 30, 1960–1, pp. 1–12, also R. Ng. Poerbatjaraka, 'Het Oud-Javaansche Rāmāyaṇa', *Tijdschrift voor de Indische Taal–, Land– en Volkenkunde* 72, 1932, pp. 151–214, Manomohan Ghosh, 'On the Source of the Old-Javanese Rāmāyaṇa Kakawin', *Journal of the Greater Indian Society* 3, 1936, pp. 113–7 and Soewito Santosa *ed.* and *tr.*, *Rāmāyaṇa Kakawin or the Indonesian Rāmāyaṇa*, 3 vols. (Satapitaka series 251–3), New Delhi, 1980.

several versions then current we may presume in Southeast Asia. Whereas the *Bhaṭṭikāvya* is intended to exemplify the rules of Sanskrit grammar, the variety of metres in Yogīśvara's poem suggests that he may have intended it similarly as a textbook of metrics. In what follows, only Yogīśvara's divergences from Bhaṭṭi's treatment will be noted. He adds a sizable dissertation on *nītiśāstra* which Rāma preaches to Bharata on his departure (perhaps a relocation of the *kaccit* sarga to suit the Javanese and Malay custom of sermons to mark major departures), Sītā's lament on being seized by Rāvaṇa (cf. Rām. 3.47), an elaborate story of Śabarī's hostility in a former birth to Viṣṇu in his boar incarnation, the deception of the Vānaras by Svayamprabhā, and a detailed description of a Śaiva temple seen by Hanumān when reconnoitring Laṅkā (significantly described in terms of a Javanese Chandi); he gives much more fully the ethical considerations surrounding Vālin's death (cf. Rām. 4.17–18), Rāma's laments on mount Mālyavān (cf. Rām. 4.27), Sītā's laments to Trijaṭā (cf. Rām. 6.38), Sītā's letter to Rāma and his reading of it, the commotion in the ocean after Rāma has shot his arrow (cf. Rām. 6.14) and Varuṇa's declaration that Rāma is an *avatāra*, and the beauty of mount Suvela in Laṅkā (cf. Rām. 6.29–30); there are also several other episodes with some amplification of detail. In the part not dependent on the *Bhaṭṭikāvya*, innovations include Rāvaṇa's spies, Śuka and Sāraṇa, being turned into a single individual, Indrajit's seven wives fighting alongside him, and the fire at Sītā's ordeal being changed into a lotus.[50]

There also exists as a separate work, composed later, the Javanese *Uttara Kāṇḍa*, describing the genealogy of the Rākṣasas and Vānaras, as well as modern adaptations of Yogīśvara's poem, the *Serāt Rām* and the *Carīt Rāmāyaṇa*. However, a rather different version of the Rāma story is contained in the *Serāt Kāṇḍa* and the *Rāma Kling*. The more important of the two, the *Serāt Kāṇḍa*, has incorporated much Islamic material, in the same way as the Malay *Ḥikāyat Srī Rāma*, with which it also agrees in making Rāvaṇa's wife Mandodarī originally the wife of Daśaratha and the mother of Sītā; from these and other similarities we may infer that both go back to a similar if not identical Indian source, if indeed the *Serāt Kāṇḍa* does not derive from the Malay version. The *Serāt Kāṇḍa* also has in common with several other Southeast Asian versions the episodes of Rāma's abduction to the

[50] The first and last of these are elaborated by the Thai *Rāmakīen*, which also narrates the incident depicted on one of the Prambanan reliefs of fish swallowing the stones of the causeway (deriving ultimately from brief hints in *Setubandha* 7.9, cf. also *Bālarāmāyaṇa* 7.52).

underworld, Sītā's banishment for drawing Rāvaṇa's portrait, the birth of one son to Sītā and the miraculous creation of the other, and conflict between Rāma and his sons.

Old Khmer epigraphy (sixth to fourteenth century AD) attests knowledge of the Rāmāyaṇa by the Khmers, at least in the court, but does not reveal the extent of this knowledge. There are then numerous versions of the Rāma story from the Middle Period onwards, all of which pass under the generic title *Rāmakerti* 'the fame of Rāma'; the oldest belongs predominantly to the seventeenth century although some parts may go back to the sixteenth.[51] It was composed by a group of talented poets, of whom the first began with Rāma's first exploit as a youth and the last, grouping together the compositions of his predecessors, co-ordinated them into a long poem of over five thousand stanzas finishing with the welter of combats following the death of Indrajit. The work is not strictly an epic poem but rather the libretto of a mimed dance-drama. It also bears an interesting relationship to the great monument of Aṅgkor Vat, which contains scenes from the Rāma story sculpted on the walls of its galleries; these are described in part of the 'Poem of Aṅgkor Vat' (*Lpoek Aṅgar Vatt*, st. 203–374), which is dated 1620 AD and which closely follows the *Rāmakerti* in its description of the events depicted, suggesting that the sculptures themselves of the twelfth or thirteenth century are related to the form of the story presented in the *Rāmakerti*.

Composed at a period when Buddhism was at its peak in Cambodia, the work presents a distinctly Buddhist outlook. Rām is frequently called Nārāy (= Nārāyaṇa, another name of Viṣṇu) and this is given more precise expression by Rām himself when he says to Paramasū (= Paraśurāma) that all the gods and ascetics, seeing how the demons were harming the religion of the Lord (Buddha), invited him to be reborn in the form of Rām (st. 211–3, cf. Bibhek's comment at 4284–5); however, there does not seem to be any real appreciation of the *avatāra* doctrine. In reality the stress is rather on Rāma as a Buddhist figure, portrayed both as a Bodhisattva and as a Buddha, but still characterised as the one who upholds dharma.[52]

[51] *Rīoeṅ Rāmakerti*, Institut Bouddhique, Phnompenh, 1937, fasc. 1–10; *Rāmakerti* (*XVIe–XVIIe siècles*), traduit et commenté par Saveros Pou, Paris, 1977, and Saveros Pou, *Études sur le Rāmakerti* (*XVIe–XVIIe siècles*), Paris, 1977. Dr Pou regards fascicules 75–80 of the Institut Bouddhique edition as representing a later version and translates the first ten fascicules, drawing also on the evidence of a manuscript in the Bibliothèque Nationale in Paris, as *Rāmakerti I*; the comments which follow are based on her translation and study.

[52] Cf. also Saveros Pou, 'Les traits bouddhiques du *Rāmakerti*', BEFEO 62, 1975, pp. 355–68.

Nevertheless, the narration of the story does not depart radically from the traditional form, though everywhere showing the influence of Buddhist sentiments. Although the story opens with Bisvāmitr seeking Rām's and Laks' help to get rid of the demon disrupting his sacrifice, the earlier events of the Bālakāṇḍa are incidentally alluded to subsequently. The demon is named as Kākanāsur (8), from her disguise as a crow, and is subsequently identified as the mother of Mahārīk (= Mārīca), when he replies to Rāb's order to become a golden deer by recounting his mother's death at Rām's hands (1487–96), not his own clash as in the original; presumably there has been conflation with the story of the crow that vexed Sītā.

Janak finds Sītā while ploughing and when she is of marriageable age offers her hand to whoever is capable of lifting a bow which he consecrates. Rām succeeds and the marriage ceremony is then described (73–128), but there is no mention of any other marriages. As they return, Rām is challenged by Rāmaparamasū (= Paraśurāma) and humiliates him, as in the original story. Then Dasarath declares his intention of transferring the insignia of royalty to Rām, which interestingly include the golden sandals (256); however, there is no Mantharā to instigate Kaikesī, who acts of her own accord.

During the night that Rām, Laks and Sītā spend with Kukhan (= Guha), while Laks and Kukhan mount guard, Laks is nearly overcome with sleep and in anger exacts from the goddess of sleep, Nidrā, the boon of never knowing hunger, illness or tiredness (403–20).[53] When they resume their journey towards Citrakūṭ, the scorched forest revives at their presence and three scenes of nature interpreted parabolically by Rāma are described (490–556). Meanwhile, following Dasarath's death, the chaplain Varasiddhi (= Vasiṣtha)[54] sends a message to Bhirut (= Bharata), which Kaikesī intercepts and alters to give a more cheerful impression (684–9); otherwise the narrative follows the original plot for the events of the Ayodhyākāṇḍa, even to the miraculous entertainment of Bharata and his troops by Bhāradvād (1060–80).

So too the encounters with Birādh, Sūrapanakhā, Dūs, Trīmukh (= Triśiras) and Khara, Sūrapanakhā's recounting of events to Rāb or Rābaṇā, Mahārīk's disguise as a deer and Rāb's seizure of Sītā from

[53] This is a simpler version—perhaps drawn from a common source—of the story in Kṛttibās' *Rāmāyaṇ* where the occasion is given simply as their first night in the forest but the implications of the boon are elaborated.

[54] Varasiddhi is the reading of the Bibl. Nat. ms., whereas the Institut Bouddhique text reads Visiṭṭh, 'qui semble être une correction exagérée et de surcroît défectueuse' as Dr Pou notes in her translation.

the hermitage follow the standard pattern, although we may note that Sītā's chiding of Laks lacks the suggestion that he improperly desires her. But, as she is being carried off, Sītā gives a message for Rām to two egrets separately (1658–66) before that to the countryside at large (1667–78). Rāb gains the victory in the ensuing fight with Jatāyu by hurling at him a marvellous ring which he wrenches from Sītā's finger (1709–19). An egret sees Rām and Laks and delivers Sītā's message to them despite initial anger by both brothers at its manner of address (1815–39).

The *Rāmakerti* then contains as a separate episode, narrated before the meeting of Rām and Laks with Sugrīb, a much expanded version of the story of Dūbhī (= Dundubhi, 1843–2106). Dūbhī's ousting of his father is recounted and then his combat with Bālī, king of Khās' Khin (= Vālin of Kiṣkindhā), who is mentioned as having once defeated and imprisoned Rābaṇā (1958), an allusion drawn from the Uttarakāṇḍa. The episode concludes with Sugrīb's installation in Bālī's place and then his banishment on Bālī's return.

As Rām and Laks wander in search of Sītā, the cry of a royal buffalo presages aid (2110–19), and shortly afterwards Sugrīb, in wonder at the sun standing still (2127–36), sends Hanumān to investigate. Hanumān, who is pure white and wears two magnificent ear-rings (2157, 2166–9, and 2174–5), recognises Rām as his master and offers him his allegiance before departing to report to Sugrīb that Rām shows the marks of a Buddha (2291–2, cf. 2141).[55] However, they actually meet Sugrīb when Laks explores the salty river, which proves to flow from Sugrīb's tears (2208–20); there are also certain differences of detail in Rām's exploits to convince Sugrīb (2294–2332), including the seven palm trees (for *sāl* trees) being supported on the back of a *nāgarāj* (cf. the *Ānanda Rāmāyaṇa*).

As in most versions Laks has to remind Sugrīb of his promise of aid and Sugrīb makes the excuse that it takes time to summon his forces and then goes to get Hanumān's help (2519–55). There is no mention of the despatch of search parties and instead the whole army marches against Laṅkā. Hanumān is then sent to reconnoitre—this episode

[55] The concept of the sun standing still so that a shadow does not move off such an exalted being may also be a Buddhist influence; it occurs for instance in relation to the Buddha in the preface to the *Vessantara Jātaka* (V. Fasubøll *ed. Jātaka* vol. 6, London, 1896, p. 479). Hanumān's whiteness is also found in the Malay and Thai versions (which also have the ear-rings) and in the constume used by the actor depicting him in Kūṭiyāṭṭam productions of Bhāsa's *Abhiṣekanāṭaka* or Śaktibhadra's *Āścaryacūḍāmaṇi* in the temples of Kerala. Since ear-rings are first associated with Hanumān in the *Pampa Rāmāyaṇa*, possibly both they and his whiteness have a South Indian source.

thus following not preceding the main expedition. Hanumān is accompanied on his leap by little monkeys (2655–8) and there is no mention of any exploits during it. When Hanumān penetrates Rāb's palace, the cry of a lizard gives a warning when he mistakes Mandogirī (= Mandodarī) for Sītā (2717); before leaving he humiliates Rāb by tying his hair to Mandogirī's in a knot which can only be released by Mandogirī striking Rāb's head thrice with her (inauspicious) left hand (2720–4; he repeats the trick at 4401–6).

As a preliminary to the construction of the causeway there is a lengthy innovation in the story of Mahājambū (3072–530). Rām decides that their forces are inadequate and turns for advice to Sugrīb, who suggests Mahājambū, a former friend of Bālī, whose ministers are Nīl and Nal. To circumvent Mahājambū's irascibility, Rām is advised to appeal to Isūr (= Śiva, 3230–41) and then reveals himself to Mahājambū in his full glory as Nārāy (3255–64). Mahājambū excuses himself from personal participation as too old but sends his ministers, Nīl and Nal. Then follows the construction of the causeway, along with Rām's threats to the ocean, which induce appeals to the goddess Maṇimekhalā (3486).[56]

The order of events from the beginning of the conflict is then rather different and Rāb does not send out spies. Instead, on hearing that the ocean has been crossed, Rābaṇā prepares for war and opens his parasol of victory, only for Sugrīb to smash it (3540–75). In anger, Rāb summons his brother Kumbhakār—described in some detail—who inflicts some damage on the monkeys before returning to his house (3553–629).[57] Rābaṇā then demands from another brother Bibhek (= Vibhīṣaṇa) a prediction of the outcome of the hostilities; Bibhek is depicted not as a warrior but as an astrologer, who now warns Rāb of the malign disposition of the stars and advises the return of Sītā (3650–65), and in the face of Rāb's anger accepts exile, joining Rām. The episode itself has been delayed and we see here also a distinct development of Bibhek's character towards the wise, dispassionate

[56] Maṇimekhalai is a goddess of the sea in South India. This may therefore indicate some acquaintance with a South Indian form of the story; cf. S. Lévi, 'On Maṇimekhalā "the guardian deity of the sea" ' and 'More on Maṇimekhalā', IHQ 7, 1931, pp. 173–5 and 371–6. The motif of the marine creatures at first removing the stones as fast as the monkeys throw them in, first occurs in Pravarasena's *Setubandha* (7.9) and is depicted on the ninth-century reliefs at Prambanan in Java (no. 41).

[57] This episode has been brought forward chronologically (in Kampaṉ's version too Kumbhakarṇa takes part in the action at an earlier point). It may be noted that both it and the previous episode are contained in a passage found in the Bibl. Nat. ms. but lacking in the Inst. Bouddhique text (3535–3634).

and essentially non-combatant adviser, first to Rāb and then to Rām.[58] Kumbhakār too is shown in a somewhat different light, as essentially upright and in contrast to Bibhek placing loyalty to his older brother and king above other considerations; thus, at a later stage in the conflict he delivers a long tirade against Bibhek for deserting his elder brother (4295–309), in the course of which he alludes to Rām's killing of Bālī as a terrible injustice.

In the course of Aṅgad's embassy Rāb, in an attempt to soften Aṅgad, declares that his mother Mandogirī is now his wife and so Rāb himself is Aṅgad's second father (4133–41). This obviously alludes to the story found in the Malay version of Vālin's seizing Mandūdākī from Rāvaṇa for a period, without narrating it at all.[59] When Indrajit binds Rām and Laks with the snake weapons, Hanumān as in other versions is sent to get the ingredients for the remedy, including the water of the Nine Pools and the urine of the king of bulls from the forest of Hemabān (4361–85); however, in this version a mortar of emerald is also needed which is in Rāb's possession, so Hanumāṇ slips in by night to appropriate it and to repeat his trick of tying Rāb's and Mandogirī's hair together (4389–406). As well as Indrajit, Rāb himself resorts to magic and, in order to foil his designs, Hanumān disguised as a brāhman enters Rāb's palace to plague Mandogirī and thus disrupt the rite (4653–70).

Next come, as in the original, Indrajit's return to the fight and death at Lak's hands, Rāb's intention to wreak vengeance on Sītā and his dissuasion by a counsellor Rakkhas (i.e. Rākṣasa, = Supārśva; 4671–745). However, the last section of the *Rāmakerti* then goes back to an earlier stage in the battle (cf. Rām. 6.57–9) to narrate the combats of Mahodar with Aṅgad (4754–79), Atikāy with Laks (4781–807), Trīsīr with Hanumān and Usabh (4808–40), Narātak with Bibidh (4844–67), Mahākpāl with Usabh (4869–92), Duramukh with Kesar (1894–925), Mukharakkhas with Nal (4929–52), Kumbhagadādhar with Nīl (4959–80) and Mahāmād with Satabalī (4986–5024). The whole poem as extant then ends with the hint of a new episode with Rāb's seeking help from his friend Mūlaphalam (5025–34).[60] The story is thus incomplete

[58] Incidentally, Sītā's guard Sujātā (= Trijaṭā) is identified by the *Rāmakerti* as Bibhek's wife (2742–3); is this because of her similarly sympathetic character? Kampaṉ had already turned Trijaṭā into Vibhīṣaṇa's daughter and the *Ānanda Rāmāyaṇa* also makes her his wife.

[59] We may note that, although the *Rāmakerti* is thus aware of the story of Mandodarī belonging to Vālin as well as to Rāvaṇa, there is no trace of the other story of her having been Daśaratha's wife nor of any complications in the parentage of Sītā in consequence.

[60] This incident is paralleled by that of Mūlapatāni in the Malay version and Mūlaphalam in the Thai version. Raghavan comments on the latter: 'Rāvaṇa then sends his "Mūla-

and we are in no position to say how the end of the story was seen in the earliest Khmer traditions. However, this first *Rāmakerti* is essentially a condensed and selective version of Vālmīki's Rāmāyaṇa with relatively little interference from popular imagination or other cultures, especially by contrast with subsequent Rāmakertis, which show Thai influence and a loosening of structure.

The later *Rāmakerti II* recounts the events of the Uttara kāṇḍa and includes several features which are standard in the Southeast Asian versions.[61] Thus, in Rām's absence Sītā is inveigled by a servant (one of Rāb's family in disguise) into drawing a portrait of Rāb, which is hidden under Rām's bed on his return and causes him such discomfort that in anger he commands Laks to execute Sītā, but Laks cannot do it and leaves her in the forest (1–215). Sītā then reaches Vajjamrik's (= Vālmīki) hermitage and there gives birth to one son, the other being created by the sage through a fire-sacrifice; they are named Rāmalaks and Japalaks (216–346). Rām releases a stallion to roam before sacrifice, under the care of his brothers Bhirut and Sutrut and of Hanumān.[62] Rāmalaks and Hanumān engage in combat in which Hanumān is worsted, but in the subsequent encounter with the boys Rāmalaks is captured (458–753).

Japalaks then goes to rescue his brother and with various supernatural help succeeds (754–952). Rām pursues them and discovers their true identity, but, despite repeated urgings, Sītā refuses to resume married life (953–1596). When she is tricked into coming back by Rāma's supposed death, on discovering the deception she calls on the Earth to take her to its bosom, where she is hospitably received by Biruṇ (= Varuṇa, 1597–774). Though ending with the Uttarakāṇḍa episode of the appeal to Earth, this gives a totally new slant to Sītā's behaviour.

A Malay version of the Rāma story, the *Ḥikāyat Srī Rāma*, represents a popular form of the story carried orally to Indonesia between the thirteenth and seventeenth centuries and it exists in several recensions showing varying degrees of assimilation to this very different cultural

bala" *i.e.* a reserve force of picked fighters, according to Vālmīki (VI. 94) whom Rāma destroys; but in Thai, Mūlabala is taken *as the name of an individual demon-ally* of Rāvaṇa, ...' (*The Rāmāyaṇa in Greater India*, Surat, 1975, p. 80, cf. p. 128). However, I have not been able to find the relevant words in the passage referred to (i.e. 6.81–2).

[61] On this version, see Saveros Pou, *Rāmakerti II*, Paris, 1982; I am grateful to Dr Pou for the use of her English summary of the text before publication.

[62] In making Rām's brothers and Hanumān joint guardians of the horse, this version seems intermediate between the puranic versions (e.g., *Padma Purāṇa*) and other Southeast Asian versions.

environment.[63] Some elements probably come from towards the south of India. Most notably the poem begins in the Shellabear recension with the past exploits of Rāvaṇa (as in effect does the *Rāmopākhyāna*), including his coming by ship to Būkit Sĕrĕndīb, which is based on the story of Vijaya the founder of Ceylon told at the end of *Mahāvaṃsa* VI; such a transfer presumably took place in Ceylon or Tamilnad. In fact the various manuscripts extant start at different points in the preliminary material, which is particularly un-Muslim in outlook and has perhaps therefore been deliberately omitted by their copyists for religious motives.[64] The fullest version makes clear that the original on which they are all based provided a background in the previous incarnation of Rāvaṇa as Hiraṇyakaśipu, defeated by Viṣṇu in one of his previous incarnations; this has obvious similarities to the way in which Tulsīdās begins his Hindī version. Signs of Muslim influence may also be seen for example in Daśaratha's ruling in Isfahā bogā and the naming of Nabī Adam as an ancestor.

Typical of the tendency to conflate different episodes and to import folk elements which serve to heighten the miraculous element is the account of Daśaratha finding his chief wife Mandū dārī in a bamboo clump (perhaps a kind of doublet of the finding of Sītā by Janaka). Daśaratha has two sons each by Mandū dārī and a concubine Balyā dārī, the latter of whom also has a daughter, Kikewī Dewī; they are born from five of the six balls of rice (corresponding to the *pāyasa*) given to Daśaratha by a sage whose aid he seeks to cure his childlessness, but the sixth is stolen by Gāgak sāra (= Kākāsura) and taken to Rāvaṇa, who eats it. Although the motif of the special food is retained, the concept of Viṣṇu's incarnation in Rāma and his brothers is suppressed.[65] Rāvaṇa then comes to Daśaratha's court disguised as a brāhman

[63] W. F. Stutterheim, *Rāma-Legenden und Rāma-Reliefs in Indonesien* 2 Bde, München, 1925, and A. Zieseniss, '*Die Rāma-Sage bei den Malaien*, Hamburg, 1928 (translated as *The Rāma Saga in Malaysia, tr.* P. W. Burch, Singapore, 1963); cf. also P. L. Amin Sweeney, *The Ramayana and the Malay Shadow-Play*, Kuala Lumpur, 1972. Of the literary versions, that edited by Shellabear is taken from a ms. presented to the Bodleian Library by Archbishop Laud in 1633. Though the oldest ms. extant, it represents a younger version than that edited by Roorda van Eysinga.

[64] See R. O. Winstedt, 'An Undescribed Malay Version of the Ramayana', JRAS 1944, pp. 62–73 and E. C. G. Barrett, 'Further Light on Sir Richard Winstedt's "Undescribed Malay version of the Ramayana" ', BSOAS 26, 1963, pp. 531–43.

[65] Nevertheless, the birth of Sītā from part of the sacred food renders concrete the idea that all involved in Rāvaṇa's destruction are divine, expressed in the *Adhyātma* and *Bhuśuṇḍi Rāmāyaṇas* through the declaration that Yogamāyā or Lakṣmī will take birth as Sītā. A parallel to, and possible source for, the daugher is the Bengali version by Candrāvatī in the sixteenth century, which introduces Kaikeyī's daughter Kukuā (who

and demands his wife, who however makes a replica of herself (Mandū dākī) which is handed over to Rāvaṇa (anticipating the motif of seizure of a substitute elsewhere applied to Sītā). Daśaratha subsequently goes by stealth to Laṅkā in order to impregnate the counterfeit Mandū dākī; although born in Rāvaṇa's household and to his wife, the child thus conceived, Sītā, is nevertheless not Rāvaṇa's but Daśaratha's. As in other versions Rāvaṇa, alarmed at her horoscope, has her abandoned in an iron box in the sea but she is rescued by a pious king, Maharīsi Kalī, and brought up by him. This version of Sītā's parentage seems a deliberate conflation of the three possible forms.

Exotic development of the parentage of various characters seems indeed one of this version's characteristics. Taking its cue from a story found in a very late part of the Rāmāyaṇa (7 App.I.3.1–120) about a change of sex through bathing in a pool by Ṛkṣarajas, the father of Vālin and Sugrīva, the Roorda recension makes Vālin and Sugrīva the offspring of Gautama's wife Dewī Indra (= Ahalyā) by two of the gods, changed into ape form as a result of Gautama's anger by bathing in two pools with clear and cloudy water. This version links this tale with the birth of Hanumān, since Dewī Indra curses the daughter, Añjanā, who has betrayed her, to remain with her mouth open for a hundred years and Rāma, seeing her thus, is enamoured of her and has two drops of his sperm conveyed to her mouth; the resulting offspring is a white ape with ear-rings, Hanumān.[66] It prefaces both stories with the tale that Vālin seized Mandū dākī from Rāvaṇa and begot Anggāda (= Aṅgada) on her, before she is restored to Rāvaṇa after the nearly full-term embryo has been removed by Caesarian section. The Shellabear recension, lacking an account of Vālin and Sugrīva, combines both motifs in its account of Hanumān's birth. Rāma and Sītā come upon the two pools, bathe in the pool with clear water and are changed into apes, indulging in the uninhibited behaviour of such animals, but Lakṣmaṇa manages to immerse them in the cloudy pool, thus changing

later in the story incites Sītā to draw the portrait of Rāvaṇa). A still more complex version of the birth of Sītā to Rāvaṇa is found in the late Javanese *Serāt Kāṇḍa*.

[66] This is evidently a reworking of the *Śiva Purāṇa* account (3.20) of Hanumān's birth from Śiva's semen. Indeed, the Wilkinson ms. gives precisely the *Śiva Purāṇa* account of Śiva spilling his semen while watching the dance of Viṣṇu in the form of Mohinī; however, it places the incident much earlier in the narrative, before other mss. begin (Barrett, op. cit., pp. 534–5). The story also occurs in the *Tattvasaṃgraha Rāmāyaṇa* and another form of the story from South India is intermediate between that and the Malay form (cf. C. Bulcke, 'An Indonesian birth story of Hanumān', JOIB 3, 1953–4, pp. 147–51). The linking of Ahalyā's adultery and Hanumān's birth to Vāyu and Añjanā is made in several popular versions, for example in the Panjab and Gujarat.

them back into human form. Lakṣmaṇa, however, fears that Sītā may nonetheless give birth to an ape, so he suggests removing the sperm from her body. This is then conveyed to Dewī Anjatī who is practising asceticism with mouth agape; again the swallowed seed produces Hanumān, the child this time of Rāma and Sītā. Then comes the story of how Lakṣmaṇa intercepts the sword intended for Śūrpaṇakhā's son, who is practising asceticism in a bamboo clump, and accidentally kills him with it, thus providing the motive for Śūrpaṇakhā's attempted vengeance on Sītā.[67]

Both versions also include an account of Rāvaṇa's journey to the sun, which he has decided to subdue because its rays have irritated him; this again is apparently derived from the incident recorded in a fourth-stage addition to the Rāmāyaṇa (7 App.I.1.15*). On the other hand some details of the trials of strength by which Rāma convinces Sugrīva and of Vālin's death may well derive from the fifth act of Murāri's *Anargharāghava*, while thereafter Rāma enters Kiṣkindhā as in the *Pampa Rāmāyaṇa*.[68] At this point both versions narrate Bharata's visit to Rāma, the timing of the incident being another divergence from the original, as is the fact that one version has it that this follows their mother Mandūdarī's death, presumably an individual innovation or misunderstanding, since the other version has Daśaratha's death.

Apart from these points, the Malay versions basically follow the original story from Sītā's abduction (although we may note that there are two gazelles involved as decoys and that Lakṣmaṇa draws a magic circle round Sītā before leaving her) until the conquest of Laṅkā, though with an increased emphasis on the magical.[69] For example, in their final duel, Rāma cannot vanquish Rāvaṇa, since his heads regrow as soon as they are severed, until he learns from Sītā through Hanumān that Rāvaṇa's vital spot is a small head concealed beneath his ear. On the other hand, the reunion with Sītā is simplified, with a reduction in

[67] This story occurs in the Jain *Vasudevahiṇḍi*, with which the Malay version also agrees in making Khara and Dūṣaṇa into one individual. There must have been influences on the Malay versions coming from the west coast of India, as well as the Bengal area. Additionally, the motif of Rāma giving Śūrpaṇakhā a note for Lakṣmaṇa is found in the relatively late *Narasiṃha Purāṇa*.

[68] Cf. Zieseniss, op. cit., pp. 124 and 146–8.

[69] This is perhaps most obvious in the episode of Miraba, found in the Raffles version, where Rāma is taken to the underworld; the Javanese *Serāt Kāṇḍa* also has this Maiyārāb incident, which is obviously based on a folk tale included in Kṛttibās' Bengali version as the story of Mahī Rāvaṇa. Another borrowing from Bengal is the episode, transferred from Aṅgada, of Hanumān coiling up his tail to make a seat higher than Rāvaṇa's.

the religious significance; there is still the ordeal by fire, with Hanumān not Lakṣmaṇa making the pyre, but Agni does not appear and instead Sītā emerges by herself when the fire has burnt down. Subsequently Mandū dākī recognises from Maharīsī Kalī's account that Sītā is her daughter.

The later events diverge considerably from the original. Rāma and Sītā remain childless until, by the aid of Maharīsī Kalī who gives them bezoar stones (a doublet of the means in the Shellabear version to relieve Daśaratha of his childless state), Sītā becomes pregnant. Before the birth, she is exiled by Rāma as the result of her sister-in-law's intrigues, and goes to stay with Maharīsī Kalī, not Vālmīki. One son (= Lava) is born to her but one day he cannot be found, which causes Maharīsī Kalī to create and animate a replica of him from *kuśa* grass (= Kuśa). One version also includes a rather modified version of the conflict between the twins and Lakṣmaṇa over the sacrificial horse (here reduced in significance to a gazelle) found in the *Padma Purāṇa* and Bhavabhūti's *Uttararāmacarita*. The silence of all animals and the sister-in-law as a result of Sītā's curse persuades Rāma of her innocence and he remarries her at Maharīsī Kalī's court. Rāma appoints Lava king in Duryā pūrī nĕgāra, the city he had built on a site discovered by Vibhīṣaṇa after his return from Laṅkā, and Kuśa king of Laṅkā, himself founding another new city Ayodyā or Andya pūrī nĕgāra (these and other episodes here obviously represent modified versions of the founding of various cities narrated in the Uttarakāṇḍa); there, according to one version, Rāma devotes himself with Sītā to the ascetic life until after forty years he passes from this transitory world to the world of eternity.

The oldest extant Laotian form of the Rāma story is the *Phra Lak Phra Lam* (more exactly, *Bṟaḥ Lak Bṟaḥ Lām*, 'lord Lakṣmaṇa, lord Rāma'), which exists in several versions.[70] It is however a relatively recent work, composed between the eighteenth and mid-nineteenth century, in all probability written in 1850 by one Phutthaphochan (possibly a misreading for Phutthakhochan, i.e. Buddhaghoṣa) on the basis of an earlier oral or perhaps written Rāma story. It is cast in the form of a Jātaka, with the Buddha identifying himself as Rāma at the conclusion

[70] There is also the slightly later *Gvāy Dvóṟaḥbī*, so named after the episode of Dundubhi, which is given some prominence. See S. Sahai *ed.*, *The Phra Lak Phra Lam or The Phra Lam Sadok; A Lao version of the story of Rama*, New Delhi, 1973, S. Sahai, *Rāmāyaṇa in Laos: a study in the Gvāy dvóṟaḥbī*, Delhi, 1976, and Vo Thu Tinh *tr.*, *Phra Lak Phra Lam* [ou] *le Ramayana Lao* (Collection 'Littérature Lao', volume premier), Vientiane, 1972. Since there is much divergence over the form of names, I have used the originals.

of the story, and in a similar fashion to the Khmer *Rāmakerti I* it makes Rāma into an ideal upholder of dharma and Buddhism. It has clearly been much influenced by other Southeast Asian versions. The opening of the Luang Prabang version seems specifically indebted to the Thai version, but all versions seem acquainted with the Javanese, Khmer and Malay forms of the story; indeed not infrequently different forms have been combined, leading to duplication of incidents or characters.

The story is given a local setting, for Daśaratha founds a city on the Mekong river, first opposite and then on the site of Vientiane, while Rāma is portrayed as a mighty king of Vientiane. Daśaratha's youngest brother rules at Indraprastha (a reminiscence of the old Khmer city Aṅgar, also called Indraprasth) as does his son Rāvaṇa after him. Much of the early part of the poem is devoted to Rāvaṇa's ancestry and past exploits, as in several versions from the *Rāmopākhyāna* onwards; he is portrayed as handsome and as possessing a deep understanding of Buddhist doctrines. Daśaratha has a daughter whom Rāvaṇa carries off; Daśaratha, unable to prevent it, prays to Indra for sons able to chastise Rāvaṇa and twins are born to his wife, who are Rāma and Lakṣmaṇa. After many adventures, the two brothers succeed in rescuing their sister, defeating Rāvaṇa's attempt to recapture her.[71] Subsequently Daśaratha abdicates in favour of Rāma and Rāvaṇa moves to Laṅkā with his brothers, Vibhīṣaṇa and Indrajit; the omission of Kaikeyī's intrigues and the figure of Mantharā, though occurring in other versions, is presumably a popular simplification.

Rāvaṇa, still nursing hatred against Rāma, goes to Indra to request magic powers but while there he seduces all Indra's harem, including Sujātā, who to gain revenge is born as Rāvaṇa's daughter, Sītā; later, she tries to stab Rāvaṇa and is then turned adrift on a raft, but rescued by a holy man, Janaka. When Sītā reaches marriageable age, Rāvaṇa tries to win her but is unable to bend the bow or to gain her by other means; however Janaka makes him a replica of Sītā as a kind of consolation prize and animates it.[72]

In its narrative of Sītā's abduction, the Lao version has Lakṣmaṇa consign Sītā to the care of the Earth before going to help Rāma and it is only Rāma's distrust of her that causes the Earth to release her hold on

[71] The idea of a daughter of Daśaratha occurs also in the *Dasaratha Jātaka* and the Malay version, but in those she is identified as Sītā, whereas here she is distinct; this is perhaps an attempt to unscramble the complex Malay narration of Sītā's parentage.

[72] These two elements of Sītā's birth to avenge herself on Rāvaṇa and Rāvaṇa's appearance at her *svayaṃvara* appear together also in the Burmese version of about the same date, which suggests a direct link between these two versions, since other versions have one or other but not both.

Sītā, allowing Rāvaṇa to carry her off. This obviously corresponds fairly closely with the magic circle motif of the *Ānanda* and *Bhuśuṇḍi Rāmāyaṇas* and the Khotanese and Malay versions, perhaps modified by remembrance of Sītā's swallowing by the Earth at the end of the story. So too its statement that Sītā was protected from molestation by a miraculous fire recalls the entry into fire of the real Sītā in the sectarian Sanskrit Rāmāyaṇas, including the *Bhuśuṇḍi*. The Lao version substitutes Garuḍa for Jaṭāyus but Rāvaṇa disables him with Sītā's ring, as in the Khmer version. During the search for Sītā, Rāma is changed for a time into a monkey by eating the fruit of a certain tree, unites with a young woman, also so changed, and thus begets Hanumān; the female monkey's father is Janaka (but she is not Sītā—this is rather a duplication, just as is the subsequent narration of a transfer of semen involving Tārā) and her mother soon after commits adultery with the Sun, producing the twins Sugrīva and Vālin. The whole episode has links with the Malay forms of this episode, with Janaka replacing Gautama. On the other hand, the emphasis placed on the story of the buffalo Dundubhi indicates borrowing from the Khmer version, whereas the transposition in some recensions of Vālin and Sugrīva is paralleled only in the Khotanese and Sinhalese versions.[73] Tārā next bears a son to Rāma, who is a double of Hanumān, for both together perform the exploits of the leap to Laṅkā, the giving of the message to Sītā, the tying together of Rāvaṇa's and his queen's hair (as in the Khmer version) and the burning of Laṅkā; the construction of the causeway is also mainly the work of Hanumān and his double. Rāma's ultimatum to Rāvaṇa causes a split which leads to the ejection not only of Vibhīṣaṇa but also of Indrajit (here brother not son of Rāvaṇa) and of Rāvaṇa's son. Among the battle incidents is included Rāma's abduction to the underworld, here by the king of the Nāgas rather than the Mahī Rāvaṇa of the Bengali version and some recensions of the Burmese, Javanese and Malay versions. After killing Rāvaṇa, Rāma triumphantly enters the palace and recovers Sītā; there is no hint of the fire-ordeal.

The two characteristic innovations of the later Southeast Asian versions, Sītā's drawing a portrait of Rāvaṇa and her giving birth to one son only with the second magically created, both occur in the Laotian version; in this version the sage involved is Janaka—again no

[73] However, it is not accompanied, as in those versions, by the conflation of Vālin and Hanumān. Possibly the feature arose in all three independently as a result of incomplete understanding of the story. So too the final happy reunion of Rāma and Sītā after her banishment and the birth of her sons is found also in the Tibetan and Thai versions but presumably occurs in each as a result of a natural desire to have a happy ending, as it does in Bhavabhūti's *Uttararāmacarita*.

doubt by simplification—as in the Malay version. The story of the conflict of Sītā's sons with the party guarding the sacrificial horse is also here much simplified—Kuśa and Lava go disguised as melon-sellers to Rāma's capital and become embroiled first with the gate-keepers, then with their captain, Hanumān, and finally with Rāma himself before their recognition, when Rāma makes them tell their story.

In Thailand the Rāma story was apparently known before the coming of the T'ai from Yunnan in the thirteenth century, but gained great popularity thereafter, with many rulers assuming the title Rāma and in some cases writing versions of the story. However, much of the story must have been taken over along with their other borrowings from Khmer culture. The sack of Ayuthaya in 1767 meant the loss of almost all older Thai literature, but the first ruler of the Bangkok period, Rāma I, commissioned the collection of all available written and oral material, resulting in the completion of the *Rāmakīen* in 1797, after incorporation also of the writers' study of Vālmīki's version and ones in Hindī, Bengali and Tamil. The work tends therefore to be encyclopaedic and eclectic. The second ruler, Rāma II, had certain scenes rearranged for the stage around 1815.

The story begins, as in the Malay version,[74] with Hiran Yak (= Hiraṇyakaśipu) menacing the world until Phra Isuan (= Īśvara, i.e. Śiva) commissions Phra Narai (= Nārāyaṇa) to remedy this; Phra Narai assumes the form of a boar and rescues the Earth. After this conflation of two stories relating to Viṣṇu's *avatāras*, the Thai version also, in its lengthy account of the history of the Rākṣasas and Vānaras, includes Phra Narai turning himself into a woman to destroy another demon and an account of the birth of the Vānaras in two stages: firstly, the siring of sons on Kala Ačana (= Añjanā), wife of Khodom (= Gautama), by Indra and Aditya, a secret betrayed by their daughter, Sawaha, to Khodom who turns them into monkeys, Kakat and Sukhrip (= Vālin and Sugrīva), and secondly the placing of his weapons into Sawaha's open mouth by the wind god Phra Phai (= Vāyu), from which comes Hanumān himself. This again has obvious similarities to the Malay version. Next comes the attempt by Rāmāsun (= Paraśurāma) to rob Maṇimekhalā of a jewel, which occurs also in some Khmer versions and must derive ultimately from a South Indian tradition. Kakat gains a new name of Phali Thirat (= Vālin) and the boon that any opponent will lose half his strength as rewards for re-establishing mount Phra Sumen (= Sumeru or Meru);[75] he also seizes Nang

[74] Certain details may, however, derive directly from Tulsīdās' version.

[75] The motif of Vālin taking half the strength of any opponent, first found in Kampan̲'s Tamil version, occurs in the *Ānanda Rāmāyaṇa*, as does the incident of Aṅgada coiling up his tail as a seat in his audience with Rāvaṇa, found also in the Bengali version of

Montho (= Mandodarī) from Thotsakan (= Daśakaṇṭha, Rāvaṇa) and has Ongkhot (= Aṅgada) by her, as in the Roorda recension of the Malay version. Other episodes included in this preliminary material are Indra piercing Thotsakan's chest with an elephant-tusk as he snatches Butsabok (= Puṣpaka), Thotsakan's son gaining the title Inthorachit by defeating Indra and the incarnation of one of Śiva's attendants as the buffalo Thorapha, father of Thoraphi (= Dundubhi).

An account of Thotsarot's (= Daśaratha's) marriage with Kaiyakesi and her help in keeping his chariot together in the fight against a demon lead into the story of the ascetic Kalaikōṭ (the Tamil name for Ṛśyaśṛṅga) and his performing of the ceremony to cure Thotsarot's childlessness. As in several versions, a crow, Ka Kanasun, steals some of the rice portion on behalf of Thotsakan; thus, Phra Laksami (= Lakṣmī) is born to Nang Montho in Longka as Nang Sīdā at the same time as Phra Narai is born as Phra Rām; the other brothers are incarnations of Ananta and Viṣṇu's weapons.[76] Nang Sīdā's birth presages evil for Thotsakan and so she is cast adrift on the sea in a glass vessel. This is found by king Chanok (= Janaka), who digs a pit in which to place the container and recovers it some time subsequently by ploughing it up; thus, there is a definite synthesis of the motifs of Sītā being washed up from the sea and appearing from the furrow.

From a balcony Nang Sīdā sees Phra Rām arrive in Mithilā for the contest to bend Phra Isuan's bow, and they fall in love on sight. This is very similar to Kampaṉ's treatment of this incident, which derives ultimately from the Sanskrit dramas and occurs also in the *Ānanda* and *Bhuśuṇḍi Rāmāyaṇas*. Other features shared with Kampaṉ are Bharata's exclusion from Daśaratha's funeral ceremonies and his and Śatrughna's preparations to die by fire as Rāma returns in triumph, while the name of Khukhan reflects the Tamil form of Guha, just as Kalaikōṭ does that of Ṛśyaśṛṅga. The Tamil version consulted by Rāma I's poets must have been either Kampaṉ's or one closely related to it.

On the other hand, the story of Lakṣmaṇa slaying the ascetic son of Samanakhā (= Śūrpaṇakhā) with the sword intended for him by Phra Phrom (= Brahmā) goes back to Vimalasūri's Jain version, probably

Nityānanda (and—assigned to Hanumān—in the Malay). Probably, therefore, the Bengali version consulted by the Thai poets, though based on Kṛttibās, included this element from Nityānanda.

[76] All these details occur also in the Luang Prabang version of the Lao *Phra Lak Phra Lam*, except that Indra replaces Viṣṇu. They can be traced back to the Purāṇas, through the *Adhyātma* and *Bhuśuṇḍi Rāmāyaṇas*. In most Southeast Asian versions they have been suppressed.

through the Kannaḍa *Pampa Rāmāyaṇa*. Agreement with other Southeast Asian versions is frequent. As noted above, from Java come the amalgamation into one individual of the two spies, Śuka and Sāraṇa, the motif of the golden lotus in Sītā's ordeal, and the queen of the fish Supanna Matcha (= Suvarṇamatsyā) hindering the building of the causeway until seduced by Hanumān (their son Matchanu subsequently helping Hanumān to rescue Rāma from Maiyarap). With the Khmer *Rāmakerti I* are shared the identification of Rāma as Narai, the figure of Ka Kanasun as the mother of Marit (= Mārīca), Sītā's message to some birds (peacocks in the Thai version but egrets in the Khmer), the disabling of Jaṭāyus with Sītā's ring,[77] the emphasis on Thoraphi (= Dundhubi), the description of Hanumān as a little white ape with ear-rings, Vālin catching Rāma's arrow before allowing it to pierce him, Hanumān stealing the mortar from Rāvana and tying his hair to Nang Montho's, and the figure of Mūlaphalam; with *Rāmakerti II* are shared Sītā's drawing of Rāvaṇa's portrait at the instigation of a servant, who is a relative of Rāvaṇa in disguise, Sītā's refusal to return to Ayodhyā and the ruse of Rāma's pretended death. Some of these are also found in the Lao version, with which the following episodes are common: Rāma's abduction by Maiyarap (also in the Malay and one Javanese version, and going back to Bengali versions), guidance of Sītā by Indra and a buffalo after her abandonment (found only in the Muongsing recension), and the happy ending in a final reconciliation of Rāma and Sītā after her swallowing by the Earth.

Other popular features include the way in which Hanumān is turned into a philanderer (common to several Southeast Asian versions but contrasting sharply with the celibacy attributed to him in Indian tradition) and the multiplicity of battle episodes with the attendant greater use of magic and the prominence of Phiphek (= Vibhīṣaṇa) to help Rāma counter it. There is also prominent use of the folk-tale motif of the external soul, not only in relation to Rāvaṇa, whose *guru* Khobut conjures Rāvaṇa's heart into a glass vessel which he guards for him until Hanumān tricks him out of it, but also to Maiyarap, whose heart is in a bee on a palm tree and is betrayed by his sister after Hanumān seduces her. One feature that seems to be peculiar to the Thai version is that the arrival of Indra's charioteer, Mātali, has been brought

[77] The Lao version has virtually the same story, substituting Garuḍa for Jaṭāyus. Remoter parallels are the Malay version, where Sītā gives her ring to Jaṭāyus, and the Tibetan and Khotanese versions, where Rāvaṇa kills the vulture by throwing down a red-hot iron ball and lumps of tin red with blood respectively; in fact, in the Tibetan version, it is Ramaṇa (= Rāma) who throws a ring at Marutse (= Mārīca).

forward to the point where Rāma and his allies cross over to Laṅkā. However, as in many Southeast Asian versions, the story is given a purely local setting with, for example, the old capital Ayuthaya taking its name from Daśaratha's capital and the old Khmer settlement of Lopburi being identified with the Vānara capital and at the same time associated with Rāma's son Lop (= Lava).

Although there is sculptural evidence of acquaintance with the Rāma story in Burma from the eleventh century, the first extant version is the *Rama Thagyin*, 'Ballad of Rāma', composed in 1775 by U Aung Phyo.[78] The basis of the Burmese version is to be found in the Thai tradition, for the ruler brought back from his sack of Ayuthaya in 1767 a troupe of actors of the Rāma play, but other sources were undoubtedly used. After narrating the birth of Dasagiri (= Rāvaṇa) and his installation as king of Laṅkā, the poem tells how he saw on mount Gandhamana a nymph who defies his attempts to seduce her, immolates herself and then emerges from the earth as a baby, who is brought to Dasagiri and set adrift by him in a box, whence she is rescued by Janaka. Dasaratha's slaying of the ascetic youth leads him on to a great ascetic, who grants him offspring through two plantain fruits for his queens; a discrepancy here is that Lakkhana (= Lakṣmaṇa) as well as Bhadra (= Bharata) is born to Kaike. In accord with Burma's Buddhist affiliation, Rāma is described as a Bodhisattva, not as an *avatāra* of Viṣṇu. Dasagiri is also a competitor at the contest for Sītā's hand, as in the *Bhuśuṇḍi Rāmāyaṇa* and the Laotian version; he lifts but fails to string the bow and so is defeated by Rāma who draws the bow so tight that it breaks.

The events leading up to Sītā's abduction are considerably simplified. Dutha and Khara molest the trio and are killed, whereupon their mother Gambi appeals to Dasagiri and also takes the form of a golden deer to aid his plans; thus, Gambi combines the roles of Śūrpaṇakhā and Mārīca. In the search for Sītā, Thugyeik (= Sugrīva) concealed in a tree sees the two brothers and, reminded of his brother Bali, weeps; his tears falling on Rāma waken him and the alliance follows; this seems a simpler form of the river of tears motif occurring in the Tibetan, Khmer and Laotian versions, but whether because derived from a more primitive form or simplified from the more elaborate form is uncertain. Hanumān is first introduced as a small monkey, before regaining his original size and strength at Rāma's touch (cf. the Chinese '*Jātaka* of an Unnamed King'). The events of the Yuddhakāṇḍa

[78] See U Thein Han, 'The Ramayana in Burma', *Studies in Indo-Asian Art and Culture*, vol. 2, New Delhi, 1973, pp. 71–83.

are described fairly briefly but one point of interest is that, although the invisible Indazita (= Indrajit) is killed by Rāma, this is rendered possible by Lakkhana who alone can see him by virtue of not having looked at a woman's face throughout their exile (cf. the Bengali version of Kṛttibās). The poem ends with Rāvaṇa's defeat by Rāma.

Later nineteenth-century Burmese versions include the episodes of Gombadipa (= Mahī Rāvaṇa) carrying Rāma off to the underworld, Sītā's banishment for drawing Rāvaṇa's portrait, and the miraculous creation of Kutha (= Kuśa), evidently drawn from one or other of the Southeast Asian versions.

A popular version of the Rāma story is preserved in Sinhalese as one of the legends narrated in the course of the Kohom̆bā Kankāriya festival.[79] According to it Rāma, who is Viṣṇu incarnate, departs for a seven-year exile alone to avoid the effect of an evil omen. Rāvaṇa seizes Sītā while he is gone and he only discovers the fact on his return; this is obviously a drastic simplification of the plot, which among other things completely omits Kaikeyī's intrigues. Rāma then roams the forest in search of Sītā, meets Vālin, who is also lamenting the loss of his wife, and befriends him; here, as in the Khotanese version, Sugrīva and Vālin are transposed and the story then also conflates Vālin with Hanumān. Vālin, after his tail has been set on fire and he has thereby set Laṅkā ablaze, seizes Sītā and carries her back to Rāma. Thus all the battle scenes are dropped. Subsequently, during Rāma's absence, Sītā, in response to a request from Umā, draws a sketch of Rāvaṇa and conceals it under the bed on Rāma's return; Rāma, discovering it, is enraged and banishes the pregnant Sītā, who is led by Saman (= Lakṣmaṇa) to the Himālayas where she is found by Vālamīga (= Vālmīki) and given shelter. There Sītā gives birth to one son, the sage one day creates another to replace him when he has fallen from his bed, Sītā soon discovers them both but only accepts the sage's explanation when he miraculously creates a third; this is a still more elaborated version of the motif found in several popular forms of the story (such as the Tibetan, Thai and Malay versions). Indeed, it is notable that this Sinhalese version shows such analogies with other popular versions but reveals no trace of influence from the *Dasaratha Jātaka* form of the story, despite its place of origin.

From Southeast Asia the Rāma story has even spread as far as the Philippines, where a version entitled *Maharadia Lawana* (i.e. Mahārāja

[79] See C. E. Godakumbura, 'The Rāmāyaṇa, A Version of Rāma's Story from Ceylon' and 'The Cult of Kohom̆bā or the Three Sons of Sītā', JRAS 1946, pp. 14–22 and 185–91. The festival is attested on literary evidence only since the fifteenth century.

Rāvaṇa) has come to light in the Maranaw language spoken on part of Mindanao.[80] It belongs to the seventeenth to nineteenth centuries and is related to the Malay folk versions, the *Sěri Rāma* and the *Ḥikāyat Mahārāja Rāvaṇa*. This Philippino version represents the furthest spread of the Rāma story from India and also one of its latest adaptations. Indeed, from the beginning of the nineteenth century there is the start of European scholarly interest, with editions and translations of the original Rāmāyaṇa into English in the first decade and into Italian and French in the middle of that century. By now, the Rāmāyaṇa has taken its place as one of the classics of world literature.

[80] J. R. Francisco, 'Maharadia Lawana', *Asian Studies* (University of Philippines, Quezon City) 7, 2, Aug. 1969, pp. 186–249, cited in V. Raghavan, *The Rāmāyaṇa in Greater India*, Surat, 1975, p. 134.

10
EVOLUTION OF THE EPIC

Here ends the story and its sequel, the prime Rāmāyaṇa, graced by Brahmā and composed by Vālmīki. (7.100.26)

While the multiplicity of adaptations of the Rāmāyaṇa extant throughout India and much of Asia amply attests the popularity and the inherent appeal of the story first made popular by Vālmīki, the evidence drawn from them, when combined with the internal evidence of the work ascribed to Vālmīki, enables us to chart more accurately the process by which its hero, Rāma, developed from a moral hero to a divine figure, whether as the *avatāra* of Viṣṇu or a Bodhisattva, as well as the decay or suppression of this deification in an Islamic environment. At the same time, it is possible to assign certain chronological limits to the successive stages of growth of the original Rāmāyaṇa and thereby to improve our understanding of the development of some aspects of ancient Indian culture.

The first stage of Vālmīki's work, its core in books 2–6, is the most difficult to date, as the wide variety of opinion on the dating of the epic noted in the first chapter indicates. Although these views relate to the whole text, the starting dates given obviously apply to the first stage. The problem is that the period involved precedes any of the really fixed points of chronology. Nevertheless, there are limits which can be established, even if only negatively. The absence of anything fully analogous to epic literature from the Vedic literature obviously precludes assigning either epic to a date very early in the first millennium BC on current assumptions about the dating of Vedic literature. On the other hand, the presence in Vedic literature of features which probably anticipate the epics suggests that they appear after no very extended interval.

The evidence of the language, collected in the second chapter, reinforces this view that the Rāmāyaṇa belongs to the period subsequent to the Vedic literature, while the fact that the pantheon discoverable in the first stage is closer to the Vedic than the puranic pattern provides corroborative evidence. The language as a whole appears similar to that of the later Brāhmaṇas and Sūtras, but there are divergences from the description of that form of the language by Pāṇini which preclude simple identification. At the same time, the language and style of the first stage are closely related to those of the oldest parts of the Mahābhārata, and this suggests that there was a distinct epic form of the language, which might well be classed as a distinct dialect. There is some simplification by comparison with Pāṇini's description, with the elimination of some of the more archaic features abandoned also in the Brāhmaṇas. This need not, however, indicate a later date, for the epic language is obviously a reflex of the speech of the kṣatriyas and the language of the court might easily be linguistically more evolved than that of contemporary brāhmans, the priestly class. Nevertheless, the language of the Rāmāyaṇa probably is somewhat younger, at any rate more developed, since the types of nominal composition present reveal a slightly more developed pattern than the oldest Upaniṣads, as well as showing certain well-marked deviations from Pāṇinian norms. Yet, for example, a definite innovation in the formation of the pseudo-desiderative adjective (of the type *vaktukāma*), unknown to Pāṇini, is recognised not much later in the grammatical tradition by Kātyāyana. Indeed, not much later again Patañjali, who is usually assigned to the second century BC, actually quotes part of a stanza found in the Rāmāyaṇa (5.32.6 = 6.114.2), but since it is proverbial in nature there is no proof that he is quoting from the Rāmāyaṇa.[1] The Mahābhārata, on the other hand, may have been known to Pāṇini, who cites the word but without any certain indication of its meaning (Pāṇ. 6.2.38).

The relationship of the Rāmāyaṇa to the Mahābhārata is of course a factor, the unravelling of which is crucial to a full understanding of the dating of either epic. The most commonly expressed view is that the Mahābhārata is older in its origins than the Rāmāyaṇa, which however developed over a shorter period, as is shown by the acquaintance of later parts of the Mahābhārata with the Rāmāyaṇa. This view appears substantially correct, though capable of some amplification. With regard to the first stage, with which we are at present concerned, the evidence of the style of the two epics, especially in the use of figures of speech and of the formulae typical of oral composition, suggests that they were possibly more independent of each other than is usually recognised, which would tend to weaken arguments based on linguistic comparison. Nevertheless, the Rāmāyaṇa does display greater homogeneity of language (and also of metrical expression) which may suggest a slightly later date for its origin than for the Mahābhārata, as well as vindicating the traditional ascription to a single author.

[1] Cf. K. T. Telang, 'The Râmâyaṇa older than Patañjali', *Indian Antiquary* 3, 1874, p. 124 and my *Proverbs*, p. 148.

Apart from their language and style, the plots of the two epics have been utilised as a means of dating their origins. Here it is fairly clear that, whatever the degree of historical reality attaching to either story, the political situation underlying them does point to a particular period. In the case of the Mahābhārata, this is the immediately post-Vedic period near the beginning of the first millennium BC, when the centre of power still lay in the Delhi region and the Doab. On the other hand, the political background to the Rāmāyaṇa reflects the shift of the power focus into the upper Gaṅgā basin which occurred somewhat later. Nevertheless, as the *Iliad* and *Odyssey* demonstrate, along with much other epic literature, there is often—even customarily—a substantial interval between the period of the events narrated and that of the composition of the epic. For the Mahābhārata this might amount to anything up to almost half a millennium, though probably not quite so much. For the Rāmāyaṇa it was presumably less, since not only is the political situation later but the names of participants in the action are not attested from Vedic literature as are some of those in the Mahābhārata; an interesting exception is that a Janaka of Videha appears as a debater in some of the early Upaniṣads.[2]

Correspondingly, an end point is provided by the fact that the type of political set-up envisaged in the Rāmāyaṇa was completely superseded in the Gaṅgā basin by the establishment of the Mauryan empire in the last quarter of the fourth century BC; indeed, some features had disappeared earlier, including the monarchical government of Videha. It is not easy to envisage a poet deliberately choosing this setting at a date significantly after its disappearance—and if we accept the tradition, supported by internal evidence, of a single author for the basic poem, this is more or less what is involved. To the extent that the authors at any period in reality depicted the conditions of their own time, this provides a relatively fixed *terminus ante quem* for the composition of the first stage.

Its upper limit is established by the need to allow some interval between the Vedic period and Vālmīki for the development of the plot, for it is improbable that Vālmīki started from scratch, even though there is much plausibility in the view which sees his greatness as lying in the bringing together into one skilfully handled narrative of several separate elements. This implies that the first stage can hardly be earlier than about the sixth century BC. On balance, the fifth century

[2] Janaka appears to have been a dynastic name used by several members of the family. The *Chāndogya Upaniṣad* (5.11.5 etc.) also includes a king Aśvapati Kaikeya, whose name is identical with that of Bharata's grandfather.

seems the most plausible date for its original composition, with some expansion and modification in the course of oral transmission during the next century also falling within the first stage.

However, right from its first recitation there must have begun the process of expansion and embellishment which turned Vālmīki's poem into the epic now extant. The next stage saw the enlargement of the core by additions and elaborations included in the Ayodhyā to Yuddha kāṇḍas. The degree of divergence in language and style noted in the second chapter argues for an interval of about two to four centuries between the first stage and at least the later parts of the second. On the other hand the cultural pattern visible in most of the second stage, though more developed than that of the first stage, does not differ from it sufficiently to suggest a very great time span between the origin of the poem and the earlier passages assigned to the second stage. Accordingly, it seems reasonable to assign the beginning of the second stage to the third century BC.

It is during the second stage that the complex inter-relationship of mutual borrowing with the Mahābhārata begins. This in itself provides some indication of date, since it is clear that in general the later parts of the Mahābhārata are familiar with the Rāmāyaṇa as it was by the end of the second stage. However, this still gives an extended period and it is possible to achieve greater precision, though scarcely to achieve the ideal of assigning a separate date to each passage. The evidence of the *Rāmopākhyāna* is naturally of particular importance but there is a significant amount to be learnt from other episodes. For example, an illustration of the complexity of the relationship is provided by the *Nalopākhyāna*, which has clearly at one point borrowed from the Rāmāyaṇa, since Sudeva's soliloquy over Damayantī imitates Hanumān's over Sītā, but has probably suggested the wording of part of Rāma's *unmada*; the natural inference is that the second stage passage containing Hanumān's soliloquy (5.12–17) is earlier than Rāma's *unmada* (3.58), even though both show considerable elaboration of language and style, for the *Nalopākhyāna* is a homogeneous insertion into the Mahābhārata.

During the second stage also the divergence into Northern and Southern recensions was taking place, and was largely complete before the fixing of the Uttarakāṇḍa in the later part of the third stage. It had already progressed significantly by the time of the Mahābhārata borrowings from the Rāmāyaṇa; the *Nalopākhyāna* follows in its borrowing a text which is nearer the present Northern recension, while the affiliation of the *Rāmopākhyāna* can be even more precisely determined as being to a text approximating to the present Northeastern recension. Indeed, the emergence of the separate recensions is obviously intimately connected with the elaboration of the epic during the second stage and cannot therefore have started very much later. It was presumably well under way by the beginning of the Christian era.

The very occurrence of the *Rāmopākhyāna* in the Mahābhārata attests the popularity of the Rāmāyaṇa by the time of its composition, which means that it must belong at least a century or two later than the original composition of the Rāmāyaṇa, as its own position as an insertion into the Mahābhārata also indicates. Equally, however, it is not among the latest additions to the Mahābhārata. In terms of the development of the Rāmāyaṇa, it belongs somewhere in the second stage, since (as just noted) it was produced some considerable time after Vālmīki and on the other hand antedates the religious views reached by the end of the second stage and during the third, for—with one exception—it sees Rāma as an exemplary but still basically human figure. In this it differs from many of the other Mahābhārata allusions to the Rāmāyaṇa, which see Rāma as divine and which stand later in the evolution of the Mahābhārata. Indeed, I have argued that it may well have provided the basis on which the third stage was elaborated. In keeping with this is the point that it lacks Sītā's fire-ordeal, which as a fairly extensive summary it might be expected to include, since it is an important feature of the plot as it had developed by the end of the second stage.

The *Rāmopākhyāna* in fact contains no reference to several of the more obvious additions of the second stage, for example Daśaratha's account of his slaying of the ascetic youth (though mentioning Daśaratha's death), Bharadvāja's entertainment of Bharata's army. Jābāli's and Vasiṣṭha's speeches to Rāma, Sītā's meeting with Anasūyā, Vālin's accusation of Rāma and his reply, Hanumān's killing the sons of Rāvaṇa's ministers and Rāma's first encounter with Rāvaṇa, to name only the most prominent episodes and thus the most likely for inclusion. It does allude to episodes which it is reasonable to infer have been elaborated rather than inserted—such as Sītā's spirited rejection of Rāvaṇa before he seizes her—but always in a way that is consistent with what may be expected to have lain behind the present expanded version. To cite just one significant example, it refers to the arrival of the trio at Śarabhaṅga's hermitage but not to Indra's previous arrival, which seems to form part of the process of enhancing Rāma's status culminating in his identification as an *avatāra*. Nevertheless, because of its own nature as a summary, it is difficult to establish with certainty how far the *Rāmopākhyāna* was familiar with passages of the second stage; the evidence is suggestive but not decisive. Most probably the *Rāmopākhyāna* was composed around the middle of the second stage, in perhaps the first century BC.[3]

The close of the second stage is very much linked with the start of the third, the addition of the Bāla and Uttara kāṇḍas. The opening of the Ayodhyākāṇḍa and the close of the Yuddhakāṇḍa (the beginning and end of the complete work prior to the third stage) reveal a religious pattern which aligns them in some ways more with the third stage than with the rest of the second. The absence of Sītā's fire-ordeal in the *Rāmopākhyāna* (which has however Rāma's repudiation of her until reassured by Brahmā) has just been mentioned as possibly significant and it is also absent from the Tibetan and Khotanese versions and the Jain versions of Saṅghadāsa and Guṇabhadra; on the other hand it is mentioned by Bhāsa, Kālidāsa and other Sanskrit dramatists, and so predates them.[4] It should therefore be assigned to the first century AD, or possibly the second.

Corroborative evidence comes from another passage which has been assigned to the end of the second stage, the account of the search parties. It was shown towards the end of the fourth chapter that the geographical data contained in them indicates a date between the second century BC and the first century AD, and more probably towards the end of that period, which is also that reflected in the geographical allusions of the third stage. However, despite the fairly close limits assignable to the search party accounts, it is worth noting that, as well as being absent from the *Rāmopākhyāna*, they appear to have been ignored by Bhaṭṭi as late as the sixth century. Whether or not this particular instance is valid, it serves to remind us that there could in some cases have been a significant interval between the composition of a particular passage and its general acceptance. While therefore the earliest external attestation of a passage establishes a *terminus ante quem*, it may be unwarranted to postulate a date for the passage little earlier than that attestation.

[3] It would thus be feasible for Aśvaghoṣa to have drawn on it, as has been argued on the basis of his mention of Vasiṣṭha and Vāmadeva rather than Bharata's mission to Rāma (so E. H. Johnston *tr.*, *The Buddhacarita*, Lahore, 1935–6, pp. xlviii–l) but the point is too slight to establish the conclusion sought (cf. V. Raghavan, 'Buddhological texts and the Epics', *Adyar Library Bulletin* 20, 1956, pp. 349–59). Aśvaghoṣa has several other reminiscences of the Rāmāyaṇa itself.

[4] The date of the plays ascribed to Bhāsa is still not settled to universal satisfaction. However, the probable date of the third century AD is not so much earlier than Kālidāsa in the fourth to fifth century and thus is not vital here.

An overlap between the end of the second stage and the beginning of the third is certainly not improbable, and both should therefore be assigned to the first century AD. However, before proceeding to examine that transition, it should be noted that there is one instance where there may be an even greater overlap. The wholly anomalous but well-supported prophecy by Niśākara (4.61) alludes to the incident of Indra reassuring Sītā and offering her divine food, added by most of the Northern recension in the fourth stage (3 App.I.12). It could be that the fourth-stage passage has been elaborated on the basis of the brief allusion by Niśākara, as clearly parts of the third stage have been developed from casual hints in the first two stages. On balance, however, it seems as likely that this second-stage prophecy by Niśākara is indeed later than or contemporary with the fourth-stage narrative, which in the prominence given to Indra, and possibly in the linking of Indra and Sītā, shows relatively early features.

The development of the third stage does seem in considerable measure to have been due to a desire to fill in lacunae in the story, and several parts of it are obviously based on briefer passages of the earlier stages, notwithstanding attempts by some traditionalist scholars to see such passages as references to the Bāla and Uttara kāṇḍas, guaranteeing them an equal antiquity and authority with the rest of the text. Thus, for example, Sītā's account to Anasūyā of her marriage (2.110) and Mārīca's of his previous encounter with Rāma (3.36) foreshadow the equivalent Bālakāṇḍa narratives (1.65–72 and 1.29), while allusions to Rāvaṇa's past exploits in the Sundarakāṇḍa (e.g. 5.2.19–20, 8.14 and 44.7–8) are amplified in the Uttarakāṇḍa. On the other hand, there is a marked lack of agreement between the listing of Rāvaṇa's previous exploits in the Araṇyakāṇḍa (3.30) and the account in the Uttarakāṇḍa (7.10–34), which forms the major part of Agastya's narrative (7.1–36) with its marked difference in style from the rest of the book, aligning it more with the second stage.

More crucial to an understanding of the development of the third stage is the question of its relationship to the *Rāmopākhyāna*, discussed in some detail at the beginning of chapter eight. The nucleus of each book is obviously the family and background of Rāma and Rāvaṇa respectively and it is precisely these parts for which there exists analogous material in the *Rāmopākhyāna*, but grouped together as a prologue. It has been argued above that the *Rāmopākhyāna* is contemporary with the middle of the second stage and precedes the addition of the Bāla and Uttara kāṇḍas, probably forming the source for their nuclei. Nevertheless, the religious attitude expressed in its narration of Rāma's birth is clearly similar to that of the third stage (and also the beginning of the Ayodhyākāṇḍa and end of the Yuddhakāṇḍa), so again there is a suggestion of some overlap between the second and third stages. Yet the *Rāmopākhyāna* is not likely to have been the innovator in this respect, since the rationale of its inclusion at that point in the Mahābhārata is that Rāma is human and that is its overall attitude. It is more probable that ideas of Rāma's divinity were beginning to be current in the milieu in which the Rāmāyaṇa circulated, without as yet being accepted into the text, and that the *Rāmopākhyāna* from outside was less inhibited about including them, despite some inconsistency with its own basic position.

The reluctance with which the Uttarakāṇḍa was accepted into the text is well shown by the internal evidence of the *phalaśrutis* at the end of the Yuddhakāṇḍa, which refer to the epic as complete at that point, and of the Bālakāṇḍa summaries, which virtually ignore it (along with much of the contents of the Bālakāṇḍa itself). External references indicate that it was becoming recognised during the Gupta period. Bhāsa's plays make no reference to any event in it or the Bālakāṇḍa (which in general is probably somewhat earlier), though viewing Rāma as divine, whereas Kālidāsa is fully acquainted with it, including some of its later sargas (*Raghuvaṃśa* 15.81–98 being based on 7.88–97), as well as with parts of the Bālakāṇḍa. The latest parts of the Mahābhārata tradition, the *Śāntiparvan* and the *Harivaṃśa*, are familiar with it; they should probably be assigned at the latest to the Gupta period, to which also belongs the reference in the *Gobhilasmṛti* to Rāma being accompanied by a golden statue of Sītā at his sacrifices. The Jain writer Vimalasūri, who may possibly belong like Bhāsa to the third century, was also acquainted with it. Indeed, it has been argued that, since the Bhārgavas only become significant in the third stage, it must antedate Aśvaghoṣa of probably the second century, who considers that Vālmīki is a descendant of Cyavana, a Bhārgava.[5]

On the other hand, relief sculptures of Rāmāyaṇa scenes, which themselves attest the growing religious signficance of the work, belonging to the Gupta period at Nācnā Kuṭhāra and Deogaṛh do not include anything from the Uttarakāṇḍa, although the four-headed Brahmā, first mentioned in the third stage, is depicted at Deogaṛh. Similarly, it is ignored by Bhaṭṭi, who seems however to be particularly conservative in his choice of material, since the list of omissions in his poem is significantly close to the passages of the second stage. Such

[5] See N. J. Shende, 'The Authorship of the Rāmāyaṇa', *Journal of the University of Bombay* 12, 1943, pp. 19–24 and U. P. Shah *ed.*, Uttarakāṇḍa, Introduction, p. 52.

negative evidence, therefore, should be taken as pointing to lack of acceptance of the Uttarakāṇḍa rather than its non-existence.

However, if the Uttarakāṇḍa was extant in substantially its present form by the fourth century, and in all probability by the third, it is scarcely feasible to assign the Bālakāṇḍa, which is in general earlier, to the end of the fourth century or later, as Kirfel seeks to do on the basis of the Sagara episode (1.37–43).[6] It may well be that certain passages, including this one, were added to the Bālakāṇḍa long after the main period of its composition, but external allusions and internal evidence alike suggest that the bulk of it was in existence by the third century AD. Two particularly late passages, on the evidence of their religious implications, are the Ṛśyaśṛṅga and Paraśurāma episodes (1.8–10 and 73–5), which quite possibly fall after this date. However, it is significant that the Northern recension has a much more developed account of Ṛśyaśṛṅga than the Southern and that the Paraśurāma episode, late as it is, must be substantially earlier than the *Viṣṇudharmottara Purāṇa* at the start of the seventh century.

Internal evidence would also support the proposed dating of the third stage to between the first and third centuries AD. For example, in addition to the geographical detail already mentioned, the musical terms occurring are similar to those employed by Bharata and Dattila in the early centuries AD. Negatively, but perhaps even more significantly, the absence of the horoscope for Rāma in the account of his birth may be contrasted with Kālidāsa's inclusion of a horoscope for Raghu.[7] The urge to include such detail may reasonably be held to have been strong and, although the zodiacal detail of the fourth-stage horoscope cannot be earlier than the later part of the second century, its composition may well not have been so much later; at any rate, such details were fashionable by Kālidāsa's time. Therefore, the fact that Rāma's horoscope lacks sufficient manuscript support to be included in the text argues again that the Bālakāṇḍa was essentially complete by around the third century.

Correspondingly, the earliest passages belonging to the fourth stage may belong to any period after the completion of the second and third stages. Although of course additions could have been made to the Ayodhyā to Yuddha kāṇḍas at any time after the end of the second stage, it seems likely that in fact the next phase of expansion of the text

[6] W. Kirfel, 'Rāmāyaṇa Bālakāṇḍa und Purāṇa', *Die Welt des Orients* 1, 1947, pp. 113–28; see also above, p. 57.

[7] At *Raghuvaṃśa* 3.13 Raghu's birth and future greatness are marked by five planets in their exaltation. Incidentally, Rāma's horoscope is given in detail in the *Agastyasaṃhitā*.

was largely concentrated in the Bāla and Uttara kāṇḍas, and therefore in broad terms the fourth stage does follow the third stage chronologically. Zodiacal terms, as just indicated, first appear in fourth-stage passages, where their introduction into Rāma's horoscope may well follow their introduction in the middle of the second century AD at no very great interval. There is no fourth-stage passage which needs to be assigned to an earlier date, and indeed another religiously motivated addition, a litany to the sun in the *Ādityahṛdaya* (6 App.I.65), must also be no earlier than the second century. On the whole, however, all that can be done is to establish the date by which individual passages are known to have been composed, although logically the fourth stage must be later than the second and third stages and may therefore be considered to begin in the fourth century AD.

Since the evidence indicates that the literary adaptations of the Rāmāyaṇa in or around the sixth century by Kumāradāsa, Bhaṭṭi and Pravarasena followed a form of the text intermediate between the present Northeastern and Southern recensions, it may be inferred that the archetype was still accessible up to that date and it is therefore not surprising that no external testimony can be adduced for dating any fourth-stage passage until some time later. However, in the eighth century Bhavabhūti, who in general follows a text resembling the Northern recension, copies from the first half of a Northern addition (2 App.I.26), the second half of which is drawn on by the *Padma Purāṇa* at the same or a slightly later date; both halves are also attested by Kṣemendra in the eleventh century. The first attestations of a Southern addition are not much later, for the Khotanese version, belonging perhaps to the ninth century, may draw on such a passage (2 App.I.14), while the *Ādityahṛdaya* (6 App.I.65), already established as later than the second century, forms the model for a *Brahmāṇḍa Purāṇa* passage of 800 AD or later, and Kampaṉ draws the motif of Bharata's vow to burn himself from a third passage (2.2304*). Considerably later, the *Adhyātma Rāmāyaṇa* attests the currency of a series of Northern additions to the Yuddhakāṇḍa (6 App.I.32, 36, 56 and 63).

Later attestations still seem to be of less well supported passages, such as Tulsīdās' mention of Hanumān nearly being shot by Bharata (6 App.I.57, read by some, mainly Northern manuscripts), and the Malay version's inclusion of Rāvaṇa's journey to the sun (7 App.I.1.15*, read by some Southern manuscripts) and the change of sex motif (7 App. I.3.1–120, read by a few Northern and a few Southern manuscripts). The poorer manuscript support for such passages may be coincidental but may equally suggest that they had been composed too recently to have gained sufficient currency to be alluded to in older works. Thus, we may infer that incidents or elaborations composed after about the twelfth century failed to spread beyond one or two manuscripts and that this date therefore marks the transition to the fifth stage. In fact, the oldest manuscript used for the Critical Edition is dated early in the eleventh century and, since it does contain passages exclusive to it, it ought perhaps to be said that the fifth stage starts no later than that. On the other hand, since the other manuscripts date from the fifteenth century and later, a compromise date of around the twelfth century seems reasonable. However, the number and extent of the passages peculiar to one manuscript or just two or three (without forming a complete group) is a very small proportion of the total material, and so both the precise dating of the fifth stage and the evidence presented by it are of less moment than for the earlier stages.

The evidence so far presented for the dating of the stages has been drawn primarily from linguistic data and comparison with other literature, including works drawing on the Rāmāyaṇa. Only limited use was made of cultural data, since, because they are often of rather uncertain date, their corroborative value is limited. Indeed, reasonably accurate dating of the Rāmāyaṇa's stages of growth should prove of value in defining more closely the cultural and social pattern at different periods. Accordingly, the main features visible in each stage will be briefly recapitulated, to demonstrate both the type of evidence available and its degree of consistency.

The first stage is that in which the heroic basis of the story is most evident, the material culture and the social pattern are at their simplest, and the geographical horizons are most restricted. The king surrounded by his court is the focus of society and he is respected rather than revered as divine; his right to levy tribute or taxes is matched by his obligation to protect his subjects, though without any explicit presentation of a social contract. The *purohita* is still the king's ritual specialist and has not yet developed the advisory functions known in later periods of Indian society. Warfare is a prominent aspect of the stage, not only because of the plot of the epic but also because of the martial and heroic outlook of the poet and his audience at the royal court. The form of combat usually described is the heroic ideal of the duel between two warriors mounted on chariots. The references are characterized also by a greater immediacy and realism than in later stages. The most prominent weapons are bows and arrows and swords, while protective armour is most frequently mentioned at this stage.

The social pattern is relatively simple, with little emphasis on the four *varṇas* but rather mention of town and country people. Similarly, there is no marked sign of inferiority for non-settled or tribal groups, such as the Niṣādas, whose depressed status is already alluded to in more brahmanically oriented literature probably as early as the fifth century BC. Also noteworthy is the apparent prominence of merchants in society revealed by incidental references. Attitudes towards women also reflect an early pattern. Marriage seems normally to have been between adults and women had a fairly free role in society, despite the polygyny of kings with the resulting women's quarters and the taking over of the harem by a successor; evidence for the seclusion of women is ambivalent but on balance negative. The remarriage of widows is readily envisaged and they are not yet regarded as inauspicious. Women could also become ascetics.

In material terms, we may note the possible conservatism of references to iron, as well as the hint that gold was obtained from the Northeast rather than the Deccan mines accessible to North India from the third century BC. This accords with the descriptions of flora, for the trees mentioned belong to the drier parts of the North, which rules out real familiarity with the lower Gaṅgā basin as well as South India. It is confirmed by the geographical data, which indicate that the real limit of settlement southwards was the Yamunā and Gaṅgā rivers, although the region from there to the Vindhya and Mahendra mountains was also vaguely known. A possible indication of an even earlier date is the absence of mention of either Rājagṛha or Pāṭaliputra in Magadha.

The descriptions of buildings suggest that there was as yet no great elaboration of layout, apart from the regular occurrence of a courtyard. Clothing was simple, as it tended to remain, and so were ornaments, of which garlands are most frequently mentioned. However, the mention of *kauśeya* as a fabric may provide a counter-indication to the early date implied by other details, for if its usual identification as silk is adhered to, it could hardly have been in general use before the first century BC. On balance, it is probably best to regard it as having undergone a change of meaning. With regard to diet, meat-eating is regarded as the normal practice, as also is hunting game for food, and the consumption of alcohol is standard; the usual sweetener employed is honey.

The absence of reference to writing (apart from limited use for marking objects) and the general use of oral communication point to an early period when the traditions of society were still orally based, as of course does the composition of the epic itself in an oral form, for the brahmanical reluctance to adopt writing for religious reasons would not have applied in a kṣatriya context. In fact the religious evidence of the first stage, though limited, is one of the strongest pointers to an early date. The pantheon alluded to is markedly nearer the Vedic pattern than the puranic, while the prominence of Indra, a natural choice for post-Vedic kṣatriyas as for Vedic Aryans, is particularly striking. Similarly, references to the dead going to Yama's abode, to the virtual exclusion of the concept of reincarnation, point to a situation which was being superseded in the earliest Upaniṣads. Moreover, the general ethos of the poem at this stage is heroic and not religious.

With the second stage, there is a certain shift of emphasis from the heroic to the aesthetic, which in part accounts for the greater elaboration visible in this stage. However, there is undoubtedly also evidence of a more developed social and economic pattern. Signs of greater economic activity are provided by the lengthy lists of occupations now included, as well as allusions to caravans of merchants, although the much more frequent mention of gold owes at least as much to the greater attention to aesthetic effect. The elaborate descriptions of fine mansions no doubt are also due in part to love of detail, but the mention of staircases for the first time does suggest greater architectural sophistication, as does the appearance of watch-towers on the generally more elaborate fortifications. Instead of the simple garlands of the first stage, personal ornament now consists usually of diadems, ear-rings, necklaces and anklets.

The geographical awareness revealed in this stage shows little extension from that of the first stage until we come to the search party accounts at its very end, probably in the first century AD. Awareness of the world of nature has apparently increased with more frequent mention of snakes, insects and the like and a wider flora mentioned, though typically in lists, where a degree of artificiality is apparent in the varied habitats of some species listed together. The buffalo is still wild, although reference is now made to ploughs, and to the wet-crop cultivation of rice typical of the lower Gaṅgā; presumably, as one simile indicates, bulls are the usual animal harnessed for ploughing, in contrast to the general use later of buffaloes in wet conditions. There are now references, though rare, to sugar, which of course takes over from honey as the main sweetener in India at an early date.

The status of the king is now enhanced through claims to divine status and his role as protector is still emphasised. The presence of dancers and actors at court and on festive occasions is an interesting feature. Warfare is becoming more elaborate, with the switch from chariots to elephants already commencing. The main weapons used by the armies (for which *sainya* instead of *senā* becomes the standard term) are also changing: arrows are less frequently mentioned, but spears and javelins become commoner, while swords continue to play a lesser role. Nevertheless, the main emphasis remains on the duel between two noted figures and indeed such duels receive some descriptive elaboration in this stage.

Socially, the most obvious change is in the position of women, with emphasis placed on a wife's subservience to her husband and on her chastity. The class system is also beginning to be more rigid, and allusion is made to the distinctive role of brāhmans in study and in ritual. Ascetics too are mentioned more, although they still practise certain rituals, and there is a little more emphasis placed on religious matters. Greater prominence is given to Brahmā, and heaven and hell are distinguished, without even now much reference to reincarnation. This perhaps indicates a more popular, or at least non-brāhman, approach to religion, which is further illustrated by the references to *caityas* as cult spots and perhaps also by the occasional references to astronomy or astrology. However, the inclusion from this stage onwards of a divine chorus or audience as spectators of crucial points in the narrative is perhaps the first sign of the increasing religious significance with which the epic came to be invested, turning it ultimately into a Vaiṣṇava work.

The religious emphasis is of course one of the most obvious features of the third stage, but it is by no means the only indicator of the more developed pattern of society reached in its period. Socially, there is now a much more pronounced emphasis on the four-*varṇa* model and correspondingly not just on the king's duty to protect but also on his duty to punish breaches of this religiously ordained social system, illustrated most graphically in the story of Rāma slaying the śūdra ascetic and thus bringing the brāhman boy back to life. With greater rigidity in ordinary society goes a definitely inferior position for those outside it, and for example the Niṣādas are now decidedly despised. The position of women has declined still further and they now sometimes occur simply as temptresses, for example in the story of Ṛśyaśṛṅga. At the same time the need for sons to continue the family and to perform the memorial rites for the father is stressed.

The combined results of the religious and social developments are seen in the greater frequency of allusions to teachers and learned men, while the more definite allusions to learning by heart perhaps implicitly distinguish the more religiously oriented works from secular activities where writing had become usual. The shift in diet from meat-eating to cereals probably reflects changed attitudes more than practice. The more detailed allusions to musical theory, particularly in relation to the myth of the epic's origin, are consistent with a dating in the early centuries AD. Such a dating is indicated by the geographical data, with the mention of various peoples in the Northwest who were prominent then only; a noteworthy feature is the growth of urbanisation, mostly in the Gaṅgā basin but including also mention of Taxila in the Northwest and in the Deccan of Pratiṣṭhāna, which had its greatest prominence in the first and second centuries AD.

In descriptions of warfare there is a marked turning away from reality. The theory rather than the practice of warfare tends to come to the fore, with more attention to the conventions of battle, including the duty of clemency toward those who surrender. General terms for weapons increase in frequency at the expense of specific terms, although there are also certain shifts in frequency of weapons or their names, such as the *gadā* superseding the *parigha* and the marked decline in mention of swords. Instead, the employment of divine or magical weapons is common, where their efficacy depends not on their nature—often ill defined—but on the power investing them. Two bows are particularly interesting: Viṣṇu's bow of horn, first mentioned in this stage, apparently represents a technical innovation in the introduction of the composite bow, attested in art as early as the second century BC, while Janaka's bow, in the second stage received from Varuṇa, is now declared to be Śiva's and thus its breaking by Rāma becomes an implicit exaltation of Viṣṇu over Śiva.

Viṣṇu and Śiva have risen by the third stage to a position challenging Indra and Brahmā for supremacy among the gods. Nevertheless, Brahmā is even more prominent than in the second stage and his characterisation is more advanced, with occasional references to his four heads and to his birth from a lotus. However, although Indra and Brahmā are prominent and still important, it is already clear that Viṣṇu and Śiva are become the only real contenders for the role of supreme deity. There is naturally also a tendency to exalt Viṣṇu over Śiva, evidenced also in Paraśurāma's remarks about Śiva's bow and certain episodes in the Uttarakāṇḍa. Possibly also the new motif of Rāvaṇa's worship of the *liṅga* points to a degree of hostility between Vaiṣṇavas and Śaivas. Other aspects of the definite religious emphasis of this stage are the extensive inclusion of mythological episodes drawn from outside the epic tradition, the greater stress on the practice and the powers of asceticism, the more elaborate descriptions of rituals, and the relative prominence of the Bhārgavas, who may have been responsible for this shift of emphasis in the Rāmāyaṇa as they certainly were for the Mahābhārata, although the discomfiture of their hero Rāma Jāmadagnya is against this.

Religious emphasis increases further in the fourth stage, which also, however, continues the more aesthetic emphasis of the second stage resulting, for example, in allusions to an even more extensive flora. Viṣṇu and Śiva are now the only claimants to the title of supreme deity, but an enlarged pantheon is alluded to with, for example, the artificial revival of Mitra; the term *mokṣa* now occurs in its usual religious sense. Alongside these features of the more formal religion, however, there occur a number of more popular features, such as the presence of temples, images and places of pilgrimage. There is even some indication of the growing importance of the Kṛṣṇa cult in the place-names mentioned.

Other new places mentioned show an enlarging of geographical horizons as well as the changed political situation after the early centuries AD. The greatest changes, however, apart from the religious, are social, for the epic has by now largely moved away from its heroic origins and most additions are made either for aesthetic effect or for didactic and religious purposes. The lack of touch with reality in warfare is typified by mention of armour made of gold; nevertheless several new weapons or names for them first appear in this stage. However, in general the substantial changes in vocabulary are a striking testimony to the very considerable time interval between the first two stages and the fourth.

The social framework is still more clearly given in terms of the four *varṇas* and there is even greater emphasis on the elevation of brāhmans and the degradation of śūdras and outcastes. The wife's position as simply an adjunct of her husband is now the normal view, expressed directly and also in the inauspiciousness of widowhood; there are accordingly a few references to a woman becoming a *satī*. Another mark of inferiority is that women eat after their men. The disfavour into which meat-eating had fallen by the third stage is joined by the disapproval now expressed for the consumption of alcohol.

A number of details are added to the relatively limited picture of cultural activities drawn in the previous stages. Several lengthy lists of subjects of study for young princes point to a fairly elaborate curriculum, which is however probably an ideal of brāhman theorists rather than actual kṣatriya practice. Elsewhere also reference to the study of grammar is found, as well as references to reading and writing, although reciters of the epic are still frequently mentioned. The increasing hold of astrology is very evident and now includes use of the zodiacal system first borrowed from the Hellenistic world in the middle of the second century AD. Further terms for dancers and for the first time one for a stage, together with the frequency of reference to actors and dancers, points to the importance of the theatre, which probably enjoyed its greatest popularity—at any rate as a high art form, envisaged in such allusions—between the fourth and seventh centuries AD.

Inevitably, the fifth stage, from its nature as a substantially smaller block of randomly added material, does not present nearly so coherent a pattern as the previous stages. In general, it continues the new emphases apparent in the fourth stage, occasionally adding new terms for existing features and less often including new concepts. For example, in the flora mentioned there occur several synonyms for trees already mentioned, as well as just a few new ones. An instance of later social customs is the allusion to the burden placed on a father by a daughter, presumably in arranging a marriage. Another random example is the first mention of the Dravidians by that general name rather than as separate groups. Various features of the religious pattern are new: a description of a Śaiva ascetic, the Gaṅgā as universal purifier, and (among frequent references to Viṣṇu) the first mention of the future *avatāra* Kalki—a curiously late attestation in view of his mention in the other epic (Mbh. 3.188.89—189.6 and Hv. 31.148).

The greatest development during the successive stages of the Rāmāyaṇa's growth and beyond is however in the character of Rāma himself. Although he is clearly a martial hero in the first stage and the climax of the whole epic is his military defeat of Rāvaṇa, from the beginning important issues of conduct are central to the plot. Rāma's calm acceptance of exile at his father's decree is not only pivotal to the action but also an impressive demonstration of the filial obedience which is one aspect of his exemplary adherence to duty. So too, in similar displays of wifely devotion and brotherly affection, Sītā and Lakṣmaṇa insist on accompanying him. Once in the forest, Rāma fulfils his duty as a kṣatriya by offering protection to the various sages living there.

The elevation of Rāma's character, combined with his standing as a prince, make it natural for him to be compared to the gods. Thus, in the first stage he is regularly compared with Indra, the king of the gods and a natural comparison for all human kings and heroes, not just Rāma, as we have seen. At this stage the tendency to compare Rāma and Lakṣmaṇa with Indra and Viṣṇu reflects the older relationship between the two gods. However, just as Indra serves as the comparison for others, so too Rāma is compared to other deities, including Śiva when he is in fighting mood.

The association with Indra to enhance Rāma's status goes further than just comparisons, especially in the second stage. Indra's visit to Śarabhaṅga's hermitage is in effect a prediction of Rāma's future greatness, even if the sages do before long allude back to the death of Khara as though this were the deed predicted (3.29.29–32). Indra's promise of release by Rāma to Kabandha and Rāma's lifting of the curse on Ahalyā brought about by Indra are other pointers to this somewhat more direct linkage, which even persists into the fourth stage with the story of Indra going to reassure Sītā in Laṅkā.

Despite his prowess and his comparison with Indra, Rāma is definitely human in the first stage. It is as the embodiment of the ideal of human conduct that he becomes so outstanding. More exactly, the ideal is that of the kṣatriya, whose duty is to ensure the maintenance of society by upholding dharma, by force if necessary; this picture of the vigorous upholder of righteousness is clearly presented in the regular epithets applied to Rāma. Incidentally, there is no warrant within the text for the name Rāmacandra which becomes so common later.[8] Admittedly, he may be compared to the moon, most notably in the metaphor where Rāma is the moon to Rāvaṇa's Rāhu (6.90.26cd), but equally he may be compared to the sun (*rāmadivākara* in another metaphor at 5.35.18b), or to both more or less side by side (6.115.27d and 30d), all these examples coming in fact from the more elaborate second stage. The earliest uses of the name Rāmacandra are apparently by Bhavabhūti and in the *Padma Purāṇa*.

At some point towards the end of the second stage Rāma comes to be viewed as divine. In the greater part of the second stage Rāma is still viewed as human and this is also the picture presented at the same period by the *Rāmopākhyāna*. Nevertheless, he is regarded as a particularly moral figure, whose ethical grandeur, already present in the first stage, is now emphasised by attempts to remove all possible blemishes. At the same time the association with Indra tends to be further stressed, but this was evidently a blind alley so far as his

[8] It does occur in many of the colophons of individual mss. (including the unusual 2.2336*), whose scribes were obviously familiar with it; it also occurs in one highly ornate passage with limited Northern support (5.754* 2), but with several variant readings. Altogether, these occurrences seem subsequent to the attestation of the title in other works.

ultimate stature was concerned. The reason no doubt was that, although Indra was the natural comparison for a martial hero, with his moral decline already begun he was no longer so apt a model for the ethical ideal presented in Rāma. Nevertheless, the link with Indra does sporadically persist even beyond the Rāmāyaṇa itself, for the *Padma Purāṇa* (4.1–68) makes both guilty of brahmanicide, Indra by slaying Vṛtra and Rāma by killing Rāvaṇa. Essentially, however, the association with Indra is a transition phase.

The ethical polarisation already apparent in the developments of the second stage, proceeding from within the plot itself, leads naturally to a stress on Rāma's activity on behalf of dharma and his defeat of evil in the person of Rāvaṇa. This receives its fullest development in the Rāmāyaṇa itself in the Uttarakāṇḍa, where Rāvaṇa's genealogy and past exploits are so presented as to turn him into an adversary of the gods; Rāma's defeat of him is thereby assigned the same cosmic significance as Indra's defeat of Namuci and Viṣṇu's of Bali. Even in the second stage, at the close of the Yuddhakāṇḍa, Rāma is recognised as divine in a series of identifications with various deities, working up through identification with Indra to his true identity as Viṣṇu. The reasons for such identification with the benevolent activity for mankind of Viṣṇu are evident enough, but the belief is expressed in terms of identity and not yet through the *avatāra* doctrine.

The account of Rāma's birth in the Bālakāṇḍa comes nearer to that in declaring that Rāma and his three brothers are born by divine intervention as incarnations of Viṣṇu, while various deities engender other leading figures of the story. Nevertheless, the rest of the Bālakāṇḍa, with limited exceptions, is nearer to the older pattern than the second half of the Uttarakāṇḍa where the prevailing attitude is that Rāma is divine. Yet Bhāsa in his plays views Rāma as divine and so do many of the later citations of the Rāma story in the Mahābhārata, which presumably means that such a view was widely current by the third century AD. On the other hand, the absence of the term *avatāra* is less surprising in view of the general sense in which it can be used by Kālidāsa to call the four brothers 'embodied *avatāras* as it were of *dharma, artha, kāma* and *mokṣa*' (*Raghuvaṃśa* 10.84).

The growth of such adaptations of the story, both in classical Sanskrit literature and in the Purāṇas, points clearly to the influence of the story, an influence which is specifically religious, despite the lack of evidence for any cult of Rāma until a much later date. As early as the Uttarakāṇḍa there is definite reference to devotion to Rāma (*rāmabhakti*) by the Vānaras (7.38.15, cf. 39.15), while even in the second stage the crow that molests Sītā takes refuge with Rāma himself from his arrow (5.36.16–33), an incident seen by later piety as an instance of saving devotion. In the fourth and fifth stages, however, there is ample expression of the attitude of devotion and self-surrender to Rāma, now regularly identified with Viṣṇu and sometimes termed an *avatāra* or *prādurbhāva*. Whether or not there was a specific cult before the twelfth century or so—and I personally am convinced that the lack of direct evidence does not mean the absence of any cult—the attitude of reverence toward Rāma as an incarnation of Viṣṇu is well established.

His eventual status as an *avatāra* of Viṣṇu inevitably invites comparisons with Kṛṣṇa, perhaps all the more so because the primary vehicle for both stories was one of the Sanskrit epics, in which respect the addition of the *Harivaṃśa* to the Mahābhārata is analogous to the addition of the Bāla and Uttara kāṇḍas to the Rāmāyaṇa. There is no real sign of influence from the Kṛṣṇa cult within the textual tradition of the Rāmāyaṇa itself, apart from the very limited one of the occurrence in the fourth stage of a few place-names associated with Kṛṣṇa. The distinction between Rāma as an ethical example and Kṛṣṇa as a teacher is a fundamental one, yet the first attempts to provide Rāma with a teaching role occur in the *Agni Purāṇa* perhaps in the seventh century, or even possibly indirectly in the *Anuśāsanaparvan* of the Mahābhārata. The major instance, however, is undoubtedly the *Rāmagītā*—its very name indicating the implicit parallel—now included in the *Adhyātma Rāmāyaṇa*, which also includes other discourses of Rāma, mainly to Lakṣmaṇa. By contrast the *Yogavāsiṣṭha*, for example, continues the older pattern of Rāma as the recipient of moral homilies. The *Adhyātma* also provides the first major example of the modelling of Rāma's youth on that of Kṛṣṇa, under the influence of the *Bhāgavata Purāṇa*. This feature is, however, taken much further in the *Bhuśuṇḍi Rāmāyaṇa*, which is heavily influenced by the Kṛṣṇa cult and also assigns Rāma a definite teaching role.

Similarly, Rāma's identification with Viṣṇu raises the question of his relationship to Śiva, which has been answered in different ways over the centuries. In the Rāmāyaṇa itself, by the third stage, Rāvaṇa's worship of the *liṅga* implicitly equates the struggle between Rāma and Rāvaṇa with the antipathy between Vaiṣṇava and Śaiva. On the other hand many Purāṇas, not only the Śaiva ones, incorporate a Śaiva element on Rāma's side by making Hanumān an *avatāra* of Śiva and stressing Rāma's erection of the Rāmeśvaram *liṅga*. This openness or receptiveness to Śaivism is mediated through the *Adhyātma Rāmāyaṇa* to Tulsīdās, who is probably the best known exponent of it, but it is also found in other North Indian versions such as that of Kṛttibās. So too the important theological innovation of the illusory Sītā, which preserves unblemished her chastity, passes from the *Kūrma Purāṇa* to the late Sanskrit Rāmāyaṇas and thence to Tulsīdās. An index of Tulsī's popularity—and a factor in it—is provided by the Rāmlīlā, staged annually at Daśahrā in most of North India. It illustrates a paradox of the Rāma tradition, for it has no strong sectarian connections and so is open to all Hindus, with the result that Rām has become one of the commonest names for the deity in North India (a trend that may indeed predate Tulsīdās and the Rāmlīlā). Thus, although Tulsīdās himself had links with the school of Rāmānanda, in all probability the first sectarian movement adoring Rāma, his great legacy was the vision of Rāma's righteous rule and the saving power of his name available to all (found in South India however as early as Kampaṉ and Eẓuttaccan).

The emphasis on Rāma's righteousness, his adherence to and protection of dharma, appears strongly in Tulsīdās, but it is of course basic to his portrayal in Vālmīki's Rāmāyaṇa, and the notion of dharma is a universal one in India and those parts of Asia influenced by Indian culture. This is how Rāma could so easily be accepted within the Buddhist tradition as a Bodhisattva and in Jainism as one of its great figures. Buddhist versions reached through Central Asia as far as Japan, and by sea the Rāma story spread into Southeast to adopt either a Buddhist flavour, as in the Khmer tradition, or a popular, folk aspect, as in the Malay. Yet the connecting link and the reason for the story's popularity is still the ethical emphasis on the figure of 'righteous Rāma'. Throughout its evolution and not just in the original epic, the key to the story lies in dharma and in Rāma as an ideal example of it. Truly Vālmīki's question to Nārada—'Who in the world nowadays is exemplary and courageous, right-minded (*dharmajña*) and grateful, truthful and resolute? Who cleaves to virtue? Who is kind to all?' (1.1.2–3b)—has found a triumphant answer in the figure of Rāma.

> Though a man commit sins day by day,
> if he reads one *śloka*, he is freed from sin. (7.1522* 5–6)

APPENDIX

It was argued in the second chapter that the process of growth of the Rāmāyaṇa can be divided into a number of stages. Within this appendix there will first be given for convenience a tabular presentation of the material assigned to each stage, together with the datings proposed in the tenth chapter from the evidence accumulated in the rest of the book. This will then be followed by a fuller examination of the sargas assigned to stage 2, presenting the detailed linguistic and stylistic evidence for their relatively later date.

Stages of growth

Stage 1 (orally transmitted from about the fifth to the fourth century BC)

All *śloka* stanzas of books 2–6 not listed below (37.10% of the text).

Stage 2 (approximately third century BC to first century AD)

The following complete sargas of books 2–6 (*śloka* material, 34.05% of the text):

2.1–30	3.1–4	4.13	5.1–8	6.4–5
46–7	8–11	17–18	12–17	23–4
57–8	13	21	26–7[l.v.]	30–1
61	15	23–4	33–7	46–8
65–9	25, 28–30	27–30	43	53
74	33	39–42	45–7	55
85	40	49	54–8	57–63
88–9	44–5	59–61		70–3
94–5	50	65–6		79–82
98	53			87
100–2	58			90–1
106–8	60			102–7
110–11	71			111–16

All verses in longer metres in books 2–6 (4.27% of the text).

Stage 3 (composed between the first and third centuries AD)

The Bālakāṇḍa (book 1) and the Uttarakāṇḍa (book 7); comprising 24.57% of the text.

Stage 4 (composed between about the fourth and twelfth centuries AD)

* passages (i.e. those passages relegated by the editors of the Critical Edition to footnotes or to Appendix I) with good manuscript support.

Stage 5 (from about the twelfth century AD)

* passages with poor manuscript support.

Examination of stage 2

2.1–30 (intrigues leading to Rāma's banishment). The opening of the Ayodhyākāṇḍa has clearly been extensively worked over and approximately the first thirty of its 111 sargas have been so altered or inflated as to bear no real stylistic relationship to the rest of the book. High proportions of long compounds, vṛddhied derivatives or similes are to be found in sargas 2, 5–6, 19–20 and 29–30, although the passage as a whole shows proportions little different from the average for the whole book.[1] Repeats and other stereotyped phrases are very frequent, and the almost complete absence of geminated words may also be noted, especially since the subject-matter might have been supposed to lend itself to their employment. Particularly striking is the fact that sixteen out of twenty instances of the periphrastic future and five out of the eight future participles found in the Ayodhyākāṇḍa occur in these first thirty sargas. There are several uncommon items of vocabulary, including ten verbal roots occurring here but nowhere else in the text of the Ayodhyā and Araṇya kāṇḍas, while use of the historic present is also somewhat commoner than in the rest of the book. Both instances of *yathā* = 'than' are found in these sargas and the great majority of instances of *yathā* in a causal sense are found here or in other later passages. Certain types of nominal composition are not infrequent in this and other passages of the second stage, but rare in the first stage. In terms of subject-matter, the number of references to Viṣṇu and also to Bṛhaspati are significant.[2]

2.46 (Sumantra's return and the crossing of the Gaṅgā) is integral to the narrative but it is very long and has clearly been greatly expanded, whereas sarga 47 (Rāma's lament) is peripheral and may well be an interpolation; it is not attested in either of the summaries in the Bālakāṇḍa (sargas 1 and 3) or in the *Rāmopākhyāna* (Mbh. 3.258–76), while the pessimism attributed here to Rāma is out of character with the usual portrayal of him. There are no less than four desiderative forms in sarga 46, as well as an instance of the past participle passive + *vat*. In the two sargas together there are instances of change of conjugation, the optative with *sma* and *mā* to express prohibition (twice); four *dvandvas* of abstract terms and other less common nominal compounds, *enam* for *etad*, unusual use of case, *yathā* in a final or consecutive sense twice, a doubled relative; metrical shortening, irregular sandhi, hiatus between pādas;

[1] For the purposes of this study, the longest 20% of sargas in each book are considered *long*; the longest 10%, *very long*; the shortest 20%, *short*; the shortest 10%, *very short*. The proportion of long compounds is considered *high* if they occur on average in 50% or more of the *ślokas* of a sarga, and *very high* if they occur in 66% or more. The proportion of vṛddhied derivatives (excluding patronymics) is *high* if such forms occur in 33% or more of the stanzas of a sarga, *very high* in 50% or more; when patronymics are included in the figures, the criterion for *high* rises to occurrence in 50% or more of the stanzas. The proportion of similes is considered *high* if they are found in 25% or more of the stanzas; if in 33% or more, the proportion is *very high*.

[2] For details see my VS pp. 2, 7, 13–14, 15 and 21, NS pp. 391, 392–3, 396, FS p. 442, *Syntax* pp. 343–4, RA p. 115; also *Proverbs* p. 142. It should also be noted that 2.30.4–21 (including S. * passages) is reproduced in Mbh. 2.App.41.6–52 (cf. V. Raghavan, *The Greater Rāmāyaṇa*, Varanasi, 1973, p. 6 (ii)).

a developed simile and multiple similes, metaphor, hyperbole, *arthāntaranyāsa*, alliteration and parallelism within the stanza, a proverb; and also much late or rare vocabulary.[3]

2.57–8 (Daśaratha's narration of his former misdeed and the curse by which he is now dying separated from his son) have certainly been much expanded, if indeed the whole passage, apart from Daśaratha's death itself, is not simply an insertion. Within it are to be found a periphrastic future, six desideratives, an unaugmented imperfect, a present participle passive with active endings and other unusual verbal forms, a periphrastic case expression, a string of relative clauses and the unusual correlatives *yathā . . . tena satyena*, stereotyped expressions from the Mahābhārata corpus, as well as a developed simile which includes a verb.[4]

2.61 (the well-known description of the evils of a kingless state) is in the main identical with Mbh. 12.67–8, plus additional parallels with Mbh. 12.15.32–3. The whole sarga shows certain traces of *svabhāvokti*, similes are common, and there is also a reference to the *matsyanyāya* at 21cd. Chiasmus is found at 10ab, though absent from the corresponding passage in the Mahābhārata . The form in which this semi-proverbial material is cast naturally produces a high degree of stereotyping in stanzas 8–21. Irregular verbal forms and less common adjectival forms occur.[5]

2.65–9 (Bharata's return and rejection of his mother's actions). Both sarga 65, which describes Bharata's return to the melancholy Ayodhyā, and sarga 66, in which Kaikeyī eventually breaks the news of Daśaratha's death and Rāma's banishment, have clearly been greatly expanded, perhaps originally forming with the present sarga 67 one sarga of normal length. The proportion of vṛddhied derivatives in 2.65 is very high; *svabhāvokti* and *utprekṣā* are noticeable, and the correlatives *yādṛśāḥ . . . tān* at 24 are unusual. The number of *avyayībhāvas* formed with *yathā* in these two sargas may be noted. Sarga 66 displays a number of highly abnormal features in its verbal forms; the high proportion of stereotyped phrases may also be noted. Sarga 67, which is short,

[3] See VS pp. 5, 10, 13, 21, 32 and 34, NS pp. 372, 375, 385, 394, 405–6, 414, SE p. 223, FS pp. 442, 450–2, 455–6, *Syntax* pp. 341 and 343n.11, *Proverbs* p. 143, also RA p. 120.

[4] See VS pp. 6, 10, 14, 16–17, 30–2, 34, NS p. 414, *Syntax* pp.341–3 and SET III. As van Daalen observes (*Vālmīki's Sanskrit*, pp. 271–2), many of these features occur in the S. recension only, leading him to suspect not '2,57–8 as such, but the S transmission of these sargas.' However, half of the desideratives are supported by effectively all the mss. (those at 57.28d / 1408* 2, 29c and 58.12c / 1440*); this point, not examined by van Daalen, in itself suggests that there is more to it than just faulty transmission.

[5] See VS pp. 9, 17 and 31, NS pp. 393 and 402, SE pp. 223 and 226, FS p. 453, and *Proverbs* p. 143. Stanza 8 is discussed by van Daalen (op. cit., p. 245) as a permissible exception to his 'Rule of Two', that no more than two items are qualified in one *śloka*; this is perhaps some evidence for the use of a more elaborate style. See Jacobi, *Das Râmâyaṇa*, p. 71 and E.W. Hopkins, 'The Original Rāmāyaṇa', JAOS 46, 1926, pp. 202–19.

contains an instance of the substitute perfect active participle, read by all the manuscripts.[6] The Surabhi episode, referred to in 2.68.15–24, was recognised as an insertion by Hopkins, being derived from Mbh. 3.10.5–18, but the closest parallels with the Mahābhārata are in fact in 2.1764*, since in the main the Rāmāyaṇa version is much shorter than, and in parts differently worded from, that in the Mahābhārata; however, the rest of the sarga is not without its late features.[7] The elaboration of Bharata's reaction to his mother's acts probably continues into sarga 69, wherein he emphatically clears himself of complicity to Kausalyā. Certainly, the use of a refrain consisting of a relative clause is a mark of lateness. There also occur an intensive and a desiderative form, the optative with *mā* and *sma* twice, less common nominal compounds, and several unusual items of vocabulary.[8] Most tellingly, however, many of Bharata's curses have close parallels in Mbh. 13.95 and 96.

2.74 (the construction of the royal road for Bharata) is another clear addition. The sarga shows very high proportions of long compounds and of similes, as well as a developed simile containing a verb and repetition of the same *upamāna*. The nature of the description tends to *svabhāvokti*. Other points to note include an augmentless imperfect, an agent noun, geminated words and several items of vocabulary.[9]

2.85 (Bharadvāja's entertainment of Bharata's army) is among the most obvious interpolations. The sarga is very long, despite which it shows high proportions of long compounds and of vṛddhied derivatives. *Svabhāvokti* is conspicuous, while *utprekṣā* and chiasmus also occur. Geminated words and repeats are found. Both nominal and verbal systems show a number of striking irregularities.[10]

2.88–9 (Rāma points out the beauties of Citrakūṭa to Sītā and expresses his happiness at living there in her company) both contain very high proportions of long compounds, which is indicative of their ornate, later character; in addition, sarga 88 contains two compounds exceeding pāda length. Multiple similes are observable at 88.4–6 and 22, and a developed simile occurs at 89.15, while *utprekṣā* is found at 88.4 and flectional rhyme at 88.8–10. The verbal forms show several unusual features, including an intensive.[11]

[6] See VS pp. 5, 8, 11, 18, 21–2 and 25, NS pp. 393–4, and *Syntax* pp. 341–2. It is worth noting that van Daalen considers that 'sarga 2,65 has been subject to later reworking' on the basis of the uncommon metrical patterns of 2cd and 11e (op. cit., pp. 69 and 165–7), as well as two breaches of his 'Rule of Two' (op. cit., p. 250).

[7] See E. W. Hopkins, 'Proverbs and Tales common to the Two Sanskrit Epics', AJPh 20, 1899, pp. 22–39, esp. p. 34, and my VS p. 12, NS pp. 376 and 412, and SE p. 226; note also the double sandhi of *kausalyāyātmasaṃbhavam* at 13d.

[8] See VS pp. 10, 17 and 32–3, NS pp. 371 and 375, and SE p. 223.

[9] See VS pp. 17 and 29, NS pp. 375 and 396, FS pp. 442 and 451, and *Syntax* pp. 343n.9 and 353; cf. also RA p. 127.

[10] See VS pp. 2, 6–7 and 21, NS pp. 374, 394, 396 and 406, SE p. 223, and FS pp. 451 and 453.

[11] See VS pp. 2, 21–2 and 33, NS pp. 396–7 and 403–4, and FS pp. 442 and 458.

2.94 (the *kaccit* sarga) is undoubtedly a later intrusion into both the Rāmāyaṇa and the Mahābhārata, where it occurs at Mbh. 2.5 in virtually identical wording. It contains a high proportion of patronymics and other vṛddhied derivatives. However, apart from the inevitable degree of parallelism within the sarga, its only divergent stylistic features are use of parataxis at 26–7, multiple similes and a geminated gerund; but notable verbal forms include a future participle.[12]

2.95 (Rāma learns of Daśaratha's death) also seems to have been greatly expanded; among its late features are frequent figures of speech (*utprekṣā*, *svabhāvokti*, and a proverb), two *avyavībhāvas* with *yathā*, an intensive adjective, a substitute desiderative adjective, and the use of the locative at 23c.[13]

2.98 (Rāma's renewed rejection of Bharata's entreaties to return) has less than half the average proportion of long compounds, but it is marked out by the nature of its similes, with no fewer than six developed similes, two of which are proverbial in nature, and two verses with multiple similes; other figures employed are *utprekṣā* and *arthāntaranyāsa*. There is also a high proportion of stereotyped phrases and the like, some drawn from the Mahābhārata, as well as several unusual features of morphology and syntax.[14] This sarga, like the next passage, is essentially an expansion on the rather brief treatment of the dialogue between Rāma and Bharata; indeed R. Söhnen suggests that possibly the dialogue between them originally consisted only of the speeches in sarga 97 and 104.9–22.[15]

2.100–2 (further attempts to persuade Rāma to return). In sarga 100 Jābāli argues on generally materialistic grounds for Rāma's return, and in sarga 101 Rāma angrily rebuffs him; in sarga 102 Vasiṣṭha adds further refutation, including a genealogy of the Ikṣvākus; the content of all three sargas clearly suggests their secondary nature. The genealogy is largely identical with that given in the Bālakāṇḍa at 69.17–30 and 1274* and must be regarded as in all probability an interpolation, although the nature of its contents precludes the application of stylistic criteria.[16] Sarga 100 shows a high proportion of

[12] See VS pp. 2, 15 and 21, SE p. 226, FS p. 442, *Syntax* pp. 352–3, and *Proverbs* p. 144; cf. also E. W. Hopkins, 'Parallel Features in the Two Sanskrit Epics', AJPh 19, 1899, pp. 138–51.

[13] See VS pp. 32–3, NS pp. 393 and 413, FS p. 451, and *Proverbs* p. 144.

[14] See VS pp. 21 and 26, NS p. 394, *Proverbs* p. 144, FS pp. 442–3 and 452, *Syntax* pp. 341–2 and 345, and SET III.

[15] Söhnen, *Reden*, p. 199.

[16] For comments on the relationship of this genealogy to others see A. D. Pusalkar, 'Genealogy of the Solar Dynasty in the Purāṇas and the Rāmāyaṇa', *Purāṇa* 4, 1962, pp. 23–33 and P. V. Kane, *History of Dharmaśāstra* vol. 1 pt. 1 rev. ed., Poona, 1968, pp. 382–3; cf. also Rai Krishnadasa, 'The Ikṣvāku Genealogy in the Purāṇas', *Purāṇa* 2, 1960, pp. 128–50. W. Ruben notes ('The Minister Jābāli in Vālmīki's Rāmāyaṇa', *Indian Studies Past and Present* 6, 1964–5, pp. 443–66, on p. 460) that Jābāli's speech is absent not only from the *Rāmopākhyāna* but also from the *Raghuvaṃśa* and the Malay version. Jacobi (*Das Râmâyaṇa*, pp. 88–9 and n.) suggested that 2.99.17—103.11 were interpolated, with Vasiṣṭha's speech forming 'einen Einschub in einen Einschub'. I have preferred to operate in sarga units but essentially my conclusions agree with Jacobi. But

patronymics and other vṛddhied derivatives, while considerable parts of Jābāli's speech and Rāma's reply are proverbial or at least traditional in character; there are also a number of less usual items of morphology, syntax and vocabulary in these three sargas.[17] Furthermore, the passage is not attested in the Bālakāṇḍa summaries or the *Rāmopākhyāna*, and when Bharata calls on Bharadvāja as he returns, he mentions a speech by Vasiṣṭha (2.105.11) but not one by Jābāli. This could well refer to Vasiṣṭha's second speech in 103.2–7 and it is significant that Rāma's speech then in 103.9–11 briefly replied to Vasiṣṭha's second speech but entirely ignores his first. It may also be noted that Rāma's reply to Jābāli in 101 is absent from the Lahore edition, though present in the Northwestern mss. used by the Critical Edition.

2.106–7 (the mourning town of Ayodhyā and the enthronement of the sandals) have provided later poets with a chance to run riot. Jacobi commented on the occurrence of 16 similes in as many stanzas in sarga 106,[18] and this sarga has by far the greatest number of similes of any in the Ayodhyākāṇḍa, as well as a high proportion of patronymics and other vṛddhied derivatives (of which one, *śauṇḍa*, occurs twice here but not elsewhere in the text). There are also a number of less usual nominal and verbal forms, as well as the striking fivefold repetition of *pra-* at 106.18.[19]

2.108 (the Citrakūṭa ascetics' fears about the Asuras) is not particularly relevant to the main narrative but on the whole the style is regular. However, there is a high proportion of patronymics and other vṛddhied derivatives, three desiderative forms occur, also a past participle passive + *vat*, and the rare correlatives *yadā prabhṛti . . . tadā prabhṛti* at 13a + c, while the verses in longer metre are extremely irregular.[20] It may be significant that in the Northern recension the Araṇyakāṇḍa begins at this point, since the beginnings and endings of the kāṇḍas seem to have been particularly subject to elaboration.

2.110–11 (Sītā's meeting and conversation with Anasūyā) have no real connection with the main narrative, unless they were inserted to explain how Sītā, having put on clothes of bark for their banishment, can be dressed in fine clothes when seized by Rāvaṇa. Sarga 110 contains three desiderative forms and a periphrastic future, sarga 111 has high proportions of long compounds and of patronymics and other vṛddhied derivatives, and both have numerous unusual features of morphology, syntax and subject-matter. Note also hiatus

van Daalen's calling in question of everything between 2.87 and 2.106 seems excessive (op. cit., pp. 134–5 and 168–72; at p. 252 he even suggests moving forward its start to 2.83); if 2.87–106 (20 sargas with 5 irregularities in 581 *ślokas*) is suspect, then why not 2.24–44 (21 sargas with 5 irregularities in 504½ *ślokas*)?

[17] See VS pp. 17, 18, 21, 31 and 33, NS p. 386, *Proverbs* pp. 144–5, FS pp. 450 and 455–6, and *Syntax* pp. 341, 343n.9, 345–6 and 353. See also RA pp. 113, 122–3 and 126–7, and SET III.

[18] *Das Râmâyaṇa*, p. 120 (cf. also p. 105).

[19] See NS pp. 381 and 393, FS p. 458, and *Syntax* p. 342.

[20] See VS pp. 21 and 32, and *Syntax* p. 344. See also p. 51n.65.

between pādas at 110.1ab, 51ab and within the pāda at 110.50c. Bulcke has also identified this episode as a late interpolation on grounds of subject-matter.[21]

3.1–4 (Rāma meets the Daṇḍakāraṇya ascetics, encounters the Rākṣasa Virādha, and visits Śarabhaṅga) seems definitely to have suffered inflation, to judge by its language and style. The description of the hermitage in Daṇḍakāraṇya in the first sarga, especially 3–10, with its string of descriptive adjectives, is exceptionally florid and may be compared to Mbh. 3.145.25–32; the sarga as a whole shows high proportions of long compounds and of patronymics and other vṛddhied derivatives, as well as a full-line simile. The Virādha episode at 3.2–3 is perhaps a clumsy anticipation of Śūrpaṇakhā's attack later; certainly the style is elaborate, with high proportions of similes in both sargas and also high proportions of long compounds and of patronymics and other vṛddhied derivatives in sarga 2. The purpose of Indra's prior visit to Śarabhaṅga's *āśrama* which is the central incident of sarga 4 seems designed to enhance Rāma's significance in a way characteristic of the second stage of growth. All four sargas show a number of later features in their language and style.[22]

3.8–9 (Sītā's attempt to dissuade Rāma from killing the Rākṣasas and his reply) are basically regular in style, but the subject-matter seems to be an attempt at an ethical justification of Rāma's conduct, and a certain number of features are visible which are unusual in the earlier Rāmāyaṇa.[23]

3.10 (Rāma's visit to Agastya) betrays its lateness by the very large number of supposedly epic forms found, the occurrence of chiasmus, and the extreme frequency of personal epithets and other stereotyped phrases.[24] The catalogue of the places in which Rāma, Sītā and Lakṣmaṇa spent the ten preceding years has obviously been inserted at a later date in the supposed interests of consistency. This sarga also contains the very late insertion of the episode of Vātāpi and Ilvala.

3.11 (Agastya's welcome and gift of divine weapons) seems to have been so heavily interpolated as to have little resemblance to its earlier form. The text of stanzas 17–18 in particular seems to have been often altered, for the text refers to ten deities, to whom seven are added by 3.203*, and there are several variant readings. The very great frequency of stereotyped phrases may again be noted, as well as certain grammatical irregularities. The frequency of mention of Viṣṇu is also noteworthy in view of the infrequency of mention elsewhere, and

[21] See VS pp. 4–5, 9 and 14, NS pp. 391, 409 and 414, *Syntax* pp. 349 and 351, and RA pp. 113, 115, 117 and 126–7; cf. also van Daalen, op. cit., p. 199 (on 2.110.51ab) and C. Bulcke, 'La naissance de Sītā', BEFEO 46, 1952, pp. 107–17.

[22] See VS pp. 2, 14 and 21, NS pp. 374, 411–2 and 414, FS pp. 442, 455, 457 and 459, *Syntax* pp. 343–4, 349 and 352–3, RA pp. 119 and 126–7, and *Proverbs* pp. 142 and 146.

[23] See VS p. 27, NS pp. 394 and 408, FS p. 454, and *Syntax* pp. 345, 347n.18 and 352; see also above, p. 136.

[24] See VS pp. 4–5, 17, 20–1 and 33, NS pp. 374, 386, 394 and 405, SE p. 226, FS p. 453, *Syntax* pp. 344 and 353, and SET III. Cf. also van Daalen, op cit., pp. 178–9.

no doubt one of the motives for the interpolations in this sarga was to give him what was later felt to be his rightful prominence.[25]

3.13 (Jaṭāyus' genealogy) has pronounced cosmogonical overtones, as well as parallels with the Mahābhārata. Despite being basically a list of names (or possibly because of it) it shows several irregular forms: an unaugmented imperfect twice, transfer of stem, and irregular agreement of a numeral.[26]

3.15 (Lakṣmaṇa's description of winter) provided an excellent opportunity for later poets to indulge their taste for *svabhāvokti*; other figures found, in addition to several similes, are *utprekṣā*, *samāsokti*, *atyantatiraskṛtavācya* and various *śabdālaṃkāras*. The language of the sarga is regular but it shows high proportions of long compounds and of patronymics and other vṛddhied derivatives.[27]

3.25 and 28–9 (the deaths of Dūṣaṇa and Khara) have definitely been expanded, although the whole passage containing the conflict with the various Rākṣasas, sargas 24–9, may well have been expanded to some extent. All these sargas show very high proportions of similes and sarga 25 in addition has a high proportion of long compounds; there are two desiderative forms in 28 and an agent noun in both 28 and 29. Several grammatical points suggest a later date for these three sargas, and they display a number of the more elaborate figures of speech.[28]

3.30 (Śūrpaṇakhā seeking vengeance goes to Rāvaṇa) is elaborate in style and has evidently been expanded; in particular, stanzas 4–20, the description of Rāvaṇa's past exploits, is superfluous. There are very high proportions of long compounds (including one over pāda-length) and of similes; elements of hyperbole are present, and there is some carelessness of language.[29]

3.33 (Rāvaṇa's journey to Mārīca) includes an obviously late insertion concerning Garuḍa's exploits at 28–34 (cf. the longer account at *Padma Purāṇa* 5.44.40–110), but the whole sarga in its present form is a late, ornate production, with a very high proportion of long compounds and a high proportion of vṛddhied derivatives, one full-line simile and other figures of speech.[30]

3.40 (the golden deer) contains considerable use of *svabhāvokti* and *utprekṣā*, although in the main the style is regular. The language also is fairly normal, although there are two instances of irregular declension and extensive use of the historic present, but the proportion of long compounds is very high.[31] From

[25] See VS pp. 4 and 17, NS p. 409, FS p. 453, and RA p. 116.

[26] See VS p. 17 (also p. 20), NS pp. 405–6, SE p. 226, and RA pp. 115n. and 122. Cf. also van Daalen, op. cit., pp. 299–301, n. 17.

[27] See NS p. 394, and FS pp. 445, 451–2 and 457n.; cf. also RA pp. 114 and 118.

[28] See VS pp. 5, 24–5 and 27–9, NS pp. 380 and 394, FS pp. 442, 448, 450–1, 454–5, 457 and 459, *Syntax* pp. 349, 351 and 354, and RA pp. 110 and 118.

[29] See VS pp. 3 and 7, NS pp. 397, 403–4, 407 and 411, FS pp. 451 and 459, and RA pp. 119 and 126.

[30] See NS p. 397, FS pp. 451 and 455, and *Syntax* pp. 341, 350 and 352. Cf. also RA pp. 114, 120 and 126.

[31] See VS pp. 4, 7 and 20, and NS pp. 397 and 405–6.

its exceptional length one may suspect that the next sarga, 3.41, has been considerably inflated, but linguistic evidence is lacking.

3.44–5 (Sītā entertains the disguised Rāvaṇa and rejects his advances) both show high proportions of patronymics and other vṛddhied derivatives and high or very high proportions of similes. There are also certain unusual grammatical points. Parts of 3.44 are clearly later, and Sītā's tirade, as it now stands, seems to be a later ornate substitute (3.45.29–45), showing great elaboration of language and imagery.[32]

3.50 (Rāvaṇa resumes his flight with Sītā) also seems to have been elaborated, for it has high proportions of long compounds and of patronymics and other vṛddhied derivatives and a very high proportion of similes, among which three occupy a full line. There are also various further indications of lateness in its language and style.[33] There has quite possibly also been some expansion of the following two sargas.

3.53 (Rāvaṇa's wooing of Sītā). This and the following sarga are similar in content to 5.18–20, of which they may be anticipations. They show high proportions of long compounds and of vṛddhied derivatives, as well as many figures of speech (piling up of similes, hyperbole, *svabhāvokti*, *arthāntaranyāsa* and *lāṭānuprāsa*). Most striking, however, are the grammatical irregularities and anomalous use of cases.[34]

3.58 (Rāma's roaming through the forest in search of Sītā) shows unmistakable signs of being an insertion, by contrast with the relatively simple but dramatic language of sargas 55–7. Indeed, this sarga is not read by the mss. V1 and B1, nor did Gorresio include it in his edition. In form and content it is merely an expansion, for artistic motives, on the preceding sargas and there are borrowings from the Nala episode (Mbh. 3.50–78) in language and imagery. The very high proportion of long compounds and high proportion of similes are indicative of its artificial nature, as is also the string of *lāṭānuprāsa*; in addition there is the use of metaphor, *utprekṣā* and parallelism of construction, as well as several unusual features of the language.[35]

[32] See VS pp. 4–5, 7–8, 11 and 25–8, NS pp. 395, 401n., 405–6, 408 and 411–14, SE p. 223, FS pp. 442n., 447, 450–2, 454 and 457–8, *Proverbs* p. 146, and *Syntax* pp. 341, 347, 350, 352 and 354. The form of *–samṛddhinī*, in *sarvakāmasamṛddhinī* at 45.4d, is considered remarkable by van Daalen but attributed to Vālmīki on the grounds that it is read by all mss. (op. cit., pp. 114 and 130); however, the compound also occurs with rather less ms. support in the parallel passage at 5.31.13d—a point which van Daalen does not mention, though discussing the two passages elsewhere (pp. 209–14)— and is not uncommon in the Mahābhārata (2.19.22d, 5.132.27d, 9.37.7d and 14.137.15b), from which it may well have been borrowed here.

[33] See VS pp. 5 and 7, FS pp. 442, 454, 457 and n. and 459, *Syntax* pp. 353–4, and also RA p. 113.

[34] See VS pp. 5 and 26, NS pp. 405, 409 and 412, SE p. 220, and FS pp. 442, 451–2 and 457n. Cf. also RA p. 128. Several of these irregularities are read by all mss. and so are to be retained even by van Daalen's standards; in fact, he would link them with the occurrence of *apaśyatī* at 52.1 to indicate the lateness of 3.52–3 (op. cit., pp. 133–5 and 155–6, cf. also pp. 245–6).

[35] See VS pp. 2, 5 and 7–8, NS p. 397, SE p. 226, FS pp. 450 and 457, and *Syntax*

3.60 (Rāma's ravings at the loss of Sītā) is also an elaboration on the preceding sarga, showing a high proportion of vṛddhied derivatives and of long compounds, including one exceeding pāda length. There is also a much greater use of figures of speech, such as metaphor, hyperbole and *utprekṣā*, in addition to the piling up of similes at stanza 51 and use of cognates. Noteworthy features of the language include an unaugmented imperfect, a desiderative present participle, a geminated gerund, and a *bahuvrīhi* with a present participle as prior member.[36]

3.71 (the final sarga of the Araṇyakāṇḍa, in which Rāma and Lakṣmaṇa reach Pampā) seems also to be later, showing as it does a very high proportion of long compounds, including two exceeding pāda length, and the presence of other figures of speech. There are also several unusual items of language, including another unaugmented imperfect, and of vocabulary. As noted elsewhere, the beginnings and ends of books seem to have been especially subject to inflation and we may note the exceptional length of the first sarga of the Kiṣkindhākāṇḍa.[37] Also, the preceding sarga 3.70, which recounts the incident of their meeting with the Śabarī ascetic girl, may be a later insertion, as some of its vocabulary suggests (incidentally, it is not alluded to in the *Rāmopākhyāna*).

4.13 (Sugrīva's description to Rāma of the Saptajana hermitage) forms a sylvan interlude between the first and second combats of Vālin and Sugrīva and presumably it was inserted to provide such a relief of tension. Its language is quite ornate, with high proportions of long compounds and of vṛddhied derivatives, as well as several more elaborate figures of speech and several rare items of vocabulary.[38]

4.17–18 (Vālin reproaches Rāma for killing him by stealth and Rāma justifies his action) provide another clear instance of a passage interpolated or at least greatly expanded at a time when ethical justification for any of Rāma's acts that deviate at all from later ideals was felt necessary. The elaboration of the style shows clearly the lateness of the passage, which was noticed by Hopkins who remarks that '. . . a formal charge and defence is inserted (just the procedure in the Mahābhārata!) in chapters which metrically belong to the classical, so close is the adherence to vipulā rule.' Sarga 17 has a high proportion of similes and multiple similes are found in both sargas, which also contain metaphor, *parisaṃkhyā*, alliteration, *yamaka* and a proverb; stereotyped phrases are very frequent and several parallels with the Mahābhārata occur. Yet another attempt to justify Rāma's actions is made indirectly in 7.34, which narrates a previous

pp. 341, 344, 347 and 353. Cf. also van Daalen, op. cit., p. 207.

[36] See VS pp. 11 and 17, NS pp. 387, 394 and 404, FS pp. 450–1 and 457, and *Syntax* pp. 348n.23 and 353.

[37] See VS pp. 9 and 17, NS pp. 397 and 404, and FS p. 451. Note metrical shortening in *–vāluka–* at 16b; see also above, p. 53 and above on 2.108. On the unsatisfactory nature of the text, see also van Daalen, op. cit., pp. 207–8.

[38] See NS p. 375, SE p. 215, and FS p. 451; cf. also RA p. 120.

pact of brotherhood between Vālin and Rāvaṇa, made like Rāma's and Sugrīva's in the presence of fire.[39]

4.21 (Hanumān consoles Tāra) is absent from some Northern mss. and displaced in others, so on textual grounds alone its authenticity is doubtful. However, it also shows a high proportion of long compounds, play on words, hiatus between pādas and rare vocabulary.[40]

4.23–4 (Tārā's lament and grief at Vālin's funeral) are clearly elaborated, with sarga 23 virtually repeating the subject-matter of sarga 19; it may also be noted that 24.2–12 are omitted in several Northern mss. Sarga 23 has a high proportion of long compounds and also contains five full-line similes; two of the long compounds are common in the Mahābhārata but occur nowhere else in the Rāmāyaṇa. There also occur instances of the more elaborate figures of speech, hiatus between pādas and grammatically irregular forms.[41]

4.27–30 (Rāma describes the rainy season and Sugrīva is reminded of his promise of aid) are clearly shown to be late by the occurrence of lengthy passages in longer metres in the middle of these sargas; moreover, sargas 28–30 anticipate the subect-matter of sargas 31 and 32, where Hanumān reminds Sugrīva of his promise and Lakṣmaṇa goes to Kiṣkindhā for the same purpose. The elaborate nature of the style and the divergences of the language from the rest of the Rāmāyaṇa are extraordinary. The figures of speech found include instances of multiple similes and reverse similes, *svabhāvokti*, *utprekṣā*, *rūpaka* and *yathāsaṃkhya*, in addition to various *śabdālaṃkāras*, such as *pādāntayamaka*, juxtaposition and repetition of an initial element; stereotyped phrases also occur in abundance. The passage as a whole has a high proportion of long compounds, with a very high proportion in sargas 27 and 30. The most noteworthy features of the verbal forms occurring are three desideratives, two intensives and a periphrastic future. There is even an instance of *mā* with the augmented aorist.[42]

4.39–42 (the four search-parties sent out by Sugrīva) clearly include only a fractional amount of original material. The links of this geographical material with other texts have been noted by previous writers and are fully discussed

[39] Hopkins, *Great Epic*, p. 19n. See SE pp. 215 and 225–7, FS pp. 442, 447–8, 450, 452, 456–7 and 459, and *Proverbs* p. 147; cf. also VS p. 32, *Syntax* p. 348n.23, and RA pp. 118 and 125. Cf. also V. Raghavan, *Ramayana–Triveni*, Madras, 1970, p. 4 and A. Wurm, *Character–Portrayals in the Rāmāyaṇa of Vālmīki; a systematic representation*, Delhi, 1976, pp. 39–46.

[40] See NS p. 403.

[41] See VS pp. 8 and 30, NS pp. 401 and 415, and FS pp. 450 and 457n.; cf. also RA pp. 124–5 and 127, and SET III.

[42] See VS pp. 11, 15 and 32–3, NS pp. 397–8, FS pp. 442–3, 450–2, 456 and 458, and *Syntax* pp. 347n.18 and 348n.23. Other striking illustrations of the lateness of this passage are the mention of Kṛṣṇa, cf. RA p. 118, and the mention of brāhmans chanting *sāmans* (see p. 183). For H. Jacobi's rejection of several parts of this passage (along with 4.31, Hanumān's reminder, and 34, Tārā's pacification of Lakṣmaṇa) on the grounds of

above (pp. 113–5). Indications of the lateness of the passage may be seen in the extensive use of repetitions and personal epithets, the nature of the similes, references to Viṣṇu, the various anomalies of language and unusual forms, and the tolerance of hiatus. All the sargas are very long. Above all the extremely high proportion of long compounds indicates a late date for this material.[43] If these sargas are regarded as completely interpolated, then 4.46 recording the return of the three unsuccessful search-parties would also have to be regarded as later, but there is no linguistic evidence for this, although the sarga is very short. However, it is not improbable that the original contained a brief allusion to searches in all directions as well as to their return, such as is found in the *Rāmopākhyāna*.

4.49 (the entry of the Vānaras into the Ṛkṣabila) seems from the nature of its language and style to have suffered considerable later expansion, which has incorporated a certain amount of *svabhāvokti*, especially at stanzas 7–9, and also *utprekṣā*. The sarga also has a very high proportion of long compounds, many of which are clearly stereotyped; in addition, the number of stereotyped phrases found is very large and there are certain anomalies in the verbal forms.[44]

4.59–61 (the Niśākara episode). The most obviously anomalous part of this passage is the prophecy contained in sarga 61. Its style is positively puranic, devoid of long compounds and similes; however, the previous two sargas contain a reverse simile and other full-line similes, as well as a large number of unusual or irregular grammatical forms.[45] It may also be noted that Niśākara's prophecy alludes at 61.8 to an incident not found in the text—that where Indra goes to reassure Sītā in Laṅkā and to offer her divine food, relegated to 3 App.I.12.35–8. Sargas 60 and 61 are very short at 16 and 15 stanzas respectively, as too is the following sarga 62, which in many respects goes with this passage and has certainly had a rather chequered manuscript transmission.

4.65–6 (preparations for Hanumān's leap). These last two sargas of the Kiṣkindhākāṇḍa in reality form a preamble to the Sundarakāṇḍa. Both sargas have high proportions of vṛddhied derivatives and sarga 66 also has a very high proportion of long compounds. Between them they contain numerous figures of speech, full-line similes, multiple similes, hyperbole, *utprekṣā* and alliteration, as well as unusual verbal forms, among them the rare future imperative.[46] There are signs that the inflation observable here had already begun in sarga 64.

repetition see 'Ein Beitrag zur Rāmāyaṇakritik', ZDMG 51, 1897, pp. 605–22; cf. also van Daalen's arguments for the lateness of 4.29 (op. cit., pp. 185–6).

[43] See VS pp. 6–9, NS pp. 397–8, 400–1 and 414, RA p. 116, and *Syntax*, p. 348 and n.23.

[44] See VS pp. 6, 8 and 17, NS pp. 398 and 401n., and FS p. 451.

[45] See VS pp. 17, 30 and 33, and FS p. 443; cf. also RA p. 120. On this and the next passage see also van Daalen (op. cit., pp. 134–5 and 175–7), who regards all the latter part of the Kiṣkindhākāṇḍa from sarga 53 as either interpolated or reworked, being possibly the work of a Hanumān poet.

[46] See VS pp. 2, 5, 15 and 33, NS p. 398, and FS pp. 442n., 451 and 458; cf. also RA pp.

5.1–8 (Hanumān's leap and his exploration of Laṅkā) have clearly been expanded and elaborated on over the centuries. It may be noted that the Introduction to the Critical Edition (pp. XXXII–XXXIII) accepts that the Surasā episode of sarga 1 is a later addition. The extraordinary length of sarga 1, along with the only slightly less lengthy sargas 2, 7 and 8, suggests that some of this expansion was quite late, an impression which is confirmed by the fact that sargas 4 and 6 are written entirely in longer metres (predominantly *triṣṭubh*) and that sarga 4 is rhymed throughout—a quite exceptional phenomenon. The passage as a whole shows very high proportions of long compounds and of similes; sargas 3 and 6 have a high proportion of vṛddhied derivatives; 8 of the long compounds exceed pāda length and there are full-line similes in most of the sargas. In addition there are a few irregular forms, an abundance of figures of speech of all types, and a large number of unusual items of vocabulary.[47]

5.12–17 (Hanumān discovers Sītā and secretly observes Rāvaṇa's approach) is the next significantly elaborated passage in what is in general a rather ornate book (as its name may well imply). There are high or very high proportions of long compounds and of similes in all of these sargas, as well as full-line similes and three long compounds exceeding pāda length. The language is in general regular, but there are four desiderative forms in sargas 14–16 and an intensive form in 12, as well as the form *prāptavat* at 14.11d. The more elaborate figures of speech and rare items of vocabulary are also frequent. Jacobi long ago drew attention to the large number of similes in sarga 17, while Bulcke has suggested that sarga 14 is a late interpolation, largely on the grounds of its mentioning Sītā's miraculous birth.[48] Sarga 11, which immediately precedes this group, is, like sargas 12 and 13, very long, and it too should perhaps be regarded as inflated, though not betraying it quite so obviously in language.

5.26–7 (Sītā's renewed lamentations followed by auspicious omens). These two sargas are entirely in longer metres (*triṣṭubh*, with one *vaṃśastha*) and sarga 27 is very short. There are high proportions of long compounds and very high proportions of similes in each, with two of the similes in each extending beyond one pāda, as well as a periphrasis for a case relationship.[49] Also, sarga 26 reverts to Sītā's grief very awkwardly after the encouragement of Trijaṭā's dream in 25. It may further be noted, with regard to the length of sarga 27, that

116 and 119n. A contrary opinion is expressed by A. Wurm (op. cit., pp. 102–6), who nonetheless admits inconsistencies here in the portrayal of Hanumān; unfortunately, the companion work to which he refers for detailed arguments has not, so far as I am aware, yet appeared.

[47] See VS pp. 2–3, 21 and 26, NS pp. 398 and 413, FS pp. 447, 456–7 and 459n., and RA pp. 115–6, 119, 121, 124 and 127; cf. *Proverbs* pp. 142 and 148.

[48] See VS pp. 3 and 21–2, NS p. 398, and FS pp. 455, 456n. and 457n., cf. also SE p. 227, RA pp. 112, 120–1, 125 and 128, and *Proverbs* p. 148. See also Jacobi, *Das Râmâyaṇa*, p. 120 (where II 19 is a misprint for V 19), and C. Bulcke, 'La naissance de Sītā', BEFEO 46, 1952, pp. 107–17.

[49] See NS p. 398, also RA p. 127.

most NE. mss. read sarga 30 (the only other sarga in the whole text as short as 8 verses) continuously with sarga 29; since 6 of its 8 stanzas are in longer metres, it is obviously simply a colophon to sarga 29 and presumably of later date.

5.33–7 (Hanumān's conversation with Sītā) have clearly been subject to considerable elaboration, of which there are probably traces in the two preceding sargas also. In particular 32.5–12 seems superfluous and is omitted by most NE. mss. Sarga 37 is in fact omitted by all NE. mss. (except Ñ1) and so is suspect on textual grounds alone, quite apart from the extensive repetition of material between it and sargas 54 and 66 (as also between sargas 36.22–6 and 65.7–12). There is a high proportion of patronymics and other vṛddhied derivatives in sarga 37, while sarga 35 has a high proportion of similes, with three full-line similes in sargas 34–5. Sarga 33 contains seven agent nouns, there are four desiderative forms in the passage and an intensive. The sargas are all unusually long—indeed, all except 34 are very long. The language, style and vocabulary all suggest a late date and the religious pattern is definitely that of a later period.[50]

5.43 (Hanumān slays the sons of Rāvaṇa's ministers) is very short; presumably the entire sarga was interpolated in order to enhance Hanumān's prowess after the form of the surrounding sargas was fixed. It contains a very high proportion of long compounds, a high proportion of similes including one full-line simile, and a desiderative form, as well as instances of transfer of verbal stem and of metaphor.[51]

5.45–7 (Hanumān displays his prowess in killing Akṣa, then allows himself to be captured by Indrajit and led before Rāvaṇa). All three sargas reveal their elaboration in a high or very high proportion of long compounds. In addition, sarga 45 is entirely in *vaṃśastha* metre and *triṣṭubh* or *vaṃśastha* verses are interspersed throughout sarga 46, while there are very high proportions of similes in sargas 45 and 47. It is almost superfluous to mention that several other figures of speech occur, as well as certain late items of morphology and vocabulary.[52]

5.54–8 (Hanumān meets Sītā again, returns across the sea to his companions, tells them his experiences and praises Sītā; Aṅgada then puts forward his ideas). These sargas have all been extensively interpolated or expanded. In fact sarga 56 lengthily anticipates sargas 65–6, in which Hanumān narrates his experiences and Sītā's message to Rāma, and are themselves quite possibly expanded; sarga 56 is the second longest sarga in the whole Rāmāyaṇa and yet Hanumān goes over his meeting with Sītā again more briefly in sarga 57. There are very high proportions of long compounds in sargas 54, 55 and 57, including three exceeding pāda length, and a high proportion of patronymics and other vṛddhied derivatives in 58. These sargas also contain several desiderative and

[50] See VS p. 30, NS p. 394, FS pp. 457nn. and 458n., RA pp. 115n., 116, 118, 126 and 128, and *Proverbs* p. 148. Cf. also Jacobi, op. cit., pp. 17–23 and 31–42, and van Daalen, op. cit., pp. 141–2.

[51] See VS p. 6 and FS p. 450.

[52] See VS p. 3, NS p. 398, and FS pp. 447 and 456n.

intensive forms, a periphrastic future and other verbal anomalies, several of the more elaborate figures of speech, and some less common items of vocabulary.[53]

6.4–5 (the muster of the Vānara army, and Rāma's despondency). In the Yuddhakāṇḍa some of the most obviously expanded portions are the descriptions of combat, but other passages, such as these two sargas, have also been inflated. Sarga 4 is very long (89 verses); its most obvious feature, despite its subject-matter, is the presence of numerous figures of speech, including elaborate similes. Sarga 5 may be compared in subject-matter to 2.47 and 3.60; it has high proportions of long compounds and of similes, as well as two full-line similes. Other features of this passage include two desiderative forms, two variants on standard personal epithets and two Mahābhārata stock pādas.[54]

6.23–4 (Sītā's lament and consolation by Saramā) seem to anticipate Sītā's lament and consolation by Trijaṭā in sarga 38 and are therefore superfluous. Indications of lateness are the occurrence of two intensive forms in 23, a high proportion of patronymics and other vṛddhied derivatives in 24, and full-line similes, other figures of speech and rare vocabulary in both. Bulcke regards the preceding sarga 22, the episode of the illusory head of Rāma, similarly as an anticipation of the illusory death of Sītā in sarga 68, but, while it may be correct, there is no linguistic or stylistic evidence to confirm it.[55]

6.30–1 (descriptions of the city of Laṅkā and of the start of the siege). Sarga 31 is very long, which in itself suggests much expansion at a late date. However, in addition, sarga 30 is marked by a high proportion of long compounds, including one exceeding pāda length, full-line similes and other figures of speech, especially *svabhāvokti*, while sarga 31 contains a high proportion of similes, including a full-line simile, two desiderative forms and two periphrastic futures, besides several exact parallels in wording with other parts of the Rāmāyaṇa.[56]

6.46–8 (Nīla slays Prahasta, Rāma spares Rāvaṇa, and the Rākṣasas in desperation rouse Kumbhakarṇa) are all of exceptional length and elaboration of language and style. There is a high or very high proportion of long compounds in each; sarga 46 contains six full-line similes and sargas 47–8 have a high proportion of similes; there are also several desiderative forms and an intensive. Sarga 47 contains *triṣṭubh* stanzas interspersed throughout its *ślokas*—a definite

[53] See VS pp. 3, 6 and 33, and NS pp. 399 and 403; cf. also RA pp. 115 and 128. See also Jacobi, op. cit., pp. 17–23 and 31–42, H.-R. Diwekar, *Les Fleurs de Rhétorique dans l'Inde*, Paris, 1930, p. 49, J. Gonda, *Stylistic Repetition in the Veda*, Amsterdam, 1959, p. 218, and van Daalen, op. cit., pp. 143 and 158–60.

[54] See SE pp. 212–3; cf. also RA p. 121, VS p. 2 and SET III.

[55] C. Bulcke, *Rām-kathā* (*utpatti aur vikāś*), 2nd ed., Prayāg, 1962, pp. 142–4. See VS p. 33, SE p. 212, FS pp. 456n. and 448, and *Syntax* p. 353n.33; cf. also RA pp. 116–17 and 126.

[56] See VS pp. 2–3, SE pp. 215 and 220, and FS p. 456 n.; cf. also RA pp. 117, 120 and 128.

mark of lateness—and, despite its subject-matter, is not attested in the *Rāmopākhyāna* or in the Bālakāṇḍa summaries. The number of references to Viṣṇu in this sarga is also noteworthy.[57] There is some evidence from vocabulary and subject-matter that this elaboration was continued in the next sarga, 6.49, but other indications of lateness are lacking, apart from two separate *triṣṭubh* stanzas within the sarga.

6.53 and 55 (Kumbhakarṇa's entry to the fray and death) are again ornate, shown particularly clearly by comparison with the much simpler style of the intervening sarga 54, which describes the havoc Kumbhakarṇa causes among the Vānaras; the contrast in length is also instructive, for 53 and 55 are both very long. Sarga 55 is still further increased in length by the longer verses occurring at intervals, one of which contains a periphrastic future. Both contain a high or very high proportion of long compounds and a very high proportion of similes, with one compound exceeding pāda length and four full-line similes. There are also several pādas that are stereotyped in the Mahābhārata but occur only here in the Rāmāyaṇa, apart from one found also in sarga 63.[58]

6.57–63 (the death of other Rākṣasa chiefs, Indrajit's immobilisation of the Vānaras and Hanumān's fetching magic herbs to revive them, the burning of Laṅkā, and the death of Kumbha) is another section of the battle which has been much inflated. All these sargas are also very long and contain high or very high proportions of long compounds or of similes or of both; no less than seven of the long compounds exceed the pāda. Again, several stereotyped pādas from the Mahābhārata are found. The frequent occurrence of Viṣṇu and Śiva is only one mark of the generally late religious pattern evident.[59]

6.70–3 (Lakṣmaṇa's tirade on the inefficacy of dharma and the value of *artha*, Vibhīṣaṇa's deliberately repeated warning about Indrajit's sacrifice, and Lakṣmaṇa's departure to interrupt it). None of this is attested by the Bālakāṇḍa summaries or the *Rāmopākhyāna*, but some proverbial matter at 70.31–2, 34 and 37–8 is paralleled in Mbh. 12.8.16 and 18–21, which was possibly its source. The passage contains two intensive forms and seven desideratives and high proportions of similes in sargas 71 and 73, of patronymics and other vṛddhied derivatives in 71 and 72, and of long compounds in 73, as well as other features.[60]

6.79–82 (Lakṣmaṇa's cure from his wounds, Rāvaṇa's mourning, Rāma's exploits, and the laments of the Rākṣasīs). The Rākṣasīs' laments are not in any way necessary to the story and include some retelling of events found early in the Araṇyakāṇḍa. Indicators of lateness include a high proportion of patronymics and other vṛddhied derivatives in 79 and a very high proportion of similes in 81, a refrain at 82.13 and 15–18 (which is in fact a Mahābhārata stock pāda), and in the passage as a whole three desideratives, a periphrastic future,

57 See VS p. 34, FS p. 458n., and RA p. 117 (also p. 114n.).
58 See FS pp. 451 and 457, RA pp. 114, 117 and 121, and SET III.
59 See FS p. 457n., SET III, and RA pp. 112–14, 117, 119–20 and 127–8.
60 See *Syntax* p. 353n.33, RA pp. 112, 120 and 128, and *Proverbs* p. 149.

eight full-line similes and other figures of speech, frequent geminated words, and several mentions of Viṣṇu and Śiva.[61] It may also be noted that sarga 80 is very long, as also is the sarga preceding this passage, sarga 78, which may therefore mark the beginning of this inflated section.

6.87 and 90–1 (the second encounter between Rāma and Rāvaṇa, culminating in Rāma again sparing Rāvaṇa). The motive for expansion here, as for the interpolation of sarga 47, was presumably to emphasise Rāma's chivalry. The style is much elaborated. Sarga 87 shows a high proportion of long compounds and a very high proportion of similes, including three full-line similes, as well as an intensive form and other unusual grammatical features, elaborate figures of speech, and rare vocabulary. Sargas 90–1 both have high proportions of long compounds and of patronymics and other vṛddhied derivatives and there is also a high proportion of similes in 91, in addition to unusual vocabulary in both.[62] Very probably there has been a certain amount of later inflation throughout sargas 87–91 and in this connection we may note that, while sarga 87 is long, sarga 88 is very long.

6.102–4 (Sītā appears before the victorious Rāma, is repudiated and undergoes the ordeal by fire) betray their later date rather by their subject-matter and vocabulary than by their style. However, it may be noted that there are high proportions of patronymics and other vṛddhied derivatives in sargas 102 and 104 and three full-line similes in 103 (also one in 102).[63]

6.105–7 (Rāma's divinity and identity with Viṣṇu are revealed to him, Sītā is restored to him, and his father Daśaratha appears from heaven to congratulate him). While these sargas possess such stylistic features as a high proportion of patronymics and other vṛddhied derivatives in all, a high proportion of similes in 106, and four desiderative forms in 107 to indicate their lateness, it is obviously their subject-matter which is most clearly at variance with the bulk of the Rāmāyaṇa.[64]

6.111–16 (the return to Ayodhyā). The last few sargas of the Yuddhakāṇḍa—originally the conclusion of the whole epic—have naturally been embroidered on in transmission, with the last two sargas in particular growing to exceptional length. In this passage is described the return to Ayodhyā: first a description of the places passed over (which provides a kind of recapitulation in reverse of the events of the story), next meetings with Bharadvāja and then Bharata, the climax in Rāma's coronation and finale in his perfect rule. There is a high proportion of

[61] See *Syntax* p. 353n.30, RA pp. 115 and 117, and SET III.

[62] See SE p. 215, FS pp. 447 and 459, and RA pp. 112, 117 and 120.

[63] Cf. my 'Rāmo dharmabhṛtāṃ varaḥ', IT 5, 1977, pp. 55–68, esp. p. 64, *Proverbs* p. 150 and Nilmadhav Sen, 'The Fire-Ordeal of Sītā—A later interpolation in the Rāmāyaṇa?', JOIB 1, 1952, pp. 201–6; also G. H. Bhatt, 'The Fire-Ordeal of Sītā—An interpolation in the Vālmīki Rāmāyaṇa', JOIB 5, 1955–6, p. 292, and van Daalen, op. cit., pp. 190–1, who concludes that '6,99—6,106 is an interpolated passage (or partly interpolated, partly reworked).'

[64] See RA pp. 117–18 and 123, also 114, 119 and 127, and my 'Rāmo dharmabhṛtāṃ varaḥ', IT 5, 1977, pp. 55–68, esp. pp. 66–7.

patronymics and other vṛddhied derivatives in most of these sargas and most contain full-line or even more complex similes and other figures of speech. The concluding passage on Rāma's righteous rule must have been an especial favourite since it is reproduced *in extenso* in the retellings of the story in the Mahābhārata (Mbh. 12.29.47–54, 2 App.21.547–74, 7 App.8.470–7, and *Harivaṃśa* 31.128–38).[65] In reality there are some signs of expansion throughout the last part of the Yuddhakāṇḍa, from sarga 99 onwards.

[65] See FS pp. 443 and 445, RA pp. 125–7, *Proverbs* p. 148, and 'Sanskrit Epic Tradition II. The Avatāra Accounts of Rāma', to be published in the proceedings of the Fourth World Sanskrit Conference, Weimar, 1979, by Akademie-Verlag, Berlin.

BIBLIOGRAPHY

of frequently cited works

J. L. Brockington, 'The Verbal System of the Rāmāyaṇa', JOIB 19, 1969–70, pp. 1–34. (Abbreviation: VS)

'The Nominal System of the Rāmāyaṇa', JOIB 19, 1969–70, pp. 369–415. (NS)

'Stereotyped Expressions in the Rāmāyaṇa', JAOS 90, 1970, pp. 210–27. (SE)

'Religious Attitudes in Vālmīki's *Rāmāyaṇa*', JRAS, 1976, pp. 108–29. (RA)

'Figures of Speech in the Rāmāyaṇa', JAOS 97, 1977, pp. 441–59. (FS)

'Vālmīki's Proverbs', IT 7, 1979, pp. 139–50. (*Proverbs*)

'Sanskrit Epic Tradition III. Fashions in Formulae', paper presented at the Fifth World Sanskrit Conference, Varanasi, 1981. (SET III)

'The Syntax of the Rāmāyaṇa', JOIB 31, 1982, pp. 340–54. (*Syntax*)

L. A. van Daalen, *Vālmīki's Sanskrit*, Leiden, 1980. (*Vālmīki's Sanskrit*)

A. Gail, *Paraśurāma, Brahmane und Krieger*, Wiesbaden, 1977. (*Paraśurāma*)

J. Gonda, *Aspects of Early Viṣṇuism*, Utrecht, 1954 (repr. Delhi, 1969). (*Early Viṣṇuism*)

P. A. Grintser, *Drevneindijskij epos, genezis i tipologija*, Moskva, 1974. (*Epos*)

E. W. Hopkins, 'The Social and Military Position of the Ruling Caste in Ancient India as represented by the Sanskrit Epic', JAOS 13, 1889, pp. 57–329. (*Ruling Caste*)

The Great Epic of India, New York, 1901. (*Great Epic*)

H. Jacobi, *Das Râmâyaṇa: Geschichte und Inhalt nebst Concordanz der gedruckten Recensionen*, Bonn, 1893 (repr. Darmstadt, 1970). (*Das Râmâyaṇa*)

S. D. Singh, *Ancient Indian Warfare with special reference to the Vedic period*, Leiden, 1965. (*Warfare*)

R. Söhnen, *Untersuchungen zur Komposition von Reden und Gesprächen im Rāmāyaṇa*, 2 vols. (Studien zur Indologie und Iranistik 6), Reinbek, 1979. (*Reden*)

INDEX

Ancient Texts and Authors

Abhinanda, *Rāmacarita*, 245, 251
Abhinava Pampa (pseudonym for Nāgacandra), *Pampa Rāmāyaṇa* (Kannaḍa), 267 n.19, 272–4, 291 n.55, 297, 303
Abhinavarāghava, see Bhīmaṭa
Abhiṣekanāṭaka, see Bhāsa
Adbhutadarpaṇa, see Mahādeva
Adbhuta Rāmāyaṇa (*or Adbhutottarakāṇḍa*), 253, 255–6, 259, 279
Adbhut Rāmāyaṇ, see Nityānanda Ācārya
Adhyātma Rāmāyaṇa, 92 n.8, 237 n.21, 238 n.23, 252–4, 256 n.57, 257–9, 274–6, 278–86, 295 n.65, 302 n.76, 316, 326
Agastyasaṃhitā, 259, 315 n.7
Agni Purāṇa, 239, 326
Aitareya Brāhmaṇa, 67
Ānanda Rāmāyaṇa, 238 n.22, 253, 254 n.52, 256–7, 271 n.25, 278, 291, 293 n.58, 300–2
Anargharāghava, see Murāri
Appaya Dīkṣita, 248 n.42
Ārṣarāmāyaṇa, see Yogavāsiṣṭha Rāmāyaṇa
Arthaśāstra, see Kauṭilya
Āścaryacūḍāmaṇi, see Śaktibhadra
Assamese versions, 278–9
Aśvaghoṣa, *Buddhacarita*, 262, 312 n.3, 314
Attiyatuma Rāmāyaṇam, see Eẓuttaccan
Aung Phyo, U, *Rama Thagyin*, 304–5

Bālarāmāyaṇa, see Rājaśekhara
Balarāmdās, *Jagamohana Rāmāyaṇa* (Oriya), 271 n.25, 279
Ballāla Sena, *Dānasāgara*, 233
Bāṇa, *Harṣacarita*, 217 n.35
Battatīśvara, *Rāmāyaṇa* (Kannaḍa), 274
Bengali versions, 256, 276–8, 300–1, 303
Bhadreśvara, *Kahāvalī* (Jain), 257, 266 n.16, 268, 278
Bhagavadgītā, 211 n.28, 222, 251 n.50, 254
Bhāgavata Purāṇa, 240, 252–3, 257–9, 279–80, 282–3, 326
Bhālaṇa, *Rāmabālacarita* and *Rāmaviraha* (Gujarātī), 285
Bharata, *Nāṭyaśāstra*, 190–2, 315
Bhāsa, 312, 314, 325; *Abhiṣekanāṭaka*, 242–3, 291 n.55; *Pratimānāṭaka*, 242, 273
Bhāskara, *Unmattarāghava*, 248 n.41
Bhāskara, Hulakki, *Bhāskara Rāmāyaṇa* (Telugu), 276
Bhaṭṭabhīma, *see* Bhaumaka
Bhaṭṭi, *Rāvaṇavadha* (*or Bhaṭṭikāvya*), 57 n.81, 92 n.8, 244–5, 287–8, 312, 314, 316
Bhaumaka (*or* Bhaṭṭabhīma), *Rāvaṇārjunīya*, 244 n.33
Bhavabhūti, 249, 316, 324; *Mahāvīracarita*, 246, 248, 256; *Uttararāmacarita*, 179 n.23, 235, 246–8, 298, 300 n.73
Bhāvartha Rāmāyaṇa, see Ekanātha
Bhaviṣya Purāṇa, 238 n.22
Bhaviṣyottara Purāṇa, 217 n.35
Bhīmaṭa, *Abhinavarāghava*, 248 n.41
Bhoja, *Campūrāmāyaṇa*, 249
Bhojpurī folk tales, 238 n.23
Bhuśuṇḍi Rāmāyaṇa, 252–3, 256–8, 279–80, 282, 284, 286, 295 n.65, 300, 302, 304, 326
Brāhmaṇas, 9, 25, 208, 307; *see also individual titles*
Brahmāṇḍa Purāṇa, 57, 217 n.35, 252, 259, 316
Brahma Purāṇa, 112, 240–1, 259
Brahmavaivarta Purāṇa, 235 n.14, 237, 240, 253, 258
Bṛhaddharma Purāṇa, 238 n.22, 241
Bṛhatkathā, see Guṇāḍhya
Bṛhatkathāmañjarī, see Kṣemendra
Buddhacarita, see Aśvaghoṣa
Burmese versions, 299 n.72, 300, 304–5

Cakrakavi, *Jānakīpariṇaya*, 245
Campūrāmāyaṇa, see Bhoja

Cand Bārdāī, *Pṛthvīrājarāso* (Hindī), 279 n.36
Candrāvatī (Bengali), 276, 278, 286, 295 n.65
Carīt Rāmāyaṇa (Javanese), 288
Caüpannamahāpurisacariya, see Śīlācārya
Chalitarāma, 235 n.17
Chāndogya Upaniṣad, 9, 309 n.2
Chi-chia-yeh, *Tsa-pao-tsang-ching* (Chinese), 263
Chinese versions, 262–4

Dānasāgara, see Ballāla Sena
Dasaratha Jātaka, 260–1, 268 n.20, 299 n.71, 305
Dattilam, 190, 315
Devībhāgavata Purāṇa, 234 n.14, 237, 241
Devīmāhātmya, 256
Dhaneśvara, *Śatruñjayamāhātmya*, 266 n.16
Dharmakhaṇḍa, 259
dharmaśāstra literature, 44, 175 n.18, 217, 232–3
Dhīranāga (*or* Vīranāga, *or* Diṅnāga), *Kundamālā*, 247, 249 n.44
Dīgha Nikāya, 261
Diṅnāga, *see* Dhīranāga
Divākara Prakāśa Bhaṭṭa (Kāśmīrī), 265 n.13, 285–6
Durgāvara, *Gīti Rāmāyaṇa* (Assamese), 279
Dūtāṅgada, see Subhaṭa
Dvija Madhukantha (Bengali), 276

Ekanātha, *Bhāvārtha Rāmāyaṇa* (Marāṭhī), 271 n.25, 284–5
Eẓuttaccan (Malayāḷam), 327; *Attiyatuma Rāmāyaṇam*, 274–6; *Uttararāmāyaṇam*, 274

Garuḍa Purāṇa, 237
Gāyatrī, 217
Girdhar (Gujarātī), 285
Gītagovinda, see Jayadeva
Gīti Rāmāyaṇa, see Durgāvara
Gobhila Gṛhyasūtra, 183
Gobhilasmṛti, 173 n.16, 233, 314
Govindarāja, commentary, 217, 271 n.25
Gṛhyasūtras, 79; *see also individual titles*
Gujarātī versions, 285, 296 n.66
Guṇabhadra, *Uttarapurāṇa* (Jain), 92 n.8, 256–7, 266, 268, 272, 312
Guṇāḍhya, *Bṛhatkathā*, 265 n.13, 266
Gvāy Dvóṟaḥbī (Lao), 298 n.70

Hanumannāṭaka (*or Mahānāṭaka*), 238 n.22, 246 n.38, 248–50, 252–3, 277, 280–1, 283, 285
Haribhadrasūri, *Upadeśapada*, 268 n.21
Haribhaṭṭajātakamālā, 261 n.3
Harimāhātmyadarpaṇa, 259
Harivaṃśa, 57, 59 n.88, 80 n.12, 113 nn.40, 43, 229–30, 231 n.6, 233–4, 240, 314, 323, 326, 346
Harivara Vipra, *Lavakuśaryuddha*, 235 n.17
Harṣacarita, see Bāṇa
Hemacandra (Jain), 257, 267 n.18, 278; *Triṣaṣṭiśalākāpuruṣacarita*, 266 n.16, 268–9; *Yogaśāstrasvopajñavṛtti*, 266 n.16
Ḥikāyat Mahārāja Rāvana (Malay), 306
Ḥikāyat Srī Rāma (Malay), 278 n.34, 288, 294–8
Hindī versions, 279–84, 301
Hiraṇyagarbhasaṃhitā, 259
Hobutsushū, see Tairano Yasuyori
Homer, *Iliad* and *Odyssey*, 11, 69, 309
Hsüan-tsang, Chinese translation of *Mahāvibhāṣa*, 262

Iliad, see Homer
Irāmāvatāram, see Kampaṉ
Itihāsasamuccaya, 259

Jagamohana Rāmāyaṇa, see Balarāmdās
Jaimini Bhārata, 235 n.17
Jaiminīya Brāhmaṇa, 19, 205 n.18
Jain versions, 256, 266–9, 279 n.36, 327
Jānakīharaṇa, see Kumāradāsa
Jānakīmaṅgal, see Tulsīdās
Jānakīpariṇaya, see Cakrakavi *or* Rāmabhadra Dīkṣita
Jānakīrāghava, 249 n.43
Japanese versions, 263–4
Javanese versions, 269, 271 n.25, 287–9, 299–300, 303
Jayaddissa Jātaka, 261 n.3
Jayadeva, *Gītagovinda*, 257

Jayadeva, *Prasannarāghava*, 246 n.38, 248 n.41, 249–50, 280–1, 283
Jñānadīpika, see Tulsīdās
Jñānavāsiṣṭha, see Yogavāsiṣṭha Rāmāyaṇa

Kahāvalī, see Bhadreśvara
Kālidāsa, *Kumārasaṃbhava*, 243; *Raghuvaṃśa*, 59, 162 n.10, 235, 240, 243–4, 248 n.41, 249 nn.44, 46, 252, 270, 312, 314–15, 325, 333 n.16
Kālikā Purāṇa, 241
Kalki Purāṇa, 240 n.26
Kampaṉ, *Irāmāvatāram* (Tamil), 92 n.8, 220 n.39, 256, 269–72, 274, 276, 287, 292 n.57, 293 n.58, 302, 316, 327
K'ang-seng-hui, *Liu-tu-tsi-ching* (Chinese), 262, 264, 304
Kānho Trimaladāsa, *Pātāḷakāṇḍa Rāmāyaṇa* (Marāṭhī), 285
Kannaḍa versions, 272–5
Kaṇṇaśśa Rāmāyaṇam, see Rāma Paṇikkar
Kāśmīrī version, 285–6; *see also* Divākara Prakāśa Bhaṭṭa
Kathāsaritsāgara, see Somadeva
Kātyāyana, *Vārtikas* on Pāṇini, 27, 308
Kauṭilya, *Arthaśāstra*, 63, 86 n.19, 99, 128, 131, 133, 135, 138 n.19, 142 n.27, 145 n.32
Kavicandra (Bengali), 276–7
Kavirāja, *Rāghavapāṇḍavīya*, 249 n.46
Khmer versions, 255 n.55, 256, 259, 273 n.28, 277 n.33, 289–94, 299–301, 304, 327; *see also Rāmakerti I and II*
Khotanese version, 180 n.24, 257–9, 264–5, 283 n.43, 286, 300, 303 n.77, 305, 312, 316
Kṛṣṇadāsa, *Puṇyacandrodayapurāṇa* (Jain), 266 n.16
Kṛṣṇadāsa Loḷyā (Marāṭhī), 285
Kṛṣṇakarṇāmṛta, see Līlāśuka
Kṛttibās (Bengali), *Rāmāyaṇ*, 238 n.22, 248, 268, 276–8, 290 n.53, 297 n.69, 300, 302 n.75, 305, 327; *Śivarāmer Yuddha*, 277
Kṛtyarāvaṇa, 254 n.52
Kṣemendra, 316; *Bṛhatkathāmañjarī*, 266 n.17; *Rāmāyaṇamañjarī*, 249 n.46
Kumāradāsa, *Jānakīharaṇa*, 243–5, 316
Kumārasaṃbhava, see Kālidāsa
Kumāra Vālmīki, *see* Narahari
Kundamālā, see Dhīranāga
Kūrma Purāṇa, 237, 240, 253, 258–9, 327
Kusa Jātaka, 261 n.4

Lalitavistara, 262 n.6
Laṅkāvatāra Sūtra, 275 n.30
Lao versions, 298–301, 303–4; *see also Phra Lak Phra Lam*
Lavakuśaryuddha, see Harivara Vipra
Lāvaṇyasamaya, *Rāvaṇamandodarīsaṃvāda* (Gujarātī), 285
Līlāśuka, *Kṛṣṇakarṇāmṛta*, 257
Liu-tu-tsi-ching, see K'ang-seng-hui
Lpoek Aṅgar Vatt (Khmer), 289

Mādhava (Marāṭhī), 285
Mādhavadeva (Assamese), 279
Mādhava Kandali (Assamese), 278–9
Mahābhāgavata Purāṇa, 238 n.22, 241
Mahābhārata, 226–32, 308–11 *et passim*; *see also Bhagavadgītā, Harivaṃśa, Nalopākhyāna, Rāmopākhyāna* and *Śakuntalopākhyāna*
Mahādeva, *Adbhutadarpaṇa*, 250 n.47
Mahānāṭaka, see Hanumannāṭaka
Mahāpurāṇa, see Puṣpadanta
Maharadia Lawana (Philippino), 305–6
Mahārāmāyaṇa, see Yogavāsiṣṭha Rāmāyaṇa
Mahāvaṃsa, 295
Mahāvastu, 261 n.3, 262 n.6, 264
Mahāvibhāṣa, 262
Mahāvīracarita, see Bhavabhūti
Malay versions, 238 n.23, 256–9, 273 n.27, 278, 291 n.55, 293–303, 305, 316, 327, 333 n.16; *see also Ḥikāyat Srī Rāma*
Malayāḷam versions, 274–6
Mantra Rāmāyaṇas, see Moropanta
Manusmṛti, 63, 82 n.14, 125, 128 n.4, 129, 131, 156 n.4, 174, 206 n.20, 211, 217
Maranaw version (*Maharadia Lawana*), 305–6
Marāṭhī versions, 284–5
Matsya Purāṇa, 113–14, 234
Māyurāja, *Uddāttarāghava*, 248
Minamotono Tamenori, *Sambo-ekotoba* (Japanese), 264
Mollā Rāmāyaṇa (Telugu), 276

Mongolian versions, 266
Moropanta, *Mantra Rāmāyaṇas* (Marāṭhī), 285
Mukteśvara, *Saṃkṣepa Rāmāyaṇa* (Marāṭhī), 285
Murāri, *Anargharāghava*, 246–9, 277, 297

Nāgacandra, *see* Abhinava Pampa
Nalopākhyāna, 27 n.17, 231–2, 310, 337
Nāradīya Purāṇa, 236–7
Nāradīyā Śikṣā Sāmavedīyā, 190 n.34
Narahari *alias* Kumāra Vālmīki, *Torave Rāmāyaṇa* (Kannaḍa), 267 n.19, 274, 277 n.33
Narasiṃha Purāṇa, 240–1, 297 n.67
Nāṭyadarpaṇa, 254 n.52
Nāṭyaśāstra, see Bharata
Nīlakaṇṭha Dīkṣita, 248 n.42
Nirukta, see Yāska
Nityānanda Ācārya, *Adbhut Rāmāyaṇ* (Bengali), 276, 278, 301 n.75

Odyssey, see Homer
Oriya version, 279; *see also* Balarāmdas, *Jagamohana Rāmāyaṇa*

Padma Purāṇa, 56, 235, 237–8, 252, 258–9, 280, 294 n.62, 298, 316, 324–5, 336
Padmapurāṇa of Raviṣeṇa, *see* Raviṣeṇa
Pampa Rāmāyaṇa, see Abhinava Pampa
Pañcadaśī, see Vidyāraṇya
Pañcatantra, 87
Pañcaviṃśa Brāhmaṇa, 205 n.18
Pāṇini, *Aṣṭādhyāyī*, 16, 18 n.4, 19–21, 24–7, 46, 55, 308
Pañjābī versions, 296 n.66
Pārvatīmaṅgal, see Tulsīdās
Pātāḷakāṇḍa Rāmāyaṇa, see Kānho Trimaladāsa
Pātāla Rāvaṇa, see Vīra Kerala Varma
Patañjali, 308
Paümacariü, see Svayambhū
Paümacariya, see Vimalasūri
Philippino version (*Maharadia Lawana*), 305–6
Phra Lak Phra Lam (Lao) 298–302, 304
Pliny, *Naturalis Historia*, 86 n.19
Prasannarāghava, see Jayadeva
Pratimānāṭaka, see Bhāsa
Pravarasena, *Setubandha* (or *Rāvaṇavaha*), 245, 288 n.50, 292 n.56, 316
Premānand, *Raṇayajña* (Gujarātī), 285
Pṛthvīrājarāso, see Cand Bārdāī
Punam, *Rāmāyaṇacampū* (Malayāḷam), 274
Puṇyacandrodayapurāṇa, see Kṛṣṇadāsa
Purāṇas, 109 n.32, 228 n.3, 233–41, 254, 256, 270, 279, 302 n.76, 325–6; *see also individual titles*
Purāṇasāra, 259
Puruṣārthasedhāsindhu, 259
Puṣpadanta, *Mahāpurāṇa* (Jain), 266 n.16

Rāghavapāṇḍavīya, see Kavirāja
Rāghavendratīrtha, 248 n.42
Raghunandana, *Rāmarasāyaṇa*, 258 n.59
Raghunandana, *Smṛtitattva*, 233
Raghunātha Mahant, *Rāmāyaṇakathā* (Assamese), 279
Raghuvaṃśa, see Kālidāsa
Rājaśekhara, *Bālarāmāyaṇa*, 246 n.38, 248–50, 288 n.50
Rāmabālacarita, see Bhālaṇa
Rāmabhadra Dīkṣita, *Jānakīpariṇaya*, 248 n.42
Rāmābhyudaya, see Yaśovarman
Rāmabrahmānanda, *Rāmāyaṇatattvadarpaṇa*, 259; *Tattvasaṃgraha Rāmāyaṇa* 238 n.22, 253, 259, 270 n.23, 296 n.66
Rāmacarita, see Abhinanda *or* Sandhyākaranandin
Rāmacaritam (Malayāḷam), 274
Rāmadāsa (Marāṭhī), 285
Rāmakathappāṭṭu (Malayāḷam), 274
Rāmakerti I (or *Rīoeṅ Rāmakerti*) (Khmer), 271 nn.24, 25, 289–94, 299, 303
Rāmakerti II (Khmer), 294, 303
Rāmakīen (Thai), 288 n.50, 301–4
Rāma Kling (Javanese), 288
Rāmānanda (possible author of *Adhyātma Rāmāyaṇa*), 252 n.51, 327
Rāma Paṇikkar, *Kaṇṇaśśa Rāmāyaṇam* (Malayāḷam), 274
Rāmarahasya Upaniṣad, 251 n.49
Rāmarasāyaṇa, see Raghunandana
Rāmatāpanīya Upaniṣad, 251 n.49, 259
Rama Thagyin, see Aung Phyo, U
Rāmavijaya, see Śrīdhara

Rāmaviraha, see Bhālaṇa
Rāmāyaṇ, see Kṛttibās
Rāmāyaṇa of Vālmīki, *passim*; *for other works so named see under author*
Rāmāyaṇacampū, see Punam
Rāmāyaṇa Kakawin, see Yogīśvara
Rāmāyaṇakathā, see Raghunātha Mahant
Rāmāyaṇamañjarī, see Kṣemendra
Rāmāyaṇatattvadarpaṇa, see Rāmabrahmānanda
Rāmāyankathā, see Viṣṇudās
Rāmcaritmānas, see Tulsīdās
Rāmopākhyāna, 57 n.81, 58, 92 n.8, 198, 200 n.39, 226–31, 235–6, 238, 267, 271 n.25, 295, 299, 310–14, 324, 330, 333 n.16, 334, 338, 340, 344
Raṇayajña, see Premānand
Raṅganātha, *Rāmāyaṇa* (Telugu), 267 n.19, 276, 277 n.33
Rāvaṇamandodarīsaṃvāda, see Lāvaṇyasamaya
Rāvaṇārjunīya, see Bhaumaka
Rāvaṇavadha, see Bhaṭṭi
Rāvaṇavaha, see Pravarasena
Raviṣeṇa, *Padmapurāṇa*, 266 n.16, 272
Ṛgveda, 9, 16 n.1, 145, 155
Ṛgvidhāna, 56 n.78
Rīoeṅ Rāmakerti, see Rāmakerti I

Śākalyamalla, *Udārarāghava*, 248 n.41
Śaktibhadra, *Āścaryacūḍāmaṇi*, 247, 291 n.55
Śakuntalopākhyāna, 57
Śaṅkaradeva (Assamese), 279
Śatapatha Brāhmaṇa, 171 n.15
Śatarudrīya, 217
Śatruñjayamāhātmya, see Dhaneśvara
Śeṣadharma, 259
Śīlācārya, *Caüpannamahāpurisacariya*, 266 n.16
Śiva Purāṇa, 237–8, 279–80, 296 n.66
Śivarāmer Yuddha, see Kṛttibās
Śrīdhara, *Rāmavijaya*, 285
Śyāma Jātaka, see Mahāvastu

Saddharmasmṛtyupasthānasūtra, 113
Sāma Jātaka, 261 n.3, 264
Sambo-ekotoba, see Minamotono Tamenori
Saṃkṣepa Rāmāyaṇa, see Mukteśvara
Sandhyākaranandin, *Rāmacarita*, 249 n.46
Saṅghadāsa, *Vasudevahiṇḍi* (Jain), 266–7, 297 n.67, 312
Satyāṣāḍhaśrautasūtra, 184 n.26
Saura Purāṇa, 238 n.24
Serāt Kāṇḍa (Javanese), 278 n.34, 288–9, 296 n.65, 297 n.69
Serāt Rām (Javanese), 288
Sěrī Rāma (Malay), 271 n.25, 306
Setubandha, see Pravarasena
Sinhalese version, 300, 305
Sītāsvayaṃvara, see Veṇābāī
Skanda Purāṇa, 236–8, 259
Smṛtitattva, see Raghunandana
Somadeva, *Kathāsaritsāgara*, 265 n.13, 266 n.17
Someśvara, *Ullāgharāghava*, 248 n.41
Subhāṣitaratnakośa, see Vidyākara
Subhaṭa, *Dūtāṅgada*, 241, 250
Sūtras, 25, 208, 307; *see also individual titles*
Svayambhū, *Paümacariü* (Jain), 266 n.16

Tairano Yasuyori, *Hobutsushū* (Japanese), 263–4
Taittirīya Brāhmaṇa, 203
Tamil version, 269–72, 278 n.34, 301; *see also* Kampaṉ, *Irāmāvatāram*
Tattvasaṃgraha Rāmāyaṇa, see Rāmabrahmānanda
Telugu versions, 276
Thai versions, 92 n.8, 256–7, 279, 291 n.55, 293 n.60, 294, 299–305; *see also Rāmakīen*
Tibetan version, 254 n.52, 255 n.55, 257, 264–6, 270 n.23, 283 n.43, 286, 300 n.73, 303 n.77, 304–5, 312
Tilaka commentary, 107, 116 n.49, 128 n.4, 235 n.18
Tirumale Vaidya, *see* Yogindra
Torave Rāmāyaṇa, see Narahari
Tripiṭaka (Chinese), 263–4
Triṣaṣṭiśalākāpuruṣacarita, see Hemacandra
Tsa-pao-tsang-ching, see Chi-chia-yeh
Tulsīdās (Hindī), *Jānakīmaṅgal*, 281 n.40; *Jñānadīpika*, 284 n.44; *Pārvatīmaṅgal*, 280 n.38, 281 n.40; *Rāmcaritmānas*, 92

n. 8, 249–50, 253, 256 n. 57, 257, 279–84, 295, 316, 326–7; *Vinayapatrikā*, 238 n. 22, 281

Udārarāghava, see Śākalyamalla
Udāttarāghava, see Māyurāja
Udhava (Gujarātī), 285
Ullāgharāghava, see Someśvara
Umāsaṃhitā, 259
Unmattarāghava, see Bhāskara *or* Vīrūpākṣadeva
Upadeśapada, see Haribhadrasūri
Upaniṣads, 25–7, 308–9; *see also individual titles*
Uttara Kāṇḍa (Javanese), 288
Uttarapurāṇa, see Guṇabhadra
Uttararāmacarita, see Bhavabhūti
Uttara Rāmāyaṇa, see Yogindra
Uttararāmāyaṇam, see Eẓuttaccan

Vaikhānasaśrautasūtra, 184 n. 26
Vaiṣṇava Upaniṣads, 251
Vājasaneyī Saṃhitā, 171 n. 15
Vāmana Purāṇa, 14 n. 17, 237
Varāha Purāṇa, 237
Vārtikas on Pāṇini, *see* Kātyāyana
Vasudevahiṇḍi, see Saṅghadāsa
Vasukalpa, 249 n. 44
Vāyu Purāṇa, 57, 234
Veṇābāī, *Sītāsvayaṃvara* (Marāṭhī), 285
Vessantara Jātaka, 261 n. 3, 291 n. 55
Vidyākara, *Subhāṣitaratnakośa*, 249 n. 45
Vidyāraṇya, *Pañcadaśī*, 252
Vietnamese versions, 287
Vimalasūri, *Paümacariya* (Jain), 234 n. 13, 248, 254 n. 52, 257, 266–9, 272–3, 285 n. 45, 302, 314
Vinayapatrikā, see Tulsīdās
Vīra Kerala Varma, *Pātāla Rāvaṇa* (Malayāḷam), 278 n. 34
Vīranāga, *see* Dhīranāga
Virūpākṣadeva, *Unmattarāghava*, 248 n. 41
Viṣṇudās, *Rāmāyankathā* (Hindī), 279 n. 36
Viṣṇudāsa (Gujarātī), 285
Viṣṇudharmottara Purāṇa, 236, 315
Viṣṇu Purāṇa, 57, 234, 243, 259
Viṣṇusmṛti, 174

Xenophon, *Anabasis*, 86 n. 19

Yājñavalkyasmṛti, 206 n. 20
Yajurveda, 181; *see also Vājasaneyī saṃhitā*
Yāska, *Nirukta*, 109 n. 32, 121 n. 55
Yaśovarman, *Rāmābhyudaya*, 249 n. 44
Yogaśāstrasvopajñavṛtti, see Hemacandra
Yogavāsiṣṭha Rāmāyaṇa (or *Mahārāmāyaṇa* or *Ārṣarāmāyaṇa* or *Jñānavāsiṣṭha*), 251, 279, 285, 326
Yogindra and Tirumale Vaidya, *Uttara Rāmāyaṇa* (Kannaḍa), 274
Yogīśvara, *Rāmāyaṇa Kakawin* (Old Javanese), 287–8

INDEX

Modern Authors

Agrawala, V. S., 113 n.41
Allchin, F. R., 279 n.37, 284 n.44
Altekar, A. S., 168 n.13, 177 n.21
Antoine, R., 14 n.15, 58 n.86
Ātreya, B. L., 251 n.50

Bagchi, P. C., 252 n.51
Bailey, H. W., 264
Balbir, J. K., 264 n.11
Barrett, E. C. G., 295 n.64, 296 n.66
Barua, B., 218 n.36
Batra, S. N., 15 n.20
Baumgartner, A., 228 n.3
Bharadwaj, O. P., 110 n.34
Bhardwaj, S. M. 116 n.48
Bhargava, P. L., 12
Bhatt, G. H., 8 n.3, 13 n.14, 56 n.76, 57 n.81, 215 n.32, 345 n.63
Bhattacharya, Bhabatosh, 233 n.12
Bloch, A., 10 n.7
Böhtlingk, O. von, 54
Botto, O., 10 n.6, 128 n.4
Brandis, D., 102 n.26
Buitenen, J. A. B. van, 10 n.6, 91 n.7, 145 n.32, 148 n.37, 237 n.20
Bulcke, C., 9 n.4, 10 n.7, 12, 14 n.18, 15 n.19, 48, 58 n.84, 238 n.22, 264 n.12, 271 n.25, 296 n.66, 335, 341, 343
Burrow, T., 148 n.37

Caland, W., 195 n.2, 208 n.23
Chakrabarti, Dilip K., 69 n.3
Chakravarthy, R. S., 89 n.2
Chanana, D. R., 67 n.2
Chandra, K. R., 266 n.15
Charpentier, J., 135 n.12
Chatterjee, A. K., 58 n.87
Chavannes, E., 262 n.8

Daalen, L. A. van, 16 n.1, 18 n.4, 21 n.9, 30 n.21, 44 n.51, 45 n.52, 57 n.82, 113 n.41, 168 n.13, 331 nn.4, 5, 332 n.6, 334 n.16, 335 nn.21, 24, 336 n.26, 337 nn.32, 34, 35, 338 n.37, 339 n.42, 340 n.45, 342 n.50, 343 n.53, 345 n.63
Damdinsüren, C., 266 n.14
Das Gupta, T. K., 148 n.36
Datta, Kali Kumar, 247 n.40
De, S. K., 249 n.44
Dharma, P. C., 129 n.5, 131 n.7, 137 n.14, 153 n.1, 191 n.35
Dimmitt, C., 237 n.20
Divanji, P. C., 251 n.50
Diwekar, H.-R., 343 n.53
Dumézil, G., 11

Emeneau, M. B., 143 n.28

Fausbøll, V., 291 n.55
Ferrari d'Occhieppo, K., 218 n.36
Francisco, J. R., 306 n.80

Gail, A., 155 n.3, 217 n.35, 229 n.5, 231 n.7, 236 n.19
Gawroński, A., 243 n.31
Gehrts, H., 12
Ghosh, J. C., 276 n.31
Ghosh, Juthika, 242 n.28
Ghosh, Manomohan, 287 n.49
Glasenapp, H. von, 252 n.51
Godakumbura, C. E., 305 n.79
Goldman, R. P., 10 n.6, 155 n.3
Gonda, J., 12, 14 n.18, 99 n.19, 137 n.16, 195 n.2, 198, 200 n.9, 343 n.53
Gorresio, G., 111 n.36, 337
Goudriaan, T., 15 n.20
Grierson, G. A., 255 n.54, 285 n.46
Grintser, P. A., 12, 37 nn.33,34, 39, 43 n.49, 45 n.52, 47, 49, 168 n.14
Guruge, A., 12, 168 n.13, 197 n.4

Hacker, P., 198, 201 n.11

Hara, M., 175 n.18, 187, 263 n.10
Hart, G. L. III, 123 n.59
Henry, V., 11
Hill, W. D. P., 279 n.37
Hiltebeitel, A., 11 n.9
Hofstetter, E., 10 n.7, 261 n.3
Hooykaas, C., 287 n.49
Hopkins. E. W., 10 n.6, 38, 45 n.52, 46, 51, 54 n.70, 80 n.12, 82 n.16, 111 n.36, 129 n.5, 131 n.6, 137, 138 nn.17, 18, 20, 21, 139 n.22, 141 nn.24, 25, 142 n.26, 144 n.31, 146 n.33, 147 nn.34, 35, 148 nn.37, 38, 202 nn.12, 13, 209, 331 n.5, 332, 338
Huber, E., 262 n.8, 287 n.48

Jacobi, H., 10 n.7, 11, 12–14, 45, 47–8, 55, 57–8, 99 n.19, 110 n.33, 159, 185 nn.28, 29, 187 n.32, 188, 195, 218, 331 n.5, 333 n.16, 334, 339 n.42, 341, 342 n.50, 343 n.53
Jain, J. C., 266 n.15
Janaki, S. S., 155 n.3
Jhala, G. C., 231 n.8
Johnston, E. H., 262 n.6, 312 n.3
de Jong, J. W., 38, 261 n.4, 264

Kane, P. V., 118 n.51, 333 n.16
Kangle, R. P., 142 n.27
Kapadia, B. H., 252 n.51
Katre, S. L., 284 n.44
Keith, A. B., 12
Khan, B., 197 n.4
Kibe, M. V., 58 n.87, 118 n.52, 120 n.53
Kirfel, W., 25 n.15, 57, 59, 315
Kirk, G. S., 38 n.35
Knipe, D. M., 199 n.7
Krishna Aiyangar, A. N., 239 n.25
Krishnadasa, Rai, 333 n.16
Kuiper, F. B. J., 201 n.12, 202 n.13, 216 n.33
Kulkarni, V. M., 266 n.15, 268 n.21

Lassen, C., 11, 56
Lesný, V., 57
Lévi, S., 113, 114 nn.44, 45, 263 n.9, 292 n.56
Lienhard, S., 98 n.18, 143 n.29
Lillie, A., 11 n.8
Lüders, H., 56, 260

Macdonell, A. A., 12
Mainkar, T. G., 251 n.50
Mankad, D. R., 113, 114 n.44
Masson, J. M., 163 n.12
Mayrhofer, M., 146 n.33, 192 n.38
Meyer, J. J., 142 n.27
Menon, C. A., 274 n.29
Mirashi, V. V., 120 n.53
Molé, M., 12 n.10
Monier-Williams, M., 106 n.30
Muir, J., 56 n.79
Mus, P., 287 n.47

Naidu, S. Shankar Raju, 269 n.22
Narayana Aiyar, R., 50 n.62
Neveleva, S. L., 33 n.26, 198 n.6, 202 n.13
te Nijenhuis, E. Wiersma-, 190, 192 n.37
Nooten, B. A. van, 10 n.6, 32 n.24

O'Flaherty, W. D., 174 n.17, 176 n.20
Oldenberg, H., 51 n.64, 261 n.3

Pandey, M. S., 115 n.47
Paramasiva Iyer, T., 111 n.37, 120 nn.53, 54
Pargiter, F. E., 118 n.52, 123 n.59
Pax, W., 11 n.8
Pingree, D., 218 n.36
Pisani, V., 47 n.57
Pocock, R. I., 93 n.10
Poerbatjaraka, R. Ng., 287 n.49
Pou, S., 289 nn.51, 52, 290 n.54, 294 n.61
Prakash, Om, 86 n.20
Printz, W., 237 n.21
Przyluski, J., 260 n.1
Pusalkar, A. D., 333 n.16

Raghavan, V., 13 n.14, 227, 231 n.7, 234 n.16, 241 n.27, 242 n.28, 251 n.50, 257 n.58, 259 n.60, 262 nn.6, 8, 293 n.60, 306 n.80, 312 n.3, 330 n.2, 339 n.39
Ratnam, Malladi Venkata, 11 n.8
Rau, W., 102 n.25, 148 n.36
Ripley, S. D., 94 nn.11, 12
Rocher, L., 211 n.29

Roy, B. P., 131 n.6
Ruben, W., 9 n.3, 13 n.14, 58 n.84, 113 n.40, 131 n.8, 223 n.44, 333 n.16

Sahai, S., 298 n.70
Sálim Ali, 94 nn.11, 12
Sankalia, H. D., 69 n.4, 76 n.8, 120 n.53, 185, 200 n.10, 247 n.40
Santosa, Soewito, 287 n.49
Schlerath, B., 148 n.36
Schlingloff, D., 56 n.78, 72 n.6, 262 n.5
Schreiner, P., 207 n.22
Sen, Dineshchandra, 276 n.31
Sen, Nilmadhav, 17 n.2, 30 n.21, 55 n.72, 215 n.32, 233 n.12, 345 n.63
Shah, U. P., 120 n.53, 243 n.30, 314 n.5
Sharma, Ramashraya, 204 n.17
Sharma, Ram Karan, 32 n.26
Sharma, Ram Sharan, 125 n.1
Shastri, Satyavrat, 56 n.79
Shende, N. J., 15 n.21, 314 n.5
Singh, S. D., 137 n.15, 138 nn.17, 18, 20, 139 n.22, 141 nn.24, 25, 142, n.26, 144 245 n.36, 249 n.46
Sircar, D. C., 115 n.46, 261 n.2
Słuszkiewicz, E., 227, 243 n.31, 244 n.33, 245 n.36, 249 n.46
Söhnen, R., 33 n.28, 36 n.32, 38 n.38, 40 n.45, 43 n.50, 212 n.30, 332 n.15
Stutterheim, W. F., 295 n.63
Sukthankar, V. S., 10 n.6, 155 n.3, 231 nn.7, 8
Sweeney, P. L. Amin, 295 n.63

Tedesco, P., 135 n.12, 192 n.38
Telang, K. T., 11, 308 n.1
Thein Han, U, 304 n.78
Thieme, P., 94 n.11
Thomas, E. J., 261 n.4

Vader, V. H., 120 n.53
Vaidya, C. V., 50 n.62
Vasilkov, Ya. V., 37 n.34, 39, 42 n.48
Vaudeville, C., 9 n.5, 94 n.11, 279 n.37, 281 nn.41, 42
Vekerdi, J., 55 n.74, 56, 58 n.87
Viennot, O., 209 n.24
Vira, Raghu, 262 n.8
Vo Thu Tinh, 298 n.70
Vogel, J. Ph., 72 n.6, 94 n.13
Vora, D. P., 158 n.6, 180 n.24
Vrat, Satya, 96 n.16

Watanabe, K., 262 n.7
Weber, A., 11–12, 237 n.21, 251 n.49, 260
Whaling, F., 220 n.39, 252 n.51, 279 n.37
Wheeler, J. Talboys, 11 n.8
Winstedt, R. O., 295 n.64
Wirtz, H., 9 n.3, 244 n.33
Wolcott, L. T., 238 n.23
Wurm, A., 15 n.20, 339 n.39, 341 n.46

Yamamoto. Chikyo, 262 n.8

Zbavitel, D., 276 n.31
Zieseniss, A., 295 n.63, 297 n.68

INDEX

General

Only the more significant references are noted

Actors, 178, 190, 193, 319, 323
adverbs, 30–1, 50, 55
Agastya, 3, 7, 45, 58, 84, 112, 118–9, 123, 126, 335–6
Agni, 6, 59, 195, 203, 215, 237, 253, 258
agriculture, 98–100, 319
Ahalyā, 6, 174, 176, 180, 215, 220, 240, 249, 252, 270, 296, 324
ahiṃsā, 224, 262–3, 267–8
alcohol, 82–3, 86–7, 318, 322
alliteration, 36, 42–3, 52, 55, 61
aloe, 81, 101, 104–5, 107–8
Anasūyā, 2, 14 n.18, 99, 177, 313, 334–5
Aṅgada, 4–5. 127–8, 137, 249–50, 256–7, 278, 293
animals, 88–93, 184
Añjanā, 15, 75, 175, 203
aorist, 20, 50
Apsarases, 204
armies, 134–5, 320
armour, 139–40, 317, 322
ascetics, 79, 81, 84, 123, 159, 177–8, 180, 205–7, 213–14, 216, 318, 320–1, 323
asses, 89, 138
astrology, 180, 185, 210–11, 218, 316, 320, 323
astronomy, 185, 210, 320
Asuras, 202–4, 212
aśvamedha, 6, 8, 12, 56, 81 n.13, 171, 183, 193, 214–5, 228, 235, 238 n.24
Aśvins, 195–6
avatāras (other than Rāma), 201, 287, 301, 323
Ayodhyā, 1–2, 7, 69–70, 79, 98, 109–10, 114, 117, 148

Bālakāṇḍa summaries, 7, 57 n.81, 200, 314, 330, 334, 344
battles, 42, 134, 136, 317, 320
bhakti, 212, 240, 253, 257, 269, 274, 282, 284
Bharadvāja, 2, 6, 49, 332
Bharata, 1–2, 6–8, 39–40, 127, 160, 163, 169, 171, 195, 228, 270, 281
Bhārgavas, 10, 15, 155, 213, 217, 314, 321–2
Bhuśuṇḍi, 252, 258, 282, 284
birds, 89, 93–5, 142
boats, 65
Brahmā, 7, 14 n.15, 59, 116, 126, 174, 188, 195–8, 200, 204, 206, 215–16, 222, 226, 228, 314, 320–1
brahmanical influence, 84, 158–9, 174, 183, 187, 213, 218, 221, 223, 318, 322; execution of śūdra ascetic, 8, 130, 158, 212 n.31, 213, 257, 320
brāhmans, 6, 40, 81, 122, 126, 132, 153–8, 183, 186, 188, 204, 207, 213, 215, 308, 320, 322
Bṛhaspati, 195, 243, 330
Buddha, 210, 262–3, 289, 291
buildings, 69–74, 318–9

caityas, 70–1, 73, 209, 320
caṇḍālas, 157–8
cases, syntax of, 24–5, 55
cattle, 34, 90–1, 98, 161, 319
cats, 91–2
causatives, 20, 22, 61
cavalry, 135
cereals, 84–5, 98–9, 319, 321
Ceylon, 93, 109, 120
chariots, 64–5, 89, 135–8, 145, 317, 319
chiasmus, 32, 36
Chota Nagpur plateau, 103, 120
cities, 69–72
Citrakūṭa, mount, 2, 104, 110–11, 118, 165, 332
climate, 108–9, 149–50
clothing, 74–7, 205, 318
coinage, 62
commensality, 82–3, 87, 121

commentators, 13, 68, 92 n.8, 131 n.7, 168 n.14, 188, 191 n.35, 217, 221 n.41
conch, 96–7, 191–2, 201
conjugation, change of, 18, 50
conventions of warfare, 136, 149–52, 224, 321
cosmetics, 80–1
court, 126–7, 129–33, 193, 317
cow, veneration of, 139–40, 157, 208, 213
craftsmen, 65–7, 319

Dairy products, 85
dancing, 190, 193, 319, 323
Daṇḍa, 8, 59, 111, 123, 126, 169, 175
Daṇḍaka forest, 2, 109, 111–12, 123
Daśagrīva *or* Daśānana, 15, 269, 273
Daśaratha, 6–7, 40, 159–61, 171, 195, 197, 223, 260–1, 270, 272, 345; killing of ascetic and curse, 2, 47, 49, 158, 169–70, 174, 210, 239, 264, 331
dating, 12, 50, 55–9, 76, 109 n.33, 113–16, 185–6, 190 n.34, 197–8, 218 n.36, 230, 233, 236 n.19, 260, 307–17, 321, 325
declension, irregularities of, 23
denominatives, 20, 23
desiderative: conjugation, 22–3, 50, 52; adjective (true), 52 n.65; quasi-desiderative adjective, 23, 27, 308
destiny, *see* fate
Devī, 241, 255–6
dharma, 194, 207, 220–3, 233, 285, 289, 324–5, 327, 344
diet, *see* food
doomsday fire, 34, 211
dress, *see* clothing
drums, 134, 191–2
Dūṣaṇa, 3, 133, 336

Earth, 8, 198, 225, 252, 286, 294
economic life, 62–4, 319
education, 180–4, 320, 322
elephants, 34, 90, 135, 137, 140, 184, 200 n.10, 319
employment, 65–7, 319
envoys, inviolability of, 132, 151
ethical values, 164, 210, 212, 222–5, 253, 267–8, 271, 273, 275, 323–5, 327, 335, 338

Family relationships, 159–64
fans, 78–9
fate, 211, 218
fauna, 88–98, 319
figures of speech, 32–7, 50, 52 n.65, 55–6, 60–1, 219, 221–2
fish, 83–4, 96–7
flags, 70–1, 135–6
flora, 100–8, 318–19, 322–3
food, 81–6, 157, 318, 320–1
footwear, 2, 75
formulae, *see* stereotyped expressions
fortifications, 69–72, 148, 319
furniture, 74
future tense, 19–20, 50, 55, 58 n.85

Gandharvas, 191, 204
Gaṇeśa (name of Śiva), 216
Gaṅgā (goddess), 6, 213
Gaṅgā (river), 65, 93, 98, 99 n.20, 103, 109–10, 114–15, 119–20, 208, 217–18, 318–19, 321, 323
Garuḍa, 5, 34, 49, 94, 96, 137, 195, 199, 336
Gayā, 109
gems, 69–71, 74, 78
genealogies, 29 n.20, 49, 58 n.84, 91 n.7, 155, 159, 189, 211, 228, 243, 333, 336
geographical data, 109–20, 312, 318–19, 321–2
gods: general, 194–203, 212, 214–17, 219–22, 319; battle with Asuras, 42, 195, 203, 239
gold, 67–8, 70–1, 74, 78, 139, 142, 145–7, 318–19
golden deer, 3, 82, 165, 180; *see also* Mārīca
Guha, 2, 82–3, 111, 120–1, 129, 284

Hairstyles, 79–80
Hanumān, 3–4, 6–7, 15, 40, 58, 92 n.8, 119, 122, 128–9, 132, 151–2, 162, 175, 195 n.2, 199, 203, 230, 237–8, 240–1, 254, 259, 263–5, 269, 277, 282–3, 291–2, 303, 326, 340–4; birth, 256, 296, 300–1
hiatus, 45, 54, 60
historicity of Rāmāyaṇa, 11–12, 309
honey, 85–6, 318
horoscopes, 185, 218, 315–6
horses, 89–90, 135–8, 140, 184; horse sacrifice, *see aśvamedha*

Images, 209, 322
imperative, 17–20, 22
imperfect tense, 20, 50
Indra, 6–8, 11, 14, 34, 122–3, 137, 143, 147, 174, 176, 195–6, 198–201, 206–7, 214–16, 219–21, 263, 313, 319, 321, 323–4
Indus, 109, 114
interrogatives, 31
Ila, 8, 59, 214
Ilvala, *see* Vātāpi and Ilvala
Indrajit, 4–5, 7, 136–7, 151, 179, 195, 198, 254, 300, 343; sacrifice, 204, 344
insects, 97–8, 319
intensives, 23, 50, 52
iron, 68–9, 139, 141, 146, 318

Jābāli, 2, 44, 162, 189, 223, 333–4
Janaka, 7, 14, 160, 196, 309
Janasthāna, 111–12
Jaṭāyus, 3, 91 n.7, 121, 136, 165, 175, 199, 203, 211, 264, 286, 336
jewellery, *see* ornaments
justice, administration of, 130

Kabandha, 3, 220, 324
Kaikeyī, 1–2, 127, 162–3, 171–2, 180, 227; boons as cause of Rāma's banishment, 11, 47, 125, 176, 223, 239, 267, 272–3
Kailāsa, mount, 7, 70, 110
kāṇḍas, division into, 8, 53, 57, 100 n.21, 189, 222, 334, 340
karma, 211, 253
Kārtikeya, 6
Kausalyā, 1, 162, 171–2, 174, 176, 178, 207, 277
Khara, 3, 89, 134, 136, 336
kingship, 124–30, 157–8, 179, 181, 223–4, 317, 319–20
Kirāṭas, 84, 114, 116
Kiṣkindhā, 3, 69–71, 109–10, 114–15, 119–22, 148
Kṛṣṇa, 117, 201, 211 n.28, 222, 257–8, 326
kṣatriyas, 83–4, 151, 153–5, 157–8, 181, 186, 194, 208, 215, 221, 224, 308, 319, 322–4
Kubera, 7, 96, 195, 197, 222
Kumbhakarṇa, 5, 7, 71 n.5, 82, 128, 137, 164, 195, 198, 254, 293, 343–4
Kuśa (Rāma's son), 7–9, 160, 162, 183

Lakṣmaṇa: characterisation, 161, 163, 222, 224–5
Lakṣmī, 195, 200
language, 187–8
Laṅkā, 3–5, 69, 71–2, 91, 109–10, 117, 119–20, 148
Lava, 7–9, 160, 162, 183
liṅga worship, 209, 215, 236–8, 241, 253, 277, 283, 321, 326
lions, 34, 92–3
lokapālas, 126, 197, 201, 217
long compounds, 28–30, 38, 48–52, 54–8, 60
longer metres, *see under* metre
lotuses, 35, 71, 101–2, 108

Madhuvana, 4, 86, 101
Magadha, 109 n.33, 115, 318
Mandodarī, 171, 176, 178, 241, 249, 254–5, 259, 285, 288, 292–3, 295, 297
Mantharā, 1, 95 n.15, 127, 172–3, 227, 235, 239, 246, 248, 253, 258
Mārīca, 3, 6, 165, 240, 253, 313, 336; *see also* golden deer
marital relationships, 164–7, 225, 320, 322
marriage, 167–73, 318
Maruts, 195
Mātali, 5, 136, 212, 220
materialism, 2, 162, 189, 223, 333–4
meat-eating, 81–4, 318, 320–1
medicine, 184
Menakā, 6, 14 n.18, 57
menstrual impurity, 176
Meru, mount, 67, 70
metals, 67–9, 139, 141, 145–7, 318
metaphor, 35, 61, 193, 324
metre: versification, 45, 50–4, 128; influence on wording, 20, 22 n.10, 23, 25, 37, 39, 50, 147 n.35; verses in longer metres, 33, 50–3, 56–8, 160
military personnel, *see* soldiers
minerals, 67–9
Mitra, 202–3, 322
mokṣa, 197 n.4, 322
monkeys, 92
music, 190–2, 315, 321

Nāgas, 121

Nala, 5, 64, 79, 119, 162
Name, efficacy of Rāma's, 241, 271, 275, 282, 327
Nārada, 212
Narmadā, 93, 114
Niṣādas, 2, 110, 120–1, 318, 320
Niśākara's prophecy, 49, 189, 214, 313, 340
nominal composition, 23, 25–30, 50, 54, 308; *see also* long compounds, patronymics and vṛddhied derivatives
nominal system, 23–30, 53, 61
non-finite verbal forms, 21–2, 27, 31, 60–1
Northern recension, 44, 56 n.78, 60–1, 66, 107–8, 113, 132 n.9, 198, 201, 202 n.14, 226, 232
numerals, 24, 27, 42–3, 60

Ocean, 111, 201–2; churning of, 6, 195, 204, 216
omens, 91, 185 n.28, 197, 210–11
optative, 19
oral composition, 37–40, 43, 47, 53, 187, 318, 322
ornaments, 67–9, 75, 77–8, 318–9

Pañcavaṭī, 3, 103, 112, 119
parallelism, 43, 52, 60–1
Paraśurāma (Rāma Jāmadagnya), 7, 11, 56, 155, 201, 213, 231, 236, 246, 248–50, 255, 265, 301, 315, 322
Parjanya, 34, 99, 195
participles, 17, 19–21, 27 n.17, 31–2, 50, 52, 55, 61
particles, 31–2
past tenses, 18, 20–1; *see also* aorist, imperfect and perfect
Pāṭaliputra, 109 n.33, 117, 318
patronymics, 39, 50
pearls, 68, 78, 97
people, 153–4, 318
perfect tense, 17, 20–1, 54–5, 61
phalaśrutis, 158, 186, 189, 216 n.34, 221, 314
political theory, 128–9
polygamy, 171–3, 318
Prayāga, 119
pregnancy, 167
prepositions, 24
present tense, 18
pronouns, 23–4, 55
prostitutes, 178, 193
proverbial expressions, 31, 34, 43–4, 48–9, 63, 87, 109, 125, 130, 162–4, 182, 211, 308
Puṣpaka, 6–7, 137 n.14, 198, 200 n.10
putreṣṭi, 6, 56, 80, 201, 214

Rājagṛha, 72, 109
Rākṣasas, 40, 78, 82, 120, 122–3, 129–30, 149, 151, 204, 209, 266–7; penances to gain boons from Brahmā, 7, 198, 213–14
Rāma: birth, 6, 55 n.75, 84, 220–1, 234, 258, 270, 280, 295, 314, 325; marriage, 7, 168–71; installation as *yuvarāja*, 127–8; ring as token, 4, 78, 113 n.41, 185–6; installation as king, 6, 176, 193, 345; righteous rule, 6–7, 99, 124, 154, 213, 229–30, 234, 285, 327, 345–6; use of golden statue of Sītā, 8, 173, 233, 314; death, 8, 116 n.49, 198, 258; characterisation, 125–6, 161–6, 222–4, 323–7; comparison with Indra, 219–21, 323–5; identification with Viṣṇu, 14–15, 212 n.31, 219–23, 229–31, 234–6, 238–41, 252, 275, 311, 325–6, 345
Rāma Jāmadagnya, *see* Paraśurāma
Rambhā, 6–7, 174, 178, 204
Rāvaṇa, 3–5, 7, 121, 125, 132, 149–50, 156, 163–4, 241, 246–9, 253, 255, 259, 275 n.30; *see also* Daśagrīva
recensions, 8–9, 59–61, 310–11, 316; *see also* Northern recension and Southern recension
refrains, 38, 43
relative constructions, 30–1, 50
repetition, 43–4, 47, 57
reptiles, 95–6
ritual, 34, 81, 85, 102 n.27, 107, 121, 157, 159, 161, 171, 183, 204–8, 214, 217–8, 320–1
roads, 64–6, 69–70
roots, verbal: usage, 17, 20–1
Ṛśyaśṛṅga, 6, 56, 170, 178, 231 n.9, 246 n.39, 315, 320

Śabalā, 6, 57, 84–5, 155
Śabaras, 110, 121
Śabarī, 3, 109, 121, 158, 177, 180, 210, 258
Sagara, 6, 57, 111, 160, 162, 214, 231 n.9, 315

sāls, 70, 101–4, 107–8
Saṃpāti, 4, 94, 121, 203, 214
saṃsāra, 197, 211, 319–20
sandalwood, 81, 101, 104–5, 107–8
Śarabhaṅga, 3, 220, 311, 324, 335
sargas, division into, 8, 46, 50, 53, 189, 341–2
Śatrughna, 1, 6–8, 127, 135, 150, 161 n.10, 169, 171, 237, 243 n.30, 270
search parties, 4, 49, 59 n.88, 84, 109–10, 112–15, 119, 201, 244, 312, 319, 339–40
secondary conjugations, 20, 22–3, 50, 52, 61
sentence construction, 30–2
servants, 67–79
seṭ/aniṭ variation, 19, 22
sexual ethics, 173–6, 320
silk, 75–6, 318
similes, 31, 33–5, 44–5, 48, 50, 52, 55–8, 61, 89–91, 96–100, 102, 137, 157, 161, 167, 176, 184–5, 192, 199, 202–3, 211, 216
singing, 190–1
Sītā: birth, 14, 98–9, 234–5, 241, 255–6, 261, 264–5, 267–8, 272, 285, 296, 299, 302, 304, 341; *svayaṃvara*, 7, 143, 168–71, 246, 248–50, 257–8, 270, 272, 280–1, 299, 302; abduction, 3, 156, 165–6, 175, 227, 237, 240–1, 258–9; fire-ordeal, 5–6, 49, 165, 175, 215, 224–5, 228, 237, 242–3, 253, 267, 286, 311–12, 345; exile, 7, 59, 125–6, 175, 223, 225, 235, 240, 246, 258, 265, 268; swallowing by Earth, 8, 198, 225, 240, 294, 303; characterisation, 164–6, 222, 225
Sītā (Vedic goddess), 14
Śiva, 7, 14 n.15, 34, 59, 136, 181, 195, 213–16, 222, 237–8, 240–1, 244, 250, 277, 321–2, 326, 344–5
slaves, 67
snakes, 34, 95–6, 199, 319
soldiers, 132–3, 136
Soma, 195, 203
Southern recension, 8, 13, 38 n.38, 46, 55 n.75, 60–1, 107–8, 200
spies, 151
Śrī, *see* Lakṣmī
Śrī Laṅkā, *see* Ceylon
stages of growth: linguistic features, 45–61, 329–46
stems, nominal: transfer, 23
stems, verbal: anomalies, 18, 20
stereotyped expressions, 37–45, 49–50, 54, 96, 144, 166, 194–5
śūdras, 130, 154–5, 158, 186, 217, 322
sugar, 85–6, 100, 319
Sugrīva, 3–4, 40, 121–2, 128–9, 133, 151, 163–4, 172, 174, 224, 254, 262, 265, 267, 271, 273, 291–2, 296, 304
Sumantra, 131–2, 162
Śūrpaṇakhā, 3, 99, 163, 173, 179, 240, 246, 248, 336
Sūrya, 217
sūtas (bards), 9, 84
Śveta, 8, 59, 83

Tamils, 123
Tārā, 4, 165, 178, 271, 339
taxation, 63, 126, 157, 317
temples, 70, 209, 322
textual history, *see* oral composition, recensions, stages of growth and transmission, textual
theatres, 177, 193, 323
tigers, 92–3
tīrthas, 116, 209, 322
toiletries, 80–1
trade, *see* economic life
transmission, textual, 9–10, 13, 46, 53, 188, 318
trees, 64, 70–1, 100–8
Trijaṭā, 4, 79, 271
Trijaṭa Gārgya, 49, 156
Triśaṅku, 6, 57, 155, 157–8, 213

Vaiṣṇava influence, 13–14, 34 n.30, 200, 204, 210, 320
vaiśyas, 154–5, 158, 186
Vālin, 3–4, 44, 49, 82, 122, 127, 152, 163–5, 172, 174, 210, 224, 246, 248, 253–4, 256, 262, 265, 267, 271, 296, 338–9
Vālmīki: composer of Rāmāyaṇa, 7, 10, 46–7, 122, 188, 234, 309; his hermitage, 177; inventor of the *śloka*, 9 n.5, 94, 121, 188, 190, 241
Vānaras, 3–6, 8, 35, 40, 69–71, 120–3, 149, 195 n.2, 224
varṇas, 153–8, 170, 213, 320, 322; *see also* brāhmans, kṣatriyas, vaiśyas and śūdras

Varuṇa, 149, 195, 201–2, 216 n.33, 222
Vasiṣṭha, 2, 6, 57, 121, 127, 130, 132, 155–6, 196, 202, 213, 251–2
Vātāpi and Ilvala, 49, 81–3, 188, 231 n.9, 335
Vāyu, 15, 195, 199, 203
Vedas, knowledge of, 122, 181–3, 204–5, 207, 217
Vedavatī, 7, 160, 169, 178, 236, 240–1, 266 n.17, 269
Vedic pantheon, 34, 195, 216–17, 319
vegetarianism, 84
vehicles, 65
verbal system, 17–23, 50, 52–3, 60–1
versification, *see under* metre
Vibhīṣaṇa, 4–7, 129, 132, 137, 146, 151, 163–4, 174, 253–4, 259, 271, 292–3, 344
Vindhyas, 70, 110, 112, 120, 318
Virādha, 2, 253, 335
Viṣṇu, 6, 14 n.15, 34, 56, 77 n.9, 110, 148, 179, 195, 198–201, 213–16, 219–22, 226, 238–41, 252, 321–3, 330, 335–6, 340, 344–5
Viśvakarman, 71, 195
Viśvāmitra, 6–7, 45, 57–8, 83, 121, 155, 181, 200 n.8, 213, 215, 251
voice, use of, 18–20, 22, 60
vṛddhied derivatives, 28, 48–50, 134
Vṛtra, 8, 34, 195, 214

Warfare, 42, 132–52, 224, 317, 319–22
weapons, 140–9, 155 n.3, 317, 319–22; worship of, 149
widows, 178, 318, 322
women, position of, 150, 166, 169–72, 176–80, 318, 320, 322
writing, 185–7, 318–20, 322

Yama, 7, 34, 128–9, 148, 195–7, 222, 319
Yamunā, 65, 110, 114, 120, 318
yoga, 214
yojana, 117–19